CROATIA & SLOVENIA

SHANN FOUNTAIN ALIPOUR

Contents

DISCOVER
Croatia & Slovenia

Croatia and Slovenia have become popular and well-known travel destinations in the past decade, with oodles of glossy magazine spreads and social media posts to swoon over. Montenegro has edged into the spotlight too, from the early fame of its much-photographed island idyll, Sveti Stefan, to its reputation as an excellent destination that costs significantly less to visit than its more touted northern neighbors. With sunny cities crisscrossed by winding cobblestone streets, blue gem lakes set amongst white-capped mountains, a crystalline sea, colorful festivals, great food and wine, and much more, all three countries have a variety of experiences to offer. Spend two weeks here and you will likely feel you need two more. For such small countries (all together they are about the size of Maine), the diversity and breadth of things to do is astounding.

Though tourists have long been frequenting Dubrovnik and Hvar and more recently discovering the charms of capital cities Zagreb and Ljubljana, there are still many places in these countries that are relatively undiscovered. Go to some of the lesser-known islands in October or to Slavonia or inland Montenegro almost any time of year, and you will find yourself quite alone in terms of tourists.

Clockwise from top left: fishing boat; entrance to the square in Motovun; snorkeling off the Croatian coast; Cathedral of St. Nicholas, Ljubljana; Old Town Dubrovnik from the Pucic Palace Hotel; view of marina on Hvar, Croatia.

Croatia and Slovenia share a past that has seen many different rulers, wars, and various foreign empires—Roman, Venetian, Austro-Hungarian—that have all added a flavorful layer to these countries. Montenegro shares a fair amount of this history too, though its long occupation by the Ottomans and its hard-fought holdout from them has given it a special flair. However, the countries have all remained distinct with their own languages, customs, and cultures as different as the topography you'll traverse. Drive a few hours and you'll see everything from a sparkling coastline and barren-rock hinterlands to rolling hills of grapevines, thick green forests, and snow-topped mountains.

The diversity means there really is something for every sort of traveler. Hit up Istria for food and wine and truffle-hunting, Zagreb or Ljubljana for a European capital vibe with a twist, Dubrovnik for Roman and Venetian history at every turn, the islands for soaking up the sun, the mountains of Slovenia for skiing and adventure sports, or Slavonia for taking the road less traveled. In Montenegro head to Kotor, a medieval walled city, or Budva, Eastern Europe's Riviera.

No matter how you plan your trip, you're likely to leave already planning your next one. Croatia, Slovenia, and Montenegro may be better known these days, but they haven't lost the wild and wonderful quality that keeps you feeling you've truly gone somewhere special.

Clockwise from top left: Slovenian countryside; boats in the harbor in southern Dalmatia; cherries in the market; Predjama Castle in Slovenia.

14 TOP EXPERIENCES

1 Sipping your way through the many **wine routes of Croatia and Slovenia** (page 31), with intimate tastings and tours at small production wineries.

2 Spotting storks and swimming pigs in **Lonjsko Polje** (page 122) and watching for the 250 bird species in the expansive **Kopački Rit Nature Park** (page 110)—inland Croatia is a wildlife lover's paradise.

3 Sampling the local cuisine, from **truffles in Istria** (page 157) to *janjetina* (lamb) in **Dalmatia** (page 233), will have you dreaming of your meals in Croatia for years to come.

>>>

4 Wandering around **Plečnik's Ljubljana** (page 330) and marveling at the imprint of one architect on the city's public spaces.

5 Traveling back to Roman times with a wander through the **amphitheater in Pula** (page 133), the **Forum in Zadar** (page 210) or the **Diocletian's Palace in Split** (page 248).

>>>

6 Bumming around on a beach in Slovenia's **Portorož** (page 394), **Croatia's Southern Dalmatian islands** (page 27), or **Montenegro's Gulf of Kotor** (page 409). With 2,300km (1,429mi) of coastline, there's bound to be a beach that's right for you—busy, nudist, rocky, or isolated.

>>>

7 Admiring the works of Ivan Meštrović, Croatia's most famous sculptor, at the **Meštrović Studio in Zagreb** (page 49) and the **Ivan Meštrović Gallery in Split** (page 252).

>>>

8 Winding your way up **Mount Sljeme** and stopping into one of the many alpine huts to share a bowl of *grah* (beans) and a mug of beer with the locals (page 71).

<<<

9 Hiking through the craggy landscape and gorge in the **Paklenica National Park** and lunching next to a rushing stream (page 219).

>>>

10 Basking in a riot of color and culture at one of the many outstanding **festivals** across Croatia and Slovenia, from the year-round **food and wine festivals in Istria** (page 141) to the summer's **Kurentovanje** (page 358).

11 Climbing to the top of the **Rinka waterfall** in the breathtaking **Logar Valley** for an astounding view of snow-capped peaks (page 369).

12 Rafting the river gorge in **Omiš** (page 256) or the rushing waters of Slovenia's **Soča River Valley** (page 384) in Bovec.

13 Spending the day at **Lake Skadar** in Montenegro, kayaking its beautiful waters, and touring some of Montenegro's best wineries afterwards (page 433).

14 Skiing, snowboarding, and sledding down a snowy slope at Slovenia's **Kranjska Gora** (page 382) or **Velika Planina** (page 368).

Planning Your Trip

Where to Go

Zagreb

Croatia's capital is the cultural and social heart of the country, and travelers have recently discovered the **buzzing vibe** of this charming city. Social life revolves around the bustling squares and streets of **Lower Town (Donji Grad).** For the softer side of town, head to **Upper Town (Gornji Grad)** with its quiet, winding cobblestone roads, stunning churches, and excellent museums. Bridging old and new are the delightful **Tkalčićeva** and **Radićeva** streets with their boutiques and cafés. **Mount Sljeme,** just out of town, has hiking trails and mountain huts where you can while away an afternoon with a beer and a bowl of bean stew.

Inland Croatia

Beginning in the mountainous **Gorski Kotar** and stretching across Croatia's long eastern arm, inland Croatia is definitely the country's undiscovered find. The region is dotted with picturesque villages, excellent restaurants, and *seoski turizam* establishments, where you can sleep like a local and wake up to the rooster's crow. Don't-miss destinations include the **vineyards** that dot the countryside, the riverside town of **Osijek,** and the stork-filled **Lonjsko polje.** The easternmost regions around **Vukovar**, still feeling the effects of the Homeland War almost 30 years ago, are full of friendly people eager to show off their towns to visitors.

Cathedral of the Assumption of the Blessed Virgin Mary, Zagreb

Roman amphitheater in Pula

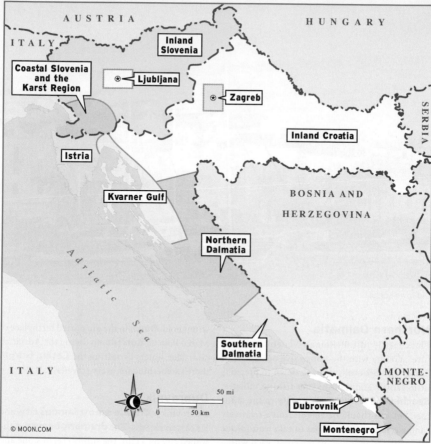

Map labels:

AUSTRIA

HUNGARY

ITALY

Inland Slovenia

Coastal Slovenia and the Karst Region

⊛ Ljubljana

⊛ Zagreb

SERBIA

Inland Croatia

Istria

Kvarner Gulf

BOSNIA AND HERZEGOVINA

Northern Dalmatia

Adriatic Sea

Southern Dalmatia

ITALY

MONTE-NEGRO

0 50 mi
0 50 km

Dubrovnik

Montenegro

© MOON.COM

Istria

This tiny peninsula, wedged between Croatia and Slovenia and only a stone's throw from Italy, packs a lot of punch into its small size. You can sun yourself on a rocky beach in the morning, retreat to the green hills for lunch, and finish off the day with dinner next to a rushing stream or in a seaside medieval town, depending on your mood. Istria is most famous for three things, and you shouldn't miss any of them: the **Roman amphitheater in Pula,** the region's **wines,** and its **truffles.** But there's more to unearth here, from almost perfect little villages like **Brtonigla** and **Hum** to a taste of faded Tito-esque grandeur in the **Brijuni Islands.**

Kvarner Gulf

Home to the grand Austro-Hungarian coastal playgrounds of **Opatija** and **Lovran** and the laid-back port town of **Rijeka,** the Kvarner Gulf is less than a two-hour drive from Zagreb. Its real jewels are the **stunning islands** just off the coast, such as **Rab,** with its preserved old town and colorful festivals; **Krk,** drawing a younger, party-loving crowd; genteel **Veli Lošinj;** and **Pag,** with its famous lace and cheese and 24-hour party beach near Novalja. The don't-miss islands are relatively undeveloped **Cres** and **Susak,** whose clay cliffs jut into the remotest portions of Croatia's Adriatic.

Old Town Korčula

Northern Dalmatia

The coast is full of Roman-Veneto architecture, starting with the impressive old towns of **Zadar** and **Šibenik,** snaking down to precious little **Trogir** and the **Kaštela** fishing villages. **Beaches** can be filled to capacity in the summer, but you should be able to find a relatively roomy one by hiring a boat to take you to one of the little islands just off the coast, each with a culture and personality all its own. Also included in this region are the stunning **Plitvice Lakes,** slightly inland, one of the most-visited destinations in Croatia for good reason.

Southern Dalmatia

Split is the boundary between north and south on the Dalmatian coast. It's important not only because it's the second-largest city in Croatia and for its dozens of connections to the Croatian islands, but also for the beautiful **Diocletian's Palace** in the heart of town. **Hvar** has already made a name for itself in the media, but along **Croatia's most stunning coastline,** it's not alone in its beauty. From the former pirate

stronghold, **Omiš,** to the purported birthplace of Marco Polo on **Korčula,** to diving the Adriatic's clear blue waters or rafting the **Cetina Gorge,** there's something for every traveler.

Dubrovnik

Dubrovnik is **Croatia's most famous city,** and it's easy to see why. The **dramatic beauty** of the walled city on a cliff, the sunny cream stone and red-tiled roofs contrasting with the blue Adriatic Sea, and the grand architecture are a few of the qualities that make Dubrovnik the equal of other European destinations. The city's popularity has translated into masses of tourists, but there's also a less-seen side of Dubrovnik, including aristocratic **Trsteno** and the shady island of **Lokrum.** The restaurants and wineries of the **Pelješac Peninsula** and the nearby islands of **Lastovo** and **Mljet,** with a lake at its center, are great escapes not far from town.

Ljubljana

Ljubljana may be small, but with a cultural menu to rival much larger capitals, a hilltop **castle,** funky nightlife, and a strong sense of self, it is a city not to be overlooked. It's impossible to ignore the influence architect **Jože Plečnik** had on the city; his touch is all over Ljubljana, including its famous **Triple Bridge (Tromostovje)**, the colonnaded market, and many of the city's tree-lined promenades. Ljubljana is the cultural and social as well as political capital of Slovenia, and it's here that you'll find an impressive selection of **museums and galleries**. If you'd like to see a more hidden part of Ljubljana, join the locals in the city's elegant **Tivoli Park.**

Inland Slovenia

Filled with mountains, lakes, rivers, and caves, Slovenia's interior is an **ideal region for sports enthusiasts.** For those interested in quieter pursuits, there is also food, culture, and history to be discovered, including wineries, Roman ruins, herding settlements, and centuries-old churches and castles. The region's most famous town is **Bled,** with a church-topped island in the center of the mountain-rimmed lake, but its gem might be the alpine **Logar Valley (Logarska Dolina)** to the east, rimmed by massive snow-capped peaks. To the east of Ljubljana is the town of **Maribor,** with a sweet historic center and amazing **wineries** all around. Those into rafting and adventure sports will be happiest around the **Triglav National Park** and **Bohinj,** with plenty of adrenaline-pumping activity.

Coastal Slovenia and the Karst Region

While not as grand as the Croatian coast, the coast of Slovenia has many charms of its own, from stunning architecture and unusual medieval frescoes to coastal walking paths and towns filled with winding cobblestone streets. Venetian-influenced **Piran** is the pride of the Slovenian coast and a starting point for those exploring the region. **Postojna Cave (Postojnska Jama)** and **Škocjan Caves (Škocjanske Jame)** are worth a visit for their underworld glory, while **Predjama Castle (Predjamski Grad),** built into a rock face high above a village, is straight out of a storybook.

If You Have...

- **FIVE DAYS:** Visit Ljubljana, Bled, Zagreb, and Plitvice.

- **ONE WEEK:** Add Zadar and Kornati Islands.

- **TWO WEEKS:** Add Split, Dubrovnik, Hvar, and Korčula.

- **THREE WEEKS:** Add Opatija, Pula, Cres, and Rovinj.

a street in Rovinj

A trip to the area wouldn't be complete without sampling the Karst's famous wind-cured *pršut* (prosciutto).

Montenegro

Montenegro is a tiny country with a wide variety of terrain and experiences. If you love beachside lounging, you will find plenty of company at the beaches in **Budva.** The **Gulf of Kotor**, with the famous walled city of **Kotor** and the island church of **Our Lady of the Rocks**, as well as the inland town of **Cetinje**, the cultural and erstwhile capital of Montenegro, are a must for culture and history buffs. **Lake Skadar** and **Lovćen National Park** are full of views, hiking, and getting away from it all. If you're really tight on time, a day trip to **Herceg Novi** from Dubrovnik can give you a little taste of the country.

town Perast in the Gulf of Kotor, Montenegro

When to Go

The coasts of Croatia, Slovenia, and Montenegro have a Mediterranean climate with hot summers (26-30°C/78-86°F) and relatively mild winters (5-10°C/41-50°F). Inland locales will bring warm to hot summers (20-30s C/70-80s F) and cold winters (-5-5°C/23-41°F), though snow accumulation has dwindled in recent years.

July and August are the busiest months on the coast—beaches and nightclubs are packed, and many of the coastal towns hold colorful festivals. But overall, they're probably the **worst months** to visit the region. Temperatures soar and hotels fill up, even at the **most expensive high-season rates,** and inland capitals are often fled by the locals, who've joined all the foreigners by the sea.

June and September are ideal for visiting the coast or cities in the interior. The waters are warm enough for swimming, and the biggest influxes of visitors are between these relatively peaceful months. If swimming's not your thing,

then **March, April, May, and October** are possibly even better—an early-morning ramble around town may make you think you're the first to discover a destination.

Autumn is a great season for visiting Istria and inland Croatia and Slovenia: Wine is harvested, leaves turn to shades of gold, and the crisp air is invigorating.

Winter, when **most hotels and restaurants are at their cheapest,** can work well for Dalmatia and Istria, when you might have some locales all to yourself. Keep in mind that some hotels and restaurants will be closed, particularly on the islands and in Montenegro. Inland Croatia and Slovenia are cold and gray in winter, but December festivities and markets bring life to Zagreb and Ljubljana. Triglav National Park and Bled in Slovenia have an entirely different side to their personalities in winter, making them destinations to put on your list not once but twice.

Before You Go

Visas and Officialdom

To enter **Croatia and Slovenia,** U.S., U.K., Canadian, Australian, and New Zealand citizens will need only a **passport;** no visa is required for stays up to 90 days. Citizens of the EU and Switzerland can visit for up to 30 days with only a **national identity card.**

To enter **Montenegro,** U.S., U.K., European, Canadian, Australian, and New Zealand citizens will need only a **passport**; no visa is required for stays up to 30 days.

Citizens of other countries should check visa regulations for Croatia and Slovenia.

Getting There

Getting to Croatia and Slovenia is easier than ever before, particularly in summer, when low-cost airlines offer flights from major European hubs such as London and Frankfurt, and ferry services connect the countries with Venice and Trieste in Italy.

If you're **flying,** you'll find Croatia and Slovenia's main air carriers (Croatia Airlines and Adria Airways, respectively), supplemented by companies such as EasyJet, Ryanair, and GermanWings, offer many flights accommodating a variety of budgets. Though the low-cost carriers generally deposit travelers in the most popular coastal regions, it's easy to get off the beaten track by taking trains or buses into the interior. Croatia's main airports are located in Zagreb and Split, though airports in Dubrovnik, Pula, and Rijeka see their share of travelers during the summer months; Slovenia's only major airport is in the capital, Ljubljana.

Montenegro has two airports, in the capital Podgorica and at Tivat, servicing the coast. Both offer daily flights to and from European destinations, with low-cost carriers like Norwegian Air, WOWair, Ryanair, and EasyJet being the most common. Another option is to fly into Dubrovnik, where organized transfer buses take tourists the 15-minute drive to the Montenegro border and beyond multiple times a day.

Train service is frequent and reliable in both Slovenia and Croatia, with at least 2-3 daily trains linking capitals Ljubljana and Zagreb with Italy, Austria, Hungary, and Serbia. Trains tend to be older than what you'll find in Western Europe, and they're often slower, too. **Bus** service is actually better, though buses have been known to deposit regular customers close to their homes, making the journey a little longer than planned from time to time.

In the summer, **ferries** connect cities like Split, Dubrovnik, and Pula in Croatia and Portorož and Piran in Slovenia with Venice and the northern Italian coast. There is a convenient ferry between Dubrovnik and the Montenegrin port of Bari for travelers adding Montenegro to their itinerary.

Getting Around

If you'll be sticking to larger towns, **public transportation** is an excellent option for getting around both Slovenia and Croatia. Buses and trains are frequent, safe, and reliable. Islands are well connected via ferry. Montenegro has frequent inter-city bus connections and an extremely cheap yet infrequent train connection between Serbia and Bar.

However, if you're planning on exploring smaller villages or following the regions' wine routes, you'll find renting a **car** to be a lifesaver. Arranging for the car before you come usually secures a better price.

As most roads lack bike lanes, and drivers are not used to sharing the road, you'll find **bicycle** use best suited to sleepy coastal islands, some devoid of cars, as well as pedestrian areas and marked bike trails.

The Best of Croatia, Slovenia, and Montenegro

Covering both capitals and many must-see stops in only two weeks, this trip combines both mountains and sea, UNESCO World Heritage sites and urban centers. If you have a couple of extra days, add them at the beginning of the trip and spend more time in Slovenia, either in Ljubljana or the Bohinj valley.

Ljubljana
DAY 1
After landing in **Ljubljana,** refresh at your hotel before heading out in the late afternoon for a stroll around the cobblestone streets of the **Old Town** and stopping for photos on the **Dragon Bridge.** After dinner, cap off the day with a view from the town's **castle.**

Inland Slovenia
DAY 2
Head to nearby **Bled** for a tour of the clifftop **castle** and a stroll around the stunning blue **lake.** Ride on a *pletna* (gondola-like boat) or in a *fijaker* (horse-drawn carriage) while admiring the scenery. Adventurous types can switch the strolling for a spot of **white-water rafting** or **hiking** around the lake. Have an afternoon coffee and *kremšnite* (cream cake) on a hotel terrace overlooking the lake, and dine on some of the area's fresh trout for dinner, preferably at a cozy fireside table.

Zagreb
DAY 3
Drive down through Ljubljana toward Zagreb, stopping for a late lunch at the **Hotel Grad Otočec,** a castle just before the Croatian border.

Cityscape of the Slovenian capital Ljubljana

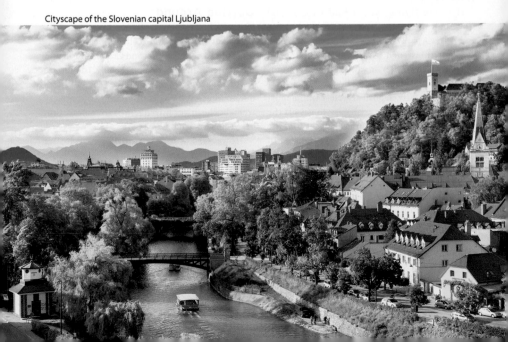

Pick Your Paradise: The Southern Dalmatian Islands

Franciscian Monastery, Hvar island

Southern Dalmatia is covered with rocky beaches, sun-washed towns, and some of the prettiest destinations in Croatia. With dozens of islands to choose from, which ones will you pick? Though each has its charms, here are four to stick on your don't-miss list.

MLJET

Legend has it this is the island that seduced Odysseus to stay for seven years on his way back from Troy, and it's not hard to see why. This **heavily forested island** near Dubrovnik has **two saltwater lakes.** An island in the larger lake holds a 12th-century Benedictine monastery. Bike rentals are available for exploring Mljet, and the island also offers **excellent diving,** with a 3rd-century Roman shipwreck and a sunken World War II German torpedo boat right off the coast.

HVAR

Since the 4th century BC many countries have laid claim to Hvar's sun-drenched stone buildings, lavender and rosemary fields, rich vineyards, and deep blue waters. These days it's the tourists who seem to have conquered. Frequented by famous actors, models, and gossip-mag regulars, Hvar Town offers **pulsing summer nightlife.** During the day, **St. Stephen's Cathedral (Katedrala sveti Stjepan),** built during the 16th and 17th centu-

ries, and the **Fortica,** a Venetian fortress with a grand view of the harbor, beckon travelers. Hvar's summer music festival is host to classical, jazz, and folk concerts. It's worth a visit to the winery of **Zlatan Plenković** in Sveta Nedelja to sample its award-winning wines.

KORČULA

Famous as the birthplace of Marco Polo and often dubbed a **mini Dubrovnik** due to its charming walled city, the island of Korčula is also home to sandy shaded coves with some of Croatia's **best beaches.** Korčula Town's 15th-century cathedral displays an early work by Tintoretto, and Moreška sword dancers give colorful performances in July and August.

VIS

First settled in Neolithic times, Vis was closed to the public shortly after World War II, when it became a Yugoslav military base. Opened to tourism in 1989, this **tranquil island** has slowly seen an increase in visitors. The town of Vis is filled with narrow leafy streets, perfect for meandering and admiring the limestone villas built by wealthy seafarers. The **Archaeological Museum (Arheološki muzej)** showcases many island treasures and offers leaflets suggesting walks past the city's ruins.

After dropping off your bags at your hotel in **Zagreb,** catch at least one or two museums in **Lower Town (Donji Grad)** before dinner and people-watching along Zagreb's buzzing **Tkalčićeva.**

DAY 4
After breakfast at the historic **Regent Esplanade** hotel (if you stayed in another part of town, have breakfast at the market), make a bee-line for **Dolac Market (Tržnica Dolac)** and then **Upper Town (Gornji Grad)** for a long morning of sightseeing and coffee-sipping. Spend the afternoon sipping wine and trying local cheeses at **Cheese Bar** before deciding which restaurant to hit for dinner.

Northern Dalmatia
DAY 5
Leave fairly early this morning to make it to **Plitvice Lakes National Park** before lunch. Take your time walking around the majestic cascading lakes, and chow down on sausage stew at **Lička kuća** before driving on to **Zadar** and

grabbing dinner at **Pet Bunara** in its stunning old town.

DAY 6
Today you can visit a few of Zadar's famous sights or hit the beaches nearby. However you spend your day, there's only one way to end it—walking down the waterfront to the **Sea Organ (Morske orgulje)** to catch the sound of the musical waves.

DAY 7
Get up early this morning for a day trip to the **Kornati Islands** to see the stark beauty of the national park, swim and soak up some sun, and eat some grilled fish. Not an early bird? Choose an excursion to the islands of **Zlarin** or **Prvić** instead. Get back to Šibenik in the early evening and immediately head out for Split to get an early start on sightseeing in the morning.

Southern Dalmatia
DAY 8
Start the day with a tour of **Split**'s major attraction, **Diocletian's Palace.** After a light lunch

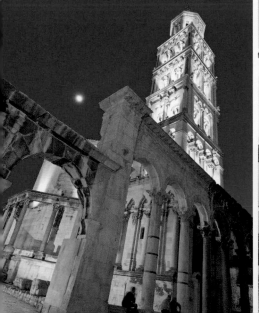
Diocletian's Palace, Split, Croatia

Dragon Bridge, Ljubljana

Plitvice Lakes National Park

head out to the **Marjan Peninsula** and absorb Meštrović's mammoth house and artwork before whiling away the evening in a lively bar crawl through the narrow, busy streets of the palace, hopefully catching a bit of jazz or live music.

DAY 9

Take the catamaran to **Hvar,** fitting in a tour of **Hvar Town's** sights before dressing up and heading to dinner or some wine-tasting at the **Pršuta Tri Wine Bar.**

DAY 10

Even if you're not a wine connoisseur, taking today to visit some of Hvar's inland **wineries** is a great way to see a less-touristed side of the island. Make sure to visit the vineyards of **Zlatan Plenković** and lunch at his waterside **Bilo Idro** restaurant. Save room for dinner in **Stari Grad,** where the historic restaurant **Jurin Podrum** will impress you with top-quality cuisine.

DAY 11

Head to **Korčula** in the morning, touring the mini-Dubrovnik's cathedral and art galleries with a break for a sweet treat from local legendary bakery **Cukarin.** In the evening dine on fresh fish and mussels.

Dubrovnik

DAY 12

Head to the **Pelješac Peninsula** this morning for laid-back beach lounging or winery-hopping before having an early dinner at **Kapetanova kuća** and heading to **Dubrovnik** for a quiet drink at your hotel. If you're still going strong, take a walk along the **Stradun** with an ice cream cone in the late evening when all the day-trippers and cruise passengers have left the city.

DAY 13

Start your day with a tour of the **town walls** before heading to the town's galleries, the **Sponza Palace (Palača Sponza),** and the **Rector's Palace (Knežev dvor).** Have a quick sandwich at **Buffet Škola,** saving a visit to the **Franciscan Monastery** for later in the day when the crowds have begun to thin. After changing at your hotel and watching the sunset from its terrace, splurge on dinner at **Restaurant 360** under a starlit sky.

Montenegro
DAY 14

Leave Dubrovnik early to cross the border to Montenegro before the crowds. Head to **Kotor** to explore the UNESCO World Heritage-protected walled city. Have a quick lunch at **Hoste**. Stop in **Perast** on your way back for a look at the island church **Our Lady of the Rocks** and have an early waterside dinner at **Conte**.

A Movable Feast

Though you'll find great food throughout Slovenia and Croatia, the **Istria** and **Kvarner** regions are the most concentrated centers of gourmet finds. From restaurants that compete with big names for Michelin stars to wineries to prized lamb specialties, every day should bring a couple of discoveries for even the most experienced palates.

Day 1

Start your tour on the **Opatija Riviera,** where you'll find a treasure trove of top restaurants. Choose from **Kukuriku** in the village of Kastav, **Konoba Tramerka**, with its innovative cuisine, and **Draga di Lovrana,** above Lovran, an excellent restaurant with a view. Spend the night at **Villa Astra** in Lovran.

Day 2

Head into Istria, stopping for lunch on the terrace of the **Humska Konoba** in Hum, supposedly the smallest village in the world. Top off your meal with a bit of the town's **mistletoe brandy,** said to aid digestion. Don't have more than a sip, since you'll need to save your tolerance for wine-tasting at the wineries of **Livio Benvenuti** and **Tomaz** near Motovun, perhaps getting in a bit of sightseeing while you're in the area. Later, have dinner

Motovun and vineyard

Vines and Wines

Slovenia and Croatia are both perfect destinations for wine aficionados. Vineyards dot the hills of both countries and the region boasts a very long winemaking history, dating from Roman times. The wines produced vary in quality and taste, but are inexpensive in general, and stopping to sample homemade vintages along the wine routes is a fun way to get to know the countryside. Some excellent wines never make it to the West, selling out their small stock locally.

CROATIA

In Croatia, mostly white wines have dominated, though red wines have had a strong showing in recent years as well. The most popular award would likely go to **Istria**'s light white **Malvazija**. Istria's other indigenous wine, **Teran,** is an earthy red, well-loved locally but little embraced by foreign palates. The small peninsula, reminiscent of Tuscany, is dotted with excellent small winemakers with dozens of varieties to try.

The **Dalmatian coast** is another well-known

Vineyards dot the hills of Croatia and Slovenia.

wine-producing region, particularly the **Pelješac Peninsula,** where the local **Plavac Mali** grape is responsible for some of the country's best red wines.

The **interior of Croatia** is perhaps the country's lesser-known wine-growing region. **Međimurje,** which hugs the Hungarian border, produces mostly whites, a bit acidic for most tastes. Some very good Croatian whites come from little-traveled **Slavonia,** from the vineyards around Slavonski Brod to the far eastern corner of Ilok, where solid reds, particularly **Burgundy,** are produced as well.

Many of the areas are covered with **marked wine routes,** though the best organized and promoted are those in Istria. More information about Istrian wine routes can be found at www.istra.hr.

SLOVENIA

Like Croatia, Slovenia's winemaking history traces its roots to Roman times. Today, the country's wines have garnered a solid reputation, but to try many of the local products, mostly produced for personal consumption and regional sales, you'll need to get out and visit the small vineyards in person. Slovenian white wines, particularly **Beli Pinot, Šipon, Chardonnay,** and **Sauvignon Blanc,** are high in quality. The country is most known for its Beli Pinot and Šipon and for the red **Kraški Teran** in the Karst. Slovenia also makes something similar to a rosé, called **Cviček,** and a couple of decent sparkling wines. The three main regions producing wine are **Podravje** (Pohorje and Pomurje regions), **Posavje** (Bela Krajina and Dolenjska regions), and **Primorska** (coastal region).

Slovenia has an excellent and well-marked **network of wine routes** for driving or cycling. More information can be found at www.slovenia.info.

at **Konoba Mondo** in Motovun before heading up to Grožnjan to spend the night.

Day 3

Get a good look around **Grožnjan** and its art galleries before slowly making your way to **Brtonigla** and the **Hotel San Rocco,** where you can sip local wines by the hotel pool before having dinner in the top-notch restaurant and taking a walk around the charming village.

Day 4

After a late checkout, drive up to the vineyards of **Moreno Coronica** near Umag for wine-tasting or take to the *vinska ceste* (wine routes) in the area for a look at some more mom-and-pop vineyards to see what's on offer. Finish the day off in **Novigrad** at **Marina Restaurant** for haute cuisine brought to you by young adventurous chefs.

Day 5

Stop in at **Poreč** for a look at the city's magnificent basilica before driving to **Pula.** Tour the

amphitheater and its interesting display on Roman winemaking, then head to **Restoran Vela Nera** for coffee and cake or a late lunch. Save room for dinner at the superb **Valsabbion,** also a great place to spend the night and enjoy walking the marina and admiring the shiny yachts.

Day 6

Head to Rijeka and take a ferry to **Cres,** where you should have lunch at the unassuming **Bukaleta** to feast on some of the island's specialties, particularly lamb. Spend the afternoon by the beach and the evening (and night) in busy little **Cres Town.**

Day 7

Head across the bridge to **Lošinj.** Walk the pretty promenade from **Mali Lošinj** to **Veli Lošinj,** stopping to admire the aristocratic homes overlooking the water, before continuing to **Trattoria Bora Bar** for dinner prepared by an Italian-born, U.S.-trained chef. Stay the night at **Hotel Dolphin Suites** in Veli Lošinj.

Old World Living

Traveling to less-touristed parts of Croatia and Slovenia, you'll be rewarded with typical village lodging, winery hotels, cozy restaurants, and quirky museums. Want to see the talked-about sights too? Just add a couple of days to peruse the capitals, Ljubljana and Zagreb, or combine it with a trip to the coast, since the tour has you headed in that direction anyway.

Day 1

Leaving Ljubljana, head to the small town of **Bovec,** at the edge of **Triglav National Park.** Spend the afternoon walking the paths around the rushing turquoise river before getting a good night's sleep at either the **Dobra Vila** hotel or the more rustic **Pristava Lepena,** in the middle of the mountains.

Day 2

Head to **Idrija,** famous for three things: the **Lace-Making School (Čipkarska šola),** the excellent restaurant **Gostilna Lectar,** and the **Kendov Dvorec,** an elegant castle hotel that happens to be one of Slovenia's best. A night at the hotel is worth the excursion alone.

Day 3

Cruise the **Upper Dolenjska Wine Route** or practice your swing at the **Hotel Grad Otočec.**

Day 4

Passing through Zagreb, head east on the highway to **Kutjevo,** where you can visit centuries-old cellars before unpacking your bags at the inn of modern-day winemaker **Enjingi.** Spend the afternoon wine-tasting, eating on the terrace overlooking the vineyards, and picking the vintners' brains on everything there is to know about viticulture.

Day 5

You've got about a two-hour drive to **Osijek,** where you'll tour the **Citadel (Tvrđa)** before eating local specialties like frog legs or stew at atmospheric **Kod Ruže.** Tonight you'll sleep in the red-themed guest house of **Crvendać,** just outside of Osijek.

Day 6

This morning take a tour of **Kopački rit** before heading to the **Baranja** for a trip through local wineries. Eat dinner at **Baranjska kuća,** having a look at the restaurant's ethnographic museum, and stay at the 1910-era **Sklepić house.**

Day 7

Don't leave the Sklepić house before riding in a typical Slavonian horse-drawn carriage (arranged in advance). After the ride, drive to **Ilok** for winery visits and dinner.

Day 8

Today you can drive to Slavonski Brod, stopping at the **Stupnički Dvori,** a combination winery, restaurant, and hotel, or continue on to the **Lonjsko polje** to search for storks and swimming furry pigs. Dine and stay at the **Ravlić** house, a thatched-roof cottage filled with antiques, sure to make you feel like you spent the night inside a fairy tale.

Day 9

Drive to **Samobor,** nowadays essentially a suburb of Zagreb, for small-town charm and a slice of the city's famous *kremšnita.* Walk around the town's museums and churches, or go for a hike in the area to stretch your legs after today's drive.

Day 10

This morning you'll drive to the **Gorski Kotar,** stopping at the picturesque village of **Fužine.** There's plenty to do in the area, but there are three things you shouldn't miss: the endearing **Museum of Frogs (Muzej Žaba)** in **Lokve,** lunch at **Konoba Volta** for local specialties, and a night at Tito's former hunting lodge **Bitoraj.** Tomorrow you can continue on to Kvarner and Istria, or turn around and return to Zagreb for a flight out.

vineyards in the Dolenjska Region

Bohinj Lake with the Church of St John the Baptist and bridge, Slovenia

Family Affair

Thought traveling through Europe with kids was hard? Think again. Croatia and Slovenia are very family-friendly (and Montenegro too, although it is not included in the itinerary), with lots of attractions that seem made for kids and laid-back locals who love to see young faces and hear the sound of happy noise.

Day 1

Starting in **Ljubljana,** tour the **Old Town** (kids tend to want a picture with the dragons on the Dragon Bridge), perhaps fitting in a child-friendly attraction like the **Railway Museum (Železniški muzej),** the **House of Experiments (Hiša Eksperimentov), The School Museum,** where you can take a class from yesteryear, or the clock at the **Puppet Theater (Lutkovno Gledališče),** which puts on a free show every hour during the day. Young children will love a trip to **MiniCity,** an entire city they can have the run of, while kids of all ages would enjoy a trip up to **Ljubljana castle** in the floor-to-ceiling glass **funicular (tirna vzpenjača)** to have the castle's **Time Machine tour** take them back in time.

Day 2

Head to **Bled,** where the castle and the deep-blue lake are the main attractions, though kids should like a horse-drawn carriage ride or taking a *pletna* boat to the lake's church-topped island. In season, taking the steam train to nearby **Bohinj** is a fun excursion as well.

Day 3

Driving to **Zagreb** in the early morning, take a tour around the **Upper Town (Gornji Grad)** and walk down the city's Brothers Grimm-like **Tkalčićeva Street,** stopping for cake and hot *kakao* (hot chocolate) at **Amelie.** If you have time, add a day to visit **Maksimir**'s tiny zoo or hike up **Mount Sljeme** with older kids to have a

Seaside town of Rovinj

hearty lunch of bean stew and roast chicken at the outdoor picnic tables. Try to schedule your trip over the summer to catch the excellent theatrical tour **Secrets of Grič (Tajne Griča).**

Day 4

Head into the **Gorski Kotar,** stopping at **Fužine.** Visit the village of Lokve's **Museum of Frogs (Muzej Žaba)** and walk along the river. Stay at the **Kuća Sobol,** in a peaceful valley populated by numerous butterfly species.

Day 5

Today is your family's introduction to **Istria,** stopping at the village of **Hum,** claiming to be the smallest in the world. Young ones will like lunch at the cozy **Humska Konoba** or in nearby **Kotlić,** where you can dine beside a rushing stream (perhaps too precarious a choice for very young children).

Day 6

Head to **Rovinj,** taking a tour of the old town. Child-friendly attractions not to miss are the **Kuća o batani,** a small but charming museum about the town's indigenous *batana* boat, and the market, a fun place to shop for homemade souvenirs. Later, make your way to the beaches, tailor-made for kids and even strollers, with lots of shady forests just behind to escape the sun if it gets too strong.

Days 7 and 8

Head south to Pula, where kids of all ages will enjoy the **Roman amphitheater.** From here you'll want to take an excursion to the **Brijuni Islands,** with a zoo safari park and lots of wild nature to fascinate the whole family.

the island of Vis, Croatia

Sailing the Croatian Islands

This itinerary is one of the most popular with sailors, with stops at some of Croatia's top destinations.

Days 1 and 2

Set sail from **Split** to **Milna** on the island of **Brač.** The next morning, take a short hop to **Bol,** lounging on the beaches at **Golden Horn (Zlatni Rat)** and noshing on *gregada*, or fish stew.

Day 3

Docking at **Hvar Town** on the island of **Hvar,** spend the day seeing the sights and the evening sipping wines at **Pršuta Tri Wine Bar.**

Day 4

Komiža on the island of **Vis** is the perfect place to rest after splurging in Hvar Town. The laid-back fishing village has a few must-sees for seafaring sorts, including the **Fishing Museum (Ribarski muzej)** and **Our Lady of the Pirates (Gospa Gusarica)** church. Dine at **Konoba Barba,** overlooking the water.

Day 5

Today it's time to sail to the islet of **Biševo** with its famous **Blue Cave (Modra špilja).** Then cruise the southern side of Vis to **Senko's,** a famous restaurant in a small cove in the middle of nowhere. It's definitely worth the mooring for some of Senko's fabulous cooking.

Day 6

Today it's up to **Vis Town,** where you can stop at some museums and a Greek cemetery before dining at **Pojoda,** one of the island's top seafood restaurants.

Days 7 and 8

Head back to Split, where in addition to **Diocletian's Palace** there's a don't-miss for sailing fans—the **Croatian Maritime Museum (Hrvatski pomorski muzej),** with lots of historical model ships, costumes, uniforms, and maritime memorabilia.

Zagreb

Zagreb is perhaps the perfect European capital.
With a charming Old Town, a lively café culture, and the requisite cathedral, but without loads of tourists, the city is easy to explore in a day before traveling on to the coast.

On the surface, Zagreb seems like a modern, bustling city. And in many ways, it is. The streets prowl with luxury cars and designer duds. Large international corporations have attached their logos to shiny new office buildings. And don't be surprised if you hear German, French, or Chinese: Over 45 embassies are located in the rather small capital of approximately 800,000 (closer to 1.1 million in the metro area).

Zagreb is the country's business capital, but as you cruise the streets you'll soon realize that much of this business is done over a cup of

Highlights

Look for ★ to find recommended sights, activities, dining, and lodging.

★ **Dolac Market (Tržnica Dolac):** Get into the thick of things, bumping shoulders and bargaining for fresh produce in the city's largest fresh market (page 46).

★ **Tkalčićeva Street:** This fairy tale-like street with cafés, restaurants, and local artisans is perfect for strolling, sitting, or window-shopping (page 47).

★ **Stone Gate (Kamenita vrata):** Inside this 13th-century gate is an ornate shrine where the faithful pray surrounded by flickering candles (page 49).

★ **Zagreb City Museum (Muzej grada Zagreba):** The city museum is well presented and the best way to get a thorough overview of the history and culture of the capital city in just over an hour (page 49).

★ **Meštrović Studio (Meštrović Atelier):** Arguably one of the finest Croatian artists, the former home and studio of **Meštrović** is now a museum dedicated to his life and work (page 49).

★ **Museum of Broken Relationships (Muzej Prekinutih Veza):** This Zagreb museum is so great it inspired the publication of a popular book and boasts an outpost in Los Angeles (page 52).

★ **Flower Square (Cvjetni trg):** You can't spend time in Zagreb without taking part in the citizens' favorite pastime: a long leisurely coffee (*kava*) on one of the streets near this square while watching the passersby. It's the busiest on a sunny Saturday morning (page 54).

★ **Marshal Tito Square (Trg maršala Tita):** Dominated by the wedding cake-like

Croatian National Theater, this beautiful square is also home to the must-see Museum of Arts and Crafts, a treasure trove of design, interiors, and objects in a stunning art nouveau space (page 54).

★ **Mount Medvednica:** Head to the park's most popular peak, Sljeme, to spend an afternoon on the mountain topped off with a mug of beer and a bowl of steaming hot beans (*grah*) with the locals (page 70).

strong coffee or a long lunch. The cafés are swarmed, particularly on pretty days when it just seems natural to take a meeting outside. At night the socializing continues, from old men in a small bar kicking back a *rakija* (brandy) to young people in a disco pulsing to the latest U.S. and European dance tunes.

As you delve a little deeper, you'll see a city that changes only what it wants to and at its own pace. At Dolac (Zagreb's main fresh market) the ritual of the daily market remains among the urbanization. Some locals stop for a quick prayer in the Stone Gate (Kamenita vrata), just as *zagrebčani* have done for over 250 years, and for the Saturday-morning promenade everyone gets dressed up to see and be seen while they stroll the streets around Flower Square (Cvjetni trg).

With a charming Old Town, a lively café culture, and the requisite cathedral, but without the loads of tourists à la Prague or Vienna, the city is easy to explore in a day before traveling on to the coast. The museums, while not housing great works of art, are well done and intimate, with exhibits on topics like naive art, local sculpture, and local history. Zagreb boasts glorious Secession architecture, some impeccably restored, some often going unnoticed on decaying gray facades.

Though the city is home to about a quarter of Croatia's population, it's easy to get off the beaten path and mix with the locals. The Paris-style parks or the hike up Mt. Sljeme for fresh air, folk music, and great cheap food are worth staying an extra day for, and several wonderful towns with culture, history, and almost no tourists are easily accessible for a day or even half-day trip.

You'll find the city easy to maneuver. It's not too large and practically everyone under 50 speaks English—often outstandingly good English, better than you'd find in nearby Italy or Germany. The people are friendly, too, and happy to lend a hand or a recommendation.

The city is what you make of it. You can live the glamorous life with the city's high rollers or wannabe high rollers, surrounded by a crowd that's probably dressed better than you are, or share a plate of fried sardines with the locals in a standing-room-only bar. There's the old and the new, and for the most part, it's all good.

Moving west instead of east, Zagreb is changing. It has been changing every year since Croatia's independence. But the core of Zagreb—the buzzing social vibe that moves like honey—remains the same. So whether you spend your time in the museums or in the nightclubs, by far Croatia's best, you can't leave Zagreb without ordering a coffee in a café. Just remember to drink it slowly. It's part of the experience.

HISTORY

In a nutshell, it's amazing that Zagreb has developed into the vibrant town it is today, having been threatened by wars (not to mention some fires and the occasional plague) in almost all nine centuries of its history.

Zagreb is thought to have been settled way back in the Iron Age, but the city wasn't officially established until 1094 when King Ladislaus of Hungary developed a diocese to gain more control over northern Croatia. A settlement called Kaptol developed around the diocese buildings, while Gradec, an area controlled directly by the Hungarian king, sprang up on the neighboring hill.

The two towns fought with each other over land and mills almost from the beginning. On top of that, they had to deal with outside invaders. In a particularly bitter fight with the Mongols in 1242, Gradec was so ravaged that King Bela IV granted Gradec an exemption from jurisdiction, even though he did not exempt them militarily. The exemption, called a "Golden Bull," freed Gradec's citizens of many taxes in order to entice others to move there.

Kaptol wasn't so happy about Gradec's good fortune and escalated the rivalry in

Zagreb

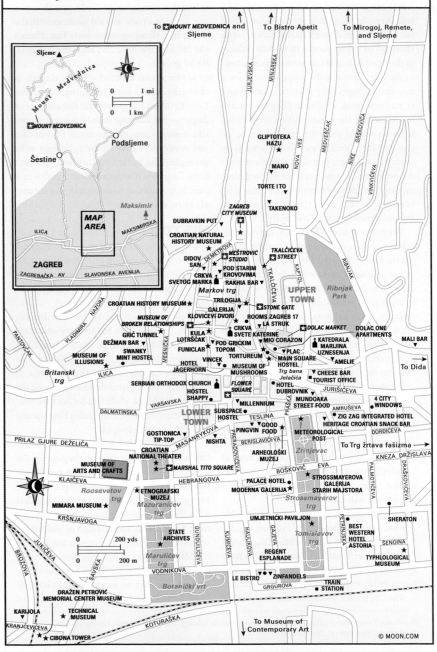

To ✚*MOUNT MEDVEDNICA* and Sljeme

To Bistro Apetit

To Mirogoj, Remete, and Sljeme

Sljeme ▲

Mount Medvednica

0 ___ 1 mi

0 ___ 1 km

✚ **MOUNT MEDVEDNICA**

Podsljeme

Šestine ○

Maksimir ↑

MAP AREA

ILICA

MAKSIMIRSKA

ZAGREB

ZAGREBAČKA AV   SLAVONSKA AVENIJA

JURJEVSKA

MINARSKA

MEDVEŠČAK   NOVA VES   GRŠKOVIĆA   NIKE   VINKVIČEVA

GLIPTOTEKA HAZU ★

MANO ▼

TORTE I TO ▼

ZAGREB CITY MUSEUM ✚   TAKENOKO

DUBRAVKIN PUT ▼

CROATIAN NATURAL HISTORY MUSEUM ★

DIDOV SAN ▼   DEMETROVA   MEŠTROVIĆ STUDIO ✚   TKALČIĆEVA STREET ✚

POD STARIM KROVOVIMA ▼

CRKVA SVETOG MARKA ▼   RAKHIJA BAR ▼

Markov trg   TKALČIĆEVA   **UPPER TOWN**   *Ribnjak Park*

TRILOGIJA ▼   RIBNJAK

CROATIAN HISTORY MUSEUM ★   GALERIJA ▼   ✚STONE GATE   KAPTOL

MUSEUM OF BROKEN RELATIONSHIPS ✚   KLOVIĆEVI DVORI ▼   ROOMS ZAGREB 17 ●

GRIČ TUNNEL ★   KULA ▲   CRKVA SVETE KATERINE ▲   ✚DOLAC MARKET   DOLAC ONE APARTMENTS

DEŽMAN BAR ▼   LOTRŠĆAK ▲   MIO CORAZON ▼   MALI BAR

SWANKY MINT HOSTEL ●   FUNICLAR ●   POD GRIČKIM TOPOM ▼   KATEDRALA MARIJINA UZNESENJA ▲

MUSEUM OF ILLUSIONS ●   HOTEL JÄGERHORN ▼   VINCEK ▼   TORTUREUM ●   PLAC ▼   MAIN SQUARE HOSTEL ●   AMELIE ▼

Britanski trg   ILICA   MUSEUM OF MUSHROOMS ▼   *Trg bana Jelačića*   CHEESE BAR ▼   To Dida

SERBIAN ORTHODOX CHURCH ♦   FLOWER SQUARE ✚   HOTEL DUBROVNIK ●   TOURIST OFFICE ★   JURIŠIĆEVA

HOSTEL SHAPPY ●   MILLENNIUM ●   MUNDOAKA STREET FOOD ▼   4 CITY WINDOWS ●

VARŠAVSKA   **LOWER TOWN**   SUBSPACE HOSTEL ●   PRAŠKA   AMRUŠEVA   ZIG ZAG INTEGRATED HOTEL ●

DALMATINSKA   TESLINA   HERITAGE CROATIAN SNACK BAR ■   ĐORĐIĆEVA

GOSTIONICA TIP-TOP ▼   NISHTA ▼   GOOD FOOD ▼   METEOROLOGICAL POST ●   To Trg žrtava fašizma →

PRILAZ GJURE DEŽELIĆA   MASANRYKOVA   PINGVIN ▼   BERISLAVIĆEVA   KNEZA DRŽISLAVA

CROATIAN NATIONAL THEATER ★   PRERADOVIĆEVA   ARHEOLOŠKI MUZEJ ●   *Zrinjevac*   EVA

MUSEUM OF ARTS AND CRAFTS ★   ★MARSHAL TITO SQUARE   BOŠKOVIĆ   PALMOTIĆEVA   DRAŠKOVIĆEVA

KLAIĆEVA   HEBRANGOVA   PALACE HOTEL ●   STROSSMAYEROVA GALERIJA STARIH MAJSTORA ★

Rooseveltov trg   ETNOGRAFSKI MUZEJ ★   MODERNA GALERIJA ★   *Strossmayerov trg*

MIMARA MUSEUM ★   *Mažuranićev trg*   GAJEVA

KRŠNJAVOGA   UMJETNIČKI PAVILJON ★   SHERATON ●

0 ___ 200 yds   STATE ARCHIVES ★   HAULIKOVA   *Tomislavov trg*   BEST WESTERN HOTEL ASTORIA ●

0 ___ 200 m   GUNDULIĆEVA   KUMIČEVA   REGENT ESPLANADE ●   PETRINJSKA   SENOINA   TYPHLOLOGICAL MUSEUM ★

JUKIČEVA   BROZOVA   SAVSKA   *Marulićev trg*   VODNIKOVA   LE BISTRO ▼   ZINFANDELS ▼▼   GRGUROVA   TRAIN STATION ■

DRAŽEN PETROVIĆ MEMORIAL CENTER MUSEUM ★   *Botanički vrt*   KOTURAŠKA

KARIJOLA ▼   TECHNICAL MUSEUM ★   To Museum of Contemporary Art ↓

KRANJČEVIĆEVA   ★ CIBONA TOWER

© MOON.COM

1247 by erecting a tower on Gradec's land; the two communities fought bitterly for decades. Several blows in the 16th century, including the loss of Kaptol lands to the Turks, the defeat of Kaptol by Hapsburg troops, and Gradec's loss of free jurisdiction, diminished the fighting and the two began to be referred to collectively as Zagreb.

Zagreb established itself as the capital of Croatia and Slavonia when the Croatian viceroy Nikola Frankopan moved his headquarters there in 1621. The 17th and 18th centuries were devastating for the city despite its new role as capital. Warfare, several fires, and two bouts of plague almost obliterated Zagreb, with the capital packing up for Varaždin to the north in 1776 and leaving less than 3,000 residents by the end of the 18th century.

The 19th century was the most prosperous for the town. The capital had centered itself in Zagreb once again and, fueled by developing industries, the city added museums, theaters, and schools.

The city continued to thrive until the formation of Yugoslavia in 1918, when the central government moved to Belgrade. And Zagreb underwent a significant transformation in the 1950s and 1960s when mayor Većeslav Holjevac built giant apartment complexes across the banks of the Sava River, adding an entire section, called New Zagreb (Novi Zagreb), to the city.

After Croatia's independence in 1991, the city struggled through the war; in the years that followed rampant corruption stagnated the country's growth. Fortunately, the city has blossomed into a vibrant and hip capital complete with tourists eager to see it.

ORIENTATION

Zagreb can be divided into dozens of neighborhoods, but the two most important for the traveler are **Upper Town** (Gornji Grad), which comprises the old town and many of the city's most charming attractions, and **Lower Town** (Donji Grad), rarely referred to as such since it *is* Zagreb—the part of the city where much of the daily hustle and bustle as well as

shopping, socializing, and business is carried out. It's also in Lower Town that you'll find most of the accommodations and restaurants as well as Zagreb's green horseshoe, a network of squares laid out in the 19th century, home to quite a few more important buildings and museums. However, recent development has reduced some of Lower Town's importance, with business towers being built slightly south of town and Western-style shopping malls popping up in the west toward Samobor and to the south in Novi Zagreb.

Novi Zagreb sprang up in the 1960s, across the Sava River, and is mostly an amalgam of soulless multistory apartment buildings, though the area has come into its own recently with the addition of a new shopping mall, relocation of a museum, and a renovation to the riverside Bundek park, a nice place for a stroll on a sunny day.

However, it's the northern suburbs, toward **Sljeme,** where the upper middle class live (and the very rich, or long ago rich, in the Tuškanac area, worth a drive if you're a fan of old houses). The hills, as they are referred to by locals, are bordered on the east by leafy Maksimir park and in the north by Sljeme, a favorite haven of city dwellers on the weekends.

PLANNING YOUR TIME

It only takes a day to get a good overview of Zagreb with a walk through Upper Town (Gornji Grad), visits to a couple of the better galleries and museums, a nice lunch, some window-shopping, and an evening out. If you have two days, though, spend the second day hiking around Sljeme or visiting one of the cities in the surrounding area, like the sugary little Samobor, on the verge of becoming a suburb of Zagreb. If you are more the city type, spend the two days in Zagreb with one day for each the Upper and Lower Town.

You'll probably want to use Zagreb as your base for exploring the area; the city's transportation system makes it pretty easy to whiz around to most of your stops by tram. The city's accommodations have finally caught up with the city's potential and there are many wonderful options in and around the city center for most price ranges.

Zagreb's main attractions are all within walking distance of each other, though you'll do a lot of walking if you want to traverse both the upper and lower towns in a day. The best plan is to see the highlights and fit in a few other stops that suit your interests, whether that's art or history or shopping, and skip the rest. Architecture buffs might really enjoy making time to see the stunning art nouveau interior at the State Archives.

Though September to May are the slowest times in terms of tourism, with summer bringing many tour groups and backpackers, Zagreb's tourist scene has increased dramatically in the past five years. Approximately 1 million tourists visit Zagreb each year. While that does mean you won't have the town to yourself, it also means that services for tourists have increased as well, making it a worthwhile tradeoff.

Remember that almost **everything is closed on Sunday** (save for most museums) and most of Upper Town's **museums are closed Monday.** In addition, most museums have shortened hours on Saturday and Sunday. Should you find yourself in town on a weekend afternoon, this is the day to head to the slopes of Sljeme or the wide promenades of Maksimir, though on a nice day it may seem the entire city had the same idea.

One of the best times to visit Zagreb is the **Advent season** (basically the entire month of December). The city has won accolades the past few years for its Advent Festival, with a winter-wonderland ice rink and many of the city's main attractions festooned and lit in a design that is more high-design than quaint. The rest of the winter is usually gray day upon another gray day, though if you happen to end up in town in winter, look on the bright side: The town's tourist attractions will be less crowded and the city looks quite romantic in winter. Be sure to head up to Sljeme, a good choice almost any time of year, for a bit of snow-packed fun.

Spring, early summer, and fall are the best times to visit Zagreb. Though fall can sometimes be rainy, it also gets its share of crisp, sunny days that somehow make the town really shine. Summer is usually bearable, but you may want to avoid town in August, when most of the locals are on the coast and the city's ratio of tourists to locals changes significantly. However, recent years have seen less of an exodus of locals in July and August, which makes the city experience that much nicer.

Itinerary Ideas

DAY ONE IN ZAGREB

1 Have breakfast at the **Regent Esplanade** hotel bright and early and imagine you're an *Orient Express* passenger from the era of luxe rail travel.

2 Wander through the stunning tree-lined **Zrinjevac** on your way to **Ban Jelačić Square (Trg bana Jelačića)**, Zagreb's main square.

3 Once there, follow the row of fresh flower stands topped with red umbrellas and climb the stairs to **Dolac Market** to join the pre-noon crowd bargaining for fresh produce.

4 After you're through with haggling, double back to historical **Tkalčićeva Street,** with its petite colorful buildings straight out of a Brothers Grimm tale. Stop into one of the many restaurants lining the street for lunch, then take a coffee and dessert at one of the cafés and do a little window-shopping.

5 From here, head to the **Upper Town (Gornji Grad)**. Stop for a photo of the colorful roof of **St. Mark's Church (Crkva svetog Marka)**.

6 Continue on to **Meštrović Studio (Meštrović Atelier)** to view over 300 of the famous artist's works and gain insight into his life.

7 Instead of taking the funicular, take the long way back down by passing through the 13th-century **Stone Gate (Kamenita vrata)**.

8 Have dinner in the lower town around **Flower Square (Cvjetni trg)**

9 For dessert, stuff your face with gelato at **Millennium,** located near the square. From here you don't need to look far to find some nightlife.

10 Sip coffee or have a beer with the hundreds of revelers sitting at outdoor cafés along Bogovićeva. If the day's history lesson hasn't worn you out, the night is young—at 10pm in Zagreb the party is just getting started.

DAY TWO IN ZAGREB

1 Have breakfast at **Le Bistro** at the Regent Esplanade.

2 Wind your way up to **Mount Medvednica's** most developed mountain, **Sljeme,** for some hiking in good weather or sledding in the winter.

3 Refuel with lunch at **Puntijarka** before heading back down to Zagreb and taking it easy the rest of the afternoon.

4 After an active day, unwind with a quiet night near the main square at **Cheese Bar** with a glass of Croatian wine.

SUNDAY ANTIQUING IN ZAGREB

1 Have a quick and early breakfast at whatever bakery you find open, and make a beeline to **Hrelić**, the city's flea market. The earlier you arrive, the better. This is the place to do some real treasure hunting, though it may take you a lot of sifting through what is truly junk, laid out on blankets on the ground, to find your bargain.

Zagreb Itinerary Ideas

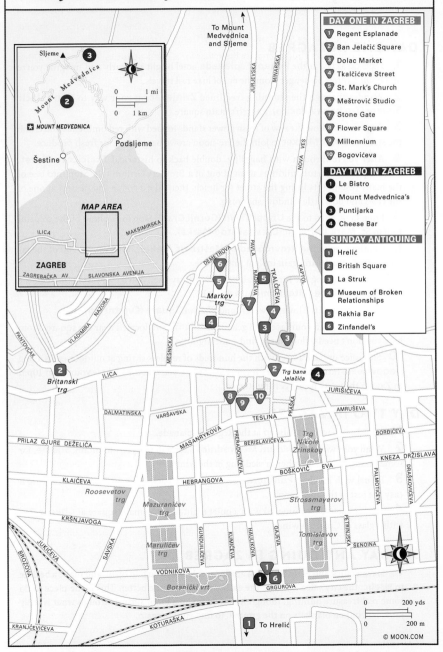

DAY ONE IN ZAGREB
1. Regent Esplanade
2. Ban Jelačić Square
3. Dolac Market
4. Tkalčićeva Street
5. St. Mark's Church
6. Meštrović Studio
7. Stone Gate
8. Flower Square
9. Millennium
10. Bogovićeva

DAY TWO IN ZAGREB
1. Le Bistro
2. Mount Medvednica's
3. Puntijarka
4. Cheese Bar

SUNDAY ANTIQUING
1. Hrelić
2. British Square
3. La Struk
4. Museum of Broken Relationships
5. Rakhia Bar
6. Zinfandel's

© MOON.COM

2 From there, head to the **British Square (Britanski trg) Antiques Market** (open until 2pm), which has a lot more high-end, and high-priced, finds to take home.

3 Have a light lunch at **La Struk** and then take a rest from your early morning jaunt.

4 In the evening, take Zagreb's antique funicular to the **Upper Town** and peruse all the junk-with-a-story at the **Museum of Broken Relationships**.

5 You might be inspired to create a backstory for all your treasures from your morning of antiquing over a glass of rakija at **Rakhia Bar.**

6 To cap off your day of bargain-hunting, splash out for a fancy meal at **Zinfandel's** in the historic Regent Esplanade, once a stop on the famed Orient Express.

Sights

BAN JELAČIĆ SQUARE AND KAPTOL

Ban Jelačić Square is the city's main square and a useful base for exploring the town. The **Kaptol** neighborhood that stretches north of the square around the cathedral is filled with restaurants, cafés, and shops, culminating in a swank shopping center, Centar Kaptol.

Ban Jelačić Square
(Trg bana Jelačića)

Ban Jelačić Square has been a meeting point for centuries of locals. Before being officially designated the main square in the 1850s, it served as a point for fairs and tax collections and was known as "Harmica" (after the Hungarian *harmincad,* which means a thirtieth).

Today the square is flanked by some beautiful, if not a little over-the-top, examples of classicist and Secessionist architecture sporting ugly signs for multinational corporations on their roofs. What the square lacks in charm it makes up for in convenience. As the city's largest tram stop, it's the perfect departure point for seeing the sights and is a popular meeting place for visitors and locals alike. Before heading off, you can stop at the main **tourist office** (Trg bana Jelačića 11, tel. 01/481-4051, www.infozagreb.hr, 8:30am-8pm Mon-Fri, 9am-6pm Sat., 10am-4pm Sun. and holidays), located on the southeastern edge of the square.

The square is rimmed with cafés that are a watering hole for Zagreb's older elite, politicians, and writers as well as unsuspecting tourists who will find the prices almost double those of other locations. Ban Jelačić Square is also the site of loud free concerts, political rallies, homecomings for sports figures, and several markets, the largest of which is held at Christmas, with wooden huts selling gifts, souvenirs, and homemade cookies.

Presiding over the square is the **statue of Ban Josip Jelačić,** sculpted by Viennese artist Antun Fernkorn in 1866. Ban Jelačić is a national hero, a Croatian count and general who abolished serfdom and broke ties with Hungary during a rebellion in 1848. The statue used to face north, with Jelačić's saber pointing in rebellion against the Austro-Hungarian empire. The Socialist government dismantled the statue in 1947 and it remained in the Academy of Arts and Sciences until 1990, when it was returned to the square, now facing south.

The **Manduševac Fountain,** on the eastern side of the square, is tied to the history of the city in several interesting ways. The site sits on a natural spring that was long a source of water for the city. Legend has it that a war leader returned to the city and asked a beautiful girl named Manda to scoop up some water for him. The story goes that the spring then got its name from the girl, and the city Zagreb got its name from the verb to scoop, *zagrabiti.*

Court records also mention the spring as the meeting point for witches, which was used as some of the evidence in their persecution.

Museum of Mushrooms

Trg bana Jelačića 3; tel.01/481-9528; 10am-4pm Mon.-Fri.; 20Kn

In Ban Jelačić Square, in the alley where the flower sellers are found before 2pm most days, is one of Zagreb's most quirky attractions, the Museum of Mushrooms. On the second floor of a fairly nondescript building you will find around 1,500 species of mushrooms and their edibility classification.

★ Dolac Market
(Tržnica Dolac)

Dolac 9; tel. 01/642-2501; www.trznice-zg.hr; mornings until 2pm daily

North of Ban Jelačić Square, follow the row of fresh flower stands topped with red umbrellas and climb the stairs to Dolac Market, the city's main market since 1930. If you're looking for the heart and soul of Zagreb, you'll find it here. Old men drink tiny glasses of brandy at the old cafés along the market's edges and watch the crowd bargaining with vendors for fresh produce, herbs, eggs, and homemade cheeses. Summer Fridays and Saturdays, you'll also spot actors dressed in traditional folk costume to remember the old days. But any time of year the atmosphere is warm and friendly, and you'll find that even those who can't speak English will try and converse and are always happy to dole out advice and recipes.

This is also a great spot to search for souvenirs. From the more predictable embroidered tablecloths, some in good taste and some not, to the quirky elixirs and health remedies, you should be able to find something worth sticking in your suitcase.

My recommendation is to buy a fresh *burek* from one of the bread shops on the edge to eat right away, and pick up some local olives or a jar of domestic honey seasoned with lavender or rosemary for the trip home.

Cathedral of the Assumption of the Blessed Virgin Mary
(Katedrala Marijina Uznesenja)

Kaptol 31; tel. 01/481-4727; 10am-5pm Mon.-Sat., 1pm-5pm Sun. and religious holidays; free

The tall, lacy spires of the Cathedral of the Assumption of the Blessed Virgin Mary can be seen from many parts of Zagreb, and though the church is grand, it seems a bit out of place with its more modest surroundings. Built on the site of a small Romanesque church constructed in 1217 by King Ladislaus, the present cathedral, constructed in the last half of the 13th century, is now a largely neo-Gothic structure.

A planned renovation to the cathedral in the 19th century became a near rebuilding of the church after a catastrophic earthquake in 1880. The Viennese architect Hermann Bollé integrated the design of the church, which had suffered from a mish-mash of styles following years of raids, various archbishops, and subsequent renovations that had all left their mark. Four Renaissance choir stalls and a few medieval frescoes are all that remain of the cathedral before the earthquake.

Other items of note: the carved panels on the side altar are by Albrecht Dürer and a subtle relief is by Ivan Meštrović, marking the grave of the controversial Archbishop Alojzije Stepinac. During the Advent season, the Cathedral is decorated with lights, making it an even more beautiful place to visit, particularly once the sun has set. Mass is at 7am, 8am, 9am, and 6pm Mondays to Saturdays, and 7am, 8am, 9am, 10am, 11:30am, and 6pm on Sundays.

Flanking the southern side of the cathedral, the 18th-century **Archbishop's Palace** is also quite different than the original structure. All that remains today are the medieval-like turrets.

Ribnjak Park

Free

Though it's slightly off the beaten tourist track, this sweet little well-maintained park

Bloody Bridge (Krvavi Most)

The street called Krvavi Most was once a bridge spanning Medveščak Creek (today Tkalčićeva Street). The creek served as a border between the settlements of Kaptol and Gradec, who rarely got along. Residents from both sides had mills along the creek and often got into skirmishes. However, the bridge really got its name from a 1667 battle in which the soldiers of Viceroy Zrinski attacked the citizens of Gradec, resulting in so many injuries and deaths that the waters of the creek supposedly ran red. The bridge was demolished in 1899 after the creek was filled in, but the tiny street's name keeps a piece of town history alive.

in the heart of the city is a nice spot to eat your finds from Dolac. Once exclusively for the use of Kaptol's priests, the park was opened to the public in 1947.

Glyptotheque of the Croatian Academy of Sciences and Arts
(Gliptoteka Hazu)

Medvedgradska 2; tel. 01/468-6050; www.gliptoteka. *mdc.hr; 11am-7pm Tues.-Fri., 10am-2pm Sat.-Sun.* *spring/summer/autumn, 10am-4pm Mon.-Fri. winter;* *20Kn*

Though this warehouse-like space, once a leather tannery, houses mostly plaster replicas of sculpture and even medieval gravestones, there are a few original pieces, and the whole collection is so well presented that it might be worth the trip if you have some extra time or are in the area. The space also has exhibits of photography, art, design, and architecture throughout the year. Check their website or the tourist office to see what's on.

★ Tkalčićeva Street

Just south of the Gliptoteka in the direction of Ban Jelačić Square, you'll find **Centar Kaptol** (Nova ves 11, tel. 01/486-0241, www. centarkaptol.hr, 9am-9pm Mon.-Sat., 9am-2pm Sun., holiday hours vary), a shopping mall that houses a multiplex cinema as well as several chic cocktail bars and restaurants frequented by the city's young elite.

As you continue further south, the street runs into Tkalčićeva Street, marked by the beginning of a pedestrian zone. Often referred to simply as Tkalča by the locals, the street is

one of the city's social hubs, packed with bars and restaurants.

But what is now a stream of people was once an actual stream bed, forming a boundary between the cities of Gradec and Kaptol. The stream was rerouted due to sewage issues and in the 18th century it became a center for manufacturing, its length lined with workshops making soap, stonework, and liquor, as well as a leather factory.

Today the street's petite colorful buildings with gingerbread windows look like something straight out of a Brothers Grimm tale. However, don't let Tkalčićeva's old-world charm deceive you. It is also home to many up-and-coming Croatian artisans. Spend some time shopping the street's jewelry ateliers, galleries, and clothing boutiques.

As you stroll, stop for a photo with the sculpture of **Marija Jurić Zagorka,** one of Croatia's first female journalists and writers. Her most famous work is *The Witch of Grič,* set amongst the 18th-century's witch hunts. The statue, by sculptor Stjepan Gračan, was erected in 1991.

Radićeva Street

Quickly becoming a rival to Tkalčićeva's history of shops and boutiques, the cobblestoned Radićeva, west of and running parallel to Tkalčićeva, slopes toward the old town and is lined with great local artisans and souvenir shops as well as some nice restaurants. The street is named after Croatian politician Pavle Radić, assassinated in Parliament in Belgrade in 1928 while debating. At the top of Radićeva is a statue of **St. George** after he

killed the dragon. Made by Austrian sculptors Kompatscher and Winder, it was brought to Zagreb in the early 20th century but didn't arrive at its current location until 1994.

TORTUREUM
(Museum of Torture)
Radićeva 14; tel. 01/645-9803; www.tortureum.com; 11am-7pm daily; 40 Kn
A recent macabre addition to Zagreb's museum scene, the Tortureum is a small but well-presented museum, with personal tablets to explain each torture device in painstaking detail. You can also enter the museum from 13 Tkalčićeva Street.

UPPER TOWN
(Gornji Grad)
Upper Town is the heart of Zagreb and the oldest part of town. The area is full of charm and character and has a good portion of the city's best museums and galleries.

★ Stone Gate
(Kamenita vrata)
Forming the eastern entrance of the city walls, the cavern-like Stone Gate, built in 1241 by the Hungarian King Bela IV, is the only gate that remains of the original four that led into the city. The gate has survived renovations, fires, and various motions by the city to tear it down. The last fire, in 1731, spared a small painting of the Virgin Mary and locals considered it a miracle. A small shrine was formed, with an intricate Baroque iron gate to protect the painting inside a small niche. Candles flicker against the dark space, lit by those who come to pray and seek help from the Virgin of the Stone Gate, whom the archbishop of Zagreb proclaimed a special protector of the city in 1991.

The rooms in the building that line the city gate were originally used as storage areas, but in the 17th century they were converted into small shops. The **pharmacy at Kamenita Street 9** continues the apothecary tradition started in the 14th century, when a pharmacy occupied the same space. A plaque on the building claims that the grandson of the famous author Dante worked in the apothecary in 1399.

★ Zagreb City Museum
(Muzej grada Zagreba)
Opatička 20; tel. 01/485-1361; www.mgz.hr; 10am-7pm Tues.-Sat.,10am-2pm Sun., closed holidays; 30Kn
Following the city's development from prehistory to the 20th century, Zagreb City Museum is definitely worth a visit to get a feel for Zagreb's origins and history. Located in the 17th-century convent of the Poor Clares, the museum houses a good mix of exhibits, including portraits, regional dress, everyday objects, socialist posters, and several scale models of Zagreb throughout the centuries. Children will enjoy the re-creations of early-20th-century storefronts and a room dedicated to Croatian animation. Most impressive, though, is the somber yet exquisite reconstructed portal of the cathedral before its 19th-century renovation. The addition of descriptions in English has made the museum a must-see during your stay for a great view of the city through the ages.

TOP EXPERIENCE

★ Meštrović Studio
(Meštrović Atelier)
Mletačka 8; tel. 01/485-1123; www.mestrovic.hr; 10am-6pm Mon.-Fri., 10am-2pm Sat.-Sun., closed holidays; 30Kn
The Meštrović Studio is in the Zagreb home where Ivan Meštrović lived between 1924 and 1942. This cozy little museum is not only home to some 300 sculptures and drawings by the famous sculptor but is also an intimate look into the life of the artist. His sunny studio is light-filled even on a rainy day and is so simple and beautiful that it may be hard to leave.

1: Marija Juric Zagorka, Croatia's first female journalist 2: Cathedral of the Assumption of the Blessed Virgin Mary 3: Ban Jelacic Square

Ivan Meštrović, Croatia's Most Famous Sculptor

The sculptor Ivan Meštrović was born in 1883 in Slavonia, though he spent most of his life in Drniš in Dalmatia. His family was poor, and daily chores left no time for him to go to school, though he managed to teach himself to read and write. He was an excellent self-taught artist and managed to land an apprenticeship with a stonemason in Split, where he was discovered and sent to study at Vienna's prestigious Academy of Art.

Meštrović's talent gained him success almost from the start, and soon his work was a part of important exhibitions, and he was receiving commissions for pieces like *The Well of Life*, in front of the Croatian National Theater. His early pieces reflect the influence of Rodin, whom he knew in Vienna, but his work quickly developed a style all his own.

Meštrović is an important figure not only for his talent as a sculptor but also for the political impact he had as an artist. Committed to the idea of a unified Slav nation, Meštrović began his artistic political statements by including a sculpture of the Serbian hero Kraljević Marko in a 1910 exhibition (today it's in his studio in Zagreb) and placing his work in the Serbian Pavilion at the Rome International Exhibition in 1911 as a statement in support of a unified Slav state.

Meštrović returned to Croatia in the 1920s, turning away from political themes and producing the Račić Memorial Chapel in Cavtat and the statue of Gregorius of Nin for the city of Split.

Imprisoned by the Ustaše in 1941, he was later freed and allowed to leave the country. Although Tito tried to get Meštrović to return to his homeland, the sculptor opted to work as a professor in the United States, where his 1924 sculpture of two Native Americans on horseback decorates Grant Park in Chicago.

Most of the work in his later life revolves around religious themes. He died in 1962 and was laid to rest in the Church of the Holy Redeemer in Otavice, which he had built as his family's resting place years before.

St. Mark's Church
(Crkva svetog Marka)

Trg svetog Marka 5; tel. 01/485-1611; 11am-4pm and 5:30pm-7pm daily, posted hours not always observed; free

St. Mark's Church just might be one of the most photographed buildings in Croatia. Its colorful roof tiles, the most unique feature of the church, depict the coat of arms of Zagreb (the white castle on a red background) and the Triune Kingdom of Croatia, Slavonia, and Dalmatia (on the left if you're facing the church). You'll probably recognize the red and white checkerboard design, called the *šahovnica,* from the modern-day Croatian flag. It has been a symbol of Croatia since medieval times. Dalmatia is represented by the three lions' heads and Slavonia by the animal, actually a marten or *kuna,* the national animal of Croatia and also its currency's namesake.

The Romanesque window on the south side of the church helps support the claim that the church may have been built as early as the 13th century, but earthquake, fire, and well-intentioned reconstructions have left little of the original structure. The simple Gothic church has a rather pretty south portal, original to the church, the work of 15th-century sculptors from Prague. Neo-Gothic elements were added by the architect Herman Bollé at the end of the 19th century. There are several works in the church by sculptor Ivan Meštrović in the 1930s, including the crucifix above the main altar, the Pieta, and the Madonna as a village woman.

Mass is at 6pm Monday through Friday, 7:30am on Saturday, and 10:30am and 6pm on Sunday.

1: St. Mark's Church 2: Zagreb's funicular, connecting the Ilica street with Strossmayer promendade 3: Zagreb's 13th-century Stone Gate

St. Mark's Square
(Markov trg)

Outside the church on Markov trg, if you have the feeling you're being watched, you probably are. The square is home to Croatia's government, and men in dark suits protecting the country's politicos are a regular fixture here, explaining the proliferation of sleek black cars parked in the square. At the corner of the square and Ćirilometodska Street is the **Town Hall,** now used only for special meetings of Zagreb's Town Council and wedding ceremonies. The **Sabor,** or parliament, is housed in the buildings on the eastern side of the square, and the **Governor's Palace (Banski dvor),** the former Baroque residence of the civil governor of Croatia, is now the official seat of the government. It was also once the home of Ban Josip Jelačić.

Croatian History Museum
(Hrvatski povijesni muzej)

Matoševa 9; tel. 01/485-1900; www.hismus.hr; 10am-6pm Mon.-Fri., 10am-1pm Sat.-Sun., closed holidays; 15Kn

Housed in a refreshed Baroque mansion, the small Croatian History Museum shows interesting and well-presented temporary exhibitions pulled from the museum's collection of over 140,000 items. However, this museum shouldn't be the first on your list unless you are a big history fan or have a lot of time.

Croatian Natural History Museum
(Hrvatski prirodoslovni muzej)

Demetrova 1; tel. 01/485-1700; www.hpm.hr; 10am-5pm Tues., Wed., and Fri., 10am-8pm Thurs., 10am-7pm Sat., 10am-1pm Sun., closed holidays; 30Kn

In what could be a great setting for a Wes Anderson film, the Croatian Natural History Museum houses mediocre temporary exhibits, but the most interesting displays are the permanent collections on the 2nd floor. Skeletons, specimens in glass bottles, and stuffed birds and mammals showcased in old-fashioned glass cabinets provide an experience from another era; it's even a little creepy if you happen to be the only visitor. The most fetching display is the eight-meter (26-foot) basking shark, found in the Adriatic in the 1930s.

★ Museum of Broken Relationships
(Muzej Prekinutih Veza)

Sv. Ćirila i Metoda 2; tel. 01/485-1021; www.brokenships.com; 9am-10:30pm June-Sept., 9am-9pm Oct.-May, closed holidays; 40Kn

Started in Zagreb as a touring exhibit, the Museum of Broken Relationships houses artifacts from failed romances around the world. Founded by two Croatian artists, the museum now has a permanent outpost in Los Angeles and an internationally distributed book showcasing the museum's exhibits. Objects that signified the end of a relationship, from toys and postcards to fuzzy handcuffs and three volumes of Proust, are accompanied by the stories they tell. You will leave with a sense of having read a hundred romances, some funny, some sad, but all quite human. With translations of the stories of the objects in English, the museum is a must-see and easy to add to an evening in the old town thanks to its extended hours.

Croatian Museum of Naive Art
(Hrvatski muzej naivne umjetnosti)

Sv. Ćirila i Metoda 3; tel. 01/485-1911; www.hmnu.org; 10am-6pm Tues.-Fri., 10am-1pm Sat. and Sun., closed holidays; 20Kn

The small Croatian Museum of Naive Art is a don't-miss, if only for the simple, almost organic art it displays. The artists, all untrained, depict sometimes lively, sometimes depressing, scenes of peasant and village life. Most of the works are by the movement's most famous painter, Ivan Generalić, though other artists—even those from outside of Croatia but who embody the naive style—are also on display.

Naive Art

The naive art movement in Croatia was started in the late 1920s and 1930s by an academically trained artist, Krsto Hegedušić, who found similarities to French naive painter Henri Rousseau in a small group of painters in the village of Hlebine. With his support, self-taught artists like Ivan Generalić and Franjo Mraz began exhibiting more widely and started using a traditional technique of painting on glass with oil.

Though their work does include a few jaunty pictures of village life, most of Generalić's and Mraz's work is dark and sometimes gruesome, portraying the hardships of peasants and the realities of war. The strong political messages and socialist exhibitions by the Hlebine painters came to an ugly end when Mirko Virius, an artist with a no-holds-barred approach to depicting rural poverty, was killed by the Ustaše in a concentration camp.

The movement then entered a surrealist phase, with works by Ivan Generalić and a new generation of naive painters that included his son Josip and another artist, Ivan Rabuzin, displaying often distorted dreamlike pieces.

Much of naive art today is more decorative than artistic, though the village of Hlebine remains a haven for the purest form of the craft.

Klovićevi dvori Gallery
(Galerija Klovićevi dvori)
Jezuitski trg 4, tel. 01/485-2117, www.gkd.hr, 11am-7pm Tues.-Sun., 40Kn

Jezuitski trg (Jesuit's Square), marked by the fountain depicting a fisherman wrestling a snake, is home to the Klovićevi dvori Gallery, once a 17th-century Jesuit monastery. It now hosts important exhibitions, often of well-known international artists such as Picasso and Chagall.

Jesuit Church of St. Catherine
(Crkva svete Katerine)

In Katarinin trg, or St. Catherine's Square—a square neighboring Jesuit's Square—is the 17th-century Jesuit Church of St. Catherine (Crkva svete Katerine) (10am-1pm daily, free), a jewel-box Baroque church that is worth a peek. Built between 1620 and 1632, it is the earliest example of Baroque religious architecture in Zagreb. The facade was damaged in the 1880 earthquake and rebuilt by architect Herman Bollé. Behind the church there is a beautiful view of the city not to be missed.

Burglars' Tower
(Kula lotrščak)
Strossmayerovo šetalište 9; tel. 01/485-1768;
www.gkd.hr/kula-lotrscak; 9am-9pm Mon.-Fri., 10am-9pm Sat. and Sun.; 20Kn

The Romanesque Burglars' Tower, dating from the 13th century, was built by the people of Gradec to protect the city from the Tatars and thieves. At the time, loud bells warned citizens of fires, storms, and the closing of the city gates every evening. In the 19th century a fourth floor was added and later a cannon, to help the churches' bell-ringers know when it was noon.

The cannon is still fired every day at noon, these days letting locals know it's time for lunch. Hike up the narrow staircase for a red-tiled-roof view of Zagreb.

In front of the tower you'll find **Strossmayer's path (Strossmayerovo šetalište)**, a promenade named after Josip Juraj Strossmayer, bishop of Đakovo. It's worth a stroll to see the magnificent city views and pose on the bench with the sculpture of poet Antun Gustav Matoš, one of Croatia's best-loved poets.

Funicular
(Uspinjača)
Tomićeva ulica; tel. 01/483-3912; every 10 minutes 6:30am-10pm daily; 4Kn one-way

At the base of Burglars' Tower, the funicular

transports passengers—some 750,000 a year—down to the lower town (and back up again if they wish). The 66-meter-long (216-foot-long) funicular, the shortest in the world, is one of the oldest forms of public transportation in the city, established around the same time the horse-drawn tram appeared on Zagreb's streets. During Advent weekends the funicular is free.

Grič Tunnel
(Tunel Grič)
Mesnička 19; 9am-10pm daily; free

The Grič Tunnel is an underground passage built as an air-raid shelter during World War II and used as a bomb shelter during the Croatian War of Independence. It connects Mesnička and Radićeva streets and takes about 10-15 minutes to walk through. It is well-lit and offers a cool respite on a hot day. During Advent, the tunnel is decorated beautifully, and you will not regret taking a few minutes to see it.

LOWER TOWN
(Donji Grad)

Though Lower Town is slightly younger and a lot busier than the cobblestoned Upper Town, the area is a must-see for its museums, its charming network of squares, and most of all, for a taste of bustling Zagreb life. Don't leave without a coffee on Flower Square among the locals.

From the bottom of the funicular that runs from the upper town it's just a short walk south to **Ilica**, a busy street filled with shops that connects the main square, **Ban Jelačić Square**, with **British Square (Britanski trg)** to the west. Cross over Ilica (watch for trams when you cross) and make your way to **Flower Square (Cvjetni trg)** and the café-lined **Bogovićeva** for a peek into the social side of the city.

★ Flower Square
(Cvjetni trg)

Locals almost never refer to this square by its official name, Preradović's Square (Preradovićev trg), but instead call it Flower Square (Cvjetni trg), because it was the site of a Parisian-style flower market until the 1980s and is still the home of several florist stands. The streets that branch off of the square are the place to be seen on Saturday mornings; sunny days seem to bring out all of Zagreb to the cafés along Bogovićeva and Preradovićeva. Before leaving Cvjetni trg to have a coffee yourself, peep inside the small **Serbian Orthodox Church (Pravoslavna crkva)** (hours vary, free). The quiet, icon-filled space is a tranquil respite from the activity outside.

Ilica Street

Ilica is Zagreb's main high street and the place locals have gone for decades to shop. While shopping centers outside the center have changed that a great deal, the street is still bustling as it not only houses shops but also connects Ban Jelačić Square with British Square (Britanski Trg), two important tram and social hubs for the city.

Museum of Illusions
(Muzej Iluzija)
Ilica 72; tel. 01/799-9609; www.muzejiluzija.com; 9am-10pm daily; 40Kn

The Museum of Illusions opened its doors in 2015 to offer more than 70 exhibits that not only play tricks on your eyes but highlight how our brain doesn't always process the truth properly. Walk in a slanted room, look in a true mirror, or take a picture of your head on a platter.

★ Marshal Tito Square
(Trg maršala Tita)

The center of Marshal Tito Square is dominated by the **Croatian National Theater (Hrvatsko Narodno Kazalište)**, a massive yellow neo-Baroque wedding cake of a building. On the western side of the square, you'll find the **Museum of Arts and Crafts (Muzej za umjetnost i obrt)**. The northern and eastern sides of the square are flanked by the beautiful buildings of Zagreb's **Law Faculty (Pravni Fakultet),** holding their own against the theater with their more austere but equally glorious Austro-Hungarian facades.

The square is also home to three sculptures. Ivan Meštrović's beautiful 1905 piece *Well of Life* is in front of the theater, while his *History of the Croats* stands in front of the yellow building in the northwest corner. And, tucked amongst the trees in the southwestern corner, is a piece by Fernkorn of St. George killing a dragon.

CROATIAN NATIONAL THEATER
(Hrvatsko Narodno Kazalište)

Trg maršala Tita 15; tel. 01/482-8532; www.hnk.hr

Built by Viennese architects Ferdinand Fellner and Herman Helmer, who designed 40 theaters in Europe, the Croatian National Theater was opened in 1895 by the Emperor Franz Josef I, who beat on the balcony above the main entrance with a silver hammer. Inside the domed ceilings, frescoes and gilt-laden balconies are just the right environment for taking in an opera or a ballet, a must if you want to get a peek at the interior. Or, just walk up and see if it happens to be open.

MUSEUM OF ARTS AND CRAFTS
(Muzej za umjetnost i obrt)

Trg maršala Tita 10; tel. 01/488-2111; www.muo.hr; 10am-7pm Tues.-Sat., 10am-2pm Sun.; 40Kn

The Museum of Arts and Crafts is a veritable wonderland for anyone who loves interiors. Its impressive exhibits range from furniture to porcelain to religious art, and the space itself, with its central atrium rimmed with intricate cast-iron handrails, is truly a don't-miss for design fans.

Mimara Museum
(Muzej Mimara)

Trg Franklina Roosevelta 5; tel. 01/482-8100; www.mimara.hr; 10am-5pm Tues., Wed., Fri., and Sat., 10am-7pm Thurs., 10am-2pm Sun. Oct.-June, 10am-7pm Tues.-Fri., 10am-5pm Sat., 10am-2pm Sun. July-Sept.; 40Kn

Housed in a sprawling 19th-century building, once a local high school, the Mimara Museum is the collection of Ante Topić Mimara, who made money abroad and donated the artwork he amassed to the nation. There's lots of controversy surrounding Mimara, from just who he was, to how he made his money, to whether

Croatian National Theatre, Marshal Tito Square

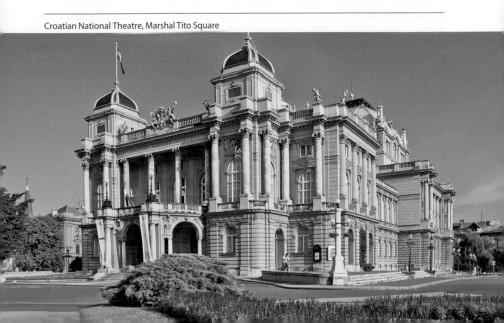

Tito Sentiment

The tiny village of Kumrovec is all but deserted on a typical day, leaving the birthplace of Josip Broz Tito, his statue in front of the barn, and the rest of the small town rather abandoned and forgotten. But come to town on May 4 (the anniversary of his death) or May 25 (the anniversary of his birthday, long celebrated in former Yugoslavia as Dan Mladosti, or Day of Youth) and you'll see a different story as people gather in the Zagorje village to remember and celebrate Tito. In 2005, in fact, 25 years after Tito's death, there were over 10,000 attendees, from Croatia, Serbia, and Bosnia.

As the years have passed since Tito's death in 1980, opinions about the former dictator of Yugoslavia have been increasingly positive. Close to half of Slovenians polled in 2000 referred to their opinion of Tito as "excellent" or "good," with only 10 percent responding "poor." There are also plenty of Croatians who remember him fondly, with 60 percent of those polled voting to have his body moved from Belgrade back to Kumrovec (which has not happened, by the way). All this enthusiasm may seem hard to imagine given all the bad things that went with his regime: The suppression of even a word against Tito, the tendency to throw people into prison over nothing, the Bleiburg massacre, the repression of the Church (state employees were not allowed to attend church if they wanted to keep their jobs), and the Croatian Spring debacle are just a few examples.

But people tend to remember the good, such as how Yugoslavians were the wealthiest and freest in Eastern Europe, putting them above their neighbors. Things haven't improved as rapidly as people hoped for since the fall of the Berlin Wall, and that makes some people nostalgic. Some also miss the security of a state job and a state-provided apartment. Yet plenty remember the hardships of living under the Tito regime. And so, for the time being, there will still be one or two news stories a year about people fighting to have the name of Tito Square changed and people fighting to keep it the way it is.

some of the pieces in his collection are real or fake.

With close to 4,000 works of art and some big names attached like Van Gogh, Rubens, Renoir, and Manet, plus prehistoric artifacts, glassware, and sculpture, the museum displays just about everything that falls under the heading "art."

Ethnographic Museum
(Etnografski muzej)

Trg Mažuranića 14; tel. 01/482-6220; www.emz.hr; 10am-6pm Tues.-Fri., 10am-1pm Sat.-Sun.; 20Kn

One of the most under-visited museums in town, the Ethnographic Museum not only has an impressive collection of regional costumes from around the country, but the building itself, with a gorgeous Art Nouveau cupola, is worth checking out. Items on exhibit have descriptions in English.

State Archives
(Državni arhiv)

Marulićev trg 21; tel. 01/480-1999; www.arhiv.hr; 8:15am-3:45pm Mon.-Wed., 8:15am-5:45pm Thurs., 8:15am-2:45pm Fri.; 20Kn

Most people would bypass the State Archives on **Marulić Square (Marulićev trg)** with only a passing nod to the beautiful building, built in 1913 as the University Library. However, if you have the time it's really worth catching the daily guided tours (times vary; see website for updated schedule) to see the interior of one of the city's most impressive art nouveau buildings. The building is full of elaborate marble and dripping, decadent crystal chandeliers. Best are the reading rooms, full of soaring ceilings and leaded-glass windows, particularly the Professor's Reading Room. A sort of chapel to academia, the cozy wood-paneled room is filled with its share of opulence, particularly the art nouveau paintings of nudes celebrating higher

Regent Esplanade Hotel

Even if a night at the Regent Esplanade is out of your budget, this landmark of rail travel deserves a stop to admire the marble and mirrored art nouveau lobby and perhaps have a drink in the piano bar before continuing on your tour of the city.

Built in 1925 for *Orient Express* passengers when Zagreb was a stop on the original Venice-Simplon *Orient Express*, the hotel has a long list of famous people who enjoyed its glory days—past guests include Josephine Baker, Charles Lindbergh, Laurence Olivier, and Louis Armstrong.

The hotel has been home to many local scandals since its debut but saw its darkest days as the last guests disappeared at the beginning of World War II, only to be replaced by hundreds of German officers when the Gestapo chose the hotel as its headquarters in the area. The hotel was neglected during its years as part of Yugoslavia but was tastefully renovated in 2004, regaining the aura it had so long ago.

learning. Behind the building, facing the Botanical Gardens, is a statue of Marko Marulić, the 15th-century poet the square is named after.

Botanical Gardens
(Botanički vrt)
Marulićev trg 9a; tel. 01/489-8066; botanickivrt.biol.
pmf.hr; 9am-sunset or 7pm, Apr.-Oct.; free
The land for the Botanical Gardens was given as a gift to the University of Zagreb from the city in 1889 on the condition that its gates would be open to the public free of charge. Over 100 years later, the university still honors the promise and provides a green oasis for locals and visitors to stop and reflect in the center of the city. Open spring through fall, the winding gravel paths pass through nicely maintained flower beds and thousands of specimens of plants. You'll see families out for a stroll, young couples meeting for a chat during their lunch break, or those who just decided to take a greener detour amid the car-packed city streets. Don't miss the beautifully restored **Exhibition Pavilion**, which as recently as 2004 was decaying into ruin.

Tomislav Square
(Tomislavov trg)
East of the Botanical Gardens and past the grand **Regent Esplanade hotel** is a long stretch of green that signals your arrival at

Tomislav Square. In this square, named for the first Croatian king, a statue of the 10th-century Tomislav on horseback greets travelers spilling out of the **Main Train Station (Glavni kolodvor)**. In December, it's home to a temporary ice-skating rink.

At the other end of the square is the yellow-hued neoclassical **Art Pavilion (Umjetnički paviljon)** (Trg kralja Tomislava 22, tel. 01/484-1070, www.umjetnicki-paviljon.hr, 11am-7pm Tues.-Sun., 30Kn), designed by Viennese architects Ferdinand Fellner and Hermann Helmer. Opened in 1898, it still hosts temporary art exhibits and special functions.

Typhlological Museum
(Tiflološki Muzej)
Draškovićeva 80/II; tel. 01/481-1102;
www.tifloloskimuzej.hr; 9am-4pm Mon.-Wed.
and Fri., 9am-8pm Thur.; 20Kn
The Typhlological Museum is a journey into the world of those without sight. The museum has some interesting interactive exhibits, like the Dark Room, where you can experience what it is like to be blind, and a typewriter on which you can type in Braille and take the paper with you as a souvenir. You can also learn about Braille, appreciate sculptures created by blind artists, and more. All exhibits are labeled in English and in Braille.

Strossmayer Gallery of Old Masters
(Strossmayerova galerija starih majstora)

Trg N. Š. Zrinskog 11; tel. 01/489-5117; 10am-7pm Tues., 10am-4pm Wed.-Fri., 10am-1pm Sat.-Sun.; 30Kn

The Strossmayer Gallery of Old Masters is a small but impressive collection of rich paintings, including works by Tintoretto and El Greco, located in the Croatian Academy of Arts and Sciences. The most important Croatian work on display is the 11th-century **Baška tablet (Bašćanska ploča),** found on the island of Krk. It is the oldest example of Glagolitic script, the writing of the medieval Croatian church. A statue by Ivan Meštrović of Bishop Juraj Strossmayer, the founder of the Yugoslav Academy for Arts and Sciences, is located behind the building.

Modern Gallery
(Moderna galerija)

Andrije Hebranga 1; tel. 01/604-1040; www.moderna-galerija.hr; 11am-7pm Tues.-Fri., 11am-2pm Sat.-Sun.; 40Kn

Across the street from the Strossmayer Gallery is the Modern Gallery, with a nice permanent exhibition entitled *200 Years of Croatian Art.*

Zrinjevac

Possibly the prettiest of Zagreb's squares, lined by giant trees with crackled white and gray bark and surrounded by some of the city's prettiest architecture, Zrinjevac was used as the city's cattle market when it was moved from Ban Jelačić Square in 1830. The square was turned into a park in 1872, the same year the now-massive plane trees were planted, using seeds from Trieste, Italy. Named for the 16th-century count Zrinski, who died fighting the Turks, it was designed by Milan Lenucij, who went on to design the other squares (Strossmayer, Tomislav, Starčević, Marulić, Mažuranić, Maršal Tito) that form the city's green "horseshoe." Soon Zagreb's elite were constructing mansions along the square; the grand buildings are a great sampling of the city's most prominent architects during the late 19th and early 20th century. In the summer, classical music concerts are often held in the music pavilion, and the fountain designed by Bollé still patters with water. However, perhaps the two most interesting features of the square are the **meteorological post,** donated by a local doctor in 1884, where you can check the ever-changing weather, and the **portrait** by Oton Iveković of the square's namesake, Nikola Zrinksi, at No. 20.

Zrinjevac

Archaeological Museum
(Arheološki muzej)

Trg N. Š. Zrinskog 19; tel. 01/487-3000; www.amz.hr; 10am-6pm Tues., Wed., Fri., and Sat., 10am-8pm Thur., 10am-1pm Sun.; 30Kn, free first Sunday of the month

The Archaeological Museum in Zrinjevac is worth a visit. Within an interesting art nouveau building is an impressive collection, from prehistory finds around northern Croatia to the pottery of Greek settlements on the Adriatic coast. The most interesting exhibits are likely the local pottery and jewelry from the Bronze Age, including the famous Vučedol Pigeon, a pouring vessel iconic to the country. There is also an interesting Egyptian exhibit and an exposed mummy, its linen wrappings laden with Etruscan text displayed on the wall beside it. In the summer months, a café serves drinks in the museum's garden. Tours are available at 3pm on Saturdays.

Victims of Fascism Square
(Trg žrtava fašizma)

If Zrinjevac is Zagreb's most beautiful square, then the Victims of Fascism Square is its most political. It was christened the Square of Great Croatians (Trg hrvatskih velikana) in 1990, but anti-fascist groups protested until the former name was returned.

HOUSE OF CROATIAN ARTISTS
(Dom hrvatskih likovnih umjetnika)

Trg žrtava fašizma 16; tel. 01/461-1818; www.hdlu.hr; hours and entry price vary depending on exhibit

The large circular structure at the Victims of Fascism Square's center, the House of Croatian Artists, was completed as an art gallery in 1938, based on a plan by Ivan Meštrović. In 1941 it was turned into a mosque, complete with three minarets, to build Bosnian Muslim support for the NDH, a pro-Nazi puppet state that was in power at the time. In 1945 it became the Museum of People's Liberation; the minarets were pulled down four years later. In 1991 the building was returned to its original purpose and currently houses excellent contemporary art exhibitions.

OUTSIDE THE CENTER
Museum of Contemporary Art
(Muzej Suvremene Umjetnosti Zagreb)

Avenija Dubrovnik 17; tel. 01/605-2700; www.msu.hr; 11am-6pm Tues.-Sun., 11am-8pm Sat.; 30Kn, free the first Wednesday of each month

Just across the river Sava, the Museum of Contemporary Art has been around since 1954, but its new location makes it seem brand new. The more than 600 permanent pieces showcase Croatian and international artwork from the 1950s to today, and temporary exhibits change every two to three months. Mobile guides in several languages and free Wi-Fi connection make for a pleasant and informative tour. In the summers there is often live music on the rooftop bar, and some of the interactive exhibits such as the ductwork-like slide are nice, but the museum seems to have a love-it-or-hate-it impression on most visitors.

Savska

Though Savska Street is still considered the center by many locals, it's a bit of a trek from the most-frequented sights. If you're at the Mimara Museum, just keep heading south along Savska towards the cylindrical window-filled **Cibona Tower** that marks the home of Zagreb's basketball team, Cibona, which plays next door in the **Dražen Petrović Basketball Center.**

TECHNICAL MUSEUM
(Tehnički muzej)

Savska cesta 18; tel. 01/484-4050; www.tehnicki-muzej.hr; 9am-5pm Tues.-Fri., 9am-1pm Sat.-Sun.; 20Kn

The Technical Museum on Savska Street houses an interesting array of machinery, engines, a transportation exhibit, and even a WWII submarine. There's also a planetarium (same hours, 15Kn) and reconstructions of a mine shaft and Nikola Tesla's laboratory. It's worth a stop if you're a big fan of science or have never made it to the Smithsonian. If the above two don't apply to you and you're short on time, feel free to skip this stop.

Nikola Tesla: A Genius for Invention

Nikola Tesla was born in the village of Smiljan, near Lika, in 1856, the son of a Serbian Orthodox priest. He studied in Karlstadt, Graz, and Prague before beginning his career as an electrical engineer in Hungary. He worked in Paris for the Continental Edison Company, then accepted an offer to work for Thomas Edison in New York in 1884.

His letter of introduction to Thomas Edison, written by a Mr. Batchelor, said, "I know two great men—one is you and the other is this young man."

Edison and Tesla later had a falling out. The reasons for the argument are unclear—some say the issue was money and others claim it was an argument of direct current versus alternating current to power long-distance transmission of electricity.

Tesla teamed up with financial support from Westinghouse, ultimately winning the battle of the currents and demonstrating the use of alternating current at the Chicago World's Fair in 1893.

Tesla realized many other achievements, such as designing the first hydroelectric power plant at Niagara Falls in 1895 and inventing the Tesla coil, widely used in radio and television sets, in 1891.

He registered over 700 patents worldwide, though much of his genius did not earn him recognition or money, largely because he did not want to reveal his secrets. For instance, Tesla was the father of long-range radio-wave transmissions but did not demonstrate this feat publicly, allowing Guglielmo Marconi to receive credit first (the U.S. patent office later recognized Tesla as the inventor). He also claimed some far-fetched inventions, like a supposed death ray, that caused many to see him as slightly delusional. Yet when Tesla died in 1943 the FBI confiscated his research, leaving his fans to speculate as to what he was really working on.

DRAŽEN PETROVIĆ MEMORIAL CENTER MUSEUM

Trg Draženo Petrovića 2; tel. 01/484-3146; www.drazenpetrovic.net; 10am-5pm Mon.-Fri.; 30Kn

Visit the Dražen Petrović Memorial Center museum for a peek at the life of one of Croatia's most beloved athletes. On display are his jerseys, awards, honors, and photographs that chronicle his rise in basketball.

Mirogoj

Aleja Hermanna Bollea 27; www.gradskagroblja.hr; 6am-8pm Apr.-Oct.; 7:30am-6pm Nov.-Mar.; free

Though it may seem morbid to spend one's holiday poking around a cemetery, Mirogoj is not only considered one of the most beautiful memorial parks in Europe, but it is also a major Zagreb landmark. It looks like a fortress for the dead, with its high brick walls topped by cupolas that appear to guard the graves beyond. Known for its grand architecture (the main building was designed by Bollé) and the famous Croatians buried there, it is also interesting for its example of

religious tolerance, with Catholic, Orthodox, Muslim, and Jewish tombstones lying side by side. The place is vast—it is the final home of some 300,000 people—but the most outstanding features are found along the arcades that extend from either side of the main building, with their haunting cast-iron lanterns and magnificent, somber sculptures watching over the graves of Croatia's most famous historical figures. To get there from the center, take bus 106 from the cathedral or tram 14 going east toward Mihaljevac and get out at the fourth stop (Gupčeva zvijezda) and walk for about five minutes uphill.

Church of St. Mary (Crkva svete Marije)

Ul. Ivana Česmičkog 1; tel. 01/450-0500; generally open dawn-dusk daily; free

Located in the leafy suburb of Remete is the Church of St. Mary, a Gothic structure with a salmon and white Baroque facade. The church is swamped with the faithful on Marian feast days, particularly August 15 (Assumption,

Dražen Petrović, Beloved Basketball Star

Croatia is a tiny country full of successful athletes, from Wimbledon-winning tennis stars to Olympic gold medalists. But basketball player Dražen Petrović was in a league of his own. Born in Šibenik in 1964, he grew up playing basketball and soon moved from Zagreb's Cibona team to Spain's Real Madrid and finally to the NBA, at a time when European players were the exception rather than the norm. He played for the Portland Trail Blazers and the New Jersey Nets, where he earned the title of team MVP.

In the summer of 1993, after his best NBA season ever, he traveled to Poland to play with the Croatian National Team in a qualification tournament. He made the fateful decision to drive back to Croatia with friends and was killed on a German autobahn in a high-speed crash on June 7, 1993.

The impact his death had on the country was intense. Seeing a wonderful player and a great person struck down in the prime of his life would have been enough cause for sadness. But the death of a role model at a time when young men were still dying for Croatia's independence on the front lines that summer brought the grief to a much deeper level.

The entire nation mourned the death of Petrović, with over 200,000 people showing up for his funeral. His tomb at Mirogoj is still visited daily by fans who will not forget him.

locally known as Velika Gospa). The interior of the church is stunning in an eclectic way, with an over-the-top marble altar, whose 15th-century wooden statue of the Madonna is said by many to bestow miracles. But the most beautiful feature of the church are the delicate, fading frescoes by Ivan Ranger, the famed monk whose artwork graces many northern Croatian churches.

Though Remete is quite close to Mirogoj, if you're lacking a navigation system or have a fear of passing giant city buses on curvy roads about the width of a pencil, the best way to get there by car is to take Bukovačka cesta from Maksimir Park and follow it to the top of the hill. By bus, hop on 226 from Mirogoj or 203 from Mirogoj's crematorium; ask the driver to alert you to the stop for Remetska crkva.

Nightlife

BARS

The most important thing you need to know about bars in Zagreb (and Croatia in general) is that they almost all get started in the early morning as cafés, and as the day turns to dusk, the ratio of coffee to alcohol switches. The atmosphere morphs from conversation to celebration, and the music gets amped up or turns live.

If you want to bar hop, **Tklačićeva** and **Bogovićeva** are great streets to do so. With dozens of bars to choose from and lots of outdoor seating in warmer weather, if you don't like one just move a few chairs to your left or right and you'll be at a different bar.

Preradoviceva street has also become something of a bar scene of its own. Though it skews twenties, you will find all ages looking for a good time around the bars that line the street.

ESPLANADE 1925
Mihanovićeva 1; tel. 01/456-6666; www.esplanade.hr; 8:30am-2am daily;40Kn-60Kn

Esplanade 1925 at the Hotel Esplanade hosts an upscale crowd with a robust list of adult beverages in the elegant bar or on the terrace. Several nights a week DJs spinning hip Euro lounge tunes or live music acts get the party going without stopping your conversation.

SWANKY MONKEY GARDEN

Ilica 50; tel. 01/400-4248; 10am-1am daily; 15Kn-40Kn

The twenty-somethings head to Swanky Monkey Garden for reasonably priced cocktails and beer in the colorful bar or on the roof terrace in summer. The bar has a relaxed vibe and good DJs.

BAR ALCATRAZ

Preradovićeva 12; tel. 091/521-3703; 7am-2am daily; 15Kn-30Kn

Bar Alcatraz is close to Cvjetni Trg (Flower Square) and is perfect if your crowd is laid-back and likes beers that don't break the bank. A bit smoky for some, the dark, small space gets larger in summer with the use of an outdoor terrace. Any time of year, though, the low-key bar is a fun place to hang with the locals, who often start the evening here due to the cheap drinks.

SPUNK

Hrvatske bratske zajednice; tel. 01/615-1528; 7am-1am Mon.-Thurs., 7am-4am Fri., 12pm-4am Sat., 6pm-1am Sun.; 20Kn-30Kn

Students might want to try Spunk, outside the National University Library, which doesn't look that promising but is still filled with laid-back people. It morphs into quite a scene at night with good music and, on occasion, live bands.

RAKHIA BAR

Tklačićeva 45; tel. 098/964-0587; 12pm-2am daily; 30Kn-50Kn

At Rakhia Bar, you can try over two dozen varieties of *rakija*, a brandy made with various fruits and sometimes nuts—it's something of a Croatian national spirit.

VIVAT FINA VINA WINE BAR

Martićeva 17; tel. 01/615-2577; 10am-11pm Mon.-Thurs., 10am-1am Fri. and Sat., closed Sun.; 30Kn-50Kn

For enjoying a glass of wine in a swanky-yet-cozy space, Vivat Fina Vina Wine Bar is the perfect choice. With a huge variety of both foreign and local wines available (they own a shop of the same name across the street if you want to buy a bottle to take home), the bar also serves excellent coffee from local roaster Hug&Punch and is strictly non-smoking.

BREWERIES

Craft beer has become a big thing in Zagreb, and there are a number of new breweries that have popped up in the last five to ten years.

CRAFT ROOM

Opatovina 35; tel. 01/484-5390; 10am-2am most days; 20Kn-40Kn

Walking distance from the main square, you'll find Craft Room, a cozy, chill bar with two patios for better weather. There are beers from a number of foreign as well as local micro-breweries available, which makes it a great place to try something new or find your reliable favorite.

THE GARDEN BREWERY

Slavonska Avenija 22F; 11am-11pm Mon.-Thurs., 11am-2am Fri., 12pm-2am Sat., 12pm-8pm Sun.; 20Kn-40kn

Further afield, The Garden Brewery is set in a huge industrial space and offers its own brews of everything from IPA to stout and everything in between. A street food partner is right outside to dish up some nice sliders should you get hungry.

LIVE MUSIC AND DANCE CLUBS

The line between café, bar, and music club is quite flexible in Zagreb, with many establishments fitting into any of the categories depending on the day of the week or time of day. However, a few places are either large enough to host a dance floor, focus on music, or at least provide some sort of music every night they're open, giving them a space in this list.

Zagreb's Solar System

Grounded Sun (Prizemljeno Sunce)

When you're having a drink or snack on Bogovićeva, make sure to look out for the large golden ball, actually a sculpture by Ivan Kožarić, titled *Grounded Sun (Prizemljeno Sunce)*. First exhibited in 1971, the ball, almost two meters (seven feet) in diameter, changed location several times before it landed in one of Zagreb's busiest pedestrian streets in 1994. In the early years of the new millennium, Dawor Preis began placing models of the planets of the solar system around town with little or no publicity. Even most locals aren't aware of his installation, entitled *Nine Views*. The size and distance of all the models are in scale with the "sun," the *Prizemljeno Sunce*. Use the **Zagreb Be There App** (www.betherezagreb.com) to track them all down.

BACCHUS JAZZ BAR

Trg Kralja Tomislava 16; tel. 098/322-804; 11am-midnight Mon.-Fri., 3pm-midnight Sat.; drinks 20Kn-40Kn

Fans of jazz will like Bacchus Jazz Bar. Located on King Tomislav Square, it is cozy and homey in winter and has a nice garden in summer. The jazz and beer are great; the wine list less so.

BOOZE & BLUES

Tklačićeva 84; tel. 01/483-7765; www.boozeandblues. com; 8am-12am Sun.-Wed., 8am-2am Thurs. Sat.; no cover most nights, drinks 20Kn-40Kn

If you like blues, Booze & Blues has live blues several nights of the week and a good drink selection. Its location next to dozens of other locales makes it a great choice for an evening of bar-hopping.

VINYL

Bogovićeva 3; tel. 01/238-5421; www.vinylzagreb. com; 8am-12am Sun.-Wed., 8am-2am Thurs., 8am-4am Fri.-Sat.; no cover charge most nights; 15Kn-40Kn

Though it is a bit overpriced and the service is not always friendly, the location of Vinyl can't be beat. The multi-story club has a good alcohol selection and a lively atmosphere on the weekends.

KSET

Unska Ulica 3; tel. 01/612-9758; 9am-4pm Mon.-Tues., 8am-12am Wed.-Thurs., 8am-4pm and 8pm-1am Fri., 10pm-3am Sat.; most covers around 15Kn, varies depending on act; drinks 15Kn-25Kn

KSET is a student club run by volunteers that turns from study bar to a venue for live music and theme nights. The drinks are cheap, and the vibe is college-age.

CONCERT VENUES

TVORNICA KULTURE

Šubićeva 2; tel. 01/457-8389; tvornicakulture.com; 8pm-2am Sun.-Thurs., 8pm-4am Fri.-Sat.

A bit of a walk from the center of town (under thirty minutes from the main square), you will find Tvornica Kulture, which is probably the best venue for rock concerts in town. Both local and some foreign bands perform

concerts, and entry depends on who is playing. You can buy tickets and see the schedule on their website, which is also in English.

BOOGALOO

Vukovarska 68; tel. 01/631-3022; 11pm-7am Fri. and Sat.

Another solid option for rock concerts and events is Boogaloo. They don't have a website but keep their Facebook page updated with a list of upcoming events.

The Arts

THEATERS AND DANCE

CROATIAN NATIONAL THEATRE
(Hrvatsko Narodno Kazalište)

Trg maršala Tita 15; tel. 01/482-8532; www.hnk.hr; box office 10am-7pm Mon.-Fri., 10am-1pm Sat., and 1.5 hours before performances

Break out the opera glasses at Croatian National Theatre, also known as **HNK,** where dramas (mostly in Croatian), operas, and ballets are staged in a beautiful gilt and frescoed atmosphere. Ballet and opera tickets range from 90 to 160Kn, while theater tickets can be had for 50-90Kn.

EXIT

Ilica 208; tel. 01/370-4120; www.teatarexit.hr; box office 4:30pm-8pm Tues.-Sat.

Exit is a small studio theater with some good contemporary plays, almost exclusively in Croatian. The theater is centrally located and continues a robust program even in summers, when many locals have made an exodus from the city.

CLASSICAL MUSIC

VATROSLAV LISINSKI
CONCERT HALL
(Koncertna dvorana Vatroslav Lisinski)

Trg Stjepana Radića 4; tel. 01/612-1167; www.lisinski.hr;

10am-8pm Mon.-Fri., 9am-2pm Sat. and 2 hours before events Sat. and Sun.

Vatroslav Lisinski Concert Hall has brought in big names like the late Cesaria Evora on occasion as well as regular performances by the Zagreb Philharmonic and the Croatian Radio Symphony Orchestra. Call or go online for a list of concerts.

FILM

The best thing about seeing movies in Croatia is that they are mostly in the original language, save for some animated features with Croatian subtitles. Check with the theater before you go regarding dubbing and/or subtitles. Zagreb has three big multiplexes, but the two located closest to the center are **Cineplexx Cental Kaptol** (Nova Ves 17, Centar Kaptol, tel. 01/563-388, www.cineplexx.hr) and **Cinestar** (Branimirova 29, tel. 01/468-6600, www. blitz-cinestar.hr).

Outside the center, you can often catch a show in town at the old **Europa** (Varšavska 3, tel. 01/487-2888, www.kinoeuropa.hr) on Cvjetni trg, which screens mostly art-house films.

1: bars and cafés on Tklačićeva 2: Festival of Lights 3: tapas in Zagreb 4: beeswax candles for sale in the market

Festivals and Events

FESTIVAL OF LIGHTS

Various locations; www.festivaloflightszagreb.com; March; free

New in 2017, the Festival of Lights (four days in March) has artists transform buildings and landmarks with lights and projector installations, turning the town into an interactive art gallery.

ZAGREB BEER FEST

Trg Francuske Republike; May; 50Kn

Who says all beer festivals have to be in October? For a long weekend in May, the Zagreb Beer Fest brings craft beer and music together with dozens of concerts.

ANIMAFEST: WORLD FESTIVAL OF ANIMATED FILMS

Kino Europa and other locations; www.animafest. hr; late May-early June; tickets from approximately 50Kn

This 30-year-old festival, now held on a yearly basis, screens excellent feature-length and short animated films from international filmmakers, including categories for student films and short films made for the Internet.

ZAGREB TIME MACHINE

Various locations; www.zagreb-touristinfo.hr; May-Oct.; free

The tourist board organizes its own Time Machine at locations throughout the city. Actors in historical costume, street performers, and concerts are all part of the pop-up shows.

SUMMER ON STROSS

Strossmeyer promenade; www.ljetonastrosu.com; June-Aug.

The romantic Strossmayer promenade comes to life with kiosks, art vendors, musicians, and more during the Summer on Stross (Ljeto na Strosu).

INMUSIC FESTIVAL

Jarun Lake; www.inmusicfestival.com; June; 420Kn festival ticket

Croatia's largest outdoor music festival draws upwards of 50,000 people to listen to a host of rock and urban bands on the shores of Zagreb's Jarun Lake.

INTERNATIONAL FOLKLORE FESTIVAL

Ban Jelačić Square; www.msf.hr; July; free

Teeming with colorful costumes from all over Croatia, Ban Jelačić Square comes alive with dance and music performances and stands selling hundreds of handicrafts during the International Folklore Festival.

ZAGREB SUMMER EVENINGS

Upper Town; www.infozagreb.hr; July; free

In the upper town, Zagreb Summer Evenings, featuring orchestral and chamber music, plays to good-sized crowds who come to enjoy the wide range of international performers.

THE COURTYARDS

Upper Town; dvorista.in; July; free

The Courtyards (Dvorišta) is one of Zagreb's most lovely and lively events. Multiple Upper Town secret gardens and courtyards are opened to the public, and are filled with bars, musicians, and a party-like atmosphere for ten evenings every July.

INTERNATIONAL FESTIVAL OF PUPPET THEATER

Various locations; www.pif.hr; late Aug.; 15-30Kn

Featuring wonderful puppet productions from all over central and eastern Europe for almost 50 years, the International Festival of Puppet Theater is a must-see for kids, and has a few shows aimed at adults as well.

ZAGREB FILM FESTIVAL

Various locations; www.zagrebfilmfestival.com; Oct.; approximately 30Kn per film

While a relative newcomer to the scene, the Zagreb Film Festival is gaining in importance and screens some 70 films from around the world in three Zagreb cinemas.

ADVENT

Various locations; www.adventzagreb.com; Dec.

While Zagreb has long had an ice rink and market stalls during the advent season, the Advent festival transforms the entire city for a month and makes December possibly the best time to visit Zagreb. The city's frilly Austro-Hungarian buildings and cobblestone streets are made to be a holiday backdrop. The Tunel Gric, parks, and squares are lit and decorated for the season, and there is a live nativity scene at Kaptol. All around town you'll find stalls selling food, hot drinks, and crafts; an ice park with musical accompaniment and skating instructors; concerts and events; and special holiday trains. Advent Zagreb has won best Christmas Market in Europe for three years running at the time of writing.

Shopping

ANTIQUES AND FLEA MARKETS

BRITISH SQUARE (BRITANSKI TRG) ANTIQUES MARKET

Britanski trg; 8am-2pm Sun.

On Sundays, hit the British Square (Britanski trg) antiques market for old postcards from the region, interesting jewelry, and various knickknacks from another era.

HRELIĆ

Sajmišna cesta 8; Sun. morning

At the British Square antiques market, you'll find items similar to, but less than half the price of, those at Hrelić, the city's flea market in Novi Zagreb, fittingly located near the trash dump, where most of the stuff should have gone before it was fished out for sale by the vendors. However, if you arrive early (the pros arrive at 7am or earlier) and are willing to peruse the items on blankets strewn about the ground, you'll probably find something worth taking home. Common finds are intricately carved brass Turkish coffee grinders and long wooden bowls used for kneading dough. Take the Sunday-only bus 295 from the Glavni Kolodvor (first bus leaves at 7:20am).

SOUVENIRS

TAKE ME HOME - CROATIAN DESIGN SHOP

Tomićeva 4; tel. 01/798-7632; www.takemehome.hr; 9:30am-8pm Mon.-Fri., 10am-3pm Sat.

Take Me Home - Croatian Design Shop has a great location near the funicular and stocks lots of great gifts and souvenirs, all from local Croatian designers.

CEROVEČKI KIŠOBRANI

Ilica 49; tel. 01/484-7417; www.kisobrani-cerovecki. hr; 8:30am-8pm Mon.-Fri., 8:30am-3pm Sat.

For a practical item that will also remind you of your trip to Zagreb, Cerovečki Kišobrani sells the same red handmade Šestine umbrellas that cover Dolac market stands.

FOOD AND WINE

PRŠUT I SIR

Radićeva 3; tel. 091/518-8342; 10am-9pm Mon.-Fri., 10am-7pm Sat. and Sun.

There are lots of places to get your gourmet on in Zagreb. Among the best is Pršut i Sir, selling all sorts of home-cured ham, similar to Serrano ham, and cheese from all over Croatia.

VINOTEKA BORNSTEIN

Kaptol 19; www.bornstein.hr; 9am-7pm Mon.-Fri., 2pm-7pm Sat.

Vinoteka Bornstein is a great wine shop in a dark Kaptol (the neighborhood, not the mall) cellar, with a strong showing of Croatian wines. The owners are also local emissaries for all things Istrian and are a great source of info if you're headed that way.

FRANJA

Vlaška 62; tel. 01/455-6391; www.franja.hr; 7am-8:30pm Mon.-Fri., 7am-5pm Sat.

Franja sells the local Franck brand of coffees, and while real coffee connoisseurs will not be impressed, it makes a decent souvenir.

KUĆA ZELENOG ČAJA

Ilica 14; tel. 01/483-0667; www.kucazelenogcaja.com; 9am-8pm Mon.-Fri., 9am-3pm Sat.

If you're dying for real tea, which is a rare find in Croatia, stop by Kuća Zelenog Čaja for a good selection of loose-leaf tea.

FASHION

CROATA

Ilica 5—inside the Oktogon; tel. 01/481-2726; www.croata.hr; 8am-8pm Mon.-Fri., 8am-3pm Sat.

Since the tie was actually invented by Croats, a necktie is a nice souvenir from the country. Croata, Croatia's "official" tie store, has a good selection, and purchases are packaged with a little history of the cravat.

LAPIDARIUM

Radićeva 10; tel. 01/553-0649; www.lapidarium.eu; 8am-8pm Mon.-Fri., 8am-3pm Sat.

For jewelry, Lapidarium carries modern artistic high-end pieces from local Croatian artists. From a sweet *licitar* (decorated folk hearts) bracelet for your niece to an heirloom necklace for someone very special, you can find something unique and memorable here.

A SHOO

Martićeva 19; tel. 01/388-6944; www.ashoo.net; 12pm-7pm Mon.-Fri., 9am-2pm Sat.

Locally designed and handmade, the shoes at A shoo would look equally at home in Paris or New York.

MUSIC

FREE BIRD

Tratinska 58; tel. 01/382-1870; www.freebird.hr; 8:30am-8:30pm Mon.-Fri., 8:30am-3pm Sat.

Music fans will love Free Bird. You will find a huge selection of albums on vinyl, mostly from the 1970s and '80s, and the records are a great souvenir since even foreign records were produced in the former Yugoslavia, with labels like Jugoton printed on the covers.

Sports and Recreation

PARKS

MAKSIMIR

Maksimir; dawn-sunset daily

While it may not be a must-see, Maksimir should make the top of your list if you have any extra time in Zagreb for a leisurely stroll. Located about a five-minute drive east of Ban Jelačić Square, the park was founded in 1774 by the Bishop Maximilian Vrhovac and was originally constructed in the Baroque French style, with three radial paths that still exist today. Subsequent Bishops Aleksandar Alagović and Juraj Haulik expanded on his design, incorporating many English features.

Despite its wide, straight promenade, there are dozens of smaller forested paths where you can lose an afternoon. When you're done with exercise, join a crowd of locals at the **Gazebo** (no phone, hours vary), rising above the end of the main promenade, for a peaceful view of the park and a little liquid refreshment. To get

1: Maksimir 2: Medvedgrad fortress

to the park from the main square, take trams 11 or 12, in the Dubrava direction.

ZAGREB ZOO

Maksimir; tel. 01/230-2198; www.zgzoo.com; ticket office 9am-6pm daily July-Aug., 9am-6:30pm Sept., 9am-4pm daily Oct.-June; 20Kn

Maksimir park is home to the small but well-thought-out Zagreb Zoo, and children will appreciate the **Echo Pavilion,** built in 1840, located near the zoo's entrance.

JARUN

tel. 01/303-1888; www.jarun.hr

A 15-minute drive west from the center (direction Samobor) will take you to Jarun, a popular spot for *zagrebčani* to while away a weekend afternoon. With two lakes and six different islands, the 237-hectare (585-acre) park complex, built for the 1987 University Games, has a variety of recreational and water sports available. There is also a nice network of flat paths, perfect for in-line skating or biking around the lakes. For those who like to fish, the lake is well stocked, and a daily fishing license is available. But Jarun is perhaps best known as a nightlife destination for Zagreb's younger crowd, with a strip of bars and clubs lining the lakeshores—perfect for party-hopping types. To get there from Ban Jelačić Square, take tram 17.

BUNDEK

Ul. Damira Tomljanovića

A lake just off the banks of the Sava River in Novi Zagreb, Bundek experienced a rebirth in 2006. The area, once ridden with unsavory types lurking about and the litter they left, is now a clean, busy, family-friendly park with impeccably maintained flower beds, great paths, one of the nicest playgrounds in Zagreb, and a pebbly beach serviced by a few waterside cafés. If it's a hot day, it's a pleasant place to take a dip. To get there from Ban Jelačić Square, take tram 14 or 6 in the direction of Novi Zagreb to the Sopot stop. From there, it's just a short walk.

★ MOUNT MEDVEDNICA

With its densely forested slopes and endless trails, an excursion to the Mount Medvednica range is great almost any time of the year. The range stretches along the northern side of town, from the western suburbs to slightly east of the center; its highest peak and most developed mountain, **Sljeme,** is reached by driving along Ribnjak out of the center until you see signs pointing right to Sljeme via Gračanska cesta. By tram, take 14 to Mihaljevac and then 15 to the last stop at Dolje. From there it's a short 10-minute walk to the **cable car station** (žičara, 8am-8pm on the hour daily, 11Kn one-way, 17Kn round-trip) or about a three-hour trek to the top. In nice weather, a hike or an outdoor lunch near the top are reasons enough to go. In snowy weather, there are some bunny slopes and spots for sledding to keep you occupied.

MEDVEDGRAD FORTRESS

tel. 01/458-6317; www.pp-medvenica.hr; May-Nov.; 15Kn

Four kilometers (2.5 miles) southwest of Sljeme is the 13th-century Medvedgrad fortress. Built to defend against Tatar attacks, it was abandoned in 1571 and remained neglected until it was rebuilt in the 1990s. A **Homeland Altar (Oltar domovine)** with an eternal flame surrounded by sculptures in the form of tears looks somewhat out of place in its medieval surroundings, though it's an important photo stop for Croatian politicians. There are some great views from here and a restaurant serving typical dishes. In July the fortress is home to **Medvedgrad Musical Evenings** and in late September to a **medieval folklore festival.** From Sljeme, follow the marked paths from the Tomislavov dom hotel or take about an hour's walk from Šeštine church.

CYCLING

Cycling on Zagreb's city streets, particularly on weekdays, is not recommended. Though the city has installed some designated bike lanes in the past few years, you'll usually find

A Day on Sljeme

As you wind your way up Mount Sljeme on a fall day, leaves trickle onto the pavement as you pass, and hikers and cyclists bask in the flickering light that filters through the forest of beech. Fall—or any other time of year for that matter—is perfect for enjoying one of Zagreb's traditional weekend outings. Since the 19th century, *purgeri* (the local name for people from Zagreb) have been visiting the mountain for rest and relaxation.

GETTING TO THE TOP

You can choose the easiest way to climb toward the summit of the highest peak of the Medvenica mountain range—a car. For those more athletically inclined, the steep hike or bike ride will still challenge your hamstrings. And if you're not afraid of heights, the **cable car** offers panoramic views of the golden treetops.

It is difficult to imagine you're only minutes from the city center, with its crowded cafés filled with designer-clad individuals wielding the latest models of mobile phones. Here you can enjoy a moment's quiet reflection, appreciate the local flora and fauna, and take a time-out from the busyness of city life.

WARMING HUTS

The most charming attractions of Sljeme are the many stops where you can replenish your reserves for the return journey. Many of these alpine-style huts, with names like Željeznički Dom (Railway Home) or Dom Grafičar (Home Grafičar), were built by state-run companies during the communist era for their workers to enjoy.

My favorite place to visit is **Puntijarka** (Sljemenska cesta 4/5, tel. 01/458-0384, 9am-7pm daily except major holidays, 45-90Kn), the restaurant of the Mountaineering Society. Old and young gather to share bowls of beans (locally called *grah*) and mugs of beer at dozens of picnic tables outfitted with holes to accommodate walking sticks. The lively sounds of the musicians' accordion and *tambura* accompany the crowd's appetite. Beginning outside, a long line forms to sample simple but enchanting entrées, including roast chicken, sausages, and walnut cake.

On a crisp day you'll see young and old as well as biking enthusiasts sharing tables with children in strollers, though it's the established set that draws the most attention. Old men with coordinating scarves, alpine hats, and pants similar to jodhpurs are out in large groups—they take their hiking seriously. Feel free to sit down at any table with a free spot and start a conversation over some mulled wine.

For those desiring to experience times past, an outing to a place like Puntijarka is not to be missed. The spirit of community and equality that infuses the cool air today is a stark contrast to the new Eastern Europe, where the middle class is a minority. In some ways it reminds one of the intriguing and romantic Croatia at the beginning of its independence. Gone are the threadbare art deco booths of Zagreb's Theater Café and the communist white shoes of its waitresses. Gray, crackling facades are being colorfully restored one by one to their Austro-Hungarian glory. Many things are changing, most for the better, in the new, more Western Croatia. Yet this sense of society, of the communing of the people, may be one remnant of the old regime worth preserving.

quite a few cars parked along them, and drivers aren't used to sharing the narrow roads with cyclists.

BLUE BIKE CITY TOURS AND MORE

Trg Bana Josipa Jelacica 15; tel. 098/288-3344; www.zagrebbybike.com; tours from 10am-5pm (summer) and 10am-2pm (winter); tours from 215Kn, approximately 100Kn a day for rental

Rent a bike or book a bike tour through Blue Bike City Tours and More. The friendly tour company has guides, referred to as waiters, in many languages and run frequent tours.

NEXT BIKE

Various locations; tel. 01/777-6534; www.nextbike. hr; 79Kn activation fee, 5Kn for 30 minutes and packages

Zagreb's bike-sharing service Next Bike *has* locations throughout the city. A helpful app and a one-time 79Kn activation fee, which can also be used as a credit toward five hours of bike rental, is all it takes to get started.

SKIING

Sljeme has decent skiing for beginners or for those that just want to keep their skills from getting too rusty. During the ski season more info can be found by calling 01/455-5827 and online at www.sljeme.hr. Local outfitter **Žuti Mačak** (Hvarska 1c, tel. 01/619-2620, www.zutimacak.hr, 9am-8pm Mon.-Fri., 10am-2pm Sat.) offers ski lessons with English-speaking instructors and equipment rental on Sljeme. Call ahead to make arrangements.

SPECTATOR SPORTS

Soccer

MAKSIMIR STADIUM

Maksimirska 128; tel. 01/484-3769; www.gnkdinamo. hr; from165Kn

The Maksimir stadium across from Maksimir Park is home to games of the Croatian National Team and the local Dinamo, whose fans deck out in the team's signature blue for loud and exciting matches. The main season is August to May (with a break in January and February).

Basketball

DRAŽEN PETROVIĆ BASKETBALL CENTER

Savska cesta 30; tel. 01/484-3333; around 30Kn at the door

Cibona draws pretty decent-sized crowds to watch quality basketball at the Dražen Petrović Basketball Center from September through April. You would be hard-pressed to watch a basketball game at a cheaper price.

WELLNESS CENTERS

Zagreb is full of spas and wellness centers, many with services on par with those in much larger cities.

BLISS STUDIO

Ilica 15; tel. 01/483-1541; www.bliss.hr; 9am-9pm Mon.-Fri., 9am-8pm Sat.

If you're looking for something central, Bliss Studio offers massages, facials, manicures, and pedicures as well as eyelash extensions and mesotherapy. You can also experience a Finnish sauna and enjoy a jacuzzi.

MURAD CENTER

Trpimirova 2; tel. 01/539-0555; www.muradcentar. com.hr; 6:30am-10:30pm Mon.-Fri., 8am-10pm Sat., 10am-7pm Sun.

A little further away in the Hotel Sheraton, the Murad Center offers a full range of massages, facials, a swimming pool, sauna, and aerobic classes. Despite its hotel location, it is a popular health club for many of Zagreb's well-heeled locals.

Accommodations

Some of the cheapest accommodations can be found by staying in a private home or renting a short-term apartment. In recent years, local owners and operators have turned to AirBnB (www.airbnb.com), Home Away (www.homeaway.com), and Booking.com (www.booking.com) to list their properties.

To ensure a happy experience, rely on good reviews, read the fine print, and check the location before booking.

Since Upper Town (Gornji Grad) is still devoid of formal accommodations, you'll need to sift through these sites' offerings to find rooms or apartments located in the oldest part of Zagreb. Be aware that not all of these apartments have air-conditioning—definitely a consideration in the height of summer. Otherwise, hotels and hostels are found in the lower part of town.

One welcome change to Zagreb over the past few years has been the addition of many wonderful choices for accommodations, particularly on the hostel end of the scale. The hostel choice is large and offers everything from your typical rowdy student hostel to something calm and quiet and more like a hotel. Below, a few of the standouts are highlighted.

BAN JELAČIĆ SQUARE (TRG BANA JELAČIĆA) AND KAPTOL

Under 700Kn

MAIN SQUARE HOSTEL

Tkalčićeva 7; tel. 01/483-7786; www.hostel-mainsquare.com; 90Kn pp

The Main Square Hostel is clean and well designed with multi-bed rooms, consisting mostly of pod-like bunk beds. There is free Wi-Fi, a washer/dryer, and a PlayStation, and you can't beat the location, just steps from the main square. The only downside is that it can sometimes be a little loud, since it is in the middle of all the nightlife action.

★ **ROOMS ZAGREB 17**
(Sobe Zagreb 17)

Radićeva 22; tel. 091/170-0000; www.sobezagreb17.com; from 405Kn d

The excellent location of Rooms Zagreb 17 is not the only reason to book here. On a picturesque little Radićeva street, which winds up to the old town, only one minute's walk from the main square, the rooms are modern and clean and decorated with attractive art. The five rooms and one apartment can fill up fast in the summer, so make sure to book ahead.

DOLAC ONE APARTMENTS

Dolac 1; tel. 99/299-0100; www.dolacone.com; 535Kn d

Dolac One Apartments are an excellent choice

due to their central location and clean and modern interiors, each with a kitchenette. Some rooms offer windows over Zagreb's main market.

700-1,400Kn

HOTEL DUBROVNIK

Gajeva 1; tel. 01/487-3555; reservations@hotel-dubrovnik.hr, www.hotel-dubrovnik.hr; 1,066Kn d, including breakfast

Though the rooms are a bit worn, the location of Hotel Dubrovnik can't be beat. It's right on Ban Jelačić Square and has a friendly staff and a decent buffet breakfast. The hotel recently revamped its restaurant to an American steak house with accompanying neon signage.

★ **ZIGZAG INTEGRATED HOTEL**

Petrinjska 9; tel. 01/889-5433; www.zigzag.hr; from 850Kn for a one-bedroom apartment

Less than a block from the main square, the ZigZag Integrated Hotel offers eleven apartments, four double bedrooms, and one single room with colorful yet tasteful modern design, LCD TVs, and air-conditioning, becoming increasingly important in Zagreb in summer. Some apartments are decorated with chalkboard walls listing restaurant recommendations or murals of maps. Who needs a guidebook?

LOWER TOWN (DONJI GRAD)

Under 700Kn

★ **SWANKY MINT HOSTEL**

Ilica 50; tel. 01/400-4248; www.swanky-hostel.com; from 90Kn pp

Only a short walk from the main square on high street Ilica, the Swanky Mint Hostel combines all the elements you might expect from a hostel—a fun place to get info and meet travelers, clean rooms, and one of the most popular hangouts in the city. It's definitely for the younger traveler, maybe creating a genre of its own, like hostels for the discerning backpacker.

★ **SUBSPACE HOSTEL**

Ulica Nikole Tesle 12; tel. 01/481-9993;
www.subspacehostel.com; from 201Kn pp

Two hundred meters (600 feet) from the main square is one of Zagreb's most interesting new accommodations. You don't need to be a sci-fi fan to appreciate the SubSpace Hostel, featuring 20 pods arranged bunk-bed style. Tuck into your own private space capsule, complete with your own TV, lights, personal safe, and headphone jack, for your night flight to Venus. The pods are great for privacy, but they can be a bit too stuffy in the heat of summer, even though the hostel is air-conditioned.

HOSTEL SHAPPY

Varšavska 8; tel. 01/483-0483; www.hostel-shappy.
com; from 325Kn d

On the higher end of hostels, perfectly acceptable for even older travelers, the Hostel Shappy is located only steps to Flower Square. Those familiar with Zagreb might feel nostalgic about the location, where the long-running Ham-Ham (the fast-food burger joint before McDonald's came to town) was located. The courtyard is nice and peaceful, and any remnants of the restaurant (though they had gone upscale before finally closing) are gone. Clean, modern rooms with nice bathrooms, free Wi-Fi, and free parking (a plus if you have a rental car in the center) make this hotel a nice reasonable choice.

4CITYWINDOWS BED & BREAKFAST

Palmoticeva 13; tel. 01/889-7999; www.4citywindows.
com; approx. 450Kn d, including breakfast

Another nice location is the 4CityWindows Bed & Breakfast, where four themed rooms are housed in a typical Zagreb downtown building. The friendly host will make you feel welcome.

BEST WESTERN HOTEL ASTORIA

Petrinjska 71; tel. 01/480-8900; info@hotelastoria.hr,
www.bestwestern.com; 568Kn d, including breakfast

The Best Western Hotel Astoria is a fairly new hotel in a convenient location to the tram station and within a 10-minute walk of Ban Jelačić Square.

700-1,400Kn
★ **HOTEL JÄGERHORN**

Ilica 14; tel. 01/483-3877; www.hotel-jagerhorn.hr;
990Kn d, including breakfast

Perhaps the best, and much-needed, high-end addition to the city's hotel offer, the Hotel Jägerhorn is an 18-room boutique hotel. Nestled at the end of a shop-lined alley off of busy Ilica, it's not only a two-minute walk to the main square but also surprisingly well situated for sightseeing the town's upper core. If you're not afraid of steps, a "secret" passageway connects the alley to the Upper Town. The rooms are luxurious and quiet, and the hotel has a charming café with a cozy interior and peaceful terrace for summer dining.

PALACE HOTEL

Strossmayerov trg 10; tel. 01/489-9600;
palace@palace.hr, www.palace.hr; 1,024Kn d,
including breakfast

The historic Palace Hotel has Secession charm, in particular the art nouveau lobby, and a super location—however, ask for a renovated room if you want to get your money's worth. That said, the rooms are still quite boring and service can be lacking at this longstanding Zagreb hotel.

★ **REGENT ESPLANADE**

Mihanovićeva 1; tel. 01/456-6666; info.zagreb@
rezidorregent.com, www.regenthotels.com; 1,074Kn d,
including breakfast

The Regent Esplanade, built for *Orient Express* passengers in 1925 and fastidiously renovated since, is not only close to the train station (though it's unlikely guests of the hotel would be coming by train today) but also home to a couple of the best places to eat in the city. And don't let the train station put you off. Unlike some European cities, the area around the train station is actually quite nice, perhaps thanks to this historic hotel. The only downside is the comparatively longer walk to the Upper Town and main square.

SHERATON

Kneza Borne 2; tel. 01/455-3535; www.sheraton.com;
1,150Kn d, including breakfast

Though the comfy Sheraton is a favorite with the business set and has a great spa and decent indoor pool, if you're looking for luxury, skip it (it's out of the way for the price and notorious with taxi drivers looking to rip off unsuspecting foreigners).

OUTSIDE THE CENTER

It used to be that leaving the center meant the best deals in accommodations. With the addition of hotels and hostels and the easy booking of apartments on websites, that's not so much the case anymore. Go out of the center to get away from the tourists, or stay near the highways if you really just want to sleep a night on your way down to the coast.

Under 700Kn
FUNK LOUNGE HOSTEL

Rendićeva 28; tel. 01/555-2707; www.funklounge.hr;
from 75Kn pp

On the super cheap end of things, Funk Lounge Hostel is located near Maksimir Park only two blocks from a tram stop. The entrance is inviting, and you might think you're entering a boutique design hotel instead of a hostel. The rooms are very small but clean and have AC. A locker is provided for each guest.

LOOP HOTEL

Župančićeva 18; tel. 01/409-3430; www.theloophotel.
eu; 402Kn d, including breakfast

The Loop Hotel just opened at the time of writing, but the modern hotel on the outskirts of Zagreb could be promising for travelers with a car wanting to get in as little traffic as possible. While it's not on the highway, it is near Zagreb's loop at Slavonska Avenija, making it easy to hit highways going in any direction out of Zagreb (be warned, though,

that the loop doesn't mean you'll technically enter any highway here, only that you will have signs easily directing you to them). The modern industrial style (read: gray and white and plain) rooms are clean and new. There's also plenty of parking and free Wi-Fi.

CAMERA FELICE

Trg Vladka Mačeka 2; tel. 091/900-0342;
www.camera-felice.com; 415Kn d, including breakfast

Camera Felice means "happy rooms" in Italian. The friendly owner and the colorful (but not loud) rooms help this "hotel" live up to its name. It's a 10-minute walk to the main square, but visitors should be aware that there is no maid service during short stays.

LOBAGOLA B&B

Bosanska 3; tel. 091/431-1070; www.lobagola.com;
489Kn d, including breakfast

A 15-minute walk from the city center, the Lobagola B&B is a friendly place with themed rooms and a communal terrace. Freshly baked bread and bike rentals are two perks of staying here.

700-1,400Kn
★ HOTEL PRESIDENT PANTOVČAK

Pantovčak 52; tel. 01/488-1480;
www.president-zagreb.com; from 800Kn d,
including breakfast

Located only 200 meters (600 feet) from British Square, perfect for antique hunters who want to hit up the Sunday market, Hotel President Pantovčak is a six-room boutique hotel. Floor-to-ceiling windows are a highlight of each elegantly designed room, which blends modern with antiques impeccably and tastefully. The neighborhood is Zagreb's ritziest (though some of the homes have still not been renovated) and if you follow the street to the top, you'll find the residency of the President of Croatia, hence the name.

Food

BAN JELAČIĆ SQUARE (TRG BANA JELAČIĆA) AND KAPTOL

Local Cuisine

★ CHEESE BAR

Augusta Cesura 2; tel. 091/888-8628; 7am-1am daily; 35Kn-100Kn; Croatian

Cheese Bar is just steps from the main square and is a great place if you're looking for a light meal of Croatian cheeses, salamis, prosciutto, and more. An excellent wine list and homemade brandies complement such finds as Pepelnik, a cheese made from the ash of the Bukova tree, and a cheese matured in a cave.

★ LA STRUK

Skalinska Ulica 5; tel. 01/483-7701; 11am-10am Mon.-Sat., 11:30am-10pm Sun.; 35-75Kn; Croatian

Try to snag a table at La Struk, a tiny restaurant devoted to all types of strukli, both sweet and savory. It's about time someone gave what is quite possibly the region's finest culinary invention the attention it deserves.

Fine Dining

MANO

Medvedgradska 2; tel. 01/466-9432; www.mano.hr; 12pm-11pm Mon.-Sat.; 75-150Kn; Steak

Mano has been around for a while, and the atmosphere—a candlelit brick-walled warehouse space—is one of the best in the city. The food doesn't always live up to the interior, but the menu is based on fresh ingredients from Dolac and changed twice a year, while focusing on the steaks the restaurant has become known for.

International

TAKENOKO

Nova Ves 17; tel. 01/486-0530; www.takenoko.hr; 11am-1am Mon.-Sat., 11am-6pm Sun.; 65Kn-120Kn; Japanese

Unless you eat dinner really early, you'll need to make reservations for Takenoko, Zagreb's first sushi restaurant and in-crowd favorite. The sashimi and wok bowls are quite nice, but the American-style rolls are a bit overpriced for what you get. No reservation? Try snagging a seat at the bar.

MIO CORAZON

Radiceva 16; tel. 091/240-1790; 10am-12am Mon.-Thur., 10am-1am Fri.-Sat.; 60Kn-100Kn; Tapas

Mio Corazon is a colorful tapas bar with excellent cocktails, decent sangria, and a small street-side terrace.

Quick Bites

For a really quick (and cheap) snack, pick up a *burek* from one of the bakeries lining **Dolac Market** or a piece of fresh fruit and a small bag of nuts from one of the vendors.

PLAC

Dolac 2; tel. 01/487-6761; www.plac-zagreb.com; 7am-11pm daily; 25Kn-50Kn; Fast food

In a slightly hard-to-find location based on its address, Plac serves up local fast food *ćevapčići*, slightly spicy ground-meat rolls eaten with doughy bread, as well as thick home fries and burgers. The modern and clean location on the lower terrace of Dolac toward the main square has a large terrace for eating on the run in nicer weather.

Cafés and Desserts

★ TORTE I TO

Nova Ves 11; tel. 01/486-0691; www.torte-i-to.hr; 9am-11pm daily; 15Kn-35Kn; Dessert

Torte i to is a bit hard to find, tucked in the back of the first floor of Centar Kaptol shopping mall, but it's worth the effort to sample the best cakes in Zagreb. *Torta ledeni vjetar* (cold wind cake) is the unofficial house specialty, though the cheesecake is stupendous too.

AMELIE

Vlaška ul. 6; tel. 01/558-3360; www.slasticeamelie. com; 8am-10pm Mon.-Thurs., 8am-11pm Fri.-Sat., 9am-10pm Sun.; 15Kn- 35Kn; Dessert

Amelie serves excellent cakes just down from the Cathedral and has a nice terrace in summer as well.

UPPER TOWN (GORNJI GRAD)

Fine Dining

★ BISTRO APETIT

Jurjevska 65a; tel. 01/467-7335; 9am-12am Tues.-Sun.; 75Kn-120Kn; Croatian and Mediterranean

Though actually a short drive out of the upper town, Bistro Apetit is a chic slow-food restaurant in a modern light-filled space. Don't let the description scare you off, though. The place is elegant but unpretentious, and the out-of-this-world food is worth the not-outrageous prices.

Local Cuisine

POD GRIĆKIM TOPOM

Zakmardijeve stube 5; tel. 01/483-3607; 11am-12am Mon.-Sat.; 90Kn-150Kn; Croatian

Pod grićkim topom serves up solid food with mediocre service just steps from Kula Lotršćak, or Burglars' Tower. The terrace is the best spot to dine in nice weather, with a great view of the lower town.

★ TRILOGIJA

Kamenita 5; tel. 01/485-1394; www.trilogija.com; 11am-11pm Fri., 11am-12am Sat., 11am-4pm Sun.; 100Kn-150Kn; Croatian

Just next to the Stone Gate, Trilogija serves Croatian staples in an innovative way alongside a wine list of over a hundred wines, with thirty of them available by the glass.

DIDOV SAN

Mletačka ulica 11; tel. 01/485-1154; www.konoba-didovsan.com; 10am-11pm Mon.-Sat., 10am-10pm Sun.; 85Kn-120Kn; Dalmatian

Didov san is filled with regional touches, from the dark-wood and embroidered-tablecloth interior to the food. Specializing

in Dalmatian cuisine, there's a good selection of fish dishes and even a couple of escargot options for gourmands. The *janjetina ispod peke* (oven-baked lamb) is worth ordering ahead.

Quick Bites

POD STARIM KROVOVIMA

Basaričekova 9; tel. 01/485-1342; 8am-11pm Mon.-Sat.; 20Kn-40Kn; Sandwiches and Snacks

Claiming to be the oldest café in Zagreb, Pod Starim Krovovima has been serving guests since 1830. Today the space is bright and friendly with a new exhibition of art on its walls every month. Have a beer and snack on *hrenovke* (hot dogs), *kranske* (a type of regional sausage), or a sandwich.

LOWER TOWN (DONJI GRAD)

Fine Dining

★ ZINFANDEL'S

Mihanovićeva 1; tel. 01/456-6644; www.zinfandels.hr; 6am-11pm Mon.-Sat., 6:30am-11pm Sun.; 150-200Kn; European

Located in the historic Esplanade hotel, Zinfandel's is currently one of the city's best restaurants. With a broad wine list, exceptional service, and elegant decor, the restaurant offers excellent European cuisine that is beautifully presented.

★ MALI BAR

Vlaška 63; tel. 01/553-1014; 12:30pm-12am daily; 75Kn-100Kn

For fine innovative dining on a budget, head to Mali Bar, where the locally famous chef serves up the local to the exotic. Pâtés, chicken wings elevated to another level, pastas, salads, and a solid wine list should leave everyone happy.

Local Cuisine

★ GOSTIONICA TIP-TOP

Gundulićeva 18; tel. 01/483-0349; 7am-10pm daily; 40Kn-75Kn; Dalmatian

Gostionica Tip-Top, locally known as Blato (mud), serves an excellent daily dish, often fish-based. If you are tiring of the upscale and want a taste of what many of the city's restaurants were like just a decade or so ago, this is the place to come. The unpretentious *kavana* was very popular with Croatian artists and has immortalized the poet Tin Ujević on the front window. The cuisine comes from the island of Korčula, with dishes like *pašticada* and *bakalar* (cod) every Friday. There's also a good selection of decent Dalmatian wines, but stay away from the table wine.

★ MUNDOAKA STREET FOOD

Petrinjska 2; tel. 01/788-8777; 8am-10:30pm Mon.-Thurs., 8am-11pm Fri., 9am-11pm Sat.; 55Kn-75Kn

For a much more modern option, Mundoaka Street Food aims to bring foodie quality to street food in a modern setting. With homemade breads, local draft beers, and locally roasted coffee, as well as a solid wine list, the menu changes daily depending on what the chef finds at market.

Vegan
NISHTA

Masarykova 11/1; tel. 01/889-7444; www.nishtarestaurant.com; 12pm-11pm Tues.-Sun.; 40-70Kn; Vegan

Vegan and gluten-free diners should visit Nishta for an array of tasty dishes and homemade juices along with a selection of beer and wine. Staff are helpful, and you'll leave full despite the restaurant's name, which means "nothing" in Croatian.

Quick Bites
PINGVIN

Nikole Tesle 7; tel. 01/481-1446; 8:30am-5am Mon.-Sat., 7pm-3am Sun.; 15-25Kn; Sandwiches

If late nights and panini-style sandwiches are your thing, Pingvin will satisfy, with huge hot circles of bread filled with basic toppings like ham, cheese, and fresh tomatoes.

GOOD FOOD

Teslina 7; tel. 01/481-1302; www.goodfood.hr; 9am-12am Mon.-Thurs., 9am-2am Fri.-Sat., 11am-11pm Sun.; 25Kn-50Kn; Sandwiches and salads

Good Food is a late-night option with plenty of variety on offer, from salads, smoothies, and sandwiches to some excellent burgers. Nice atmosphere, too.

★ HERITAGE CROATIAN FOOD SNACK BAR

Petrinjska Ulica 14; tel. 097/684-2306; 11am-8pm daily; 30Kn-80Kn; Croatian

Heritage Croatian Food Snack Bar serves Croatian food and wines from various regions of the country. It's a great place to learn more about local cuisine from the knowledgeable staff. The restaurant also runs a shop, where you can purchase a gastro-souvenir to take home.

LE BISTRO

Mihanovićeva 1; tel. 01/456-6666; 9am-11pm daily; 60Kn-100Kn; European

A bit on the pricey side for quick bites, but worth a mention for the sunny French bistro-style atmosphere and super brunch-type dishes, Le Bistro in the Regent Esplanade hotel is a great way to while away a Sunday morning.

Cafés and Desserts
VINCEK

Ilica 18; tel. 01/483-3612; www.vincek.com.hr; 8:30am-11pm Mon.-Sat.; 15-35Kn; Dessert

If you're window shopping on Ilica, stop at Vincek, a long-running Zagreb institution, for cakes, cookies, and ice cream.

MILLENNIUM

Bogovićeva 7; tel. 01/481-0850; 8am-11pm daily; 8Kn-25Kn; Dessert

Pass on the cakes at Millennium. They're good, but they can't come close to the creamy gelato-style ice cream in dozens of flavors.

OUTSIDE THE CENTER
Fine Dining
★ DUBRAVKIN PUT

Dubravkin put 2; tel. 01/483-4975; 10am-12am daily; 100Kn-180Kn; Seafood

Dubravkin Put is the city's nicest fish restaurant with food to match. The decor is simple, but the vibe is luxe to the extreme.

Quick Bites
DEŽMAN BAR

Dežmanova 3; tel. 01/484-6160; www.dezman.hr; 8am-12am Mon.-Sat.; 20Kn-40Kn; Sandwiches and snacks

If you are near British Square, pop into

Dežman Bar, a chic bar with a good coffee and wine selection as well as tasty sandwiches and appetizers.

KARIJOLA

Kranjčevićeva 16a; tel. 01/366 7011; 9am 12am daily; 45Kn-75Kn; Pizza

Near Cibona Tower, Karijola serves pizza, but not the kind you order at 2am for sustenance during a study session. Their clay oven-baked pizzas have a thin crispy crust and super-fresh ingredients. The pizza with mozzarella, tomato, and fresh basil hits the spot on a hot summer day.

Information and Services

TOURIST AND TRAVEL INFORMATION
Tourist Office

Trg bana Jelačica 11; tel. 01/481-4051; www.infozagreb.hr; 8:30am-8pm Mon.-Fri., 9am-6pm Sat., 10am-4pm Sun. and holidays

The main tourist office is located on Ban Jelačić Square and provides some nice color brochures, featuring maps and walks around town, free of charge. You will also find branches at the airport, the bus station, the train station, and Lotrsčak tower. The office also provides information on events and happenings around town and sells the **Zagreb Card** (www.zagrebcard.com, 270Kn for 24 hours), which includes free city transport as well as free admission to seven popular attractions and discounts on many other places, goods, and services all over town.

Guided Tours
SECRETS OF GRIČ
(Tajne Griča)

Corner of Ilica and Mesnička; tel. 091/461-5677; www.tajnegrica.hr; 9pm Sat. (English tour); approx. 150Kn pp

The tour that you absolutely must take if you

are in town from May to September is the Secrets of Grič. A theatrical nocturnal tour of the Upper Town, costumed actors guide you through historical sites, mixing facts with the fiction of famed writer Zagorka. The tour takes approximately one hour. Be sure to book tickets in advance online. At the time of writing, the tour is on hiatus due to construction on its path. It will start up again as soon as the road repairs are complete.

CITY TOUR ZAGREB

tel. 097/720-9390; zagrebcitytour.com; 115Kn

If you'd like someone to take you around town, the tourist office can hook you up with a private guide or you can catch a ride on the city's hop-on/hop-off City Tour Zagreb bus. Buy tickets and check the schedule of stops online.

SEGWAY CITY TOUR

Ul. Antuna Mihanovića 1; tel. 01/301-0390; www.segwaycitytourzagreb.com; from 300Kn

A slightly quirkier option is the Segway City Tour, which offers several pre-planned tours or custom tours depending on your interests.

BANKS AND CURRENCY EXCHANGE

It's best to avoid changing money at hotels due to the usually poor exchange rate; most banks will exchange money, as will exchange offices (look for the *mjenjačnica* signs), who take about a 1.5 percent commission. Major banks are Zagrebačka Banka, Privedna Banka (PBZ), and Raiffeisen. If you need to exchange money outside of business hours, head to the bus station or the post office next to the train station for 24-hour service. Also, ATMs (labeled *bankomat*) around town accept most major cards. There's one conveniently located on Ban Jelačić Square, as well as many other locations around the center. Don't expect to find one in Upper Town, however.

INTERNET ACCESS AND COMMUNICATIONS

If you have an unlocked cell phone or tablet, the best deal is **Croatian Telekom's** (www.hrvatskitelekom.hr) unlimited surfing packages for tourists. For around 85Kn for seven days (longer packages also available) you can get a SIM card and unlimited internet for surfing on the go or posting those Instagram photos.

More and more hotels and hostels are offering free internet connections, as are many restaurants, bars, and even nightclubs. In a pinch, find a café offering free Wi-Fi, order a coffee, and ask for the password.

The main **post office** (Branimirova 4, 7am-12am daily) is located next to the train station. Here, as well as at the post office at Jurišićeva 13 (7am-8pm Mon.-Fri., 7am-1pm Sat.), there are metered booths for international telephone calls. Other post offices are located around town—just look for the yellow Pošta signs.

LAUNDRY SERVICES

WASHNGO

Mesnička 5; tel. 091/987-6543; www.zagrebwashngo.com; 7am-10pm daily

For free Wi-Fi and mobile phone charging while you wait for your clothes to get clean, try Washngo.

LEFT LUGGAGE

The main **bus station** (Avenija M. Držića bb, tel. 060/313-333, www.akz.hr, 6am-10pm daily, 5Kn for up to 15 kg per hour) and **train station** (Trg Kralja Tomislava 12, tel. 060/333-444, 24 hours) have left-luggage offices with cheap rates for stowing your bags.

EMERGENCY SERVICES

Croatia's emergency number is 112. The main **police station** (tel. 01/456-3311) is at Petrinjska 30. If you find yourself in need of a doctor in the middle of the night, the clinic of the **Sveti Duh hospital** (Sveti Duh 64, tel. 01/371-2111) is open 24 hours. There are several all-night pharmacies in Zagreb, though the most central is **Central Pharmacy** (Trg bana Jelačića 3, tel. 01/481-6198) on the main square.

Getting There and Around

GETTING THERE
Air
Located 17 kilometers (10.5 miles) from the center, Zagreb has a beautiful new airport, **Franjo Tuđman** (http://www.zagreb-airport. hr/en), which was named after Croatia's first president. **Croatia Airlines** (*tel. 01/487-2727 or 01/616-0215,* www.croatiaairlines.com) is the major carrier serving the city.

From the airport, a taxi to the center should cost around 200-250Kn. If you take a taxi, make sure the driver starts the meter, and ask for a receipt. A cheaper option is to take the **Croatia Airlines bus,** which leaves the airport every half hour or hour (check the schedule at www.plesoprijevoz.hr). The price is only 40Kn, payable to the driver, and takes about 30 minutes to the main bus station.

Train
Zagreb's main **train station** (Trg Kralja Tomislava 12, tel. 060/333-444, www.hzpp. hr) is conveniently located in the center of the city; unlike in many European cities, it is located in a safe area. Trains, run by **Hrvatske željeznice** (Croatian Railways, tel. 060/333-444, www.hzpp.hr), are usually on time and are a great way of getting around the Zagreb area. You can also pick up multiple daily connections to regions around Croatia and Slovenia. Eurail passes can include Croatia and Slovenia depending on the combination you choose.

Tickets should be purchased at the ticket counter to save a little money; tickets bought from the conductor will be slightly higher. You should also be aware that there are slow trains (*putnički*) that stop at every station along the way, and inter-city trains (IC), which are more expensive but usually worth the money in time savings.

You can purchase a timetable at the station, though your best bet is to check out Croatian Railways' website. Make sure to give yourself a few extra minutes to board since the Zagreb train station can be more than a little confusing at times.

Bus
The city has a large and busy **bus station** (Avenija M. Držića bb, tel. 060/313-333, www. akz.hr) with lots of connections. Though the inter-city buses are run by multiple companies, the system actually runs pretty smoothly.

Car
Highways into Zagreb from Slovenia are quite good, with a major highway connecting Ljubljana to Zagreb (A3, approximately 1.5-2 hours between the two capitals). From the Ljubljana border, drive straight until you see white signs marked with the word Centar, directing you toward the center of town. If you're traveling from Zagreb to Maribor, take the A2, also about a two-hour journey between the two cities.

GETTING AROUND
Tram and Bus
Since Zagreb's trams only operate in the central zone of the city, you need not worry about getting too lost. The main hubs for trams are at the train station and Ban Jelačić Square, with large maps displayed at these major stops to help you find your way. Buses will take you into the suburbs of Zagreb.

Regular service for both buses and trams is 4am-12am, when night services take effect and the number of lines is significantly reduced. During the day, tram service is very frequent (around every 10-15 minutes), though night trams and buses are terribly confusing to figure out, with crazy schedules and different routes than those on the regular service route. If you find yourself needing a bus or tram late at night, the best thing to do is ask. As Croatians are usually friendly people and a large percentage of the population speaks English, you shouldn't have a problem.

To travel on buses and trams, buy tickets at newspaper stands or directly from the driver. You can buy tickets per journey (10Kn, valid one-way for 90 minutes) or per day (*dnevne karte,* 30Kn), or buy a **Zagreb Card** from the tourist office—this includes city transport for 24 or 72 hours as well as discounts to museums. Once you board the tram or bus, simply validate your ticket by punching it in the machine onboard.

Taxi

There are numerous taxi stands in Zagreb. The two most central and convenient taxi stands are on Ban Jelačić Square next to the Varteks department store and on Gajeva next to the pedestrian zone. You'll also find them in front of the main train and bus stations as well as in front of hotels. Alternatively, call 970 or 01/660-0671 to reserve a taxi. (You will not find taxis driving around waiting to be flagged down—the person wildly gesturing at cabs from the sidewalk is easily pegged as a tourist.)

Taxi services in Zagreb have improved tremendously due to multiple companies having entered the market. Uber entered the Croatian market in 2015, was then banned, and at the time of writing is allowed as long as the cars are under seven years old. This has risen the price of an Uber somewhat, but they still tend to be cheaper than taxis.

Eko Taxi (tel. 099/456-0455, www.ekotaxi. hr) is the choice for eco-conscious travelers, with a fleet of hybrid vehicles and the best rates in town. You can also reserve online. Another option is **Radio Taksi** (www. radio-taksi-zagreb.hr). While tipping is not standard, it is customary to round up when paying your fare.

Car

While driving on Croatia's highways is quite easy and comfortable, driving in town is often stressful. Traffic in Zagreb is nearly always bad 8am-6pm or 7pm, unless of course you visit in July and August when it seems like the entire city is at the coast. The major tips for in-town driving: Pay attention and remember that drivers don't necessarily obey the rules.

If you need to rent a car in Zagreb, **Dollar**

Zagreb tram

(www.dollar.com) and **Hertz** (www.hertz.hr) have locations at the airport and the center of the city.

Parking in Zagreb is scarce and not for those averse to parallel parking, so you'll want to find somewhere to leave the car and traverse the city center by foot or with the help of trams. If you do need to park in Zagreb, remember that each zone is subject to different rules, with first-zone areas allowing a maximum of only one hour. Find a parking meter, placed at intervals along the street, and pay, then place the receipt on your dashboard from inside the car. Or pay your parking via cell phone—send your license plate number via a text message to 101 (Zone 1, red, one-hour maximum), 102 (Zone 2, yellow, two-hour maximum), or 103 (Zone 3, green, three-hour maximum). It is charged to your cell phone immediately; it's either added to your bill or, if you have a prepaid card, deducted from the balance. Unfortunately, even if your U.S. cell phone has free data, it will not work to pay from a U.S. phone. The city can be quite tow-happy, so make sure the place you park is legal.

An easy option is to leave your car in a parking garage. Prices vary 4-10Kn an hour. The most central parking garage to the main square is Langov Trg. Another good option is to park at Centar Kaptol and walk down Tkalciceva.

Around Zagreb

SAMOBOR

Since the early 19th century, Samobor has lured travelers to its charming streets and the tranquil mountains that surround it. Though today it is mainly a destination for Zagreb residents looking to get away from it all, in the past its importance and culture rivaled that of its much larger neighbor.

There are a few things in this gingerbread town that are considered typical Samobor. The most famous is the *kremšnita (cream cake)*, a flaky square of crust topped with vanilla custard, though its name suggests the origin may be Austrian (but don't mention that to the locals). They also make a big deal over their crystal, though you'd probably be better off toting home some local *bermet,* touted as an aperitif—or a digestif, which might be a better term given how strong it is, or *samoborska muštarda,* a very sharp mustard with a hint of grape.

Sights

Admire the pretty buildings and the mountains from **King Tomislav Square (Trg Kralja Tomislava),** the main square and center of the tiny town. Afterward, head to the **Town Museum (Gradski muzej)** (Livadićeva 7, tel. 01/336-1014, 9am-3pm Tues.-Thurs., 9am-7pm Fri., 10am-2pm Sat., 10am-5pm Sun. winter, 2pm-7pm Sun. summer, 20Kn) next to the Hotel Lavica. The museum was home to composer Ferdo Livadić, who once hosted his friend Franz Liszt here. There's not too much to see here, besides some furniture and decorations from local families and a decent exhibit of agricultural tools.

The **Photo Gallery Lang (Fotogalerija Lang)** (Langova 15, tel. 01/336-2884, www.fotum.hr, 11am-1pm and 4pm-7pm Sat.-Sun. and by appt.), tucked in an alleyway, hosts surprisingly good contemporary photography exhibits. A short walk away, on the northeastern side of the square, is the **Gallery Prica (Galerija Prica)** (Trg Matice hrvatske 3, tel. 01/333-6214, www.pousamobor.hr, 9am-3pm Tues.-Thurs., 1pm-7pm Fri., 10am-1pm Sat.-Sun., 10Kn), which displays paintings by primary-color fan and local artist Zlatko Prica, and haunting photography from his equally talented daughter Vesna.

The town has two nice Baroque churches worth a peek if you have the extra time: the 17th-century **Church of St. Anastasia**

(**Crkva Sv. Anastazije**) and the 18th-century church of the **Franciscan Monastery** (**Franjevački Samostan**).

Hiking

If you're tight on time, make a beeline for the **Anindol** forest on Tepec Hill. It's full of paths to explore, but the best two are the winding **Stations of the Cross** (**Križni put**), which puts you at the tiny **Chapel of St. George** (**Kapelica sv. Jurja**) in less than half an hour, or the path to Samobor's **Old Town** (**Stari Grad**). Stari Grad is really just the ruins of the town's 13th-century castle, but the view is worth the hike, and the ruins are quite peaceful. The shortest route from the Old Town is to take Jurjevska Street to Anindol (15 minutes). From here, it's another 15-20-minute walk.

If you really want to explore the excellent hiking options around town, pick up a *planinarska karta* (mountain map) from the tourist office on King Tomislav Square.

Samobor is the entrance to the **Žumberak region** of inland Croatia, with a wonderful nature park (www.ppzsg.org) and some great ecotourism sites.

Festivals

One of the best times to come is during **carnival** (**Samoborski fašnik**) **in February,** when the town hosts hundreds of revelers with all kinds of performances and lots of activities for kids. Samobor's version of carnival is decidedly more family-friendly than its better-known cousins.

If you miss *fašnik,* there are several other festivals worth checking out. The **Samobor spring fair** (**Samoborski proljetni sajam**) features stands with local food products and handiwork, while the square is popping with fireworks on **Day of the Town** (**Dan Grada,** July 26), and Samobor's **autumn music festival** (**Samoborska glazbena jesen**) brings some excellent musicians to town. Check with the **tourist office** (Trg Kralja

Tomislava 5, tel. 01/336-0044, www.samobor. hr, 8am-4pm Mon.-Fri., 10am-1pm Sat.) for more information.

Accommodations

Relatively new on the scene, the **Hostel Samobor** (Obrtnička 34, 01/337-4107, www. hostel-samobor.hr, from 130Kn pp) is clean and has a central location.

The **Hotel Livadić** (Trg Kralja Tomislava 1, tel. 01/336-5850, www.hotel-livadic.hr, 465Kn d, including breakfast) is the nicest accommodations in Samobor, with quaint rooms right on King Tomislav Square, the main square.

The **Hotel Lavica** (Ferde Livadića 5, tel. 01/336-8000, www.lavica-hotel.hr, 300Kn d, including breakfast) is somewhat more basic, but the price is better and the creekside location is only a few steps away from the main square.

If you are interested in staying and eating in a typical house, ★ **Etno kuća pod Okićem** (Podokića 40, tel. 01/338-2335, www.etno-kuca.hr, 400Kn d) is only eight kilometers (five miles) from Samobor. The gingerbread house has a spacious loft room, and the restaurant serves delicious hearty meals in a rustic setting.

Food

For local flavor at lunch or dinner, **Krcma Gabreku 1929** (Starogradska 46, tel. 01/336-0722, www.gabrek.hr, 12pm-12am daily, 80Kn) serves comforting soups and local dishes like young boar roast. Portions are generous.

For a quicker bite, try the **Pizzeria Napoli** (Grada Wirgesa 6, tel. 01/336-0072, 12pm-10pm Mon.-Sat., 40Kn) for pizzas and pasta dishes.

And for dessert, don't miss ★ **Medenko** (Mirka Klescica 1, tel. 01/336-6848, 11am-9pm daily, 15Kn), serving wonderful homemade ice creams from the everyday to the occasional elderflower or linden and sunflower seed. Though the town is known for

---

1: Samobor's Town Museum 2: Samobor river and old streets

its kremšnita, so you might have to save room for a slice from one of the cafés on the square.

Information and Services
TOURIST OFFICE
Trg Kralja Tomislava 5; tel. 01/336-0044; www.samobor.hr; 8am-4pm Mon.-Fri., 9am-5pm Sat., 10am-5pm Sun.
Located conveniently on King Tomislav Square, the tourist office sells maps, including special versions for hiking. They also hand out free brochures and information and can help you arrange accommodations.

Getting There and Around
Samobor is a little over 20 kilometers (12 miles) west of Zagreb. If you're driving, take the A3 toward Ljubljana. The trip should take about 30 minutes, but heavy traffic on the road sometimes makes it a bit longer. Buses run by the **Samoborček** company (tel. 01/333-5170, www.samoborcek.hr) leave Zagreb's main bus station and the Črnomerec tram terminal. There are dozens of connections daily, taking about 45 minutes, and costing around 40Kn each way depending on where you get on. When you get to Samobor, from the bus station it is only a five-minute walk to the main square, Trg Kralja Tomislava.

PLEŠIVIČKA WINE ROUTE
The best wine route in the area is the **Plešivička Wine Route.** You can pick it up at Rude, a few kilometers southwest of Samobor. The roads are well marked and you can download a map at http://www.tzgj.hr/en/maps/plesivica_wine_road_map.html; you can get additional information and a list of wineries online at www.zagrebacka-zupanija.hr/vina/eng. However, it's best not to plan too much and just enjoy the drive of around 20 kilometers (12 miles) through vineyards and villages. The wineries are marked with little signs declaring *vino*. Though none of them hold regular opening hours, despite some claiming they

do, it's a nice drive hunting down a spot to buy some wine.

Most of the growers will offer you a tasting before you buy, which is important given that the quality of the wine will vary greatly. However, it's pretty cheap, and if you happen to be traveling the road in autumn, you'll run into Portugizac Plešivička, the local version of Beaujolais Nouveau.

A nice place to stop for lunch along the way is **Restoran Ivančić** (Plešivica 45, tel. 01/629-3303, www.restoran-ivancic.hr, 9am-11pm Tues.-Sun., 12pm-8pm Mon., 90Kn), with its vineyard-view terrace.

ZAPREŠIĆ
The main attraction in the small town of Zaprešić, 18 kilometers (11 miles) northwest of Zagreb, is the **Jelačić New Palace (Jelačić Novi dvori),** a well-preserved feudal estate that covers 20 hectares (50 acres). There's also a small museum, the **Matija Skurjeni Museum (Muzej Matija Skurjeni)** (Aleja Đure Jelačića 8, tel. 01/331-0540, www.muzej-matija-skurjeni.hr, 9am-3pm Tues. and Thurs., 12pm-5pm Wed. and Fri., 10am-2pm Sat., and 10am-12pm Sun., 20Kn), with a cheerful display of naive art, an impressive manor house, a chapel, and the grand **Jelačić family tomb.**

Nearby is a well-maintained **golf complex,** though it's really little more than a driving range. A short drive south, the **Zajarki Lake** has a nice fish farm and fishing society.

Zaprešić is accessible by bus and train, with frequent connections since many people work in Zagreb. It's a 30-minute drive from Zagreb (take Ilica out of town and follow the signs for Zaprešić).

MARIJA BISTRICA
About 32 kilometers (20 miles) north of Zagreb is Marija Bistrica, whose hilltop **Pilgrimage Church of St. Mary of Bistrica (Hodočasnička crkva Marije**

Bistričke) (tel. 049/468-380, www. marijabistrica.hr, contact tourist board for hours and pilgrimages) has turned into a destination for the devout, particularly between Whitsunday (Pentecost) and the end of October. The church itself is attractive, designed in the late 18th century by Bollé, who built Zagreb's cathedral. But the pilgrims come not so much for the church as for the **Black Madonna,** a 15th-century dark wooden statue of the Virgin. Legend has it that the statue was bricked into the church wall in the 17th century to protect it from the Turks. Some three decades later, a beam of light revealed its hiding place. Locals declared it a miracle and the bishop of Zagreb spread the news, hoping to promote the town as a spiritual center for pilgrims. His efforts paid off, and today the Black Madonna, who also survived an 1880 fire that only added to her aura, brings busloads of tourists to the otherwise tiny town.

Behind the huge **amphitheater,** built for a visit by the pope in 1998, a path leads up **Calvary Hill (Kalvarija),** passing the Stations of the Cross to a very nice view of the town at the top.

If you have time and your own car, take a leisurely drive north to **Belec** to visit the gorgeous 1675 Baroque church of **Our Lady of the Snow (Marija Snježna).** The outside is plain and unassuming, but the inside is filled with paintings, gilt, and heavily carved statues and altars. Though the church is only officially open on Sundays, knock at the white house just below the front gate of the church and ask for Ivo, the bell ringer. It's his job to unlock the church for visitors, so don't be embarrassed to ask.

Bluesun Hotel Kaj (Zagrebačka bb, tel. 049/326-600, www.hotelkaj.hr, 898Kn d, including breakfast, parking, and Wi-Fi) is a new hotel with modern well-appointed rooms, a restaurant, and a spa.

If you'd like to visit Marija Bistrica, there are multiple connections by bus daily to and from Zagreb (40 minutes). To visit the church at Belec, about 15 kilometers (nine miles) north of Marija Bistrica, follow the road to Zlatar and then follow signs for Belec.

Inland Croatia

With nary a tourist—despite charming Baroque

enclaves, funky art galleries, and outstanding wineries—inland Croatia offers enticements as varied as its landscape.

Zagreb is within this area, divided into several regions, each with distinct culture and geography. For avid sightseers, Zagorje has plenty of castle-topped hills to visit, and Međimurje is filled with Baroque palaces and festivals. Slavonia's little villages are great places to get into deepest Croatia, the version you would likely have found 60 years ago: Farmhouses hug the main road, many displaying signs for fresh eggs, lamb, wine, or even hogs. Where Slavonia stretches toward the Danube are some of the best wineries in the country, plus the area's

Highlights

Look for ★ to find recommended sights, activities, dining, and lodging.

★ **Varaždin:** In this gentle Baroque city there's lots for lovers of the style, even a parklike Neo-Baroque cemetery (page 98).

★ **Hlebine:** Artists still keep tradition alive in this charming town, birthplace of the Croatian naive art movement. The galleries show off the masters while locals work in their studios (page 104).

★ **Osijek's Citadel (Tvrđa):** The fortress in Osijek is crisscrossed with centuries-old cobblestone streets and hopping with chic cafés and restaurants. It's also at the heart of the city's cultural rebirth (page 108).

★ **Kopački rit Nature Park (Park prirode Kopački rit):** One of Europe's best wetlands, this park is a must-see for bird-watchers (page 110).

★ **Ilok Wineries:** This tiny medieval town is home to several old wine cellars, and the surrounding countryside is just right for getting out on the open road. Join a guided cycling tour to explore the region (page 115).

★ **Fužine:** Smack dab in the middle of nowhere, this often overlooked village on the road to Rijeka has some great food and a hotel in a former Tito hunting lodge. It's also a great jumping-off point for adventure sports (page 120).

★ **Lonjsko polje:** Wildlife fans shouldn't miss this nature preserve, not far from Zagreb, where you can see hundreds of nesting storks and furry swimming pigs (page 122).

largest towns, including Osijek and Vukovar, still struggling with the economic stagnation caused by the war.

For the more active traveler, the Žumberak, not far from Zagreb, has a network of winding trails for hiking, or the Gorski Kotar's mountainous, almost alpine, geography makes way for skiing, climbing, and rafting excursions. Lonjsko polje and Kopački rit are two nature preserves with loads of wildlife, worth taking a boat or jeep tour to spot wild storks and swimming swine.

While each area is distinct, one thing they all have in common is their impressive range of *seoski turizam* (village tourism), where visitors can stay overnight and get a real taste of village life. They are also brimming with homemade wines (though you'll find the best in Slavonia), with vineyards and wine producers open to the public for tastings and occasionally lodging, where you can chat with the owners and learn all about the making of wine. Another common thread are the people—hospitable, friendly, and welcoming to visitors—who assure the traveler a memorable visit and a taste of local culture.

PLANNING YOUR TIME

Most locations in inland Croatia are an easy day trip from Zagreb. In one day you can easily fit in three stops in Zagorje by car, or one or two if you're taking public transportation,

although it's harder on weekends when connections are scarcer. Varaždin and Karlovac are nice day or even half-day trips from the capital. And if you're already in Samobor, outside Zagreb, the Žumberak is right around the corner. You'll need to plan at least one overnight in Slavonia, though, to make the best use of your trip.

If you're traveling onward to the coast, you have to pass through Karlovac if you're headed to Istria, the Kvarner Gulf, or Dalmatia. It's a good place to stop and have lunch. On your way to or from Opatija, Rijeka, and Istria, you'll have to cross the Gorski Kotar. The leafy, mountainous region is a restful prescription when you've had too much sun and sailing.

Slavonia requires a special trip, with at least one overnight in the area. If you pick one of the *seoski turizam* hotels, that overnight should be part of the whole experience itself. And it's possible to spend your entire tour of Slavonia without seeing another person from abroad.

How you plan your time also depends on your interests. Wine lovers will want to rent a car and take to the wine routes of Slavonia for two or three days, while adventure fanatics should head straight to the Gorski Kotar for rock-climbing and rafting. There are even a couple of crazy film festivals for artsy sorts, and all the castles and ancient churches history buffs could dream of.

Previous: view of Krapina; Varaždin; Kumrovec, birth place of Josip Broz Tito, former leader of Yugoslavia.

Inland Croatia

SLOVENIA

BOSNIA AND HERZEGOVINA

CROATIA

HUNGARY

SERBIA

Risnjak National Park
HOTEL BITORAJ
FUŽINE
Delnice
Bjelolasica
Ogulin
Josipdol
Senj
Krk
Pag
Jablanac
Zuta Lokva
Gospić
Prijeboj
Slunj
Bruvno
Vrtoće
Bos. Krupa
Bosanska Dubica
Banja Luka
Doboj

Novo Mesto
Velenje
Celje
Maribor
Dravograd
Ptuj
Krško
Bregana
Samobor
Zumberak
Pribić
Velika Gorica
Ozalj
Karlovac
DUBOVAC
Gornja Stubica
ZAGREB
Krapina
Lepoglava
Trakošćan
VELIKITABOR
Kumrovec
VARAŽDIN
Čakovec
TERBOTZ MALA HIŽA
Štrigova
Mačkovec
ŠHAMPER BISTRO AND WINERY
MALA WINERY
HLEBINE
Koprivnica
Bjelovar
Đurđevac
Virovitica
Sisak
Čigoč
RAVEC
LONJSKO POLJE
Muzilovčica
Glina
Velika Zdenci
Slatina
Požega
Vetovo
Kutjevo
ENJINGI
Dilj
Brodski-Stupnik
STUPNIČKI DVORI
Slavonski Brod
Đakovo
Vukovar
Osijek
CITADEL (TVRĐA)
Bilje
Dalj
VINARIJA ANTUNOVIĆ
ILOČKI PODRUMI
ILOK WINERIES
Ilok
BARANJA WINERIES
BARANJSKA KUĆA SKLEPIĆ HOUSE
Karanac
Zmajevac
Suza
KOPAČKI RIT NATURE PARK (PARK PRIRODE KOPAČKI RIT)
Pécs
Sásd
Bátaszék
Baja
Fadd

Sava River
Drava River
Dunav River
Dunav
Drina River

E65
E71
E57
A4
A2
A5
A1
A6
A3
1
2
3
22
20
32
25
30
37
14
6
5
7
2
M5
E761
E66
M16
M17
E73
E70
E71
E661
E70
E59
E65
E59
6
55
57
6
61
66
61
56

0 20 km
0 20 mi

© MOON.COM

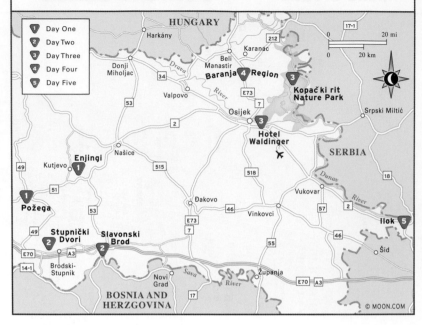

Slavonia Wine Route

Itinerary Idea

SLAVONIA WINE ROUTE

Day 1

- Drive from Zagreb to **Požega** and wander around the pretty town.
- Head out to the **Enjingi** winery, one of Croatia's best, for some serious kicking back with a bottle and some local *kulen*.

Day 2

- Slowly make your way to **Slavonski Brod,** where you should stop for a coffee at the town's central **Navigator.**
- Then head on to **Stupnički Dvori,** whose vineyards were the inspiration for famed Croatian writer Ivana Mažuranić's Hlapić storybook character. The Slavonian home cooking here might even be good enough to make you forget about the wine for a few minutes.

Day 3

- Spend the day touring the giant nature reserve of **Kopački rit.**
- Hole up for the night in Osijek's historic **Hotel Waldinger.**

Day 4

- Wind your way through the wineries of the **Baranja,** arriving at the **Sklepić house** in the early afternoon for a ride in a typical Slavonian horse-drawn *fijaker,* a great meal, and a night in the 1910 village cottage.

Day 5

- Spend your last day roaming around the medieval town of **Ilok** and the surrounding wineries.

Those traveling by bus or train should take note that the castles of Veliki Tabor and Trakošćan are not the easiest to access via public transportation. The same goes for most of the wine routes listed here. If you'd like to see some of these places without a car, contact the tourism boards in the area to find out about guided tours, organized bike trips, and other arrangements to avoid losing too much precious travel time.

Whatever your choice may be, taking two or three days to see inland Croatia is a great decision. You'll get to see a side of the country that few visitors bother to explore. People are friendly all over the country, but perhaps even more so in towns like Osijek and Vukovar, where the area is just beginning to recover from the war and the kind locals are thrilled to share the best of the region with visitors.

Zagorje

Bucolic little villages, winding hillside roads, and medieval storybook castles . . . When traveling in Zagorje it's hard to believe you're just a stone's throw from the bustling capital of Zagreb.

Zagorje is also home to a rather distinguished political history. The launching spot for the 1573 Peasants' Revolt and the birthplace of Josip Broz Tito, the leader of Yugoslavia from 1945 to 1980, are both located here.

It's a nice place for cycling if you're so inclined. Well-marked paths between the major sights like Veliki Tabor and Kumrovec make taking to a bike a nice way to see the area; rentals are available in Zagreb.

Zagorje is the place to really relax, slowly browsing a castle and then going for a long lunch of local specialties like *štrukli* (a pasta-ish dough filled with creamy cottage cheese) and *purica z mlincima* (turkey with *mlinci,* a sort of thick baked noodle).

For souvenirs, pick up the little *licitari,* or bright-red gingerbread hearts, that are meant as an ornament rather than a sweet. They're synonymous with the area and have been adopted by Croatia as one of the country's iconic symbols.

The **Tourist Board of Krapina-Zagorje County** (Magistratska 3, Krapina, tel. 049/233-653, info@visitzagorje.hr, www. visitzagorje.hr) can provide more information for planning your visit.

KUMROVEC

Though it's famous as the birthplace of Yugoslavian leader Josip Broz Tito, Kumrovec's **Old Village Museum (Muzej Staro Selo)** (www.mss.mhz.hr, 9am-7pm daily Apr.-Sept., 9am-4pm daily Oct.-Mar., 25Kn) is intriguing in its own right. Some 20 cottages and outbuildings, including Tito's childhood home, have been restored and opened to the public; the museum starts behind the large parking lot on the right if you're coming from Klanjec. The best thing about the museum is that while the displays are interesting and informative, it bears no resemblance to most tourist villages. Here you actually feel like you are in an early 20th-century village, with chickens and geese running wild and occupied homes that are only distinguishable from the museum ones by the paraphernalia and occasional child in the yard.

If you're interested in **cycling,** there's a nice marked trail from here to Veliki Tabor, about 15 kilometers (9 miles) north.

The **Pansion Zelenjak** (Risvica 1, Kumrovec, tel. 049/550-747, zelenjak@zelenjak.com, www.zelenjak.com, 389Knd, including breakfast) has clean rooms on the shores of a rushing mountain stream and some good freshwater fish dishes in the restaurant.

Kumrovec is 40 kilometers (25 miles) northwest of Zagreb. To reach Kumrovec, take a train from Zagreb to Savski Marof, where five buses continue to Kumrovec's train station, a little less than half an hour's walk from the museum complex. The train and bus take around an hour and cost approximately 35Kn. By car, take the A4 toward Maribor, exit at Krapinske Toplice, and follow signs to Kumrovec. The drive takes about 45 minutes.

VELIKI TABOR

When most people think of a medieval castle, something like **Veliki Tabor** (Košnički Hum 1, Desinić, tel. 049/374-970, www.veliki-tabor.hr, 9am-5pm Mon.-Fri. and 9am-7pm Sat.-Sun., Apr.-Sept., 9am-4pm Mon.-Fri. and 9am-5pm Sat.-Sun., Oct. and Mar., 9am-4pm Wed.-Sun., Nov.-Feb., 25Kn) is what comes to mind. It's the sort of castle you drew in school, with huge circular towers looking over the surrounding countryside from a hilltop. The main structure, a pentagon-shaped tower, was built in the 12th century; the cone-roofed circular towers were added in the 15th and 16th centuries. Some historians claim the castle sits on the site of an earlier Roman fortress from the 2nd century.

There are several varied exhibits, including medieval weaponry, glazed sections of old stove tiles, and a smattering of furniture. The real draw here is the architecture of the castle, which looks like the setting for a movie about knights and fair maidens. There's also the castle's most famous exhibit, the purported **skull of Veronika Desnićka,** a local beauty who caught the count's son's eye. They ran off together, but the count disapproved of the marriage and had his son imprisoned. The unlucky Veronika was drowned and her

statue of Josip Broz Tito in Kumrovec

Matija Gubec and the Peasants' Revolt

In 16th-century Zagorje, peasants were stretched thin between ever-increasing feudal obligations and constant battles with the Ottoman Empire. They complained, but the emperor didn't listen, so in 1573 they decided to rebel.

When the rebellion broke out, they elected the charismatic Ambroz Matija Gubec as leader in a plan to develop a government, led by peasant officials, that would answer only to the emperor. Their revolutionary ideas alarmed the nobility, who raised armies to defeat them.

The poorly armed peasant army fought hard but eventually lost a decisive battle at Stubičko Polje in February 1573 when the bishop of Zagreb, Juraj Drašković, defeated Gubec and his men in a bloody battle, capturing Gubec, who was executed in St. Mark's Square in Zagreb. On the accusation that he had been elected "king" by his followers, he was crowned with a scalding ring of iron.

The revolt and execution of Gubec became the stuff of legend in Croatia, inspiring poets and writers and even politicians. Tito and his partisans embraced Gubec's cause as their own, naming one of their brigades in World War II after the famous peasant leader.

The village of Gornja Stubica, where the revolt was launched, has the **Peasants' Revolt Museum (Muzej seljačkih buna)** (Samci 64, tel. 049/587-880, www.mdc.hr/msb, 9am-5pm daily Oct.-Mar., 9am-7pm daily Apr.-Sept., 20Kn), which presents items that give a sense of everyday feudal life, with captions in English, as well as a hilltop statue of Matija Gubec.

body walled up inside the castle. In 1982, renovations uncovered a skull, now displayed in the castle's chapel.

Not all sections of the castle have been restored. Long-term renovations are ongoing, and it is difficult to say which rooms will be next. In the summer months there are performances of sword-fighting and hawking, particularly interesting for children.

There's a restaurant nearby, **Grešna Gorica** (tel. 049/343-001, www.gresna-gorica. hr, daily, 50Kn), though the hilltop setting is far better than the food. Even so, it's usually packed on the weekends with day-trippers having lunch among the turkeys and chickens that wander around. Near the village of Desinić, a short drive away, is the lovely **Seljački Turizam Trsek** (Trnovec Desinićki 23, tel. 049/343-464, josip@trsek.hr, www. trsek.hr, 275Kn d, including breakfast), a rustic bed-and-breakfast sort of place with excellent food and cozy charm.

About 50 kilometers (31 miles) northwest of Zagreb, Veliki Tabor can be reached via the A4 highway toward Maribor. If you're taking the bus, there are several daily connections from Zagreb to the nearby village Desinić (2.5

hours). It's about a five-kilometer (three-mile) walk from the station to the castle.

KRAPINA

The busy border town of Krapina, with a small historic core, lies next to the Slovenian border in a region of rolling hills. The city is the largest in the county but is most famous for the 1899 discovery of Neanderthal remains. Today, a modern **Krapina Neanderthal Museum (Muzej Krapinskih Neandertalaca)** (Šetalište Vilibalda Sluge bb, tel. 049/371-491, www.mkn.mhz.hr, 9am-7pm Tues.-Sun. Apr.-Oct., 9am-5pm Tues.-Sun. Nov.-March, 60Kn) displays nice exhibits of Stone Age life in the area. A short path takes you to the exact spot where the bones were found, marked by some statues depicting a Neanderthal family—a good spot to take a photo.

Just north of town is **Gostionica Preša** (Tkalci bb, tel. 049/372-664, 7am-10pm Sun.-Thurs., 7am-11pm Fri.-Sat., 55Kn), where you can munch on Zagorski specialties while taking in some great views of Krapina and the surrounding hillsides lined with vineyards. A short drive out of Krapina, **Pansion Vuglec**

Breg (Škarićevo 151, tel. 049/345-015, info@ vuglec-breg.hr, www.vuglec-breg.hr, 658Kn d, including breakfast) is a slightly more upscale form of rural lodging. The re-created village offers clean rooms, nice meals, and home-made wines from the surrounding vineyards. It's less authentic and pricier than some other *seoski turizam* establishments in the area, but it has a nice atmosphere.

Krapina, 56 kilometers (35 miles) north of Zagreb, is easily reached via the A4 highway toward Maribor; it takes about one hour. The town is also easily reached by train (1.5 hours) for around 39Kn. From the train station (F. Galovića 8, tel. 049/371-012), it's a short walk north to the town center.

LEPOGLAVA

Though Lepoglava's main claim to fame is being home to the country's largest prison, the little town has some interesting tourist stops. The city's **tourist office** (Hrvatskih pavlina 7, tel. 042/494-317, turizam@lepoglava-info. hr, www.lepoglava-info.hr, hours vary, call for assistance) can help with maps and infor-mation as well as arrange guided tours. The **prison,** located in a former Pauline mon-astery that sustained substantial damage in World War II, counts dozens of famous his-torical figures including Tito; Croatia's first president, Franjo Tuđman; and the Cardinal Stepinac as former inmates.

However, Lepoglava was also home to painter-monk Ivan Ranger, who left his touch on churches across northern Croatia. The **Church of the Immaculate Conception of Blessed Virgin Mary (Crkva Blažene Djevice Marije)** (Hrvatskih pavlina bb, tel. 042/792-566, hours vary, open daily, free) is a beautiful Gothic church with lots of Baroque touches, including some outstanding frescoes by Ranger. You can visit the church's **Gallery of Ivan Ranger (Galerija Ivana Rangera)** (inside the Crkva Blažene Djevice Marije, hours vary, open daily, donation appreciated) to see photos of his other frescoes if you don't have time to travel Ranger's Way, heading north out of Lepoglava.

Lepoglava Lace

The art of lace-making was introduced to Lepoglava by 15th-century Pauline monks. The local village population started mak-ing the lace using narrow strips of linen thread. It became a mini industry for Lepoglava, supported by local aristocracy, the Paulines (who used the lace for church clothing and decoration), and the sale of pieces at local fairs.

A lace school, the Banovinska čipkarska škola, kept the tradition alive by teaching the art in the first half of the 20th century while introducing new techniques to the women who practiced the skill. Lepoglava bobbin lace is still made the way it has been for centuries—on a cylindrical pillow, wind-ing the thread around small wooden sticks, or bobbins. The most common designs are geometrical or depict plants and animals.

The town is working hard to keep the tradition alive, with lace-making classes in elementary schools, the found-ing of a society, and the county fair-style **International Lace-Making Festival (Međunarodni festival čipke)** (late Sept., contact Lepoglava tourist office, tel. 042/494-317, turizam@ lepoglava-info.hr, www.lepoglava-info.hr), which brings exhibitions of European laces, workshops, and cultural performances to the little town every September.

Lepoglava is also very famous for its lace and the **Lepoglava Lace Gallery,** located in the tourist office (Hrvatskih pavlina 7, www. lepoglavska-cipka.hr), not only serves as a museum but also as a retail shop.

It's somewhat quirky, but perhaps the most interesting exhibit of artwork in Lepoglava is that created by the prisoners. Their work is displayed in the **Gallery of Prisoner's Work (Galerija zatvorskih radova)** (by arrange-ment with the tourist office, 20Kn).

Lepoglava is approximately 70 kilometers (43 miles) north of Zagreb. There is at least one daily bus from Zagreb (2 hours 10 min-utes, 76Kn), but traveling to Lepoglava is easi-est via Varaždin, 26 kilometers (16 miles) to

Traveling Ranger's Way

Ivan Ranger was born in 1700 in Tyrol. Joining the Paulist Monastic Order as a child, he began painting at a young age in northern Italy and in southern Germany. In his 20s he moved to Lepoglava and became a prolific painter of Baroque frescoes in churches throughout northern Croatia, decorating their walls with his colorful and stylistically original murals. He died in Lepoglava in 1753 and is buried inside the church.

From Lepoglava, traveling **Ranger's Way (Rangerov put)** is a nice way to see the countryside. With five stops in chapels and churches, the 8.5-kilometer (5 mile) journey can be taken by car or as a pleasant two-hour journey on foot. The stops include:

- Monastery and Church of St. Mary (Crkva Sv. Marije), Lepoglava

- Chapel of St. John (Kapelica Sv. Ivana), Gorica

- Chapel of St. Juraj (Kapelica Sv. Juraja), Purga

- Chapel of God's Mother of Snow (Kapelica Majke Božje Snježne), Žarovnica

- Chapel of Visitation of the Blessed Virgin Mary (Župna crkva Pohođenja Blažene Djevice Marije), Višnjica

The **Lepoglava tourist office** (Hrvatskih pavlina 7, tel. 042/494-317, www.lepoglava-info. hr) offers maps that can help guide you in following Ranger's footsteps.

the northeast; it has many more connections via train and bus, taking about 45 minutes. The train is the cheaper method, running around 25Kn each way.

TRAKOŠĆAN

Trakošćan castle (tel. 042/796-281, www. trakoscan.hr, 9am-6pm daily Apr.-Oct., 9am-4pm daily Nov.-Mar., 40Kn) is a bit of a national icon. This is the castle you'll find on many postcards from Croatia—it's a must-see field trip for Croatian schoolchildren, and certainly the country's most famous. Built in the 13th century as a small and rather unimportant fortress, the castle was given by King Maximillian to the Drašković family in the 16th century. They owned the castle for almost 400 years and remodeled it to more closely resemble Bavarian castles of the day. The interior exhibits consist mainly of possessions of the great family, including weaponry, paintings, furniture, and a nice display of lead soldiers.

Outside, there's a beautiful Romanticist park designed in the 19th century. In nice weather, it's a great place for a leafy walk around the lake.

At the entrance to the castle, there's a small café offering drinks and a light lunch.

Trakošćan is 80 kilometers (50 miles) northwest of Zagreb. The only way to reach Trakošćan is by car (via Krapina) or by bus from Varaždin. By car, head out of Zagreb on the road to Ljubljana, and exit on the road for Maribor/Krapina. At Krapina, you'll head northeast toward the village of Bednja, just one kilometer (0.6 miles) or so from the castle. The drive should take around 1.5 hours. By bus, there are multiple daily connections from Varaždin, taking about 45 minutes.

Međimurje

Hugging the borders of Slovenia and Hungary, Međimurje has a flavor all its own and plenty of pretty countryside to explore. The region technically begins above Varaždin, in Čakovec, a small town that was once home to a powerful family, the Zrinskis. The regional distinction for Varaždin is not clear, even among locals, who don't consider themselves to belong to Međimurje or Zagorje and will heatedly debate their side. And to be fair, Varaždin is certainly a city of its own. The chocolate-box town is filled with immaculate Christmas-village buildings and is a must-see in the area. But getting out into the countryside is worthwhile, too. The low rolling hills of the area are covered with vineyards and tiny villages, perfect for a sunny day's drive, topped off with a leisurely late lunch and a bottle of local wine.

★ VARAŽDIN

A neat little Hapsburg town 80 kilometers (50 miles) north of Zagreb, the city of Varaždin was first mentioned in 1181. The town was always an important military outpost, occupying a prime spot on the Hungarians' route to the sea and key for fending off later attacks by the Turks on Hapsburg and Hungarian lands. The wealthy city was even Croatia's capital from 1765 to 1776, when a disastrous fire forced the government to move back to Zagreb. After the fire, the town rebuilt its palaces, their intricate Baroque facades creating an almost amusement-park feel to the refined provincial town.

Sights
FREEDOM SQUARE AND NORTH
(Trg slobode)
A good starting point on a sightseeing tour is the Gothic **Church of St. Nicholas (Crkva svetog Nikole)** on Freedom Square. It is thought to date from Romanesque times (11th-12th centuries), though the current structure is a 15th-century rebuild of the original. Farther up the street is the **Entomology Museum (Entomološki muzej)** (Franjevački trg 6/I, tel. 042/210-474, www.gmv.hr, 9am-5pm Tues.-Fri., 9am-1pm Sat.-Sun., 25Kn) in the Herzer Palace, with an exhibit of over 4,500 insects. Even if you're not into bugs, the World of Insects, as the permanent display is named, is arranged in a variety of old cabinets and drawers that might make you feel like you are on a movie set rather than a museum.

Heading up Uršulinska, the **Ursuline Church (Uršulinska crkva)** is worth a quick look. Though it doesn't house any important works behind its pink Baroque facade, the interior is a pretty blend of Gothic and Baroque touches.

OLD TOWN CASTLE
(Stari Grad)
A little farther north of the Ursuline Church is **Stari Grad** (Strossmayerovo šetalište bb, tel. 042/658-754, www.gmv.hr, 9am-5pm Tues.-Fri., 9am-1pm Sat.-Sun., 25Kn), better known as **Varaždin's castle,** which is also home to the **town museum** (9am-5pm Tues.-Fri., 9am-1pm Sat.-Sun., admission included with Stari Grad). The museum is home to a decent collection of weaponry, local crafts, and old furniture, helpfully captioned in English. The castle was built as a fairly standard Hungarian fort in the 12th century and transformed in the 16th century into a Renaissance castle complete with two concentric moats. At the end of the 16th century it was acquired by the counts Erdödy, who made significant structural changes to turn it into a residence, where the family lived until 1925.

If you have time to take a short detour, a leisurely five-minute walk west takes you to the **City Cemetery (Gradsko Groblje)** (Hallerova aleja, dawn-dusk daily, free). It is one of the most beautiful cemeteries in

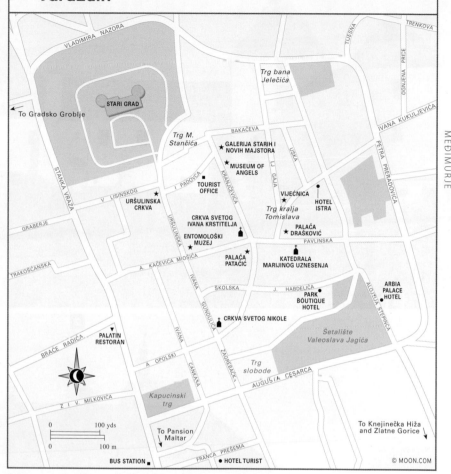

Varaždin

To Gradsko Groblje →

STARI GRAD

Trg bana Jelečića

Trg M. Stančića

★ GALERIJA STARIH I NOVIH MAJSTORA

■ MUSEUM OF ANGELS

■ TOURIST OFFICE

★ URŠULINSKA CRKVA

CRKVA SVETOG IVANA KRSTITELJA

★ ENTOMOLOŠKI MUZEJ

★ PALAČA PATAČIĆ

★ VIJEĆNICA

Trg kralja Tomislava

● HOTEL ISTRA

★ PALAČA DRAŠKOVIĆ

KATEDRALA MARIJINOG UZNESENJA

● PARK BOUTIQUE HOTEL

ARBIA PALACE HOTEL

CRKVA SVETOG NIKOLE

Šetalište Valeoslava Jagića

▼ PALATIN RESTORAN

Trg slobode

Kapucinski trg

To Pansion Maltar

To Knejinečka Hiža and Zlatne Gorice ↘

0   100 yds
0   100 m

■ BUS STATION   ● HOTEL TURIST

© MOON.COM

Street labels: VLADIMIRA NAZORA, TLESNA, TRENKOVA, OGNJENA PRICE, IVANA KUKULJEVIĆA, PETRA PRERADOVIĆA, BAKAČEVA, USKA, GAJA, I PADOVCA, KRANJČEVIĆA, STANKA VRAZA, V. LISINSKOG, GRABERJE, URŠULINSKA, TRAKOŠĆANSKA, A. KAČEVIĆA MIOŠIĆA, IVANA GUNDULIĆA, ŠKOLSKA, J. HABDELIĆA, PAVLINSKA, ALOJZIJA STEPINČA, BRAČE RADIĆA, A. OPOLSKI, A. CANKARA, ZAGREBAČKA, AUGUSTA CESARCA, Z I V. MILKOVIĆA, FRANCA PREŠERNA

Croatia and worth a visit if you enjoy gardens. Laid out in the early 20th century and inspired by Versailles, the cemetery has rows of tombstones lined with 7,000 trees and shrubs and somber sculptures, making it feel more like a park than a graveyard.

Not far from the cemetery, you might want to visit the **Museum of Angels (Muzej Andjela)** (Silvije Strahimira Kranjvije S 14, www.angelsmuseum.com, 10am-1pm and 5pm-8pm Mon.-Fri., 10am-2pm Sat., free), the gallery and museum of local artist Željko

Prstec. There is also a gift shop where you can pick up a secret map to find angels hidden all over the town center.

M. STANČIĆ SQUARE
(Trg M. Stančića)

Slightly east of the Stari Grad castle complex, walk through the 15th-century **Watchtower (Kula stražarnica),** which has an interesting ethnographic collection, to M. Stančić Square. If the weather's nice, stop for a coffee on the square for a nice view of the castle.

When you're finished, head to the tricolored **Sermage Palace (Palača Prassinsky-Sermage)**, a 17th-century palace unlike most of that period's architecture (the facade seems rather Shakespearean) that houses the city's **Gallery of Old and New Masters (Galerija starih i novih majstora)** (Trg Miljenka Stancica 3, tel. 042/214-172, www.gmv.hr, 9am-5pm Tues.-Fri., 9am-1pm Sat.-Sun., 25Kn) to view seasonal art exhibits from the city's vast collections.

FRANCISCAN SQUARE
(Franjevački trg)

Near M. Stančić Square is Franciscan Square, which isn't square at all but rather a very wide rectangular street. On the northern end is the **Franciscan Church of St. John the Baptist (Crkva svetog Ivana Krstitelja)**, a pleasing 17th-century edifice with a gilded altar and a copy of the statue *Grgur Ninski* by Ivan Meštrović.

Just across the square is the frothy rococo **Patačić Palace (Palača Patačić)**, one of the city's most impressive mansions from the late 18th century.

KING TOMISLAV SQUARE
(Trg kralja Tomislava)

Located at the eastern end of Franciscan Square, King Tomislav Square is Varaždin's unofficial main square. The **Drašković Palace (Palača Drašković)**, on the eastern side, is the former home of Suzana Drašković, a woman who had a significant impact on Varaždin's history. When her husband died in 1765, the viceroy of Croatia moved his court to the city (purportedly to be closer to her, though Zagreb had also been declining in the 18th century), making Varaždin the capital of the country. The palace itself is rather ho-hum, save for its heavy stone portal presided over by a shiny gold crest.

The **Town Hall (Vijećnica)** at the northern end of the square acquired its present appearance after renovations in the late 18th

---

1: Old Town Castle **2:** Varaždin

century. The structure was actually built in 1523, though parts of the building are Romanesque, likely remnants of a previous building. The town hall lends a theme park-like appearance to the square, with its crisp white facade and neat flower-filled balcony topped by a huge clock tower. Between 11am and noon every Saturday the **changing of the town guard** takes place, with uniformed volunteers bringing back a bit of Austro-Hungarian flair to Varaždin.

At the southern end of King Tomislav Square, turn onto Pavlinska headed east toward Varaždin's cathedral, built in 1647. Despite the imposing name, the exterior of the **Cathedral of the Ascension (Katedrala Marijinog Uznesenja)** (Pavlinska 5, free) doesn't look much grander than the other churches in town, though its gilt-laden interior tries hard to live up to its name; it's usually open during the day, and there are morning and evening masses daily.

Entertainment and Events

On Saturday from April to October, Franciscan Square turns into the **Square of Olden Trades and Crafts,** featuring everything from potters to weavers and ironsmiths, plus musical performances and a children's puppet show. The city's arts festival, **Špancirfest** (late Aug., www.spancirfest. com), holds street and open-air theatrical and musical performances as well as some interesting costume parades. And during September there's the refined **Varaždin Baroque Evenings (Varaždinske barokne večeri)** (late Sept., www.vbv.hr) with lovely Baroque music concerts performed by both local and international musicians. The town's Baroque settings make the concerts all the more satisfying.

But if a Baroque concert is a little too cultural for your tastes, September is also the month the city hosts the small, off-beat **Trash Film Festival** (www.trash.hr), focusing on low-budget and sometimes flat-out weird action movies.

Any time of the year you can check out the

city's **concert** schedules at the Erdödy Palace or the Croatian National Theater.

For sports enthusiasts, the city's first-division soccer team, **Varteks** (www.nk-varteks.com), has home games that can really get you into the spirit of the town.

Accommodations

Though the rooms aren't as promising as its charming exterior, the **Hotel Istra** (Ulica, Ivana Kukuljevića 6, tel. 042/659-659, www.istra-hotel.hr, 500Kn d, including breakfast) has an excellent location steps off King Tomislav Square. The rooms are a bit bland and on the small side for the price, but the hotel is new and has flat-screen TVs and air-conditioning for the warm summer months.

The **Hotel Turist** (Aleja kralja Zvonimira 1, tel. 042/395-395, www.hotel-turist.hr, 420Kn d, including breakfast) might be exhibit B under communist hotels from the outside, but the rooms inside are fresh and clean after a renovation.

The **Pansion Maltar** (Prešernova 1, tel. 042/311-100, info@maltar.hr, www.maltar.hr, 375Kn d, including breakfast) is a nice little bed-and-breakfast a short walk from King Tomislav Square.

There are two new and more luxurious additions to the town's hotels in the last few years. The boutique **Arbia Palace Hotel** (Ulica Alojzija Stepinca 7, tel. 042/302-104, www.arbiapalace.com, 770Kn d, including breakfast) is located in a renovated building in the center of town. Spacious rooms, parking, and a very nice breakfast make it worth the splurge. The attractive **Park Boutique Hotel** (Ul. Juraja Habdelića 6, tel. 042/420-300, www.park-boutique-hotel.eu, 620Kn d, including breakfast) is in a central location next to the city park. Some rooms are very modern, others a modern take on the traditional, and there is a small sauna for chilly nights.

Food

In town head to **Palatin Restoran** (Brace Radic 1, tel. 042/398-300, www.palatin.hr, 11am-11pm daily, 90Kn) for solid food served in a cozy setting. But if it's real atmosphere you're craving, head a couple of kilometers out of town to either **Kneginečka Hiža** (Toplicka 136, Gornji Kneginec, tel. 042/690-793, 11am-10pm, 80Kn) for hearty local dishes served in a wooden house worthy of a storybook or **Zlatne Gorice** (Banjščina 104, Varaždin Breg, tel. 042/666-054, www.zlatne-gorice.eu, 12pm-9pm Tues.-Sat., 12pm-6pm Sun., 85Kn) set overlooking the vineyards for well-prepared local dishes and wines.

Information and Services

The **tourist office** (Ivana Padovca 3, tel. 042/210-987, info@tourism-varazdin.hr, www.tourism-varazdin.hr, 8am-5pm Mon.-Fri., 9am-1pm Sat.) has maps, and the staff is happy to answer questions.

Getting There and Around

The **bus station** (Zrinskih i Frankopana, tel. 060/333-555, www.ap.hr) is about a five-minute stroll from the town center. Buses connect almost hourly with Zagreb (about 100Kn), a little under two hours away. The **train station** (Kolodvorska 17, tel. 042/213-740) is slightly farther out on the conveniently named Kolodvorska ("Railway Street"). Slow trains to Zagreb (about 90Kn) take about 2.5 hours but are very scenic, and the price is hard to beat. If you're driving from Zagreb to Varaždin, the trip is about 80 kilometers/50 miles (about 1.5 hours) on the A4 highway.

Around town, the best form of transportation is your feet. The city is rather small, particularly the touristed sections, and much of it is pedestrian-only. If you do find yourself in need of a taxi, simply dial 970.

ČAKOVEC

There's not a lot to see in this largely modern town except the 17th-century **castle,** famous because it was home of the Zrinskis, one of Croatia's most powerful noble families. All over Croatia—from street names to restaurants—you'll see the Zrinski name, attached to a family of powerful warrior barons, once favorites of the Hapsburgs. Unassuming little Čakovec was their home from 1546, when the castle was given to Nikola Šubić Zrinski by Emperor Ferdinand I. The Zrinski line came to an unfortunate end when their loyalty to Austria wavered and Petar Zrinski was executed in 1671.

A Baroque palace inside the castle walls houses the **Museum of Međimurje (Muzej međimurja)** (Trg Republike 5, tel. 040/313-499, www.mmc.hr, 8am-6pm Mon.-Fri., 10am-1pm Sat.-Sun. summer, 8am-3pm Mon.-Fri., 10am-2pm Sat.-Sun. winter, 20Kn). There are some exhibits about the Zrinskis, as well as Iron Age finds and brightly embroidered regional dress.

Today Čakovec is the departure point for a wine-roads tour of the region. Right in the Old Town, though under renovation until May 2019, ★ **Shamper Bistro and Winery** (Trg republic 5, tel. 040/390-777, www.shamper. hr, 10am-11pm daily, 75Kn) serves excellent homemade food along with their own wine. Superior service makes for a pleasant experience. **Trattoria Rustica** (I. G. Kovačića 6, tel. 040/311-207, www.trattoriarustica.hr, 8am-11pm Mon.-Fri., 8am-12am Sat.-Sun., 55Kn) is a good choice for Italian staples. A hip and also very reasonable place to fill up, the **Mundoaka Bistro and Wine Bar** (Trg Republic 5, tel. 040/385-035, 9am-11pm Mon.-Sat., 10am-5pm Sun., 50Kn) has good continental food and occasionally really excellent creative dishes depending on the day or season.

Four kilometers (2.5 miles) north of town, ★ **Mala Hiža** (Mačkovec 107, tel. 040/341-101, www.mala-hiza.hr, 9am-9pm daily, 75Kn) looks like a gingerbread house in the middle of nowhere, but the flashy cars out front will tip you off to the well-known restaurant inside that brings people from miles around to munch on gourmet dishes in rustic surroundings. In the summer, the terrace on the 1887 house is also nice for a glass of wine and a leisurely lunch.

Čakovec is 12 kilometers (7.5 miles) northeast of Varaždin. You can get to Čakovec by bus or train from Varaždin (15-20 minutes) or Zagreb (2.5 hours by bus, 3.25 hours by train). The **bus station** (Tome Masaryka 26, tel. 040/313-947) is only a two-minute walk north of King Tomislav Square (Trg Kralja Tomislava). The **train station** (Kolodvorska 2, tel. 040/384-333) is slightly farther away, about a 10-minute walk to the southwest. If you're driving, simply follow the roads to Čakovec from Varaždin.

MEĐIMURJE WINE ROUTES

Driving northwest out of Čakovec in the direction of Štrigova, you'll start to see signs for *vinska cesta* (wine route), leading you through peaceful countryside with rolling hills strung with rows of vineyards. Before heading out, visit the **tourist board (Turistička zajednica Međimurske Županije)** (Ruđera Boškovića 3, tel. 040/390-191, www. visitmedimurje.com) in Čakovec for maps and directions. You'll need a car to navigate the routes, though the brave might be able to travel by bicycle (with a lot of safety gear).

The wines you'll find will be of varying quality, but most people will let you taste before you buy. And if you're the type who feels guilty trying and not buying, bottles are usually available for a not-too-steep 30-40Kn. If you get stuck with a bad one, just add some fizzy mineral water to your glass and say *življeli* (cheers).

Sights

Though the main attractions are the lovely winding roads and vine-covered hillsides, in the middle of the small village of Štrigova, northwest of Čakovec and almost at the Slovenian border, is a nice dual-towered church, the 18th-century **Church of St. Jerome (Crkva Sv. Jeronima).** If you're lucky enough to find the church open, check out its beautiful frescoes by Ivan Ranger.

Wineries

It seems every other house along the route has a hand-painted *vino* sign, alerting you to homemade wine. You can stop and try your luck if you feel like it, but there are a couple of wineries on the routes worth singling out. **Vinogradarstvo i podrumarstvo Bobnjar** (Robadje 130, Štrigova, tel. 040/851-431, call for hours) is run by a lovely couple who have been producing wine since 1952. With a great selection of whites (all made without additives, so they're a bit acidic), the couple counts at least two Croatian presidents as customers. **Vino Lovrec** (Sv. Urban 133, Štrigova, tel. 040/830-171, www.vino-lovrec. hr, call for hours) produces a very honest wine with no added sugars, and has a great rustic tasting area.

On the internationally acclaimed side of wineries, **Vinarija Jakopić** (Železna Gora 113, Štrigova, tel. 040/851-300, www.vina-jakopic.hr) is something of a star in the area, with multiple winners of the Decanter World Wine Awards. In operation since 1908, the family winery showcases their wine at the **Terbotz restaurant** (see Accommodations and Food below).

Accommodations and Food

Međimurski Dvori (Vladimira Nazora 22, Lopatinec, tel. 040/855-763, info@medjimurski-dvori.hr, www.medjimurski-dvori.hr, 65Kn), northwest of Čakovec in Lopatinec, is a destination restaurant, the sort of place you can easily spend several hours lingering over the chef's duck specialties or a more common north Croatian dish like turkey with *mlinci*.

★ **Terbotz** (Železna Gora 113, Štrigova, tel. 040/857-444, www.terbotz.hr, 11am-11pm Fri., 11am-1am Sat., 75Kn), amidst seemingly endless vineyards on the surrounding hills, has some nice local dishes, with a good selection of game and a collection of regional wines to choose from (make sure to try the

quite lauded graševina). The wine cellar area is probably the best spot to sit and order up a few glasses.

Just out of town is the family-run **Mamica Pansion** (Čakovečka 47, tel. 040/373-433, www.mamica.com.hr, 490Kn d), with clean, quiet rooms and a good restaurant.

★ HLEBINE

The small town of Hlebine is where the naive art movement was born. It's not hard to find your way away around the town's one main street. The **Generalić Gallery** (tel. 048/671-920, www.generalic.com, call or email via website ahead of time to arrange a visit) is located in the former studio of Ivan Generalić, the genre's best-known painter, though it also exhibits work by his son Josip and grandson Goran. The gallery is open by request only, so call in advance if you would like to visit.

There's not really anywhere to eat in Hlebine, so head to the nearby **Podravska Klet** (Starogradska cesta bb, tel. 048/634-069, 10am-10pm daily, 70Kn) in Koprivnica. It is one of the best restaurants in the entire region, with a warm local atmosphere and homey dishes like beef goulash on the menu. On weekends, it's a good idea to book ahead.

Almost at the Hungarian border, Hlebine is approximately 80 kilometers (50 miles) northeast of Zagreb and is accessed via Koprivnica, about 16 kilometers (10 miles) away. Monday to Friday there are six buses a day from Koprivnica to Hlebine (30 minutes, 20Kn), but service is highly irregular on the weekends. Koprivnica is connected by bus with Zagreb (1.5 hours, 80Kn) and Varaždin. Even simpler is to take the slow train to Koprivnica (1.5 hours, 46Kn) and then take the bus for Hlebine. If you're traveling by car, the simplest route is to take the A4 toward Varaždin and exit Koprivnica and follow the signs.

Slavonia

A vast stretch of rich agricultural land, Slavonia (Slavonija) doesn't get many of Croatia's tourists, who typically turn west toward the coast and skip this part of eastern Croatia, stretching out its green arm leisurely toward the Danube. Its geographical position, sharing borders with Bosnia, Serbia, and Hungary, has led Slavonia to be bounced between different rulers and kingdoms on and off since the 11th century. The Homeland War, Croatia's fight for independence from Yugoslavia in the 1990s, affected the area significantly with some towns, like Vukovar, suffering mass destruction and loss of life. While the war is now firmly behind them, Slavonia's economic prospects have been slow to recover, and many of its youth have left to work in more prosperous areas of Croatia or other European countries.

But you won't find friendlier and more welcoming people anywhere, and Slavonia is doing a great job of promoting the things that make it unique. This is the place to stay in a *seoski turizam* hotel, get a ride in a *fijaker* (carriage), and explore the local cuisine, heavy in pork but also characterized by freshwater fish. *Fiš paprikaš* is a must-eat while you're here, but also be sure to try some of the spicy *kulen* (salami) and sausages made after the annual pig slaughter in November.

POŽEGA

Požega is one of Slavonia's prettier small towns, with a long row of one-story typical homes lining the main road in and out of town. On the town's main **Holy Trinity Square (Trg svetog Trojstva)**, the **Church of the Holy Spirit (Crkva svetog Duha)** was once used as a mosque by the Turks, who occupied the town between 1536 and 1691. The 14th-century **St. Lawrence's Church (Crkva svetog Lovre)** has some nice Gothic frescoes, and the **Town Museum (Gradski muzej)** (Matice Hrvatske 1, tel. 034/272-130,

www.gmp.hr, 10am-12pm and 6pm-8pm Mon.-Fri., 10am-12pm Sat., 10Kn) has a small collection that's worth a look if you're in town, along with a souvenir store called the Mali Salon that has longer hours than the museum. For a quiet escape, the **Old Town Promenade (Šetalište Stari Grad)** is a nice walking path through the ruins and site of the early-13th-century town.

In May, Požega hosts a quirky **Croatian Festival of One-Minute Films (Hrvatska revija jednominutnih filmova)** (www. crominute.hr), with creative takes on 60 seconds from around the globe.

Wineries

Twenty-seven kilometers (17 miles) from Požega is ★ **Enjingi** (Hrnjevac 87, Vetovo, tel. 034/267-200, www.enjingi.hr, 391Kn d, including breakfast), one of Croatia's best wineries. It's open to the public for tastings (8am-5pm Mon.-Fri., 8am-3pm Sat.) but it's even better to spend a night here, chatting with the owners over a glass of wine and some local kulen with fresh bread. Rooms are fairly basic, but the experience can't be beat.

Nearby are the 800-year-old **Kutjevo cellars** (Kutjevo, www.kutjevo.com, tel. 098/299-588, call for reservations for a tour and/or tasting), where you can taste several wines as well as learn a bit about local wines in the guided introduction. Kutjevo produces several varieties of wine, but be sure to sample its specialty, ice wine, made from grapes harvested when the temperatures are well below freezing, giving it a distinct flavor, as well as its aged wine, de Gotho. It bills itself as the oldest operating cellars in Croatia.

Accommodations and Food

Once again, the **Enjingi** (Hrnjevac 87, Vetovo, tel. 034/267-200, www.enjingi.hr, 391Kn d, including breakfast) winery is a great location for a room. **Hotel Grgin Dol**

(Grgin Dol 20, tel. 034/273-222, www.hotel-grgin-dol.hr, 370Kn d) is a family-run hotel with dated but clean rooms and friendly service. There is a restaurant on site and it is a short walk to the center of town. **Zlatni Lug** (Donji Emovci 28A, tel. 098/472-483, www.zlatnilug.hr, 380Kn d) is both a restaurant and hotel located in a historic building. The food is quite possibly the best in town, and the rooms, while very basic, are clean and convenient.

Getting There and Around

You can reach Požega by **bus** (Industrijska 2, tel. 034/273-133) or **train** (Franje Cirakija 7, tel. 034/273-911); both stations are at the northern end of the town. There are several bus and train connections daily—the bus takes 2.5 hours, the fast train takes three hours, and the slow train takes up to five hours, though the trains are a bit cheaper—a one-way ticket on the train is 88Kn versus 110Kn by bus. By car from Zagreb, it's about 150 kilometers (93 miles) east. Take the Autocesta (highway) A3 toward Slavonski Brod and exit Nova Gradiška. From here you'll find road signs that will point you into town.

SLAVONSKI BROD

Though there's not a lot to see in this mainly industrial town, the city's small 19th-century waterfront center is a nice place to stop for a bite to eat, and there are a couple of good options for overnight stays before moving on through Slavonia. If you're here mid-June, be sure to stop for the **Brodsko Kolo Festival** (www.brodsko-kolo.com) for the superb displays of folk dance, *tamburaše* musicians, and exhibits of village life.

Sights

The main **I. B. Mažuranić Square (Trg I. B. Mažuranić)** faces the Sava River and the town of Bosanski Brod, today a peaceful place on the other bank—though less than two decades ago, shots rang across the river into town. Walk down the riverside walkway **Radić Promenade (Šetalište braće Radić)**

to the Baroque **Franciscan monastery (Franjevački samostan).** On the western side of the square are the remnants of the **Brod Fortress,** once a giant star-shaped edifice built in the early 18th century to defend Slavonia against the Turks.

Going out of town, **Dilj mountain** is a lovely place to take a hike, with some beautiful old weekend homes, including one once occupied by Croatian children's author Ivana Brlić Mažuranić, and several nice spots for picnicking. Ask at the **tourist office** (Trg pobjede 30, tel. 035/231-939, www.tzgsb.hr) for more information.

Wineries

★ **Stupnički Dvori** (Vinogradska 65, Brodski Stupnik, tel. 035/427-775, 400Kn d) is a bit of a one-stop shop, just 15 minutes west of Slavonski Brod in Brodski Stupnik, with a winery, restaurant, and hotel, all with traditional Slavonian flavor. The place is a must-visit in nice weather, when you can dine overlooking the vineyards on the restaurant's terrace. To get here, exit the highway at "Slavonski Brod Zapad" and follow the signs toward Nova Gradiška/Požega. In the village of Slatinik, follow the road toward Nova Gradiška for six kilometers (3.7 miles) until you reach the village of Brodski Stupnik.

Accommodations and Food

Navigator (Trg Ivane Brlić Mažuranić 13, tel. 035/123-456, 7:30am-12am daily) is a cafe that turns into a nightclub as the evening wears on. It's where the hip go to meet up and be seen. **Pizzerija Uno** (Nikole Zrinskog 7, tel. 035/442-107, 9am-12am daily, 45Kn), with its dark brick and wood interior and flower-filled summer terrace, is a great option for food in town.

Located in the guesthouse of a family house, **Sobe Levicki** (Ante Starčevića 4, tel. 035/444-666, www.sobe-levicki.com, 315Kn d) is more hostel with private rooms than hotel, but the location is good, the furniture is new, and it is clean and comfortable. The small hotel offers free Wi-Fi as well as free pickup from the bus and train stations and is located right on the main square. The new luxury hostel **Hostel Levicki** (Trg Stjepana Miletića 11, tel. 098/365-1000, www.hostel-levicki.hr, from 130Kn pp) is a centrally located, nicely decorated and very clean hostel if you are not opposed to sharing a room. Another option for overnight is the **Hotel Savus** (Dr. A. Starčevića 2a, tel. 035/405-888, info@savus-hotel.com, www.savus-hotel.com, 825Kn d, including breakfast). Right in the center of town, it has a rather gaudy lobby but the rooms are comfortable.

For cheaper options, contact the **tourist office** (Tourist Information Center Slavonski Brod, Trg pobjede 30, tel. 035/231-939, www.tzgsb.hr) to see about small pensions and private accommodations.

Getting There and Around

Slavonski Brod is one of the largest towns in Slavonia, approximately 200 kilometers (124 miles) east of Zagreb. The city is easily accessed by bus or train. The **bus station** (Trg hrvatskog proljeća, tel. 035/441-200) has multiple daily connections with Zagreb (three hours, 110Kn), as well as Osijek (two hours, 63Kn) and Đakovo (45 minutes, 37Kn). The **train** (Trg hrvatskog proljeća, tel. 035/441-082) is faster and cheaper; from Zagreb it takes only about 2.5 hours and costs around 110Kn. If driving from Zagreb, simply take the Autocesta A3 in the direction of Slavonski Brod.

ĐAKOVO

Đakovo, 95 kilometers (59 miles) east of Slavonski Brod, is a town of around 30,000 people and an important trading center in Slavonia due to its location and history. The city has long been a market town, a place where local farmers and craftspeople met to buy and sell, and Đakovo maintains that feeling even today. The most striking feature of Đakovo, which you'll spot before you even come close to the town, is the giant 84-meter (275-foot) brick **cathedral** (Trg Josipa Jurja Strossmayera 6, tel. 031/802-225, 7am-12pm and 3pm-7pm daily, free) that seems to dwarf everything by comparison. It was built between 1862 and 1882 by the Bishop Juraj Strossmayer, famed for his mission to unite the Slavs, in the Gothic Revival style.

If you've ever been to Vienna, you've heard of the Lipizzaner horses. Đakovo has one of the few Lipizzaner stud farms, **Ergela Stud Farm** (Augusta Šenoa 47, tel. 031/813-286, www.ergela-djakovo.hr, tickets start at 20Kn), a 10-minute walk from the cathedral. The farm puts on shows for large groups, but individual visitors can still see the horses and a small collection of historical photographs. Call ahead to see what times the horses might be training that day if you'd like to see them in action.

Đakovo is very well connected with Osijek, with over a dozen buses (45 minutes, 30Kn) and half a dozen trains (45 minutes, 28Kn) daily. You can also connect with Zagreb by bus (3.5 hours, 115Kn) or train (3 hours, 94Kn).

OSIJEK

It's worth spending a day in the riverfront town of Osijek, just 20 kilometers (12 miles) from the Serbian border, to walk around its famous fortress, the Tvrđa, a collection of Habsburg-era buildings that sit on the site of a much older Roman stronghold.

Osijek was damaged badly in the war, and you'll see some of the scars on buildings today. However, the city has started to regain some of its prosperity of days past.

One of the nicest walks in Osijek is to follow the peaceful walkway **Promenade Cardinal Franjo Šeper (Šetalište Kardinala Frane Šepera)** along the riverfront to the **winter harbor (Zimska luka),** where waterfront cafés hug the small marina.

Upper Town
(Gornji Grad)

Osijek's small Upper Town is centered around the **Ante Starčević Square (Trg Ante Starčevića),** dominated by the town's brick **Parish Church of St. Peter and Paul**

(**Župna crkva svetog Petra i Pavla**) (Trg Ante Starčevića, tel. 031/310-020, www. svpetaripavao.hr, open daily, mass at 7am and 6:30pm Mon.-Fri., 7am Sat., 6:30am, 8:30am, 10am, 11:30am, and 6:30pm Sun., free), built in the 1890s for the growing city. The interior of the church seats 3,000 and is covered in striking frescoes, painted between 1938 and 1942 by Croatian artist Mirko Rački.

The nearby **Europska avenija** starts off with the architecturally interesting, and still in operation, 1912 **Urania Cinema,** just off the beginning of Europska toward the river. The pink facade topped by a mournful mask resembles a giant organ. Back on Europska, you can take a look at the **Gallery of Fine Arts (Galerija likovnih umjetnosti)** (Europska avenija 9, tel. 031/251-280, www. mlu.hr, 10am-6pm Tues.-Fri., 15Kn), the town's art gallery, with lots of decadent 19th-century portraits by Slavonian painters. From there, Europska becomes a wide tree-lined street, hugged by glorious art nouveau homes, some decaying, some restored.

Agatha Christie

Famed mystery author Agatha Christie had more than one connection with Croatia. In 1928, after a painful divorce, she set out from London to Baghdad, taking the Venice-Simplon *Orient Express.* She said she had always wanted to take the famous train. She described it as *"Allegro con fuoco,* swaying, and rattling and hurling one from side to side in its mad haste to leave Calais and the Occident."

The original Venice-Simplon *Orient Express* traveled through Zagreb as well as Slavonia on its way to Belgrade. Agatha Christie set the majority of her book, *Murder on the Orient Express,* on a train stuck in a snowdrift between Vinkovci and Brod (the name for Slavonski Brod and Bosanski Brod when they were considered one town).

And this wasn't the only time Agatha Christie came to Croatia. After meeting her archaeologist husband, Max, they took a second honeymoon to Dubrovnik and Split, on the Dalmatian coast.

★ Citadel
(Tvrđa)

The 17th-century **Citadel (Tvrđa),** at the end of Europska's grand portion, is Osijek's best-known attraction and social hub. The Austro-Hungarian fort is actually a giant complex of buildings crisscrossed with nice little cobblestone streets. The area is also Osijek's cultural center, and the city is currently renovating more and more buildings for schools, the university, and the public.

The heart of the Tvrđa is the huge **Holy Trinity Square (Trg svetog Trojstva),** punctuated by the **plague column (Zavjetni stup),** a 1729 thank-you from those who survived an outbreak that killed one-third of the city's population. The cloaked figures at the Baroque pillar's base are saints added in 1784 after several more bouts of plague had struck the city. The square's **Museum of Slavonia (Muzej Slavonije)** (Trg Svetog Trojstva 6, tel. 031/250-730, www.mso.hr, 10am-6pm Tues.-Sat., 20Kn)

has some interesting exhibits of local history and artifacts.

Entertainment and Events

For nightlife, head to the Tvrđa, where Osijek's university students and young professionals drink until the wee hours. If you'd prefer to take it easier, there are some nice cafés at the **winter harbor (Zimska Luka)** that have great outdoor seating in summer, or take in a movie at **Europa cinema** (Šetalište Petra Preradovića 2) or the **Kino Urania** (Vjekoslava Hengla 1), both within walking distance of Upper Town. The Kino Urania is particularly beautiful due to its stunning art deco architecture.

Croatian National Theater (Hrvatsko narodno kazalište) (Županijska 9, tel. 031/220-700) hosts performances of classical music and theater throughout the year.

On the first Saturday of each month, **Holy Trinity Square (Trg svetog Trojstva)** is overrun with antiques dealers from Croatia

Osijek

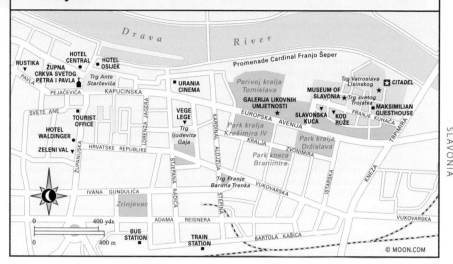

as well as neighboring Hungary, Bosnia, and Serbia. You'll get a better deal here than you would at the market's equivalent in Zagreb.

Accommodations

Surprisingly, Osijek has several options for accommodations on the upper end of the scale but little to offer in terms of budget hotels. Travelers watching their wallets should head to the **tourist office** (Županska 2, tel. 031/203-755, www.tzosijek.hr, 7am-4pm Mon.-Fri., 8am-12pm Sat.), where they can tell you all about renting private rooms. One nice option is the ★ **Maksimilian Guesthouse** (Franjevačka 12, tel. 031/497-567, www.maksimilian.hr, 330Kn d, including breakfast). Located in a charming old town building, the cozy rooms come with friendly owners who are happy to make local recommendations.

The **Hotel Central** (Trg Ante Starčevića 6, tel. 031/283-399, www.hotel-central-os.hr, 768Kn d, including breakfast) is located in a pretty old Secession building in Upper Town. The rooms aren't as charming as the building, but they are fresh and clean, and it's hard to beat the location. The nearby ★ **Hotel Waldinger** (Županska 8, tel. 031/250-450, www.waldinger.hr, 931Kn d, including breakfast) has more charming rooms and the same great location at slightly higher rates; the waterfront **Hotel Osijek** (Šamačka 4, tel. 031/230-333, www.hotelosijek.hr, 1,023Kn d, including breakfast), despite its soulless exterior, is considered the nicest hotel in town.

Food

The vegetarian restaurant **Vege Lege** (Gajev Trg 4, tel. 031/445-440, www.vege-lege.com, 9am-7pm Mon.-Fri., 10am-3pm Sat., 20Kn) has good tacos, veggie burgers, and falafel, while meat eaters will find **Zeleni Val** (Županijska 22, tel. 031/200-864, 8am-11pm Mon.-Fri., 10am-11pm Sat., 11am-11pm Sun., 30Kn) is the best place in town for the Croatian meat staple čevapčići. For something reasonable but higher quality than fast food, try **Rustika** (Ulica Pavla Pejačica 32, tel. 031/369-400, www.rustika.hr, 11am-11pm daily, 80Kn) for excellent pizzas, local beef dishes, pastas, and even rooms. ★ **Kod Ruže** (Kuhačeva 25a, tel. 031/206-066, 9am-10pm Mon.-Sat., 75Kn) in the Tvrđa serves up gourmet local dishes (even frog legs are on the

Land Mines

The Homeland War may be a piece of history, but land mines left by the conflict continue to do damage around Croatia. An estimated 13 of Croatia's 21 counties are thought to contain land mines, with the area covering close to 1,700 square kilometers (656 square miles).

Croatia ratified the Mine Ban Treaty in 1998 and is working hard to clean up the mines, but the process is slow and expensive, and even after demining, some mines can still remain. Since 1991, land mines have hurt thousands of people in Croatia and killed more than 100 since 1998.

Before hiking in rural areas, you should educate yourself to be safe. One of the best sources of information is the **Croatian Mine Action Center (Hrvatski Centar za Razminiranje)** (www.hcr.hr). Their website has maps for all regions of Croatia with danger areas marked in red. Also be on the lookout for red signs with the words *Pazi Mina* (Danger Mines) and a skull and crossbones.

Croatia is working on new methods to detect land mines, with a promising study in using the country's tradition of bee-keeping by training bees to sniff out mines. In the meantime, if you'd like to help the country's fight against land mines, visit **Adopt-a-Minefield** (www.landmines. org) to donate toward the cause.

menu) in a quaint space loaded with atmosphere and a heavy dose of chic. For a great *fiš paprikaš,* a sort of freshwater fish stew that is a local specialty, and other Slavonian specialties, try **Slavonska Kuća** (Ulica Kamila Finigera 26, tel. 031/369-955, 9am-11pm Mon.-Sat., 60Kn), a casual but cozy spot for a hot meal.

Getting There and Around

Both the **bus** (Bartula Kašica 70, tel. 060/353-353, www.app.hr, ticket office 5am-9pm daily) and **train** (Trg Lavoslava Ružičke 2, tel. 060/333-444, www.hzpp.hr, ticket office 5am-9:30pm Mon.-Fri. for domestic lines) stations are close to the center of town, with a 10- to 15-minute walk landing you on the main square. There's a fast InterCity train to Zagreb that takes about three hours and costs approximately 113Kn. Buses take closer to four hours, but the connections are frequent, and the trip costs around 125Kn to or from Zagreb. If you have a lot of bags, a tram ride (buy tickets at newspaper kiosks, about 8Kn) will take you there faster. The tram is also a great way to zip around town if you're too lazy to walk, although there are only two lines, so you'll be relying mostly on your feet or your rental car. Walking is preferred around the narrow Tvrđa.

TOP EXPERIENCE

★ KOPAČKI RIT NATURE PARK
(Park prirode Kopački rit)

On a floodplain created by the Danube and Drava Rivers, **Kopački rit** (tel. 031/285-370, http://pp-kopacki-rit.hr, 8am-4pm daily winter, 7am-3pm daily summer, 80Kn) is a giant nature reserve just 10 kilometers (six miles) northeast of Osijek. The park spans close to 23,000 hectares (56,000 acres), with lakes and swampy marshes filled with fish and over 250 species of birds. The forests of the **Tikveš** area of the park are filled with wild boar, deer, and the occasional black stork.

The highlight of Tikveš forest is the lovely **Dvorac,** actually a hunting lodge built by Archduke Franz Ferdinand that later passed into the hands of the Serbian royal family and then Tito. Some of the areas have yet to be cleared of land mines, so watch for signs warning you to steer clear. An English-language guide and more information are available at the visitors center at the entrance to the park. They can also let you know about boat tours, which depart almost daily in warmer months, or help you organize a jeep tour of the park with a local guide.

Accommodations and Food

Within the park, toward Tikveš, **Kormoran** (Podunavlje bb, tel. 031/753-099, www.belje. hr, 11am-10pm daily summer, call for winter hours, 75Kn) serves fresh local fish either grilled or as a part of a *paprikaš* stew cooking over glowing coals.

The red-and-white-themed house of **Crvendać** (Biljske satnije ZNG RH 5, tel. 031/750-264, pansion@crvendac.com, www. crvendac.com, 300Kn d, including breakfast), literally meaning "redbird," is clean and happy, and the owners make some great food at reasonable prices. With loads of space for exploring and two clay tennis courts, **Hotel Lug** (Šandora Petefija 64, tel. 031/628-028, www.ekolug.com, 390Kn d, including breakfast) has simple but clean rooms and a good restaurant. The best feature? It's located close to the main entrance of the park.

Getting There and Around

By car from Osijek, drive to Bilje and turn right at the main intersection. From there, simply follow the signs to the park. Buses leave every half hour to one hour from Osijek to Bilje (20-30 minutes). At the end of the line, it's about a four-kilometer (2.4-mile) walk to the visitors center. For those who have bikes, there's a bicycle path of approximately 16 kilometers (10 miles) on the Osijek to Bilje road.

THE BARANJA

At first glance the Baranja is just a lonely stretch of plain, but look closer and you'll uncover some of Slavonia's best finds. Discovering local wineries is also a great way to get to meet the people, and the hospitable owners of bed-and-breakfasts around the area make visitors feel like they have their own personal guided tour.

Wineries

The Baranja has been known for its wines since Roman times. If you have time to visit only one winery in the region, the ★ **Vinarija Josić** (Planina 194, Zmajevac, tel. 098/252-657, www.josic.hr, restaurant 1pm-10pm Tues.-Sun.) should top your list. The family makes award-winning wines in a brick wine cellar that dates from 1935. The bottles make nice souvenirs as well, not only for the great red or white wine inside, but for the labels, decorated with endangered bird species from nearby Kopački rit. The restaurant is lovely and worth the visit. The **Kolar wine cellar** (Maršala Tita 141, Suza, tel. 031/733-184, call to arrange a visit) also has some rooms available. Last but not least on the list of stops: the **Gerštmajer wine cellar** (Šandora Petefija 31, Zmajevac, tel. 091/351-5586, call for hours), where you can drop by to sample wines or call ahead to arrange a lunch of local specialties.

Accommodations and Food

★ **Baranjska kuća** (Kolodvorska 99, Karanac, tel. 031/720-180, www.baranjska-kuca.com, 11am-10pm Tues.-Thurs., 11am-1am Fri.-Sat., 11am-5pm Sun., 80Kn) offers great meals with local wine and a few rooms as well in an authentic setting. Just down the road, the ★ **Sklepić house** (Kolodvorska 58, Karanac, tel. 031/720-303, www.sklepic.hr, 320Kn d, including breakfast) is possibly one of the nicest experiences in the region. The 1910-era village house is pleasingly authentic, the stay includes a lovely breakfast, and the owner can arrange for typical Slavonian horse-drawn carriage rides as well as tours of Kopački rit and the wine routes of the Baranja. There is no air-conditioning, and you should expect simple accommodations, but it will be among the most authentic places you stay.

Getting There and Around

The region is about 30 kilometers (18 miles) north of Osijek. Follow the A7 to Beli Manastir and then follow the signs for the villages, located east of the highway. Public transportation is infrequent—you'll need a car to get around the region.

VUKOVAR

Once a happy and prosperous multicultural community, the city of Vukovar was heavily

The Siege of Vukovar

On September 14, 1991, the Croatian National Guard cut off the Yugoslav People's Army (JNA) barracks, leaving them without electricity, food, water, or phone lines. Serb paramilitaries responded by launching a fierce attack, killing civilians as they went, and forcing some 2,000 refugees into the center of Vukovar. During the next two weeks, 15 to 80 wounded civilians were brought to the Vukovar hospital each day.

This clearly marked a new phase in the war. On October 4 the JNA attacked—this time fiercely, with air attacks, artillery, and mortar, dropping two bombs on the packed hospital. Most of the hospital was operating out of the basement by this time, protecting most of the patients but making it hard to find room for the 92 additional wounded that poured in that day.

October had hardly begun, and most people moved into public bomb shelters protected by the Croatian National Guard. The Serb forces were experiencing morale issues as they weren't able to bring down the small and comparatively unarmed town. The group was suffering from a lack of organization, so a new general took over the Vukovar "operation" and launched another serious attack on November 3, advancing to within just a few hundred meters of the town center.

Vukovar felt betrayed by the leadership in Zagreb, whom they felt had sold them out by agreeing to an internationally brokered cease-fire. Tuđman reportedly offered no help, worried more about diplomacy than about Vukovar.

Finally on November 18 the town fell, with Serb forces throwing the patients and hospital personnel onto trucks, killing them, and depositing them in a mass grave at Ovčara. Two thousand Croatian civilians and soldiers died defending Vukovar, and another two thousand (mostly men who were bused out of town that late fall day) remain missing.

INLAND CROATIA
SLAVONIA

damaged during the Homeland War. Today Vukovar is only beginning to recover, though the Croat and Serb populations remain divided, and while there's not a lot of sightseeing, there are plenty of reasons to visit.

For one, the city is a great jumping-off point for touring the wine country just outside town, but more importantly, it's great to show support for Vukovar's economy and to get to know the people, who are welcoming and friendly despite the recent suffering and the lingering wounds of war.

For more information, you can contact the **tourist office** (J. J. Strossmayera 15, tel. 032/442-889, www.turizamvukovar.hr). The local agency **Danubium Tours** (Trg Republike Hrvatske 1, tel. 032/445-455, danubiumtours@vu.t-com.hr, www.danubiumtours.hr) can arrange for private rooms as well as very reasonable bike trips, walking tours, and trips through the local wine region, all including excellent lunch

stops. They also run a nice **boat tour**, with a glass of local wine, that passes most of the important buildings of Vukovar.

Sights

The **Town Museum (Gradski muzej)** (Županijska 2, on Strossmayera near the market, tel. 032/441-270, www.muzej-vukovar.hr, 10am-6pm Tues.-Sun., 40Kn) is housed in the early-18th-century **Eltz Castle (Dvorac Eltz).** Many of the town's permanent exhibitions were seized by the Serbs, with some being officially transported to Serbia and others disappearing altogether. However, an agreement in 2001 has helped many items return to the museum, and the city is in the process of restoring Eltz Castle, which was badly damaged in the Homeland War, to its former glory. It is an extremely well done museum and worth a visit.

As Strossmayera crosses the river it becomes Dr. Franje Tuđmana, which leads through Vukovar's old town. One of the prettiest buildings here is the Grand Hotel. Built in 1897, it was Vukovar's finest hotel until it

---

1: Ilok defense walls and church **2:** reminders of war, Osijek **3:** Kopački rit Nature Park

was sold in 1919 to the Worker's Union and renamed the **House of Workers (Radnički Dom)**. It was here that the Yugoslav Communist Party was founded in 1920.

Many of the buildings in Vukovar's **Old Town (Stari Grad)** (along and around the street Dr. Franje Tuđmana) were built in the Baroque period, with lovely arched arcades on the ground floors. Most were badly damaged in the war, though some have been restored and some left with the reminders of the violence that disrupted the peaceful city streets.

Southeast of the old town, the 18th-century **Franciscan monastery (Franjevački samostan)** (Samostanska 2) was Vukovar's oldest preserved Baroque monument prior to its almost total destruction in 1991. However, Zagreb county contributed to its wonderful and almost exact reconstruction.

Vukovar has several war monuments, but the most moving is the **Ovčara Memorial Centre** (tel. 032/512-345, www.hdlskl. hr, 10am-5pm daily, free) a few kilometers south of the city on the Ovčara Bravo road. Remembering the 263 men and 1 woman who were executed in 1991, the photos of those who died won't soon be forgotten.

Opened in 2015, the incredibly well-designed **Vučedol Culture Museum** **(Muzej Vučedolske Kulture)** (Vučedol 252, tel. 032/373-930, www.vucedol.hr, 10am-6pm Tues.-Sun., 45Kn) displays artifacts and re-creations of life in the ancient Vučedol culture, which flourished around 3000 B.C.

Accommodations and Food

The fairly new **Hotel Lav** (Strossmayera 17, tel. 032/445-100, info@hotel-lav.hr, www. hotel-lav.hr, 900Kn d, including breakfast) is a point of pride for Vukovar's residents, marking a new chapter in the life of the city. Its rooms are sleek, though perhaps a little bland. But what the rooms lack in personality, the magnificent Danube views make up for. Try **Megaron** (Dalmatinska 3, tel. 098/896-507, 2pm-9pm daily, 60Kn) for local specialties like Slavonian salami and *kulen*.

Getting There and Around

Vukovar is 35 kilometers (21 miles) southeast of Osijek. By car from Zagreb, take the A3 highway toward Slavonski Brod, exiting at Vinkovci, where you'll follow the signs for Vukovar. The drive from Zagreb takes about seven hours. The **bus station** (Olajnica bb, tel. 032/441-829) has multiple daily connections with Osijek (45 minutes, 50Kn) as well as Zagreb and Slavonski Brod. Although it

House of Workers, Vukovar

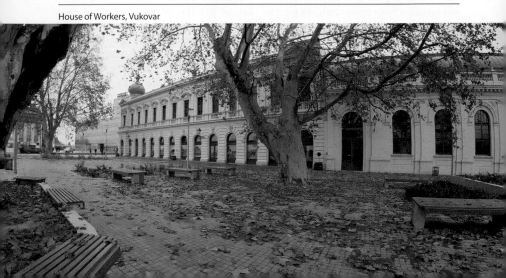

is not the fastest route, the **train** (Priljevo 2, tel. 032/430-340) is perhaps the nicest way to travel from Zagreb (around 3.5 hours, inter-city ticket 115Kn) and from Osijek (two hours, 25Kn).

AROUND VUKOVAR
★ Ilok Wineries

The town of Ilok is a largely undiscovered lit-tle gem with a charming, if small, medieval old town. It's famous for its wines, particu-larly the gold-tinged Traminac, served at the coronation of Queen Elizabeth II. If you're in the mood for wine-tasting, start with the 17th-century cellars of **Iločki Cellars (Iločki Podrumi)** (Šetalište o. M. Barbarića 4, tel. 032/590-088, www.ilocki-podrumi.hr, call for reservations).

It's also worth checking out local produc-ers **Julius Stipetić** (S Radića 16, tel. 032/591-068, call for hours) and **Ivan Čobankovic** (V Nazora 59, tel. 032/593-382, call for hours), of-fering a selection of solid white and red wines.

The **Ilok tourist office** (Trg Nikole Iločkog 2, tel. 032/590-020, info@turizamilok. hr, www.turizamilok.hr) can provide you with

maps and info on the local wine routes if you'd like to explore more vineyards and wine producers. An interesting souvenir is a bottle of wine from Ilok's **high school,** founded in 1899 to teach wine cultivation, a tradition it continues today.

If you'd like to stick around a while, try the **Hotel Dunav Ilok** (Julija Benešića 62, tel. 032/596-500, www.hoteldunavilok.com, 500Kn d, including breakfast), a small fam-ily hotel furnished with antiques; it has a res-taurant as well. If you're in town at the end of September, the town hosts a **wine harvest festival** with cultural performances and lots of yummy wine-tastings.

Dalj

In this tiny village on the eastern border of Croatia, winemaker Jasna Antunović Turk has made a name for herself both nationally and internationally and is known for her su-perb white grasevina wines. The **Vinarija Antunović** (Ul. Braće Radić 17, tel. 031/590-350, www.vina-antunovic.hr, call for hours) has a tasting room and offers local cuisine if you find yourself in the area.

Karlovac Region

The region around Karlovac is an easy stop-off on your way to the coast. Whether you're headed to Istria, the Kvarner Gulf, Dalmatia, or the Plitvice Lakes, you'll have to pass through Karlovac, and it's a nice place to have lunch and a quick look around before con-tinuing on your way. Driving to Istria or the Kvarner Gulf, you'll pass through the Gorski Kotar, a region that gets few tourists but has lots of activities for fans of adventure and other obscure attractions, like the Museum of Frogs in the village of Lokve.

While the Lonjsko polje isn't quite on the route to anywhere, fans of nature will want to make a detour to see the nature park and its interesting wildlife, particularly the large community of storks that nest here every year.

KARLOVAC

If you're driving from Zagreb to the Dalmatian coast, you'll pass the exit for Karlovac on the highway. It's actually a worth-while stop, if only for a couple of hours, to see the pretty center of town and maybe have a riverside coffee.

Situated on a delta between four rivers—the Korana, Kupa, Mrežnica, and Dobra—Karlovac was built in the 16th century by the Austrians to help defend their territories from the Turks, explaining the city's neat grid of streets, wide compared with other old Croatian towns. The town once had walls in the shape of a six-pointed star; they were de-molished in the 19th century.

Karlovac became an important trade city

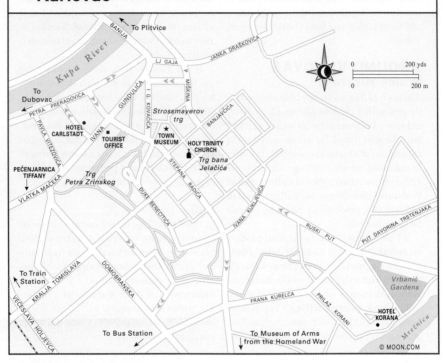

Karlovac

To Plitvice

BANIJA

Kupa River

LJ GAJA

JANKA DRAŠKOVIĆA

To Dubovac

PETRA PRERADOVIĆA

PAVLA VITEZOVIĆA

GUNDULIĆA

I. G. KOVAČIĆA

MIŠKINA

BANJAVČIĆA

0   200 yds
0   200 m

HOTEL CARLSTADT

IVANA

TOURIST OFFICE

Strossmayerov trg

★ TOWN MUSEUM

HOLY TRINITY CHURCH

PEČENJARNICA TIFFANY

Trg Petra Zrinskog

VLATKA MAČEKA

STEPANA RADIĆA

Trg bana Jelačića

DUKE BENEČTIĆA

IVANA KUKLJEVIĆA

RUSKI PUT

PUT DAVORINA TRSTENJAKA

To Train Station

KRALJA TOMISLAVA

DOMOBRANSKA

VEČESLAVA HOLJEVCA

Vrbanić Gardens

FRANA KURELCA

PRILAZ KORANI

HOTEL KORANA

Mrežnica

To Bus Station

To Museum of Arms from the Homeland War

© MOON.COM

on the route to the coast in the 18th and 19th centuries. Even as part of former Yugoslavia, Karlovac was relatively prosperous, with a good base of industries in the area. The city was badly damaged in the Homeland War, when it was on the defensive front lines. It's finally recovering and has restored a significant amount of the charming center.

Sights

A good starting point for exploring the town is the main square, **Ban Jelačić Square (Trg bana Jelačića).** Its wide expanse is surrounded by refined Baroque buildings, some of which have been restored. In the square's center is a **plague column,** built after an outbreak in 1691. From the square, you can see the steeple of the **Holy Trinity Church (Crkva presvetog Trojstva).** The church is the oldest building in Karlovac, built as a part of the Franciscan monastery in the 17th century. Its interior is gilt and Baroque like so many church interiors, but its lower ceilings, which make it more intimate, add to its appeal.

On nearby **Strossmayer Square (Strossmayerov trg)** is the **Town Museum (Gradski muzej)** (Strossmayerov trg 7, tel. 047/615-980, www.gmk.hr, 8am-4pm Tues.-Fri., 10am-4pm Sat., 10am-12pm Sun., 10Kn), a nice permanent exhibition of town history presented in the 17th-century palace of Vuk Frankopan, a general who came from a powerful noble family.

If the weather's nice, a stroll through the **Vrbanić gardens** on the banks of the Korana River is a nice way to stretch your legs. Be sure

1: Windows on wooden house in the village Krapje, Lonjsko Polje Nature park **2:** Central Square, Karlovac

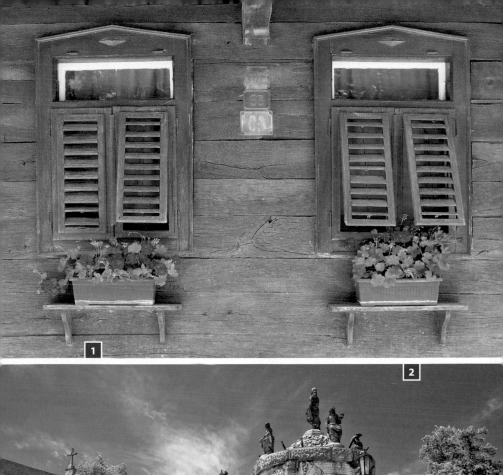

to stop at the **Hotel Korana's restaurant** for a light lunch or snack on the riverside terrace.

Just out of town overlooking the Kupa River is the medieval fortress **Dubovac** (tel. 047/615-980, www.gmk.hr, 10am-7pm Tues.-Sat., 2pm-7pm Sun.-Mon. Apr.-Oct., 10Kn), owned in the 15th and 16th centuries by the Frankopans and the Zrinskis. It's about a 30-minute hike up (take Ulica Vladka Mačeka west and uphill to the left) to see a small exhibition and a superb view of all of Karlovac.

A short drive south of town on the road to Plitvice is the **Museum of Arms from the Homeland War (Muzejska zbirka naoružanja Domovinskog rata)** (dawn-dusk daily, free), also known as the **Turanj Military Complex,** an exhibition of tanks and weaponry used during the conflict, when the front lines were here in Turanj. The collection is displayed around the ruins of four buildings, once Hapsburg army barracks.

Sports and Recreation

There are some great cycling routes in the area of Karlovac. For maps and more information, contact the **tourist office (Turistička Zajednica Grada Karlovca)** (Petra Zrinskog 3, tel. 047/615-115, www.karlovac-touristinfo.hr).

Accommodations

The **Hotel Carlstadt** (A. Vraniczanya 1, tel. 047/611-111, carlstadt@ka.t-com.hr, www.carlstadt.hr, 455Kn d, including breakfast) has basic rooms and is located smack in the center of town, while the **Hotel Korana** (Perivoj J. Vrbanića 8, tel. 047/609-090, info@hotelkorana.hr, www.hotelkorana.hr, 850Kn d, including breakfast) is a nicer option, nestled on the banks of the Korana River in a shady park. The **tourist office (Turistička Zajednica Grada Karlovca)** (Petra Zrinskog 3, www.karlovac-touristinfo.hr, tel. 047/615-115) can also point you in the direction of private rooms and apartments for an overnight stay; if you'd like to rough it, there's a nice campsite, **Slapić** (Mrežnički Brig bb,

tel. 047/854-700, www.campslapic.hr, 50Kn pp plus 45Kn for a tent site), about 15 kilometers (nine miles) southwest of town.

Food

In the city center, **Pečenjarnica Tiffany** (Vladka Mačeka 6/1, tel. 047/614-666, 7am-10pm Mon.-Sat., 1pm-11pm Sun., 35Kn) has sandwiches, grilled dishes, and pizzas in a very casual setting. **Lovački Rog** (Pojatno bb, tel. 047/637-675, www.lovacki-rog.hr, 10am-11pm daily, 75Kn), on the road to Plitvice, specializes in venison and local fish dishes, and its outdoor terrace is great in nicer weather. On a hill just outside the city, the cozy **Restoran Kalvarija** (Vucjak 3, tel. 098/699-001, 12pm-12am Fri.-Sun., 55Kn) is a great choice for both excellent atmosphere and food.

Getting There and Around

Karlovac is approximately 50 kilometers (31 miles) southwest of Zagreb. The city's **bus station** (Prilaz Vjećeslava Holjevca 2, tel. 047/614-729) is on one of the main thoroughfares a short walk from the center. There are six connections with Zagreb on weekdays, four on Saturday, and three on Sunday. Tickets cost approximately 36Kn each way. The **train station** (Vilima Reinera 3, tel. 047/646-244) is just 1.5 kilometers (almost one mile) north on the same street (though it has a different name). There are multiple connections daily, and a one-way ticket costs around 35Kn. Generally, the bus has been the fastest mode of transportation, reaching Zagreb in about one hour. However, road construction might make the train a faster option, particularly if you are traveling during rush hour. By car from Zagreb, simply take the Autocesta A1 toward Karlovac, about one hour's journey southwest.

Karlovac is a great place to stop off on a longer journey, with great connections to the Plitvice Lakes, Zadar, Split, and Rijeka, and actually just about any city in Croatia. There are several daily connections to almost any larger city in the country, with buses to Zagreb leaving almost every half hour. If you are traveling from Istria, it's the easiest connection hub for Plitvice.

ŽUMBERAK

Filled with densely forested hills and the weekend homes of Zagreb city-dwellers, the Žumberak has some of the best easy hikes around and is convenient for a day trip from Zagreb. Starting about 30 kilometers (18 miles) west of the capital, you can reach the area by connecting in Samobor (Slani Dol, about 6 kilometers/3.5 miles from Samobor, is a good entrance point). Though Samobor is not technically part of the Žumberak, its **tourist office** (Trg Kralja Tomislava 5, tel. 01/336-0044, www.samobor.hr, 8am-7pm Mon.-Fri., 9am-7pm Sat., 10am-7pm Sun.) is the place to go to find out more about hiking in the area. It's easy to get around the region by car, though the bus company **Samaborček** (tel. 01/333-5170, www.samaborcek.hr) has good connections within the region.

Ozalj

The wonderful **castle** (no phone, 8am-3pm Mon.-Fri., posted hours not always observed, 10Kn) on the banks of the Kupa River is a nice stop, particularly if you can find someone to open the doors. Inside is a great exhibition depicting Croatia's history in English, harder to find than you might think. Below the castle is another tiny pretty building that looks like a mini castle on the edge of the river. It was actually a working hydroelectric plant built in 1908. The **tourist office** (Kurilovac 1, tel. 047/731-196, www.ozalj-tz.hr) should be able to help you with more details. In nearby Vivodina, north of Ozalj, the restaurant **Frlan** (Vivodina 3, tel. 047/753-111, call for hours) can hook you up with a good meal and has its own selection of wines.

Pribić

If you're in the area, and particularly if you love old buildings, it's worth a visit to the hauntingly beautiful **Church of the Annunciation (Crkva svetog Blagovijesta).** The neo-Byzantine Greek Catholic church and monastery is now abandoned and rarely open to the public, but its architecture, an interesting mix of Orthodox and art nouveau, is stunning in itself.

Northern Žumberak

Filled with great **hiking** (contact the Samobor tourist office, Trg Kralja Tomislava 5, tel. 01/336-0044, www.samobor.hr, 8am-7pm Mon.-Fri., 9am-7pm Sat., 10am-7pm Sun.), the northern Žumberak has a couple of super *seoski turizam* hotels and restaurants. Try the 19th-century **Kurija Medven** (Medvenova Draga 13, tel. 01/627-0347, 469Kn d, including breakfast) for cozy authentic rooms and cuisine.

A short drive outside of Samobor in the border town of Bregana is **Eko-Selo Žumberak** (Koretići 13, tel. 01/338-7472, 391Kn d, including breakfast), a hamlet of wood and stone cottages in a bucolic setting next to a rushing brook. The rooms are very basic, but clean, and it's the perfect spot if you love riding (the Eko-Selo also runs a horse ranch) and other outdoor pleasures.

GORSKI KOTAR

Entering this mountainous and thickly forested region, you might think you fell asleep and ended up in a valley in Austria. Even in the summer the air here is noticeably cooler, and in the winter the area is often covered in a blanket of white. If you like adventure sports or great food, you'll certainly want to visit the area, conveniently located on the road from Zagreb to Rijeka. It's a great stopping-off point before heading to Istria that is virtually overlooked by travelers and full of adrenaline-fueled pursuits.

It is important to note that parts of the Gorski Kotar are impassable in winter, so this is a trip best made in spring, summer, or fall. The area really shines in summer, when its noticeably cooler temperatures and lack of

Jasenovac in World War II

The concentration camp at Jasenovac was set up in the summer of 1941 in a small village south of Zagreb. The camp was one of several in Croatia, though the atrocities committed at Jasenovac caused it to secure an even more sinister place in history.

Jasenovac held Croatian political prisoners (some of whom were thrown in for offenses as small as having been on the guest list for the Serbian king's wedding), though it mainly served as a death camp for Serbs, Jews, and gypsies. The respected archbishop of Zagreb during World War II, Alojzije Stepinac, compared Jasenovac to the mark of Cain, a sin that would sully Croatia forever.

Certainly it has caused the nation loads of shame, though the usual response has been to downplay or cover up what happened. Franjo Tuđman was a prime example, estimating the death toll at only 40,000 and even callously suggesting that the victims of Jasenovac and World War II fatalities (including the pro-Nazi Ustaše) be buried in a common grave with a memorial. Yugoslav historians had the tendency to inflate the numbers to one million. Though it's hard to reach a precise figure, Yale professor and surprisingly unbiased Croatian historian Ivo Banac puts the figure at about 120,000.

Whatever the number, the facts are shocking and deplorable. One of the camp's former leaders, Dinko Šakić, was finally extradited from Argentina in 1998 and sentenced to 20 years in prison. It was too little, too late. Perhaps future Croatian politicians will bring the reality of this tragic past to light to help teach a lesson for the future and to memorialize precious lives lost.

visitors make it a welcome respite after some time on the busy coast.

Ogulin

The town of Ogulin, 58 kilometers (36 miles) southwest of Karlovac, has an early-16th-century castle with a small but disappointing museum. However, Ogulin is a great starting point to explore **Klek mountain.** Make your way by car or bus to the nearby village of Bijelsko, seven kilometers (four miles) west of Ogulin, to start your two-hour round-trip journey on foot. Klek is not the highest of the mountains in the area—it stands a bit less than 1,200 meters (4,000 feet)—but it is certainly the most impressive in the Gorski Kotar region. The sheer rock jutting above the green forested hills has long been the source of local legends involving witches, as well as a princess supposedly locked inside the ominous-looking rock. There's a hut on the mountain that serves refreshments on the weekends, and the views at the top are worth the climb if you're the sporting type. Note, though, that this steep hike is not for those with a fear of heights.

Risnjak National Park

If you're looking for hiking, **Risnjak National Park** (www.risnjak.hr) has better trails than Bjelolasica. It's only a short bus ride from the town of Delnice, the main transportation hub for the area, 60 kilometers (37 miles) west of Karlovac. Pick up maps and information at the **Pansion Nacionalni park Risnjak** (tel. 051/836-133) in Crni Lug before heading to the park entrance. The park offers a good network of trails of varying difficulty, from a relatively easy nature walk, the Poučna staza Leska, to a steep hike up the Veliki Risnjak mountain, not for the faint of heart.

★ Fužine

Fužine, 132 kilometers (82 miles) southwest of Karlovac, is one of the prettiest towns in the Gorski Kotar, with a nice lake and an interesting cave, the **Špilja Vrelo.** The town is a great jumping-off point for active vacations, with most accommodations helping you arrange fishing, rock climbing, and rafting trips. Most of all, the town has some great homemade specialties to sample. Have a slice of the local *štrudla šumsko voće* (blackberry strudel) and pick up some honey and a bottle of Goranski Jaeger for the trip home.

If you have a warm spot in your heart for amphibians, check out the nearby village of Lokve and its **Museum of Frogs (Muzej Žaba)** (Šetalište Golubinjak 50, tel. 051/831-099, call ahead to arrange a visit, 15Kn). The quirky, small museum has a simple display of frog photos, live local frogs, and frog paraphernalia. It's not impressive but is still a must-see for those who like to dip into a bit of local culture and support the small community. Lokve even has a yearly frog festival in May, called **Žabarska noć (Frog Night)**, serving frog specialties and filled with songs and small-town charm.

★ **Bitoraj** (Sveti križ 1, tel. 051/830-005, info@bitoraj.hr, www.bitoraj.hr, 654Kn d, including breakfast) is one of the nicest places to stay in the Gorski Kotar, and historical too, as it was once the hunting lodge of Josip Broz Tito, leader of Yugoslavia for over three decades. **Konoba Volta** (Doktora Franje Račkog 8, tel. 051/830-830, 6am-10pm Mon.-Fri., 7am-11pm Sat.-Sun., 40Kn) is great for heartwarming local meals.

If you'd like to get the feeling of living in the mountains, rent the charming **Kuća Sobol** (Vučnik 27, tel. 051/812-371, www.sobol.hr, 994Kn), which accommodates up to six, located near Fužine in Butterfly Valley, where a purported 500 species of butterflies can be found. The owners can also arrange fly-fishing expeditions and have some rooms for rent if your party isn't large enough for a whole house.

Tight on cash? Check with the **tourist office** (tel. 051/835-163, info@tz-fuzine.hr, www.tz-fuzine.hr), which rents cheaper mountain houses in the surrounding countryside as well as private rooms in town. The tourist office can also help arrange excursions to the cave and other activities in the area.

Getting There and Around

The Gorski Kotar region is southwest of Zagreb and west of Karlovac. The Karlovac-Rijeka highway passes right through the best of the region, including Fužine, while the Karlovac-Split highway touches the southern edge, with good access to Ogulin. Each town is around one hour and 45 minutes away from Zagreb by car.

If you'd prefer to travel via rail, the train makes stops at Ogulin (1.5 hours, 53Kn) and Fužine (2.75 hours, 78Kn). Ogulin's train station is about a 10-minute walk to the center of town.

Delnice, 60 kilometers (37 miles) west of Karlovac, is the main transportation hub for the area, with buses connecting pretty much everywhere in the Gorski Kotar region. Buses going from Zagreb to Istria stop in Delnice (Delnice bus station, tel. 051/812-060), taking almost three hours and costing around 110Kn. Buses run from Zagreb to Ogulin (2.75 hours, 100Kn—making the train a much better option); to Fužine you'd need to connect in Delnice (30 minutes, 27Kn).

SISAK

Though Sisak was founded in Roman times, you can still see remnants of a **2nd-century tower** on Ban Jelačić Square (Trg bana Jelačića). There's little to interest visitors here except a small **Town Museum (Gradski muzej)** (Kralja Tomislava 10, tel. 044/811-811, www.muzej-sisak.hr, 10am-6pm Tues.-Fri., 9am-12pm Sat.-Sun. summer, 15Kn) and a 16th-century **Old Town castle (Stari Grad)** (inquire at museum for more information) a few kilometers south of town. Worth a mention is the excellent restaurant called **Cocktail** (Dr. A. Starčevića 27, tel. 044/549-137, www.cocktail.hr, 10am-11pm daily, 60Kn), a small modern space that offers local dishes as well as a few Italian favorites.

Sisak is 50 kilometers (31 miles) south of Zagreb. The train to Sisak takes about one hour and costs 28Kn, with over half a dozen daily connections on weekdays, slightly fewer on weekends. The bus takes around one hour as well but is slightly more expensive.

★ LONJSKO POLJE

Though best known for the **Lonjsko polje Nature Park (Lonjsko Polje Park Prirode)** (tel. 044/715-115, www.pp-lonjsko-polje.hr, 25Kn), the region is also filled with storybook wooden houses, most of which date from the 19th and early 20th centuries. **Čigoč,** 30 kilometers (18 miles) southeast of Sisak, is a traditional village of wooden houses within the park; it's also designated the European Village of the Stork, with a stork's nest on almost every roof. If you'd like to see the storks, try to visit between the end of March and the end of August—although a few make their home here year-round, too lazy to migrate after feedings by the locals. There's even a **stork ceremony** on the last Saturday in June that brings a load of visitors to town. A **park information point** (Čigoć 26, tel. 044/715-115, 8am-4pm daily) sells tickets to the park, and the village has a small visitors center and a private **Ethnographic Collection (Etnološke zbirke)** (tel. 044/715-184, by advance arrangement, 10Kn), which are most likely to be open on summer weekends.

The floodplain is filled with wildlife, including Posavina horses, furry Turopolje swimming pigs, and numerous birds. If you'd like to arrange a **tour** of the park, call the park manager (tel. 044/672-082).

Staying in the nature park is an experience in itself. Jakša and Zlata **Ravlić** (Mužilovčica 72, tel. 044/710-151, 341Kn d, including breakfast) offer rooms in their ivy-covered 200-year-old timber house in Mužilovčica. With its fairy-tale charm and cozy antique-filled rooms, you may want to move in. But if you just want to eat some of their great home cooking, you'll need to call ahead and let them know.

Istria

Sunlit rolling hills, miles of vineyards, charming stone cottages, and lined with crystal clear, cool water and rocky shores . . . If you have to pick only one region of Croatia to visit, Istria seems to wrap up the best and present it in a neat, easy-to-travel little package.

Travelers flock to the coast for picturesque port towns littered with remnants of the Roman and Byzantine periods, and former fishing villages turned tourist meccas. However, the interior of the peninsula is beginning to hold its own, with travelers realizing it rivals Tuscany or Provence—with cuisine to match. Culinary travelers can discover the region's local black and white truffles, homemade olive oil, and wine roads. This hinterland paradise is also dotted with medieval hilltop

Highlights

Look for ★ to find recommended sights, activities, dining, and lodging.

★ **Pula's Amphitheater (Amfiteatar):** Pula's Roman amphitheater is one of the best preserved (page 133).

★ **Veli Brijun:** Once the playground of both European aristocracy and Josip Broz Tito, this nature park and popular day-trip destination is experiencing a rebirth as a luxe haven for celebrities and politicos (page 142).

★ **Golden Cape (Zlatni Rt):** A forested nature park on the edge of the picturesque town of Rovinj, Golden Cape is full of beaches, all easily accessible on foot (page 146).

★ **Basilica of Euphrasius (Eufrazijeva basilica):** This 6th-century Byzantine church, filled with sparkling mosaics and a big dose of history, is hidden on a side street in Poreč's ancient center (page 149).

★ **Novigrad:** A small seaside town with some outstanding food, the laid-back Novigrad is a great location from which to explore some of Istria's best wine country (page 153).

★ **Grožnjan:** Participants in this hilltop village's young musicians' summer school give heartwarming performances all summer long. And the views aren't half bad either (page 161).

★ **Hum:** Whether its claim of being the smallest town in the world is true or not, Hum is

a delight, with pretty views, good food, and mistletoe liquor to pick up as a signature souvenir (page 162).

towns to explore, from Motovun's backdrop for an impressive international summer film festival to Grožnjan's artsy core.

Though the Istrian beaches aren't quite as stunning as their Dalmatian neighbors to the south, they're often easier to access, with flat, fine pebbled paths accommodating a bicycle or a stroller. It's just one example of how Istria's tourism is far more developed than in Dalmatia, making Istria easy to travel and navigate. The region has clearly marked roads for sampling wine and olive oil, and information and brochures at every turn. There's almost always some cultural or culinary festival going on and an impressive selection of hotels and restaurants to choose from.

There are other advantages to Istria, too. As Croatia attracts more and more visitors, especially to its coastal regions, many towns are having a hard time hanging on to what makes them unique. But if you're looking for something besides your typical fish restaurant with its tourist-oriented menu, or a boutique hotel that doesn't try too hard, or a yachting community without the bling, Istria is where you'll find it. Overall, it's refined yet full of laid-back character (except when it comes to truffles, which they tend to get overly excited about, but that's another story).

The Italian influence in the area is strong and adds another dimension to traveling in Istria. Many of the street signs are marked in Italian as well as Croatian. You'll find this region has long been discovered by European travelers, but there are still enough hidden locales (like secluded villa accommodations or restaurants serving only one party of guests at a time) and rocky coves to escape to.

The worst of Istria is that to see it in its glory you absolutely must rent a car. The best of Istria is that packed within such a small peninsula you've got everything—a giant Roman amphitheater where you can catch a concert, wine and olive oil roads, beaches, water sports, tiny character-filled villages, superb restaurants, and solid museums—making it easy for a week to fly by before you know it.

PLANNING YOUR TIME

It's tempting to want to just move to Istria and savor each little corner slowly (and if you feel that way, the real estate offices in every village will make it clear you're not the first), but Istria is very doable with two nights on the coast and one overnight in the interior to get a good overview. The best thing about Istria in terms of time is that everything is very close, and you can traverse the distance between the two farthest points in less than two hours. But you'll need a car to do it quickly or thoroughly, whatever your preference may be.

If you have a car, you can really choose to stay in any town; you'll usually get better deals in the interior than on the coast, where the majority of tourists book hotels. If you're traveling by bus you may want to stick to the bigger towns if you're pressed for time, since connections to some of the villages are scarce or even nonexistent. Biking is possible, though you'd want to take lots of safety precautions since the roads are still relatively narrow and sans bike lanes. Additionally, the biking culture is not well established, so drivers aren't really expecting to encounter cyclists as they come around a turn.

Try to squeeze in the region's highlights or tailor your trip to specific interests, such as food, wine, or sacred art. If you have a week you can see the peninsula at leisure and traverse the best villages and towns without a problem.

Summer is the busiest time of year, with prices and the number of fellow travelers peaking in August, when it seems like every Italian in Italy has driven over the border. However, summer is also the time when Istria holds the most festivals and some excellent concerts with international opera and pop stars holding court in the larger coastal towns.

Istria

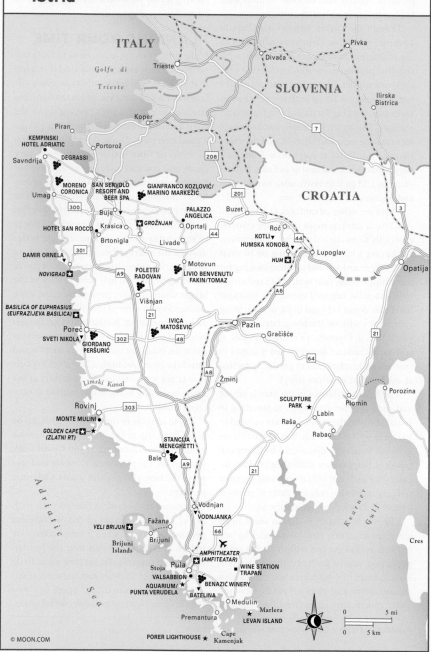

ITALY

Golfo di Trieste

Trieste

SLOVENIA

Divača

Pivka

Ilirska Bistrica

Piran

Koper

7

KEMPINSKI HOTEL ADRIATIC

Portorož

208

Savndrija

DEGRASSI

MORENO CORONICA

SAN SERVOLO RESORT AND BEER SPA

GIANFRANCO KOZLOVIĆ/ MARINO MARKEŽIĆ

201

CROATIA

Umag

300

Buje

PALAZZO ANGELICA

Buzet

Roč

3

HOTEL SAN ROCCO

Krasica

GROŽNJAN

Oprtalj

KOTLI

HUMSKA KONOBA

44

44

Brtonigla

Livade

Lupoglav

DAMIR ORNELA

301

Motovun

HUM

Opatija

NOVIGRAD

A9

POLETTI/ RADOVAN

LIVIO BENVENUTI/ FAKIN/TOMAZ

A8

Višnjan

BASILICA OF EUPHRASIUS (EUFRAZIJEVA BASILICA)

21

IVICA MATOŠEVIĆ

Pazin

Poreč

SVETI NIKOLA

302

48

Gračišće

64

21

GIORDANO PERŠURIĆ

A8

Limski Kanal

Žminj

Porozina

SCULPTURE PARK

Plomin

Rovinj

303

Labin

MONTE MULINI

Raša

GOLDEN CAPE (ZLATNI RT)

STANCIJA MENEGHETTI

Rabac

Bale

A9

21

Kvarner Gulf

Vodnjan

VODNJANKA

66

Cres

VELI BRIJUN

Fažana

Brijuni

Brijuni Islands

AMPHITHEATER (AMFITEATAR)

WINE STATION TRAPAN

Stoja

Pula

VALSABBION

BENAZIĆ WINERY

AQUARIUM/ PUNTA VERUDELA

BATELINA

Medulin

Marlera

Premantura

LEVAN ISLAND

PORER LIGHTHOUSE

Cape Kamenjak

Adriatic Sea

0   5 mi

0   5 km

© MOON.COM

ISTRIA

Fall and spring are the prettiest times, with far fewer tourists and asparagus harvests (spring), truffle hunting season (fall), and the grape harvest (fall) to make Istria even more interesting. Winter is doable and you will have most places to yourself, but also be aware that some restaurants and hotels close between November and the beginning of March.

Itinerary Ideas

FOODIE TOUR OF ISTRIA

Day 1
- Start your tour in **Pula**, with breakfast at the city's art-nouveau style **market hall**.
- For the rest of the morning, take in the exhibits at the **Museum of Olive Oil Production.**
- After lunch, visit the **Trapan Wine Station,** a short drive out of town, for an afternoon of wine-tasting.
- Enjoy a delicious seafood dinner at **Batelina** back in Pula.

Day 2
- Drive to **Rovinj** to enjoy the sights, particularly the charming **Batana House Museum**. Purchase one of their cookbooks as a souvenir.
- Have dinner at the Michelin-starred **Monte**.

Day 3
- Spend the day at the **San Servolo Resort and Beer Spa** in Buje, enjoying their therapeutic beer baths. Have dinner at the resort's steakhouse accompanied by a glass of truffle beer.

Day 4
- Head to **Motovun,** where you can spend the day with more winery visits or take a pasta-making class at the **Kaštel Cultural Center**.
- Have dinner at **Konoba Mondo**.

Day 5
- Start your day with a **truffle hunting expedition** near Motovun.
- Spend the night in the ultra-quiet **Oprtalj** at the **Palazzo Angelica** to experience Istria without the tourists.

ISTRIA HISTORY TOUR

Day 1
- Start your day in **Pula**, visiting the many Roman and Byzantine monuments and ruins, as well as the city's museums.

Istira Itinerary Ideas

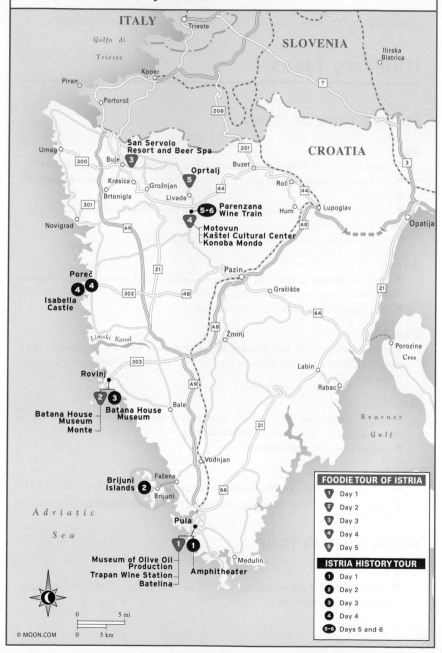

ITALY

Trieste

SLOVENIA

Golfo di
Trieste

Ilirska
Bistrica

Piran

Koper

Portorož

208

300

CROATIA

201

Umag

Buje

San Servolo
Resort and Beer Spa

3

Buzet

Roč

3

7

Oprtalj

5

44

Krasica

Grožnjan

44

Brtonigla

Livade

Lupoglav

Parenzana
Wine Train

5-6

Novigrad

301

A9

4

Hum

A8

Opatija

Motovun
Kaštel Cultural Center
Konoba Mondo

Poreč

4

4

21

Pazin

302

48

Isabella
Castle

Limski Kanal

Gračišče

21

64

A8

Žminj

Porozina

Cres

303

Labin

Rovinj

A9

Rabac

Batana House
Museum
Monte

2

3

Batana House
Museum

Bale

Kvarner
Gulf

21

Brijuni
Islands

2

Fažana

Vodnjan

Brijuni

66

Adriatic

Sea

Pula

1

1

Museum of Olive Oil
Production
Trapan Wine Station
Batelina

Amphitheater

Medulin

0   5 mi

0   5 km

© MOON.COM

FOODIE TOUR OF ISTRIA	
1	Day 1
2	Day 2
3	Day 3
4	Day 4
5	Day 5

ISTRIA HISTORY TOUR	
1	Day 1
2	Day 2
3	Day 3
4	Day 4
5-6	Days 5 and 6

- If it's summer, hit the **Amphitheater** in the evening to experience gladiator fights and a variety of historical experiences.

Day 2

- Head to **Brijuni Islands** for a day discovering Tito's summer escape and safari park. Stay overnight at one of the island's hotels or, if you really want to splurge, rent one of the island's villas.

Day 3

- Spend your day wandering around **Rovinj's** old town.
- In the evening, head to the **Batana House museum** for a history lesson, followed by a batana ride to a traditional dinner accompanied by local folk music.

Day 4

- Drive north to **Poreč** to savor the beautiful 6th-century mosaics in the **Basilica of Euphrasius**.
- Stay at the historic **Isabella Castle** on **Sveti Nikola island**.

Days 5 and 6

- Drive to the Istrian interior for winery-hopping and a ride on the historic **Parenzana Wine Train**, built in 1902. Stay overnight at one of the *agroturizam* hotels in the interior to experience traditional Istria at its best.

Labin

The peaceful hilltop town of Labin is actually one of the region's most political cities. Labin belonged to the Byzantines, Lombards, Franks, Italy, and the Germanic marquisate—all before the 15th century. The Venetian Republic ruled the town from 1420 to 1797 and left the most indelible mark upon the town, whose medieval core will remind you of walking through Venice without the canals. After the fall of Venice, it was ruled by the French, the Austrians, and the Italians, and finally became a part of Croatia after World War II.

Its downhill suburb, the 20th-century Podlabin (literally, beneath Labin), was the country's coal-mining capital, and a center of pro-worker and pro-Tito sentiment. Driving into town you may notice the "Tito" spelled on the mountaintop with stones or the ax-and-sickle stencils on a wall in the old town.

Today, coal mining has died out and the city has become an artists' haven, attracting a mound of tourists from nearby **Rabac** (a seaside resort town a few kilometers east of Labin) in the summer months. From June to August, Labin welcomes the hordes with its **Art Republika festival,** bringing dozens of performing and visual artists to the city streets.

Since there's little in the way of accommodations in Labin proper (unless you want to rent a room or apartment), lose the crowds by getting there in the early morning to wander the cobblestone streets—though you'll need to stick around until 10 if you want to pop in to the city's galleries and sights. If you're staying in Rabac, you can drive to Labin, or go green and hike the marked walking trail between the two towns. It's a very doable seven kilometers (4.3 miles) or so (about 45 minutes)—or you can take the bus.

SIGHTS

Start your tour of Labin at the old town's **Tito's Square (Titov trg);** the 16th-century town **loggia** was the spot of town meetings and peasant dances in centuries past. Climb the cobblestone path to the 14th-century **Church of the Birth of the Blessed Virgin Mary (Crkva rođenja blažene djevice Marije).** The simple stone front hides an elegant interior, worth a peek if mass is in session (11am Sun.).

Just up the street is the bright reddish Palazzo Lazarini, now the **Labin National Museum (Narodni muzej Labin)** (1 svibnja 6, some still refer to it as 1 maja 6, tel. 052/852-477, tulio-vorano@pu.htnet.hr, 8am-2pm Mon.-Fri. winter, 10am-1pm and 5pm-8pm Mon.-Sat. June and Sept., 10am-1pm and 6pm-10pm Mon.-Sat. July-Aug., 15Kn), housing a small ethnographic collection, paintings, and Roman relics. The most distinguishing feature of the museum is its small re-creation of a coal mine in the basement, probably the closest most of us will get to experiencing the feel of working underground. Just across the street from the museum, a modern facade tips you off to the **City Gallery (Gradska galerija)** (Titov trg 11, Ulica 1, maja 5, tel. 052/852-464, 10am-2pm and 6pm-9pm Mon.-Sat., free), housing revolving contemporary (mostly local) art exhibitions.

At the top of 1 svibnja street (or 1 maja, as it used to be called), the **fortress (Fortica)** has a nice view of Rabac, the peaks of Velebit, and the Island of Cres. From here, walk down Giuseppine Martinuzzi to the **Chapel of Our Lady of Carmel (Crkvica Gospe od Karmene),** today the **Gallery Alvona** (Giuseppina Martinuzzi 15, tel. 098/183-0901, www.galerija-alvona.hr, free), which houses some well-known contemporary artists, particularly during the summer season.

The last stop in Labin, before wandering through some of the city's other galleries, is the birthplace of Matija Vlačić Illyricus, a prominent Protestant theologian and friend of Martin Luther. The **Memorial Collection of Matija Vlačić Ilirik (Matija Vlačić Illyricus Memorijalna zbirka)** (Giusepinna Martinuzzi 7, tel. 052/852-477, open on request, 20Kn) holds interesting memorabilia, but more curious is the celebration of Protestantism in heavily Catholic Croatia.

BEACHES

Labin is, of course, inland, but nearby Rabac has lots of beaches, the best of which is **Maslinica.** Though it shares its shores with tourist developments, the beach is public. It's not a hidden beach and is usually crowded with tourists in season, but it does have a pebbly (read: won't kill your bare feet) shore and lots of services, from cafés and snack bars to personal-watercraft rental and mini-golf. Rabac bills itself as the "pearl of the Adriatic." However, loads of oiled bodies and plastic sand pails can't help but sully the marketing angle. If you're looking for luxe or a quiet, natural escape, it's best to head elsewhere in Istria.

ENTERTAINMENT AND EVENTS

While you'll find a sprinkling of bars and cafés near Titov trg and lots of performances during the summer **Art Republika festival** (www.labin-art-republika.com) that runs in July and August, you need to head out of town to find more edgy or more raucous nightlife. If it's edgy you're after, head to Podlabin's **Lamparna Cultural Centre** (Rudarska 1, tel. 052/855-289, www.labinary.org/lamparna, call for event program), in an abandoned coal-mine building (actually the place the miners stopped to pick up their lamps before going underground, hence the name), where interesting exhibitions and concerts are held. Rabac is the place for the typical touristy beachside discos and clubs, which get a bit better during the **Rabac Open Air Festival** (www.rabacopenair.com), now a three-month-long program of cinema and theatre,

1: view of Rabac, a seaside resort town near Labin
2: old streets of Labin

street music, a summer carnival, a jazz fest, and performances for all ages.

ACCOMMODATIONS

In the old town of Labin, the **Hotel Peteani** (Aldo Negri 9, tel. 052/863-404, www.hotelpeteani.hr, 1,125Kn d, including breakfast) is a boutique hotel in a converted early-20th-century villa. Rooms are on the small side but are beautifully decorated, and the location can't be beat. For cheaper centrally located accommodations, AirBnB (www.airbnb.com) and Booking (www.booking.com) have some reasonable options, even some in the old town. Rabac is also convenient: there are multiple bus connections to Labin, or it's about a 45-minute walk between the towns.

Campers can pitch a tent at the woodsy beachfront **Oliva campsite** (P.P.2, tel. 052/872-258, www.maslinica-rabac.com, 75Kn campsite without electricity) in Rabac. Recently the camp has added some air-conditioned mobile homes for up to six people.

The **Palača Lazzarini** (Kort, Sv. Martin, tel. 052/856-006, www.sv-martin.com, 391Kn d) is 10 kilometers (6.2 miles) from Labin (best for those who have a car, though the hotel does rent bikes). The cozy apartments, located in an 18th-century summer palace, are a great respite during the busy tourist season.

Another peaceful option for those with transportation is the **Villa Calussovo** (Ripenda, Kras 18, tel. 052/851-188, www.villacalussovo.com, 400Kn d, including breakfast), a big yellow country house set on six acres of bucolic bliss. Only four kilometers (2.5 miles) from the beach, the hotel has comfortable rooms and a good restaurant.

In Rabac, the waterfront **Apartmani Adoral** (Obala M. Tita 2a, tel. 052/535-840, www.adoral-hotel.com, 1,000Kn d) are luxe, modern flats with great sea views, but little place to lay your towel on the rocks out front. If a beach resort is more your style, try the renovated **TUI Family Life Bellevue Resort** (Rabac bb, tel. 052/465-200, www.valamar.com, 1,700Kn d), with pools and a playground for the kids. Set away from the tourist hustle

and bustle, all of the suites at **Villa Annette** (Raška 24, tel. 052/884-222, www.villaannette.hr, 1,389Kn d, including breakfast) have magnificent sea views. Though the hotel is not beachfront, it does have a nice pool for lounging in warmer months, a good restaurant (ask for room service, since the restaurant is low on ambience), and super-helpful service.

FOOD

Though not technically a restaurant, it is worth stopping in **Palazzo Negri Olive Gallery** (Dolinska 3, tel. 052/875-280, www.negri-olive.com) for an olive oil- and wine-tasting complete with loads of information from the delightful owners.

In Labin, the centrally located **Velo Kafe** (Titov trg 12, tel. 052/852-745, www.velokafe.com, 11am-11pm daily, 45Kn) has good pasta dishes and a nice terrace for prime people-watching. **Due Fratelli** (Mantozi 6, tel. 052/853-577, www.due-fratelli.com, 12pm-11:30pm Mon.-Sat., 12pm-5pm Sun., 80Kn) has good seafood (freshly caught by the owners) and Istrian staple dishes. For more seafood, head to Rabac, where the bland atmosphere at **Noštromo** (Obala maršala Tita 7, tel. 052/872-601, www.nostromo.hr, 7am-11pm daily late Apr.-Oct., call for winter hours, 80Kn) is lifted by the superb views of the bay on the open-air terrace. The restaurant serves up solid fish, shrimp, and salads, perfect for a scorching day.

INFORMATION AND SERVICES

The main **tourist office** (Aldo Negri 20, tel. 052/855-560, tzg.labin@pu.htnet.hr, www.rabac-labin.com) will supply you with tourist brochures and maps for both Labin and Rabac. In season, there's an additional outpost at Titov trg 2.

GETTING THERE AND AROUND

Buses from Pula (one hour) and Rijeka (1.25 hours), as well as local routes, stop at the **bus station** (tel. 052/855-220) in Podlabin.

One-way tickets from Rijeka and Pula cost about 50Kn and travel multiple times daily. From the bus station, it's a 15-20-minute walk uphill into the old town.

Between Rabac and Labin, more than a dozen buses run daily, costing around 20Kn each way.

If you're driving to Labin, take care where you park and make sure you pay the appropriate amount to avoid a ticket. Some parking spots, especially those near the entrance to the old town, have a time limit.

AROUND LABIN

Die-hard art fans or those looking to escape the tourists might want to make an outing to the open-air **Sculpture Park (Park skulptura)** (tel. 052/852-464, dawn-dusk daily) in Dubrova, with more than 70 stone sculptures by contemporary artists who have participated in the Mediterranean Sculpture Symposium (Mediteranski kiparski simpozij). Dubrova also hosts an interesting festival, the **Labin Stories (Labinske konti),** on the last Saturday in July, featuring folk songs and dances as well as typical local instruments.

The picturesque perch of **Plomin** is somewhat sullied by the giant smokestack of the thermal power plant in the valley below, but its 11th-century **Church of St. George (Crkva Sveti Juraj),** home of an early Glagolitic inscription, and the sleepy ancient streets are a nice escape from the hustle of Labin and Rabac in the high season. The tavern **Dorina** (Plomin 54, tel. 052/863-023, 8am-11pm daily, 50Kn) is a good place to stop and have a bite.

Another interesting destination, about 5 kilometers (3 miles) west of Labin, **Raša** is an industrial town built by Mussolini in 1936. Its **St. Barbara's Church (Crkva svete Barbare)** (open periodically, free) was designed to resemble a coal cart and lantern.

Pula

Pula is a love-it-or-hate-it sort of city. A busy port town surrounded by communist-style high-rises, the city has a rough-around-the-edges quality that, depending on your personality or your mood, can come as a shock or a welcome change after Istria's mostly slow, charming little villages. Of course, discovering its tender side among the salty remnants of the Eastern Bloc period can be very rewarding.

No matter what your impressions of Pula, though, you can't ignore its impressive sights. Pula's past can be traced back to prehistoric times, but it's the Romans (who left the huge amphitheater) and the Hapsburg era (when the city was the Austro-Hungarians' main, and really only significant, port) that left the strongest marks on the city.

It's best to see Pula in a day and then move on, at the very least to the beaches only a short drive away. The city also has a couple of superb restaurants, possibly some of Istria's best, and summer brings an impressive roster of international opera and pop stars to perform in the town's amphitheater.

SIGHTS

★ Amphitheater
(Amfiteatar)

The crowning jewel of Pula tourist stops, this Roman **amphitheater** (Flavijevska, tel. 052/219-028, www.ami-pula.hr, 9am-5pm daily late Oct.-Mar., 9am-7pm daily Oct. and Apr., 8am-9pm daily May, June, and Sept., 8am-12am daily July-Aug., 50Kn) is the world's sixth-largest Roman arena, and one of the best-preserved. Dating from the reign of Emperor Augustus in the 1st century BC, the arena was reconstructed over the years until the version you see today was erected by Vespasianus. The arena survives thanks to

Pula

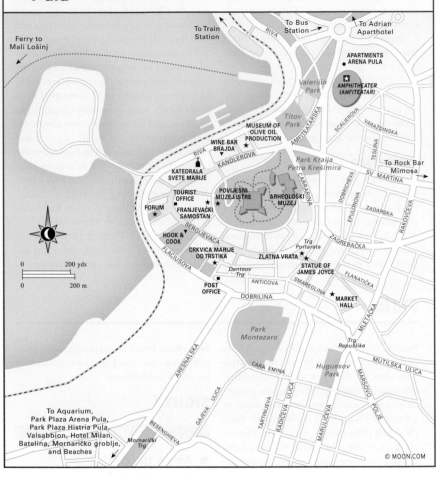

To Train Station

To Bus Station

To Adrian Aparthotel

Ferry to Mali Lošinj

RIVA

APARTMENTS ARENA PULA

Valerijin Park

AMPHITHEATER (AMFITEATAR)

SCALIEROVA

VARAŽDINSKA

Titov Park

AMFITEATARSKA

MUSEUM OF OLIVE OIL PRODUCTION

WINE BAR BRAJDA

RIVA

KANDLEROVA

Park Kralja Petra Krešimira

TESLINA

To Rock Bar Mimosa

SV. MARTINA

KATEDRALA SVETE MARIJE

DOBRICHEVA

EPULJDNOVA

ZADARSKA

RAKOVCEVA

CARRARINA

TOURIST OFFICE

POVIJESNI MUZEJ ISTRE

ARHEOLOŠKI MUZEJ

FORUM

FRANJEVAČKI SAMOSTAN

HOOK & COOK

SERGIJEVACA

ZAGREBAČKA

Trg Portarata

CRKVICA MARIJE OD TRSTIKA

FLACIUSOVA

ZLATNA VRATA

STATUE OF JAMES JOYCE

FLANATIČKA

Danteov Trg

ANTICOVA

SMAREGLINA

POST OFFICE

DOBRILINA

MARKET HALL

MILETAČKA

0   200 yds

0   200 m

Park Montezaro

CARA EMINA

Trg Republike

Huguesov Park

MARSOVO POLJE

MUTILSKA ULICA

ARSENALSKA

GAJEVA ULICA

BESENGHIEVA

Mornarički Trg

TARTINJEVA

RADIČEVA ULICA

MARULIĆEVA

To Aquarium, Park Plaza Arena Pula, Park Plaza Histria Pula, Valsabbion, Hotel Milan, Batelina, Mornaričko groblje, and Beaches

© MOON.COM

local architect and Venetian senator Gabriele Emo (who is remembered in an inscription on the second tower), who convinced Venice not to move the arena piece by piece across the Adriatic in the 16th century. Originally built to seat over 20,000 spectators, the amphitheater was built of limestone, which was plundered by locals in the centuries following the fall of Rome (the last time was in the 18th century, when the arena's stone was used in the city's cathedral).

Today the arena seats 5,000 for concerts and events. The underground rooms are also worth a peek, particularly if you're fond of winemaking. The display will tell you all about Roman viticulture. From June to September, except during the film festival, the arena hosts evening gladiator fights, workshops, and education presentations on Roman life. Tickets run around 80Kn per person for adults.

Museum of Olive Oil Production
(Museum Olei Histriae)

A new museum in Pula, the small **Museum of Olive Oil Production** (Ulica sv. Teodora 1a, tel. 052/661-235, www.oleumhistriae.com, 10am-6pm daily Mar.-May and Oct.-Dec., 9:30am-8pm daily June-Sept., 9:30am-10pm daily July-Aug., 50Kn) has an excellent display of the history of olive oil production, how olive oil is produced today, and how the experts taste oils. You can end your time by partaking in an olive oil tasting for an additional fee and can buy a souvenir bottle of your favorite from the museum's shop.

Golden Gate
(Zlatna vrata)

South of the amphitheater on the Via Sergia, the soaring **Golden Gate** or the "Triumphal Arch of Sergia" still reminds visitors of an important Roman family, called Sergia, who built the monument to themselves around 27 BC. The Corinthian arch is impressive, its huge ancient stone bulk standing solitary in the street, but the best thing about it is that it leads you into the ancient, and probably prettiest, parts of the city.

Chapel of St. Mary of Formosa
(Crkvica Marije od Trstika)

Near the Zlatna vrata on Maksimilijanova is the little **Chapel of St. Mary of Formosa,** a sweet 6th-century chapel that was once part of a large Benedictine abbey. It was once covered in Byzantine mosaics, today on display in the Archaeological Museum. A short walk north from the chapel will bring you to a stunning 2nd-century **floor mosaic** in a rather strange location for ancient relics, behind an apartment building. The large mosaic is protected by a metal fence, but free to view and always open since it sits outdoors. The mosaic depicts the punishment of Dirce, tied to the horns of an angry bull by the twins Amphion and Zethos, and was uncovered (and miraculously unharmed) by Allied bombs during World War II.

Franciscan Monastery
(Franjevački samostan)

If you haven't had your fill of stone relics yet (and the museum at the Temple of Augustus, your next stop, has some of the city's best), the nice little museum beside the austere 13th-century **Franciscan Monastery** (Balde Lupetine, 10am-1pm and 4pm-7pm daily in summer, 10Kn) has a few more, some dating back to Roman times.

Forum

Built between 2 BC and AD 14, the **Temple of Augustus** dominates Pula's Forum, still a major hub of activity in the old town. The Roman temple is one of the best-preserved outside of Italy, though it had to be painstakingly reconstructed after a WWII bomb all but destroyed it. Today it houses a wonderful display (www.ami-pula.hr, 9am-11pm daily July-Aug., 9am-9pm daily May, June, and Sept., 9am-7pm daily Apr. and Oct., 10Kn) of Roman stone and bronze sculptures. Long ago, the Temple of Diana mirrored it, but today only the back wall of that temple survives. The wall became a part of the **town hall (Gradska vijećnica)** in the 13th century.

Cathedral of St. Mary
(Katedrala svete Marije)

Not far from the Forum, the 5th-century **Cathedral of St. Mary** (Flavijevska, 7am-12pm and 4pm-6pm daily, free) is worth a peek. Though some parts were tacked on after various fires, many original elements survive, including some nice pieces of 5th- and 6th-century mosaics in front of the main altar.

Historical and Maritime Museum of Istria
(Povijesni muzej Istre)

The **Historical and Maritime Museum of Istria** (Gradinski uspon 6, tel. 052/211-566, 8am-9pm daily in summer, 9am-5pm daily in winter, 20Kn) is not really worth a visit for its exhibits (unless you're into displays of maritime history, postcards, and uniforms) but for the *kaštel* (castle fortress) that houses it. Built in 1630 for the Venetians by a French military architect, it has a four-pronged star shape that provides a great perch for enjoying some of the best views in the city.

A fun activity the museum started offering is the **Zerostrasse: Pula's Underground Tunnels (Zerostrasse: Pulski podzemni tunnel)** (Carrarina 3, 9am-10pm daily in summer, 9am-5pm daily in winter, 15Kn), where you can traverse underneath the city in tunnels built during the period of Austro-Hungarian rule.

Archaeological Museum
(Arheološki muzej)

The blink-or-you'll-miss-them remains of Pula's smallest Roman theater (it had three, back in the day) are in the shadow of the **Archaeological Museum** (Carrarina 3, tel. 052/218-603, www.ami-pula.hr, closed at the time of writing due to renovations), housed in a pretty building that was once the German Royal Gymnasium, or high school. The museum started undergoing renovation in 2013 and is still closed at the time of writing, but exhibits include Roman relics and remnants of classical buildings and displays from pre-history to medieval times, with an assortment of weaponry, fossils, and such. Information is provided in English.

Statue of James Joyce

Perhaps more of a photo op than anything else, the statue of author James Joyce, Pula's most famous expat, is seated in front of the Uliks coffee bar, ready for you to order a round.

Market Hall
(Tržnica)

Markets are always a great place to get a taste of city life, but Pula's **market hall** (Narodni trg bb, 7am-1pm daily) is something of an architectural delight as well. Built in 1903, the giant iron-and-glass structure is similar to Paris's famous Les Halles. Take an hour to browse the lively fish stalls and have a coffee in the glass art nouveau space.

Naval Cemetery
(Mornaričko groblje)

Located on the edge of the leafy Stoja district, the **Naval Cemetery** (Arsenalska, dawn-dusk, free) is a pretty Hapsburg-era graveyard, where more than 150,000 Austro-Hungarian military personnel are buried. It's actually quite park-like, with towering cypresses and peaceful sculptures. From here you can head off to lunch or some of the beaches in Stoja.

Aquarium
(Aquarium Pula)

The town's **Aquarium** (Fort Verudela, tel. 052/381-402, www.aquarium.hr, 9am-9pm daily June-Sept., 9am-8pm daily May and Oct., 9am-4pm daily Nov.-Apr., 100Kn) is a bit pricey for the small size, but the installation is well done, and the historic fort it's located in makes it a great outing for families. Exhibits showcase Croatia's underwater life as well as some tropical displays, totaling over 200 species in residence.

BEACHES
In Town

If you just want to take a seaside stroll, or if you're not too picky about your beach, you can hop one of the dozens of daily buses to **Stoja** (bus 1 or bus 4, 11Kn), just 3.5 kilometers (two miles) from the city center. From here there's a great promenade from Stoja to **Valkane** (a mostly run-down concrete beach area) and **Valsaline,** which has some decent spots to lay down your towel; Valkane and Valsaline are four kilometers (2.5 miles) and five kilometers (three miles) from the center, respectively.

South of Valsaline, you'll find **Punta Verudela** (take bus 2A or 3A, dozens of connections daily, 11Kn), six kilometers (3.7 miles) from the center, to be the pick of locals when it comes to taking a dip, though the beaches get packed on a nice day.

1: Pula's Roman amphitheater 2: safari park on Veli Brijun 3: beach near Pula 4: pedestrian street in Pula's city center

Premantura

Ten kilometers (six miles) south of Pula, the small town of Premantura (bus 26 from Pula, at least five connections on weekends, 10 on weekdays, more in summer, 15Kn) is a must-visit for windsurfing aficionados, even beginners. **Stupica** beach is the best place for catching a gust if the infamous *bura* happens to be blowing. **Windsurfing Centar Premantura** (tel. 091/512-3646, bivancic@yahoo.com, www.windsurfing.hr, contact for more info) rents equipment (140Kn for two hours) and gives daily courses (from 300Kn) during the summer from a hut on the beach at Autocamp Medulin.

Cape Kamenjak

Located at the southern tip of Istria (bus 25 from Pula, at least seven on weekends, 14 on weekdays, more in summer, 15Kn), the long narrow peninsula of Kamenjak is home to some of Istria's best beaches. The whole area is a nature preserve (you'll pay around 20Kn to get in) and is covered with dirt paths perfect for hiking or biking and also for finding hidden coves and deserted beaches (watch for strong currents when swimming, though). The Safari Bar is the only place to get a snack or a drink, so you might want to pack a picnic lunch.

Other Beaches

From the village of Marlera, southeast of Medulin, you can take a boat in the summer to **Levan Island** (contact Slaven for boat taxi pickup, tel. 098/182-0719, www.levan.hr), which has a restaurant and sandy beach. Ask a local how to get to the beaches below the Svetica Hill (accessible by boat or gravel road—check the insurance policy on the rental car), basically a set of miniature coves perfect for stealing a little privacy; they're to the east of Medulin below Svetica. If you are looking for a taxi boat, ask about options at the Medulin harbor.

ENTERTAINMENT AND EVENTS
Nightlife

Though the center of the city is low on hotels and restaurants, nightlife is a different story. Cruise the streets around the arena and you're bound to run across bars and cafés hopping with people. Low key options include **Wine Bar Brajda** (Kandlerova Ul. 34, tel. 052/383-747) to discover local wines or **Rock Bar Mimosa** (Vukovarska 13, tel. 098/963-6171) for rock, jazz, and blues depending on the night and a great selection of beer. Or head to Premantura and Medulin for a serious summer party scene.

Festivals

Pula has many festivals, from the musical variety like the **Dimensions Festival** (August, www.dimensionsfestival.com), an electronic music festival, and **Seasplash Festival** (July, www.seasplash-festival.com), focusing on dubstep and reggae, both located a few kilometers from town in Stinjan, to the historical **Days of Antiquity** (June, www.pula-superiorum.com), which explores what it was like to live in the days of Rome. The longest running, for over 60 years, is the **Pula Film Festival** (July, www.pulafilmfestival.hr), during which Croatian films are screened at the arena. In September, the **Visualia Festival of Light** (September, www.festival-visualia.com) brings artistic light displays to the city.

ACCOMMODATIONS

On the cheaper end, there's not much to recommend in Pula. If you're determined to stay in the center, the one good (read: clean) option is the **Apartments Arena Pula** (Flavijevska 2, tel. 052/516-207, www.pula-apartments.com, 398Kn d) for nice service, a central location, and basic creature comforts.

The best bet for budget travelers is to check what's available on **AirBnB** (www.airbnb.com) and **Booking** (www.booking.com) for a variety of rooms and apartments, many at very affordable prices.

On the upper end, however, Pula has added several great options to its luxury hotels. For those looking for a family resort vacation, the **Park Plaza Histria Pula** (Verudella 17, tel. 052/590-000, www.parkplaza.com, 950Kn d, including breakfast) is a large hotel with a waterfront pool and modern, tastefully decorated rooms. The spa and the kids and teen clubs are popular with guests who jockey for space on the lounge chairs in summer.

The nearby **Park Plaza Arena Pula** (Verudella 31, tel. 052/375-000, www.parkplaza.com, 792Kn d, including breakfast) was renovated in 2015 and boasts not only a waterfront pool but direct beach access as well.

In Stoja, the family-owned and -operated **Hotel Milan** (Stoja 4, tel. 052/300-200, www.milan1967.hr, 700Kn d, including breakfast) dates from 1967, but from the sleek, modern building you'd never know it. The leafy, quiet location is a 10-minute bus ride from the center of town and a short walk from the sea.

In the Pješčana Uvala yachting district, ★ **Valsabbion** (Pješčana Uvala IX/26, tel. 052/218-033, www.valsabbion.hr, closed Jan., 1,279Kn d, including breakfast) is certainly Pula's chicest boutique hotel. From its much-lauded lobby restaurant to the lush rooms and waterfront yacht-filled location, this is where the beautiful people go.

Though it is six kilometers (3.7 miles) from the city center, the bright and cheery **Adrion Aparthotel** (Puntižela 40, tel. 052/330-077, www.adrion-aparthotel.hr, 600Kn d) consists of multiple small apartments and studios and is only a 10-minute walk to the beach.

If you're not afraid of a 30-minute bike ride or you have your own car, the beach areas south of town have a couple of great options for travelers. For those on a budget, you can rent your own lighthouse room in the ★ **Porer lighthouse** (via Adriatrica Agency, Heinzelova 62a, Zagreb, tel. 01/610-2000, www.adriagate.com, 600Kn d) or stay the night at **Camping Brioni** (tel. 052/465-010, www.camping-adriatic.com, 150Kn hostel bed, including breakfast), where you can pitch a seaside tent or share a room with fellow travelers at the camp's hostel.

FOOD

Fast food is rarely inventive, but don't miss **Hook&Cook's** (Ul. Seršjevaca 18, 10am-11pm daily, 50Kn) hot tuna steak burger when you break from sightseeing for lunch.

Restoran Vela Nera (Pješčana uvala, tel. 052/219-209, www.velanera.hr, 8am-12am daily, 90Kn) has a pretty oceanfront location and boasts its knowledge of wine as an added bonus to the delicious seafood dishes. The best fish restaurant in Pula is closed in August because the owner of ★ **Batelina** (Čimulje 25, tel. 052/573-767, 5pm-11pm daily in summer except Aug., call for winter hours, 100Kn) says there is no good fish and too many people to serve them properly. Suffice to say that anything you order here is high quality and prepared lovingly. Reservations are a must, and even hardcore foodies will not leave disappointed.

WINE

A young winemaker with a strong offering, ★ **Trapan Wine Station** (Giordan Dobran 63, tel. 098/244-457, www.trapan.hr, contact to reserve tasting, though generally 11am-7pm in summer, 75Kn) offers flights of wine in their cozy and modern building just south of Pula.

Near Pula, the **Benazić Winery** (Valdebecki put 36, tel. 099/634-8156, www.vinabenazic.com, contact via email or website to arrange a reservation) offers degustation menus from 50Kn and up. The winery produces Malvazija, Teran, muscat, and cabernet sauvignon.

INFORMATION AND SERVICES

Lots of information, from brochures to information about tours and excursions, can be found at the Pula **tourist office** (Forum 3, tel. 052/219-197, www.pulainfo.hr, 8am-8pm Mon.-Sat., 9am-8pm Sun. in summer, call for winter hours) on the Forum. The tourist office also sells a Pula Card (90Kn) that offers discounts at six local attractions.

Need to connect with someone back home? The central **post office** (Danteov trg 4, tel. 052/215-955, 7am-8pm Mon.-Fri., 7am-2pm Sat.) can help you send a postcard back home or make a phone call.

Most aches and pains can be solved at the all-night **pharmacy** (Giardini 15, tel. 052/222-551, 24 hours). In summers, the city has a **tourist health clinic** (Dom zdravlja, Clinic 16, Flanatička 27, tel. 052/210-805, 10am-6pm except Wed. in June, 9am-9pm July-Aug.). For something more serious, Pula's **hospital** (Zagrebačka 30, tel. 052/214-433) should be able to help.

Luggage can be stored at the **bus station** (Istarska 3, tel. 052/219-074, 5am-10pm daily, around 2Kn per hour) or the **train station** (Kolodvorska 5, tel. 052/541-733, 9am-4pm Mon.-Sat., around 15Kn per day).

GETTING THERE AND AROUND

Pula's **airport** (tel. 052/530-105, www.airport-pula.com) is Istria's main hub. The airport is only six kilometers (3.7 miles) from the center and a shuttle bus (www.fils.hr, 30Kn to Pula center) connects the airport with Pula as well as most major stops along Istria's west coast (prices are higher than to the center).

Pula has good train and bus connections. The **train station** (Kolodvorska 5, tel. 052/541-733) is about a 10-minute walk from the center of town, while the central **bus station** (Istarska 3, tel. 052/219-074) is only about five minutes away. There's another **bus station** (Trg Istarske Brigade, tel. 052/502-997) slightly north of the amphitheater that serves mostly local routes, with connections to the beaches and small towns near Pula.

There are several daily trains to Zagreb (seven hours, 131Kn) and at least one to Ljubljana (four hours, 130Kn).

There are several daily buses connecting Pula with Rijeka (2.25 hours, 84Kn) or Zagreb (five hours, around 215Kn depending on the time of departure).

Pula is 292 kilometers (181 miles) southwest of Zagreb. From Zagreb, take the highway toward Rijeka and then go through the Učka tunnel, at which point you'll follow the signs to Pula.

If driving to Pula is pretty simple (there's a sign pointing you to the city from most everywhere in Istria), parking is likely to be a wholly different matter. There are few parking spots, and most require tricky parallel parking maneuvers. Best to drop off the car at the hotel and continue your sightseeing using public transportation.

Local buses (www.pulapromet.com) can get you around Pula from stops all over the city. You can buy tickets at newspaper kiosks for 7Kn or onboard for 11Kn to most places around town. Prices are slightly higher to the beaches around Medulin.

AROUND PULA
Vodnjan

Vodnjan, home to the **Vodnjan mummies,** is 11 kilometers (seven miles) north of Pula (hop on a city bus 22 in Pula, takes about 30 minutes, 7 or more buses on weekends and 16 or more weekdays, 15Kn). The mummified bodies of six saints who have never decomposed—due to preservation or miracles, your call—are housed in the **Church of St. Blaise (Crkva svetog Blaža)** (tel. 052/511-420, 9am-7pm Mon.-Sat., 2pm-7pm Sun. in summer, call ahead for a winter visit, 35Kn). There are about 14 other churches in or around town, though perhaps more interesting are the some 3,000 *kažuni*, or stone huts, in the surrounding countryside.

Run4Ham (early April) combines running and gourmet tastings. The **Olive Oil and Wine Day** (May) is worth a trip for anyone who enjoys olive oil and wine. The exhibition's highlight is a judging of olive oils and wines by local producers. Snatch a few bottles of the winners for the flight back home.

A must-stop for lunch or dinner is the superb family restaurant ★ **Vodnjanka** (Istarska bb, tel. 052/511-435, www.vodnjanka.com, 11am-11pm Mon.-Sat., 6pm-12am

Festivals for Foodies

- **Oleum Olivarum,** Krasica (March), and **Olive Oil Exhibition (Smotra maslinovog ulja)** (April), Vodnjan: Lectures, exhibitions, and tastings plus competitions for the best local olive oil.

- **Vinistra** (April or May), Poreč: A festival of all things culinary; local products like grappa, olive oil, cheese, and prosciutto are on display culminating in a judged ranking of Istrian wines.

- **Fažana School of Sardine Salting (Fažanska škola soljenja sardela)** (May), Fažana: One day of presentations and workshops in sardine salting with various local advice on the right combination of salt, oil, and spices. Even if you're not in the mood to learn, you can still judge by tasting the recipes.

- **Wine Day (Dan Vina)** (end of May): Cellars all over Istria open their doors 10am-6pm for tastings. Plan your itinerary by picking up a map of participating wineries from the Istrian Tourist Board.

- **Istrian Malvasia Festival (Fešta istarske malvazije)** (end of May or early June), Brtonigla: The festival celebrates the most famous indigenous wine, with tastings, gourmet presentations, and entertainment.

- **Fisherman's festivals (Ribarske fešte)** (varying dates throughout the summer), Medulin, Savudrija, Novigrad, Umag, Vrsar, Funtana, and Fažana: Local mariners entertain the crowds with song and feed them grilled fish and seafood, with sides of wine, cheese, and olives.

- **Maneštra Festival (Maneštrijada)** (bi- or tri-annually), Gračišće: The main square comes alive to prepare the area's typical stew, *maneštra*, a pasta-based dish that varies according to the season's ingredients.

- **Subotina with giant truffle omelet (Subotina uz divovsku fritadu s tartufima)** (September), Buzet: A giant truffle omelet made of over 2,000 eggs in a 2.5-meter-wide (8-foot-wide) pan kicks off Buzet's traditional festival filled with crafts, folk groups, and food. You can follow special food- or wine-based "trails," stuffing yourself with the best the region has to offer.

- **Festival of New Wine (Fešta mladega vina)** (October), Svetvinčenat: A tasting of the Istrian Beaujolais in a beautiful old Venetian palace.

ISTRIA
PULA

Sun. in summer, 11am-11pm Mon.-Sat. in winter, closed Jan., 75Kn), famous for its Istrian sausages, prosciutto, and escargot.

Bale

Bale, northwest of Vodnjan, is a charming village dating from 983. Wander the perfect meandering streets or peek in some of the churches, but don't miss two very interesting (and two very different) places to stay. On the uber-luxe end is the ★ **Stancija**

Meneghetti (Bale, tel. 091/243-1600, www. meneghetti.info, 1,200Kn d hotel), a beautiful villa with an equally wonderful **restaurant** (12pm-11pm daily, 160Kn) and winery.

On the conservation, and frankly hippie and trippy, side is the **Eia Eco Art Village** (San Zuian 13, tel. 098/916-0650, www.eia. hr, around 50Kn pp campsites), which hosts visitors for next to nothing in its peaceful and ecofriendly space (exhibit A: showering with collected rainwater).

Brijuni Islands

A small archipelago of islands off the Istrian coast, the Brijuni Islands were once an aristocratic playground created by Austrian industrialist Paul Kupelweiser, later a hunting retreat of Yugoslavian leader Josip Broz Tito, and today a national park. If you want to see the islands, you can either book a day trip through the **Brijuni National Park office** (tel. 052/525-882, www.np-brijuni.hr, 8am-10pm daily July-Aug., 8am-8pm daily June and Sept., 8am-3pm Mon.-Sat. Oct.-Apr., four-hour tour 210Kn) or book a hotel or excursion (such as golf or diving) through the park office in Fažana. Booking a hotel room or villa offers you the most freedom around Brijuni, since day-trippers are generally herded in a neat little jaunt around the island. Avoid all the waterfront placards hawking Brijuni tours. Only tickets purchased through the park office allow you to go on Veli Brijun. The other boats can only travel around them and are not allowed to dock.

★ VELI BRIJUN

Veli Brijun, the largest of the islands, and one of only a couple of the 14 islands open to the public, holds the majority of the sights. The rough-around-the-edges island contains some stunning scenery, refined villas, wild animals, and even dinosaur footprints. In short, it's the perfect setting for a science fiction movie. Day-trippers to Veli Brijun will take a small tourist train that runs through the **safari park,** which was once stocked with game for Tito's hunting fetishes. You might spot some elephants and zebras as well as animals native to the Istrian landscape. Animals that have died are now on display in the island's Natural History Museum. The train also passes the **White Villa (Bijela vila),** Tito's haunt and overnight destination of many a well-known guest, and stops at the ruins of a Byzantine fortress. If you're on the day tour,

you'll probably also see a 15th-century church and the exhibition **Tito on Brijuni (Tito na Brijunima)** (8am-8pm daily July-Aug., 8am-7pm June and Sept., 8am-6pm daily May and Oct., included with excursion to the island), with a fascinating set of photographs of the Yugoslav leader with high-level politicos from 60 countries as well as a smattering of Hollywood stars. Downstairs is an exhibition of many of the former animal inhabitants of the island, well-preserved in taxidermy behind glass.

The tour also includes the stone quarries and a small church. You can stay longer on the island as long as you leave by the end of the day. Rent a golf cart or a bicycle to scoot around the island (rentals available from the sports center near the Neptun-Istra hotel, carts around 500Kn half day, bicycles around 120Kn full day), perhaps visiting some of the Roman ruins and Kupelwieser's grave. Even more interesting is an underwater "trail" that explores Roman ruins with snorkel gear in a pristine bay.

If you're staying on Veli Brijun, there's also a **golf course** (greens fees 200Kn for the day, 180Kn if you're staying on the island, 100Kn for a set of clubs for the day) if you'd like to keep your swing from getting rusty.

OTHER ISLANDS

The office also runs trips to **Mali Brijun,** with an old Austro-Hungarian fort as part of the tour. Other than that, Mali Brijun's only other attraction is its quiet, pebbly shores—quite impressive, particularly if you fancy yourself a bit of a Robinson Crusoe. **Sveti Jerolim** and **Kotež** are also open for swimming and fish picnic excursions. Boats are allowed to moor on Mali Brijun and Sveti Jerolim only with previous permission and the payment of a fee to the park office. Small boats are allowed freely and without payment on Kozada.

Brijuni's Luxe Past

Though most people associate Brijuni with Tito, it was Austrian industrialist Paul Kupelwieser who brought the islands to life. Once the retreat of wealthy Romans, the islands had deteriorated to malaria-ridden wastelands when Kupelwieser bought them in 1893. Within just a few years he brought in a Nobel Prize-winning scientist to get rid of the malaria and built a harbor and hotel with a heated seawater swimming pool. Four to five connections with the mainland a day brought in Europe's elite, including the Archduke Franz Ferdinand, the Duke of Spoleto, and Kaiser Wilhelm II.

The resort was popular with the polo circuit but it never did turn a profit. In 1930, Paul Kupelweiser's son committed suicide on the islands. After World War II, Tito took it over and built the Bijela Vila (White Villa), where he entertained stars attending the Pula Film Festival, like Elizabeth Taylor, Richard Burton, and Gina Lollobrigida, and heads of state like Queen Elizabeth II.

Today, a touch of past glamour is beginning to return to the islands. There's a 22-hole environmentally friendly golf course, and the yearly Brioni Polo Classic has brought the tradition of polo back to Brijuni. Brioni planned on building a resort on the island, but for the moment plans have apparently been put on hold. Still, the islands have become a secret of the yachting set, welcoming a new crop of stars and politicos to Brijuni's shores, most of whom rent one of the island's secluded private villas.

ACCOMMODATIONS AND FOOD

There are two hotels on the island, the expensive and unimpressive **Neptun-Istra** (tel. 052/525-807, 1,030Kn d, including breakfast) and **Karmen** (tel. 052/525-807, 900Kn d, including breakfast). The hotels also have restaurants and cafés where you can get a bit of nourishment. The Neptun-Istra is the nicer of the two, but either one will do if you make sure to get one of the rooms with terraces facing the sea (a feature of the majority of rooms in both hotels). Or, splurge by renting one of the **villas** (www.brijuni.hr, 7,500Kn to 13,500Kn per night), which come with private transport to and from the island, bikes, and an electric cart. They also offer plenty of privacy and come with your own personal maid and a private beach, a celebrity-esque touch apropos to the island's past.

GETTING THERE AND AROUND

Your departure point for Brijuni will be the town of Fažana, about a 10-minute drive north from Pula. If you're relying on public transport take bus 21 (at least seven connections on weekends, 15 on weekdays, more in summer, 15Kn) from Pula. The Brijuni National Park office on Fažana's small harbor sells trips to the island (eight daily May-Oct., one daily the rest of the year except Jan. when the park is closed). You can also book a trip through your hotel (usually around 250Kn, including transportation to Fažana and lunch), though tours booked at unofficial spots in the Pula harbor may not give you as much for your money as going directly through the park's office.

Rovinj

Rovinj's Luxe Past

Rovinj is one of Istria's most charming coastal towns. This also means it's one of its busiest. The town's almost untouched medieval core is sunny, sometimes quite hilly, and filled with bars, cafés, and galleries for poking around. The shady beaches just out of town or across the water are some of the best in Istria, too, making Rovinj a great all-around stop.

Rovinj was once an island; during the 18th century the strait between Rovinj and the mainland was filled in, creating a profitable little port city. Rovinj is still quite profitable, not only from the tourist trade, but from the town's tobacco factory, **Tvornica Duhan Rovinj,** which has made the town's inhabitants some of the wealthiest in Croatia. That prosperity and popularity translates into a wide offering of hotels and restaurants to service the artsy sun-washed stone enclave.

SIGHTS
Marshal Tito Square
(Trg maršala Tita)
The harborside **Marshal Tito Square** is Rovinj's main square and a great starting point for touring the old town. You can branch out onto any of the surrounding streets for some atmospheric wandering or follow the narrow little street called Grisia up to the St. Euphemia's Church (Crkva svete Eufemije). As you're climbing up Grisia, take some time to pop in the **art galleries** and shops selling local crafts and colorful paintings; the street is also home to its fair share of touristy knickknacks.

Rovinj Heritage Museum
(Zavičajni muzej Rovinj)
On the northern end of Marshal Tito Square, the **Rovinj Heritage Museum** (Trg Maršala Tita 11, tel. 052/816-720, www.muzej-rovinj.hr, 10am-11pm daily in summer, 60Kn) is housed in a Baroque palace next to the **Balbi Arch,** the town's gate back in medieval times. The museum is most proud of its impressive Old Masters collection (with lots from the Italian school), but the place really hits its niche with the displays of Croatian contemporary painting and local artists.

old town, Rovinj

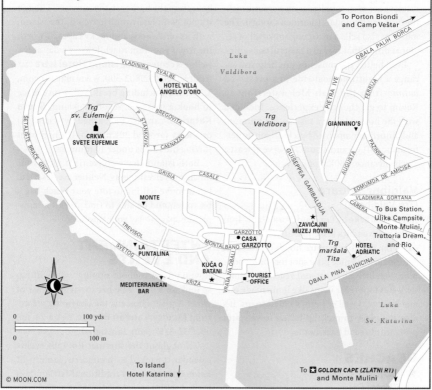

Rovinj

Luka Valdibora

HOTEL VILLA ANGELO D'ORO

VLADINIRA · SVALBE

Trg sv. Eufemije

CRKVA SVETE EUFEMIJE

ŠETALIŠTE BRAĆE GNOT

P. STANKOVIĆ · BREGOVITA · CAENAZZO

GRISIA · CASALE

MONTE ▼

TREVISOL · SVETOG · MONTALBANO

▼ LA PUNTALINA

KUĆA O BATANI ★

MEDITERRANEAN BAR ▼

KRIZA

0   100 yds
0   100 m

Trg Valdibora

GIANNINO'S ▼

GUISEPPEA GARIBALDIJA

GARZOTTO
● CASA
GARZOTTO

ZAVIČAJNI MUZEJ ROVINJ ★

VRATA NA OBALI

★ TOURIST OFFICE

Trg maršala Tita

HOTEL ADRIATIC ●

OBALA PINA BUDICINA

To Porton Biondi and Camp Veštar →

OBALA PALIH BORCA

PIETRA IVE · FERRLIA

PAZINSKA

AUGUSTA

EDMUNDA DE AMICISA

VLADIMIRA GORTANA

CARERA

To Bus Station, Ulika Campsite, Monte Mulini, Trattoria Dream, and Rio →

Luka Sv. Katarina

To Island Hotel Katarina ↓

To ❖ *GOLDEN CAPE (ZLATNI R1)* and Monte Mulini ↓

© MOON.COM

ISTRIA
ROVINJ

St. Euphemia's Church
(Crkva svete Eufemije)

Towering over Rovinj's old town at the end of Grisia, **St. Euphemia's Church** (Garibaldijeva 1, tel. 052/815-615, 10am-2pm and 3pm-6pm daily, free, small fee to walk up the bell tower) is named for the town's patron saint, a Christian martyr from the era of Diocletian, who fed her to the lions in 304. The building dates from the 18th century, though its facade was added later. The most interesting parts are the statue of St. Euphemia, who turns atop her perch to show the direction of the wind, and her 6th-century stone coffin behind the altar. The bell tower climb is worth the effort for the magnificent view.

Batana House
(Kuća o batani)

The **Batana House** (Obala P Budicin 2, tel. 052/805-266, www.batana.org, 10am-2pm and 7pm-11pm daily June-Sept., 10am-1pm and 4pm-6pm daily Mar.-May and Oct.-Dec., by arrangement only Jan.-Feb., 20Kn) is a miniature (just over 93 square meters/1,000 square feet) "ecomuseum" devoted to the local *batana* boat. The name of the boat likely derives from the Italian *battere*, meaning to strike or hit, an onomatopoeic reference to the sound made when the waves hit the wooden watercraft. Some form of the flat-bottomed boat has been in use since the 14th century, though the true heyday of the *batana* was in the 1960s, when motors were added and almost every local family had one for fishing or for excursions to the islands around Rovinj. The well-presented displays are even supplied with a soundtrack, the *bitinada* (regional fishermen's songs). The museum also sells a nice cookbook full of regional dishes that makes a tasteful souvenir.

Even better, the museum can help you arrange a nighttime boat ride in a preserved *batana* from the Mali Mol waterfront in Rovinj to get the true experience. Included with the boat ride are a visit to the museum and dinner accompanied by a local music performance (Tues. and Thurs., reserve at least a day in advance, 260Kn pp).

Valdibor Square
(Trg Valdibora)

Rovinj's **market** (Trg Valdibora, 7am-4pm daily, best vendors leave just after 12pm), located on Valdibor Square north of Marshal Tito Square, is a nice little spot for some shopping. Vendors sell fruits and vegetables along with good souvenir items like homemade oils and honeys as well as herb-scented soaps. It's also the place to pick up beach towels and postcards to send back home.

BEACHES
★ Golden Cape
(Zlatni Rt)

Just a kilometer (0.6 mile) south of Rovinj's harbor, most easily accessed by foot or bike from the old town, you'll find the nature park of **Golden Cape,** with great forested paths leading to dozens of rocky and pebbly beaches. These beaches are convenient, easily accessible by foot, bike, and even stroller. The park extends for over seven kilometers (four miles); the busiest beaches are on the western side, and the shores at the tip of the Skaraba Cape are much less frequented. Though the beaches aren't officially nudist, don't be surprised if you run across a few nude sunbathers in the little coves along the way.

Islands Offshore

Crveni Otok, literally "red island" (also known as Otok Sv. Andrija), is a tiny escape just 15 minutes by boat from Rovinj (20Kn), with approximately two boats departing every hour from the harbor in the summer. Though it's not completely undiscovered, the island, with its pinewoods and rocky capes, is worth the trip if you want to while away a day at the wellness center in the **Island Hotel Istra** (Sv. Andrea, tel. 052/802-500, www.maistra.com, 1,294Kn d, including breakfast), a nice place to book a massage. Another island, **Sveta Katarina,** can also be reached by water taxi or a ferry (around 20Kn) from the harbor at Rovinj; the ride is under 10 minutes.

Both islands have convenient places for lunch and refreshments. Neither are deserted, but if you're willing to tote your beach bag a bit you should be able to find at least a semi-private space to lay your towel.

ENTERTAINMENT AND EVENTS

Rovinj proper is about sipping, not swilling, so look for a cozy café bar to savor a glass of wine. A great choice is the charming waterfront **Mediterranean Bar** (Sv. Kriza 24, tel. 091/532-8357, 9am-2am daily).

Throughout the summer Rovinj's events calendar is packed with concerts, lantern-lit *batana* parades, and traditional Istrian days loaded with typical crafts, foods, and costumes. Also interesting are summer's twice-monthly fishermen festivals, with grilled fish and the a cappella *bitinadas.*

ACCOMMODATIONS

Rovinj has dozens of package-type hotels in its environs; the center offers several good boutique options, heavy on charm. For those who want to rough it, try the beachfront campsite **Porton Biondi** (Aleja Porton Biondi 1, tel. 052/813-557, www.portonbiondi.hr, from 47Kn pp), less than one kilometer/mile east of town, and the more tourist-friendly **Camp Veštar** (Veštar bb, tel. 052/829-150, www.maistracamping.com, from 37Kn pp for a pitch), which has a bar, a pool, and boat and bike rentals only six kilometers (3.7 miles) east of town. Camp Veštar is right on a nice pebble beach, and even has dog showers for campers' furry friends.

A campsite that's definitely more glamping than camping, **Ulika Campsite** (Polari 5, tel. 052/817-320, www.dn-rovinj.com, 592Kn for a mini-mobile home) is a good choice whether you have a tent or not. The campsite has nice showers and a pool for guests.

Though the rooms and facilities could do with an update, the location of ★ **Island Hotel Katarina** (Otok St. Katarina 1, tel. 052/800-250, www.maistra.com, 550Kn d) is phenomenal. A tiny island just a 10-minute boat road from central Rovina (boats leave hourly and are free for hotel guests), a large pool, pristine beaches, and a tranquil setting are hard to beat.

Don't let the narrow-alley location of the **Hotel Villa Angelo d' Oro** (Via Švalba 38-42, tel. 052/840-502, www.angelodoro.com, 878Kn d, including breakfast) fool you. It's had more than its share of press, though sometimes the service fails to live up to the luxe reputation. **Casa Garzotto** (Via Garzotto 8, tel. 098/616-168, www.casa-garzotto.com, 995Kn d, including breakfast) gives consistent great service and has very charming rooms, though walking-weary travelers should be warned of the stairs you'll need to climb to get to your room.

The ★ **Hotel Adriatic** (Obala Pina Budicina, tel. 052/800-250, www.maistra.com, 1,800Kn d) brings luxe boutique accommodations to a historic building in the old town. The 18 suites are beautifully outfitted, and the restaurant and bar are sleek to match.

Out of town, a complete overhaul of hotel ★ **Monte Mulini** (Šetalište uvale Lone, tel. 052/800-230, www.maistra.hr, 3,065Kn d, including breakfast) has turned the former Tito-era relic into the most upscale of the Maistra Group's hotels, complete with shady swimming pools, a beach, and a spa.

FOOD

Restaurant Trattoria Dream (Joakima Rakovca 18, tel. 052/830-613, 11:30am-10pm daily, 65Kn) is a bit more flair than substance.

Still, the trendy restaurant on a side street has lots of tasty seafood as well as good pastas and a few dishes that could pass as vegetarian.

But since Rovinj is on the sea, it's worth the splurge to try out some of Rovinj's better restaurants. **Rio** (Aldo Rismondo 13, tel. 052/813-564, 7:30am-1am daily in summer, call for winter hours, 90Kn) is owned by the same family that owns Rovinj establishment restaurant Giannino's. Excellent local food for reasonable prices in a waterfront location, the restaurant is also the perfect breakfast spot.

Now with its own Michelin star at the time of writing, ★ **Monte** (Montelbano 75, tel. 052/830-203, www.monte.hr, 6:30pm-11:30pm daily in summer, closed mid-Oct.-mid-Apr., 400Kn) is often lauded by guidebooks and hotels (you won't be the only tourists, but the food is great), with quality seafood dishes and a nice location near Sv. Eufemija. One of the first to do molecular gastronomy in Croatia, they are still one of the most adventurous.

At first glance the prices at **Giannino's** (Augusto Ferri 38, tel. 052/813-402, www. restoran-giannino.com, 11:30am-3pm and 6pm-11pm daily, 100Kn) might seem a little high for a *gostionica* (bistro), but the food will change your mind. This place is very popular with visiting Italians and local businessmen. Giannino's has haute seafood dishes (think sole with truffles or grilled lobster) in a slightly shabby atmosphere with real soul (though it has been said the dishes for regulars are often prepared with more care).

If you're looking for a romantic meal, try the cliff-top ★ **La Puntulina** (Sv. Križa 38, tel. 052/813-186, 12pm-3pm and 6pm-12am daily, no credit cards, 90Kn), with solid Italian-Istrian cuisine and a knockout downstairs waterside cocktail bar and terrace.

INFORMATION AND SERVICES

Rovinj's **tourist office** (Pina Budicina 12, tel. 052/811-566, www.rovinj-tourism.com, 8am-9pm daily mid-June-mid-Sept., 8am-3pm Mon.-Sat. rest of the year) is located near Trg maršala Tita to provide you with lots of maps, brochures, and information on bike and boat rentals and scuba diving.

GETTING THERE AND AROUND

If you're taking the **bus**, the **station** (Trg na lokvi 6, tel. 052/811-453, note the hectagon-shaped 13th-century Romanesque church next door) is only a five-minute walk from the center of town with good connections to Zagreb (approx. 5.5 hours, 220Kn) and Pula (40 minutes, 34Kn). The nearest **train station** is in Kananfar, 20 kilometers (12.4 miles) east of Rovinj; there's bus service to Rovinj. A ticket to Zagreb on the train from Kananfar takes approximately six hours and costs around 125Kn. If you're driving, be aware that you'll need to park somewhere and leave your car; parking is scarce and cars are not allowed inside the old town. For taxis, dial 052/811-100.

If you'd like to connect via boat, **Venezia Lines** (tel. 052/422-896, www.venezialines.com, €70) runs day trips to Venice, including a guided tour. The trip takes a total of about nine hours.

AROUND ROVINJ
Limski Kanal

A Mediterranean fjord cutting a sparkling blue line into Istria between Rovinj and Poreč, the **Limski Kanal** was once the haunt of pirates attacking Venetian ships. Today the Limski Kanal is the perfect spot for a boat trip as well as for visiting **Romuald's Cave,** where St. Romuald lived for two years, and for sampling local oysters and mussels. Romuald's Cave, a 105-meter-long (345-foot-long) cave in a hillside, was a solitary refuge for the 11th-century saint. Currently due to safety issues, the cave is closed, but when it is open again, guided **tours** (arranged through Natura Histrica, Obala A. Rismondo 2, Rovinj, tel. 052/830-582, www.natura-histrica.hr, 10-30Kn) are the only way to see the cave. Tours of the fjord are easily booked through tourist offices in Rovinj, Poreč, or from the harbor in Vrsar. Trips can last a couple of hours or a whole day including a fish picnic, and cost 100-250Kn per person. If you're looking to form your own opinion of the region's famous oysters and mussels, everyone will point you toward **Viking** (Lim bb, tel. 052/448-223, 11am-4:30pm and 6:30pm-11pm daily, 85Kn).

Wineries

Slightly inland from Vrsar, head to the wineries of **Ivica Matošević** (Krunčići 2, Sv. Lovreč, tel. 052/448-558, www.matosevic.com, call to reserve a tour), a young winemaker and the director of Vinistra, who produces top-rate Malvazija and a good sauvignon blanc.

Poreč

Poreč is a charming seaside town, once a Roman colony, with traces of Romanesque, Venetian, and—more interesting—Byzantine architecture. Called Parenzo in Italian and Parentium in Latin, Poreč was an important Roman town, with the largest Roman temple on the Adriatic's east coast. The Byzantine emperor Justinian I also found the city important, building the stunning Eufrazijeva basilica in town, though historians have failed to explain why he found the city so alluring. Remaining under the Venetian Republic for 500 years, Poreč was a trade and military port, and the Austro-Hungarians established it as a capital of the Istrian region.

In modern times it's a major tourist destination, its outer edges filled with large package hotels. The town's most famous attraction is the 6th-century basilica, though the town has several places of interest to tourists. During most of the year, it's really a don't-miss stop, though summer makes it one of Istria's most-packed cities as the dozens of hotels and tourist complexes nearby dump thousands

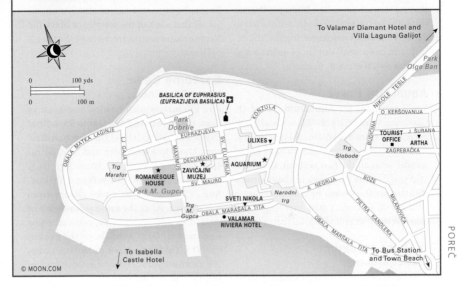

Poreč

into the little place. When the place is really overrun with tourists, visitors often miss the charm and remnants of grandeur that make it special. The upside of visiting in summer is getting to enjoy all of the events taking place, particularly the classical music concerts performed in the stunning basilica.

The best thing about Poreč is the location. Even in the high season, you can dip into town for sightseeing or events and then escape to a town slightly inland or the more upscale Novigrad to the north to get away from the throngs. It's also near the beginning of some nice wine roads, ripe with producers of Istria's outstanding Malvazija.

SIGHTS
★ Basilica of Euphrasius
(Eufrazijeva basilica)

If you have time to see only one thing in Poreč, it should be the 6th-century **Basilica of Euphrasius** (Eufrazija utica 22, tel. 052/451-784, 9am-4pm daily Nov.-Mar., 9am-6pm daily Apr.-June and Sept.-Oct., 9am-9pm daily July-Aug., 40Kn). Unlike most grand churches, its position is almost hidden, in the center of town though slightly off the main thoroughfare on Sveta Eleuterija. The complex was built around 553, during the Justinian period, by the Bishop Euphrasius, whose signature and likeness can be seen in multiple locations. Visitors enter through a stone portal, completed in 1902 and topped with an ancient mosaic depicting Jesus and inscribed in Latin, "I am the gate. Who enters through me, will be saved." The rest of the church is quite well preserved, with one of the few additions being the 13th-century baldachin, or canopy, above the altar, so well integrated that it looks original as well. The still-sparkling Byzantine mosaics were created by artisans shipped in from Constantinople and Ravenna and are by far the most arresting feature of the sight. The mosaics depict biblical stories and saints, as well as a number of female saints.

Euphrasius even put himself and his family in the apse. To the far left is his brother Cladius, a small boy depicting Cladius's son, and Euphrasius, holding a scale model of the basilica in his hands.

If you have plenty of energy, make the hike up the bell tower of the octagon-shaped

Bapistry (Baptisterijum) (10am-5pm daily, 10Kn), also part of the original complex, for the best views in town. The **Bishop's Palace (Biskupska palača)** (included with ticket to Bapistry) was built much later, in the 17th century, and has a small display of mosaics and Baroque sacral art in its museum.

Aquarium Poreč

You'll see signs for **Aquarium Poreč** (F. Glavinica 4, tel. 052/428-720, www.akvarij-porec.com, 10am-5pm daily, till 11pm in summer, 40Kn) everywhere, and it's hard not to wonder what all the fuss is about. One local said you'd see as many fish in the *ribarnica* (fishmonger's)—though he may have been a little harsh, you won't miss anything if you skip this small sampling of local fish in tanks.

District Museum
(Zavičajni muzej)

Housed in an 18th-century Baroque palace, the **District Museum** (Dekumanska 9, tel. 052/431-585, www.muzejporec.hr, currently closed due to renovation) is the oldest museum in Istria, dating from 1884. The permanent collection is a nice mix of Roman and Greek stone monuments and pottery as well as a nice display of 17th-century Baroque portraits and art objects. There are occasional temporary exhibits open to the public during renovation.

Romanesque House
(Romanička kuća)

At the end of Dekumanska you'll find the sweet little stone **Romanesque House** with an interesting wooden wraparound balcony, built in the 13th century.

Marafor Square
(Trg Marafor)

At the very end of the peninsula, **Marafor Square** is the location of the old Roman forum. The square's name likely derives from the words *Mars* and *Forum*, since the large square, rivaling the size of the squares in Pula and Salona, centered around a 1st-century temple to Mars. The sides of the square were home to small temples of Neptune and Diana. Today, some carved stone remnants are all that's left of the temples of Mars and Neptune, and nothing remains of the temple of Diana.

Baredine Cave
(Jama Baredine)

Five kilometers (three miles) northeast of town, the **Baredine Cave (Jama Baredine)** (Nova Vas, tel. 052/421-333, www.baredine.com, 11am-3pm daily Mar. and Nov., 10am-4pm daily Apr. and Oct., 10am-5pm daily May, June, and Sept., 10am-6pm daily July-Aug., 75Kn) could be a nice change from sun and sea. After the underground tour of stalactites and stalagmites, you can enjoy a restaurant, farm animals, or the exhibition **TraktorStory** (www.traktorstory.com, 30Kn), which showcases local antique tractors and agricultural machines.

BEACHES

Poreč's profusion of hotels and tourist complexes doesn't help its beach scene. The most popular is the **Town Beach (Gradsko kupalište)**, an unappealing mass of concrete slab. **Sveti Nikola island** (taxi boats 7am-11pm, 25Kn) is prettier, with lots of trees and paved and pebble beaches, though these can also get packed in the summer. If you want to make the trip, there's a boat at the harbor that can take you there every half hour during the summer in less than 10 minutes. Another option is the **Zelena Laguna** tourist resort, six kilometers (3.7 miles) from the center of town, with more concrete-slab bathing options. To get there you can either walk the pedestrian path or take the small tourist train leaving regularly from Trg Slobode (May-Sept.).

WINERIES

Giordano Peršurić (Istarske divizije 27, Poreč, tel. 098/195-7037, www.misal.hr, call

1: Marafor Square in Poreč 2: Basilica of Euphrasius

Istrian Wine

Though the history of wine in Istria dates back to Roman times, much of the area's production suffered during the World Wars and the era of Tito. However, the past 20 years have seen a rebirth of viticulture on the small, sunny peninsula. Istrian vineyards produce a number of wines, but only two are indigenous—the red earthy **Teran** and **Malvazija,** a smooth, slightly sweet white that traces its popularity back to 13th-century Venice.

Istria holds several festivals revolving around wine, but if you can only make one, try to attend the **Vinistra Festival** in Poreč for four days in late April or early May. Dozens of tastings, judging, and exhibits of local olive oil and cheese make for some tasty testing of the Istrian culinary landscape. At the end of May, you can catch **Dan Vina,** or Day of Wine, when dozens of local vineyards hold an open house from morning till evening, perfect for some serious wine-cruising. And Malvazija fans will appreciate Brtonigla's **Malvazija Festival** in early June.

There are dozens of wine routes for those who'd like to savor the vintages as they see the countryside. Since many wineries' production is small, lots of excellent wines never make it past the border, so this is your chance to discover what Istria has to offer. For more information about Istrian wine routes, check out www.istra.hr.

for wine-tasting appointment) produces the only sparkling wine in Istria—a surprisingly good one too, known as Misal. The father died and the daughters have taken over the winery. While there have been some consistency issues, they seem poised to carry on the tradition. Make sure to try their excellent pink sparkling wine.

ENTERTAINMENT AND EVENTS

Though Poreč's claim to fame might be its basilica, the **Vinistra** (Apr. or May, www. vinistra.com) festival comes in a close second. The most respected wine fair in Croatia, Vinistra is marked by a competition of Istrian wines, though travelers will likely appreciate the wide variety of culinary offerings during the fair. Local cheeses, olive oils, and other products complement the guests of honor, the local wines.

The best entertainment in Poreč in summer are the weekly **concerts** (June-Aug., check with the tourist office for details, tickets around 30Kn) in the atrium of the basilica (classical) and behind the District Museum (jazz). In August the town hosts a great **Street Art Festival** with music, visual arts, and even a bit of acrobatics.

ACCOMMODATIONS

You can search online for private accommodations on **AirBnB** (www.airbnb.com) or **Booking** (booking.com), especially if you'd like to stay on a budget in the old town. Otherwise, especially if you have kids in tow, the **Villa Laguna Galijot** (Plava laguna, www.lagunaporec.com, 750d) is a hotel and bungalow complex set amongst parklike grounds. With rocky beaches, a playground, and a sports complex, it's only a 15-minute walk to Poreč, or you can take the hotel's little train/shuttle.

A 15-minute walk from the center of town is the **Valamar Diamant Hotel** (Naselje Brulo 1, tel. 052/465-000, www.valamar.com, 750Kn d, including breakfast), a big tourist complex that was renovated in 2007. The hotel has beaches, indoor and outdoor pools, a spa, and a fitness center. It's another great choice for families, with a kids club if you want to sunbathe alone.

Out on Sveti Nikola island, the ★ **Isabella Castle** (Otok Sv. Nikola, tel. 052/465-100, www.valamar.com, 1,400Kn d, including breakfast) has been recently renovated. The island location is nice, and you have access to two pools for taking a dip. The hotel offers free five-minute boat trips to Poreč.

A nice option if you are traveling without children is the **Valamar Riviera** (Obala Marsala Tita 15, tel. 052/465-120, www.valamar.com, 1,000Kn d), an adults-only hotel located a short stroll from the old town. A free five-minute boat ride takes you to the hotel's sister property, Valamar Isabella Resort, on Sveti Nikola island, to use the resort's pool and beach.

FOOD

Even if you don't go for the vegan and vegetarian menu at **Artha** (Jože Šurana 10, tel. 052/435-495, 10am-11pm Mon.-Sat., 10am-3pm Sun. in summer, 45Kn), then go for the tasty breakfast, sandwiches, and more at this friendly restaurant near the city market.

In the center, ★ **Sveti Nikola** (Obala Maršala Tita 23, tel. 052/423-018, www.svnikola.com, 12pm-12am daily, closed Jan.-Feb., 110Kn) serves artful truffle-laced dishes in a swank space. Fans of carpaccio will find fish and beef varieties with creative twists like the addition of parmesan or truffles. Though it looks like a tourist trap, **Ulixes** (Decumanus 2, tel. 052/451-132, 12pm-12am daily, 90Kn) has surprisingly great food and friendly service in a cozy stone courtyard just off a busy pedestrian street.

INFORMATION AND SERVICES

The helpful **tourist office** (Zagrebačka 9, tel. 052/451-293, www.istria-porec.com, 8am-10pm Mon.-Sat. and 9am-1pm and 5pm-9pm Sun. July-Aug., 8am-8pm Mon.-Sat. and 9am-1pm and 5pm-8pm Sun. Sept.-Oct. and mid-Apr.-June, 8am-4pm Mon.-Sat. Nov.-mid-Apr.) can provide brochures, maps, and listings of local accommodations and private rooms as well as help with details about concerts and events. International information, with operators who speak English, can be reached by dialing 902.

GETTING THERE AND AROUND

Poreč's **bus station** (Rade Končara 1, tel. 052/432-153) has good connections to Pula

(around 10 buses daily, 1 hour 10 minutes, 50Kn) and Rovinj (around five buses daily, mostly in the mornings, 50 minutes, 37Kn); it also connects to Zagreb (four hours, 196Kn). Driving to Poreč is easy—just follow the signs from Rovinj or Pazin, in the interior. Parking is another matter. You'll likely circle a while to find a space—just mind the parking fees and maximum times.

AROUND POREČ
★ Novigrad

Novigrad, 17 kilometers (10.5 miles) north of Poreč, is a precious little town right on the seafront. Driving out of Poreč, simply follow the signs for Novigrad or take one of eight buses daily to Novigrad's **bus station** (Murvi bb, about an eight-minute walk to the town center). The town itself has a couple of sights, a nice parish church, and a small museum, but it's not so great for wandering about since the tiny streets are open to cars. Check out the **Museum Lapidarium** (Veliki trg 8A, tel. 052/726-582, www.muzej-lapidarium.hr, 10am-1pm and 6pm-10pm Tues.-Sun. in summer, 10am-1pm and 5pm-7pm Tues.-Sun. in winter, 10Kn) for Roman relics, and the excellent **Gallery Rigo** (Velika ulica 5, tel. 052/757-790, call for hours, free) for great expos of contemporary Croatian art. For sunbathing, the beaches north of town are much better than anything Poreč has to offer.

Though there are two choices of waterparks in Istria, **Istralandia Aquapark** (Partizanska 4/1, tel. 098/249-119, www.istralandia.com, 10am-6pm early June-mid-Sept., 180Kn) is by far the most professionally done. From an array of pools and slides as well as snack bars, restaurants, lounge chairs, and a beach volleyball area, you might think you were at a waterpark in the U.S., which could be a good or a bad thing, depending on your mood. Transport is available from Pula, Rovinj, Umag, Poreč, and more by calling for a reservation and paying an extra fee.

Reasonable family-friendly accommodations can be found at the **Aminess Maestral**

Hotel (Tere 2, tel. 052/858-600, www. aminess.com, 480Kn d, including breakfast). The hotel is on the beach and it has a kids club, electric car charging, an indoor pool, and separate outdoor pools for kids and adults.

A family-run hotel, **Cittar** (Prolaz Venecija 1, tel. 052/757-737, www.cittar.hr, 880Kn d, including breakfast), is smack in the old town, and the newer **Hotel Villa Cittar** (tel. 052/758-780, www.cittar.hr, 1,010Kn d, including breakfast) is a 2008 addition to Novigrad, with more upscale rooms than its sister property and an indoor pool for year-round swimming. The most luxurious place in town is the **Hotel Nautica** (Sv. Antona 15, tel. 052/600-400, www.nauticahotels.com, 1,450Kn d, including breakfast), slightly removed from town on a marina populated with moored yachts.

You'll find lots of places to eat in town, from the seafront seafood restaurants to the more gourmet **Damir i Ornella** (Zidine 5, www. damir-ornella.com, tel. 052/758-134, 12pm-3pm and 6pm-11:30pm Tues.-Sun., call ahead for reservations, 200Kn), offering great local takes on sushi, grilled seafood, and a standout kiwi flan. Book at least a day in advance.

The young chefs at ★ **Marina Restaurant** (Sv. Antuna 38, tel. 098/969-0492, 12pm-3pm and 7pm-11pm Wed.-Mon., 300Kn) offer extremely innovative cuisine that is keeping this small town on the culinary map.

There are a couple of fun bars in town, like hip **Cocktail Bar Code** (Gradska Vrata 20A, no phone, 3pm-12am Sun.-Thurs., 3pm-2am Fri.-Sat.) and **Vitriol** (Ribarnička 6, tel. 052/758-270, 8am-12am daily), also a great place for a coffee or pre-dinner cocktail on the seaside terrace.

Brtonigla

The neat little village of Brtonigla, about six kilometers (3.7 miles) northeast of Novigrad, charms travelers from the start. Surrounded by meticulous vineyards, the center of the small, sun-washed stone nucleus is presided over by a picturesque church and the town's hotel and restaurant, which are likely responsible for the discovery of the town by foreigners. The ★ **Hotel San Rocco** (Srednja ulica 2, Brtonigla, tel. 052/725-000, www.san-rocco.hr, 1,208Kn d, including breakfast) is highly recommended for its small but cozy rooms, nice pool area, and superior restaurant (which has been awarded two stars from Gault Millau) serving sheep's cheese, organic fruits and vegetables, and regional specialties.

Malvazija is arguably Istria's best wine,

seaside town of Novigrad

a gentle white that goes with nearly everything. The **Istrian Malvasia Festival (Fešta istarske malvazije)** (end of May or early June) in Brtonigla is a don't-miss for fans of the variety. Highlighting local growers, it's a great time to sample a few producers and choose which ones to add to your suitcase.

Since there's only one bus a day from Novigrad to Brtonigla (45 minutes, 32Kn), it's best to drive to this small town. On the road between Poreč and Novigrad, look for the road to Buje, and after turning, follow the signs to Brtonigla. You can also call a cab from Novigrad (tel. 052/757-224).

Savudrija

North of Umag (which unless you are craving a lackluster tourist town filled with souvenir stands is completely skippable), lies Savudrija, at the Slovenian border. For those looking for a five-star family beach resort, the ★ **Kempinski Hotel Adriatic** (Alberi 300A, tel. 052/707-000, www.kempinski.com, 2,010Kn d, including breakfast) has a kids club, clean private beach, spa, and golf course. It's a great option for those wanting to combine a beach vacation with touring the Istrian wine roads, and it's a quick day trip to Slovenia as well.

Wineries

Take a trip to **Višnjan,** 12 kilometers (7.5 miles) east of Poreč (you'll need a car—head north from Poreč toward Novigrad and then follow the signs for Višnjan), to visit two of Istria's best winemakers. **Poletti** (Markovac 14, Višnjan, tel. 052/449-251, www.vina-poletti.hr, call for hours) has won awards for his Malvazija, but his most interesting wine is a Muškat ruža, a variety that used to be native to the area and Poletti is now reviving. You can even rent a villa on the property of this six-generation winemaking family. **Radovan** (Radovani 14, Višnjan, tel. 052/462-166, www.vinaradovan.com, call for hours) is another young winemaker, equally impressive in reds and whites, particularly his Malvazija, chardonnay, cabernet sauvignon, and Teran.

Fans of food and wine, particularly those who stayed in Brtonigla, should drive to **Momjan** (head northwest of Buje and follow signs for Momjan; it's about a 30-40-minute drive). **Gianfranco Kozlović** (Valle 78, Momjan, tel. 052/779-177, info@kozlovic.hr, www.kozlovic.hr, 10am-7pm Mon.-Sat. but call ahead or check the website to make sure no private event is being held) was one of the pioneers of the Istrian wine revolution of the early 1990s. His wines are solid, though the old winemakers consider him a bit of a rebel for bringing new techniques and equipment, like stainless steel vats, to a very old trade. The excellent restaurant of winemaker **Marino Markežić** (Kremenje 96B, Kremenje, tel. 052/779-047, 12pm-10pm Wed.-Mon., closed Jan. and last two weeks of June), in the nearby village of Kremenje, specializes in truffle-based dishes. Make sure to try his Muscat and elegant gray Pinot while you're there.

Though it's a bit of a drive north of Poreč and Novigrad, the northwestern corner of the Istrian peninsula is home to two excellent wineries (and conveniently located close to the Slovenian border if you're headed that way). The best winery in Istria, perhaps, is **Moreno Coronica** (Koreniki 86, Umag, tel. 052/730-196, www.coronica.eu, call for hours), a small winemaker with the highest-quality wines. His Malvazija is outstanding, winning numerous awards, but you should also try his aged Gran Teran, from which he is trying to create a world-class red. **Degrassi** (Podrumarska 3, Savudrija, tel. 052/759-250, www.degrassi.hr, call for hours) produces what are arguably Istria's best red wines, but his whites aren't bad either. He was also among the founders of the new Istrian wine movement, along with Gianfranco Kozlović and Ivica Matošević. When touring the cellar take note of his ancient amfore, or clay jugs, a very old method of producing wine.

Beer Spa

If you've ever wanted to literally bathe yourself in beer, head to Buje for a truly different experience. The **San Servolo Resort and Beer**

Spa (Momjanska 7, Buje, tel. 091/477-2400, www.sanservoloresort.com, 990Kn d) is a craft brewery that also offers cozy hotel rooms and a spa centered around therapeutic beer baths. The hotel also offers a good steakhouse and, of course, beer. Craft beers—lager, APA, and IPA, including a beer made with truffles (this is Istria!)—are available for tasting and purchase.

Istrian Interior

Though the coastal towns get the bulk of the tourist trade, the beautiful interior of Istria, not unlike Tuscany or Provence, is becoming more hip. Some towns, like Motovun, have become a bit too popular, but the advantage to the increased tourism is a wave of new restaurants and small hotels to meet demand. Of course, if you really want to get away from it all, visit the region in spring or fall, or try out towns like Pazin or Beram, rarely tread even by the most enthusiastic of tourist groups.

No matter when you come, the highlight of interior Istria is its gastronomic offerings. To enjoy the serious vineyards producing high-quality wines and the restaurants that serve lots of creative versions of truffles, local cured ham, and asparagus in season, it's best to forget about the diet while you're visiting.

PAZIN

Though Pazin is a somewhat provincial town without a lot of atmosphere, the "capital" of Istria does have a few interesting stops, and the added bonus of being off the tourist path. The main attraction is the city's *kaštel* (castle stronghold), which dates back to the late 10th century. Today it is the home of the **Ethnographic Museum of Istria (Etnografski muzej Istre)** (Trg Istarskog razvoda 1275. br. 1, tel. 052/622-220, www.emi.hr, 10am-6pm daily, 25Kn), with a good showing of Istrian costumes and housekeeping tools. From here, make the short walk down the street to the bridge, the perfect place from which to admire the **Pazin cave,** which inspired both Dante and Jules Verne, whose Mathis Sandor character escapes from the castle by swimming in the underground waterway to the shore.

About six kilometers (four miles) northwest out of town in the village of Beram, the **Chapel of Our Lady on the Rocks (Crkvica Majka Bojža na škriljinah)** (free, though a donation would be very kind) in the Beram graveyard is a must-see if you're in the area. You can obtain the keys to the unassuming little church by asking the **tourist office** in Pazin (Ulica Franine i Jurine 14, tel. 052/622-460, call for hours) to arrange a visit for you. The 15th-century chapel (the loggia was added in the 18th century) is decorated with outstanding frescoes created by Vincent of Kastav in 1474. The *Adoration of the Kings* is the largest, but the *Dance of Death* is by far the most famous, with its eerie skeletons parading with mortals right above the entrance. There's a tavern in town, **Vela Vrata** (Beram 41, tel. 091/781-4995, 4pm-11pm daily, 45Kn), where you can order up some *fuži* (a type of local homemade pasta) and a glass of local wine.

There are two super *agroturizam* hotels in the area around Pazin. First up is **House Ivela** (Pariži 109 A, tel. 052/686-271, also bookable through www.airbnb.com, 732Kn), about 10 kilometers (six miles) southwest of Pazin on the road to Kanfanar. If you think the charming cottage and perfectly decorated rooms look like they jumped out of an interiors magazine, you're right: The fairytale house was featured in a local edition of *Elle Décor*. The owners also offer painting courses for the artistically inclined. **Agroturizam Ograde** (Lindarski katun 60, tel. 052/693-035, www.agroturizam-ograde.hr), about 10 kilometers (six miles) south of Pazin, has a typical little stone house for rent or a double apartment with friendly owners and super meals. Even if

Istrian Truffles

Most people are familiar with truffles—those ugly, bumpy tubers that fetch hundreds of dollars at market. Istria is full of them, both the black and white varieties (though the white is more common). The white variety, or *tuber magnatum,* is particularly precious, selling for €2,000-4,000 per kilogram.

They thrive in the grayish clay soil of Istria's interior, particularly in the area around **Motovun**, near the roots of the majestic oak, most common near Livade and Buzet. The hunting season runs from the last days of summer to the end of January, when lots of old men and their highly trained hounds can be found around Motovun forest, sniffing for black or white gold.

Istria does all sorts of things with its truffles, from shaving them on pasta to cooking them with meats to putting them into cheese. The white truffles are quite strong in flavor, and are best used to complement plain foods like pasta. Though Istria has its moments with truffles, it can sometimes get a little too tuber-happy, overusing the truffle and falling far short of culinary genius. Look for the *Izvorni Tartuf* or *Tartufo Vero* sign in restaurants, which indicate the use of real truffles and not just essence of truffle.

In October the town of **Livade** spends weekends debating over the biggest and best truffles as well as auctioning off a few and holding cooking classes on how to use them. It's here that Istria really got on the truffle map in 1999, when Zigante found a truffle that entered *Guinness World Records* as the largest truffle in the world.

you're not overnighting here, it's a great place to have a meal—call ahead for hours.

You can get to Pazin by train from Pula (1 hour 10 minutes) or Rijeka (1 hour), both around 40Kn, arriving at the **train station** (Stareh Kostanji 1, tel. 052/624-310), about a 10-minute walk to the center of town. By **bus** (tel. 052/624-364) there are connections with Pula (two or three daily, one hour, 40Kn) and Rijeka (six or more weekdays, two on weekends, one hour, 49Kn). There are also multiple daily connections to Poreč (45 minutes, 33Kn), Rovinj (weekdays only, one hour, 36Kn), and Zagreb (four hours, 172Kn). Going to Beram or the agro-tourism hotels, you'll really need your own car.

GRAČIŠĆE

The 12th-century village of Gračišće is a quiet little place with some impressive cut-stone Venetian homes, including the **Palace Salomon,** lining the main square. The church **St. Mary's-on-the-square (Majka Bojža na Placu)** has some nice 15th-century frescoes. If the church is locked, you can ask at the parish office (tel. 052/687-115) or peek

through the windows for a view. Perhaps more interesting than the frescoes are the nails stuck in the church walls: Local legend said that if women hammered them into the wall it would help them become pregnant.

Gračišće is also worth a visit for the **St. Simon's Walking Trail (Pješačka staza sv. Šimuna),** an 11.5-kilometer (seven-mile) walking trail around town. It takes about 2.5-3 hours; you'll pass a peaceful waterfall, the nests of birds who like to feast on bees, and the small stone cottage-filled village of Lovrići.

Gračišće's **Maneštra Festival (Maneštrijada)** brings out dozens of chefs vying for the title of best *maneštra*, a pasta-based stew that varies with the seasons. If you're lucky enough to be in town during a festival (held at least twice a year), head to the main square to sample what's on offer.

Konoba Marino (Gračišće 75, tel. 052/687-081, www.konoba-marino-grascisce.hr, 50Kn) has some good meat and pasta dishes and has rooms to offer as well if you'd like to stay in town.

About six kilometers (four miles) southeast

of Pazin, Gračišće is best reached by car, though there are at least two connections by bus from Pazin on weekdays (20 minutes, 21Kn).

MOTOVUN

Istria is filled with picturesque hilltop towns; seen from below, Motovun seems to win top honors, its stone buildings winding their way up the slopes like a well-placed dollop of whipped cream on top of the vineyard-filled valleys below. A small, well-preserved medieval town, Motovun was mostly Italian-speaking until the mid-20th century, by which point the majority of townspeople had left seeking better opportunities. Motovun has since been repopulated by artists and people seeking a bit of Istrian charm. It used to be somewhat of an undiscovered gem; then the town made the most of its wonderful film festival and marketed itself as a must-see for every visitor to Istria. While the streets can get crowded during the day when tour buses bring in groups and during the film festival, other times the town is peaceful. Several private offerings are clean and very reasonable (just make sure they offer parking if you have a car) and the town makes a great base for seeing other towns in the region.

Sights

The **St. Stephen's Church (Crkva svetog Stjepana)** (open most days, free) on the town's main square is a relatively plain yellow Baroque structure, with a somewhat incongruent Romanesque-Gothic bell tower tacked onto its side. Inside, you'll find a pretty Venetian painting of the Last Supper above the altar. Passing the large municipal building, climb up to a path that encircles the old town walls. From here you have some great views of the valleys and vineyards below. For more information and free brochures, contact the Motovun **tourist office** (Trg Andrea Antico 1, tel. 052/681-758, www. tz-motovun.hr).

Wineries

If you're in Motovun and you're a fan of the grape, make time to stop at **Livio Benvenuti** (Kaldir 7, Motovun, tel. 098/421-189, www. benvenutivina.com, call for hours). The young winemaker has already won multiple awards for his Malvazija. Another international award-winner, **Fakin** (Bataji 20, Brkac, tel. 092/239-9400, www.fakinwines.com, call for hours) is a must-try for their Malvazija La Prima, a dry white aged twelve months. Also on the must-see list: **Tomaz** (Kanal 36, Motovun, tel. 052/681-717, www.vina-tomaz. hr) for the Malvazija.

Gastronomic Experiences

The hills around Motovun are famous for their truffles, so why not take a truffle-hunting expedition? **Truffle Hunting Istra** (tel. 091/569-6835, trufflehunting.weebly.com) takes individuals and groups truffle-hunting in the nearby forest. Or try a cooking class to learn how to make local pasta at the **Kaštel Cultural Center** (Trg Andrea Antico 7, tel. 052/681-607, www.hotel-kastel-motovun.hr), part of one of the old town's hotels.

Entertainment and Events

The **Motovun Film Festival** (July, www.motovunfilmfestival.com) has only been going on since 1999, but already the festival is the most prestigious in Croatia. It gathers a good group of European actors and directors (and the occasional Hollywood B-lister) as well as fans of cinema and party-circuit types who come for the glamour-by-osmosis. It's a much more accessible film festival for those who've always dreamed of rubbing shoulders with the artsy set, and the open screenings are both laid-back and elegant at the same time. If you'd like to be a part of the action, book well in advance to score a room.

Accommodations and Food

There are several rooms and apartments for rent in the old town via Booking.com. **Villa Borgo** (Borgo 4, tel. 052/681-708, www.

villaborgo.com, 654Kn d, including breakfast) is a friendly hotel with clean and modern rooms, an excellent common terrace overlooking the valleys, and a good breakfast. The best in-town options are the **Bella Vista** (tel. 052/681-724, www.apartmani-motovun.com, 585Kn d), with two apartments in an atmospheric stone townhouse, and the **Hotel Kaštel** (Trg Andrea Antico 7, tel. 052/681-607, www.hotel-kastel-motovun.hr, 590Kn d, including breakfast), its jaunty facade disguising somewhat less jaunty but clean rooms in a couldn't-be-better old-town location. The hotel also recently opened a small wellness center. The Hotel Kaštel also has a **restaurant** (8am-10pm daily, 80Kn) with many solid local dishes and a terrace on a charming square.

For food in town, try **Konoba Mondo** (Barbacan 1, tel. 052/681-791, hours vary, call ahead, no credit cards, 75Kn), with olive-truffle tapenade for a starter followed by an expertly done homemade pasta dish. There are other restaurants in town, some with a view, but you'll just wish you'd come back here.

A six-kilometer (3.7-mile) drive southeast away from Motovun, **Agroturizam Štefanić** (Štefanići 55, tel. 052/689-026, www.agroturizam-stefanic.hr, call ahead, 90Kn) makes all dishes with ingredients that come straight from their farm. It's a great choice for traditional staples, fresh cheese, and roasted meats.

Getting There and Around

You can catch a bus to Motovun from Pazin (at least two connections on weekends, more in summer, 45 minutes, around 25Kn) all year. The bus from Pula to Buzet stops in Motovun as well. The station is at the bottom of the hill in Kanal, the more modern part of town. If you're driving, there are a few parking spaces up near the old town (usually there are a couple available early mornings and out of season). Otherwise, you'll have to park at the lot in Kanal and hike up for about half an hour. If you're lazy, proceed to Grožnjan.

OPRTALJ

If you're coming from Motovun, you'll come to a large crossroads (large for the Istrian interior, anyway). Go left for Buje or the beach, right for Buzet, or straight for Oprtalj. Driving to Oprtalj, you'll pass through the village of **Livade,** less than a kilometer from the crossroads, worth a stop for lunch or for stocking up on truffle souvenirs at the **Zigante Tartufi restaurant** (Livade 7, tel. 052/664-302, www.zigantetartufi.com, 12pm-11pm daily in summer, 12pm-10pm daily in winter, 95Kn). Livade developed as a stop on the Parenzana, a railroad that connected Italy with Istria. The town has an annual Truffle Fest (Oct.). From here you'll head up to Oprtalj—it's only a few kilometers, but due to the winding narrow roads, with plenty of pretty scenery to gawk at, the trip will take about 20 minutes.

Oprtalj is quickly being transformed into a proper little tourist town. On the upside, there are plenty of nice spots for refreshments, and many of the homes have been lovingly restored. On the downside are those darn tourist buses, but if you can manage to visit when none of them are parked in the lot coming into town, you'll feel like you have the place to yourself. The town has three interesting churches, dating from the 15th and 16th centuries with some attractive frescoes (though the churches are often closed). The main church, the **Parish Church of St. George (Župna crkva sv. Juraj),** dates from the 14th century. There is also a nice town loggia and lapidarium. However, the best part of Oprtalj is simply taking in the view beside the town loggia, with sunny rolling hills and stone houses, and strolling around one of Istria's prettiest hilltop villages.

If you can visit on the second Sunday of the month, you can catch an **antiques fair (sajam antikviteta)**, or come in October for the town's **Chestnut Festival (Kestenijada).**

You can ask in town about a room or you can rent a room at the **Palazzo Angelica**

Parenzana Train

The Parenzana was a 123.1-kilometer-long (76.5-mile-long) narrow-gauge railroad that connected Italy, Slovenia, and Croatia. Built in 1902, the train made its first voyage from Buje to Trieste, Italy, and eventually began stopping at 33 cities in Istria (fast it was not).

Its main purpose was to ferry local salt, olive oil, Istrian stone, and wine to nearby Italy. Though the railroad ceased operation in 1935, the tradition remains alive today with several interesting attractions. The **Parenzana Museum (Muzej od Parenzani)** (tel. 052/644-150, open by appointment) in Livade has an interesting collection of photographs and memorabilia from the Parenzana line. In Vižinada you can see a full-scale locomotive from the railroad.

Most interesting, though, are two activities that make use of the train's former route. The **Parenzana Wine Train** (www.parenzana.hr, 130Kn pp) is a small train running between wineries and agro-tourism establishments.

Part of the former train route has been turned into a lovely bike trail, passing below Motovun. Learn more about the trail at **Istria Bike** (www.istria-bike.com).

(Matka Laginje bb, tel. 051/619-862, www.palazzoangelica.com, 550Kn d, including breakfast), a historic 19th-century villa with a pool. In addition to Zigante's place down in Livade, Oprtalj's **Konoba Oprtalj** (M. Laginje 11, tel. 052/644-130, 12pm-10pm Tues.-Sun., 55Kn) has hearty meat and pasta dishes in a cozy atmosphere.

You'll need a car to reach Oprtalj. Otherwise, try booking a tour or day trip from one of the tourist offices on the coast.

★ GROŽNJAN

The postcard-perfect streets of this quaint medieval hilltop town were all but abandoned when artists started setting up their studios here in the 1960s. Currently, there are close to 30 galleries and ateliers in Grožnjan. Even the street signs are artistic, made of hand-painted ceramic instead of the ho-hum metal in most towns. Summer brings more tourists, but for the moment it's still not swamped even at the height of the season, and most of the artists are in town as well as the **Jeunesse Musicales International Cultural Centre** (Umberta Gorjana 2, tel. 052/776-106, www.jmi.net). A training ground for young musicians, the center puts on a **student concert** almost every night in season (Musical Summer, www.hgm.

hr). Out of season, Grožnjan is still lovely, with views that can easily rival those of Motovun and a much less touristy feel.

Sights

The 18th-century parish **Church of Sts. Vitus and Modestus (Župna crkva Sv. Vida i Modesta)** is not all that impressive if you've seen others in Croatia. However, the large expanse of courtyard next to its bell tower is a nice place to sit and reflect. The town's 16th-century **Church of Sts. Cosmas and Damian (Crkvica Sv. Kuzmana i Domjana)** has some colorful frescoes, though their provenance is much more recent, having been painted in 1989 by Croatian artist Ivan Lovrenčić. The town has over 30 art galleries. A couple worth checking out are the **Fonticus Gallery** (Trg Lože 3, tel. 052/776-357, hours vary), the town's largest, and **Pharos** (Gorjana 8, tel. 091/767-9818, 10am-8pm daily in spring and summer), with a range of furniture and small paintings.

The **tourist office** (Umberta Gorjana 3, Grožnjan, tel. 052/776-131, www.groznjan-grisignana.hr) is a useful place to stop for more information.

Accommodations and Food

Centrally located **Rooms Svalina** (Vincenta iz Kastva 5, tel. 052/277-6237, www.

1: Motovun 2: Grožnajan 3: church in Oprtalj
4: the village of Hum

roomssvalina.com, 370Kn d) are basic but clean.

Kaya Energy Bar (Vincenta iz Kastva 2) is a welcome addition to town, with comfy seating on the terrace near the parish church. It's perfect for savoring a glass of wine and perusing their quirky, high-quality collection in the small shop that's part of the bar. You can also grab a meal at **Bastia** (1 Svibanja 1, tel. 052/776-370, 8am-2am daily mid-June-Aug., 9am-10pm out of season, closed mid-Jan.-Feb., no credit cards, 60Kn), with local dishes and a small bar; it's also an unofficial place to ask about private rooms.

A short drive from town in the village of Momjan, ★ **Stari Podrum** (Most 52, tel. 052/779-152, www.staripodrum.info, 12pm-11pm Thurs.-Tues., 200Kn) is a family-owned restaurant with a long history of serving excellent cuisine. The refined yet cozy atmosphere is the perfect setting to tuck into local boškarin beef, truffles, wild asparagus, and tiramisu with seasonal fruit.

Getting There and Around

Getting to Grožnjan is difficult without a car. If you'd like to try, take the bus from Buzet to Buje (or Buje to Buzet, three or more a day, 30 minutes, 33Kn) and ask the driver to drop you off at the nearby village of Bijele Zemlje, from where you must hike a couple of kilometers uphill.

★ HUM

Conveniently located on the way into or out of Istria, the little village of Hum claims it's the smallest town in the world, with less than 20 full-time residents. Whether it is or not, it would be a shame to miss the tiny little walled village and all the gems it has to offer.

Passing through a large gate, you'll likely hear the laughter and footsteps of patrons of the Humska Konoba above. But once you pass the *konoba,* the town becomes quiet, even deserted, depending on the time of year you happen to visit. The **Church of**

Kažuni: Istria's Stone Shelters

Dotted throughout the rural landscape of Istria are small circular stone structures with cone-like roofs. You'll also find more modern versions in urbanized areas, used as kiosks or tourist info points. Indigenous to local architecture, the *kažuni* were originally built as shelters for those out tending the fields and vineyards. Though you could be bold and hunker down in one yourself for the night, there's always the chance an upset shepherd could disturb your rest.

the **Blessed Virgin Mary (Crkva blažene djevice Marije),** the village's main feature, is rarely open, but there is a woman in town who has the key if you absolutely must see inside. Ask at the *konoba,* which also holds the key to the **Chapel of St. Hieronymus (Crkvica svetog Jeronima),** a Romanesque chapel in the cemetery, worth a look inside to admire the ancient frescoes. Hum has two gift shops that are a good spot for buying the town's own specialty, a mistletoe liquor used since the Middle Ages for killing off a variety of ailments.

Any time of the year, the ★ **Humska Konoba** (Hum 2, tel. 052/660-005, www.hum.hr, 11am-11pm daily, 60Kn) is not only the local source for tourist information but a favorite with locals for the cozy Istrian food and the great views of the green valleys from its terrace. While you're in the area, the small restaurant ★ **Kotlić** (Kotli 3, no phone, 2pm-10pm Sat.-Sun., 50Kn) is a nice place to stop on the banks of a rushing stream. Just park before crossing the river and walk over the bridge on foot, since its sturdiness is not guaranteed.

You'll need a rental car to get to Hum. Not too far from the Učka tunnel, which connects Kvarner and Istria, less than 10 kilometers (six miles) from the village of Roč, you'll see signs directing you toward Hum.

Kvarner Gulf

Lying at the northern end of Croatia's spectacu-
lar coast, the Kvarner Gulf starts things off with laid-back but edgy
Rijeka, the luxe Opatija Riviera, and beautiful islands off the coast.

The Kvarner region is geographically defined as its gulf and the surrounding three sides of steep mountain ranges. Historically, the area
was all but cut off from the rest of Croatia by its terrain. The isolation
certainly has given Kvarner a culture of its own, different from Istria
to its west, Lika to the east, and Dalmatia to the south.

Although destinations in this region will satisfy beach lovers, many
also offer something more. Islands such as Rab, Lošinj, and Pag are
rich cultural locales, with festivals and handicrafts in addition to

Highlights

Look for ★ to find recommended sights, activities, dining, and lodging.

★ **Opatija:** Only a couple of hours from Zagreb and situated near the entrance to Istria on the Kvarner Gulf, Opatija was once a playground for the Austro-Hungarian elite. Today it's regaining some of its aura, with boutique hotels and world-class restaurants along its riviera, particularly in the former fishing village of Volosko (page 176).

★ **Cres:** The relatively undeveloped island of Cres is home to step-back-in-time fishing villages and charming little towns (page 186).

★ **Veli Lošinj:** This laid-back town on the island of Lošinj has a faded-glory vibe, a dolphin preserve, and wonderful new hotel options. Spend some time looking through the garden gates of the captains' villas and strolling the waterfront promenade (page 193).

★ **Susak:** Though it gets its share of day-trippers, mornings and evenings in Susak are almost devoid of tourists. Hike the island's 11-kilometer (seven-mile) trail, stopping for a dip at a beach surrounded by the clay cliffs, a geographical feature distinct in the Adriatic's mostly rocky archipelagos (page 194).

★ **Rab Town:** The medieval core of Rab Town is charming any time of year, but even more so during the annual Rab Fiera, a celebration of old-time crafts and trades. The rest of the year it's a

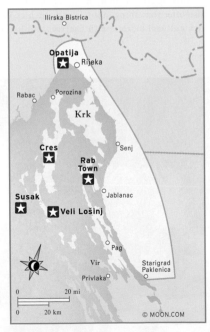

nice place to wander around, stopping for an ice cream or a souvenir and walking along the old city walls (page 195).

beaches made for lounging. There are places for those looking for a nonstop club scene, for history (the Greeks, Romans, and Venetians all left their mark), for sports like scuba diving and hiking, and for natural beauty and wildlife, with a sanctuary for vultures on the island of Cres and a dolphin preserve at Veli Lošinj.

There's plenty for foodies and a few gems for wine lovers, though Kvarner is by no means as heavily into wine as other locations in Croatia and Slovenia. Gourmet cuisine is a different story. Food lovers shouldn't miss the area around Opatija and Lovran, where several of Croatia's top restaurants serve up award-winning cuisine, much of it with a view thrown in for extra value.

Most of the islands are connected by ferries and catamarans in the summer, making it easy to wind your way through them. Pag, which technically belongs to Northern Dalmatia, has been included in Kvarner because of the number of connections with the gulf and its islands.

PLANNING YOUR TIME

The relative ease with which you can fit a lot into a short period of time is one of the features that makes Kvarner so special. From liberal port-city life in quirky Rijeka to a sheep farm on Pag or party-hopping with the masses on Krk, you should always be entertained. Most European tourists come to one spot and camp out for the week, parking their towels on the beach during the day and going out for dinner at night, possibly squeezing in a tiny bit of sightseeing. But the fact that there's not too much to see in any one place makes it easy to see most, if not all, of Kvarner. You can get a great overview of the place in a week, spending one or two nights around Rijeka or Opatija and then heading to the islands for a few days. Two weeks and you can see everything at leisure, even spending an entire couple of days soaking up the sun.

If you're just skirting the region on your way to Istria (the Učka tunnel, entrance to Istria, is just northwest of Rijeka), still make time for a quick visit to Rijeka or at least a leisurely lunch at one of the excellent restaurants around Opatija.

KVARNER GULF

Kvarner Gulf

SLOVENIA

CROATIA

★ OPATIJA
Kastav
Volosko
Pazin
A8
Lovran
Rijeka
E65
3
DRAGA DI
LOVRANA ★
Medveja
Rijecki zaljev
★ ZURKOVO
COVE
Stubica
E65
64
Mošćeniće
Tuk
Mrkopaljski
21
Brestova
Omišalj
42
Labin
Porozina
102
32
Ogulin
Beli
Porat
Malinska
A1
104
Krk
Vrbnik
NADA'S
Valbiska
Krk
E65
Koromačno
8
Merag
Cres
KANAJT
Punat
ROOMS PIAZZETTA
102
Valun
Loznati
Baška
Jezerane
Lubenice
BUKALETA
Stara Baška
Senj
23
Prvić
Zeča
★ CRES
Goli
Otok
Belej
Lopar
100
Rab
Otočac
Unije
Osor
106
A1
52
Lošinj
★ RAB TOWN
HOTEL
ARBIANA
Barbat
▼ VILLA BARBAT
Tovarnele
Cunski
Mišnjak
Jablanac
VINARIJA
COSULICH
ARTATORE JANJA
Prizna
Mali Lošinj ▼
★ VELI LOŠINJ
HOTEL AND
WINERY BOŠKINAC
★ SUSAK
HOTEL
DOLPHIN SUITES
Orjule
Žigljen
TRATTORIA
BORA BAR
Novalja
BOŠKINAC
Ličhi Osik
Ilovik
Karlobag
Gospić
Olib
Metajna
25
LUN OLIVE
GARDENS
Silba
Pag
TRAPULA WINE
AND CHEESE BAR
A1
Maun
Pag
Premuda
E65
8
50
Dinjiška
Škarda
Vir
Ist
Vir
Paklenica
National Park
Molat
Privlaka
106
Sestrunj
306
Soline
Starigrad
Paklenica
Dugi Otok
A1

© MOON.COM

0   10 mi

0   10 km

Kvarner Gulf

KVARNER GULF

Itinerary Ideas

A QUICK TOUR OF THE KVARNER MAINLAND

Day 1

- Start your morning in **Rijeka,** with breakfast at its historically interesting **market** before climbing the 538 stairs to Trsat castle.
- Have lunch at **Trsatika** and enjoy the view.
- In the evening, stop by the **Peek&Poke Computer Museum** to take a look at the history of computers.
- Sample *rakija* at **Rakhia Bar** before moving on to dinner.

Day 2

- Enjoy the morning in **Opatija**, admiring the Austro-Hungarian villas while strolling the **Lungomare**.
- Head to the village of **Kastav** for a long lunch at **Kukuriku.**
- After lunch, lounge by the pool at **Villa Astra** until dinner.

BEST OF THE KVARNER ISLANDS

Day 1

- Start your tour in **Vrbnik** on the island of **Krk,** spending the day on the beach and having lunch and a glass of homemade wine at **Nada's.**

Day 2

- Connect to **Cres** in the morning. Head to **Bukaleta** for an early lunch and then spend the afternoon on the beach near **Cres Town**, capping off the day with dinner and wine next to the harbor.

Day 3

- In the morning, continue to **Mali Lošinj** to walk around town and peruse the art at the **Art Collections in the Fritzy Palace.**
- After lunch, walk the promenade to the even more charming **Veli Lošinj,** where you can admire the grand villas and stop in at a couple of the town's sights and shops.
- Have dinner at the sophisticated but unpretentious **Trattoria Bora Bar** before turning in at the Hotel Dolphin Suites, located in one of the city's old villas.

Day 4

- Head to the island of **Susak** for some quiet relaxation, cycling, and a leisurely seafood lunch before returning to the mainland via Mali Lošinj.

Kvarner Gulf Itinerary Ideas

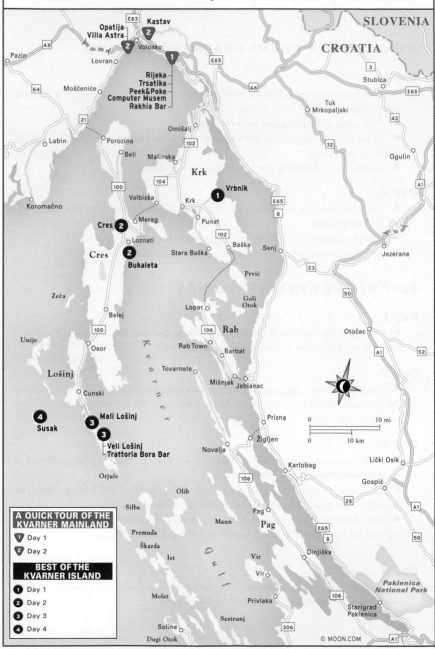

SLOVENIA

CROATIA

Opatija
Villa Astra
Kastav
Volosko
Pazin
Lovran
Rijeka
Trsatika
Peek&Poke
Computer Musem
Rakhia Bar
Moščeniće
Labin
Porozina
Beli
Malinska
Omišalj
Krk
Vrbnik
Valbiska
Krk
Koromačno
Merag
Punat
Cres
Loznati
Baška
Cres
Stara Baška
Senj
Bukaleta
Prvić
Zeča
Belej
Lopar
Goli
Otok
Unije
Osor
Rab
Rab Town
Barbat
Lošinj
Tovarnele
Cunski
Mišnjak
Jablanac
Prizna
Mali Lošinj
Susak
Žigljen
Veli Lošinj
Trattoria Bora Bar
Novalja
Karlobag
Orjule
Olib
Silba
Pag
Premuda
Maun
Pag
Škarda
Ist
Vir
Dinjiška
Vir
Molat
Privlaka
Sestrunj
Soline
Dugi Otok

Stubica
Tuk
Mrkopaljski
Ogulin
Jezerane
Otočac
Lički Osik
Gospić
Paklenica
National Park
Starigrad
Paklenica

Kvarner

Gulf

© MOON.COM

A QUICK TOUR OF THE KVARNER MAINLAND
1 Day 1
2 Day 2

BEST OF THE KVARNER ISLAND
1 Day 1
2 Day 2
3 Day 3
4 Day 4

0   10 mi
0   10 km

Rijeka

Most tourists view Rijeka only as a destination point for getting somewhere else. And it's true that the port city of 150,000 has lots of ferry connections and is close to the airport for making a quick entrance and exit. But the town has a personality all its own, with a heavy dose of hip and a very open mind—probably owing to the fact that it is the country's largest port, which has opened it up to new ideas for centuries.

The city was originally settled by the Romans and ruled by the Hapsburgs, though it's the Hungarians who had the most influence on Rijeka. Coming to power in the late 18th century, they quickly established it as their harbor and built a whole mass of infrastructure to support it. During the first half of the 20th century Rijeka was a center of turmoil, with locals fighting for a united Slav nation, falling to Italian control, then German, then as a part of Yugoslavia, and finally to its current status as Croatia's third-largest city. Though industry suffered at one point, the construction of a highway connecting Rijeka and Zagreb in about a two-hour journey has

brought new life to the city's economy, and a giant project to grow the port within the next decade promises even more.

SIGHTS

Riva

Unlike in many of Croatia's coastal cities, Rijeka's waterfront promenade, locally dubbed the **Riva,** is not the center of social life in town. But it's still worth a stroll down the street to get a peek at the city's largest showing of 19th-century buildings, which remained after the city was heavily bombed in World War II.

Korzo

One block inland from the Riva, you'll find **Korzo,** a pedestrian-only street lined with cafés and shops. This is the heart of Rijeka and definitely the place to stop for a coffee and some people-watching. Here you'll find a small gallery of the larger Museum of Contemporary and Modern Art called the **Mali Salon** (Korzo 24, tel. 051/492-611, www. mmsu.hr, 11am-8pm Tues.-Fri., 11am-2pm

Rijeka main square and fountain

and 6pm-9pm Sat.-Sun., free), with revolving exhibitions of 20th-century and present-day artwork.

On the Korzo you'll also find the **City Tower (Gradski toranj),** a medieval gate topped with a frothy Baroque city coat-of-arms and a useful clock. It was located on the water until the 18th century, when landfills extended the city's area and relegated the tower to an interior position.

Old Town
(Stari Grad)

The entrance to Stari Grad is the City Tower on the Korzo. Despite its charming name, the area is largely unimpressive save for a couple of landmarks and museums, the most stunning of which is **St. Vitus's Church (Crkva svetog Vida)** (Trg Grivica 11, tel. 051/330-879, 6:30am-12pm and 5pm-7pm daily, mass at 7am and 6pm Mon.-Sat., 8am, 9:45am in Italian, 11am Sun., free). On the way up to the church, notice the simple Roman arch, which once served as the entrance to the city's Praetorium, or local headquarters of the Roman military. Construction of the church began in 1638, took more than a century, and bled the city's resources. It is still not completed, as some surfaces of the church were never covered in stone. The exterior is rare among Croatian churches, with a vast rotunda fashioned after the Santa Maria della Salute in Venice. The interior is straight-up Baroque, the marble ostentation incongruous with the altar's centerpiece, a 13th-century Gothic crucifix. Placed above the main altar, it was saved from an older church that stood on the site. Legend has it that in 1296 a certain Petar Lončarić, angered over a gambling loss, threw a stone at the crucifix and it bled.

Near the church you'll find something entirely different. **Peek&Poke Computer Museum** (Ivana Grohovca 2, tel. 091/780-5709, www.peekpoke.hr, 2pm-9pm Mon.-Fri., 11am-4pm Sat. May-Oct., 11am-4pm Sat. Nov.-Apr., 30Kn) sounds much more adult than it actually is. This family-friendly computer museum displays working models of really old computers. It's a fun stop for a bit of nostalgia or to show your kids what it was like back in the day (circa 1989, for instance).

Museum Square
(Muzejski trg)

Positioned northwest of St. Vitus's Church (if you're walking from the church, walk north and turn left on Žrtava fašizma), Museum Square is home to three of Rijeka's most important museums. The largest of these is the **History and Maritime Museum of the Croatian Littoral (Povijesni i pomorski muzej hrvatskog primorja)** (Muzejski trg 1, www.ppmhp.hr, 9am-4pm Mon., 9am-8pm Tues.-Sat., 4pm-8pm Sun., 15Kn), with an extensive collection of local maritime history, including ship's instruments, model ships, logs, and old postcards. The museum also has a decent showing of archaeological artifacts as well as small displays of subjects as diverse as poetry, weaponry, and ethnography. The ornate 19th-century building that houses the museum, the **Governor's Palace (Guvernerova palača),** has its own history as well. It's here that Gabriele d'Annunzio, an Italian right-winger who declared Rijeka as part of Italy in 1919, clashed with Italian military and supporters of Rijeka's independence, forcing d'Annunzio and his *arditi* (a faction that claimed his right to lead the city) to leave. As a matter of fact, it's worth the visit just to admire the palace's grand rooms.

Just outside the museum is the **lapidarium** (same hours as the museum, included in ticket price), housing various tombstones and a row of stone heads known as Adamić's Witnesses, paid for by a local 18th-century merchant to ridicule those who accused him of a crime he didn't commit.

On the western side of Museum Square is the **Rijeka City Museum (Muzej grada Rijeke)** (Muzejski trg 1, tel. 051/336-711, www.muzej-rijeka.hr, 10am-8pm Mon.-Sat., 10am-3pm Sun., 20Kn), housed in a block-like building supposedly inspired by Mondrian where a small permanent collection (photographs, weaponry, jewelry) and changing temporary exhibitions chronicle the city's history.

Slightly northeast of Museum Square, the **Natural History Museum (Prirodoslovni muzej)** (Lorenzov prolaz 1, tel. 051/553-674, www.prirodoslovni.com, 9am-7pm Mon.-Sat., 9am-3pm Sun., 10Kn) is a well-presented museum with a nice little collection of flora and fauna from the region, including an aquarium and pint-sized botanical garden.

Republic of Croatia Square
(Trg Republike Hrvatske)

South of Museum Square, down Frana Supila, is the University Library at Republic of Croatia Square. A former 19th-century girls' school, the building now houses the **Glagolitic Script Exhibition (Izložba glagoljice)** (Dolac 1, tel. 051/336-911, 8am-3pm Mon.-Fri., 15Kn) for those interested in learning more about the area's medieval common language.

Trsat

East of the city center, quite a walk from Rijeka's old-town tourist attractions, lies Trsat, a suburb of Rijeka. Long a pilgrimage site for locals, the importance of Trsat dates back to the 13th century, when legend has it that the house of Mary and Joseph rested here for three years during its journey from Nazareth to Loreto, in Italy. The devoted (or the active) will want to climb the 538 steps of the **Trsat stairs (Trsatske Stube)**, started in 1531 by the Uskok commander Petar Kružić and added to over the years, to reach the Franciscan monastery. Those with less time or less endurance can take bus 1 from the Riva (every 15 minutes, 15.50Kn).

The **Church of Our Lady of Trsat (Crkva gospel trsatske)** (open most days, free) is said to be built on the spot where the house of Mary and Joseph rested. The church and the **Franciscan monastery (Franjevački samostan)** were built, added to, and rebuilt over the years and today represent several architectural styles, including Gothic, Renaissance, Baroque, and Biedermeyer. Our Lady of Trsat was built in the 15th century, only to be almost completely reconstructed in the early 19th century. The altar is topped by an image of the Virgin Mary from 1367. Definitely worth a visit in the complex is the moving **Votive Chapel (Kapela zavjetnih darova)** (open most days, free) where candles illuminate paintings and tapestries given by people whose prayers were answered.

If you drove into Rijeka on the highway from Zagreb, you likely passed **Trsat Castle (Trsatska gradina)** (Petra Zrinskog bb, tel. 051/217-714, www.trsatskagradina.com, 9am-11pm daily Apr.-Nov., 9am-3pm daily Dec., Feb., and Mar., 15Kn for guided tour) as you came into town. Just across from the monastery, the decaying castle holds an amazing position on the rocks above Rijeka. On a clear day there's a magnificent view of the Kvarner Gulf. Parts of the castle date from Roman times, when a lookout tower occupied the spot; then the powerful Frankopan family built a castle here in medieval times. Trsat Castle was given a final overhaul by Laval Nugent, an Austrian count, who made it his final home and added several romanticist touches, like a classicist mausoleum in the castle's main courtyard. In the summer, the castle is often the location for open-air concerts. Find yourself in need of lunch? Stop at **Trsatika**, which offers filling, reasonable meals with a great view as well.

Croatian National Theater
(Hrvatsko narodno kazalište)

A bit out of the way on the Mrtvi Kanal (on the far eastern end of the Riva, dubbed Ivana Zajca Street), the grand Austro-Hungarian **Croatian National Theater** (Uljarska 1, tel. 051/355-900, www.hnk-zajc.hr, open for performances, box office 9:30am-12:30pm Mon.-Sat. and one hour before performances), built in 1885, is fronted by two sculptural compositions by Venetian sculptor Benvenutti. Nearby, the town's **market** (open mornings daily) is housed in three striking pavilions, the first two built in 1880 of iron and large panels of glass, heralding a new age of architecture. Unfortunately, the original interiors of the older pavilions have been all but destroyed, but the third pavilion, built in 1920 and home to the city's **fish market,** is home to some pleasing stone decorations, mostly centered around sea life, as well as the original open roof and gallery construction.

BEACHES

Though Rijeka's not famous for its beaches, there are a few places to take a dip (and you're likely to find fewer tourists than at Opatija's more popular beaches). The only in-town location is the suburb of **Pećine** (bus 2, eight minutes, 15.50Kn). The beaches are pretty clean, though they are rocky. Architecture buffs will appreciate the grand Austro-Hungarian-era villas in the area. The beach bar **Pajol** (Pećine bb., 097/761-9799, hours vary) is a nice place to eat and drink between dips, though parking is nearly impossible unless you arrive very early in the day. Traveling even further east, try Kostrena's **Žurkovo cove** (bus 10, 15-20 minutes, 21Kn).

ENTERTAINMENT AND EVENTS
Nightlife
In the Trsat area, **Beertija** (Slavka Krautzeka 12, tel. 051/452-183, 8am-12am Sun.-Thurs., 8am-4am Fri.-Sat.) is everything you could want in a pub and more: a huge selection of beers, a courtyard, frequent live music acts, and a friendly crowd.

Finally giving *rakija* (generally homemade brandy) the respect it deserves, ★ **Rakhia Bar** (Andrije Medulića 5, tel. 095/514-6599, 5pm-2am Fri.-Sat., 5pm-12am Mon.-Thurs.) offers up 50 varieties, including rare finds flavored with elderflower or truffles, right in the heart of the city.

Tunel (Školjić 12, tel. 051/327-116) is a club actually in a tunnel. It's the spot for electronic music and a crowd that doesn't conform.

Concerts and Theaters
The **Croatian National Theater (Hrvatsko narodno kazalište)** (Uljarska 1, tel. 051/337-114, www.hnk-zajc.hr, box office 9:30am-12:30pm Mon.-Sat. and one hour before performances) hosts opera, classical concerts, and occasional theater performances in Croatian and Italian. Children will enjoy the **City Puppet Theater (Gradsko kazalište lutaka)** (B. Polića 6, tel. 051/325-688, www.gkl-rijeka.hr), a small puppet theater with nice plays for the younger set.

Slightly out of the center, Rijeka's Tower Center shopping mall houses a big multiplex, **Cinestar** (Ul. Janka Polića Kamova 81a in Tower Center, tel. 060/323-233, www.blitz-cinestar.hr), for the latest Hollywood blockbusters.

Carnival
Rijeka's carnival season is by far its most famous event. Starting the Sunday before Lent, the city organizes dozens of performances, presentations, and concerts leading up to the carnival parade, led by lots of people in hideous masks meant to scare away evil spirits. The carnival has a long tradition in the area, though Rijeka's version, begun in 1982, is a fairly recent addition to the world carnival scene. Today it draws more than 10,000 people to town for the colorful celebrations. You can find out more information (though for the moment most of it is in Croatian) at www.rijecki-karneval.hr, or contact the **tourist office** (Korzo 14, tel. 051/335-882, rijeka@visitrijeka.hr, www.visitrijeka.hr, 8am-7:30pm Mon.-Fri., 8am-1:30pm Sat. winter, 8am-8pm Mon.-Sat., 8am-2pm Sun. summer).

ACCOMMODATIONS
Located in the center of town, the **Lounge Hostel Carnevale** (Jadranski Trg 1, tel. 051/410-555, www.hostelcarnevale.com, 355Kn d, with basic breakfast) is clean and friendly and also offers air-conditioning and free Wi-Fi as part of your stay.

Another option is the **Hostel Rijeka** (Korzo 32, 3rd floor, tel. 051/215-415, www.hostel-rijeka.com, from 170Kn pp or 450Kn d), centrally located in the heart of the action. The hostel offers free Wi-Fi and a shared kitchen and entertainment area. Be advised that this hostel is located on the third floor with no elevator, so you might want to skip it unless you are traveling light.

Apartments Villa Nora (Podkoludricu 4, tel. 099/215-8511, www.villanora.info, 750Kn d) are about four kilomenters (2.5 miles) from Rijeka's city center, but have a beautiful position right on Kvarner Gulf in an old villa. The rooms aren't quite as atmospheric as the villa itself, but they are clean, comfortable, and air-conditioned and have satellite television and Internet access. The best part is the location, where you can take a dip right in front of the hotel.

Located in a modern 1920s-era "skyscraper," the 14-story **Hotel Neboder** (Strossmayerova 1, tel. 051/373-538, www. jadran-hoteli.hr, 578Kn d, including breakfast) has small and rather lackluster rooms, but the location close to the city center and sea-facing rooms (not all are) make it an option if you don't find something else.

A much better option is the totally different **Botel Marina** (Riva 1, 051/410-162, www.botel-marina.com, 128Kn pp or from 400Kn d). This floating hotel is actually a boat moored right on the centrally located Riva. The rooms are clean and modern, and the hotel is sort of half-hostel, half-hotel, but still suitable for families. There is also a restaurant on board for a nice breakfast or meal.

The **Jadran Hotel** (Šetalište XIII divizije 46, tel. 051/216-600, www.jadran-hoteli.hr, 706Kn d, including breakfast), fully renovated in 2005 and part of the Best Western chain, is on the water's edge in Pećine, about two kilometers (one mile) east from Rijeka's center (bus 2, 15.50Kn). Though it's certainly within walking distance of town, the route is a bit perilous, so plan on taking a bus or a cab. The exterior is rather nondescript, but a sea-view room with a balcony and magnificent vistas across the gulf to Cres more than makes up for the bland architecture.

Considered the swankiest hotel in Rijeka, the **Grand Hotel Bonavia** (Dolac 4, tel. 051/357-100, www.bonavia.hr, 1,134Kn d,

including breakfast) is a nondescript glass block from the outside, but the rooms inside are well designed. The hotel, just a short walk from the Riva, has a very good breakfast; its nice restaurant, the Bonavia Classic, is located next to lots of shops and cafés.

FOOD

Croatia has recently experienced a gourmet burger trend, and Rijeka has a few good options. One of the best is **Submarine Natural Burgers** (Koblerov arg 2, 051/581-363, www.submarineburger.com, 11am-11pm Mon.-Thurs., 11am-12am Fri.-Sat., 12pm-11pm Sun., 50Kn), which has locally sourced and organic burgers and a good selection of craft beers.

Just across the square, **Maslina na Zelenom Trgu** (Koblerov trg, 051/563-563, www.pizzeria-maslina.hr, 7am-11pm Mon.-Fri., 12pm-11pm Sun., 50Kn) offers beyond your standard pizza, with toppings like truffles, shallots, and even tofu, though you can always order the standard offerings if you are feeling less than adventurous.

Though **Konoba Tarsa** (Josipa Kulfaneka 10, tel. 051/452-089, 11:30am-12am daily, 95Kn) is a bit large to officially be called a *konoba*, it's popular with locals for the warm atmosphere and hearty dishes, from seafood platters and black risotto to grilled meats and rib-sticking stews.

If the walk up to Trsat has your tummy growling, grab a table at **Trsatika** (Šetalište J Rakovca 33, tel. 051/217-455, 11am-11pm Thurs.-Tues., 75Kn), preferably one on the terrace that offers a great view. The menu is average—plenty of grilled meats and pizzas—but the location is stunning as well as convenient.

Also in Trsat, **Gvardijan Pizzeria** (Frankopanski Trg 9, tel. 051/403-642, 7am-12am Sun.-Thurs., 7am-2am Fri.-Sat., 75Kn) offers giant pizzas in a cozy setting.

For seafood, one of the most reasonable spots in town is ★ **Na kantunu** (Demetrova 2, tel. 051/313-271, 8am-10pm Mon.-Sat., 70Kn), a bit low on atmosphere but high in quality fish dishes and a great wine list.

The unassuming exterior masks the high-end fare you will find at **Konoba Nebuloza** (Titov trg 2b, 051/374-501, www.konobanebuloza.com, 11am-12am Mon.-Fri., 12pm-12am Sat., 70Kn). Set next to a river, the cozy restaurant has a very creative menu with a number of standout risottos, sous vide fish, local game, and desserts like green apple panna cotta.

INFORMATION AND SERVICES

For more information on rooms and apartments, tours, and maps, you can contact the local **tourist office** (Korzo 14, tel. 051/335-882, rijeka@visitrijeka.hr, www.visitrijeka.hr, 8am-7:30pm Mon.-Fri., 8am-1:30pm Sat. winter, 8am-8pm Mon.-Sat., 8am-2pm Sun. summer).

You'll find a **post office** (Korzo 13, 7am-9pm Mon.-Fri., 7am-2pm Sat.) conveniently located on the Korzo.

An all-night **pharmacy** is conveniently located on the Korzo (Korzo 22, tel. 051/211-036, 24 hours), and a **hospital** (Krešimirova 42, tel. 051/658-111) near the train station can take care of more serious ailments.

Rijeka's **train station** (Krešimirova 5, tel. 060/333-4444 or 051/211-638) has a left-luggage office open 24 hours and charging 15Kn per day.

GETTING THERE AND AROUND

Getting to Rijeka is quite easy, with excellent bus, ferry, and train connections from Croatia's major cities letting passengers off a walkable distance from the city center. In the summer some discount airlines offer connections to Rijeka's small **airport** (tel. 051/842-040, www.rijeka-airport.hr), actually located on Krk. Take the Autorolej bus, which meets most planes, for the slightly less than an hour ride (50Kn). Otherwise you'll be forking over upwards of 300Kn for a ride into town in a cab (tel. 051/332-893).

There are also boat connections from Rijeka to Cres, Mali Lošinj, Rab, and Novalja as well as the Dalmatian ports of Hvar, Korčula, and Dubrovnik. The Riva-located office of **Jadrolinija** (Riva 16, tel. 051/211-444, www.jadrolinija.hr, 7am-6pm Mon.-Fri., 8am-2:30pm Sat., 12pm-3pm Sun.) can let you know more about times and ticket prices. Ferries from Rijeka are a great option for connecting to Kvarner islands (prices to islands like Cres, Rab, and Mali Lošinj run around 50Kn). Ferries to Split (12.5 hours overnight, around 90Kn pp for a two-bunk berth, including breakfast) are quite long, though the price can't be beat for an overnight with breakfast along the coast.

Though the trip by train is much longer than the bus, it is a bit cheaper, making it a good option for those with more time than money. Rijeka's **train station** (Krešimirova 5, tel. 060/333-4444 or 051/211-638) is about a 10-minute walk west from the city center; it offers connections to major hubs like Zagreb (four hours, 96Kn) and Pula (two hours with transfer, 59Kn).

Rijeka's main **bus station** (Žabica 1, tel. 060/302-010, www.autotrans.hr), where intercity connections arrive and depart, is a 5-10-minute walk west of the center on Trg Žabica. Frequent connections are available to towns such as Pula (eight or more buses daily, two hours, 84Kn), Zagreb (over a dozen buses daily, 2.5 hours, 144Kn), and Split (four or more buses daily, 7.5 hours, 285Kn).

Around town you can easily walk or take a city bus to Trsat (bus 1, five minutes, 15.50Kn) or the beaches at Pećine (bus 2, eight minutes, 15.50Kn) from the Riva. Bus 32 travels to Opatija (30 minutes, 26Kn).

1: Lungomare promenade near Opatija **2:** Korzo street in Rijeka **3:** St. Vitus's Church in Rijeka **4:** café in Lovran

Opatija Riviera

Though the attractive Opatija Riviera (Opatijska rivijera) tends to attract an older crowd, that's not to say there's nothing for the hip and trendy (unless you're looking for a hopping nightlife scene, in which case look elsewhere). The line of coast, hugged mostly by grand old villas built by Vienna's elite in the 19th century, has some excellent boutique hotels and more than its fair share of superb restaurants to keep those chasing the finer things in life entertained for at least a couple of days. The downsides are that some of the most charming parts, like Lovran, are notoriously unwalkable (few sidewalks and busy roads) and almost unparkable.

★ OPATIJA

An Austro-Hungarian gem on the coast, Opatija is not the place to go if you want to party till dawn, but if you'd like a spot on the coast that isn't packed with a zillion tube-topped youngsters, the genteel charm of the city should win you over.

Sights

The standout of Opatija, the nearly 12-kilometer-long (7.5-mile-long) **Franz Joseph Path (Šetalište Franza Josefa),** or **Lungomare,** running north toward Lovran, is a wonderful wide seafront promenade, perfect for leisurely strolls. Shaded by trees, you can take in the rocky beaches and the opulent old villas—some painstakingly restored, some decaying in neglect. The most famous of these villas is the **Villa Angiolina,** not only one of the city's finest, but also its first. Built by merchant Higinio von Scarpa in 1844 in honor of his late wife, the grand home and its stunning gardens are periodically open for concerts and performances. Ask at the **tourist office** (Obala m. Tita 101, tel. 051/371-310, www.opatija-tourism.hr, 8am-9pm Mon.-Sat., 6pm-9pm Sun. June-Sept., 8am-3pm Mon.-Fri., 8am-2pm Sat. Oct.-May) for more details.

If you would like to peek in an old villa and see an interesting exhibition as well, the **Croatian Museum of Tourism (Hrvatski muzej turizma)** (Park Angiolina 1, 051/603-636, www.hrmt.hr, 10am-8pm daily, 15Kn) tells the history of Croatian tourism. The small museum is well done and a nice stop for history buffs.

The pretty **Juraj Šporer Art Pavilion** (Park Sv. Jakova 1, tel. 051/272-225, prices and opening times vary with exhibitions) has revolving art exhibitions, mostly contemporary.

If the Lungomare seems too tame, the nearby **Učka Nature Park (Park prirode Učka)** (tel. 051/293-753, park.prirode.ucka@ inet.hr, www.pp-ucka.hr) has dozens of hiking trails on the mountain that separates Kvarner from Istria. The tourist office can provide detailed maps and guides of the various routes.

Beaches

If you're looking for a swim or just some beachside lounging, you'll need to head slightly south toward Lovran for the best spots. **Ičići** is only about a three-kilometer (two-mile) walk on the Lungomare from the center of Opatija. You could also hop a bus to **Medveja** (bus 32, 25 minutes), which has some nice shingle beaches and an outpost of the locally famous Hemingway franchise to wet your whistle in between swims. If you're a fan of windsurfing, head to **Preluk Bay** in Volosko, one of the best spots for early-morning windsurfing in the summer and early fall. For information on equipment rental and courses, contact Opatija's **tourist office** (Obala m. Tita 101, tel. 051/271-310, www.opatija-tourism.hr, 8am-9pm Mon.-Sat., 6pm-9pm Sun. June-Sept., 8am-3pm Mon.-Fri., 8am-2pm Sat. Oct.-May).

Accommodations

For those who don't mind roughing it,

Opatija Riviera

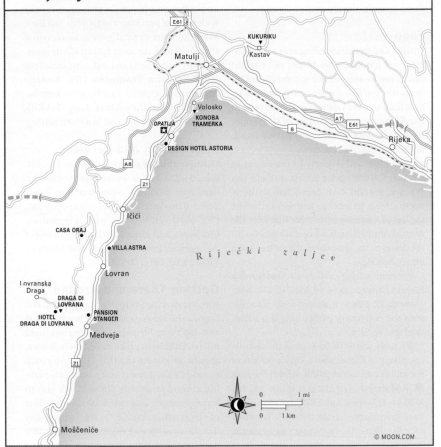

© MOON.COM

there's a great **campsite** (Liburnijska 46, tel. 051/704-836, info@rivijera-opatija.hr, www. rivijera-opatija.hr, 50Kn pp) in Ičići, conveniently located near the beach.

The renovated **Design Hotel Astoria** (Obala Maršala Tita 174, tel. 051/706-350, www.hotel-astoria.hr, 900Kn d) is located in a turn-of-the-20th-century villa decorated with a sleek modern touch. You'll also find all the conveniences of this century, like powerful air-conditioning and high-speed Internet access.

The sleek **Hotel Navis** (Ivana Matetića Ronjgova 10, www.hotel-navis.hr, 1,216Kn d, including breakfast) is the place to stay if you want to be assured a sea view, as every room has one. There is also a pool, a small spa, a great restaurant, and a small private beach. The hotel also has a shuttle service to downtown, which will allow you to leave your Tesla charging at one of the hotel's charging stations.

A villa-hotel with its own rocky beach, the **Hotel Miramar** (Ive Kaline 11, tel. 051/280-000, www.hotel-miramar.info, 943Kn d) has nice rooms, all air-conditioned and with their own balcony or terrace. The hotel also has a small spa facility and a parking garage, a huge boost for travelers with a rental car trying to find a space in already-packed Opatija.

Food

Opatija and the surrounding area are a goldmine for foodies, with dozens of tasty but pricey restaurants servicing tourists and locals alike. You'll find more variety and quality here than in most cities, even tourist meccas like Dubrovnik, particularly in the former fishing village of Volosko, which boasts some of Croatia's finest restaurants.

For coffee and desserts in the center of Opatija, **Café Wagner** (Obala maršala Tita 109, tel. 051/202-071, 7am-12am daily) is worth a stop. Its interior and service invoke the feel of Viennese-style cafés that were the norm on the Riviera over a century ago. Go for the desserts, the chocolates, the coffee, and a hint of nostalgia.

For moderately priced meals, **Gostionica Kaneta** (Nova cesta 64, tel. 051/712-222, 7am-12am daily, 80Kn) is an excellent place for meat and potatoes or pasta dishes in a warm, local atmosphere.

It's truly worth the detour to the charming village of Kastav, above Rijeka, for lots of atmosphere and an excellent meal at the cozy ★ **Kukuriku** (Trg Matka Laginje 1A, tel. 051/691-417, www.kukuriku.hr, 1pm-12am Tues.-Sun. Sept.-Easter, 250Kn). Roosters are everywhere (the restaurant's name means "cock-a-doodle-doo"), though the menu is heavy on grilled meats and local flavor. The restaurant recently opened a lovely hotel with sleek modern rooms so you can go from dinner to bed in no time.

A trip to Opatija wouldn't quite be complete without splurging on some seafood or more gourmet cuisine, something the tiny area is famous for. Volosko, a suburb of Opatija, is brimming with choices. The dishes get even more inventive, though the decor's decidedly local, at **Plavi Podrum** (Obala Frana Supila 4, tel. 051/701-223, dkramari@ inet.hr, 12pm-12am daily, 300Kn), winner of multiple "world's best" and fancy French awards. Dishes like St. Jacques shells on a reduction of apples and monkfish with truffles and coffee powder, or desserts such as cake with a hint of port wine and tobacco, will leave even the most cynical gourmets adjusting their belts to make room for just a little more.

Newer on the scene but also excellent is ★ **Konoba Tramerka** (Dr. Andrije Mohorovica 15, 051/701-707, www.konoba-tramerka.com, 1pm-12am daily, 250Kn), which serves fresh seafood in a rustic setting.

Information and Services

Opatija's **tourist office** (Obala m. Tita 101, tel. 051/271-310, www.opatija-tourism.hr, 8am-9pm Mon.-Sat., 6pm-9pm Sun. June-Sept., 8am-3pm Mon.-Fri., 8am-2pm Sat. Oct.-May) can help out with information, brochures, and maps. Rent boats from one of two agencies in the **Hotel Admiral** (Obala m. Tita 139, tel. 051/271-533).

Getting There and Around

If you're driving to Opatija from Rijeka, just hop on the main coastal road heading west and don't stop for about 15 kilometers (nine miles). Otherwise, take bus 32 from Rijeka, about a 30-minute trip that will set you back around 26Kn. Even if you have a car, parking around Opatija is difficult. It's best to leave your car and continue on foot (lots of places are accessible via the Lungomare) or take a taxi (more expensive but possibly worth it to avoid the frustration of locating the hillside restaurants and dealing with tricky parking).

Water taxis (50Kn-70Kn) are a cheaper and more atmospheric option for getting to the beaches and Lovran. They have notoriously unreliable schedules but can be picked up at the harbors of the hotels **Millennium** (Obala m. Tita 109) and **Admiral** (Obala m. Tita 139).

LOVRAN

Once a playground for rich Austro-Hungarians with the massive villas to prove it, Lovran is once again attracting Europe's well-heeled. The crowd is slightly younger than Opatija, but no less refined. The tiny harbor is ringed by massive villas, many of which have been turned into boutique hotels and private retreats. There's not too much in the way of actual sights, though you might want to attempt the picturesque climb through Lovran's older section (starting behind the main street, Maršala Tita) to the **St. George's Church (Crkva svetog Jurja),** a 14th-century church with pretty frescoes if you happen to find it open.

Beaches

Beaches in Lovran are fairly nonexistent. The best bets are the beaches at **Medveja** (three kilometers/two miles away, bus 32, five minutes) or back at **Ičići.** If you're staying at one of the villas along the waterfront, you'll likely have access to the water via some stairs.

Accommodations

Some of the best hotels in Lovran are owned by one small firm, which has tastefully converted a few of the area's old villas and farmhouses into refined accommodation. Among these properties, the standouts are likely ★ **Villa Astra** (Viktora Cara Emina 11, tel. 051/294-589, www.hotelvillaastra.com, 1,915Kn d, including breakfast), a 1905 waterfront villa with a pool and a great restaurant. The company's ★ **Casa Oraj** (Tuliševica 64, tel. 051/294-604, www.hotelvillaastra.com, 2,500Kn), a house that sleeps eight, is perched on a hilltop high above the sea, about a 10-minute drive from Lovran. The authentic century-old property is filled with antiques and lots of peace and quiet in its sprawling gardens.

Villa Eugenia (Maršala Tita 34, tel. 051/294-800, www.villa-eugenia.com, 1,034Kn d) is another nice choice in Lovran, with attractive fresh rooms, a whirlpool tub, a billiards table, and a decent list of spa treatments and massages. Balconies have a nice view of the sea below. The **Hotel Park** (Maršala Tita 60, tel. 051/706-200, www.hotelparklovran.hr, 700Kn d) is located in a bright blue building with smallish but sleek rooms, many of which have balconies. High above Lovran, with an amazing view and even better salt-touched breezes, ★ **Hotel Draga di Lovrana** (Lovranska Draga 1, tel. 051/294-166, www.dragadilovrana.hr, 900Kn d, including breakfast) offers pretty rooms in a quiet location with an excellent restaurant. Though bus 36 travels between Lovranska Draga and Lovran, it's easier to take a taxi or a car to shuttle you to the beach or to Opatija since the roads are steep and curvy.

If you can't afford the luxury villas, your best bets are private apartments in the area. One reliable option is the **Pansion Stanger** (M. Tita 128, tel. 051/291-154, www.pansion-stanger.com, 558Kn d, including breakfast), with attractive sea-view rooms and friendly owners.

Food

Najade (Maršala Tita 69, tel. 051/291-866, 11am-12am daily, 95Kn) has been a staple on the Lovran restaurant scene since 1990. Within its homey stone walls, diners chow down on fresh fish and grilled meats.

Though you'll need a car or cab to get there, some of the best food and vistas are north of town. ★ **Draga di Lovrana** (Lovranska Draga 1, tel. 051/294-166, www.dragadilovrana.hr, 12pm-12am daily, 100Kn) has two choices for a good meal: the highly acclaimed restaurant and the more laid-back taverna, both with views of the Kvarner Gulf and the surrounding mountains that alone are worth the trip. The restaurant offers top-notch seafood and international cuisine, while the taverna has simple but filling dishes like minestrone or scrambled eggs with asparagus in season, and a good wine list.

Also a bit of a drive, the charming family-run **Konoba Kali Medveja** (Kali 39a, 051/293-268, www.konobakali.hr, hours vary, 80Kn) has beautiful views and dishes such as homemade ravioli, roast dishes, and even dried fruit snacks you can purchase for your trip home.

For something heartier, climb toward Učka Nature Park, where **Dopolavoro** (Učka 9,

Ičići, tel. 051/299-641, 12pm-11pm Tues.-Sun., 95Kn) doles out meat dishes enhanced by wild mushrooms and fresh vegetables in season. It's a great choice if you enjoy game like wild boar, deer, and bear.

Information and Services

Lovran has a small **tourist office** (Obala m. Tita 63, tel. 051/291-740, www.tz-lovran. hr, 8am-2pm and 5pm-8pm Mon.-Sat., 8am-2pm Sun. June-Sept., 8am-2pm Mon.-Sat. Oct.-May) with maps, brochures, and local information.

Getting There and Around

If you don't have a car, buses are the easiest way to get to and from Lovran. Take bus 32 to Opatija (15 minutes, around 20Kn) and Rijeka (45 minutes, 26Kn). Lovran is west of Opatija along the coastal road.

Kvarner Islands

Far less publicized than the Dalmatian Islands, the Kvarner Islands have their own beauty, turquoise waters, and cultural finds. Many of the islands, such as Rab and Krk, are easier to access from the mainland, though these islands are also the most developed for tourists, which translates into lots of hotels and restaurants, but also lots of fellow sun-worshippers when it comes time to hit the beaches. Cres and Susak are decidedly more untouched and are great destinations if you're looking for natural attractions and peace and quiet. Partiers will find their groove on Krk and in the 24-hour club hub of Novalja on Pag. Like pretty much all of Croatia, Kvarner has something for every personality and mood. As for the seasons, many of the restaurants and hotels close in the winter, though not quite to the extent of the islands in Dalmatia. If you do visit in winter, you're sure to get a sense of the local culture and people with nary a tourist to compete with for attention.

KRK

Krk is the largest of Croatia's islands and it is extremely popular with tourists, mostly Croatians and Europeans who flood the large package hotels and beaches. The most popular spots are the sandy beaches at Baška, packed to capacity in August, and Krk Town. Quieter spots like Vrbnik and Malinska have some great boutique hotels and little restaurants.

Krk has been a tourist destination since the mid-19th century, though the island's history dates back to Roman times, when Caesar purportedly camped at the military outpost located there.

For all the tourists and souvenir shops that go along with them, there are still lots of cultural and gastronomic traditions, particularly Vrbnička Žlahtina, a white wine from Vrbnik, and a local version of the bagpipe, the *mijeh*, fashioned from a goat's stomach. You'll find the most colorful traditions on display during the **Krk Folklore Festival (Smotra folklore otoka Krka)**, held in July or August in a different town on the island each year.

Krk Town

The heart of Krk Town is a beautiful little walled city, filled with narrow alleyways, though many are now inhabited by shops selling T-shirts and bric-a-brac. The town walls have protected Krk since pre-Roman times, and the oldest tower at Kamplin Square (Trg Kamplin) was built in the 12th century.

SIGHTS

Don't-miss sights in Krk include the **Ban Jelačić Square (Trg bana Jelačića)**, where the 13th-century **guard tower** is enhanced by a recycled Roman gravestone depicting the deceased, who now overlook all the action on the town's main square; a tower at the adjoining Main Square (Vela placa), at Ban Jelačić Square's western end, sports a 16th-century 24-hour clock.

The Romanesque **Cathedral of the Assumption (Katedrala Uznesenja)** (Trg sv. Kvirina, 9:30am-1pm and 5pm-7pm daily, free) was built in the early 13th century, though its bell tower was added between the 16th and 18th centuries. Inside the church you'll see more recycling of Roman ruins (this time it's columns) as well as some Renaissance Venetian paintings on the church's altars. Next to the cathedral you'll find the **St. Quirinus's Church (Crkva svetog Kvirina),** which houses a **Collection of Sacral Art (Izložbena zbirka sakralne umjetnosti)** (tel. 051/221-341, 9:30am-1pm daily Apr.-Oct., 15Kn) filled with sacred objects spanning the 14th-18th centuries. The star of the collection is a paneled golden altarpiece centering on the Virgin.

East of the cathedral hugging the waterfront walls is the **fortress (Kaštel).** The round tower belonged to the Frankopan family, who ruled Krk from the 12th to the late 15th century.

To escape all the touristy action, head north of J.J. Strossmayera, where quiet streets are punctuated by the occasional cat or elderly woman standing in her doorway. Follow Dr. Dinka Vitezića to the 11th-century **Church of Our Lady of Health (Crkva majke božje od zdravlja)** (open sporadically, free), which made use of old Roman relics in its construction.

ENTERTAINMENT AND EVENTS

At night, head to a bar for some people-watching or catch a **concert** (check with the tourist office for details) in the summer. After hours, check out the completely unique **Volsonis** (Vela Placa 8, tel. 051/880-249, www.volsonis. hr, 7am-2am Sat.-Sun. winter, 7am-5am daily summer), housed within a 2,000-year-old archeological site complete with two altars to Venus. A cafe and pizzeria during the day, it turns into a packed club at night, often with live music acts. Another option, **Casa di Padrone** (Šetalište sv Bernadina, tel. 091/229-4602, 8am-12am daily late Apr.-Sept.), keeps the music spinning and the crowd dancing. It's the place to see and be seen—just make sure your wallet is full.

ACCOMMODATIONS AND FOOD

Hotel Bor (Šetalište Dražica 5, tel. 051/220-200, www.hotelbor.hr, 553Kn d, including breakfast) is only an eight-minute walk east from the center of town and a minute away from a rocky beach. The rooms are basic but clean and have televisions.

The most luxe choice in Krk Town is the recently renovated **Hotel Marina** (Obala Hrvatske mornarice bb, tel. 051/221-128, www.hotelikrk.hr, 1,135Kn d, including breakfast). The circa 1925 hotel underwent an overhaul in 2008 that created a sleek space right on the seafront. In addition to air-conditioning, satellite TV, and Internet access, every room has a sea view.

For food, don't expect to be blown away in this heavily touristed area. If you don't have the time or energy to explore around the island, try **Konoba Nono** (Krčkih iseljenika 8, tel. 051/222-221, nono@nono-krk.com, 11am-12am daily Apr.-Oct., 90Kn). Krk specialties rule the menu, like *šurlice,* a type of pasta, and lamb and seafood dishes. **Citta Vecchia** (Josipa Jurja Strossmayera 36, 095/506-3179, 12pm-12am daily summer, winter hours vary, 85Kn) has good food in a pleasant atmosphere. The restaurant also offers rooms for bed-and-breakfast accommodations.

INFORMATION AND SERVICES

The **Krk Island tourist office** (Trg sv Kvirina 1, tel. 051/220-226, www.krk.hr, 9am-9pm daily summer, call for winter hours) offers plenty of helpful information, from accommodations to maps and more.

You can hop on the Internet at **Krk Sistemi** (Šetalište sv Bernadina 3, tel. 051/222-999, www.krksistemi.hr, 15Kn for 30 minutes), though these days it is fairly easy to plop down in the multiple cafés offering free Wi-Fi and order a coffee.

KVARNER GULF
KVARNER ISLANDS

GETTING THERE AND AROUND

The airport on the tip of Krk also serves **Rijeka**. Unfortunately, public transportation is not a convenient option from the airport (you'd have to go to Rijeka and then get a bus to Krk Town). Even for those watching their pennies, a taxi is well worth the splurge, around 250Kn.

Getting to Krk by bus is quite easy, with good connections from Rijeka (around 10 per day, 1.5 hours, 51Kn) and Zagreb (at least two per day, five hours, 181Kn). The bus is also the way to get from town to town on the island, with good connections to Baška and Malinska. The **bus station** (Obala Hrvatske Mornarice, tel. 051/679-051) in Krk Town is less than a five-minute walk west of the town center.

Northern Krk

If you're looking for something a little more sophisticated, head to northern Krk, where wine and food go hand in hand with a couple of good choices for accommodations. First up is **Vrbnik,** known for its local white wine. You can get a taste at ★ **Nada's** (Glavica 22, tel. 051/857-065, www.nada-vrbnik. hr, 12pm-11pm daily summer, 12pm-11pm Fri.-Sun. spring and fall, closed Nov.-end of Feb., 95Kn), a restaurant famous with local Croatians and tourists alike. The decor is far from fancy, but it has soul. Home-cured hams hang from the ceiling, and diners cram the outdoor benches to savor the great seafood. Don't miss the restaurant's sea bass in salt or lamb stew if it's available, washed down with a prerequisite glass of the restaurant's Vrbnička Žlahtina, made from the owner's grapes.

The most popular beaches in Vrbnik are **Zgribnica,** protected from winds by the cliffs that surround it, and **Potovosce,** a pebble beach with a small bar and restrooms. **Risika** is about six kilomteters (four miles) away but has a nice sandy beach on Sv. Marko Bay. If you're looking for something more private,

just pick a little rocky cove and claim it as your own.

Slightly northwest in Dobrinj, **Villa Rustica** (Sv. Ivan Dobrinjski 42, tel. 051/868-110, 700Kn) sleeps four and has sprawling gardens, a pool, and lots of country charm just a short walk away from a good beach.

In Malinska, on the western coast, the **Hotel Pinia** (Porat bb, tel. 051/866-333, www. hotel-pinia.hr, 900Kn d, including breakfast and one other meal) has renovated rooms, sea views, an indoor pool, and a beach just in front, though it is outside the village proper. Another option is the **Hotel Vila Rova** (Rova 28, tel. 051/866-100, www.hotel-vila-rova. com, 920Kn d), a boutique hotel right on the beach. Even better is the seaside promenade that runs in front of the hotel, perfect for a sunset stroll.

Cheap and tasty, **Fisch&Chips Popaj** (Put Radici 1, tel. 051/550-150, 7am-11pm daily, 40Kn) is the place to go for a plate of fried fish and other dishes that come from the neighboring fish market. The rustic **Konoba Bracera** (Kvarnerska 1, tel. 051/858-700, www.konoba-bracera.com, 10am-11pm daily, closed Jan., 60Kn) is a popular option serving hearty portions of fish stew and pasta dishes.

Malinska has some nice beaches to the west of the town's marina. If you want even more privacy, walk or drive west to Porat, where lots of rocky coves provide calm and quiet.

Punat

Punat is a mostly touristy town, with a small gem of an islet only 800 meters (half a mile) out in the water and a good restaurant. The only must-do in town is to take a water taxi to **Košljun,** where a 15th-century **Franciscan monastery (Franjevački samostan)** (tel. 051/854-017, 9:30am-6pm Mon.-Sat. May-Sept., call for winter hours, 15Kn) takes center stage. There are some pretty works of art in the monastery's church (fans of naive art should look out for Ivan Lacković's drawings) and there's a quirky little museum (with exhibits like a pickled two-headed lamb), but the real draws are the quiet sprawling gardens of

---

1: Baška, Krk island **2:** the old city of Cres **3:** sunning on Krk

the monastery, perfect for a leisurely stroll. Special events such as concerts are sometimes held. The whole excursion takes about two hours, and the water taxi will set you back about 20Kn in each direction.

The **Hotel Kanajt** (Kanajt 5, tel. 051/654-340, www.kanajt.hr, 960Kn d, including breakfast) has rooms with unexciting standard hotel furniture, but the location directly in front of a marina is what makes it special. Lots of seafaring types get their bearings at the Hotel Kanajt.

Even better is the hotel's super restaurant, ★ **Kanajt** (Kanajt 5, tel. 051/654-340, www.kanajt.hr, 7am-1pm and 5pm-11pm daily, 90Kn), which serves a variety of seafood and meats, the best of which are prepared *ispod peka* (oven baked), including octopus, lamb, and veal. You will need to order these oven-baked dishes ahead of time; call or stop by for more details.

Punat has some good spots for beginning windsurfers, depending on which way the wind is blowing. Nudists will appreciate the beach at Konobe naturist camp, also known as **Acapulca,** a huge clothing-optional beach with tennis and volleyball.

You can get more information about activities and beaches in town from the Punat **tourist office** (Obala 72, tel. 051/854-860, www.tzpunat.hr, 8am-3pm Mon.-Fri., longer hours in summer). You can also find out the schedule and destinations of the small tourist train that ferries travelers to some of the busier beaches. The town also has a convenient **medical clinic** for tourists (Pod Topol 2, 2:30pm-9pm Mon., Wed., and Fri., 7am-1pm Thurs., 9am-12pm and 6pm-8:30pm Sat.-Sun. May-Sept.) near the bus station.

The **bus station** (tel. 051/222-111), a 10-minute walk to the southeast of the center, connects with both Krk Town (15 minutes) and Baška (30-40 minutes).

Stara Baška

Stara Baška, 12 kilometers (7.5 miles) south of Punat, is a small fishing village hugging a rocky cliff, parts of which are beautiful and parts of which have been taken over by garish villas. Its most striking feature is its beaches. If you're coming by car, you'll need to park above the beach and walk down a very steep path to reach the pretty coves. It's not to be attempted by the out-of-shape or unsteady, but if you do go, pack a picnic basket—you won't want to climb back up for a drink. There's a nice restaurant in town, **Nadia** (Stara Baška 253, tel. 051/844-663, novice.mladenovic@ri.t-com.hr, call for hours, 100Kn), serving lots of fresh fish specialties. Buses are infrequent to Stara Baška, so it's best reached by car.

Baška

At the height of the season, in July and August, you might think the only sights in Baška are the thousands of bodies fighting for attention and space along the beach. But just a 2.5-kilometer (1.5-mile) walk northwest along the road to Krk Town, the village of **Jurandvor** holds an important spot in Croatian culture as the site where the **Baška tablet (Bašćanska ploča)** was discovered. Dating from the 11th century, this oldest known text of Glagolitic script was found at the village's 9th-century **St. Lucy's Church (Crkva svete Lucije)** (tel. 051/860-184, www.azjurandvor.com, approx. 10am-3pm and 5pm-9pm in summer, check hours with tourist office in Baška, 25Kn). A replica of the tablet is on display (the real tablet is in Zagreb).

The most famous sight in Baška, though, is its **Great Beach (Vela Plaža),** a mix of tiny pebbles and sand that stretches for about 1,800 meters (1.1 miles). In the hottest summer months, its 4,000 spaces can be almost filled to capacity. What makes Vela Plaža so nice? Situated right in the center of town, it's easy to get to; it's rimmed with bars, restaurants, and cafés; and it's relatively shallow, making it great for kids.

The **Hotel Zvonimir** (Emilia Geistlicha 34, tel. 051/656-810, www.valamar.com, 700Kn d, including breakfast) has clean, comfortable rooms and a seaside location. The **Atrium Residence Baška** (tel. 051/656-890, www.valamar.com, 1,127Kn d, including

Baška Tablet (Bašćanska Ploča)

Anyone who has dealt with real estate in Croatia will probably see the humor in the Baška Tablet, the oldest proof of Croatian literacy and essentially an early land title for a church. It was found in the church it served to protect, Sv. Lucija in Jurandvor near Baška. The abbot writes that the land was given by King Zvonimir to the church and that anyone who refuted it should be "cursed by the twelve apostles and four evangelists and St. Lucy"—perhaps not a bad clause to add to modern-day contracts.

Humor aside, the tablet dates from about 1100 and is one of the most important archaeological finds in Croatian history. The tablet, which weighs nearly 800 kilograms (1,760 pounds), was written in Croatian Glagolitic script. This alphabet, approved by the Roman Catholic Church (who normally opposed languages other than Latin), was used for translating the gospels into Slavic languages. Priests along the Adriatic were quick to adopt it.

The Glagolitic script persisted until the 18th century, when Austrian and Venetian ruling forces heavily discouraged it. They finally banned its use in official documents in 1818, and it had died out by the late 19th century.

Today, the famous Baška Tablet rests in the Academy of Arts and Sciences in Zagreb. Much smaller, but generally quite heavy, knock-offs can be found as souvenirs in shops across Croatia.

---

breakfast) is right on the beach. With fresh and sleek interior design and all the modern conveniences like high-speed Internet access, it became the new crown jewel of local hotels when it opened in 2008.

New in 2015, the **Heritage Hotel Forza** (Kralja Zvonimira 98, tel. 051/864-036, www. hotelforza.hr, 900Kn d, including breakfast) is the best value in town. The family run boutique hotel has tastefully decorated rooms, most with sea views, and it is a short walk to the beach. The hotel also runs a restaurant downstairs that has good meals for any time of day.

Bistro Francesca (Zvonimirova 56, tel. 099/654-7538, www.bistrofrancesca.com, 12pm-3pm and 6pm-12am daily mid-May-Sept., 100Kn) is a newer gourmet addition to town. A cozy enclosed courtyard and jazz music compliment the menu, filled with Croatian dishes, often with a twist, like cold beetroot soup or fried figs with ice cream.

Baška is well connected by bus from Krk Town (at least four buses daily, 45 minutes, 27Kn). The **tourist office** (Kralja Zvonimira 114, tel. 051/856-817, www.tz-baska.hr, 8am-3pm Mon.-Fri.) can help with brochures and maps, including a good hiking map of the area.

Sports and Recreation

Squatina Diving (Zarok 88A, Baška, tel. 051/856-034, www.squatinadiving.com, Apr.-Oct.) offers introductory diving courses and trips for certified divers.

Pretty much anywhere you see a larger marina, there are likely boats for rent or water taxis for hire. It's a great way to get off the beaten path and discover your own little private paradise.

You can find hiking maps and more information on outdoor activities at Krk's tourist offices. The **Baška tourist office** (Kralja Zvonimira 114, tel. 051/856-817, www.tz-baska.hr) has an extensive supply of maps and brochures. The **Krk Town tourist office** (Trg sv Kvirina 1, tel. 051/220-226, www.krk. hr, 9am-9pm daily summer, call for winter hours) can also provide you with lots of ideas for active day trips and brochures of hiking paths in the area.

Getting There and Around

Low-cost carriers such as Ryan Air (www. ryanair.com) and Eurowings (www. eurowings.com) usually offer at least weekly direct flights to Krk from Europe during the summer. If you do fly into Krk's **Rijeka Airport** (tel. 051/842-132, www.

rijeka-airport.hr), you'll need to take a taxi (250-300Kn) to Krk Town, since the bus will route you to Rijeka before depositing you back on Krk. Check with airport information about taxis.

There are many daily **buses** connecting Rijeka with the island, usually stopping in Krk Town and Malinska before a final stop at Baška. There are around 10 connections a day from Rijeka (1.5 hours, 51Kn) and at least two a day from Zagreb (five hours, 181Kn).

Krk is well connected with **ferries** (www.jadrolinija.hr), particularly in the summer, when you can hop a boat to Cres (from Valbiska, 30 minutes), Rab (from Baška, one hour), or Crikvenica (from Šilo, 20 minutes, summer only) on the shore.

★ CRES

Cres is one of Croatia's largest islands and surprisingly one of its most unspoiled. The 80-kilometer-long (50-mile-long) island has a shady northern section known as Tramuntana, long a native home of the Eurasian Griffon and the lovely fishing village of Cres Town. In the south there's Osor, the oldest city on the island, with a history full of Roman artifacts. Looking on the map you'll notice a large lake, Lake Vrana. Since Cres and neighboring Lošinj are dependent on the freshwater lake for water, the lake is strictly off-limits to the public. But there's still plenty of beauty and culture to explore, including summer musical performances in Osor and in the almost abandoned village of Lubenice.

Cres Town

Nestled next to a small medieval harbor, the quaint fishing village of Cres Town has a maze of picturesque streets perfect for getting lost in for a couple of hours.

SIGHTS

Start your tour at the main square, **F. Petrić Square (Trg F. Petrića).** The waterfront square is bordered by a simple town loggia dating from the 16th century. Cres Town has several pretty churches, though the

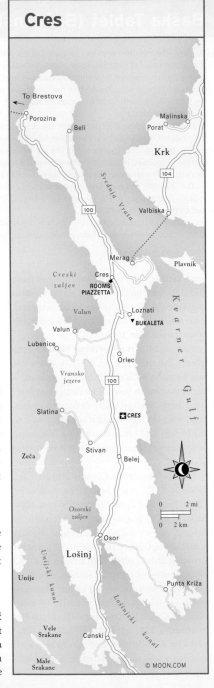

Cres

To Brestova
Porozina
Beli
Malinska
Porat
Krk
104
Srednja Vrata
Valbiska
100
Merag
Plavnik
Creski zaljev
Cres
ROOMS PIAZZETTA
Loznati
BUKALETA
Valun
Valun
Lubenice
Orlec
Vransko jezero
100
Kvarner Gulf
Slatina
CRES
Zeča
Stivan
Belej
Osorski zaljev
Osor
Lošinj
Unijski kanal
Unije
Punta Križa
Lošinjski kanal
Vele Srakane
Cunski
Male Srakane

0   2 mi
0   2 km

© MOON.COM

late-Gothic **Church of St. Mary of the Snow (Crkva Sveta Marija Snježne)** (Pod Urom, 9am-6:30pm daily, free) is certainly one to keep on your don't-miss list. The 15th-century simple stone building (the bell tower was added in the 18th century) is decorated with a few striking reliefs. Though the painting on the main altar dates from the 19th century, there are a couple of 15th-century works like the painting *St. Sebastian with the Saints,* by Alviseo Vivarini, and a wooden mourning scene. Nearby, the **Church of St. Isidor (Crkva Sv. Izidora)** (check with tourist office for hours, free) is worth a quick stop as well. Built in the 12th century, it is said to be Cres Town's original parish church. Inside the church you'll find several 15th-century wooden sculptures.

Outside the remains of the southern town walls you'll find an early 14th-century **Franciscan monastery (Franjevački samostan)** (open for mass on Sun.) with a pretty cloister, housing a small graveyard holding the city's most important families and a well, adorned with the oldest known coat of arms of the town. The monastery also has a small **museum** (tel. 051/571-217, by appt. only, donation necessary) with a few old portraits and paintings, some dating to the 15th century.

On the northwestern side of town you'll find a circular 16th-century Venetian **defense tower,** the last one remaining from the town's old defense system.

For a few days every summer, the **CREScendo Music Festival** brings both domestic and foreign jazz musicians to stages around town.

ACCOMMODATIONS

There aren't a lot of options for hotel accommodations on Cres. The **tourist office** (Cons 10, tel. 051/571-535, www.tzg-cres.hr, 8am-8pm Mon.-Sat., 9am-1pm Sun. summer, 8am-3pm Mon.-Fri. winter) should be able to help arrange private rooms and apartments. **Camp Kovačine** (Melin 1/20, tel. 051/573-150, www.camp-kovacine.com) offers campsites, mobile homes (550Kn d), and air-conditioned rooms (596Kn d, including breakfast) in a nice beachfront location only a short walk north from Cres Town.

In the center of Cres Town, ★ **Rooms Piazzetta** (Pjaceta 20, tel. 098/215-548, 450Kn d) has clean modern rooms for those who would rather stay in the town than on the beach. Cres Town has only one hotel, the **Hotel Kimen** (Melin I 16, tel. 051/571-322, www.hotel-kimen.com, Easter-Oct., 596Kn d, including breakfast in the main house). The rooms have been renovated and are quite nice, with sleek bathrooms, air-conditioning, and satellite television. Avoid the half board or full board options as the food is underwhelming.

FOOD

Cres may be lacking in lodging options, but eating is an entirely different story—there are dozens of good restaurants and *konobas.* The most famous staple on the Cres restaurant scene is the unassuming **Belona** (Šetalište 23. travnja 24, tel. 051/571-203, 9am-12am daily summer, 9am-10pm daily winter, 85Kn). Housed in a small tavern just outside the town walls, Belona's has been serving seafood since before World War II, when the *osteria* took its name from a beautiful and witty barmaid who worked there. Today the barmaid is gone, but the excellent food, like seafood risotto and oven-baked sea bass in summer and sauerkraut with garlic sausages in autumn, keeps diners coming back. ★ **Bukaleta** (Loznati bb, tel. 051/571-606, 12pm-12am daily Apr.-Oct., 90Kn) is about a 10-minute drive southeast to the tiny hilltop village of Loznati. The restaurant is famous for its lamb, prepared in all sorts of ways: baked, roasted, stewed, and more. Lambs on the islands are known to be tastier, marinated from birth by the herbs they graze on, and Bukaleta is something of an expert at preparing them. The family's homemade olive oil is a special treat as well.

INFORMATION AND SERVICES

Cres Town's **tourist office** (Cons 10, tel. 051/571-535, www.tzg-cres.hr, 8am-8pm

Mon.-Sat., 9am-1pm Sun. summer, 8am-3pm Mon.-Fri. winter) has lots of helpful information as well as brochures and maps.

GETTING THERE AND AROUND

If you're coming straight from the mainland, at least two buses (more in summer) link Cres Town with Rijeka (two hours, 102Kn). Taking the ferry from Krk you'll land in Merag, connected by at least two buses a day with Cres Town (20 minutes, 23Kn). You can also hop a bus to the island of Mali Lošinj (two buses per day, more in summer, 1.25 hours, 47Kn) or to Osor on Cres (up to seven per day in summer, two during winter and on weekends, 45 minutes, 33Kn).

Beli

The small town of Beli is one of the oldest villages on Cres. Located 15 kilometers (nine miles) north of Cres Town, Beli has two Romanesque churches, one with several interesting Glagolitic inscriptions and the other, St. Marija, with a small museum.

The three-star **Pansion Tramontana** (tel. 051/840-519, www.beli-tramontana. com, 450Kn d, including breakfast) has long been a source of clean, comfortable rooms in Beli. The owners also own a diving company and can arrange for super diving excursions and nature walks around the area. The hotel has a good restaurant where you can fill up on local specialties, whether you're staying there or not. **Gostionica Beli** (tel. 051/840-515, www.beli-cres.com, 300Kn d) has super meals of local lamb and fresh seafood as well as several apartments for rent.

There is at least one daily bus to Beli from Cres Town on weekdays (30 minutes, 20Kn), leaving in the morning and returning in the early evening.

Osor

Though the port village of Osor seems pretty quaint these days, it has a much grander past. The oldest town on the island, Osor was known as Apsoros in Roman times and was an important port in the Adriatic. Only a few meters from the island of Lošinj, Osor rises above the narrow channel likely dug by the Illyrian Liburni tribe before the Romans arrived. Today a small bridge connects the two islands. There is a small **Archaeological Museum (Arheološki muzej)** (Gradska vijećnica, tel. 051/237-346, www.muzej.losinj.hr, 10am-12pm and 7pm-9pm Tues.-Sat., 35Kn) in the town hall with some interesting Roman finds and a scale model of the town as it was in medieval times. If it's open, the **Bishop's Palace (Biskupska palača)** houses a lapidarium of finds from local churches.

Osor has a very pretty campsite, **Bijar** (Osor 76, tel. 051/237-027, www.camp-bijar.com, 67Kn pp), right by the water. **Apartments Mikulec** (Osor 37, tel. 091/564-0111, www.apartmanimikulec.com, 450Kn d) are a short walk to the beach and offer clean and comfortable rooms and small apartments with private baths. There are several restaurants in town. Try **Konoba Bonifačić** (Osor 64, tel. 051/237-413, 10am-11pm daily, 85Kn) for good seafood and a peaceful atmosphere.

Osor also holds **musical evenings** (www.osorfestival.eu) during July and August, with many performances of local Croatian musicians and composers held in the Crkva Uznesenja (Church of the Assumption of the Virgin Mary). The **tourist office** in Mali Lošinj (Riva Lošinjskih Kapetana 29, tel. 051/231-547, www.visitlosinj.hr, 8am-8pm Mon.-Sat., 9am-1pm Sun. June-Sept., 8am-1pm Mon.-Fri. Oct.-May) should have more details.

Buses conveniently connect Osor with Mali Lošinj (at least two daily, 30 minutes, 27Kn) and Cres Town (up to seven per day in summer, two during winter and on weekends, 45 minutes, 33Kn).

Lubenice

The beautiful, tiny village of Lubenice, a stone town 378 meters (a quarter of a mile)

1: Veli Lošinj harbor **2:** towers of Rab **3:** ruins of the Church and Convent of St. John the Baptist in Rab Town **4:** Lubenice town, Cres island

above the water, holds **Lubenice Musical Evenings (Lubeničke glazbene večeri)**, classical music concerts on the main square, on Fridays in July and August. Tickets cost around 50Kn with transportation from Cres Town; you can buy tickets in Cres Town at **Autotrans** (tel. 051/572-050, www.autotrans. hr). Another great secret of Lubenice is its beach, located at the foot of the town, called **Sveti Ivan** (St. John). It's a 45-minute walk down (quite steep, so be careful and make sure you're wearing shoes with treads) and about an hour's climb back up, but if you like beautiful beaches, with clear water ideal for snorkeling (you can see the fish from above the water as well), it's worth the hike. If the day has made you hungry, fill up on local wine and cheese at **Lubenička loza** (Lubenice bb, tel. 051/840-427, 9am-10pm daily May-Sept., 80Kn). There are only a few buses a week to Lubenice, so you'll need a car to get the most out of your visit.

Valun

Valun, 13 kilometers (eight miles) southwest of Cres Town, is another destination for beach lovers, with two nice pebble beaches, the best of which is **Mali Valun** beach, surrounded by mountains and normally quite secluded. If you happen to come on a busy day, rent a kayak at the harbor and find your own spot of paradise. Valun is also served only sporadically by buses, so it's best to have a car to enjoy it fully. If you find yourself in Valun, you won't go hungry as there are two waterside restaurants: **MaMaLu** (Valun 13A, tel. 051/525-035, 12pm-11pm daily in summer, winter hours vary, 100Kn) and **Na Moru** (Valun 65, tel. 051/525-056, 12pm-11pm daily in summer, winter hours vary, 100Kn), where you can fill up on fish and local wine.

Getting There and Around

Hourly ferries connect Cres with the villages of Brestova (Istria, 30 minutes) and Valbiska (Krk, 30 minutes). There's also a daily catamaran from Rijeka (1 hour and 20 minutes).

The **bus station** (Zazid 4, tel. 051/571-810) links Cres Town with Mali Lošinj (2 per day, more in summer, 1.25 hours, 47Kn) and Rijeka (two hours, 102Kn). You'll also find at least a couple of buses linking Cres Town with Osor (up to seven per day in summer, two during winter and on weekends, 45 minutes, 33Kn), though connections can be scarce in the off-season months.

LOŠINJ

Just across the small bridge from quiet Cres, the island of Lošinj is far more developed and busy. In fact, Mali Lošinj is the largest town on the Croatian islands, though it didn't grow that large on tourism alone—the shipbuilding industry was responsible for its development in the 18th and 19th centuries.

At one time Veli Lošinj (which means big Lošinj) was bigger than Mali (which means small). Today the situation is reversed, with Mali Lošinj catering to the bulk of the tourist trade. There's lots to see and do on the island, though not so much that you can't relax. After viewing the dolphin colony that lives offshore and visiting a couple of small museums, it's easy to fill up your time strolling the waterfront promenade and gawking at the pastel-colored houses of wealthy captains and merchants of long ago, preening over the water.

Lošinj is connected with Italy via ferries, which makes it possible to continue on a European journey from the island. It also means that thousands of Italians flood the hotels in Lošinj each summer to experience the island's charms. If you happen to be around in September, when the place is significantly quieter, don't miss the island's **Fishermen's festival.**

Mali Lošinj

Though there's not much to see in Mali Lošinj in terms of actual tourist attractions, the town itself is quite pretty, with steep winding streets and a busy Riva (harbor-front walkway) filled to the brim in summer with bronzed limbs stretching out at the café tables.

Lošinj

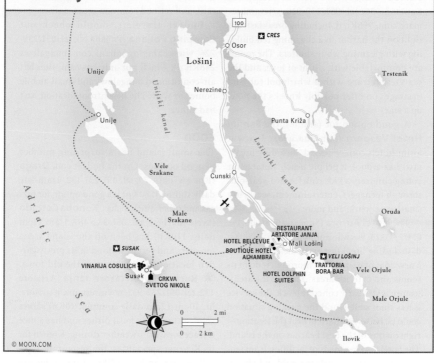

The **Art Collections in the Fritzy Palace (Umjetničke zbirke)** (Vladimira Gortana 35, tel. 051/231-173, www.muzej.losinj.hr, 10am-1pm and 6pm-8pm Mon.-Fri., 10am-1pm Sat. summer, 10am-1pm and 5pm-7pm Mon.-Fri., 10am-1pm Sat. winter, closed Jan.-Feb., 35Kn) display a nice selection of paintings, mostly 17th- and 18th-century Italian pieces and a decent showing of modern Croatian art as well.

Though it's hard to imagine a museum devoted to one statue could be so interesting, the **Apoxymenos Museum (Muzej Apoksiomena)** (Riva lošinjskih kapetana 13, tel. 051/734-260, 9am-5pm Tues.-Sun., last entry at 4pm, 50Kn) is surprisingly well presented. The Greek statue of the athlete was discovered underwater, and the museum provides displays with information on the history and the process of rescuing the statue, but centers around the remarkably well-preserved statue itself.

If you're searching for a beach, the **Sunčana uvala** beach in front of the Hotel Aurora is one of the best in Mali Lošinj. With relatively small pebbles and a forested space with a playground, sports facilities, and restaurants, the wind-protected cove is a good all-around choice for beaches. Just north of town, the stunning **Čikat Bay** is another nice choice, with a beachfront promenade separating the pebbly shores and a handful of Austro-Hungarian villas. The area has cafés and a few places where you can rent snorkeling gear. The nicest walk on the island is the four-kilometer-long (2.5-mile-long) **promenade** south of town connecting Mali and Veli Lošinj, winding its way through forests and coves with plenty of pretty views in between.

ACCOMMODATIONS

Suites Mare Mare (Riva Losinjskih Kapetana 36, tel. 051/232-010, www.mare-mare.com, 998Kn d, including breakfast) are right on the harbor in a charming red building with gleaming white shutters. The rooms are comfortable with a hint of luxe, and the sea-view terrace with a whirlpool tub and massages on offer possibly knocks the hotel up a star.

A good option for families, the **Family Hotel Vespera** (Sunčana uvala 5, www.losinj-hotels.com, 990Kn d, including breakfast) has a pool, a pebble beach suitable for young children, a kids club for two-year-olds through teenagers, entertainment, access to a small water park, and more.

The **Hotel Aurora** (Sunčana uvala bb, tel. 051/231-324, www.losinj-hotels.com, 1,200Kn d, including breakfast and lunch) has gotten a new coat of paint and a thorough redo of its rooms and exterior areas. Though the architecture is still early concrete block, the service is less than stellar, and the parking situation could be better, it's hard to beat the location—right on one of the best beaches on the island. The hotel also has loads of facilities, from tennis and volleyball courts to a pool and a bowling alley.

The **Hotel Apoksiomen** (Riva Lošinjskih kapetana I, tel. 051/520-820, www.ohm.hr, 1,170Kn d, including breakfast) is a small boutique establishment right on the town's harbor promenade. The hotel has a nice little terrace restaurant with great views, and the rooms all display art by Croatian painters. The sleek modern architecture of the ★ **Hotel Bellevue** (Čikat 9, tel. 051/679-000, www.losinj-hotels.com, 1,278Kn d) somehow works perfectly amongst the old Austro-Hungarian elegance of pristine Čikat Bay. Combining the best hotel on the island with the best beach, the hotel also offers a spa, a pool, restaurants, bars, and a pillow menu.

Another high-end addition to the island's accommodations, the ★ **Boutique Hotel Alhambra and Villa Augusta** (Čikat 16, tel. 051/260-700, www.losinj-hotels.com, 1,800Kn d) offers seaside lounging, a small but well-done spa and indoor pool, an elegant restaurant, and refined common areas.

Budget travelers should check out **Camping Poljana** (Poljana bb, tel. 051/231-726, www.campingpoljana.com, bungalows 248Kn d), which not only has campsites but air-conditioned bungalows and small mobile homes as well. The beachfront location isn't bad either.

FOOD

The small island has a surprising number of good options. On the budget end, **Draga** (Braće Vidulić 77, tel. 051/231-132, 11am-late daily summer, 30Kn) is a good option for pizzas and other quick dishes. **Konoba Corrado** (Svete Marije 1, tel. 051/232-487, 11am-11pm daily, 110Kn) has been on the island scene for years and serves seafood in its pretty garden location in the heart of the old town. ★ **Restaurant Artatore Janja** (Artatore 132, tel. 051/232-932, www.restaurant-aratore.hr, 10am-12am daily summer, 90Kn) serves solid seafood and local dishes and has a nice terrace for warm-weather dining. Known for its Kvarner specialties, the restaurant typically serves up dishes like lobster in *buzara* sauce, lamb with gnocchi, and many types of risottos.

Restaurant Rosemary (Čikat 15, tel. 051/231-837, 11am-11pm daily, 300Kn) is set in a cozy villa amongst the trees. Fresh local dishes won't disappoint, and the chef-run attention to detail is evident.

A decidedly fine dining experience on the island, ★ **Restaurant Alfred Keller** (Čikat 16, www.losinj-hotels.com, 12pm-11pm daily Apr.-Nov., 370Kn) in the Hotel Alhambra is new to Mali Lošinj. The restaurant is known for its quality ingredients and the chef's creative interpretations of local dishes. There is a nice wine cellar stocked with options for pairing.

INFORMATION AND SERVICES

Mali Lošinj has a **tourist office** (Riva Lošinjskih Kapetana 29, tel. 051/231-547, www.visitlosinj.hr, 8am-8pm Mon.-Sat., 9am-1pm Sun. June-Sept., 8am-1pm Mon.-Fri. Oct.-May) with lots of information. Their website has downloadable brochures on private accommodations, restaurants, and events.

★ Veli Lošinj

Veli Lošinj is the smaller but grander of the two towns on the island, with dozens of towering villas with pretty walled gardens. Peek through the *portuni* (garden gates) and get a glimpse of what life was like for the upper class of the island (mostly ship owners and captains) many years ago.

Other highlights of the island are the large **St. Anthony's Church (Crkva svetog Antuna)** (Trg Sveti Antun, open for Sun. mass, free), with its 15th-century painting *Madonna with Saints* by early Renaissance painter Bartolomeo Vivarini, and in a 15th-century Venetian tower a small **museum** (tel. 051/231-173, www.muzej.losinj.hr, 10am-12pm and 7pm-9pm Tues.-Sat. June-Sept., 35Kn) displaying paintings and artifacts of the island as well as a Roman statue discovered off the coast in 1999.

Veli Lošinj is home to the **Blue World Institute of Marine Research and Conservation (Plavi Svijet)** (Kaštel 24, tel. 051/604-666, www.plavi-svijet.org, 10am-9pm daily July-Aug., 10am-2pm daily off-season, 20Kn), housing an interesting display of Adriatic marine life with a special focus on the institute's Adriatic Dolphin Project, studying the indigenous bottlenose dolphins. In addition to providing touch-screen info points, a documentary film with English subtitles, and a children's section, the center informs visitors how they can help protect the dolphins. For example, learn the safe distance to maintain between the dolphins and your boat and how you can become an eco-volunteer.

ACCOMMODATIONS

For private accommodations and apartments on the island, the **Palma Travel Agency** (V. Nazora 2, tel. 051/236-179, www.losinj.com) can arrange for an overnight in a number of residences, including stone houses and decaying grand villas. The **Youth Hostel Veli Lošinj** (Kaciol 4, tel. 051/236-234, 170Kn pp, including breakfast) is an older building, and though the rooms are basic, it is clean, the staff is friendly, and there is free Wi-Fi. The **Vitality Hotel Punta** (Sestavine bb, www.losinj-hotels.com, 665Kn d) is the nicest hotel on the island. The modern facilities include a spa, a waterfront pool, and wonderful sea views. However, the ★ **Hotel Dolphin Suites** (Slavojna 14, tel. 051/236-409, www.dolphinsuitescroatia.com, 1,200Kn d) are probably the best experience on the island. Located only two minutes from the harbor in a fully renovated historic villa with a pool, the modern rooms are luxe and fresh.

FOOD

The promenade that stretches from Mali Lošinj continues beyond Veli Lošinj to the quaint fishing village of Rovenska, where you'll find the island's only natural sandy beach and a gem of a restaurant, the ★ **Trattoria Bora Bar** (Rovenska 3, tel. 051/867-544, www.borabar.net, 9am-2am daily Apr.-Nov., 100Kn), which serves up creative dishes like tuna carpaccio with celery root and truffles alongside local sausages. The Italian-born chef Marco Sasso owned a restaurant in the United States before falling in love with Croatia's islands and opening the trendy restaurant, which has Wi-Fi and houses a book exchange for literature-thirsty travelers.

Getting There and Around

Summer connections to the island are the best, with a daily catamaran between Mali Lošinj and Rijeka (1 hour and 20 minutes) and Pula (2.5-3 hours) and a car ferry from Zadar (seven hours). You can also connect directly to Venice (www.venezialines.com, four hours, €70).

Buses link Mali Lošinj with Cres Town (two per day, more in summer, 1.25 hours, 47Kn) and Osor (at least two per day, 30 minutes, 27Kn).

If you don't feel like walking the promenade between Mali Lošinj and Veli Lošinj, close to 10 buses a day make the 10-minute trip for around 15Kn.

★ SUSAK

Sixteen kilometers (10 miles) southwest of Lošinj, Susak is a delightful, mostly overlooked island with a completely different composition than the other Kvarner Islands, hence the clay ocher-colored cliffs. The islanders have a culture uniquely their own and their own dialect. Only 150 people call the four-square-kilometer (1.5-square-mile) island home year-round. You'll find more natives in the United States, where 2,500 people claim roots from the small island. The island hosts a yearly Emigrant's Day the last Saturday of July, when many people revisit their roots and celebrate.

The settlement of Susak is the only village on the island, and it is divided into two parts: the **Upper Village (Gornje selo),** the oldest part of town, and the **Lower Village (Donje selo).** In the Upper Village you'll find the 1770 **St. Nicholas's Church (Crkva svetog** **Nikole),** built on the remains of an 11th-century Benedictine monastery; if it's open you're free to go in.

There's a great 11-kilometer (seven-mile) **track** around the island that takes about three hours to walk. You can stop off for a swim wherever you feel like it. Make sure to take some water and perhaps a snack for the journey.

The beaches on Susak are completely different from what you will find in the rest of Croatia, with sandy shores and grassy knolls. On the northwest side of the island, near the village, the beaches are quite shallow, and two bays, **Spiaža** and **Bok,** also have wonderful natural sandy bases. Bok Bay is traditionally clothing optional. The southwest side of the island is a better choice for those looking for absolute privacy, though it's exposed to a lot more wind, and getting to a flat rock surface in one of the coves is not for the unbalanced.

Wineries

Susak has some nice wines, particularly Pleskunac, a nice red, and Trojišćina, a rosé. To have a taste, try **Vinarija Cosulich** (tel. 051/239-070, call for hours), the cellars of an Italian winemaker who bought up vineyards on the island in the 1990s.

Susak village and harbor

Accommodations and Food

The only lodging on Susak is through private rooms and apartments. You can get a list from the **Mali Lošinj tourist office** (Riva Lošinjskih Kapetana 29, tel. 051/231-547, www.tz-malilosinj.hr, 8am-8pm Mon.-Sat., 9am-1pm Sun. June-Sept., 8am-1pm Mon.-Fri. Oct.-May) or via the website www.otok-susak. org. **Apartmani Grgac** (Podgorska 125, tel. 01/339-0358, www.apartmani-grgac-susak. com, info@apartmani-grgac-susak.com, 520Kn) offers attractive, clean apartments and rooms surrounded by stone walls a short walk to the seafront. **Susak Sansego** (Susak 622, tel. +386 040/562-749, www.susak.si, from 1,100Kn) is a group of old stone houses for rent with daily maid service. You can eat and sleep at the **Buffet Palma** (Susak 127, tel. 051/239-068, 8am-12am daily May-Sept., call for prices), which serves up local fish dishes and clean, basic rooms. Susak's small harbor has a few more *konobas* and pizzerias for lunch or dinner. If you would like to buy some bread for the day, keep in mind that all purchases must be preordered through the local store. Don't miss getting a *burek* at the Osman Patissiere (summers only).

Getting There and Around

Susak gets its share of day-trippers from the multiple ferries run by Jadrolinija that deposit tourists on the island during peak season. The ferry connects with Mali Lošinj (2.5 hours, 50Kn). On Susak you'll have to get around on foot or rent bikes from the **Sunbird Agency** (eight hours for 75Kn, ask about longer periods) near the Hotel Bellevue in Mali Lošinj or the **ASL Travel Agency** (Obala m. Tita 17, tel. 051/236-257) in Veli Lošinj.

RAB

Rab was originally settled by the Illyrians, but the Greeks and the Romans also staked a claim here. The island was then ruled by the Venetians, who used the island as a place for refugees of the plagues to come and start a new life in the 15th century. The island started to make a name for itself in tourism in the late 19th century, most notably for its naturist (aka nude) beaches that even drew a king of England.

Today the highlight of Rab for history buffs and charm seekers is its small fortified Rab Town, filled with the cobblestone alleyways and tiny squares prerequisite to a proper Adriatic island town. The island also has some excellent beaches, filled in the summers by Europeans coming from the north for a bit of sun and surf.

★ Rab Town

If you're looking for a place with medieval charm and twisting, narrow alleys, Rab Town is the perfect fit.

SIGHTS

Positioned on a narrow peninsula jutting out into the sea, the picturesque walled city is punctuated by four church towers. If you're interested in visiting these towers, start with the largest at the **Church of St. Mary the Great (Crkva svete Marije Velike)** (Kaldanac, tel. 051/724-195, 10am-12pm and 7:30pm-9pm daily summer, free), built in the 12th century, with many additions and renovations parlaying a bit of Renaissance flair on the Romanesque church. A cathedral until 1828, it's still known locally as the Katedrala. To the west of the church is the **Great Bell Tower (Veli zvonik)** (Ivana Rabljanina, 10am-1pm and 7:30pm-10pm daily summer, 5Kn), worth the climb for some stunning views.

The nearby 11th-century **Church of St. Andrew (Crkva svetog Andrije)** (Ivana Rabljanina) has the oldest bell tower, dating from 1181. The third tower is located at the **Church of St. Justine (Crkva svete Justine)** (Gornja ulica, open daily, ask at tourist office for hours, often 7:30pm-9pm June-Sept., 10Kn), which also houses a small collection of paintings and sacral art. The star attraction here is the box made of precious metal that holds the skull of St. Christopher. The casket, made in the 12th century, is

Leave the Bathing Suit at Home

Rab has an interesting history of naturism, or nudist-friendly beaches. Old articles mention the practice on Rab as early as 1907, though it saw its biggest increase when Viennese Richard Erhman, then president of a naturist union, opened an official nude beach on the island in 1934. But it was Edward VIII, visiting with Wallis Simpson in August 1936, who made Rab famous. Stopping on the island during their scandalous yachting trip down the Adriatic, Edward and Wallis had a dip sans clothing at Kandarola Cove, on the Frkanj Peninsula west of Rab Town.

Kandarola Cove is still the most popular and well-known nude beach on the island. It is also one of two official nude beaches, the other being Ciganka in Lopar. Still, there are plenty of other unofficial spots for naturists around Rab. If you're interested in pursuing the naturist lifestyle with fewer spectators, try other coves along the Frkanj Peninsula or the nearby island of Dolin.

filled with reliefs depicting St. Christopher's beheading.

At the **Church and Convent of St. John the Baptist (Bazilika svetog Ivana Evanđeliste)** (Gornja ulica), the 12th-century tower is all that remains among the ruins of the Benedictine cloister, said to date from the 6th century. It's worth walking the **town walls** for some nice views of town. At the highest part of the walls, **St. Christopher's Church (Crkva Sveti Kristofor)** (Gornja ulica, 9am-12pm and 7:30pm-9pm daily summer, ask tourist office for off-season hours, donation required) has a small lapidarium next door. It's here that Rab Town's peninsula joins with the mainland, becoming the **Komrčar,** a peaceful park with wide paths winding through the forested hills and depositing locals and tourists alike at the city's beaches.

The **Promenade (Šetalište Fra Odorika Badurine)** is a waterfront walkway reached on foot through Komrčar Park, with some shaded areas and pretty, clean water for taking a dip if you don't mind the concrete beneath your towel.

If you'd like to find a more secluded beach out of town, rent a boat at the western end of the old-town harbor or **Kristofor** (Palit bb, tel. 051/725-543, www.kristofor.hr, around 350Kn per day). You'll want to bring supplies, though, unless you don't plan to stay very long.

ENTERTAINMENT AND EVENTS

In the summer months you'll find lots more to do on Rab, with galleries opening their doors to the public until late in the evening and a few festivals and events. Among these are **Rab Classical Music Evenings,** held every Wednesday at 9pm in the Church of the Holy Cross (Sveti Križ) on Gornja ulica from June to September.

The annual **Rab Fiera** (end of July) showcases medieval costumes, handicrafts, and culture in a colorful festival that transforms Rab Town's cobblestoned streets.

ACCOMMODATIONS

The waterfront **Tamaris Pension** (Palit 285, tel. 051/724-925, www.tamaris-rab.com, 596Kn d, including breakfast) is located near Rab Town on the edge of Komrčar Park. The rooms are fairly basic but clean and comfortable, with balconies overlooking the park or the sea and a good restaurant with nice fish dishes.

The finest accommodation in Rab Town is the ★ **Hotel Arbiana** (Obala Petra Krešimira 12, tel. 051/775-900, www.arbianahotel.com, 1,205Kn d, including breakfast), a boutique hotel set in an old villa right on the waterfront. The hotel has a peaceful walled garden area where you can dine in good weather. The rooms are full of luxurious details and the service is excellent. The only drawback (or an extra charming detail, depending on how you look at it) is its proximity to the church bells.

FOOD

Even though Rab is a busy tourist destination, you'll still manage to find some good food any season of the year. Budget-watchers can start with a *konoba,* like the rustic **Konoba Rab** (Kneza Branimira 3, tel. 051/725-666, 10am-12am Mon.-Thurs., 5pm-11pm Fri.-Sun. mid-Feb.-Oct., 100Kn), which specializes in lamb, though seafood and other meat entrées are also on offer. Call one day ahead to order the delectable *janjetina ispod peka* (brick oven-baked lamb). The most beautiful place to eat on the island has to be **Agatini Vrtovi** (Obala Petra Krešimira 12, tel. 051/775-900, www.arbianahotel.com, 12pm-11pm daily, 250Kn), located at the end of the harbor. High-end cuisine sometimes comes with high-end prices, so be sure to ask for the price of the catch of the day in advance.

Around Rab

There's honestly not much to see in terms of tourist stops beyond Rab Town. Other parts of the island have been primarily developed with Central European tourists in mind. Most anywhere you go you'll find signs for *apartmani* and restaurants with multilingual menus. The real draw outside of Rab Town is the beaches, usually packed with tourists, though they certainly aren't Croatia's best.

The most popular beach is the two-kilometer-long (one-mile-long) **Paradise Beach (Rajska plaža)** in **Lopar,** on the northern tip of the island. Though its position near the San Marino hotel complex and a huge camping spot means it's hardly private, the sandy shores, clear shallow water (extending over 500 meters/a quarter mile before it reaches your waist), and a pine forest edging the beach, if you need a bit of shade, make it one of the island's best. The beach also has cafés and bars, and sports activities like volleyball courts and table tennis. Lopar has 22 beaches, and 3 of them are nudist. The prettiest, even worth a trip for non-naturists if you don't mind sharing the sands with unclothed loungers, is **Sahara,** so named for its sandy shores and out-of-the-way location; a 30-minute walk over the hill or a short boat ride from Lopar's harbor (the better choice) mean there's less activity than Paradise Beach, with pretty views, rock edging the cove, and shallow, clear water.

Hotel Epario (Lopar 456A, tel. 051/777-500, www.epario.net, 705Kn d, including breakfast) in Lopar was built in 2007 and has 25 basic but fresh double rooms with air-conditioning, satellite TV, and balconies, but it's not on the beach. **Camping San Marino** (Lopar bb, tel. 051/775-133, www.camping-adriatic.com, tent camping 150Kn for two people) has an idyllic location along Paradise Beach and lots of facilities, including showers, bathrooms, a tennis court, mini-golf, a playground, a small market, and more.

Getting to Lopar is simple, with close to 10 daily buses making stops at the San Marino beach and in Lopar proper. A small **tourist office** (tel. 051/775-508, www.lopar.com) can help with information and brochures.

A few kilometers/miles south of Rab Town, beer-swilling partying types will want to check out **Pudarica,** two kilometers (1.25 miles) from the village of **Barbat.** There is a lackluster beach shack-style club on the edge of the beach, **Santos,** that is useful in case of thirst or hunger.

Though the hotel is not worth the mention, the restaurant at **Villa Barbat** (Barbat 362, tel. 051/721-858, www.hotel-barbat.com, 12pm-10pm in summer, call for winter hours, 95Kn) is a nice spot for a seafood lunch or dinner on the attractive stone terrace.

Over a dozen buses daily link Barbat with Rab Town, less than a 10-minute journey.

If you have a car, it is worth checking out **Suha Punta,** a bit rocky but with very clear water, in Komar.

Getting There and Around

If you're driving to Rab from the mainland, you'll need to connect with the car ferry at

Goli Otok: A Yugoslavian Alcatraz

view on Goli Otok

Goli Otok means "naked island," and its geography certainly confirms the name—arid, no trees, lots of rocks. However, it has been said that the landscape is not how the island got its name. Instead, the name came about because the island used to be a popular spot for naturists to bathe.

But Goli Otok's fame comes from its history as a prison, the Alcatraz of Yugoslavia, from 1949 to 1988. Instead of housing hardened criminals, though, it held political prisoners. These prisoners were ostensibly former Nazi loyalists or those that sided with Stalin when Tito decided to sever ties with the Soviet Union. However, many people, perhaps betrayed by a jealous neighbor, were thrown in for offenses that would seem small to those used to freedom of speech.

Life on Goli Otok was full of hard labor in the island's quarry, and new prisoners were tortured, beaten, forced to dunk their heads in bodily waste, and more. Not many people talk about their life on Goli Otok—so horrific were the conditions that most choose only to forget.

In the 1950s the island started housing fewer political prisoners and more regular criminals. The hardships also lessened, with prisoners having a music room and a football team.

Slightly north of Goli Otok is Grgur, another island that functioned as a women's prison. The existence of Goli Otok was not officially admitted until after Tito's death, and the island was abandoned in 1989.

If you'd like to visit the island, you'll see many advertisements for excursions from the island of Rab.

Jablanac (look for signs off the Magistrala) to the southern tip of Rab, about eight kilometers (five miles) from Rab Town. Lines for the ferries can get quite long in summer—try to hit them when the fewest people are coming or going: weekdays, early morning, and late evening.

There is a summer ferry to Baška on Krk Island (links with Lopar, one hour, 45Kn), and the summer-only catamaran links Rijeka and Novalja on Pag with Rab (two hours to Rijeka, 40Kn). There are multiple daily buses from Rijeka (2.5 hours, 121Kn) and Zagreb (five hours, 230Kn) to the island. The **Autotrans line** (www.autotrans.hr) runs most of the bus connections.

PAG

Though the island is famous for its cheese, its lamb, and its lace, most tourists descend on the arid island of Pag for partying at the 24-hour club scene near Novalja. But there's much more to see, including ancient limestone Pag Town, an excellent winery, and the local cuisine. The cheese (called *paški sir*) and the lamb owe their distinct and delicious flavor to the herbs that grow wild on the island. The sheep graze on sage, tinged with the salt from the nearby sea, soaking all their products with a delicate aroma. Pag lace makes a great souvenir, often sold directly in front of a lace-makers house, who has carried on the tradition of generations before her.

Pag Town

Pag Town is full of old stone buildings, but few with much historical or architectural interest besides those on the main square, **Petar Krešlmir IV Square (Trg kralja Petra Krešimira IV)**. It's home to two 15th-century buildings by famous Dalmatian architect Juraj Dalmatinac. The **Duke's Palace (Knežev dvor)** served as the seat of island government until 1905, and the **Parish Church (Zborna crkva)** (Trg Kralja Krešimira IV, tel. 051/611-576, 9am-12pm and 5pm-7pm daily June-Sept., Sunday mass only Oct.-May, free), diagonally across the square, was built in a grand scale in order with cathedrals of the day, but the church never got to fulfill its purpose. Particular to the church are the reliefs of local women in traditional headdress surrounding the Virgin Mary above the entrance. The interior is mostly from the 18th century, when the church was refitted in grand Baroque style.

On nearby Zvonomirova is the **Town's Tower (Kula skrivanat)**, a 15th-century fortification with an arched gate in its center. It's the only remaining tower of Pag's original nine.

Summer in Pag brings in two additional stops. First up is the summer art festival at St. George's Church (Crkva Sveti Jurja) (Trg Sveti Jurja, evenings June-Sept., check with tourist office for schedule), which is full of art exhibits and concerts, and the must-see **Lace Museum (Galerija paške čipke)** (Trg Kralja Krešimira IV, 9:30am-6:30pm June-Sept., 10Kn), which shows off Pag's tradition of lace-making.

Pag Town has a decent if unimpressive pebbly **town beach (gradska plaža)** across the causeway from the center on the western side of the bay.

ENTERTAINMENT AND EVENTS

Pag's **carnival** runs the first Saturday after the Epiphany to the first day of Lent. Filled with typical masked parties and a smattering of folklore, the party culminates with the burning of a cloth dummy named Marko, blamed for all the bad in the town during the year. The town holds a second one-day carnival for tourists during the summer. Typically held on the last Saturday in July, the event highlights a lot more culture, including the traditional *tanac* dance, costumed performers, and a parade.

ACCOMMODATIONS AND FOOD

There are dozens of apartments and rooms available for rent on Pag. The hotels in Pag are not currently recommended, so these are a much better option. Try **Agencija Perla** (Josipa Bana Jelačića 21, tel. 023/600-003 in summer and tel. 023/612-077 in winter, www.perla-pag.hr), or check online at Booking (www.booking.com) or AirBnB (www.airbnb.com).

For food, try ★ **Trapula Wine and Cheese Bar** (Trg Kralja Petra Kresimira IV, tel. 099/271-9014, 50Kn), located right on the main square, for local Pag cheese, wine, olives, and more. More substantial fare can be found at the excellent **Na Tale** (Stjepana Radića 4, tel. 023/611-194, www.ljubica.hr, 8am-12am daily, closed Christmas-mid-Jan., 100Kn), located at the edge of the town walls. Serving grilled fish, octopus lasagna,

Birthplace of Nikola Tesla

If you're traveling down to Dalmatia and are a fan of Tesla (the man, not the cars), a stop at the **Nikola Tesla Memorial Center (Memorijalni Centar Nikola Tesla)** (www. mcnikolatesla.hr, 8am-3pm Tues.-Sat., 10am-3pm Sun. winter, 8am-8-pm Tues.-Sat., 9am-8pm Sun. summer, 50Kn), is worth a quick visit. Though most of the original buildings have been destroyed, the center has lovingly built replicas in their place. The complex includes a small museum chronicling his achievements, and a tour at one-hour or so intervals gives more detail on his life. While the museum is a must for big fans of Tesla, others might feel let down, especially with the museum. On the upside, visitors with small children could find it a much-needed stop on the way down to Dalmatia, and there is plenty of space and freedom for kids to run around, as well as a small playground. Exiting from the A1 highway at Gospic, the village of Smiljan is located about seven kilometers (four miles) away.

and top regional wines, the restaurant is possibly Pag Town's best and has a shady courtyard to boot.

INFORMATION AND SERVICES
Pag's **tourist office** (Katine, tel. 023/611-286, www.tzpag.hr, 8am-10pm daily June-Sept., 8am-3pm Mon.-Fri. Oct.-May) can help out with brochures, maps, and hiking routes.

Novalja
Novalja, north of Pag Town, enjoys its reputation as a party destination, packing in young tourists to the local discos and DJ bars. For those not into the party scene, Novalja still has a couple of gems. The only real tourist sight in town is the small **Town Museum (Gradski muzej)** (Ul. kralja Zvonimira 27, tel. 053/661-160, www.muzej. novalja.hr, 9am-1pm and 6pm-10pm June-Sept., 15Kn), showing exhibits on local life, culture, and history as well as highlighting finds from a 1st-century Roman ship just off the coast. Licensed divers can explore the site, now protected by a giant iron cage, free of charge.

Pag's most popular beaches are centered around Novalja, with something for almost every type of tourist. Novalja's **Zrće** beach is round-the-clock party central with

poolside lounging and beach volleyball during the day and DJ-fueled dancing by night. The clubs there offer a free shuttle from Novalja's waterfront, so it's easy to get there even without a car.

Just north of Novalja in Stara Novalja is the sandy **Trincel** beach, often overcrowded but packed with services and restaurants.

Nudists will find a portion of **Straško** beach reserved just for them. Families will appreciate the other parts of the two-kilometer (one-mile) stretch, bordered by pine forests plus cafés and snack stands for hungry swimmers.

ENTERTAINMENT AND EVENTS
Partygoers will appreciate the summer's full schedule of live concerts and DJs, with activities focused in Zrće beach. You can reach clubs **Papaya, Aquarius,** and **Kalypso,** which operate 24 hours a day in season, by hopping on a free shuttle on Novalja's seafront, usually in front of the **Cocomo** bar.

ACCOMMODATIONS AND FOOD
Budget travelers should check out the beachfront **Kamp Straško** (tel. 053/661-226, www.kampstrasko.com, 1,100Kn for a mobile home, 217Kn for a pitch) with camping spots and mobile homes that can sleep up to four people. The hotels in Novalja are

largely overpriced. If you're determined to stay in town, try renting a room or apartment through a local agency like **SunTurist** (Kranjčevićeva bb, tel. 053/661-226, www.sunturist.com).

The nicest hotels are outside of Novalja. The lovely **Hotel Luna** (Jakišnica bb, tel. 053/654-700, www.lunaislandhotel.com, 900Kn d, including breakfast) is a 20-minute drive to the north, in a beautiful location with sleek modern rooms, indoor and outdoor pools, and a sauna. Closer to Novalja, on a hillside just far enough away from town for peace and quiet, you'll find the ★ **Hotel and Winery Boškinac** (Novaljsko polje bb, tel. 053/663-500, www.boskinac.com, 1,420Kn d, including breakfast), a statuesque tile-roof villa with cozy rooms and a terrace perfect for relaxing with a glass of wine from their vineyards.

The hotel's restaurant ★ **Boškinac** (Novaljsko polje bb, tel. 053/663-500, www.boskinac.com, lunch and dinner Tues.-Sun., closed Jan.-mid-Feb., reservations required, 120Kn) is also one of the best in the area, with traditional dishes made with ultra-fresh ingredients and access to the large wine cellar, stocked with house and international varieties.

Around Pag

The eastern side of the island has several pretty beaches, though some may say the landscape is more lunar than beach-like. **Ručica,** two kilometers (1.25 miles) from the village of Metajna, is one of the nicest, and even has a small restaurant on the hillside above that signals lunch and dinner with the ringing of a bell. You'll need a car to enjoy a day here.

Sv. Duh, located on the eastern side of the island about 10 kilometers (six miles) from Novalja, is a good choice if you're looking for sand. Half of the beach is used by nudists, and the beach charges a small entrance fee (around 5Kn).

A beautiful walk through the ★ **Lun Olive Gardens (Vrtovi lunjskih maslina)** (Lun bb, tel. 053/665-067, www.vlm.com.hr, 8am-3pm Mon.-Fri.) is a wonderful way to spend an hour amidst the olive trees, many of which are over 1,000 years old.

the island of Pag

Getting There and Around

If you're driving to Pag, you can either cross the bridge (almost 30 kilometers/19 miles north of the village of Posedarje) just off the Magistrala, connecting you with the southern end of the island, or take the hourly ferry from Prizna (look for signs off the Magistrala) to Pag's northern tip, close to Novalja.

Those without a car can rely on buses connecting Rijeka and Zadar that stop on the island of Pag. Rijeka to Pag Town takes about four hours and costs around 150Kn, while Zagreb to Pag Town takes around six hours and costs approximately 250Kn. These buses are the island's only form of public transportation connecting Novalja and Pag Town, though there are almost 10 daily in the summer and they cost around 35Kn.

A catamaran run by Jadrolinija (daily in summer, three times a week Oct.-May, www.jadrolinija.hr) connects Novalja with Rijeka (three hours, 80Kn) and Rab Town (one hour, 45Kn).

Northern Dalmatia

Northern Dalmatia does not have the block-
buster destinations of its southern counterpart, but its charming
coastal towns are full of Roman-Veneto architecture and make great
departure points for discovering private retreats.

The real standouts of Northern Dalmatia are Zadar, with lots of
Roman relics and a culture all its own, and the Kornati Islands, a small
wild archipelago with national park status. As for overlooked highlights, Šibenik's old town is a must-see that's also a good place to get
out of the way of many of the summer's tourists. There's also tiny but
lovely Trogir, full of fine well-preserved structures from the Middle
Ages, though it fills to capacity with holidaying Europeans in the summer months, making it a bit harder to see the charm.

Highlights

Look for ★ to find recommended sights, activities, dining, and lodging.

★ **The Forum in Zadar:** The forum is the central attraction in a town filled with Roman ruins and local culture. The giant square is littered with ancient columns and surrounded by churches and museums (page 210).

★ **Sea Organ (Morske orgulje):** Walk along Zadar's waterfront and listen to the sounds made by the waves (page 211).

★ **Dugi Otok:** A great choice for beach bums, this island's Telašćica Bay nature park is filled with spots for swimming and sunning (page 218).

★ **Hiking and Tours in Paklenica National Park:** Trek through the rocky karst landscape or take an off-road photo safari—and then reward yourself with sausages and beer for lunch at the creek-side Forest Hut (page 219).

★ **Lower Lakes (Donja jezera) in Plitvice Lakes National Park:** The pooling and cascading lakes in Plitvice are bordered by well-marked paths and lush forests. The lower lakes, closest to the main entrance, are highlighted by the park's biggest waterfalls—a must-see on the way to or from the coast (page 222).

★ **Kornati Islands:** Made up of a string of scruffy islands, this national park is filled with wildlife, deserted stone houses, and a flotilla of top-quality fish restaurants (page 224).

★ **St. Jacob's Cathedral (Katedrala svetog Jakova):** Juraj Dalmatinac's stunning cathedral is the highlight of Šibenik's sun-washed medieval core (page 226).

★ **Krka National Park:** Whether you only scratch the surface by visiting the stepped rushing falls at Skradinski Buk or continue on to the fairy-tale Byzantine monastery, this park's beauty makes it obvious why it's one of the region's most-visited destinations (page 231).

And cities aren't the only gems of the region. Natural beauty abounds in the area's national parks, in the karst landscape of Paklenica, the stunning Plitvice Lakes, the limestone cliffs of the Kornati, and the beautiful Krka, a rushing river punctuated by waterfalls. Though technically inland, the Plitvice Lakes, one of Croatia's busiest tourist destinations, make a great stop-off on your way to or from the coast or as a day trip from the Northern Dalmatian coastal towns.

It is a bit harder to find a good beach in this area, but they do exist, especially on some of the uninhabited islands just off the coast.

Good food is not at all hard to find here, with dozens of seafood restaurants and places serving spit-roasted lamb, one dish with which the region has lots of expertise.

PLANNING YOUR TIME

If you have only 2-3 nights, try to fit in Zadar, a trip to the Kornati Islands, and perhaps a stop at Jurlinovi Dvori for a taste of traditional Dalmatia and at the famous restaurant Torcida near Šibenik for some *janjetina* (lamb)—this will give you a nice overview of the region. If you have another day or two, spend the night in Šibenik's old town,

squeezing in a quick tour around town and a ferry to one of the islands just off the coast for a bit of relaxing. Trogir is close to Split, and even closer to Split's airport, making it convenient to spend half a day in transit.

Not surprisingly, the coastal towns and islands are busiest in July and August. Despite potential crowds around attractions and shops in Zadar and Trogir, you won't find yourself overwhelmed on some of the off-the-coast islands, where you can keep walking until you get to a patch of undiscovered pebble shore. However, the best times to visit are May, June, and September, when the limestone is warm with the sun, but not so warm you're immediately running for the shade. The tourist numbers are dramatically lower in these months, though if you're planning to party, spring and fall aren't the time for it. Most of the visitors during this time of year are retirees.

Winter can be either an excellent time to visit (some days turn out sunny and warm enough for only a light jacket) or an awful one (if the infamous *bura* is blowing). Some establishments, particularly on the islands, are closed during the winter months. However, it can be a good time to come if you want to have the entire region to yourself.

Previous: Šibenik; Lower Lakes of Plitvice Lakes National Park; hiking Paklenica National Park

Northern Dalmatia

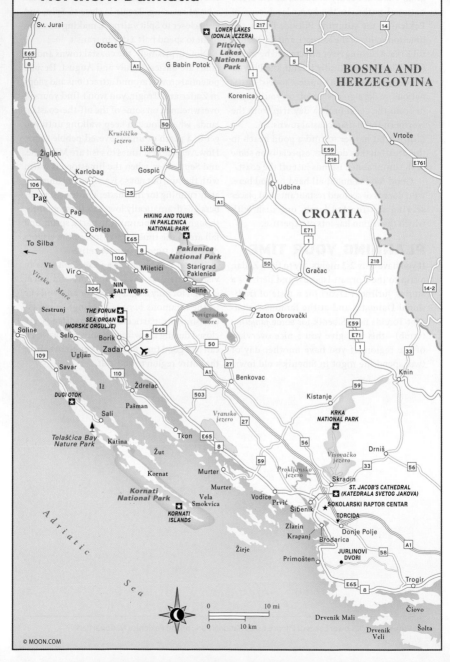

Sv. Jurai

Otočac

**LOWER LAKES
(DONJA JEZERA)**

217

*Plitvice
Lakes
National
Park*

14

G Babin Potok

E65
8

A1

5

14

1

Korenica

**BOSNIA AND
HERZEGOVINA**

50

*Kruščićko
jezero*

Žigljen

Ličko Osik

Vrtoče

E59
218

E761

Karlobag

Gospić

106

Udbina

Pag

25

Pag

A1

CROATIA

Gorica

**HIKING AND TOURS
IN PAKLENICA
NATIONAL PARK**

E71
1

To Silba

E65
8

*Paklenica
National Park*

Vir

Vir

Miletići

Starigrad
Paklenica

50

Gračac

218

14-2

106

*Virsko
More*

306

**NIN
SALT WORKS**

Seline

Sestrunj

**THE FORUM
SEA ORGAN
(MORSKE ORGULJE)**

*Novigradsko
more*

Zaton Obrovački

E59
E71
1

Soline

Selo

8
E65

33

Ugljan

Borik

Zadar

50

Knin

109

Savar

110

Benkovac

A1

27

59

Iž

Žddrelac

Pašman

503

Kistanje

59

DUGI OTOK

Sali

*Vransko
jezero*

27

**KRKA
NATIONAL PARK**

*Telašćica Bay
Nature Park*

Katina

Žut

Tkon

E65

8

56

Drniš

*Visovačko
jezero*

33

56

Kornat

Murter

59

*Prokljansko
jezero*

Skradin

*Kornati
National Park*

Murter

Vela
Smokvica

Vodice

Prvić

**ST. JACOB'S CATHEDRAL
(KATEDRALA SVETOG JAKOVA)**

**KORNATI
ISLANDS**

Šibenik

SOKOLARSKI RAPTOR CENTAR

TORCIDA

Zlarin

Donje Polje

A1

Krapanj

Brodarica

Žirje

**JURLINOVI
DVORI**

58

Primošten

Trogir

A d r i a t i c

E65
8

Čiovo

Sea

Drvenik Mali

Šolta

Drvenik
Veli

0   10 mi

0   10 km

© MOON.COM

Itinerary Ideas

BEST OF NORTHERN DALMATIA

One week is enough to see all the highlights of Northern Dalmatia, with plenty of time to stop and enjoy some sun and sea. This trip is easiest with a car, but not impossible by public transport if you are traveling in summer and plan your connections carefully (you may have to travel the evening before instead of the morning of, for example).

Day 1: Plitvice Lakes National Park

- Spend the day hiking and exploring the terraced lakes and waterfalls at **Plitvice Lakes National Park**, a UNESCO World Heritage site.

Day 2: Paklenica National Park

- Arrive at **Paklenica National Park** in the morning.
- Hike through the gorge to the **Forest Hut Lugarnica** for a light lunch.
- After exploring the park's cave, end the day with dinner at **Taverna Konoba Marasović**.

Day 3: Zadar

- Start your day in Zadar by entering the city at the port gate and buying breakfast provisions from vendors at the city's **market**.
- Head over to **The Forum** and St. Donat's Church for a peek into Zadar's history.
- Stop into **Bistro Kalelarga** for lunch.
- In the evening after dinner, head to the **Sea Organ** to sit and listen to music created by the sea.

Day 4: Dugi Otok

- Take a ferry from Zadar to **Dugi Otok** for a day relaxing on the beach and swimming.

Day 5 Kornati Archipelago

- Book a boat tour from Zadar to the **Kornati Islands**, making sure you stop to snorkel or swim in the surrounding fantasy-blue water.

Day 6: Šibenik

- Take your time this morning, but be sure to reach **Šibenik** by early afternoon and visit **St. Jacob's Cathedral.**
- Make a beeline for the **Medieval Mediterranean Garden of St. Lawrence's Monastery** for a coffee among the fragrant herbs.
- Head to **Pelegrini** for dinner, a local restaurant that has garnered international acclaim.

Northern Dalmatia Itinerary Ideas

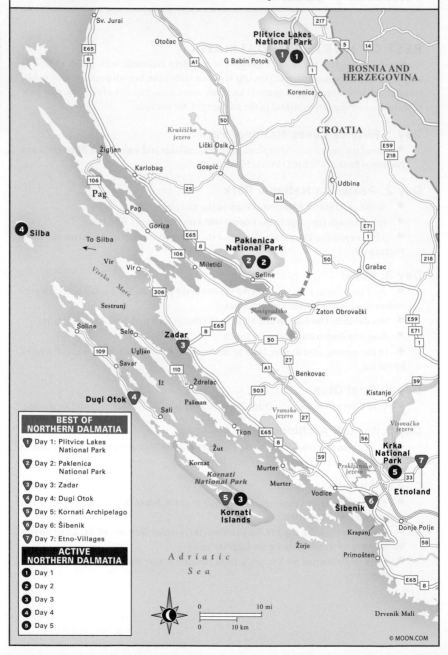

BEST OF NORTHERN DALMATIA

1 Day 1: Plitvice Lakes National Park
2 Day 2: Paklenica National Park
3 Day 3: Zadar
4 Day 4: Dugi Otok
5 Day 5: Kornati Archipelago
6 Day 6: Šibenik
7 Day 7: Etno-Villages

ACTIVE NORTHERN DALMATIA

1 Day 1
2 Day 2
3 Day 3
4 Day 4
5 Day 5

© MOON.COM

Day 7: Etno-Villages

- Leave Šibenik to visit **Etnoland** and get a taste of Dalmatian village life.

ACTIVE NORTHERN DALMATIA

For adventure seekers, Northern Dalmatia has lots of active pursuits, from hiking to rock climbing to scuba diving, to keep you entertained and on the go.

Day 1

- Get to the **Plitvice Lakes National Park** early so you can get a look at the Lower Lakes before taking the five-kilometer (three-mile) uphill trek to the Upper Lakes, where you will find fewer tourists. Don't forget your water bottle!

Day 2

- **Paklenica National Park** has good rock climbing, but you can also hike, or explore the park's **Manita Peć** cave.

Day 3

- From Zadar, book a scuba diving (or snorkeling, if you let your license lapse) trip to the **Kornati Islands** and explore the pristine waters of the archipelago.

Day 4

- Take a boat from Zadar to the island of **Silba,** where you can explore the car-free island by bike.

Day 5

- Combine hiking with a boat tour of the **Krka National Park**.

Zadar

Zadar is one of Dalmatia's larger cities, though it never feels big. The town has real soul—likely derived from all the hardships it has faced over the years. It was bombed over 70 times by the Allies in World War II, the reasons for which are still unclear, and held under siege during the Homeland War. Zadar has lots of interesting architecture—from the Roman to Austro-Hungarian municipal buildings. The city is home to Croatia's oldest university, established by Dominican monks in 1396, making it quite a vibrant town when school is in session. At other times, student numbers are replaced and tripled by tourists who pile in from the beach resorts nearby. The city is a great location from which to explore the area. While you'll find plenty of beach resorts in the surrounding areas, staying in the old city is a wonderful experience, a short jaunt to the beaches during the day and packed with things to do and places to eat at night.

HISTORY

Zadar (called Zara in Italian) was long under Venetian rule, and the Italian influence in town has always been strong. The city was even given to Italy in 1921 before being returned to Croatia as a part of Tito's Yugoslavia in the late 1940s.

Buildings ruined in World War II were replaced with a crop of modern structures,

Zadar

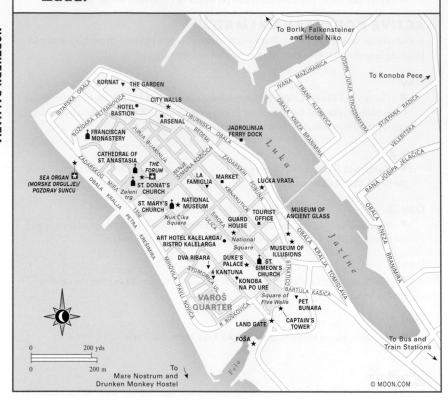

To Borik, Falkensteiner and Hotel Niko

To Konoba Pece

KORNAT THE GARDEN

CITY WALLS

HOTEL BASTION

ARSENAL

JADROLINIJA FERRY DOCK

FRANCISCAN MONASTERY

CATHEDRAL OF ST. ANASTASIA

THE FORUM

SEA ORGAN (MORSKE ORGULJE)/ POZDRAV SUNCU

ST. DONAT'S CHURCH

Zeleni trg

LA FAMIGLIA

MARKET

LUČKA VRATA

ST. MARY'S CHURCH

NATIONAL MUSEUM

Nun Čika Square

GUARD HOUSE

TOURIST OFFICE

MUSEUM OF ANCIENT GLASS

ART HOTEL KALELARGA/ BISTRO KALELARGA

ŠIROKA ULICA

National Square

MUSEUM OF ILLUSIONS

DVA RIBARA

DUKE'S PALACE

4 KANTUNA

ST. SIMEON'S CHURCH

KONOBA NA PO URE

VAROŠ QUARTER

Square of Five Wells

PET BUNARA

LAND GATE

CAPTAIN'S TOWER

FOŠA

To Bus and Train Stations

0   200 yds

0   200 m

To Mare Nostrum and Drunken Monkey Hostel

© MOON.COM

Luka

Jazine

Foša

giving the old town an organic feel as mid-century apartment blocks share walls with Austro-Hungarian buildings, discarded Roman columns less than a block away. The city received even more damage when Serbian paramilitaries and the Yugoslav People's Army (JNA) surrounded the city in 1991, not completely retreating until 1995.

It has taken Zadar some time to recover economically from the siege. However, the fishing industries, the ferry port, and the appeal of the old-town core, with its museums and Roman architecture, are bringing *kuna* and tourists back in droves as Zadar once again becomes a destination for those in the know.

SIGHTS

TOP EXPERIENCE

★ The Forum
(Trg Rimskog Foruma)

Zadar's main square is referred to as **The Forum,** though it looks a bit more like a graveyard for old Roman columns (only one of the Forum's original columns remains standing). You'll find a lot of the pieces recycled inside **St. Donat's Church (Crkva svetog Donata)** (Poljana pape Ivana Pavla II, 9am-5pm daily Apr., May, and Oct., 9am-9pm daily June, 9am-10pm daily July-Aug., closed Nov.-Mar., 20Kn), today only a tourist stop and a musical venue (due to the excellent acoustics). The stark Byzantine church was built at the beginning of the 9th century with remnants of columns, plaques, and other stone pieces the Romans left behind. In July and August the **St. Donat Musical Evenings** (www.donat-festival.com) are held inside.

At the northern end of the Forum, steps away from St. Donat's Church, is the **Cathedral of St. Anastasia (Katedrala svete Stošije)** (Trg Sv. Stošije, 8am-6pm daily summer, 8am-12:30pm daily winter, free), a late Romanesque church from the 12th and 13th centuries that displays some magnificent stonework. The interior has some beautiful 13th-century frescoes as well as the 9th-century sarcophagus of Saint Anastasia. For some super views of town, you can climb up the 56-meter (184-foot) 19th-century **bell tower** (9am-8pm daily summer, 10Kn), built by English architect T. G. Jackson.

Nun Čika Square
(Trg Opatice Čike)

Across from St. Donat's Church, Nun Čika Square connects to the southern side of the Forum. Here you'll find the **Archaeological Museum (Arheološki muzej)** (Trg Opatice Čike 1, tel. 023/250-613, www.amzd.hr, 9am-2pm Mon.-Fri., 9am-1pm Sat. Nov.-Mar., 9am-3pm Mon.-Sat. Apr., May, and Oct., 9am-9pm daily June and Sept., 9am-10pm daily July-Aug., 30Kn), whose plain building offers a stark modern contrast to the ancient relics around it. Inside, over 100,000 pieces from prehistoric times to the Romans to medieval times can be found on the museum's three floors, including a model of the Forum as it once was.

Next to the Archaeological Museum is the 11th-century **St. Mary's Church (Crkva svete Marije)** (Trg Opatice Čike, tel. 023/250-496, 8am-12pm and 5pm-8pm daily, free), with a 16th-century facade that was bombed during Allied raids on Zadar. The church is pleasant, and is a mish-mash

of styles, from original recycled Roman columns to ornate Baroque balconies added in the 19th century, but the real finds are in the church's museum. The exhibit **Gold and Silver of Zadar (Zlato i srebro Zadra)** (Trg Opatice Čike, tel. 023/250-496, 10am-1pm and 5pm-7pm Mon.-Sat., 10am-1pm Sun. summer, 10am-12:30pm and 5pm-6pm Mon.-Sat., 10am-12:30pm Sun. winter, 30Kn) is a treasure trove of sacred art, caskets, icons, and Byzantine crafts housed in the *samostan* (convent) next door to the church.

Franciscan Monastery
(Franjevački samostan)

Zadar's **Franciscan Monastery** (Zadarskog mira, tel. 023/250-468, www.svetifrane.org, 9am-6pm daily, 20Kn) is said to have been founded by Saint Francis in 1219. Thought to be the oldest Gothic church in Dalmatia, it has an interior that is mostly Renaissance. There's not much to see beyond a few graves, though the well at the center of the courtyard garden is rather poignant given it was one of the few sources of drinking water for the city during the Homeland War of the early 1990s.

★ Sea Organ
(Morske orgulje)

Built in 2005, the **Sea Organ,** located on the Obala kralja Petra Krešimira IV, is the inventive idea of local architect Nikola Bašić. The organ looks like a set of giant steps; the power of the waves forces interesting organic sounds out of the openings between the stairs. At night you can watch a stunning light show, **The Greeting to the Sun (Pozdrav Suncu),** also by Bašić, where a 22-meter (72-foot) circle soaks up sun in its solar panels during the day and starts to emit a glowing amalgam of colors at night.

City Walls

From the Sea Organ you can walk along the 16th-century city walls down the Liburnska obala to the southeastern **Port Gate (Lučka vrata),** fashioned from a Roman triumphal arch into a Renaissance grand entrance topped with the Lion of Venice. There's a wonderful morning **market** (7am-1pm daily, tourist stalls stay open later) near here on Krnarutića, where you can buy fresh produce and bread for a makeshift picnic lunch as well as a smattering of touristy souvenirs.

National Square
(Narodni trg)

Past the market on Krnarutića, make a right onto Jurja Barakovića toward National Square, now more of a main square than the larger Forum, which was once center stage. Here you'll find a 16th-century **Guard House (Gradska straža)** with a big clock tower and the **Town Loggia (Gradska loža)** (Poljana Pape Aleksandra III, tel. 023/251-851, www.nmz.hr, 9am-10pm daily summer, 9am-8pm Mon.-Fri., 9am-1pm Sat.-Sun. winter, 80Kn), now an art gallery and concert venue for the town. Admission to the gallery also gets you into the **National Museum (Narodni Muzej)** (Poljana Pape Aleksandra III, tel. 023/251-851, www.nmz.hr, 9am-10pm daily summer, 9am-8pm Mon.-Fri., 9am-1pm Sat.-Sun. winter, 80Kn). The well-presented museum, located back toward the Port Gate (follow Široka to Poljana Pape Aleksandra III and turn right), has a display chronicling Zadar's history, paintings and relics from nearby towns, and scale models of Zadar through the centuries.

St. Simeon's Church
(Crkva svetog Šimuna)

Most people come to the 17th-century **St. Simeon's Church** (Trg Šime Budinića, tel. 023/211-705, 8am-12pm and 4pm-7pm daily summer, 8am-12pm daily winter, free) to see the opulent casket of Saint Simeon. Fashioned of some 250 kilograms (550 pounds) of silver, supported by four equally ornate bronze angels, it holds the body of Saint Simeon, one of Zadar's patron saints. There are various legends surrounding the body and its casket. The body supposedly came to Zadar when a merchant shipping it from the Holy Land to Venice fell ill and died here. The identity of the body was said to be revealed to local priests in a dream. The casket, commissioned by Elizabeth, Queen of Hungary, in the late 14th century, some centuries after the death of Saint Simeon in the 5th century, has a legend of its own. The story goes that she had the casket built in remorse after she stole one of the saint's fingers and it began to decompose. Once the digit was returned to its proper place, the decay miraculously stopped.

A short walk away, the **Museum of Ancient Glass (Muzej antičkog stakla)** (Poljana zemaljskog Odbara 1, tel. 023/363-831, www.mas-zadar.hr, 9am-9pm daily summer, 9am-4pm Mon.-Sat. winter, 30Kn) displays primitive and ancient glass with occasional displays of glassblowing. If you like glass or are craving powerful air-conditioning, it's worth a stop.

Museum of Illusions
(Muzej Iluzija)

A popular addition to the list of touristy things to do in Zadar, the **Museum of Illusions** (Poljana Zemaljskog Odbora 2, tel. 023/316-803, www.zadar.muzejiluzija.com, 9am-12am daily June-Sept., 10am-8pm daily Oct.-Nov. and Apr.-May, 10am-4pm daily Dec.-Mar., 60Kn) is a fun-for-all-ages experience showcasing how the eyes and the mind can play tricks on you. Multiple exhibits make for fun photo ops, and the tunnel that makes you feel as if you are walking upside down is quite interesting.

Duke's Palace
(Kneževa Palača)

The **Duke's Palace** (Poljana Sime Budinica 3, tel. 023/627-765, www.knezeva.hr, 9am-12am daily summer, 10am-8pm daily winter, 80Kn), built in the 13th century, was the historic building to have suffered the most extensive damage during the Homeland War. Carefully restored and reopened in 2017, the

---

1: Sea Organ, Zadar 2: the archaeological site of the Roman Forum in Zadar 3: Narodni trg square in Zadar 4: Zadar's market

museum has an interesting permanent exhibition called "Six Salon Stories," which uses historical rooms to chronicle the history of Zadar. Temporary exhibitions can be excellent as well and have included pieces from renowned international artists such as Marc Chagall.

Square of Five Wells
(Trg pet bunara)

The Square of Five Wells was once Zadar's main source of drinking water. These days it's frequented by young locals looking for a bit of recreation—summer brings frequent concerts and performances to the square. Here you'll find the **Captain's Tower (Kapetanova kula)** (10am-1pm and 5pm-8pm Mon.-Fri., 10am-1pm Sat. summer, 10Kn), a five-sided tower built by the Venetians to defend the city against the Turks. Currently it's being used as an exhibition space for Croatian artists.

Nearby you'll find the **Land Gate (Kopnena vrata)** near the Foša harbor, lined with eerie-looking cattle skulls, supposedly to scare off attackers during the days when it served as the main entrance to the city.

Varoš Quarter

On the way back toward the Forum from the Square of Five Wells, the Varoš quarter is one of Zadar's prettiest neighborhoods, filled with winding streets and little shops. The winding **Stomorica street** is packed with cafés for an afternoon coffee.

Around Zadar

The **Nin Salt Works (Solana Nin)** (Ilirska Cesta 7, tel. 023/264-021, www.solananin.hr, 8am-12pm and 5pm-8pm daily summer, call for winter hours, 40Kn) produces salt the old-fashioned way—with sun, sea, and wind. A tour takes visitors through the salt flats and salt harvesting. Learn about flower salt, an unprocessed salt rich with seaweed that is said to provide numerous health benefits. The salt works also has a small museum shop where you can purchase the products.

BEACHES

There's not a lot to choose from in terms of beaches in Zadar. Some people swim offshore where the Sea Organ is located, but most head to **Borik,** a package-hotel mecca a short drive away (take bus 5 from Zadar, about 10 minutes). Better yet, take a ferry excursion to one of the **islands** in Zadar's archipelago.

ENTERTAINMENT AND EVENTS
Nightlife

Low-key evenings can be found in the bars and cafés around the Stomorica in the Varoš quarter, worthy of a little pub crawl. Another option is the **Arsenal** (Trg Tri bunara 1, tel. 023/253-833, www.arsenalzadar.com, 7am-3am daily summer, call for off-season hours), which bills itself as a multipurpose arts venue. Located in a renovated 18th-century warehouse, the expansive space with soaring ceilings is the perfect place for sipping wine or a cocktail, browsing the small gallery, or listening to a local band of jazz or *klapa* singers. Arsenal also has small shops selling clothing, crafts, and local wines.

For something livelier, head to the crazy buzz-worthy The Garden and The Garden Zadar, which also host a summer music festival. **The Garden** (Liburnska obala 6, tel. 023/364-739, www.thegardenzadar.com, 10am-1am daily summer) is a British-owned club bringing in live bands and well-respected DJs to an outdoor space that's bustling day and night. Choose from cocktails, tapas, and a solid beer list. The owners of The Garden opened **The Garden Zadar** (Punta Radman put 8, Petrčane, tel. 023/364-739, www. thegardenzadar.com, 10am-1:30am summer) in 2008. The seaside location is more of an upscale young beach bar than a lounge club like The Garden.

Festivals and Events

The highlight of Zadar's summer season is the **St. Donat's Musical Evenings** (July and Aug., www.donat-festival.com), with outstanding classical concerts from international performers. Even better is the location, in St. Donat's Church. **Zadar Theatrical Summer (Zadarsko kazališno ljeto)** (late June-Aug.), a mostly Croatian group of performers, stage theater and dance performances all over the city's historic core during the summer season.

ACCOMMODATIONS

For students and those stretching their *kuna* as far as possible, the **Drunken Monkey Hostel** (Ulica Jure Kastriotica Skenderberga 21, tel. 021/314-406, www.themonkeytroophostels.com, 150Kn pp) can get a little rowdy, but its location, a 20-minute walk to the old town and near some nice beaches, is wonderful. There is also a small pool and a bar on-site, and it's a good choice if you consider yourself a member of the young party crowd. If you'd like to rent a room or apartment in or around Zadar (there are even a handful in the old town), try **Jaderatours** (Poljana Pape Aleksandra III 5/1, tel. 023/250-350, www.jaderatours.hr).

Mare Nostrum (Sveti Petar, tel. 023/391-420, www.marenostrum-hr.com, 750Kn d, including breakfast) is very simple and no-frills, but a great location right on a nice pebbly beach between Zadar and Biograd elevates it a bit. The hotel is small, so it fills up quickly during the high season into the early fall.

The outside looks like any old restaurant, but the **Hotel Niko** (Obala Kneza Domagoja 9, tel. 023/337-880, www.hotel-niko.hr, 1,306Kn d, including breakfast), located in Puntamika, a suburb north of Zadar, is a great place to stay with cozy rooms upgraded from the standard of most Croatian family hotels. It's only a few meters from the sea and it takes about 20 minutes to get into the heart of Zadar from the bus stop in front.

Though saying **Falkensteiner Club Funimation Borik** (Majstora Radovana 7, tel. 023/206-636, www.falkensteiner.com, 1,564Kn d) is a bit of a mouthful, the all-inclusive hotel about 10 minutes from Zadar by car is perfect for families, with sleek rooms and family suites, a huge kids club, a playground, and a mini water park. Room rates include three meals and use of facilities. Guests without kids can enjoy the hotel's spa services and consider booking a room in the quieter and more luxe **Adriana wing** (1,846Kn d).

Built on the remains of a medieval fortress, the **Hotel Bastion** (Bedemi zadarskih pobuna 13, tel. 023/494-950, www.hotel-bastion.hr, 1,600Kn d, including breakfast) opened in 2007. The boutique hotel is pleasant, bordering on luxurious, with a waterside terrace restaurant and a small cellar-like spa. Located steps from the Sea Organ and other sights in Zadar's old town, it's convenient, pretty, and the best value in Zadar proper.

Quite possibly the best accommodations in Zadar, ★ **Art Hotel Kalelarga** (Majke Margarite 3, tel. 023/233-000, www.arthotel-kalelarga.com, 1291Kn d) is a boutique design hotel with rooms out of a magazine. Centrally located in the old town and above one of the city's best restaurants, you can't go wrong.

FOOD

Had enough fish during your coastal visit? Head to **4Kantuna** (Varoska 1, tel. 091/313-5382, www.restaurant4kantuna.com, 11am-10pm daily in season, call for off-season hours, 80Kn) for excellent wood-fired pizza, but also pastas and risottos in a great atmosphere. **La Famiglia** (Knezova Šubića Bribirskih, tel. 091/140-7005, 8am-12am daily, 50Kn) is a great spot for burgers and *ćevapi*.

Kornat (Liburnska obala 6, tel. 023/254-501, 11am-11pm daily, 90Kn) is a refined place without the attitude. The wine list is excellent and the menu is peppered with gourmet features like truffles and monkfish. Don't miss the restaurant's fish stew, *na gregadu*.

On the chic and trendy side of Zadar's gastronomic offerings are two restaurants with the same owner. The first, **Dva Ribara** (Blaža Jurjeva 1, tel. 023/213-445, 10am-11pm daily, 95Kn), means "two fishermen," but the menu is actually stronger on the meat side of things. In the heart of town, it has a minimalist interior that contrasts nicely with the ancient surroundings. Ask for a glass of the house wine, much cheaper than the wines listed in the *vinska karta*. Dva Ribara's swankier sister, **Foša**

(Kralja Dmitra Zvonimira 2, tel. 023/314-421, 12pm-12am daily, 140Kn), has been a staple of the restaurant scene for some time now, but the food does not match the atmosphere or the prices. Go for a glass of wine and an appetizer and then head to ★ **Pet Bunara** (Stratico 1, tel. 023/224-010, www.petbunara. com, 11am-11pm daily, reservations recommended, 110Kn) for top-notch local cuisine in an attractive setting next to the city's Square of Five Wells (Trg pet bunara).

Another high-end option at reasonable prices, **Bistro Kalelarga** (Majke Margarite 3, tel. 023/233-000, www.arthotel-kalelarga. com, 8am-10pm, open later in summer, 90Kn) offers excellent seasonal dishes—cold cucumber soup, fennel, homemade pastas—in a chic old-town setting.

A bit out of the way in Vinjerac but worth the trek is ★ **Konoba Pece** (Draga 2, tel. 02/327-5069, 4pm-11pm daily, 80-120Kn), off the main road near the Maslenica bridge. The food is out-of-this-world good—grilled octopus done to perfection, prawns in mustard seed sauce—and it has a great terrace. It can get insanely busy in season and sometimes it is hard to get a table at all, which is the only drawback anyone could find to the restaurant.

INFORMATION AND SERVICES

You can find more information, maps, advice, and free brochures from Zadar's **tourist office** (Narodni Trg, tel. 023/316-166, www. tzzadar.hr, 8am-12pm daily July-Aug., 8am-8pm daily June and Sept., 8am-3pm Mon-Fri. Oct.-May).

Zadar's main **post office** (Kralja S Držislava 1, tel. 023/316-552, 7:30am-9pm Mon.-Fri., 7:30am-8pm Sat.) can help you send a postcard home.

There are three spots in town for left luggage. Try the **bus station** (Ante Starčevića 1, tel. 023/211-555, www.liburnija-zadar.hr, 6am-10pm Mon.-Fri., 15Kn per day), the **train station** (Ante Starčevića 4, tel. 052/212-555, www.hzpp.hr, 24 hours daily, 15Kn per day),

or the **Jadrolinija ferry dock** (Liburnska obala 7, tel. 023/254-800, www.jadrolinija.hr, 7am-8pm Mon.-Fri., 15Kn per day).

In the old city, the clean and comfortable **Laundry Lounge** (Jurja Biankinija 9, www. self-service-laundry-zadar.com, 8am-8pm daily) is not only convenient but offers free Wi-Fi as well.

GETTING THERE AND AROUND

Zadar Airport (ZAD, tel. 023/313-311, www. zadar-airport.hr) is about a 10-minute drive east of town. Croatia Airlines runs buses (25Kn) into town that coincide with their flights. If you're flying with another carrier, you can wait for the next bus or take a **taxi** (tel. 023/251-400, 180-220Kn).

Zadar is a large ferry port with connections to Pula (five hours), Ancona in Italy (seven hours), and multiple points in the Zadar archipelago. **Jadrolinija** (Liburnska obala 7, tel. 023/254-800, www.jadrolinija.hr) runs almost all of the ferry connections.

The **bus station** (Ante Starčevića 1, tel. 023/211-555, www.liburnija-zadar.hr, ticket office 6am-10pm daily) and **train station** (Ante Starčevića 4, tel. 052/212-555, www. hzpp.hr, ticket office 7:30am-9pm daily) are located next to each other about a 15-minute walk southeast of the old town center. You can also take local bus 5 or hop in a taxi (about 75Kn). Buses tend to be faster than trains for getting to Zagreb or Split. Bus connections are plentiful: Zagreb (almost two dozen buses daily in summer, five hours, 220Kn), Rijeka (six daily in summer, five hours, 200Kn), Split (eight daily in summer, three hours, 120Kn) and Dubrovnik (seven daily in summer, eight hours, 275Kn). You can also take a fast train to or from Zagreb (two daily, seven hours, 160Kn); the advantage of the bus is that it's quicker and stops at Plitvice, although getting on again is slightly more difficult.

Around town, you can take the rowboats, located between the Liburnska obala and Obala kneza Trpirmia shores. Just show up and they'll shuttle you back and forth for about 10Kn. Buses to Borik are marked "Puntamika." Buses to the harbor next to the old town are marked "Poluotok." Bus tickets run 6Kn each way if bought from a newspaper kiosk and 10Kn if purchased on board.

Islands Around Zadar

If you're looking for a bit of lounging seaside, some of Northern Dalmatia's most beautiful coastline is only a short ferry ride away. The islands of the Zadar archipelago are some of the least touristed in Croatia, leaving you with lots of unspoiled beauty to enjoy. Most of the islands are an easy day trip during the summer, when daily ferries connect them with Zadar's harbor. In winter it might be necessary to make an overnight trip in order to visit these wild islands.

UGLJAN

So close to Zadar it's almost a part of the city, the relatively undeveloped island of Ugljan fills up on weekends as locals head to its shores. The island has two marinas for boaters. The **Olive Island Marina** (tel. 023/335-809, www.oliveislandmarina.com) offers a pool, a playground, and a restaurant, while the ecofriendly **Preko Marina** (tel. 023/286-169, www.marinapreko.com) is close to Preko's ferry port, where buses haul travelers out to the island's villages. Hourly ferries from Zadar take about 30 minutes and cost around 20Kn.

Beaches near the ferry dock get very crowded. Ask the **tourist office** (tel. 023/286-8388, tzpreko@preko.hr, www.preko.hr) in Preko about renting a bike to explore the less-developed western side of the island, or find a water taxi to take you out to the islet of **Galevac,** just offshore, for some of the best swimming. Galevac has a 15th-century monastery and nice beaches backed by thick woods to provide a bit of shade.

Your best option for accommodations on Ugljan is a private room or apartment, booked by visiting the local tourist office on Preko's main square or via their website (www.preko.hr).

PAŠMAN

The sleepy little island of Pašman has some friendly fishing villages and a 12th-century fortress, now a monastery, in the village of Ugrinći. For swimming, try the coast south of **Tkon,** the busiest town on the island. Here you'll discover plenty of sandy shores near the Sovinjc nudist resort. If you'd rather your fellow bathers stay clothed, the pebbled beaches of Lučina, on the northern side of the island near Pašman Village, are another option.

You can inquire about campsites or book a private room through the **tourist office** (tel. 023/260-155, www.pasman.hr). There are a couple of friendly, clean pensions in town, such as the **Vila Kruna** (Kraj 122a, tel. 023/285-410, www.vila-kruna.com, 425Kn d). The **Lanterna** (Pašman Village, Obala bb, tel. 023/260-179, www.lanterna.hr, 382-786Kn) has a good restaurant (10am-10pm, 80-110Kn) with fresh fish, most of which is cooked in a stone oven.

Get to Pašman by taking the ferry from Zadar to Ugljan and then taking a bus (almost 10 daily in summer, 25 minutes). The bus first stops in Pašman Village and ends at Tkon, the island's official center.

IŽ

Iž is a tiny, slightly unkempt-in-a-good-way island with two main villages, Veli Iž and Mali Iž. There's not much to do here besides swim, eat, and hike the paths cutting through the slightly wild olive trees. Iž is also near Zadar and is served by a daily car ferry, which drops you in Bršanj, not the best village if you don't have a car, or the weekly ferries, which drop you in the much more developed Veli Iž. The island is relatively undeveloped, leaving private rooms and apartments the best options for lodging. Try the **Apartmani Strgačić** (tel. 023/319-484, www.apartmani-strgacic.hr, 450Kn d) in Veli Iž, which also organizes fishing expeditions.

The **Hotel Korinjak** (tel. 023/277-064, www.korinjak.com, 490Kn d) is a typical relic of the Tito days, a big concrete block in a good location with basic rooms and basic service. Though the hotel hasn't updated its facilities, it has updated its marketing angle, now focusing on vegetarianism and wholesome living.

There's a smattering of restaurants down by the harbor, where you can get a good meal or a strong coffee.

★ DUGI OTOK

With a name that literally means "long island," and at 50 kilometers (31 miles) long and 4.5 kilometers (2.7 miles) wide, Dugi Otok is the largest of the islands forming the Zadar archipelago. Dugi Otok is arguably its prettiest as well, with quirky geography forming dozens of indented coves and a cliff-backed coastline. The biggest draw of the island is the **Telašćica Bay nature park** (Ulica Danijela Grbin bb, Sali, tel. 023/377-096, www.pp-telascica.hr, 40Kn), where you'll find some nice swimming and a saltwater lake, **Mira Lake (Jezero mira).** The park is just a few kilometers from the village of Sali, a great distance for a bike ride if you don't have a car (and perhaps even if you do).

If you're looking for something a little less quiet, try the sandy **Sahuran beach** just south of Veli Rat.

The best lodging on the island is in private rooms and apartments, which can be booked through the island's **tourist office** (Obala Perta Lorinija bb, tel. 023/377-094, tz-sali@zd.t-com.hr, www.dugiotok.hr, 8am-9pm daily July-Aug., 8am-3pm Mon.-Fri. Sept.-May), located in the village of Sali. Try the **Picić Guesthouse** (Luka 5, tel. 091/1762-450, 280Kn d) for clean rooms, a waterfront location, and excellent food. The **Hotel Maxim** (tel. 023/291-291, www.hoteli-bozava.hr, 1,165Kn d, including breakfast and dinner) is another option for an overnight. Reconstructed and decked out with a slightly garish facade, the hotel has a nice swimming pool and is located directly on the sea. For a nice tavern atmosphere and good local fish specialties, try **Kod Sipe** (Sali 174, tel. 023/377-137, 10am-12am summer, call for off-season hours, 80Kn).

Dugi Otok's Telašćica Bay nature park

Taking a day trip to Dugi Otok is really only a possibility in summer (June-Aug.), since ferry connections from Zadar (1.5 hours) get rather sporadic the rest of the year. There are at least two ferries daily in summer (check with the Jadrolinija office in Zadar's harbor, tel. 023/254-800, www.jadrolinija.hr), letting you off at points like Brbinj, Božava, and Sali. Buses between the towns are few and infrequent, so if you're traveling without a car, try to get a ferry that docks in Sali, the best entry point to the Telašćica Bay park, or Zaglav, where a bus to Sali meets the ferry.

SILBA

This car-free island, the northernmost island of the Zadar archipelago, is filled with lots of peaceful coves and beaches, perfect for cyclists and families. The peaceful part is somewhat altered in summer when the year-round population of several hundred is augmented by lots of visitors that descend on the elegant little Silba, lined with patrician merchants' houses and courtyard gardens from its seafaring days. Beaches west of Silba Town are definitely the prettiest and offer some spectacular sunsets. The island's **tourist office** (tel. 023/370-010, www.silba.net, 8am-12pm Mon.-Sat. July-Aug., call for off-season hours) has a list of private rooms and apartments. For nourishment try **Konoba Mul** (Port mul, tel. 023/370-351, 11am-11pm daily July-Aug., call for off-season hours, 75Kn), serving good fish dishes and salads in pleasant surroundings next to the bobbing boats in the little harbor.

There are several boat connections daily with Silba in the summer months. Zadar has the most, though note that the catamarans (1.75 hours) are the fastest. The car ferries can take around 3.5 hours since they have other stops to make. It's also possible to connect with Pula (six connections weekly in summer), Rijeka (one connection weekly in summer), and Lošinj (six connections weekly in summer). Contact **Jadrolinija** (www.jadrolinija. hr) about current schedules and prices.

Paklenica National Park

TOP EXPERIENCE

Paklenica National Park, founded in 1949, is the best place for trekking through the craggy karst landscape of Northern Dalmatia. Just a couple of kilometers from beaches and package-holiday hotels, nature lovers can lose themselves (hopefully not literally) in the park's gorges, peaks, and caves. The park also offers wonderful opportunities for rock-climbing fans, and the less-active traveler can still take advantage of the rocky wilderness on an off-road safari.

The small town of **Starigrad Paklenica** is the best base for seeing the park and as a center for lodging and food. Buses connecting Rijeka and Zadar usually stop in Starigrad Paklenica (note that many locals refer to it simply as Starigrad, but it's best to add the Paklenica to keep it from getting mistaken for another Starigrad, near Senj). The park is about two kilometers (1.2 miles) north of the town.

At the ticket booth at the entrance to the park, you can buy **tickets** (one-day high season 50Kn, plus 15Kn for entrance to Manita Peć cave) and pick up a free map of the park's trails, or visit the **park office** (Dr. F. Tuđmana 14a, tel. 023/369-202, www. np-paklenica.hr, call for hours) in Starigrad Paklenica before setting out. The office sells detailed maps and can help you plan your trip.

SPORTS AND RECREATION
★ Hiking and Tours

Paklenica is filled with some 150 kilometers (93 miles) of mapped hiking routes. Most routes will take at least two hours round-trip, though you can wind your way through the park for a few days if you like. Just after

Bura Winds

You'll hear it talked about all over Croatia's Adriatic coast. The *bura* is a cold—sometimes bitterly so—northerly or northeasterly wind that can chill you even on a sunny winter's day on the islands. That's not to say the *bura* can't blow any time of year, but it's that extra cold gusting wind in winter that really gets attention. The Velebit mountain range is the hardest hit by the *bura;* Kvarner is second. The *bura* can come out of nowhere. One moment it's calm and clear, and a few hours later winds in the range of 200 kilometers per hour (124 miles per hour) are whipping against sailboats and bridges, making all forms of transportation hazardous.

However, the *bura* actually contributes to a lot of the character of the coastal regions. Most of the towns are built densely, with narrow streets to counteract the winds. And it's the winds that cure the area's top-quality *pršut* as well.

you leave the ticket booth, you'll see the **Paklenica Mills (Paklenički mlinovi)** (8am-7pm daily summer, by arrangement with the park office off-season). The seven corn- and grain-grinding mills were in use until the 1960s, serving the area and even the outlying islands. Today there are demonstrations of the water-driven mills as long as the water flow is heavy enough to operate them.

Continuing up the main trail, following the Velika Paklenica gorge, you'll find a series of underground **tunnels** built by the Yugoslav government to shelter high-level officials in the event of an emergency. At the time of this writing, the tunnels are closed for construction, but the park plans to open them in the future for events and exhibitions.

Serious hikers will not be put off by the challenging climb to reach the **Manita Peć cave.** The cave must be visited with a park **guide** (guided tours 10am-2pm Sat. Apr., 10am-2pm Mon., Wed., and Sat. May-June and Oct., 10am-2pm daily July-Sept., by arrangement Nov.-Mar., 15Kn). The trip will take about 1.5 hours one-way to see the 175-meter-long (109-mile-long) cave filled with lots of dripping stalactites and stalagmites.

The mountain has a superb small rest stop for lunch, the **Forest Hut Lugarnica** (10:30am-4:30pm May-Oct. daily, 30Kn), about a two-hour walk from the parking lot, depending on which path you take. The location is beautiful, next to a rushing stream,

though you will need to watch small children carefully. Sausages, bean stew, and beer are offered along with sodas, coffees, and doughnuts.

For those who don't want to go it alone, the park offers half-day and full-day guided tours as well as specialized tours for bird-watchers. Tours can be arranged in advance through the park office.

There are several options for those who don't want to trek for hours at a time but want to see the beauty of the Velebit Mountains. The **Starigrad Paklenica tourist office** (Trg Tome Marasovića 1, tel. 023/369-245, www.rivijera-paklenica.hr) can hook you up with agencies providing **boat trips** up the Zrmanja River, and the owner of the Hotel Rajna organizes **photo safaris** (tel. 023/369-130, www.hotel-rajna.com) through the Velebit in 4WD vehicles.

Climbing

Paklenica National Park is a great spot for rock climbers, with some 400 routes, both single-pitch and multi-pitch, available. The park office also sells a detailed climbing guide. It's often best to forget about climbing in the winter months, when strong *bura* winds might just blow you off the cliff.

ACCOMMODATIONS

Most accommodations are found in the village of Starigrad Paklenica, though the park has its own **Camp National Park** (Dr. F. Tuđmana 14a, tel. 023/369-202, www.np-paklenica.hr, from 40Kn pp), located on a stretch of pebbly beach next to the main park office in Starigrad Paklenica. Due to the small size of the camp, reservations are not possible.

For slightly cushier digs, the friendly family **Hotel Rajna** (Ul. Dr. F. Tuđmana 105, tel. 023/369-130, www.hotel-rajna.com, 340Kn d, including breakfast) is quite a comfy two-star hotel with most basic creature comforts. If you're traveling with friends or want to splurge a bit, the owner also has a charming stone cottage ★ **Varoš** (tel. 023/369-130, www.hotel-rajna.com, 2,340Kn), which sleeps 15, a 15-minute walk to Paklenica National Park. The 1850-era building is furnished tastefully and traditionally.

FOOD

The restaurant at the **Hotel Rajna** (Jadranska cesta 105, tel. 023/359-121, 6:30am-11pm daily Jan. 15-Dec., 85Kn) has good grilled fish and meats and fish stew. However, the real treat is ★ **Taverna Konoba Marasović** (Trg Marasović, near Entrance 1 to the park, 1pm-9pm daily summer, 100Kn) in a rustic setting near the entrance of the national park. The restaurant has a lovely terrace, tasty local dishes, and dramatic ambience. It also has a small ethnographic museum and souvenir shop. It's highly recommended to eat in the late evening when the stars start to appear in the sky.

GETTING THERE AND AROUND

Paklenica National Park is located about 200 kilometers (124 miles) south of Rijeka and 45 kilometers (28 miles) north of Zadar on the coastal road. If you're driving, head to Starigrad Paklenica and then follow the brown signs labeled "N.P. Paklenica" to the entrance of Paklenica Park, about two kilometers (one mile) north of Starigrad Paklenica. Parking is available at the entrance to the park; a better option is another lot, past the info point.

Buses between Rijeka and Zadar often stop at Starigrad Paklenica to pick up passengers (unless they're full, which can happen often in the summer); they'll drop you off if you ask. From Zagreb, the best bet is to take a bus to Zadar and connect with Starigrad Paklenica (1.25 hours, 28Kn). There is no public transportation to Paklenica National Park; those without a car will have to walk the two kilometers from Starigrad Paklenica to the park.

Plitvice Lakes National Park

One of the country's biggest attractions, the 16 lakes of Plitvice Lakes National Park are some of Croatia's most stunning scenery. Though the park is technically inland, travelers most often stop off on their way to or from the coast or via excursions offered from coastal towns.

Plitvice has long been a destination; visitors started to arrive in the late 19th century to admire the natural wonders. The park was under Serb control from 1991 to 1995, with forces using the hotels as barracks. It didn't take long to repair the damage to the buildings and flood the area with travelers once again.

The color of the lakes is turquoise blue or deep green, and the park is filled with giant trees and lots of wildlife. Formed by thousands of years of calcium carbonate deposits, the lakes are held by a natural travertine dam that grows a little each year. The lakes were declared a national park by Yugoslavia in 1949. A UNESCO World Heritage site since 1979, with close to one million tourists seeing the lakes every year, the park is definitely worth a visit. It's also easy to visit, with dozens of paths, lots of information, and an organized system of shuttle buses and boats included in the entrance fee.

SIGHTS

Plitvice Lakes National Park (tel. 053/751-015, www.np-plitvicka-jezera.hr, 7am-7pm daily, ticket sales 7am-5pm, 250Kn summer, 150Kn spring and fall, 55Kn winter) has two entrances from the old Zagreb-Split road, both with helpful information centers, though Entrance 2 (closest to local accommodations) used to be closed in winter. As you walk along the paths and bridges, keep an eye out for wildlife, particularly birds; there are over 100 species.

In summer 2018, the lakes were so popular that the park was occasionally closed during peak visiting hours due to overcrowding. It may be advisable to arrive either before 9am or later in the day, around 4pm, depending on how long you want to spend in the park.

★ Lower Lakes
(Donja jezera)

Entrance 1 (Ulaz jedan) on the northern end of the park is considered the main entry point. It's here that you're closest to the most-touristed spot, the **Big Waterfall (Veliki Slap),** about 78 meters (256 feet) tall. It's about a 10-minute walk to the Big Waterfall; paths from there can take you to other waterfalls or to the shuttle boat toward Entrance 2.

The lower lakes include Kaluđerovac Lake, Gavanovac Lake, and Milanovac Lake, small lakes punctuated by waterfalls and a couple of caves (near Kaluđerovac Lake). These feed into the large Kozjak Lake, the largest of Plitvice's bodies of water and the boundary between the lower and upper lakes.

At the top of Kozjak you'll have the option of taking a shuttle (included in the entrance fee) to Entrance 2, at the southern end of Kozjak, or to continue along the footpath on the eastern shore.

Upper Lakes
(Gornja jezera)

Reached by trekking about five kilometers (three miles) from Entrance 1 or south from Entrance 2 (Ulaz dva), the upper lakes are some of Plitvice's most beautiful, and also

not quite as busy. Near the park's hotels, you'll find Gradinsko Lake and then Galovac Lake, where the water descends like stairs, dropping into a series of sparkling blue pools. Galovac is followed by Okrugljak Lake, where waterfalls take center stage, and then Ciginovac Lake and Prošćansko Lake. If all the uphill walking is too much, a good option is to take the shuttle from Entrance 2 to Okrugljak Lake and then walk down.

ACCOMMODATIONS AND FOOD

A good choice for budget travelers, **Camp Korana** (tel. 053/751-888, www.np-plitvicka-jezera.hr, bungalows 227Kn d, including breakfast) has spots for tents as well as small private bungalows (actually huts) with communal baths. The main downside to the camp is that it's about six kilometers (3.7 miles) from the park entrance. Rooms at **Hotel Degenija** (Selište Drežničko 59, tel. 047/782-143, www.hotel-degenija.com, 1020Kn d) are pricey in the high season, but they are very modern and well-appointed. The service is friendly, and the restaurant is nice as well. Even though the Degenija's rooms are nicer, the **Plitvice Hotel** (tel. 053/751-100, www.np-plitvicka-jezera.hr, 700Kn d, including breakfast) has an excellent location, just a five-minute walk to the park; its time-warp communist era vibe has unfortunately been eliminated in an update, which is clean and fresh but nothing special. Don't stay here for the rooms or the subpar food—run elsewhere for dinner—but for the convenience.

There are several restaurants around Entrance 2, though the best is across from Entrance 1, the **Lička kuća** (Entrance 1, tel. 053/751-024, 11am-11pm daily Apr.-Oct., 85Kn), with lots of regional specialties and traditional hearty food like spicy sausage stew. The place is touristy but it's also very good. Even better is to buy some bread and fresh tomatoes from the supermarket and local

---

1: Plitvice Lakes National Park **2:** Paklenica National Park is particularly popular among climbers.

homemade cheese from the usually present vendors. The rounds are typically sold whole, but if you ask for half *(pola)* you'll probably strike a deal. The cheese has a slightly nutty, smoky flavor that hits just the right chord on a crisp night.

GETTING THERE AND AROUND

Plitvice is located about 90 kilometers (56 miles) south of Karlovac and 160 kilometers (100 miles) northeast of Zadar. If you're driving to Plitvice, just follow the signs from the highway or the old coastal road. Arriving by bus is fairly easy—most buses going from Zagreb (2.5 hours) to Split (3.5 hours) or other Dalmatian cities will stop here as they pass by; they'll drop you off if you ask, stopping in front of either of the two entrances. Getting back on a bus can be trickier since there's not much in the way of schedules and they won't stop if they're full. As a result, if you don't have a car, it's probably best to book a Plitvice excursion trip (around 350Kn), advertised widely at travel agencies all along the coast.

Murter and the Kornati Islands

If you've ever wondered what it would be like to live on a deserted island, you can probably find a spot in the Kornati archipelago, a largely wild national park, to answer any lingering questions. The town of Murter is the gateway to the islands and also a spot for lodging before embarking on your journey.

MURTER

There's nothing much to say about Murter except that it's the handiest point of departure for the Kornati archipelago. Since Kornati doesn't have a lot in the way of lodging, you're more likely to have luck here, planning your trip from the **Kornati National Park office** (Butina 2, tel. 022/435-740, www.np-kornati. hr, 8am-3pm Mon.-Fri. June-Sept., call for off-season hours), which sells permits for diving and fishing as well as maps, or from local agencies where you can rent a boat or book an excursion. **Eseker Tours** (Majnova bb, tel. 022/435-669, www.esekertours.hr) rents all sorts of things like bikes (60Kn per day), scooters (45Kn per hour), boats (from 300Kn per day for a simple fishing boat to 2,900Kn per day for an extra-fancy motorboat), and personal watercraft (75Kn for 10 minutes).

For dining try **Tic-Tac** (Vlade Hrokešina 5, tel. 022/435-230, 12pm-11pm daily May-Sept., reservations recommended, 85Kn), on a small street not far from the main square. The decor is simple but the menu is nothing less than gourmet. Dishes like tuna carpaccio, cuttlefish in black sauce with polenta, and gnocchi with fish roe and prawns are surprisingly sophisticated for such an unassuming little place. It has been a staple in Murter for years, though in the height of summer the quality can diminish when the tiny restaurant tries to keep up with demand.

A more reliable choice in season, the always-excellent **Fine Food Murter** (Mainova 5, tel. 091/121-0093, 10am-12am daily in summer, call for off-season hours, 110Kn) is decidedly gourmet: think truffles, fish carpaccio, and some of the best fish soup you will have on the coast.

Getting to Murter is easiest from Šibenik or Vodice. Buses (7-10 per day) connect to the island, conveniently disembarking at Murter's main square. There are also several ferries connecting from Šibenik and Zadar—check with **Jadrolinija** (www.jadrolinija.hr) for fares and prices.

★ KORNATI ISLANDS

The Kornati Islands stretch out south of Zadar's coast. The archipelago was declared a national park in 1980 and remains one of the most stunning landscapes in Croatia.

The islands were once covered with oak trees, burned to make way for sheep pastures. Instead of taking away the beauty of the islands, it might have made them prettier. The bright-white, slightly scruffy karst rock formations are a beautiful contrast with the clear blue waters, which are home to lots of local fish, such as bream, eel, sea scorpion, and cuttlefish. The waters around the islands, particularly the eastern edges if the sea is not too rough, are a wonderful place to snorkel or scuba dive.

There's proof of Illyrian and Roman settlements on the islands, though the islands were mostly uninhabited, owned by Zadar's aristocracy, until the 19th century. After that, locals from the islands of Murter used them to raise sheep. Sheep aren't tended on the islands today, but you'll see some wild descendants, although 1,300 died during the drought of 2007, as well as a number of abandoned stone cottages, mostly dating from the early to mid-20th century, occasionally inhabited in summer by their owners from Murter, who defected long ago. Other than the sheep, there's not a lot of wildlife save for the occasion lizard, snake, or bird.

The islands are immensely popular with yachters, so even though there's not a lot of lodging, there are multiple places for an amazing seafood lunch or dinner. If you'd like to stay on Kornati, you can rent one of the abandoned stone cottages through an agency in Murter, who will leave you there for several days with a stash of supplies, in case you ever wanted to see for yourself what it's like on one of those survival reality shows.

Food

Whether it's thanks to the number of yachts and fancy sailboats that cruise around Kornati, occasionally mooring in the coves and harbors, or simply a local sensibility for good food—or both—the fact remains that Kornati is a treasure trove of excellent restaurants. There are at least 17 restaurants in the uninhabited island chain, almost one for every nautical mile. Not fancy restaurants, mind you—you're likely to sit on plastic chairs—but you'll have an awesome view and cuisine that would satisfy even the toughest food critic. Best of all, you can tie your boat up right in front, eat to your heart's content, and then keep on sailing. One note: The restaurants don't really have menus; they basically fix whatever they've caught. Figure on paying 80Kn-120Kn for a main dish, much more for lobster.

Katina Island: Mare's (Vela Proversa, tel. 098/273-873, 10am-12am daily, cash only) has been a fixture on Kornati since the 1950s; the family who owns it has been on the island since the 19th century. The family still tends a grove of olive trees, producing sweet organic oil, and they grow the vegetables served alongside the main dishes. If it's available, try the *Brudet od ljutice i janjetina s krumpirom* (shallot soup and lamb with potatoes).

Strižnja Bay, Kornat Island: The menu at ★ **Darko's,** also known as **Konoba Strižnja** (Uvala Strižnja, www.konoba-striznja-kornati.hr, 8am-12am daily Apr.-Sept., cash only), is quite simple—you'll get whatever it is that Darko caught that day, baked or broiled, alongside fish soup and octopus salad. In fact, the owner makes it a principle to never serve less than the best quality, so if you want lamb, you'd better come in the spring when it's at its most tender.

Vrulje, Kornat Island: Ante's (Uvala Vrulje, tel. 022/435-025, 10am-12am daily, cash only) is a back-to-basics restaurant run by a true fisherman. The octopus *(hobotnica)* à la Veneziana, a thick tomato-based stew with more than a hint of red wine, is highly recommended. However, prices can be high for what you're offered.

Opat Cove, Kornat Island: A stone house with green shutters nestled on a rocky, barren hill is the location for **Opat** (Uvala Opat, Luke 47, tel. 022/435-061, 9am-12am daily), a family restaurant known for its brick oven-baked seafood, like scorpionfish with potatoes. The atmosphere of the restaurant is the main draw.

Vela Smokvica Island: Located in a deep blue cove, **Piccolo** (Obala Smokvica Vela, tel.

022/435-106, 7am-12am daily May-Sept., cash only) is one of the islands' most popular restaurants. It's a family-run business: The wife cooks what the husband catches. Dine on lots of fresh grilled seafood, or fish stew seasoned with paprika.

Getting There and Around

There are no ferries to Kornati. To visit, you have two choices: Travel on your own boat (you'll need an international captain's license) or take an organized tour of the islands. Tours can be booked through the many agencies in Murter or by signing up with one of the clipboard-wielding young people along Murter's harbor. Most of the excursions include a tour, a swim, and lunch for around 250Kn pp. If you'd like to explore the island with more freedom and you don't have a captain's license, inquire in Murter at the **Kornati National Park office** (Butina 2, tel. 022/435-740, www.kornati.hr, 8am-3pm Mon.-Fri. June-Sept., call for off-season hours).

Šibenik

One of the most overlooked towns in the country, Šibenik has a wonderful old town, not too packed with visitors even at the height of the season and with some great lodging finds. An important location in Venice's fight to hold off the Turks, the town flourished in the Middle Ages, and in modern times as well, when a big aluminum plant kept the locals employed. However, the war in the 1990s changed all that, with the plant closing (it's now a decaying relic along the Magistrala) and the city falling on hard times.

Most Croatians would probably wrinkle their noses if you mention Šibenik, since it has never really been an attractive destination. There are no resorts to speak of or real beaches. So why would you go? The old town center, for one, is totally charming and almost perfectly preserved, yet it doesn't have any of the made-for-travelers feel that many other cities with lots of historic buildings have. Though you won't find any mega-resorts, the center is packed with character-filled apartments where you can live like a local during your vacation, heading down to one of the town's best cafés for breakfast and a coffee with the other regulars. And who needs a town beach when you can walk down to the ferry dock and hop on a boat for a 20-minute or one-hour ride to an island almost devoid of cars, with wild natural beaches that are much less crowded than any near the resorts?

Basically, if you know how to work Šibenik, you'll love it, particularly if you're a contrarian who likes to stay away from tourist-laden spots.

SIGHTS

★ St. Jacob's Cathedral
(Katedrala svetog Jakova)

Outshining all of the town's pretty architecture and churches, the 15th-century **St. Jacob's Cathedral** (Trg Republike Hrvatske, tel. 022/214-899, 9:30am-8pm Mon.-Sat., 1pm-8pm Sun. July-Aug., 9am-6:30pm Mon.-Sat., 1pm-6pm Sun. Sept.-May, free) glows over Šibenik's old-town waterfront. The church was built by local architect Juraj Dalmatinac, among others, since it took over 100 years to complete. The inside is luxurious, with lots of gilt and a soaring ceiling topped by an octagonal dome. The most interesting features, however, are on the Gothic and Renaissance facade. The building is encircled by 71 stone heads—according to legend the faces of those townspeople who didn't pony up for the construction, making the addition of the dog head all the more humorous. The top of the dome itself is beautiful, with a gilt-topped cupola and four somber statues guarding the town and sea below, but it's

Šibenik

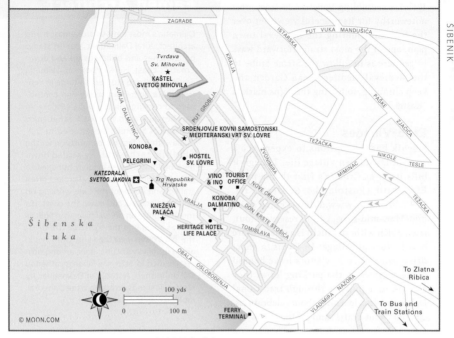

hard to catch a glimpse of them unless you climb the steps next to the loggia (above the Republic of Croatia Square) and look back from the top.

Duke's Palace
(Kneževa palača)

To the south of St. Jacob's Cathedral down a small alleyway, you'll come to the 15th-century Duke's Palace. Inside, the **City Museum (Muzej grada Šibenika)** (Gradska vrata 3, tel. 022/213-880, www.muzej-sibenik.hr, 10am-8pm Mon.-Sat. summer, 10am-1pm Mon.-Sat. winter, 30Kn) has exhibits on a variety of historical periods and people, such as architect Juraj Dalmatinac, as well as interesting temporary exhibits.

Republic of Croatia Square
(Trg Republike Hrvatske)

The large square to the eastern side of St. Jacob's Cathedral is the Republic of Croatia

Square, flanked by the town hall and its 16th-century **loggia,** today home to a café.

Medieval Mediterranean Garden of St. Lawrence's Monastery
(Srdenjovje kovni samostanski mediteranski vrt Sv. Lovre)

Opened in 2007, the **Medieval Mediterranean Garden of St. Lawrence's Monastery** (Strme stube 1, tel. 022/212-515, www.spg.hr, 8am-11pm daily summer, call for off-season hours, 15Kn) recreates a medieval garden, heavy on herbs and indigenous plants. A must for gardeners, it's also the perfect place to have a coffee or a drink among the fragrant lavender and thyme on your way to or from the city's old fortress.

St. Michael's Fortress
(Kaštel svetog Mihovila)

From pretty much anywhere in the old town,

you can climb up to the northeast to find **St. Michael's Fortress** (about 9am-dusk daily, 10Kn), a crumbling Venetian fortress most noteworthy for its peaceful views out over the bay. Considering the medieval town plan, one of the most straightforward ways to get here is to follow the Strme Stube to the Medieval Mediterranean Garden and keep climbing, following the signs marked "Kaštel."

Etno-Villages

Šibenik has two options to experience a taste of Dalmatian village life. Though it bills itself as Croatia's first theme park, **Etnoland** (Postolarsko 6, Drniš, tel. 099/220-0205, www.dalmati.com, daily mid-Mar.-mid-Nov., call to reserve a tour, from 30Kn without lunch) is actually more of a historical village. In Drniš, a short drive from Šibenik, visitors leave behind modern times in the parking lot as they embark on a journey through traditional Dalmatian life, learning about celebrations, customs, and crafts, and seeing mock-ups of houses from a century ago. Though you can wander through the park alone, most guests book a tour that lasts 3.5 hours and includes a traditional Dalmatian lunch. The park opened in 2007 and is well planned if a bit touristy. The Jurlinovi dvori complex on the hills of nearby Primošten is more authentic in feel.

Even more touristy but nice and especially fun for kids is the **Dalmatian Ethno Village** at the Solaris Resort (Hoteli Solaris 86, tel. 022/361-001, www.solarishotelresort.com, call for reservations and cost) just outside of Šibenik, featuring an entire working Dalmatian village just steps from the beach. A mill, an olive oil producer, a pastry shop, a weaver, traditional musicians, and even a mini vineyard give a condensed overview of Dalmatian culture, and the complex also has a good restaurant and bar. Combined with time on the Solaris beach and a playground for kids, water park, and mini golf, it's an easy day out for the family.

Juraj Dalmatinac, Famed Architect

Dalmatia's most famous stonemason and architect, Juraj Dalmatinac, put his stamp on churches and buildings up and down Croatia's coast. He was born in Dalmatia around 1400 and studied his trade in Venice, where he had an atelier and contributed to carvings on the Doge's Palace. In Italy he was known as Giorgio da Sebenico (George of Šibenik); he returned to Dalmatia with his first big commission for the **Šibenik cathedral.** He settled down here, building a house in town, but due to a lack of funding, the cathedral project often stalled, and he spent the time working on other projects up and down the coast. His touch is found on several palaces in Split as well as an altar in the **Split cathedral,** the **Minčeta Fortress** in Dubrovnik, and a loggia in Ancona, Italy, among others. He died in 1473, the Šibenik cathedral still unfinished. A statue of Dalmatinac by Meštrović stands across from the cathedral, looking over the water.

BEACHES

Šibenik itself has nothing in the way of beaches, but there are plenty of nearby spots for sun and surf, making the city an easy point of departure. A few beaches are accessible by car, though unless you're with the kids, there's little to recommend them. The Solaris hotel complex (drive south of town on the Magistrala and look for the signs, or take bus 6) has a sandy beach, a new bar area constructed of authentic stone huts, and plenty of video games and bouncy castles for the little ones. However, the best beaches are a short water taxi or ferry ride away. The first, closest to Šibenik's center, is the tiny island of **Zlarin,** known for its coral jewelry; it's about 20 minutes across the water. There's an excellent *konoba* at the end of the marina's dock and two shops specializing in expensive (or overpriced, depending on your view) coral jewelry; they fill to capacity as soon as every ferry lands. Otherwise the island is very quiet, with a small pebbly beach to the left of the marina when you're facing the island and concrete bathing areas farther on. Keep walking around to find a really wild and beautiful stretch of deserted beach—not so good for swimming, given the winds and the rocks, but perfect for wading and lounging in solitude.

Another choice of island excursions is the slightly farther afield **Prvić** (45-minute ferry ride from Šibenik), a car-free island covered with pines and herbs sprouting out of rocky stretches. The best beach on the island is at **Šepurine.** If you'd like to stay overnight, unlike the hordes of day-tripping visitors, the simple but lovely 16-room **Hotel Maestral** (tel. 022/448-300, www.hotelmaestral.com, 920Kn d, including breakfast), located in an old stone house in Prvić Luka, is a great spot.

Šibenik's harbor is the spot to catch the usually twice-daily ferries to the islands. Check with the Jadrolinija office at the harbor for schedules and prices, since even the schedule posted outside the office is not always correct.

ENTERTAINMENT AND EVENTS
Festivals and Events

If you're looking for a bit of Dalmatian flavor in Šibenik, Thursday evenings in July and August bring out local *klapa* **groups;** contact the **tourist office** (Obala Dr. Franje Tuđmana 5, tel. 022/214-411, www.sibenik-tourism.hr) for more details. The end of August is heralded by two days of varied musical performances during the **Dalmatian Chanson Evenings (Večeri Dalmatinske Šansone)** (www.sansona-sibenik.com), though the city's biggest event is the **International Children's Festival (Međunarodni Dječji Festival)** (www.mdf-sibenik.com), held for two weeks from the end of June to the beginning of July every year since 1958. The town hosts dozens of performances, art exhibitions, and hands-on educational exhibits, all revolving around children.

Shoppers will appreciate the weekly **antiques fair** (8am-3pm Sat.) around the St. Francis Church (Crkve Svetog Frane). The antiques fair operates additional days in the summer.

ACCOMMODATIONS

Šibenik has some beautifully renovated apartments and homes for rent on websites like Airbnb (www.airbnb.com) and Booking.com (www.booking.com) that are not only a great deal but can also land you a spot in the old town. The **Konoba** (Andrije Kacića 8, tel. 091/198-8989, www.bbdalmatia.com, 533Kn d) is owned by a lovely Dutch family and decorated simply but tastefully. One of the apartments has a wonderful balcony with a view over the old town's rooftops, though it does lack air-conditioning.

The **Hostel Sv. Lovre** (Andrija Kacića 11, tel. 022/212-515, www.hostelsvlovre.com, 186Kn pp) is a lovely, clean hostel set next to the herbal gardens. The hostel also offers a variety of language and culture courses for visitors, often sold as a package with accommodations.

A wonderful addition to the town's hotel offerings, the ★ **Heritage Hotel Life Palace** (Trg Sibenskih Palih Boraca 1, tel. 022/558-128, www.hotel-lifepalace.hr, 1,200Kn d, including breakfast) is close to the cathedral. This boutique hotel, located in an expertly renovated historic building, has beautifully decorated rooms and heated bath floors for winter mornings. The hotel also has a whirlpool tub and a small sauna on the rooftop.

FOOD

In the heart of the old town, try **Konoba Dalmatino** (Fra Nikole Ružića 1, tel. 091/542-4808, generally 11am-10pm daily summer, call for off-season hours, 75Kn), nestled in a narrow alleyway with a handful of outdoor tables serving good cheese, salads, and fish dishes alongside the potable house wine—not the finest, but homemade by the restaurant's owner, who often doubles as a waiter. A welcome addition to town, hip little **Vino & Ino** (Fausta Vrancica bb, tel. 099/827-8893, www.vinoiino.hr, 8am-12am daily, 80Kn) serves excellent local wines alongside cheese plates

and snacks. However, the best table in town has to be at ★ **Pelegrini** (Jurja Dalmatinca 1, tel. 022/213-701, www.pelegrini.hr, 11am-12am daily, 200Kn), just across from the gorgeous St. Jacob's Cathedral. In good weather you can dine at the few outdoor tables overlooking the water (ideal for wine and a snack) or in the open-air courtyard just beyond the restaurant. In the winter, dine inside the restaurant's pretty stone-clad space. Any time of year, the excellent menu, from snacks of olives, cheese, and salted anchovies to mains of roasts, risotto, and seafood ravioli, never fails to satisfy. It recently earned a well-deserved Michelin star for its attention to detail.

If you have a car or you're willing to foot the bill for a water taxi (actually a nice way to spend a few minutes), **Zlatna Ribica** (Krapanjskih Spužvara 46, tel. 022/350-695, www.zlatna-ribica.hr, 11am-11pm daily, 100Kn), in the seaside village of Brodarica, a few kilometers/miles south of Šibenik on the Magistrala (drive, hop a water taxi, or take bus 7), is considered one of the area's finest. The decor is average, but the fish is always fresh, and the view to the tiny island of Krapanj is very nice. The restaurant also rents rooms. It has been a staple in the area for decades.

INFORMATION AND SERVICES

The **Šibenik tourist office** (Obala Dr. Franje Tuđmana 5, tel. 022/214-411, www.sibenik-tourism.hr) has some information on the area, but the travel agencies on the Republic of Croatia Square, **Atlas** (tel. 022/330-232) and **Cromovens** (tel. 022/212-515, www.cromovens.hr), may be more useful at hooking you up with private rooms and excursions in the region.

GETTING THERE AND AROUND

Šibenik's **bus station** (Draga 14, tel. 060/368-368) is close to the ferry terminal and a short

five-minute walk south from the old town. The bus heads frequently to Split (close to two dozen buses per day, two hours, 60Kn), Zadar (close to four dozen per day, 1.5 hours), Dubrovnik (several per day in summer, six hours), Rijeka (around a dozen per day in summer, six hours), and Zagreb (over a dozen per day in summer, 6.5 hours, 235Kn). Tickets on city buses cost around 10Kn. Bus schedules can be found online (www.atpsi.hr).

Šibenik also has a **train station** (Fra Jeronima Milete 24, tel. 022/333-699) with a couple of daily connections to Zagreb (6.5 hours, 150Kn) and Split (two hours, 43Kn). Ferries in town only travel to nearby islands and have no major connections to places like Split.

By car, you can connect with Split (south) or Zadar (north) by simply following the Magistrala or getting back on the highway (a little quicker but less scenic).

AROUND ŠIBENIK
★ **Krka National Park**

Krka National Park (www.npkrka.hr, 110Kn May-June and Sept.-Oct., 200 Kn July-Aug., 30Kn Jan.-Mar. and Nov.-Dec.) follows the rushing Krka River between Knin and Skradin. Skradin is located only a 15-minute drive northeast of Šibenik. Local buses connect Šibenik with Skradin (around eight connections Sat.-Sun., two or three Mon.-Fri., 30 minutes), and the excursion is an easy day trip from Šibenik.

The entrance, at the village of Skradin, is where you can pick up **boat tours** (Mar.-Nov., 70Kn) run by the national park, while at the Lozovac entrance, a shuttle bus goes down to the river. Keep in mind that if you want to go farther up the river from Visovac to the Krka monastery (additional 70Kn Mar.-Nov.), as described here, you should depart early in the morning—the tour takes around four hours round-trip and schedules make it into a whole-day affair. If you'd like to do the longer tour, it's a good idea to stop in Šibenik at the **Krka National Park office** (Trg Ivana Pavla II 5, Šibenik, tel. 022/217-720, www.

1: islands of the Kornati National Park **2:** old town Šibenik **3:** the Cathedral of St. Jacob (Sv. Jakova) in Šibenik **4:** Krka National Park

npkrka.hr) for more information, or book a package tour through one of the travel agencies in Šibenik.

Boat tours departing from Skradin first stop in the village of **Skradinski Buk,** where a series of small **waterfalls** rush over the craggy outcroppings of limestone. One of the falls spills into a nice pool where you can swim, though you certainly won't be the only one taking a dip. You'll also find some peaceful **hiking trails** through the forests and over the river. From here, you can catch the bus to Lozovac, or continue farther upriver on a boat, visiting the fairy-tale **Franciscan monastery** on the tiny island of Visovac; **Roški slap,** another set of waterfalls; and finally the **Krka monastery,** a Byzantine-style Serbian Orthodox church and monastery filled with icons and art dating as far back as the 14th century.

You can arrange for private accommodations through Skradin's **tourist office** (Obala bana Šubića 1, tel. 022/771-306, www.skradin.hr) or stay at a guesthouse such as the **Malin Guesthouse** (Aleja Skradinskih Svilara 15, 280Kn d, including breakfast). If you must have a hotel, the **Hotel Skradinski Buk** (Burinovac bb, tel. 022/771-771, www.skradinskibuk.hr, 684Kn d, including breakfast), has rather bland rooms, but the value for money is better than most hotels in the area. There are several good restaurants around the village of Skradinski Buk. Try **Restoran Skala** (Rukovaca 7, tel. 095/884-5801, www.restoran-skala.com, 9am-12am summer, 11am-11pm winter, 140Kn), with a beautiful, quiet location and a nice terrace.

Wineries

The ★ **Bibic Winery** (Zapadna ulica 63, Plastovo, Skradin, tel. 022/775-597, www.bibich.co, tasting 10am-7pm daily summer, call for winter hours) in Skradin is a must-visit to taste the local wines, which get their unique flavor from wood and are among the best in the region.

Sokolarski Raptor Center (Sokolarski Centar)

The **Sokolarski Raptor Center** (Škugori bb, tel. 091/506-7610, www.sokolarskicentar.com, 9am-7pm daily summer, contact for winter hours, 45Kn), located eight kilometers (five miles) from Šibenik, rehabilitates falcons and owls. An educational presentation and a chance to meet the feathered residents is not only fun but environmentally friendly, too.

Krapanj Island

If you're a good swimmer, you could technically swim from the coast in Brodarica (a few kilometers south of Šibenik, take bus 7 or a water taxi) and reach the shores of tiny Krapanj Island, just several hundred meters offshore. Its claim to fame is as the smallest inhabited island in Croatia, but it's really known for its sponge diving, the trade that kept it alive for decades. Today, sponge diving has largely died out, but the 15th-century **Franciscan monastery (Franjevački samostan)** has a simple **museum** (9am-12pm and 5pm-7pm Mon.-Sat. June-Sept., 15Kn) following the history of sponge divers on the island. It gets packed in July and August with day-trippers (take a taxi boat from Šibenik or Brodarica), but if you're lucky enough to visit in the off-season, it's a sleepy island with its own personality.

Southeast of Šibenik

Thirteen kilometers (eight miles) southeast of Šibenik (take the Magistrala toward Split, and soon turn off on the road toward Vrpolje) is legendary restaurant ★ **Torcida** (Donje Polje 42, tel. 022/565-748, www.restoran-torcida.hr, 8am-11pm daily, 80Kn), famous for its *janjetina,* or spit-roasted lamb. On weekends you'll find it hard to get a table; it's enormously popular with the local population. It's definitely worth the detour for a taste of true Dalmatia. Don't expect amazing service, don't order anything besides lamb and sides (it's what they do best), and go with the flow of the locals.

Acquiring a Taste for *Janjetina*

Janjetina, or spit-roasted lamb, is a sacred food to many Croatians, particularly those along the coast. Consumed on special occasions and de rigueur at Easter, the best lamb is found in ramshackle roadside establishments on the way to the beach.

Janjetina can be a bit of an acquired taste. In my case, it just seemed sort of, well, fatty, I guess, and not very flavorful. When they served it, I felt like I was in a medieval court, with the pieces of meat seemingly hacked off at random and piled on a platter and people digging in without forks or knives. Word got around about me not being a fan of lamb, and suddenly friends and family had made it their mission to introduce me to this food of foods. We were invited to every *roštilj* (cookout) for miles around, with a plate of lamb coming to me first, to see if this would be the one that would succeed in the collective mission to convert me.

Approximately 14 years after I'd first tried *janjetina,* we were spending the week in Šibenik, and after having consumed fish for five days straight, my husband mentioned to our friend Mickey that he'd like some *janjetina.* And between Šibenik and Split there is only one real place to go for *janjetina:* **Torcida** (Donje Polje 42, tel. 022/565-748, www.restoran-torcida.hr, 8am-11pm daily, 80Kn). Torcida is also the name of Split's soccer fan club, so chances were pretty good it would be excellent, since Dalmatians do not take anything relating to their soccer lightly. Torcida is in the middle of nowhere, way up the hill from the coast. Once you think you have certainly passed it and are hopelessly lost, keep going until you see about four dozen cars parked in the arid landscape. Torcida tries to be more than a cinder-block establishment with granite-tile floors, but sophisticated it is not.

Out back is a veritable factory of lamb-on-a-spit, with a dozen spits spinning a dozen lambs. Inside, the tables are packed with families, young and old, most wearing some Italian designer or other, pulling meat off the bones with their teeth, wiping their hands every once in a while on a napkin, taking toothpicks from the handy container in the middle of the table.

The waitress came out to take our order, no menu or pad and pen in sight—because what else would we order anyway? Our table ordered a bottle of white wine, a bottle of mineral water (you mix the two together to make *gemišt*), and lamb.

It was summer and the restaurant was hot. A sign on the front door boasts that it is *klimatazirano* (air-conditioned), but with 500 bodies squished table to table inside, the air-conditioning unit was on the losing end. We refreshed with a couple of glasses of *gemišt* and the waitress came with a basket of bread, a plate of tomatoes and spring onions, and a platter of lamb, still warm from the fire.

Everyone started with forks and knives, but five bites in we were all using fingers to pull and turn and get the sweet meat into our mouths any way possible.

"This is not lamb," I said.

"Ah, but it is." Mickey smiled. "The best lambs are from Dalmatia. And you should see the ones from the islands." In Dalmatia, and on islands like Pag, the sheep and lambs feed on little aromatic herbs that grow between the rocks. "It's like marinating them from birth," Mickey explained.

Whatever it is, that was all I needed to convert. Torcida was what I was looking for. Like my favorite barbecue restaurants back home, it has no pretensions. The decor is nothing special—except, perhaps, for the large framed painting of the Mona Lisa smoking a joint (removed the last time I visited). I faded into a food-induced coma. And I wondered: Just what herbs are those lambs feeding on after all?

Primošten

Once a hopping party town before the Croatian in-crowd moved to Hvar, Primošten has some good restaurants and bars they left behind. The old town is precious, a little island connected by a thin stretch of land to the mainland, and worth a quick walk around before heading out of the now mostly lower-end tourist trade.

SIGHTS

Though there's nothing specific to see in Primošten proper, it's nice to walk around the cobblestone-paved old town before heading up into the hills to the wonderful **Jurlinovi dvori complex** (Draga bb, tel. 022/574-106, info@jurlinovidvori.org, www.jurlinovidvori.org), in the preserved village of Draga. Call to reserve a visit; if you can't get anyone who speaks English, have a local tourist office or your hotel call for you. Stone houses are clustered around a central courtyard, and each small home is part of the museum, showcasing a traditional Dalmatian kitchen, living room, cellar, sleeping quarters, and a domestic chapel. One home also holds a collection of sacred objects. Nearby is a 13th-century Romanesque chapel, the church of St. George. The whole place has a laid-back air, preserving history and showing it off to visitors without being gimmicky. It's also one of the few places in Dalmatia where you can get a look at the history and culture of the people.

WINERIES

Wine lovers and foodies will find a couple of gems in town. The local Babić wine has a specific salty taste, certainly worth a try, and lobster prepared in the local style is a must-try at one of the better restaurants in town. Check with the **tourist office** (Trg biskupa Josipa Arnerića 2, tel. 022/571-111) for excursions and tours of the local wine trails, through the rocky villages of Burnji in the hills above Primošten.

BEACHES

There's a big beach fronting the cafés and tacky souvenir shops along the street connecting the parking lot and the old town. It's usually quite crowded, though the convenience of a nearby coffee is not a bad feature. Better beaches can be found by walking along the promenade north of town.

ACCOMMODATIONS AND FOOD

Book private rooms from **Agency Nik** (Trg Stjepana Radića 1, tel. 022/571-200, www.nik.hr). Another option is the Tito-era package hotel **Zora** (Raduča bb, tel. 022/581-022, www.hotelzora-adriatiq.com, 1,200Kn d, including breakfast), with an ugly unpromising exterior but clean, basic rooms a 10-minute scenic walk to the old town. The location is superb, but the price in high season makes private accommodations a better bet.

An absolute must-eat is the charming step-back-in-time **Jurlinovi dvori** (Draga bb, tel. 022/574-106, info@jurlinovidvori.org, www.jurlinovidvori.org, call for hours, 90-150Kn), with excellent local cuisine, warm hospitality, and a one-of-a-kind experience in the hills above Primošten. Call to arrange a meal, and if you can't get anyone who speaks English, have a local tourist office or your hotel call for you. Back in town, you'll find lots of konoba-style restaurants and pizzerias. For a really great view and filling food, try **Konoba Babilon** (Težačka 15, tel. 022/570-769, 12pm-2pm and 6pm-8pm daily May-Sept., 85Kn) and its charming open-air dining.

GETTING THERE AND AROUND

Take buses 14, 15, or 16 from Šibenik on weekdays (on weekends take bus 16, at least once daily, 30 minutes) to get to Primošten. If you're driving, it's about 20 kilometers (12 miles) south of Šibenik. Exit off the

Finding Your Own Private Paradise

If you really want to find a stretch of deserted beach, it's not that hard to do in Croatia, with hundreds of uninhabited islands just off the coast. The first thing to do is to ask the locals, though keep in mind that another person's idea of paradise may be very different from your own. If you're used to navigating a boat, rent one from the marina and set out to find your own spot, either mooring offshore or parking one of those inflatable types right on the beach. Not confident with taking to the high seas? Rent a water taxi with a captain who can take you there, perhaps even negotiating a fish picnic in the deal. Of course, you'll see lots of advertisements for these fish picnics, but unless you want to share them with 20 other hungry travelers, it's better to hire your own private boat. If all else fails, walk. Usually just beyond the beach where everyone is packed in is a beach where everyone isn't. It's probably harder to get to, just short of requiring rock-climbing skills (at least remember to wear a pair of thick-soled shoes), but you're usually rewarded for your efforts.

Because a private beach usually means a remote one, make sure you don't go so far that you get lost, and bring plenty of supplies, because if you're hungry or thirsty, even paradise doesn't seem so great.

Magistrala (well, it's more of a turn than an exit). Once you're in town, there are at least two small lots where you can pay to park (around 10Kn per hour in summer). From the lot, walk south along the waterfront to reach the old-town area.

Trogir

A postcard-perfect prosperous fishing village with a lively Riva for strolling after dark, Trogir also has some charming architecture. Beaches are just across the bridge on the island of Čiovo, though the best ones are found by boat, on some of the almost uninhabited islands offshore. Trogir fills up at the height of summer, making it hard to walk, let alone enjoy the full beauty of the place. Its proximity to Split and Split's airport, however, make it a worthwhile stopping-off point if you're in transit.

SIGHTS
Land Gate
(Kopnena vrata)

When you enter Trogir, passing the little market on the right and crossing the small bridge, you'll see the big 17th-century Land Gate. The guy on the top is the town's Saint John (Sveti Ivan), a local 12th-century bishop that locals claim was blessed with miracle-working powers. Following the road leading through the gate, you'll arrive at the **Town Museum (Gradski muzej)** (Gradska vrata 4, tel. 021/881-406, www.muzejgradatrogira. blogspot.com, 9am-2pm Mon.-Fri. Oct.-May, 10am-1pm and 5pm-8pm daily June and Sept., 10am-1pm and 6pm-9pm daily July-Aug., 20Kn). Inside is a small display of photographs, documents, local costumes, and a few pieces of artwork and archaeology. It's only a small view of Trogir's past, but the courtyard is charming and the museum sometimes has *klapa* concerts during the summer, making it a worthwhile stop.

St. Lawrence's Cathedral
(Katedrala svetog Lovrijenca)

On **John Paul II Square (Trg Ivana Pavla II),** arguably Trogir's nicest square, are the must-see early-13th-century (though it wasn't completely finished until the 15th century)

Trogir

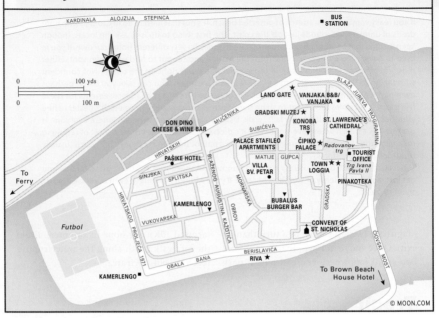

© MOON.COM

St. Lawrence's Cathedral (tel. 021/881-426, 9am-7pm Mon.-Sat., mass Sun. summer, 9am-12pm daily winter, hours not always observed, free) and its much later addition, the **Venetian bell tower** seen peeking above Trogir's red-tiled roofs. If the tower is open, you can climb the almost 50 meters (164 feet) to the top for about 10Kn and get some nice views of Trogir.

The most stunning feature of the church is the western portal, where wonderful reliefs by the 13th-century stone carver Radovan compete for attention in a busy amalgam of reality and fantasy. The interior of the church depicts scenes from the life of Saint Ivan of Trogir. Opening off the north of the interior, **St. John of Trogir's Chapel (Kapela svetog Ivana Trogirskog)** has an impressive ceiling populated by angels carved by apprentices of the renowned Dalmatinac. Beyond the chapel you'll find a small **treasury** *(riznica)* (9am-7pm Mon.-Sat., 10Kn) with a smattering of gilt and carvings.

Čipiko Palace

Just across from the cathedral on John Paul II Square is the **Čipiko Palace,** a decaying Venetian-style home that's pretty to admire from the outside, but with nothing to see on the inside. It's significant to the city since it was the home of the Čipiko family of nobles, who were important to Trogir in the Renaissance. The family dabbled in seafaring military life and literary pursuits, as well as funding some of the cathedral's stash of art and sculpture.

Town Loggia
(Gradska loža)

You'll also find the **Town Loggia** on John Paul II Square. Though the loggia was restored in the late 1800s, many of its ornate reliefs date back to the Middle Ages. The one that doesn't was actually carved by Meštrović, of the Bishop Petar Berislavić, on the loggia's south wall. Next door in a former bishop's palace is the **Pinakoteka** (tel. 021/881-426,

9am-8pm Mon.-Sat., 3pm-7pm Sun. June-Sept., call for off-season hours, 20Kn), which houses an attractive collection of Trogir's sacred art, including a 15th-century altarpiece by local painter Blaž Jurjev of the Madonna and Child with the saints.

Convent of St. Nicholas
(Samostan svetog Nikole)
South of John Paul II Square, the **Convent of St. Nicholas** (Gradska 2, tel. 021/881-631, 8am-1pm and 3pm-7pm daily summer, for off-season hours contact the tourist office, Ivana Pavla II broj 1, tel. 021/881-412, 15Kn) is worth the trip for its Greek relief of Kairos from the 3rd century and for its treasure-chest haul of icons and art from the 13th to 17th centuries. Most touching are the hope chests carried by young girls entering the convent.

Riva
Along the water is the wide café- and yacht-lined Riva, which fills with tourists and locals on summer evenings. At the far end you'll see the 15th-century **Kamerlengo** (9am-7pm daily summer, 30Kn), a medieval fortress that has nice views from the top and hosts open-air movies and concerts during the hottest months.

BEACHES
The best beaches right around Trogir are on **Čiovo Island,** just across the bridge from the old town. Turning to the left after the bridge, you'll see a few convenient, but usually crowded, beaches. The best are found by driving until the road turns to gravel and continuing farther—all the way until the old quarry, if you like—and finding a stretch of beach backed by a few trees for some quiet lounging. If you see a couple of kids charging an entrance fee, feel free to hand them a few *kuna.* You can also inquire at the **tourist office** (Ivana Pavla II broj 1, tel. 021/881-412) or the harbor about boats to take you out on fish picnics. Some are more touristy and carry large groups, while private boats and captains are also available for hire.

ENTERTAINMENT AND EVENTS
Though Trogir's not really a party town, there's a decent selection of spots to drink and dance. Quieter sorts should try the bars in **Radovan Square (Radovanov trg),** behind the cathedral. Those looking for something louder should hit the cafés along the Riva, often hosting live bands in the summer.

In summer the city of Trogir plays host

Čiovo Island

to a number of music groups, from pop to classical to folk, during its **Trogir Cultural Summer (Trogirsko kulturno ljeto)** (July-Aug.). Check with the tourist office (Ivana Pavla II broj 1, tel. 021/881-412) to see what's playing.

ACCOMMODATIONS

If you plan on roughing it, **Camp Seget** (Hrvatskih žrtava 121, tel. 021/880-394, www.kamp-seget.hr, 120Kn) is located two kilometers (one mile) north from Trogir. The camp has space for tents and RVs plus a handful of hostel-type rooms. For private rooms, try **Travel Agency Portal** (Obala bana Berislavića 3, tel. 021/885-016, www.portal-trogir.com), with a decent selection of old town lodging as well as beachfront rooms, apartments, and villas. It's advisable to book ahead for the best spots.

In the old town there are several nice boutique hotels. The **Vanjaka B&B** (Radovanov Trg 9, tel. 021/884-061, www.vanjaka.hr, 675Kn d) has three well-done rooms in a renovated 17th-century house. The **Pašike Hotel** (Sinjska bb, tel. 021/885-185, www.hotelpasike.com, 800Kn d, including breakfast) is located down a narrow little street in Trogir's medieval core, furnished with wonderful antiques in an organic fashion. The rooms are small but the location in the old town is wonderful and the staff are friendly, sometimes adding to the experience by dressing in local costume. It's a family hotel, and most of the antique furniture has been passed down through the generations.

The **Palace Stafileo apartments** (Budislavičeva 6, tel. 091/731-7607, www.trogironline.com/stafileo, 426Kn d) offers excellent value for money. The rooms in the 15th-century center-of-town palace don't have a lot of character, but they have satellite TV, air-conditioning, and small kitchens.

Villa Sv. Petar (Ivana Duknovica 14, tel. 021/884-359, www.villa-svpetar.com, 820Kn d) is another convenient option in a stone building in the heart of the old town. The furnishings are fairly simple, but the service is great. Ask for a room with exposed stone walls for the most authentic charm.

On the island of Čiovo, but only a short walk to the old town, is the charming **Brown Beach House Hotel and Spa** (Put Gradine 66, tel. 021/355-450, www.brownhotels.com, 2,500Kn d, including breakfast). Billing itself as sophisticated yet unpretentious, the 42-room property located in an old tobacco factory is well designed. Its waterside pool is perfect for a dip in the heat of the afternoon.

FOOD

For a casual meal, try **Bubalus Burger Bar** (Ribarska 12, tel. 099/299-1984, 11am-12am daily summer, call for off-season hours, 60Kn) for gourmet burgers and sandwiches alongside an impressive beer list.

The prices are quite high, but **Don Dino Cheese and Wine Bar** (Hrvatskih Mucenika 12, tel. 021/881-574, 8am-12am Mon.-Fri., 8am-2am weekends, 90Kn) has an excellent selection of Croatian wines with a knowledgeable staff. Round out your choice with a cheese plate, sausage and pates, or an octopus salad for a light meal or appetizer. **Kamerlengo** (Vukovarska 2, tel. 021/884-772, www.kamerlengo.hr, 9am-12am daily, 90Kn) is a reliable choice, especially in the winter when many places are closed, for grilled fish in the center of the old town. For something different and a little gourmet, try **Vanjaka** (Radovanov Trg 9, tel. 021/882-527, www.restaurant-vanjaka.com, 8am-11:30pm, 90Kn) instead, for an upmarket take on local specialties. **Konoba Trs** (Matije Gupca 14, tel. 021/796-956, www.konoba-trs.com, 12pm-11:30pm daily, 100Kn) offers mixed grills, seafood, and risottos in a peaceful courtyard setting.

INFORMATION AND SERVICES

Trogir's **tourist office** (Ivana Pavla II broj 1, tel. 021/881-412, 8am-9pm daily June-Sept., 8am-2pm Mon.-Fri. Oct.-May) can provide maps, brochures, and information on private accommodations. The bus station has a **left-luggage office** (9am-10pm daily, 15Kn a day).

GETTING THERE AND AROUND

It's easy to get to Trogir from Split's airport. Take bus 37, which runs every 20 minutes and takes about 20 minutes. Trogir's small **bus station** (tel. 021/881-405), across from the market, has multiple connections with Split daily (buses leave every 20 minutes, about 1.5 hours due to all the stops). There's also a ferry for Split, which takes an hour and runs four times per day in the summer. Check with the tourist office for more information on schedules. It's easy to walk around Trogir's main town, and it's possible, but a bit risky due to vehicular traffic, to stroll to some of the first beaches on Čiovo Island. To get to the best beaches, you'll need to have a car or hire a boat.

AROUND TROGIR
Kaštela

Hugging the shoreline between Trogir and Split is a series of villages referred to as Kaštela. There's some pretty architecture here as each village is formed around a castle built centuries ago to protect crops and property. Today the villages are decidedly more local than most towns on the Dalmatian coast, even in the height of summer. The prettiest village is **Kaštel Gomilica,** though **Kaštel Luksic** is now home to the recently opened **Štacija Hotel and Restaurant** (Šetalište Miljenka

i Dobrile 34, tel. 099/384-7553, www.stacija-hotel.com, 700Kn d, including breakfast), an attractive hotel on the water with a very good restaurant. The villages are great for walking from bar to bar in the evenings along the waterfront promenade, starting in **Kaštel Štafilić** and ending in **Kaštel Stari.** Bus 37 to Split makes stops at each village.

Drvenik Mali and Drvenik Veli

A daily morning ferry connects Trogir with Drvenik Veli and Drvenik Mali Islands (connections tend to be in the early morning and evening, since the ferry serves people who live on the islands but work in Trogir). The best beach is on Drvenik Veli at **Krknjaši Bay,** a stretch of pebbly beach and clear water backed by a simple seafood restaurant with very expensive prices, **Krknjaši** (Uvala Krknjaši, tel. 021/893-073, 11am-11pm daily summer, 120Kn), open only in the summer. If you can get past the cost, the location is idyllic and the cook's husband is a fisherman who catches the restaurant's offerings fresh daily.

The beach is about a 45-minute walk from the ferry stop, so give yourself time to make the boat's early-evening departure, around 6pm. Drvenik Veli is also a nice place to hike through the rural roads and olive trees. Drvenik Mali is the smaller and wilder of the two islands, with some excellent beaches (the sandy one at **Vela Rina** is likely the best), though you won't find any restaurants or cafés nor much in the way of shade, so pack a picnic and a small umbrella.

Southern Dalmatia

As you get deeper into Croatia's Dalmatian

coast, you'll find some of the most stunning coastline and picturesque islands of the Adriatic.

Cities like Hvar have graced the pages of dozens of magazines and newspaper articles, while islands like the beautiful Mljet are significantly less hyped. Split has plenty of historic interest and also serves as a port gateway to most of Croatia's islands. The Makarska Riviera is usually packed with European tourists at its large package hotels, Korčula is a must-see for fans of Dubrovnik, and islands like Vis are perfect for getting away from it all.

The Adriatic's clear blue waters are the main draw here, whether your preferences tend toward island hopping, sunbathing, diving,

Highlights

Look for ★ to find recommended sights, activities, dining, and lodging.

★ **Diocletian's Palace:** The palace is impressive not only for its Roman relics, immense size, and art treasures, but also for its place at the center of modern Split. Small apartments, restaurants, bars, shops, and even a couple of hotels occupy the space once inhabited by the despot ruler (page 248).

★ **Ivan Meštrović Gallery (Galerija Ivana Meštrovića):** The family home of Croatia's most famous artist houses hundreds of his impressive sculptures and drawings (page 252).

★ **Hvar:** With a celebrity-packed nightlife and top-end hotels and restaurants, Hvar's been rated, overrated, and underrated. Expect the unexpected, from wineries to small villages and a restaurant without electricity (page 265).

★ **Vis:** This former military base is the destination for those that want to break from the crowds and step back in time (page 271).

★ **Korčula:** Often called a mini-Dubrovnik, this island is known for its sandy beaches near the village of Lumbarda (page 275).

★ **Mljet:** Mljet is a small paradise with two saltwater lakes at its center, one topped with a 12th-century monastery (page 280).

or dining in restaurants with views worth traveling halfway around the world for. However, all the region's advantages have translated into loads of travelers. There are still out-of-the-way spots to get away from all the tourists—particularly the islands of Mljet, Lastovo, and Vis—but it's worth braving the crowds to get a look at the birthplace of Marco Polo, the pirate stronghold of Omiš, a riverside meal on the Cetina Gorge, or making a compromise, like the hidden away but popular Senko's, a restaurant in a tiny hamlet on the shore of Vis.

PLANNING YOUR TIME

To get a really thorough overview of Southern Dalmatia, with time to do some prerequisite lounging on the beach and lingering over a long lunch, you'll need about two weeks. Start your tour in Split, convenient because it's pretty much the departure point for all the islands. Then start an island-hopping tour that fits in as much as you feel comfortable with—doing an island every 48 hours should allow you to visit several while still having time for lounging by the sea. That said, you can take more time in any one place, discovering its nooks and crannies even further until you know exactly which cove is your favorite.

Whatever you choose, keep in mind that Split is a must-see, particularly given its convenience, and the other islands should be chosen based on your interests and tastes and not how many times you've read about it in a magazine. All of the islands are stunning, and each has its own personality. While it is true you won't find a manicure and a massage or high-thread-count sheets on all of them (if that's your style, head straight to Hvar), you will find excellent restaurants, friendly people, and film-worthy sunset views in each and every port.

And when in Southern Dalmatia, don't forget how close you are to Bosnia-Herzegovina—it's a great chance to take a day or longer to see another country.

Previous: harbor on the island of Brač; gladiator at Diocletian's Palace in Split; town of Komiza on Vis island

Southern Dalmatia

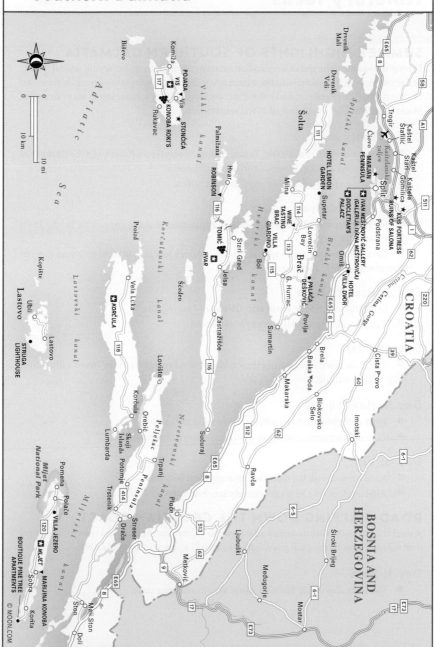

Itinerary Ideas

SUMMER HIGHLIGHTS OF SOUTHERN DALMATIA

During the summer, the glut of ferry and catamaran connections makes seeing several islands in less than a week quite doable. In the winter you will need to be more creative; hire your own boat or stay longer in order to make this itinerary work. Either way, seeing so many beautiful places in such a short time is bound to feel transforming.

Day 1: Split

- Spend your day in **Split's Old Town,** visiting **Diocletian's Palace** and the **Cathedral** in the morning, and a museum or two in the afternoon.
- End the evening with a great meal at **Villa Spiza.**

Day 2: Split to Brač

- Spend your morning on the Marjan Peninsula, making sure to fit in the **Ivan Meštrović Gallery.**
- Take the 3pm catamaran to Brač (under an hour's journey) to settle into your hotel in **Supetar** and enjoy the evening.

Day 3: Brač to Hvar

- Spend the morning at **Wine and Olive Oil Tasting Brač.**
- Take the afternoon catamaran to **Hvar Town.**

Day 4: Hvar

- Spend the morning exploring Hvar, but save some energy for **Hvar Town's nightlife,** which starts buzzing after the sun sets.

Day 5: Hvar to Vis

- Walk to **Robinson** for lunch, then take a dip in the bay.
- Take the afternoon catamaran to **Vis,** and have dinner at **Pojoda.**

Day 6: Vis

- Book a trip to visit the island's **underground tunnels.**
- Afterward, enjoy a long and leisurely lunch at **Senko's.**

ROAD-TRIPPING DOWN THE CROATIAN COAST

A road trip down the Croatian coast allows you to explore more places and have more control over how long you stay in each place, but you can still squeeze in an island visit.

Day 1: Split

- Spend the day seeing **Split's** historic sites to suit your taste.

Southern Dalmatia Itinerary Ideas

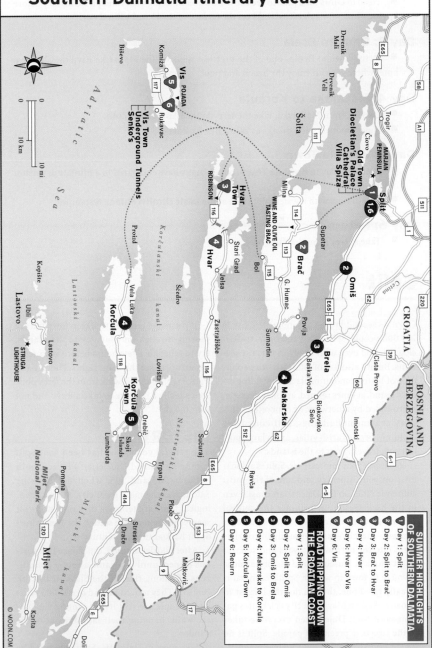

SUMMER HIGHLIGHTS OF SOUTHERN DALMATIA

- ▼ Day 1: Split
- 2 Day 2: Split to Brač
- 3 Day 3: Brač to Hvar
- 4 Day 4: Hvar
- 5 Day 5: Hvar to Vis
- 6 Day 6: Vis

ROAD TRIPPING DOWN THE CROATIAN COAST

- 1 Day 1: Split
- 2 Day 2: Split to Omiš
- 3 Day 3: Omiš to Brela
- 4 Day 4: Makarska to Korčula
- 5 Day 5: Korčula Town
- 6 Day 6: Return

© MOON.COM

Day 2: Split to Omiš

■ Head to **Omiš** for a hike to see the town's breathtaking views and pirate history before having dinner (or at least a drink) on the terrace of the **Hotel Villa Dvor.**

Day 3: Omiš to Brela

■ Drive down to **Brela,** one of the prettiest spots on the Makarska Riviera. Choose a hotel where you can enjoy the beach and pool.

Day 4: Makarska to Korčula

■ Leaving from Makarska, take the ferry to the island of **Korčula.**

■ Have appetizers and drinks at **Wine Bar Bokart**

Day 5: Korčula Town

■ Spend the day in **Korčula Town**, which many have compared to a miniature version of Dubrovnik.

■ End the day with a waterfront table at the **Lesić Dimitri Palace** restaurant.

Day 6: Return

■ Take a ferry from **Korčula** back to Split.

Split

Croatia's second-largest city, home to close to 250,000 people, Split is big and busy, traffic-clogged, and even a bit seedy in certain sections. But it's also full of loud and fun people, tons of historic monuments and buildings—once grand, at times refined, at times decrepit, surrounded by a network of concrete multi-story apartment buildings, half-completed buildings beside garish villas, and a large port ferrying travelers out to the islands.

Whatever your impressions, Split is a don't-miss on your itinerary and one of the most authentic cities on the Dalmatian coast, even in the high season. In summer the central historic section around Diocletian's Palace is packed—literally—as thousands of tourists cram into the narrow alleyways and squares to get a look at museums and historical sites. If you're in town in winter, Split's carnival is a really good one, though not the largest in Croatia. And on May 7 the city celebrates patron saint Sveti Duje, when everyone takes to the streets to preen and parade. Split is no longer undiscovered, but it's no less magical.

If you're not inclined to stay in town but are passing through on your way to the islands, try to schedule a few hours before your ferry departure to see the main sights. Diocletian's Palace is only a short walk from the ferry port, so it's really a mistake to take a ferry and not tour the city.

HISTORY

The general consensus has been that Split sprang up around Diocletian's Palace, built between 295 and 305, when neighboring Salona was the main local city. But archaeological finds are telling a different story—it seems the Romans had settled the area at least as far back as the 2nd century.

After Diocletian died, the palace had various owners until it became a refuge for citizens of Salona fleeing the Slavs in the 7th century. They moved in, and over 1,000 years later, people are still living among the palace walls, hanging their laundry out of the windows.

Like most of Dalmatia, Split was ruled by

Split

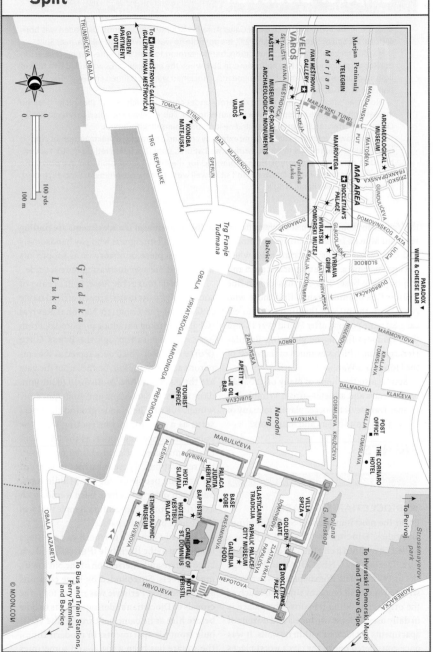

MAP AREA

TRUMBICEVA OBALA

To ★ IVAN MEŠTROVIĆ GALLERY
(GALERIJA IVANA MEŠTROVIĆA)

GARDEN APARTMENT HOTEL

Marjan Peninsula

Marjan

VELI VAROŠ

TELEGRIN ★

IVAN MEŠTROVIĆ MUSEUM

ŠETALIŠTE IVANA MEŠTROVIĆA

KAŠTELET

ARCHAEOLOGICAL MUSEUM

MANDALINSKI PUT

MATOŠEVA

ŽRISKO-FRANKOPANSKA

GUNDULIĆEVA

TOMIĆA STINE

VILLA VAROŠ ●

PUT MEJA

MARJANSKI TUNEL

MUSEUM OF CROATIAN ARCHAEOLOGICAL MONUMENTS

Gradska Luka

DOMOVINSKOG RATA

DOMOVINSKOG RATA

ARCHAEOLOGICAL MUSEUM

MAKROVEGA ▼

★ DIOCLETIAN'S PALACE

HVRATSKI POMORSKI MUZEJ

DOMAGOJA

GLAGOLJAŠKA

MATICE HRVATSKE

KRALJA ZVONIMIRA

TVRĐAVA GRIPE

SLOBODE

DUBROVAČKA

PARADOX ▼
WINE & CHEESE BAR

Bačvice

BAN MLADENOVA

KONOBA MATEJUŠKA ★

ŠPERUN

TRG REPUBLIKE

Trg Franje Tuđmana

Gradska Luka

OBALA

HRVATSKOGA

NARODNOGA

PREPORODA

Trg Franje Tuđmana

MARMONTOVA

NIGEROVA

OBROV

ZADARSKA

APETIT ▼
LJE OIL BAR

Narodni trg

ŠUBIĆEVA

TVRTKOVA

KRUŽIĆEVA

COSMILJEVA

DALMADOVA

KRALJA TOMISLAVA

KLAIĆEVA

KRALJA TOMISLAVA

POST OFFICE

THE CORNARO HOTEL

TOURIST OFFICE

MARULIĆEVA

BUVRINA

ALIŠINA

PALACA JUDITA HERITAGE

HOTEL SLAVIJA

BAPTISTRY

SEVERNA

ETHNOGRAPHIC MUSEUM

HOTEL VESTIBUL PALACE

CATHEDRAL OF ST. DOMNIUS

BASE SOBE

SLASTIČARNA TRADICIJA

PAPALIĆ PALACE/ CITY MUSEUM

PAPALIĆEVA

ZLATNA VRATA

GALERIJA FOOD

DIOCLETIAN'S PALACE ★

NEPOTOVA

DOMINISOVA

GOLDEN GATE

VILLA SPIZA ▼

KREŠIMIROVA

Poljana G. Ninskog

To Pervoj ➤

Strossmayerov park

To Hvratski Pomorski Muzej and Tvrđava G Gripe

ZAGREBAČKA

HOTEL PERISTIL ●

HRVOJEVA

OBALA LAZARETA

© MOON.COM

To Bus and Train Stations,
Ferry Terminal,
and Bačvice

0 ___ 100 yds
0 ___ 100 m

Emperor Diocletian

Though he died with the fancy name Gaius Aurelius Valerius Diocletianus, Diocletian was born Diocles, the son of slaves, around AD 237. It's possible he was even born in Salona, near Split.

He didn't receive much of an education, barely learning to read and write, but his prowess in the Roman military made him his fortune. In 284, when the emperor Carus was killed by a bolt of lightning (or perhaps by more human means), Diocletian was proclaimed emperor after Numerian, son of Carus, mysteriously died.

Diocletian's first goal was to bring the army under control, which he did, though he became increasingly more like a despot than a Roman emperor. Subjects were required to refer to him as Dominus Noster, or Lord and Master, and he identified himself with Jupiter.

He did, however, share power to some extent by creating a tetrarchy, dividing territories among hand-picked leaders. The tetrarchy worked well at first, until Diocletian retired in 305—an unheard-of move for an emperor. He had planned for the line of succession to move down the tetrarchy, but the division of power didn't sit so well with the new government. Diocletian died, possibly by his own hand, in Split.

the Venetians from the 15th century, suffered repeated attacks from the Ottoman Empire, and then came under Austrian rule, when the city became a more important port and shipbuilding base. The city has grown due to an influx of immigrants, first those who came from the hills of the hinterland to escape extreme poverty after World War II, and then refugees fleeing neighboring Bosnia-Herzegovina, which saw much of the worst of the Homeland War.

Split is also the home of many of Croatia's biggest stars and athletes—from Wimbledon winner Ivanisević to soccer players to many of Croatia's biggest singers and musicians.

SIGHTS

TOP EXPERIENCE

★ DIOCLETIAN'S PALACE

By far the most important of Split's buildings and relics, **Diocletian's Palace** is more a walled city within a city than an actual structure. Declared a UNESCO World Heritage site in 1979, the late Roman palace was reconstructed and built on many times, so much of the original building remains. The palace is in daily use—at least two hotels and dozens of apartments are located within its walls. It was once considered one of the city's worst places

to live, but some of the apartments are finding new life with foreigners who pay handsomely to live in a piece of history or as shopfronts catering to the ever-increasing tourist trade.

Start your tour at the **Riva,** Split's center of social activity. Its lesser-known official name is Coast of the Croatian National Revival (Obala hrvatskog naradnog preporoda). From here, you'll pass through the **Brass Gate (Porta Aenea),** which once served as the emperor's access to the sea. To the left of the gate are the palace **cellars *(podrumi)*** (8am-8pm daily summer, 8am-12pm and 4pm-7pm daily winter, 10Kn). These underground chambers serve as a map for reconstructing what the palace was once like above, as the basement exactly mirrored the ground floor prior to all the renovations. These substructures served for housing people during the Middle Ages, but much older relics have been found, such as a frieze from a 2nd-century temple that was likely here before the palace.

On the basement's northern end are steps leading up to the **Peristyle (Peristil),** today a large square and intersection of the old town's main streets. Surrounded by huge columns and arches, the Peristyle was meant for large crowds of Diocletian's adoring subjects to bow before him as he came out through the vestibule from his apartments. In modern times, the square has been a social and sometimes political center in Split. In the late 1960s students painted the floor of the Peristyle red, a move that angered authorities, who labeled it vandalism. In 1998, on the 30th anniversary of the Red Peristyle, a black circle was painted on the stones, an artistic statement against the government at the time. Today, the Peristyle is often used as a concert venue, for both classical and rock performances.

CATHEDRAL OF ST. DOMNIUS
(Katedrala svetog Dujma)

To the east of the Peristyle, at the foot of what is today's church belfry, you'll find two lions and a black granite sphinxlike figure to the right. Around 3,500 years old, the sphinx supposedly once had a twin. The building that is today's cathedral was once Diocletian's mausoleum. Octagonal from the outside, the mausoleum is round on the inside, with red granite Corinthian columns. Converted into a Christian church at the beginning of the 5th century, the building became the **Cathedral of St. Domnius** (Kraj Sv. Duje 2, 8am-8pm daily June-Sept., 8am 12pm and 5pm-7pm daily May and Oct., 8am-12pm daily Nov.-Apr., 20Kn) in the 7th century, dedicated to one of Diocletian's victims, the bishop of Salona. Huge 13th-century walnut doors depicting the life of Christ serve as the entry to the cathedral. The belfry (same hours as the cathedral, 5Kn), started in the 14th century, though it wasn't finished until 1908, is a must-climb if you're willing to trade the effort for some great views of the city.

The interior of the cathedral is a heady gilded and marble mix of reliefs, saints, and altars. The most impressive of the altars is the **Altar of St. Anastasius,** where the bones of Saint Domnius are held in a sarcophagus looked over by the stunning and graphic *Flagellation of Christ* by the famous stonemason Juraj Dalmatinac. To the right of the delicately wood-carved choir stalls is the treasury, a display of sacred art. Don't leave without looking closely around the dome for the frieze with two medallions, thought to be portraits of Diocletian and his wife, Prisca.

It's believed that Diocletian's body was here for almost two centuries before it disappeared.

BAPTISTRY
(Krstionica)

Though it's now known as the **Baptistry** (8am-8pm daily June-Sept., 8am-12pm and 5pm-7pm daily May and Oct., 8am-12pm daily Nov.-Apr., 15Kn), this converted building was once the temple of Jupiter in Roman times, likely around the 5th century. Located slightly northwest of the cathedral, it's one of the best-preserved Roman temples in Europe. With an impressive barrel-shaped coffered ceiling covered in reliefs, it's certainly worth a look. The ceiling, original to the temple, is covered in motifs of flowers and heads that seem to be either laughing or screaming, depending on your interpretation. Turned into a Christian baptistry, the temple also has a simple statue of Saint John the Baptist by Meštrović and a cross-shaped baptismal font, decorated with a carving of a Croatian king, probably Krešimir IV or Zvonimir, dating from around the 11th century. The carving was once part of an altar partition in the cathedral and was incorporated into the baptismal font, likely around the 13th century.

ETHNOGRAPHIC MUSEUM
(Etnografski muzej)

The **Ethnographic Museum** (Iza Vestibula 4, tel. 021/344-164, www.etnografski-muzej-split.hr, 9:30am-8pm Mon.-Sat., 9:30am-1pm Sun. summer, 9am-4pm Mon.-Fri., 9am-1pm Sat. winter, 15Kn) was founded in 1910. The stone-enclosed space is filled with various regional costumes and a nice presentation of local trades. The streets past here are best traversed during the day, as it's one of the poorest and shadiest parts of town, long a meeting place for illicit transactions.

PAPALIĆ PALACE
(Papalićeva Palača)

The 15th-century late-Gothic **Papalić Palace** was built by Juraj Dalmatinac for a local aristocrat. Within the palace is Split's **City**

Museum (Gradski muzej) (Papalićeva 1, tel. 021/360-171, www.mgst.net, 9am-9pm daily summer, 9am-5pm Mon.-Sat., 9am-2pm Sun. winter, 20Kn), where Split's history is told in manuscripts, photographs, and artwork. The exhibit also displays fragments of sculptures, old buildings, and an homage to the first Croatian poet, Marko Marulić, who was a friend of the Papalić family and a frequent guest at the palace.

GOLDEN GATE
(Porta Aurea)

On the northern end of the palace complex, you'll reach the **Golden Gate,** also called **Zlatna vrata,** the grandest of the four gates into the palace. The gate is surprisingly intact, save for some missing statues that once filled the empty niches and the columns that surrounded them. It's thought that the pedestals at the top of the wall once held statues of the four tetrarchs (Diocletian, Maximian, Galerius, and Constantius Chlorus). Next to the gate on the outside of the palace is the menacing **statue of Grgur Ninski,** a 10th-century bishop, sculpted by Ivan Meštrović. Unveiled in 1929, the work was meant to commemorate Ninski's fight for the use of Croatian instead of Latin, making it a nationalist statement. Also next to the Golden Gate is the miniscule 6th-century **Church of St. Martin (Crkvica Sv. Martina),** once a passage for watchmen guarding the gate that was turned into a Christian church in the 9th century. Standing only a little over 1.5 meters (five feet) wide and 10 meters (32 feet) long, it's likely one of the smallest Catholic churches in the world.

Archaeological Museum
(Arheološki muzej)

Located just north of the town center, Split's **Archaeological Museum** (Zrinsko-Frankopanska 25, tel. 021/329-340, www.armus.hr, 9am-2pm and 4pm-8pm Mon.-Sat. June-Sept., 9am-2pm and 4pm-8pm Mon.-Fri., 9am-2pm Sat. Oct.-May, 20Kn) is the oldest museum in Croatia, founded in 1820. Many artifacts were found in nearby Salona, with thousands of pieces of carved stone, a nice selection of Greek and Roman ceramic and glass, and a courtyard filled with sarcophagi and statues. There are also relics from the Illyrian and medieval periods.

Marjan Peninsula

West of the old town, accessed by walking up Senjska, you'll find the old quarter of **Veli Varoš,** a must-see for those who'd like to get off the beaten path and see a bit of the soul of Split. Here you'll find the **Vidilica** (Nazorov prolaz 1, tel. 021/589-550) café and restaurant, behind which you'll see a small 16th-century Jewish graveyard. From here you're entering the Marjan Peninsula, filled with lush forests and winding paved paths perfect for strolls or bike rides. The green peninsula was actually built in the mid-19th century, when locals started planting pine trees here, and in 1903 even formed an early eco-society called the Marjan Society, which is still responsible for the peninsula's well-being.

The highest point on the peninsula is **Telegrin,** rising some 175 meters (574 feet) above the Adriatic and offering excellent views. Marjan is also home to the 13th-century **St. Nicholas's Chapel (Sveti Nikola)** and the modest **St. Hieronymous's Chapel (Sveti Jere),** backing a cliff.

It's a 20-minute walk from the center to the **Museum of Croatian Archaeological Monuments (Muzej hrvatskih arheološki spomenika)** (Stjepana Gunjace bb, tel. 021/323-901, www.mhas-split.hr, 9:30am-1pm and 5pm-8pm Mon.-Fri., 9am-2pm Sat. summers, free), founded in 1893, though the current location was opened in 1976. The displays focus on Split's medieval history, and the 3,000 pieces on display range from weaponry to jewelry, tools to sculpture.

1: statue of Grgur Ninski at the Golden Gate
2: clock tower in historical center of Split
3: Diocletian's Palace, Split

★ IVAN MEŠTROVIĆ GALLERY
(Galerija Ivana Meštrovića)

A short walk down the street from the Museum of Croatian Archaeological Monuments leads to the **Ivan Meštrović Gallery** (Šetalište Ivana Meštrovića 46, tel. 021/340-800, www.mestrovic.hr, 9am-7pm Tues.-Sun. May-Sept., 9am-4pm Tues.-Sat., 10am-3pm Sun. Oct.-Apr., 40Kn). The huge palace was built by Meštrović, Croatia's most famous sculptor, between 1931 and 1939 as a family home. Though it took him eight years to build, he lived in it less than 10 years, from 1932 to 1941, and donated the home to the people in the early 1950s as a gallery of his work. Today the mammoth house displays some 190 sculptures and over 500 drawings from the artist. Near the gallery you'll find the **Kaštelet** (Šetalište Ivana Meštrovića 46, tel. 021/340-800, www.mestrovic.hr, 9am-7pm daily May-Sept., call to arrange a visit off-season, 40Kn), originally built as the 16th-century summer home of a local noble family and later used as a quarantine home and a tannery, among other things. Restored by Meštrović in 1939 to be used as a gallery for his 28 wooden reliefs depicting the life of Christ, it serves that purpose today, resulting in a powerfully moving display no matter what your spiritual inclinations. The museums are definitely worth a visit even if you've never heard of Meštrović.

Bačvice

Officially the city's beach since 1919, Bačvice is not nearly as pretty as some of the island beaches, but it will do if you're up for a swim. Given Croatia's Blue Flag Award for cleanliness, the beach is usually crowded with locals, and it received a much-needed injection of life in the form of a modern pavilion housing a handful of popular cafés and restaurants. If you notice a bunch of men in Speedos throwing themselves at a small rubber ball, don't be alarmed; it's just *picigin,* a local game with no winners or losers, just a lot of fun.

Gripe Fortress
(Tvrđava Gripe)

On the northeastern side of town you'll find the **Gripe Fortress,** built in the 17th century to defend the city against the Turks. One of the fortress's former barracks is home to the **Croatian Maritime Museum (Hrvatski pomorski muzej)** (Glagoljaška 18, tel. 021/347-788, www.hpms.hr, 9am-8pm Mon.-Sat. summer, 9am-3pm Mon.-Wed. and Fri., 9am-7pm Thurs., 9am-3pm Sat. winter, 20Kn) with an interesting display of commercial and military seafaring in the area. Costumes, statues, model ships, and old flags are a sample of what you'll find.

ENTERTAINMENT AND EVENTS
Nightlife

Coffee sipping and club hopping are a way of life for Splićani young and old, and you won't have to go far to find nightlife to your taste. Close to the Riva you'll find the eccentric and artsy **Academia Ghetto Club** (Dosud 10, tel. 021/346-879, 10am-1am daily). **Marcvs Marvivs Spalatonsis** (Papalićeva 4, 5pm-12am daily) is a mouthful, but this centrally located (across from the City Museum) jazz bar also serves wines, whiskies, and snacks. There are plenty of other bars along the Riva and around, but as the evening wears on, head to **Judino Drvo** (Kopilica 24, tel. 091/234-5494, 11pm-5am Fri.-Sat.), which features local and international DJs as well as occasional live acts.

Festivals and Events

The best festival in Split is its **Split Summer Festival (Splitsko ljeto)** (mid-July-mid-Aug., www.splitsko-ljeto.hr), when theater, classical music, and opera converge on the city; many performances are held in the Peristyle.

SHOPPING

There are several spots for wines, oils, and other local gourmet products. Try **Oleoteka Uje** (Marulićeva 1, tel. 021/342-719, www.

uje.hr, 10am-10pm Mon.-Sat., 10am-5pm Sun.) for a huge selection of olive oils as well as pampering soaps and other Dalmatian goodies. Perhaps one of the best take-homes from Split is a jersey from the local soccer team, Hajduk. The nicest ones can be found at **Cro Fan Shop** (Trogirska 10, tel. 021/343-096, www.cro-fan-shop.com, 10am-9pm Mon.-Sat.). **Studio Naranča** (Majstora Jurja 5, tel. 021/344-118, 9am-8pm Mon.-Fri., 9am-1pm Sat.) is a small gallery showcasing the work of graphic designer Pavo Majić and his wife as well as other Croatian artists and artisans.

SPORTS AND RECREATION
Spectator Sports

There's only one real word you need to know around Split: **Hajduk** (www.hajduk.hr). The local soccer club is more like a religion than a sport. Local fans, who refer to themselves as *torcida,* can be whipped into a frenzy over a victory against their biggest rival, Zagreb's Dinamo. If you'd like to experience the excitement, you can purchase tickets at the box office at **Poljud Stadium** (8 Mediteranskih Igara 2).

ACCOMMODATIONS
Under 700Kn

The **Kamena Lodge** (Don P. Perosa 20, tel. 021/269-910, www.kamenalodge.co.uk, 500Kn d) is an excellent budget place run by a friendly couple from London. Located in a traditional stone house just outside of Split's center (15-minute drive), the hotel has a pool and a minibus service that runs several times daily to the heart of town.

The **Garden Apartment Hotel** (Solurat 22, tel. 098/171-1730, www.gardenapartmenthotel.com, 600Kn d) offers wonderful rooms with en suite baths and cottages located a five-minute walk from Diocletian's Palace. The furnishings are rather basic but the surroundings are peaceful and authentic. Make sure to book the apartments and rooms at the Solurat address—the company has a few apartments at a beach location farther away.

Located within the walls of Diocletian's Palace, ★ **Base Sobe** (Kraj Svetog Ivana 3, tel. 098/234-855, www.base-rooms.com, from 453Kn d) may be the best deal in Split. You can't get more central, and the rooms are way better quality than you'd expect for the money. They're not fancy, but they're clean, and many have exposed stone walls that lend character. The location, of course, cannot be beat, and the staff is friendly.

Five minutes from Diocletian's Palace, **Villa Varoš** (Miljenka Smoje 1, tel. 021/483-469, www.villavaros.hr, 600Kn d) is a family-owned hotel in a pretty little neighborhood of Split. The simple rooms are extremely clean and tidy, and the hotel owns a nearby restaurant where you can grab a reasonable breakfast.

700-1,400Kn

Hotel Slavija (Buvanina 2, tel. 021/323-840, www.hotelslavija.com, 976Kn d, including breakfast) is the oldest hotel in Split, founded at the turn of the 20th century in a 17th-century building in the center of Diocletian's Palace. The history, however, can be traced even farther back—there's a preserved Roman spa in the basement of the hotel. The rooms are bland but clean and have air-conditioning and cable TV. Try to avoid the rooms over the narrow alley, where partying-related noise carries on until the wee hours.

The **Hotel Peristil** (Poljana kraljice Jelene 5, tel. 021/329-070, www.hotelperistil.com, 1,150Kn d) is a bit on the pricey side for a three-star, relying on its location within Diocletian's Palace to bring in the tourists. The standouts of the hotel are the friendly service and the flat-screen TVs.

One of the chicest spots in the old town, the ★ **Hotel Vestibul Palace** (Iza Vestibula 4, tel. 021/329-329, www.vestibulpalace.com, 1,180Kn d) could have stepped out of an interiors magazine, getting the mix of minimalist modern and ancient architecture just right. The hotel is small—only seven rooms—and pricey, but then again, how often do you stay in a 1,700-year-old palace?

Over 1,400Kn

Located in a 16th-century palace in the center of town, the ★ **Palace Judita Heritage Hotel** (Narodni Trg 4, tel. 021/420-220, www. juditapalace.com, 1790Kn d, including breakfast) offers eight rooms with wood floors, exposed stone walls, and beds with Egyptian cotton sheets. What elevates the hotel in particular is the level of service that really does make you feel quite royal.

The Cornaro Hotel (Sinjska ulica 6, tel. 021/644-200, www.cornarohotel.com, 1,770Kn d) opened in 2014 and is located at the entrance to Diocletian's Palace. The modern rooms are comfortable and the hotel has a rooftop bar and a restaurant right in the heart of the tourist action.

If you're looking for a large full-service hotel, including a restaurant, a spa, and a place to moor your yacht, try ★ **Le Meridien Grand Hotel Lav** (Grljevačka 2A, tel. 021/500-500, www.lemeridien.com/split, 1,890Kn d, including breakfast), about six kilometers (3.7 miles) from Split in the suburb of Podstrana; the hotel offers a shuttle into town. One of Croatia's few five-star hotels, it pulls out all the stops—an infinity pool, a champagne bar, a spa with truffle- and gold-based treatments, foodie-quality restaurants, and, of course, the marina for dozens of shiny yachts.

FOOD

For a quick snack or dessert, ★ **Slastičarna Tradicija** (Bosanska 2, tel. 021/361-070, 8am-11pm Mon.-Sat.) has been doling out cakes and ice cream for over 70 years. Just before Easter, you'll see dozens of locals lining up outside the small bakery, down the alleyway, for *pinca*, a type of bread eaten on Easter morning. Best of all, the shop has a special case of "historic" cakes and cookies, like *mandolat* (a cookie made with almonds) and *kotonjada* (quince jelly), once ubiquitous around the area and today rare outside local homes.

Vegans and vegetarians will appreciate

Makrovega (Leština 2, tel. 021/394-440, www.makrovega.hr, 9am-7pm Mon.-Fri., 9am-5pm Sat., 55Kn, cash only). The small place has macrobiotic and vegetarian options, with a menu that includes a great selection of soups, salads, mains like burritos and lasagna, and some quite tempting desserts.

There are two great wine bars in town. Start the evening with wine and cheese at ★ **Paradox Wine and Cheese Bar** (Poljana Tina Ujevica 2, tel. 021/395-854, www.paradox. hr, 9am-12am Mon.-Sat., 4pm-12am Sun.), arguably Dalamatia's best wine and cheese bar. The waiters are knowledgeable about the wines on offer, and they are a great resource to explore and learn about Dalmatian wines. Have a glass of wine and appetizers at **Uje Oil Bar** (Dominisova 3, tel. 095/200-8008, www.uje.hr, 7am-12am daily, 60Kn), which bills itself as the first Croatian oil bar. While it's best to skip this spot for dinner at the moment, the bar is the perfect place to sample Croatian olive oils and tapas with a glass of wine.

Apetit (Šubićeva 5, tel. 021/332-549, www. apetit-split.hr, 12pm-12am daily, 130Kn) is located in the beautiful Papalić Palace. The restaurant lives up to its space, buying ingredients fresh daily from the city's markets and making its pasta in-house.

The shabby chic look of **Galerija Food** (Dominisova 9, tel. 098/939-5418, 9am-10pm Mon.-Sat., 4pm-10pm Sun., 50-90Kn) is different from most establishments that have truly standout cuisine. The cozy, laid-back atmosphere is refreshing, as is the menu, with lots of vegetarian options on offer. It's a great spot for breakfast, too, and has nice outdoor seating for summer dining.

If it's local flavor you're looking for (although you may not find a local crowd in summer), **Konoba Matejuska** (Tomica Stine 3, tel. 021/355-152, www.konobamatejuska.hr, 11am-12am daily, 100Kn) is the place to book. And book you must, several days in advance to get a seat at one of the restaurant's seven tables. It's worth the wait for the excellent fish dishes at reasonable prices.

For a fine-dining meal, head to ★ **Villa**

Spiza (Kružićeva 3, tel. 091/152-1249, 9am-12am Mon.-Sat., 70-110Kn), located in the old town and serving outstanding local specialties, including fish and prawns. The restaurant is very small and very popular due to the great cuisine and the features of the place. This can translate into slow service as the few staff try to keep up with the demand, so if you go, be ready to savor a glass of wine while you wait, and to enjoy the experience.

Sometimes you need a break from the hustle and bustle of the tourist center, and ★ Perivoj (Slavićeva 44, tel. 021/785-875, www.restoran-perivoj.com, 8am-11pm daily, 120Kn) is just far enough out without being a hassle. The setting is magnificent: an old Split family house with a manor-style garden centered by a calming fountain. The food is just as great, and make sure to leave room for dessert; the restaurant's dedicated pastry chef is a master at her art.

INFORMATION AND SERVICES

For information and a few free maps, visit Split's **tourist office** (Peristil bb, tel. 021/345-606, www.visitsplit.com, 9am-8pm Mon.-Sat., 9am-1pm Sun. summer, 9am-5pm Mon.-Sat. off season) on the Peristyle.

The main **post office** (Kralja Tomislava 9, 7am-8pm Mon.-Sat., 8am-1pm Sun.) offers mail and telephone services as well as money exchange.

Clean your clothes at a coin-operated laundry (a rarity in Croatia), **Modrulj Laundrette** (Šperun 1, tel. 021/315-888, 8am-8pm daily), only 45Kn for wash and dry, or splurge for their turn-key service (ironing not included) for 75Kn per load.

Drop your luggage at Split's **bus station** (Obala Kneza Domagoja 12, tel. 060/327-327, www.ak-split.hr, 6am-10pm daily, 3Kn per hour).

GETTING THERE AND AROUND

Split Airport (SPU, tel. 021/203-555, www.split-airport.hr) is located 20 kilometers (12 miles) north of town near Trogir. Croatia Airlines runs a reasonable **bus service** (tel. 021/203-119, 30Kn) to Split. Call the office to check for departure times; they meet all Croatia Airlines flights. You can also take a **taxi** (try Radio Taxi, 970, or Taxi Riva, tel. 021/347-777). There's also a local bus, but it's not worth the time or hassle to get from the airport to Split's center. Wait on the Croatia Airlines bus, only 10Kn more, or splurge on a taxi (an alarming 250Kn trip) instead.

Long-distance bus connections are frequent, since Split is one of the main transportation hubs for Dalmatia. The **bus station** (Obala Kneza Domagoja 12, tel. 060/327-327, www.ak-split.hr) is located next to the ferry terminal on Split's harbor. There are good connections with Zagreb (over two dozen daily, eight hours), Dubrovnik (about 12 daily, five hours), and Rijeka (about six daily, eight hours). If you're traveling by bus to Dubrovnik, remember you'll need your passport—a portion of the journey goes through Bosnia.

The train (especially fast ones, labeled *"brzi"*) is a great option for getting to and from Split. Fast trains to Zagreb (about three daily, 160Kn) take about six hours, while trains to Šibenik (about five connections daily, two hours, 45Kn) and Zadar (3-4 connections daily, 4.5 hours, 90Kn) are also convenient. The **train station** (Zlodrina poljana 20, tel. 021/338-525, www.hznet.hr) is a short walk to the harbor or the main bus station.

Split's **ferry terminal** is a short walk from the Riva, and it can take you for day trips to Hvar (1.5 hours) and Brač or a longer trip (around two hours) to Vis. Catamarans and hydrofoils, which have the quickest journey times (one hour to Hvar), can be picked up from the Riva. At the marina end of the Riva are kiosks for **Jadrolinija** (Gat Sveti Duje bb, tel. 021/338-333, www.jadrolinija.hr) and **Split Tours** (tel. 021/352-533, www.splittours. hr), which also books trips to Ancona in Italy.

Around Split you can rely on walking to get anywhere you want to go. Hikes out to the Marjan Peninsula can be circumvented by taking local bus 12 from Trg Republike. A bus ticket costs about 10Kn, payable to the driver, or pick one up at newspaper kiosks.

AROUND SPLIT

Largely part of a neighboring suburb of Split, Solin, the ruins of **Salona** (tel. 021/211-538, 9am-7pm Mon.-Fri., 10am-7pm Sat., 4pm-7pm Sun. June-Sept., 8am-3pm Mon.-Fri. Oct.-May, 30Kn) are all that's left of the city, a giant for its time with some 60,000 inhabitants, established around the 2nd century BC and an important center of early Christianity. Though many of the prettier statues and pieces were excavated in the 19th century and taken to museums, the remains of the amphitheater, the aqueduct, the bishop's complex, and the Forum are still worth a look for fans of the Roman period. You can get more information from the **Tourist Board of Solin** (tel. 021/210-048, www.solin-info.com).

To reach Solin from Split, drive north on the Magistrala toward Trogir or take city bus 1. The main information booth and ticket center is just behind the parking lot for Salona.

Northeast of Split in Klis, *Game of Thrones* fans should not miss the **Klis Fortress (Tvrđava Klis)** (57 Megdan, Klis, tel. 021/240-578, www.tvrdaklis.com, 9:30am-4pm daily though hours vary, 40Kn), though non-fans will also appreciate the views if not the significance. Dating from the 9th century, the fortress is accompanied by stills from the show that made it famous.

Omiš

TOP EXPERIENCE

A pretty town at the mouth of the Cetina river gorge, Omiš is most famous for having been a pirate stronghold against mighty Venice in the 13th century. The city is quite stunning: Craggy rocks give way to narrow streets and old stone houses, and finally to the crystal-blue waters of the Adriatic.

SIGHTS

The best sights are the remains of medieval fortresses built by the nobles of Kačić and Bribir, which harbored the pirates who moored their ships slightly up river. **Mirabela** (8am-12pm and 4:30pm-8:30pm daily, 10Kn) is the most accessible—just follow the many stairs behind the parish church to climb the tower for a nice view. Farther up, the **Fortica** (dawn-dusk daily, free) is a bit of a hike, about 1.5 hours, for vistas and great photo opportunities.

Omiš has a wonderful *klapa* **festival** (www.fdk.hr), founded in 1967 and now attracting some 80 groups every July. The deep a cappella rhythms were once mocked but are now being reclaimed as an integral part of Dalmatian culture. If you'd like to find out more about *klapa* in English, try the website www.klapa-trogir.com.

ACCOMMODATIONS

Private rooms and apartments can be booked through **Active Holidays** (Knezova kačića bb, tel. 021/861-829, www.activeholidays-croatia.com) in Omiš.

There's only one downside to the ★ **Hotel Villa Dvor** (Mosorska 13, tel. 021/863-444, www.hotel-villadvor.hr, 800Kn d, including breakfast): You'll need to climb about 100 stairs to reach the pretty hotel from the parking lot (staff will help you with your bags). If you can get past the climb, the views over stone ruins, the canyon, and the sea are spectacular. The rooms are nicely furnished, though they tend to run on the small side.

Right on a stretch of sandy beach in town and very popular in summer, **Hotel Plaža** (Trg kralja Tomislava 6, tel. 021/755-260, www.hotelplaza.hr, 750Kn d, including breakfast and dinner) is tastefully decorated and has a small spa. The terrace becomes an ice skating rink in winter.

A new boutique hotel on the city scene is **Hotel Damianii** (Poljička cesta Golubinka IIA, tel. 021/735-557, www.hoteldamianii.hr, 1,774Kn d, including breakfast). The decor of the 12 rooms is far nicer than the exterior, which is clean and fresh. The hotel also has an elegant restaurant with excellent food, a bar, and an indoor pool, and it can organize excursions in the area.

FOOD

It's worth the climb to have dinner on the terrace of Villa Dvor's restaurant ★ **Knez** (Mosorska 13, tel. 021/863-444, www.hotel-villadvor.hr, 5pm-11pm daily, 80-150Kn). Overlooking the Cetina Gorge and the sea, it's particularly beautiful in twilight—you may not even notice the food, good renditions of local Poljica specialties, focusing on meats and vegetables with a few creative takes on traditional fish dishes. Save dessert for ★ **N-ice** (Ribarska 2, tel. 095/883-0718, 3pm-10pm daily, 25Kn), an ice-cream shop that stands out even in a country full of excellent gelato. Here, your ice cream is made to order and is as fresh as it is delicious.

INFORMATION AND SERVICES

The Omiš **tourist office** (Trg kneza Miroslava, tel. 021/861-350, www.visitomis.hr) can provide you with lots more information, from festival info to rafting excursions.

GETTING THERE AND AROUND

Omiš is about 25 kilometers (15 miles) south of Split. From Split, take bus 60 from the Lazareti bus stop on the Riva or an intercity bus to Omiš. If you're driving, just follow the Magistrala south from Split.

CETINA GORGE

The Cetina Gorge is full of stunning karst rock formations, dotted with deep-green scraggly forest, and cut through by bright-blue water. You'll find some of the gorge's prettiest scenery just upstream from Omiš. In the summer, boat trips a few kilometers up the gorge are widely advertised at the harbor for very reasonable prices. You can also drive along the gorge, all the way to Zadvarje about a half an hour or so on, where a **waterfall (vodopad)** (follow the signs) culminates a nice scenic drive.

view of Omiš

The Pirates of Omiš

The geography of Omiš—large flat rocks that overlook the mouth of the Cetina Gorge on one side and the sea on the other—is to thank or to blame for the pirates that once hung out there. It offered perfect protection for their fleet of light and fast ships that preyed on those who happened to sail by. The Venetians and the Kingdom of Naples, who generally thought they ruled the Adriatic Sea, considered the city of Omiš a pirate town. The people of Omiš generally saw themselves as simply extracting tolls from those who were using their part of the sea.

In defense of the Venetians and the Kingdom of Naples, the pirates, ruled by the Kačić Dukes, were quite violent, and they weren't altogether fair, even attacking ships heading on crusades, which outraged Pope Honorius III, who brought his fleet into battle with the pirates in 1221. The Kačić won that battle, but a later fight in 1228 ended their approximately century-long reign of terror.

Sports and Recreation

One of the best ways to see the gorge is to go on a rafting trip on the Cetina. The trip is pretty mild unless there has been a lot of rain recently. Try **Active Holidays** (Knezova kačića bb, tel. 021/861-829, www. activeholidays-croatia.com) or **Rafting Pinta** (Duce, Rogac 1/10, tel. 021/734-016, www. rafting-pinta.com) to book a trip, which lasts 3-4 hours.

Food

The **Restoran Radmanove Mlinice** (Kanjom cetine, tel. 021/862-073, www. radmanove-mlinice.com, 8am-12am daily Apr.-Oct., 85Kn) is in a peaceful location on the Cetina River about six kilometers (3.7 miles) from Omiš. Many boat trips end here anyway, but don't let its touristy popularity throw you off. It's perfect for cooling off on a hot summer day and for tucking into fresh trout and frog's legs on the shady terrace.

Makarska Riviera

Packed with tourists in the summer, particularly from neighboring Bosnia, it can be hard to find a spot for your towel on the Makarska Riviera's great pebbly beaches. For the most part, it's a jumble of package hotels, kids looking for a party, and families interested in relaxing by the sea. The area is also popular with Germans and Hungarians spending a couple of weeks in the sun. It is possible to use it as a comfortable overnight stop and offers a handful of hotels and good restaurants. There are also some outstanding beaches, particularly in Brela, though they are best savored outside the busiest months of July and August.

BRELA

South of Split and north of Makarska, Brela is set on a six-kilometer (3.7-mile) stretch of pebbly beach rimmed by olive and fig trees. The sea slopes gently here, making it great for young children and hesitant swimmers.

Beaches

Punta Rata is Brela's most popular beach, a long white-pebbled strip backed by lots of facilities, including restaurants, lifeguards (generally 8am-8pm daily summer), and changing areas. The 400-meter (1,300-foot) **Berulija** beach has a few more secluded spots, since the coastline dips into three different coves. If you're looking for a romantic beach, **Vrulja** is a hidden cove slightly north of town. The best

A Side Trip to Bosnia-Herzegovina

Just across the border from the Southern Dalmatia coast is Bosnia-Herzegovina (BiH). It would seem wrong to write about Croatia without mentioning Herzegovina, where most of the residents are actually Croats. You don't even need to bother with changing money, as the locals are happy to accept Croatian *kuna*. The Roman Catholic pilgrimage site of Međugorje is here in the heart of Herzegovina. The site is popular with tourists and includes a simple church and a 15-minute hike up a very rocky path to Apparition Hill, where the Virgin Mary was spotted.

Going further into Bosnia, you'll find the stunning capital, Sarajevo, as well as Mostar; they're definitely worth the visit, though plan for at least a couple of nights. There are still relatively few visitors even during the summer.

Sarajevo was hit very hard during the war in the 1990s. Today the city has been almost completely rebuilt and is filled with museums, bars, and restaurants to explore. If you would like to stay awhile, you can also explore the Bijambare caves, Bosna Springs, and Mount Bljesnica Jahorina, site of the 1984 Winter Olympics and a great place to ski. While you're in town, grab a warm beverage at the Čajdžinica Džirlo Teahouse (Kovaci Cilcma 6, www. teahousesarajevo.info, 8:30am-11pm daily). Bosnian coffee and tea served in the traditional way make this warm Bohemian café a must-stop.

Mostar is a must-see on the banks of the almost unreal-blue Neretva River. The city arguably suffered the fiercest fighting during the war, and much of the Old Town and the city's famous Old Bridge (Stari Most) were destroyed. Today, the city has been rebuilt, and the bridge reopened in 2004.

There are two must-dos in Mostar, besides a stroll in Old Town and on the bridge. A short trip from the city, the Blagaj Dervish House (Tekija Blagar Pidan) (Blagaj bb, www. blagajtekija.ba) is a 15th-century monument in an idyllic location against a mountain. It has been an important historic site since Ottoman times, and dervishes still perform the Zikr ritual. As this is still a religious site, make sure to dress conservatively; women should bring a scarf to cover their hair. Back in town, the Bosnian National Monument Muslibegovic House (Osmana Džikića 41, tel. 387/36-551-379, www.muslibegovichouse.com) is not a must-see but rather a must-stay. Though you can visit the house as a museum, it also has 12 luxury rooms only steps from the Old Town. While you shouldn't expect five-star amenities, the experience is absolutely priceless.

If you'd like to visit the country for a day or longer, you can cross the border without a visa if you're a U.S., European Union, Australian, or New Zealand citizen. There are trains from Ploče to Mostar (two hours) and Sarajevo (four hours), and buses leave Zagreb, Split, and Dubrovnik daily for Bosnia-Herzegovina's main cities (Dubrovnik to Mostar, three hours; Dubrovnik to Sarajevo, six hours; Split to Sarajevo, seven hours; Zagreb to Sarajevo, nine hours).

Bosnia-Herzegovina is safe except for the large number of land mines still lying in the fields, so it's best not to go hiking or trekking without a local guide. If you'd like to see the country in more detail or see remote parts of the country without worrying about land mines, contact the excellent ecofriendly travel agency GreenVisions (Radnička bb, Sarajevo, tel. 387/33-717-290, sarajevo@greenvisions.ba, www.greenvisions.ba), a friendly company specializing in guided trips through Bosnia-Herzegovina.

approach is by boat. You can rent a small one at Brela's marina. Don't be surprised to find a few skinny dippers in the quieter stretches of beach.

Accommodations and Food

Brela is home to two charming bed-and-breakfasts, both with waterfront swimming pools, small rocky beaches with great water, and excellent service. Abuela's Beach House (Jardula 20, tel. 091/155-5044, www. abuelasbeachhouse.com, 1000Kn d, including breakfast) has apartments and studios with kitchenettes and sea-view balconies as well as a great breakfast. From the seven-room Villa Paulina (Ivana Gundulica 48b, tel. 021/619-940, www.villa-paulina.com, 850Kn d, including breakfast) you can walk to the center of Brela along the waterside promenade.

For hotels, the chain of Blue Sun Hotels is the best choice for accommodations in Brela. The **Berulia** (Frankopanska 22, tel. 021/603-190, brela@bluesunhotels.com, www.bluesunhotels.com, 1,200Kn d, including breakfast) is a good choice if you want large hotel amenities. Basic but comfy rooms in the stark modern building overlook a sparkling pool and a gentle slope to the beach. The **Soline** (Trg Gospe od Karmela 1, tel. 021/603-190, brela@bluesunhotels.com, www.bluesunhotels.com, 1,000Kn d), has swish rooms with wood floors and a giant spa as well as indoor and outdoor pools.

Indoors or out, dining at the **Ivandića Dvori** (Banje 1, tel. 021/618-407, www.konoba-ivandicadvori.com, 5pm-1am daily, 90Kn) is a lovely experience. Sitting on a stone-floored terrace overlooking the water or beside a roaring fire inside in the winter, you can choose from a good variety of grilled fish and meat dishes.

Information and Services

You can pick up information from Brela's **tourist office** (Alojzija Stepinca bb, tel. 021/618-455, www.brela.hr, 8am-9pm daily summer, 8am-3pm Mon.-Fri. winter), but the posted hours aren't always observed.

Getting There and Around

Getting to Brela by car is easy—just follow the Magistrala. By bus it's somewhat more difficult. Buses from Split run regularly to Makarska, though you should alert your driver you want to be dropped off near Brela. If you're trying to catch the bus here, you may need to flag it down to stop, though in the high season you likely won't be the only one waving.

BAŠKA VODA

Low on charm but filled with lots of services for travelers (think mid-range hotels, souvenir shops, and loads of postcards), Baška Voda is best as an overnight on your way elsewhere.

Accommodations and Food

Rooms at the **Hotel Villa Bacchus** (Obala sv. Nikole 89, tel. 021/695-190, www.hotel-bacchus.hr, 600Kn d) all have nice mountain or sea views and access to an indoor pool.

Centrally located **Hotel Croatia** (Iza Palaca 1, tel. 021/695-900, www.hotelcroatia-baskavoda.com, 400Kn d, including breakfast) has modern clean rooms and great service.

Grand Hotel Slavia (Obala Sv. Nikole 71, tel. 021/604-894, www.hoteli-baskavoda.hr, 850Kn d, including breakfast) was recently renovated, and has a spa, beach view, and central location.

There are plenty of pizza and seafood restaurants along the waterfront, with something for everyone. Try **Del Posto** (Obala Sv. Nikole 71, 11am-11pm daily, 110Kn) for tasty dishes presented with flair in an attractive setting.

Information and Services

The town has a small **tourist office** (Obala svetog Nikole 31, tel. 021/620-713, www.baskavoda.hr, 8am-9pm daily summer, call for off-season hours) that can help you with advice about the area.

Getting There and Around

There's no proper bus station in town, so some buses traveling from Split to Makarska will drop you conveniently near the water, while others will drop you off on the Magistrala. If it's the latter, you've got about a 15-minute walk into town. Driving, of course, is simple. Just follow the Magistrala south from Split.

MAKARSKA

Makarska is a good spot for people looking for a party. It's usually packed in summer, leading the town to have a bustling nightlife.

There are also a couple of interesting stops for those wanting quieter pursuits.

1: Golden Horn beach on Brač **2:** view of Makarska

The **Veprić Shrine (Svetište Veprić)** (tel. 021/616-336, www.vepric.net, free) located near Makarska is a pilgrimage site with the stunning backdrop of the Biokovo mountains. Small shrines in the recesses of the rocks are a replica of the famous Lourdes pilgrimage site and are a peaceful spot for meditation no matter your religious leanings.

The **Biokovo Nature Park (Park Prirode Biokovo)** (www.pp-biokovo.hr, 50Kn) is a rocky mountain range eight kilometers (five miles) from Makarska with plenty of viewing spots and photo ops overlooking the Adriatic. There are also many places for rock climbing and hiking, with some that get so deep there's even a mountain house where you can spend the night if needed.

Makarska's main **beach** is slightly to the west of the center of town, rimmed by loads of package hotels. For fewer crowds, rent a boat from the marina, or hike from the Riva toward the east, where you'll find signed paths leading to **Nugal,** about three kilometers (one mile) on, where it's much quieter and the scenery is spectacular.

Accommodations and Food

Rooms at the **Dalmacija** (Kralja Petra Krešimira IV bb, tel. 021/615-777, 794Kn d, including breakfast) are extremely simple, but the hotel is relatively convenient and has swimming pools, a restaurant, and a decent array of facilities.

The **Maritimo Hotel** (Put Cvitačke 2a, tel. 021/619-900, www.hotel-maritimo.hr, 900Kn d, including breakfast) is a new boutique hotel with a restaurant and direct beach access.

Wine Bar Grabovac (Kačićev trg II, tel. 098/934-226, 9am-11pm Sun.-Thurs., 9am-2am Fri.-Sat.) is a cozy wine bar with a nice selection of Croatian wines and local appetizers. It's perfect as a pre- or post-dinner spot. **Street Food La Strada** (Setaliste Dr. Franje Tudjman 1, tel. 098/887-419, 11am-11pm daily summer, call for off-season hours, 70Kn) has a selection of good, cheap hamburgers when you need a break from all the seafood.

Don Antonio (Cvjetna 2, tel. 021/678-086, 5pm-12am daily, 100Kn) has an owner who is passionate about his restaurant and personally gives recommendations to diners. The passion is present in the good quality dishes presented, from meats to seafood and more.

Restoran Jež (Petra Krešimira IV 90, tel. 021/611-741, 12pm-12am daily Feb.-Dec., 90-150Kn), literally Hedgehog Restaurant, has long been considered one of Makarska's top spots for fish dishes, seafood appetizers, and a solid wine list.

Information and Services

The town has a helpful **tourist office** (Obala kralja Tomislava bb, tel. 021/612-002, www.makarska-info.hr, 8am-9pm daily summer, 9am-3pm Mon.-Fri. winter).

Getting There and Around

Makarska's **bus station** (Ante Starčevića 30, tel. 021/612-333) is only a few minutes' walk from the water. From here you can catch one of several daily buses to Dubrovnik (three hours) or Split (1.5 hours). Driving to Makarska, just take the Magistrala south from Split.

Southern Dalmatian Islands

BRAČ

Brač is Croatia's third-largest island, and arguably one of its most popular. Stemming from the bustling beach life of towns like Bol and Supetar and fueled by its proximity to the mainland (only one hour), Brač sees thousands of visitors every summer. If you're seeking peace and quiet, though, it's easily found in the semi-abandoned interior. Neglected vineyards are the only remnants of the once large winemaking trade on the island. Many plants succumbed to disease in the early 20th century, forcing winemakers to abandon their fields and their livelihoods.

Supetar

Given that Supetar has a fairly small old town, there aren't a lot of visit-worthy places. The best historic sight in Supetar is actually the **town cemetery,** a peaceful cypress-lined park beyond the town's beaches. The impressive sculptures that decorate the graves and mausoleums were carved by two of Croatia's leading 19th- and early 20th-century sculptors, Ivan Rendić and Toma Rosandić.

Supetar is the main tourist center of the island, with plenty to keep beachgoers and young families busy. Stretching to the west of Supetar are lots of pebbly beaches with clear water perfect for snorkeling. The best beach can be found by driving to **Lovrečina Bay,** with the remains of an old basilica.

Campers can check out **Autocamp Aloa** (Marka Marulića 3, tel. 098/776-484, www.camping-bol.com, 67Kn pp), situated on a beach three kilometers (1.8 miles) out of town. **Pansion Palute** (Put Pašika 16, tel. 021/631-730, palute@st.htnet.hr, 380Kn d) is a small family hotel with clean, cozy rooms and air-conditioning.

Aparthotel Bračka Perla (Put Vele Luke, tel. 021/755-530, www.perlacroatia. com, 1,631Kn d) is an adults-only hotel with eight suites and three rooms, all decorated in bright colors and modern furnishings. At this upmarket stone hotel, the pool area is enveloped by comfy wicker loungers. Inside, a fireplace makes for homey dining in cooler weather. The **Villa Adriatica** (Put Vele luke 31, tel. 021/343-806, www.villaadriatica.com, 1,400Kn d, including breakfast) is a 24-room boutique hotel with plain but fresh rooms and a much more luxe garden and pool area. Near the beach, the hotel also has a restaurant and small wellness center.

The **Hotel Osam** (Vlačica 3, tel. 021/552-333, www.hotel-osam.com, 600Kn d, including breakfast) has a rooftop bar and seaside swimming pool with a beach a few steps away. Most of the rooms have sea views and private balconies.

Even if you've come straight off the beach, **Punta** (Punta 1, tel. 021/631-507, www. vilapunta.com, 8:30am-12am daily Apr.-Nov., 85Kn) is the sort of place you can plop down for a relaxed lunch. Food is the typical grilled meats and fish, though there are a couple of options for vegetarians as well, and the location is great—a quiet spot a short walk from the hustle and bustle of busy Supetar.

Vinotoka (Jobova 6, tel. 021/630-969, 12pm-12am daily, 90Kn) is a family restaurant in Supetar. In addition to the seafood dishes, be sure to sample some of the owners' homemade olive oil and wines.

Bol

The popular resort town of Bol has two worthy stops. The first is the **Branislav Dešković Gallery** (Porat b. pomoraca bb, tel. 021/635-270, hours and prices vary by exhibit), a modest museum that manages to include some of the biggest names in 20th-century Croatian art. Bol is also home to a 15th-century **Dominican monastery (Dominikanski samostan)** (10am-12pm and 5pm-8pm Mon.-Sat. summer, mass only off-season, 15Kn) that looks out over the town. Inside

Brač

you'll find some Greek artifacts and a tender painting by Tintoretto, the *Madonna with Child*. The gardens here are also worth a look.

The biggest draws to Bol are the beaches, most notably **Golden Horn (Zlatni Rat),** a long stretch of tiny-pebble beach known for windsurfing and a partying crowd. To get here, follow the path west of the center, about a 20-minute walk; once here, you'll find cafés and basic services. If you're interested in a full-body tan, visit the more remote clothing-optional **Pakleni naturist beach** on the western end of Golden Horn.

Among package-hotel destinations, the **Hotel Borak** (Zlatni Rat d.d., tel. 021/635-210, www.bluesunhotels.com, 1,060Kn d, including breakfast) is a good choice, located steps from Golden Horn, with large outdoor pools, tennis courts, and children's activities, although rooms are stuck in a 1980s hotel time warp.

The **tourist office** (Bol harbor, tel. 021/635-638, www.bol.hr) has free maps as well as a brochure outlining private lodgings around the town, the best choice for budget travelers.

Possibly the best value for money in Bol, the ★ **Villa Giardino** (Novi put 2, tel. 021/635-900, www.dalmacija.net/bol/villagiardino, 700Kn d, cash only) truly lives up to its villa status. Tastefully furnished antique-filled

rooms, a genteel garden, and ceiling fans (it also has air-conditioning) deck out the old home where Emperor Franz Joseph once laid his head (room 4).

Overhauled in 2008, the **Hotel Kaštil** (Frane Radića 1, tel. 021/635-995, www.kastil.hr, 740Kn d, including breakfast) has a convenient waterfront location in an old building. Most of the plainly furnished but brand-new rooms have sea views. The building also houses two hotel-owned restaurants and a bustling bar, which make for plenty of late-night noise.

Mali Raj (Put Zlatni Rat, tel. 098/756-922, www.maliraj-bol.com, 110Kn) means "little paradise," and the lush patio setting is quite idyllic. Serving well-prepared local cuisine, you won't leave hungry.

Around Brač

A short drive from Supetar (or take one of the three daily buses), you'll find the village of **Škrip,** an ancient village that's home to the **Museum of Brač (Brački muzej)** (for hours and admission cost, check with the tourist office in Supetar, tel. 021/630-551, www.supetar.hr). The small museum has an interesting collection of Roman artifacts and a small Roman mausoleum outside, where locals claim one of Diocletian's relatives is buried.

If you're near Škrip, then head to Dol for

a great meal in a beautiful setting at **Kastil Gospodnetić** (Dol 13, tel. 091/799-7182, 2pm-10pm daily, 90Kn). Set in a historic village house, this *agroturizam* restaurant offers local dishes prepared with love.

If you're traveling with friends, **Limunovo Drvo** (Bunta, Sutivan, UK tel. 44/1225-865-591, www.croatiancottage.co.uk, £800 per week in high season), whose name translates to "lemon tree," is a charming rental villa that sleeps up to 11 in the village of Sutivan.

The ★ **Hotel Lemon Garden** (Perića Kala 1, tel. 021/660-0062, www. lemongardenhotel.com, 2,200Kn d, including breakfast) in Sutivan is a luxury boutique hotel for adults only. The swimming pool seems like it came from a movie star's backyard, lined with palm trees and chic loungers. The hotel has a private beach, free bicycles, a spa, and an excellent restaurant.

The most luxe hotel on Brač, the 15th-century ★ **Palača Dešković** (Pučišća, tel. 021/778-240, www.palaca-deskovic.com, 1,702Kn d, including breakfast) has all the amenities you'd expect from a fine boutique hotel, plus a library and a game room, a good restaurant, an art gallery and studio, and parking spaces for cars or yachts.

Wineries

Wine and Olive Oil Tasting Brač (Zrtava Fasizma 11, tel. 098/195-0559, www. winetastingbrac.com, call to arrange visit) in the village of Nerežišća may not be award-winning, but the experience of learning about winemaking firsthand from the owners of the young winery can't be beat. It's a lovely way to while away the afternoon.

Getting There and Around

Brač is most often accessed via ferries from the Split mainland (one hour); they dock at Supetar. **Jadrolinija** (tel. 021/631-357, www. jadrolinija.hr) and **Split Tours** (tel. 021/352-481, www.splittours.hr) run close to two dozen ferries a day in high season. There's also a catamaran, run by Jadrolinija, linking Split with Bol, and the small **Bol Airport** (BWK,

tel. 021/631-370, www.airport-brac.hr) a few kilometers from Bol, with flights to Zagreb.

Around the island, buses link Supetar with Bol, Milna, and Sumartin. The **bus station** (tel. 021/631-122) is east of the harbor.

★ HVAR

If you're looking for a quiet Dalmatian experience, Hvar Town is not what you're searching for. That said, Hvar has advantages that brought the tourists, and the services those tourists have demanded have increased the town's advantages. It's one of the few places in Dalmatia where you'll find multiple chic bars, hotels, and restaurants, loads of yachts, and the occasional celebrity sighting. The island is fairly young, drawing foreigners and Croatians alike, though more and more Croatians are being priced out of their own playground. Year after year newspaper articles decry the outrageous prices of burgers, beer, and a simple coffee, which in Hvar's summer season can easily run 30Kn.

However, there are a few spots to escape the crazy prices and crowds so that you can have the best of both worlds, choosing where you want to go and when, depending on your mood.

Hvar Town

Most of the year, Hvar Town is a quiet fishing village with about 3,000 residents. But by the time July swings around, tourists are descending on the place at a rate of about 30,000 a day. This translates into packed bars and restaurants and lots of jockeying to be noticed by seriously fashion-coordinated young people. Before you worry about the nightlife, there are a few things to see during the daylight hours.

Hvar Town was sacked by the Turks in the late 16th century, and the island capital was rebuilt by the Venetians in the early 17th century. Its hub is **St. Stephen's Square (Trg sv Stjepana)**, known as the **Pjaca** (pronounced "piazza"). The square's namesake is the church at the eastern end, the **St. Stephen's Cathedral (Katedrala sveti Stjepan)** (open most mornings and for mass), with its very

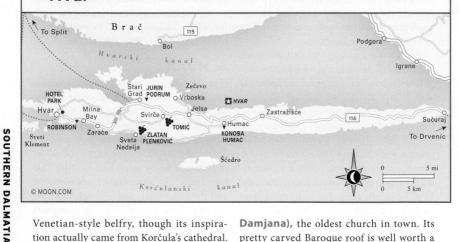

Venetian-style belfry, though its inspiration actually came from Korčula's cathedral. The interior, which has no set hours, shelters a pretty Venetian painting of the Madonna and Child from the early 13th century. Next to the church you'll find the **Bishop's Treasury** *(riznica)* (9am-12pm and 5pm-7pm daily summer, 10am-12pm daily winter, 15Kn), displaying a colorful array of liturgical vestments and sacred art.

The square is flanked on its southern side by the Arsenal, built in the early 16th century. A **theater** (under renovation at the time of writing) was built in the Arsenal in 1612. It was one of the first theaters of its day open to the public; the present interior dates from the 19th century. Next door is the **Arsenal Gallery of Modern Art (Galerija Suvremene Umjetnosti Arsenal)** (tel. 021/741-009, www.mhb.mdc.hr, 10am-12pm and 7pm-11pm daily June-Sept., 10am-12pm daily Oct.-May, 20Kn, includes admission to the theater), which displays works by contemporary local artists.

The northern end of the old town within the city walls is referred to as the **Groda.** Here you'll find the **Church of the Holy Spirit (Crkva svetog Duha),** whose facade was decorated with fragments from other Hvar churches, and the **Church of Sts. Cosmos and Damian (Crkva svetog Kozme i Damjana),** the oldest church in town. Its pretty carved Baroque roof is well worth a look. Many of the houses in the Groda were built between the 14th and 17th centuries, though two stand out from the rest: the shell of the never-completed **Užičić Palace** (often mistakenly referred to as the Hektorović Palace) and the **Leporini Palace** (identifiable by the rabbit carving on its facade). Both palaces are located on Matije Ivanića.

From Groda, follow Ivanića until you arrive at a winding path, which leads to the **Fortress (Fortica)** (8am-12am daily June-Sept., 9am-dusk daily Oct.-May, 10Kn). The Fortress is often referred to by locals as the Španjola, since the Spanish helped the Venetians construct it in the 16th century. On a clear day there's a great view from here all the way to Vis.

ENTERTAINMENT

Hvar Town's best-known bar is certainly **Carpe Diem** (Riva, tel. 021/742-369, www.carpe-diem-hvar.com, 9am-3am daily summer, 9am-12am daily winter). New and more popular places have opened up over the years (and seem to change every year), but it is still hanging on. You may want to check out **Ka'Lavanda Music Bar** (Ulica Dr. Mate Miličica 7, tel. 099/447-7799, www.kalavanda.com, 9am-2am daily in summer,

Hvar Off the Beaten Path

Hvar can get quite crowded in the peak season, and if you were looking for sleepy fishing villages and almost-secluded rocky beaches, sometimes the throngs can really get to you. Try the following spots on Hvar for a taste of peace and quiet away from all the buzz along Hvar Town's streets.

- The island of **Palmižana,** just off the coast of Hvar Town, is not completely quiet—it's host to fashion shows and art exhibits in high season—but it's full of lush forests and gardens, created at the turn of the 20th century by Eugen Meneghello, who also opened his namesake hotel, today with 14 romantic bungalows and a great restaurant.

- **Jelsa** and **Stari Grad** are both less touristed, yet no less interesting, than Hvar Town. And why not explore the tiny villages, like the remote port of **Sućuraj** or charming **Sveta Nedelja,** if you have a car and really want to get away? Rent a moped or a car from **Luka Rent** on Hvar Town's harbor.

Jelsa

- You'll need to walk for close to an hour to get from the center of Hvar Town to **Robinson** on Mekićevica Bay, but it's well worth the trek. The restaurant has no water or electricity, but it's a great place to eat, with all organic, fresh-catch, and homegrown products, and to bathe in the bay out front.

call for winter hours), where DJs accompany solid cocktails in a chill setting.

Excellent music, great cocktails, and friendly people give **Lola Bar** (Sveti Marak 8, tel. 092/285-8260, 8pm-late summer, call for winter hours) a laid-back vibe. Mellower evenings can be had at the ★ **Pršuta Tri Wine Bar** (Petra Hektorovića, Groda, tel. 098/969-6193, 6pm-2:30am daily summer, call for off-season hours), with over 50 open bottles behind the bar for a wide selection of wines by the glass. It's the perfect place to try local vintages.

ACCOMMODATIONS

Only five minutes' walk to the beach or to the center of Hvar Town, **House Gordana** (Glavica bb, tel. 021/742-182, www.house-gordana-hvar.com, from 355Kn d off-season, 1,100Kn d summer) is a bit like staying at a friendly grandmother's house. Also a short walk from town or the shore, **Apartments**

Ana Dujmovic (Zastup bb, tel. 021/742-010, www.hvar-croatia.com/dujmovic, 780Kn d) are bright and sunny, many with balconies. The 14th-century **Villa Nora** (Petra Hektorovića, tel. 021/742-498, www.vila.villanora.eu, 1,950Kn d, including breakfast) has all the modern conveniences like Internet access and air-conditioning in a central location.

The boutique ★ **Hotel Park** (Hvar Town, tel. 021/718-337, www.hotelparkhvar.com, 1,400Kn d, including breakfast) opened in 2007. The 14 airy apartments and one room have pretty sea views, Internet access, and plasma TVs.

The **Adriana Hotel** (Fabrika bb, tel. 021/750-200, www.suncanihvar.com, 2,837Kn d, including breakfast) got a refresh in 2018. For the not-so-budget price, you get a location overlooking the marina and the old city center, with indoor and outdoor pools, a spa, and a swank rooftop lounge. The Sunčani

Hvar chain (which runs the Adriana) has another luxe hotel in town, the **Amfora Grand Beach Resort** (Majerovica bb, tel. 021/750-300, www.suncanihvar.com, 2,100Kn d, including breakfast), with a cascading pool, private 1930s stone cabanas for relaxing, and light, sleek rooms. Unfortunately, the service does not match the hype.

FOOD

Dalmatino (Sveti Marak 1, tel. 091/529-3121, www.dalmatino-hvar.com, 5pm-1am Sat.-Sun., 12pm-1am Mon.-Fri., 150Kn) serves very traditional Croatian dishes—pastas, shrimp, and grilled meats—with modern flair.

If you've had it with traditional, head down the street to **Lola Street Food and Bar** (Sveti Marak 8, tel. 092/233-1410, 3pm-11pm daily, 75Kn), a buzzing little restaurant that offers some good vegetarian options alongside burgers, steamed pork buns, and spring rolls. They also have good cocktails from the bar.

Cozy **Agava** (Ulica Ivana Bozikovica 17, tel. 091/622-7788, www.agava-hvar.com, 11am-10pm daily, 150Kn) serves local dishes prepared by a team with attention to detail.

The nearby **Konobo Menego** (Petra Hektorovića, Groda, tel. 021/742-036, www.menego.hr, 11:30am-2pm and 5pm-12am daily Apr.-Nov., 120Kn) has a traditional interior and a slightly out-of-the-ordinary menu. Serving up tapas-size portions of local dishes, this restaurant has a big following.

Another option is the out-of-the-fray ★ **Robinson** (Mekičevića Bay, tel. 091/383-5160, www.robinson-hvar.hr, 11am-sunset daily June-Sept., 85Kn, cash only), an hour's walk from Hvar Town. There's no water and no electricity, but plenty of local organic food and grilled seafood, plus a nice bay where you can take a dip before or after lunch. Don't expect things to go quickly—this is a place to chill and enjoy the entire experience.

INFORMATION AND SERVICES

The Hvar Town **tourist office** (Trg sv Stjepana bb, tel. 021/741-059, www.tzhvar.hr, 8am-1pm and 5pm-9pm Mon.-Sat., 9am-12pm Sun. June-Sept., 8am-2pm Mon.-Sat. Oct.-May) is located on the corner of the Pjaca.

Palmižana

A short water-taxi ride away from Hvar Town, the over-100-year-old **Villa Meneghello** (Palmižana, Sv. Klement, Pakleni Islands, tel. 021/717-270, www.palmizana.hr, Apr.-Oct., 1,100Kn d) on Palmižana is like a vacation within a vacation. The quiet island is worlds away from the constant buzz of nearby Hvar, and the gorgeous rooms and suites, decorated with a mix of antiques, modern art, and well-placed splashes of color, have a style best defined as peaceful, laid-back luxe. The family-run hotel hosts special events during the summer, often involving themed art exhibitions. If you don't want to stay overnight, you can still come for lunch and a swim.

Stari Grad

Stari Grad is the point of entry for many ferries from Split, but there's plenty to see in this town that gets a lot less traffic than the island's capital, Hvar Town; it's also home to a growing art scene. Aficionados will enjoy cruising the narrow alleys looking for galleries and artists during the summer months. The most popular sight in Stari Grad is the **Tvrdalj** (tel. 021/765-068, 10am-1pm and 6pm-8pm daily June-Sept., 10Kn), the summer home of Hvar's 16th-century poet Petar Hektorović. Though the home is largely unimpressive, bits of the preserved gardens, a pretty fish pond, and dozens of inscriptions on the walls—all the work of Hektorović—make for a restful, contemplative meander. There's a 15th-century Dominican monastery nearby with a small **museum** (10am-12pm and 4pm-7:30pm Mon.-Sat. summer, 10Kn) where you'll find some Greek tombstones, Hektorović artifacts, and a Tintoretto.

The town also has a small museum, the **Stari Grad Museum (Muzej Staroga**

1: view from Hvar Town **2:** village Velo Grablje in the hills of Hvar **3:** Koiza waterfront, island of Vis **4:** Stinva bay beach on Vis island

Grada) (Ulaz braće Biankini 2, tel. 021/766-324, www.msg.hr, 10am-1pm daily May-June and Sept.-Oct., 10am-1pm and 7pm-9pm Mon.-Sat., 7pm-9pm Sun. July-Aug., 20Kn) highlighting Greek and Roman artifacts from around the town as well as art, antiques, and a small ethnographic collection.

There are plenty of beaches in Stari Grad, though the best ones are on the southern side of the Riva toward Borić.

When you need to grab a bite, Stari Grad has two excellent options. **Nauta Restaurant** (Ive Dulcica 10, tel. 098/555-120, 10am-11pm Mon.-Fri. and 11am-12am Sat.-Sun., 150Kn) has wood-fired pizzas and oven-baked lamb (order a day ahead) as well as other regional cuisine. In the heart of the old town, ★ **Jurin Podrum** (Donja kola 8, tel. 021/765-804, 12pm-2:30pm and 6pm-12am daily summer, 110Kn) has been famous with Europe's elite since it opened in the 1930s (Edward VIII and Wallis Simpson dined here the year of his abdication). The restaurant offers dishes from a simple starter of new goat cheese topped with grilled vegetables to an unexpected spaghetti with octopus and zucchini, a featured dish on the menu.

The Stari Grad **tourist office** (Nova Riva 2, tel. 021/765-763, www.stari-grad-faros.hr, 8am-9pm daily June-Sept., 8am-2pm Mon.-Fri. Oct.-May) can help hook you up with private lodging, generally a much better option than the overpriced concrete resorts in the area.

Jelsa

Though Jelsa sees more and more tourists every year, it's nothing like Hvar Town. Take an hour or so to wander the old alleyways, admiring the stone buildings and the 16th-century **Church of St. John (Crkva svetog Ivana)**. Though the beaches in Jelsa tend to get a bit crowded, the local **Mina** beach, next to the Hotel Mina, is good for kids. Just 1.5 kilometers (one mile) away is **Grebišče beach**, with a small bar and restaurant, or take a water taxi from the Jelsa harbor to nudist **Zečevo** island or the usually not nudist **Glavica Peninsula.**

A charming little family-run hotel conveniently located near the bus station, the **Pansion Murvica** (Jelsa 373, tel. 021/761-405, www.murvica.net, 350Kn d, including breakfast, cash only) offers clean rooms and a good restaurant. **Huljić** (Banski Dolac, tel. 021/761-409, www.wines-restaurant-huljic.com, 12pm-3pm and 7pm-12am daily mid-Apr.-Oct., 95Kn, cash only) serves plenty of dishes that are a departure from the ever-present grilled fish, plus tastings of the owners' own red and white wines. Eight kilometers (five miles) southeast of town, ★ **Konoba Humac** (Humac, tel. 091/523-9463, 12pm-10pm daily summer, 90Kn, cash only) is a restaurant in a practically deserted village. All the dishes are cooked on the fire—there's no electricity in town—and romantic candle-light is provided.

Jelsa has a **tourist office** (Riva bb, tel. 021/761-918, www.tzjelsa.hr).

Sveta Nedelja

On the southern side of the island, almost due south of Stari Grad (although it's better connected to Jelsa), is the village of Sveta Nedelja, a must for wine lovers.

Visit winery **Zlatan Plenković** (Sveta Nedelja, tel. 021/745-725, www.zlatanotok.hr, call for tours) and sample some of his Grand Cru wine, made from Plavac Mali grapes. The Grand Cru is most similar to an excellent Barolo, but with its own flair. He also has a guesthouse where you can stay.

Svirče

A worthwhile excursion from either Jelsa or Vrboska, this small interior village is not only a way to get off the beaten path, but is also home of the **Tomić** (tel. 021/768-160, www.bastijana.hr, call for hours and visits) winery. They produce a variety of wines and brandies, but it's most famous for its dessert prosecco called Hectorovich, named after Hvar's most famous poet.

Vrboska

Vrboska is a quiet little town and a great location for beachgoers. The village has two interesting churches: **St. Mary's Church (Crkva svete Marije)** (10am-12pm and 6pm-7pm Mon.-Sat., free), whose floor is largely made up of tombstones, and the Baroque **St. Lawrence's Church (Crkva svetog Lovre)** (10am-12pm Mon.-Sat., free), with a couple of pretty Italian paintings inside.

The most popular beach is **Glavica,** about one kilometer (0.6 mile) from Vrboska. If you have a car, you can park at the Soline parking lot. **Soline** is the main beach here, drawing sun worshippers from around the island. Walking 5-15 minutes from the parking lot to the north, you'll find the nudist beaches, with big flat rocks perfect for roasting in your birthday suit, or continue to the romantic coves of Maslinica and Palinica.

Right in Vrboska, family-run **Villa Darinka** (tel. 021/774-188, Apr.-Oct., 355Kn d) has comfortable rooms with sea-facing balconies and neat-as-a-pin decor. For sustenance, try the **Restoran Gardelin** (tel. 021/774-280, 8am-12am daily summer, 85Kn) for grilled fish, stewed fish, and baked fish.

Sućuraj

On the far eastern side of the island, the fishing village of Sućuraj is one of Hvar's quieter towns. A great place for beach lovers, the town is surrounded by lounging options. A short walk from the center of town you'll find sandy Cesminica to the south or pebbly Bilina to the north. You can rent a boat or hop in a water taxi from the small harbor to the sandy bays of Mlaska (north) or Perna (south).

Getting There and Around

Stari Grad is the main port serving ferries from Split (around seven daily in high season, 1.5 hours), Rijeka (13 hours, stops in Split), and Dubrovnik (7.5 hours, stops in Korčula). You can link to Makarska via the ferry at Sućuraj (only viable if you have your own car on the ferry, since there are no buses from the small village).

If you're traveling without a car, the best way to get to town is the hydrofoil from Split, run by **Jadrolinija** (tel. 021/631-357, www.jadrolinija.hr), which takes less than an hour into Hvar Town, the center of all the action. There's also a catamaran (at least one daily in summer) linking Brač (from Bol) to the town of Jelsa on Hvar.

Buses are waiting for the larger ferries and link Hvar Town and Stari Grad (30 minutes). Buses from Stari Grad also connect with Vrboska and Jelsa (each 30 minutes). Keep in mind that buses on the island can be highly unpredictable.

You can rent mopeds and cars from **Luka Rent** (Hvar Town's harbor, tel. 021/742-946, www.lukarent.com) or **Pelegrini Tours** (Riva bb, Hvar Town, tel. 021/742-250, www.pelegrini-hvar.hr). Mopeds cost around 300Kn per day. The agencies are also good sources for boat and bicycle rentals.

★ VIS

A military base under Tito for some 40 years, Vis is a relatively new addition to the Croatian tourist trade. The island has long been filled with farmers and fishermen, who know a thing or two about good food, making Vis something of an unassuming gourmet destination. Though you'll still find your share of tourists in July and August, it's much quieter than many of the surrounding islands and coastline.

Vis Town

Located on the northeast side of Vis, Vis Town is the largest village on the island. Though it's popular with yachters—the main marina is located here—its history is more agricultural, with much of the produce and wines grown in the hills outside town having supplied trade for the little port. These days you'll find top-quality restaurants and a handful of fun bars with a seafaring edge.

SIGHTS

There's not too much to see here, but the **Archaeological Museum (Arheološki**

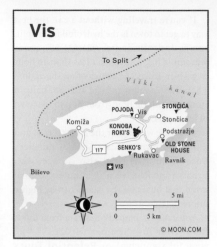

Vis

To Split

Viški kanal

POJODA Vis STONČIĆA
Komiža   Stončica
KONOBA   Podstražje
ROKI'S
117   SENKO'S   OLD STONE
Rukavac HOUSE
Ravnik
Biševo
★ VIS

0   5 mi
0   5 km

© MOON.COM

muzej) (tel. 021/711-729, 10am-1pm and 5pm-8pm Tues.-Sun. summer, 20Kn), located in the **Baterija,** an old Austrian fortress, has a nice collection of objects from Vis's Greek past. In Kut, the yachting section of town, the old patrician palaces, **St. Cyprian's church (Crkva svetog Ciprijana),** and a **British naval cemetery** are the main attractions. The cemetery is about a 20-minute walk from Kut, but just beyond it you'll find a wonderful gem of a beach at **Grandovac.** A 20-minute walk northwest of Vis Town's ferry landing are a few crumbling graves at the **Ancient Greek Cemetery (Helenističko groblje)** (afternoons daily in summer, free) and what's left of a few old Roman baths with some attractive mosaics.

One interesting excursion is to visit the secret **underground military tunnels** created by former Yugoslav leader Josip Broz Tito. Realizing the military importance the island had during the Austro-Hungarian period and World War II, he excavated the island to create a labyrinth of bunker-like underground tunnels and submarine hideouts. To visit the tunnels, book a tour through local outfitter **Alternatura** (www.alternatura.hr).

ACCOMMODATIONS
Hotel San Giorgio (Petra Hektorovića 2, tel. 021/711-362, www.sangiorgiovis.com, 890Kn

d, including breakfast) is a 35-room hotel in Kut, within Vis's old section. The stone building, with a peaceful courtyard and a good fish restaurant, houses simple but comfortable rooms with air-conditioning and satellite TV.

You could also look into booking a room or apartment through one of the agencies in town. Try **Navigator** (Šetalište stare Isse 1, tel. 021/717-786, www.navigator.hr), which also rents cars and scooters.

FOOD
You can certainly eat well—very well, in fact—in Vis Town. The artsy **Kantun** (Biskupa Mihe Pusića 17, tel. 021/711-306, 6pm-12am daily, 90Kn, cash only) mixes traditional and modern in the decor as well as the menu. It's a solid choice for dinner with a phenomenal smoked tuna carpaccio, a variety of well-prepared pasta dishes, and some good-quality meat and fish as well.

One of the few pizza places with a good wine list, **Karijola** (Šetalište Viskog Boja 4, tel. 021/711-433, 12pm-late daily July-Aug., 5pm-11pm daily June and Sept., 70Kn) serves up superb oven-baked pizza on a terrace with a pretty view of the water.

★ **Pojoda** (Don Cvjetka Marasovića 8, tel. 021/711-575, 12pm-3pm and 5pm-12am daily summer, 4pm-11pm daily winter, 120Kn) is one of Croatia's most famous fish restaurants. Located in an old house complete with cloistered garden, the restaurant is beautiful—but the creations of chef-owner Zoran Brajčić are the star attractions. Brajčić infuses the native Dalmatian cuisine with his Slavonian roots; dishes like the *manistra na brudet,* a bean and pasta soup, and the grilled belted bonito, treated to a spice rub and weighted down for 10 hours before cooking, provide diners with a stunning gourmet performance. *Hib,* a traditional biscuit made from ground dried figs, is a sweet ending to the evening.

INFORMATION AND SERVICES
Vis's **tourist office** (Šetalište stare Isse 5, tel. 021/717-017, www.tz-vis.hr, 9am-1pm and

Hiking Safely on Vis

Though there wasn't a war on Vis, there are potentially land mines left over from the old military base. If you're going to hike, make sure to follow the rules. Watch for signs with a skull or crossbones that say *"Pazi Mina."* It's also not a bad idea to check with the tourist office in Vis Town before doing any hiking or trekking in the wilderness.

6pm-9pm Mon.-Sat. summer, 9am-1pm Mon.-Fri. winter) can help with maps, brochures, and information on hiking in the area.

Komiža

On the western end of Vis, ten kilometers (six miles) from Vis Town, Komiža is a fishing village extraordinaire, slightly stubbly, laid-back, rather quiet, and washed with sun, much like many of the older fishermen in town. You'll find the 13th-century Venetian **Castle Fort (Kaštel)** by the sea, where the **Fishing Museum (Ribarski muzej)** (9am-12pm and 6pm-10pm daily in summer, 30Kn) will help you get more in touch with the local culture and historical livelihood. There are great views from the Kaštel's 16th-century tower as well.

The most interesting of the town's churches is the **Our Lady of the Pirates (Gospa Gusarica)** near the Biševo Hotel, named for the legend that claims a painting of the Virgin Mary stolen by pirates made its way back to shore after a shipwreck.

Konoba Barba (Gunduliceva 4, tel. 098/577-994, www.konoba-barba.hr, 6pm-1am daily summer, 100Kn) has nice seafood dishes in a beautiful setting with a choice of two terraces overlooking the water. Make sure to reserve in the high season.

The simple and beautiful apartments at **Villa Nonna** (Ribarska 50, tel. 098/380-046, www.villa-nonna.com, 496Kn d, cash only) are an excellent value—pleasingly furnished and only a minute's walk to the marina. If rooms here are booked, ask the owners for recommendations around town.

Approximately half a dozen buses connect Komiža and Vis Town daily, taking about 25 minutes.

Stončića

Rent a boat or take a water taxi to Stončića, about six kilometers (3.7 miles) from Vis Town. You can also go with a car, but it's a bit of a hike down to the beach—it's not far, but not recommended for the elderly or those without sure footing. The beaches in this sandy bay are heavenly, and there's a lighthouse and a restaurant. Set in a romantic cove, ★ **Stončica** (Stončica 1, tel. 021/711-669, 1pm-11pm or 4pm-11pm daily in summer, 100Kn), which lists summer hours as "open" and winter hours "by agreement," is a family restaurant serving their own homegrown and daily-catch specialties. The menu varies according to what's fresh, but you'll always find grilled fish and vegetables. Dive into the *pašticada nona* when it's available and sample the homemade spicy lamb salami *(kulen)* and dark red prosecco while sitting under the shade of palm trees and meandering vines.

Though ★ **Senko's** (Mola trovna, tel. 098/352-5803, 12pm-12am daily, 110Kn, cash only) is no longer undiscovered, it's still an experience. Located in a cove on the southern side of Vis, between Stončica and Stupišće, is chef-owner Senko Karuza's laid-back restaurant, filled with wooden tables and benches on a stone terrace overlooking the water. The fruits and vegetables come from Senko's organic garden. The menu is whatever's available and whatever he feels like making, and all of it is good—including smoked fish soup with rosemary, smoked eel soup, fish or bean and pasta stew, grilled fish and shrimp flavored with wild herbs—and wash it down with some of Senko's wine. The downsides? It is very difficult to find the place (take a taxi), and sometimes Senko is slow to get dishes to the table. But again, it's an experience, and one you won't have back home.

A Spot of Cricket, Perhaps?

Visiting Vis, the last thing you might expect to find is the traditional English pastime of cricket. While travelers flock to Vis today for fun and sun, back in 1809 the English captain William Hoste, who was stationed here for six years, didn't feel the same. He wrote, "We have established a cricket club at this wretched place, and when we do get anchored for a few hours, it passes away an hour very well."

When the British departed, the club ceased to exist, but a returnee turned it all around. Nik Roki had emigrated to Australia in the 1950s and became a huge cricket fan, passing on his love to his son Oliver. When the family returned to the island to establish their excellent restaurant and winery, they were excited to learn this tidbit of the island's past, and they reestablished the cricket club. The club has a number of enthusiastic players, including expatriates and diplomats that travel all the way from Zagreb to take part.

Interested in finding out more? Visit www.viscricket.com.

Rukavac and Biševo

In Rukavac village, 10 kilometers (six miles) south of Vis Town on the southern side of the island, you'll find **Silver Beach (Srebrena plaža),** arguably the best beach on the island. It's not hard to get to, with a short relatively level walk from a parking lot, and it has a snack bar that serves a basic lunch and rents out lounge chairs. Get there early in summer to snag a good spot.

Another piece of paradise is just across the water on the islet of **Biševo,** home to the legendary **Blue Cave (Modra špilja)** (30Kn), reached only from the sea. The only way to describe the grotto is that it's an otherworldly mix of bright blue that seems to be lit from below, covered by a canopy of dark rock. However you see it, it has been a major attraction since the 1880s. If you'd like to visit the cave, take a trip from either the Komiža or Vis Town harbors (the excursions are heavily advertised) or take a water taxi.

You'll need to book early to get one of the rooms at ★ **Old Stone House** (Rukavac, tel. 098/131-4179, UK tel. 44/1834-814-533, www.wearactive.com, 9,040Kn per week) in the miniscule village of Rukavac; weekly rates include breakfast daily, four lunches, and three dinners. The home is very stylish, and best of all, rates include an invigorating customized activity program that can consist of mountain biking, kayaking, hiking, and even yoga.

Rukavac is easily reached from Vis Town on a good asphalt road. You can also take a water taxi.

Wineries

Eleven kilometers (6.8 miles) east of Komiža or seven kilometers (4.3 miles) south of Vis Town, ★ **Konoba Roki's** (Plisko Polje 17, tel. 021/714-004, www.rokis.hr, 12pm-late daily Apr.-Oct., 120Kn, cash only) is a winery and restaurant a short drive from Vis Town by taxi or car; the restaurant will pick up parties of four or more from Vis Town. Not only is the food good, but it's fun to sample the red and white wines produced by the owners.

Getting There and Around

Vis is served year-round by at least one daily car ferry from Split (2 hours 20 minutes, 45Kn). In the summer, there are one or two more catamarans from Split (1 hour 15 minutes, 60Kn).

Komiža is connected with Vis Town by a bus that runs according to the ferry schedules. In the summer it's quite reliable, but off-season you may need to wait (bring a book).

To get around the island, it's not a bad idea to rent a small car or a scooter. **Navigator** (Šetalište stare Isse 1, tel. 021/717-786, www.navigator.hr) offers cars and scooters, and **Ionios** (Obala Svetog Jurja 36, tel. 021/711-532) offers scooters and bicycles.

Korčula

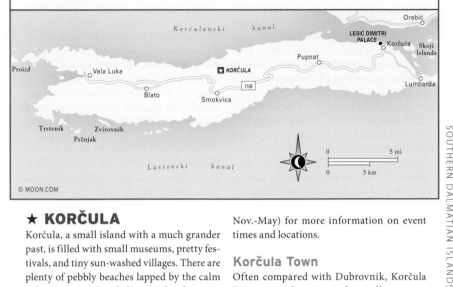

Orebić

Korčulanski   kanal

LESIĆ DIMITRI
PALACE • Korčula   Skoji
                        Islands

Pupnat

Proizd   Vela Luka   ★ KORČULA

Blato   Smokvica   [118]   Lumbarda

Trstenik   Zvirovnik
Pržnjak

Lastovski   kanal

0   5 mi
0   5 km

© MOON.COM

★ KORČULA

Korčula, a small island with a much grander past, is filled with small museums, pretty festivals, and tiny sun-washed villages. There are plenty of pebbly beaches lapped by the calm Adriatic waters, and the island is home to some quality white wines and top olive oils, famous for their rich flavor, from the town of Vela Luka. Korčula was settled by the Greeks in the 6th century BC, when it was known as Black Corfu. The island was relatively unimportant until the Venetians came in the 10th century, using it as a naval base. Korčula thrived from the 13th to the 15th centuries, but an outbreak of plague in 1571 brought an end to the island's importance. Korčula began to find life again as a tourist destination in the 1920s, and by the 1970s the island was burgeoning with hotels and restaurants to serve the summer visitors.

One of the highlights of Korčula is its colorful **festivals.** The Moreška sword dancers that perform throughout the summer for visitors, the processions held during Easter week, and the reenactment of the 1298 Battle of Korčula (early Sept.) all lend a bit of local flavor to a stay on the island. Contact the Korčula **tourist office** (Obala Franje Tuđmana, tel. 020/715-701, www.visitkorcula. eu, 8am-3pm and 4pm-10pm Mon.-Sat., 8am-1:30pm Sun. June-Oct., 8am-2pm Mon.-Sat.

Nov.-May) for more information on event times and locations.

Korčula Town

Often compared with Dubrovnik, Korčula Town reminds visitors of a smaller version of the seaside walled city. But at closer glance you'll find the Venetians, who built Korčula, did a much better job of planning. Streets are laid out to make use of summer winds and to keep out the bitter northeasterly *bura*. Still, the Venetians seem to get lost in the limelight created by the town's most famous citizen, Marco Polo, purported to have been born here in 1254. You'll see his name used in everything from pizzas to hotels to desserts.

SIGHTS

While the claim that Marco Polo was from Korčula—or that he existed at all—is mired in controversy, the idea that the circa-17th-century house touted as the **Marco Polo Museum (Muzej Marka Pola)** (Plokata 14. travnja 1921. br 33, tel. 098/970-5334, www. marcopolo.com.hr, 9am-11:30pm daily summer, 60Kn) was actually his house is a very big stretch. The museum offers an audio self-tour of seven periods of Marco Polo's life and travels; it's a fun, air-conditioned history lesson.

Heading south toward the small space known as the main square, called **St. Mark's**

Square (Trg Sv. Marka) or the Pjaceta, you'll find the Town Museum (Gradski muzej) (Trg Sv. Marka bb, tel. 020/711-420, 10am-9pm Mon.-Sat. summer, call for off-season hours, 15Kn), housed in a 16th-century Venetian palace. The star exhibits are a 4th-century Greek tablet, the earliest proof of civilization on the island, and a mock-up of a peasant kitchen.

Across from the museum is St. Mark's Cathedral (Katedrala svetog Marka) (Trg Sv. Marka bb, tel. 020/711-049, 9am-2pm and 5pm-7pm daily Apr.-Oct., 25Kn). The imposing building is considered one of the most beautiful Croatian churches. Inside, look for the two works by Tintoretto, particularly the restored 1550 painting of Saint Mark between Saint Bartholomew and Saint Jerome, and the frothy stone canopy carved by local stonemason Marko Andrijić in the late 15th century. Next door you'll find the treasury (riznica) (tel. 020/711-049, 9am-2pm and 5pm-7pm daily Apr.-Oct., call for winter hours, 20Kn), filled with a wonderful but modest art collection of Dalmatian and Italian Renaissance painters.

West of the old town, fans of more modern works will appreciate the Memorial Collection of Maksimiljan Vanka (Galerija Maksimiljana Vanke) (Put Sv. Nikole, 9am-12pm and 6pm-9pm daily July-Aug., 15Kn), with paintings from art nouveau painter Maksimiljan Vanka as well as occasional exhibits by other Croatian artists.

ACCOMMODATIONS

A minute's walk from the ferry stop, rooms at Roberta's Guesthouse (Put Sv. Nikole 24, tel. 020/711-247, robertamk@hotmail.com, 290Kn d, including breakfast) are cozy, and the hostess, Roberta, is a delight. Try to book the room with the small waterfront balcony.

The Royal Apartments (Trg Petra Segedina 4, tel. 098/184-0444, www.korcularoyalapartments.com, June-Oct., 690Kn d, cash only) aren't fancy, but they're clean, the owner is very kind and helpful, and

the location, slightly west of the old town on a small waterfront square, is wonderful.

The renovated Hotel Marko Polo (Šetalište Frana Kršinića, tel. 020/726-100, www.korcula-hotels.com, 1,017Kn d, including breakfast) has sleek and trendy but incredibly small rooms. The hotel has indoor and outdoor pools and access to a pebbly beach about one kilometer (0.6 mile) from the bus station. The property has recently received an overhaul, but unfortunately the service has not.

Opened in 2009, the ★ Lesić Dimitri Palace (Don Pavla Poše 1-6, tel. 020/715-560, www.ldpalace.com, from 3,400Kn per night) is the gem of Korčula hotels. The small luxury retreat, with just six mega-suites nestled within the walls of an 18th-century bishop's palace in the center of town, also includes a spa and a restaurant.

FOOD

The island offers a plethora of seafood restaurants, but the pastry shop Cukarin (Hrvatske bratske zajednice bb, tel. 020/711-055, www.cukarin.hr, 8:30am-12pm and 6pm-9pm daily) is the island's true culinary gem. Make sure to try the Marko Polo bombica, a chocolate-encased cream delight, or the walnut-filled klašun, and take home a bottle of one of the dessert wines made from the local grk grape. Wine Bar Bokar (Ul. Antuna Rozanovica, tel. 099/404-1052,12pm-12am daily, 80Kn) is a homey wine bar with knowledgeable owners and nice snacks to pair with your wines.

The outdoor terraces of the rustic Konoba Belin (Zrnovo Prvo Selo, tel. 091/503-9258, 10am-12am daily high season, 100Kn, cash only), some two kilometers (one mile) away from town in First Village Zrnovo (Zrnovo Prvo Selo), are the best part of the busy restaurant. The food is solid, too, with wind-cured ham and cheese appetizers, seafood risotto, and grilled fish.

Adio Mare (Sv. Roka 2, tel. 020/711-253, www.konobaadiomare.hr, 5pm-12am daily summer, call for winter hours, 135Kn) is a staple on the Korčula restaurant scene and generally declared one of the island's best. To get a table in high season, it's imperative to reserve ahead for dinner at this seafood restaurant, just steps from the main square. That said, the high season might be the time to skip this restaurant, since the quality can suffer.

The best table in town has to be at the ★ **Lesić Dimitri Palace** (Don Pavla Poše 1-6, tel. 020/715-560, www.ldpalace.com, 250Kn). Snag a waterfront table and enjoy the modern and innovative take on traditional Croatian staples.

Call in advance to order *peka* (oven-baked dishes) at **Ranč Maha** (Zrnovo-Pupnat Rd., tel. 098/494-389, www.konoba-maha.com, 1pm-11pm daily summer, call for winter hours, 95Kn, cash only), a family farm in the hills above town where hikers and tourists converge to eat the clay oven-baked meat and seafood washed down with some seriously strong homemade herbal grappa. In winter, a crackling fire makes dining here even better.

Lumbarda

The village of Lumbarda, six kilometers (3.7 miles) from Korčula Town, is best known for its sandy beaches. A short drive south of the village is Holy Cross Church (Sveti Križ), set amongst vineyards, where you'll veer left to **Bilin Zal,** a fairly quiet beach with rocky sections. For lunch there's a good little *konoba* here in the ruins of an old summer residence. Keep driving southeast to reach **Vela Pržina,** facing the Italian coast, about 15 minutes away. Pržina is a long beach but quite popular, and it fills early.

One and a half kilometers (one mile) from Lumbarda, the **Apartments Val** (Uvala Račišće bb, tel. 020/712-430, 600Kn d) are situated on a quiet bay. Each apartment has a sea-facing terrace and satellite TV, and the hosts can rent you bicycles and a small boat for cruising around the island. The casual, quiet restaurant **More** (Lumbarda, tel. 020/712-068, lunch and dinner daily summer, call for winter hours, 110Kn) has a shady vine-enveloped terrace. The specialty of the chef is the melt-in-your-mouth lobster accompanied by pasta in tomato sauce.

Vela Luka

A 20-minute walk from town is the **Vela Špila cave** (Ulica 26 br. 3, tel. 020/813-602 10am-1pm and 4pm-7pm daily summer, 20Kn), a limestone cave inhabited by various people since 18,000 BC. Archaeological finds from the site can be found in Vela Luka's small **Town Museum (Gradski muzej)** (ask at tourist office for hours, 15Kn).

The town **tourist office** (Ulica 41 br. 11, tel. 021/813-619, www.tzvelaluka.hr, 8am-9pm Mon.-Sat. June-Sept., 8am-3pm Mon.-Sat. Oct.-May) can direct you to private rooms, good restaurants, and where to buy some of the town's famous olive oils.

You'll find two small islands just off the coast of Vela Luka. Water taxis can take you to **Proizd** (20 minutes, 35Kn) or **Ošjak** (30 minutes, 60Kn), where pretty pebbly beaches and small restaurants are the perfect spot to get away; don't be shocked by the nudists.

Getting There and Around

The island's two major ferry ports, Korčula Town and Vela Luka, have good connections to the mainland. **Jadrolinija** (www.jadrolinija.hr) runs the majority of the ferries, with a daily car ferry in summer (check with Jadrolinija for winter transport) connecting both ports with Split (around three hours, 50Kn), often making a stop in Hvar as well. There's also a ferry connecting Korčula Town with Dubrovnik (three hours). Catamarans link Dubrovnik and Korčula Town (four weekly, 2.5 hours, 130Kn) as well as Split (daily, 2.25 hours, 160Kn).

Korčula has excellent connections with the Pelješac Peninsula, with connections from Orebić on the mainland and Korčula Town in just 15 minutes. There's at least one daily car ferry and one passenger ferry on summer weekdays.

Buses regularly connect Korčula Town with Lumbarda and Vela Luka (six on weekdays, fewer on weekends, one hour, 35Kn).

Water taxis are another good way to get between Korčula Town and Lumbarda.

There's a daily bus to Dubrovnik (twice daily in summer, once daily in winter, three hours, 95Kn), but it often fills up in summer, so it's a good idea to make a reservation in advance.

SKOJI ISLANDS

To really get away, rent a small boat on Korčula—you can try **Rent a Djir** (Trg Kralja Tomislava 4, tel. 020/711-750, www.korcula-rent.net), which also rents cars and scooters—and navigate your way to the Skoji Islands, a group of 19 small islands just off the coast of Lumbarda. The two largest islands, **Badija** and **Vrnik,** have places for a light lunch as well as beaches. The other, uninhabited islands are just the place to find your own stretch of pebbly perfection.

LASTOVO

The island of Lastovo was chosen by settlers as a safe harbor from the constant raids of Uskok, Turkish, and Genoese pirates. Built in the crater of a former volcano, the town is almost invisible from the tall cliffs that surround it. In 2006 the island was declared a national park, and it's a great place to see Dalmatia as it once was. It's served by only one ferry per day from Split, and the narrow alleyways of the old village are relatively uncrowded, especially outside high season. In between chilling out, you can visit the 15th-century **Church of Sts. Cosmos and Damian (Crkva svetog Kuzme i Damjana)** or hike up to the 19th-century fort for some stellar views, and then try to find a **water taxi** (ask at the tourist office or the marina) to take you to the small island of **Šaplun** for even more waterfront peace and quiet.

Festivals

The island of Lastovo is famous for its **Poklad festival,** a winter carnival centering around a giant effigy of a Turk (from the medieval era, when the island suffered constant pressure from the invading Ottomans) that is carried around town and treated quite poorly before being lifted by rope above the town and burned. It's loud, it's a little strange (lots of drunken shouting is involved), and it's quite interesting—it's one of those festivals completely unaware of any visitors who might have ventured to the island in winter to see it. As with Mardi Gras, the biggest celebration is on the Tuesday before Ash Wednesday (usually in Feb.). Contact the Lastovo **tourist office** (in Ubli on the main square, tel. 020/801-018, www.tz-lastovo.hr, 8am-12pm Mon.-Fri.) for more information.

Accommodations and Food

The **Vila Antica** (Sv. Kuzme i Damjana 3, tel. 098/447-311, www.vila-antica.com, 600Kn d), in Lastovo village, is a pretty old stone house, simply but tastefully outfitted, that's walking distance to the bus station, restaurants, and the beach, accessed via a shady path.

There's only one real hotel on the island, the **Hotel Solitudo** (Pasadur bb, tel. 020/802-100, www.hotel-solitudo.com, 450Kn d, including breakfast). Offering a restaurant and fitness center, the best parts of the hotel are the large rooms and the beach in front of the hotel.

A much better option is **Guesthouse Augusta Insula** (Ulica Zaklopatica 21, www.augustainsula.com, 900Kn d, including breakfast) It's clean, and it has a swimming pool and quite possibly the best restaurant and bar in town.

If you're not the hotel sort, the circa-1837 ★ **Struga Lighthouse** (Skrivena luka 110, tel. 01/245-2909, www.adriagate.com, 298Kn d) has several simply furnished apartments run by the lighthouse keepers, who also cook filling meals for guests. From here you can explore Lastovo's villages and festivals.

And to really live like Robinson Crusoe, **Mrčara Island** (tel. 021/384-279 or 098/328-238, www.lastovo-mrcara.com, 922Kn d), just off the coast of Lastovo, is the place to

---

1: seascape on the island of Korčula **2:** monastery on the island of Mljet

Lighthouse Accommodations on the Croatian Coast

Some lighthouses on the Croatian coast are a bit out of the way, while others are totally remote, but all of them offer cheap, interesting lodging on islands all over Croatia. One of the more famous lighthouses is on Palagruža, an island whose rocky shores are rumored to be the resting place of Greek hero Diomedes; the island's sunlit coves are fringed by the Adriatic's most startlingly blue waters. Many of the lighthouses are the ultimate in secluded escapes, with lots of flora and fauna to discover and abundant marine life, perfect for divers and snorkelers. It's imperative to bring your own provisions, though you may be able to arrange for meals or at least fresh fish from the lighthouse keeper. Check out **Adriagate.com** for more information and reservations for lighthouses on the coast.

go. Six rooms in a stone house and three little "cabins" (a nice word for shacks) offer back-to-basics lodging and facilities. There's no electricity, and washing and cooking are done with rainwater. In return, you get some beautiful nature and a fun, friendly atmosphere with like-minded guests.

The **Konoba Augusta Insula** (Zaklopatica Bay, tel. 020/801-167, www.augustainsula.com, 100Kn) serves up lobster spaghetti and a good white wine, made by the owners, on a waterfront terrace. Wherever you eat, Lastovo is famous for its lobster, so it's a must-try on the island.

Getting There and Around

A daily car ferry connects the island with Split via Hvar Town and Vela Luka on Korčula. The ferry takes about three hours from Split (about 60Kn) and docks at the village of Ubli on Lastovo. Taxis wait here to ferry you to various spots around the island.

★ MLJET

There's not much to see on Mljet besides the natural beauty of one of Dalmatia's most unspoiled islands. Just across from Dubrovnik, this heavily forested national park has a unique feature—two sparkling saltwater lakes. The largest lake has its own island, on which stands a 12th-century Benedictine monastery.

Sights and Recreation

Mljet National Park (Pristanište 2, tel. 020/744-041, www.np-mljet.hr, 8am-8pm daily Apr.-Oct., by arrangement Nov.-Mar., 80Kn) is the biggest draw on Mljet, covering one-third of the island. The crown jewels are the saltwater **Big Lake (Veliko jezero)** and **Small Lake (Malo jezero)**. The Big Lake has a small island within the lake, topped by the **Benedictine St. Mary's (Svete Marije)**, a church and 12th-century monastery, originally built in the Romanesque style, although subsequent additions and rebuilding incorporate Renaissance and Baroque styles as well. The monastery was used as a hotel from 1960 to 1991, when it fell into serious neglect. The Diocese of Dubrovnik, to which it belongs, is working to restore the historic venue to its former glory.

The village of **Polače,** which dates back to the Illyrian period, is home to a fort that was used to protect against pirates. Other than that, the biggest attractions of the island are sport and relaxation. **Cycling** the island is the best way to get around (rent bikes from the Polače harbor, the Hotel Odisej, or the park's ticket office, all around 90Kn daily). You can also rent a **canoe** or **kayak** (try Adriatic Kayak Tours, www.adriatickayaktours.com) or go **windsurfing** or **diving** (arranged through the Hotel Odisej). The diving is interesting, since a 3rd-century Roman shipwreck and a sunken World War II German torpedo boat are right off the coast.

Accommodations

At the mouth of the Big Lake, the **Srsen Apartments** (Soline bb, tel. 020/744-032, sandra.srsen@du.t-com.hr, 375Kn d) have pretty water views and a large communal terrace. In the heart of Mljet National Park you'll find the beautiful ★ **Villa Jezero** (Njivice 2, tel. 020/744-019, www.apartmani-jezero.com, apartments from 528Kn), a huge old limestone building that has served guests since 1934. The rooms are simple (come here for the location, not luxury) and the meals are lovingly prepared by the owners by arrangement. This is out-of-the-way peace at its best.

If you are looking for something more swish, the ★ **Boutique Pine Tree Apartments** (Saplunara 17, tel. 020/420-059, www.pinetreemljet.com, 3,843Kn d, including breakfast) are more like a boutique hotel. Located in Saplunara, the apartments are spacious and pristine, and there's a waterfront infinity pool and great food as well.

It's plain, and it's a 1970s communist relic, but the **Hotel Odisej** (Pomena, tel. 020/744-022, www.hotelodisej.hr, 795Kn d, including breakfast) does meet basic requirements for shelter. Actually, it's not all that bad. Some rooms have nice waterfront balconies, and the staff is a pretty friendly bunch.

Food

★ **Marijina Konoba** (Prožura, tel. 020/746-113, www.marijinakonoba.com, 8am-12am daily summer, call for winter hours, 95Kn) in Prožura is the definition of a family restaurant. The owners grow or catch everything on the menu, as well as prepare the food and serve the guests. Boats can be tied to the moorings in front. On the shaded terrace overlooking the bay, the restaurant serves homemade cheese marinated in oil and brick oven-baked lobster with potatoes along with a selection of wines from their well-stocked cellar.

Though there are plenty of tourist-oriented restaurants preying on visitors to St. Mary's Island, **Melita** (St. Mary's Island, tel. 020/744-145, 10am-12am daily May-Sept., 120Kn, cash only) is the real deal, located inside the monastery near the church. It's not cheap, but the location is prime and the food is decent. Just remember, this is a place to go if you need lunch, not a place you go out of the way to eat at.

In Babino Polje you'll find the bar **Komarac** (Sršenovići 44, tel. 098/728-532, 8:45am-12am daily, cash only), a mosquito-themed bar with an eccentric vibe, perfect for a laid-back drink.

Getting There and Around

You can visit Mljet as a day trip from Dubrovnik during the summer, taking the passengers-only catamaran (www.atlantagent.com) from Gruž in the morning, usually around 9am or 10am. The boat stops at Sobra and Polače before heading back from Gruž in mid- to late afternoon. You'll have to stay overnight if you take the Jadrolinija car ferry, also departing from Gruž harbor, leaving in the afternoon and returning the following morning. It docks in Sobra, a 20-minute drive from the national park.

Buses meet ferries in Sobra and connect to Polače and Pomena (both take over an hour), but they're not always reliable, particularly outside the busiest months of July and August. To get around and explore the island, it's really helpful to have a car. **Mini Brum** (tel. 020/745-260 or 098/285-566, www.rent-a-car-scooter-mljet.hr) rents cars from several locations on Mljet. Renting a bicycle is another option. Try the Polače harbor, the Hotel Odisej, or the park's ticket office, all charging around 90Kn daily.

Dubrovnik

Ragusa . . . Dubrovnik . . . no matter what the city's been called over the centuries, it has never failed to inspire. Within its ancient walls lies a tangle of creamy stone structures and alleyways filled with stunning relics of its past.

The city's rich history has created a vibrant cultural and musical scene, with concerts and galleries hiding in the most unexpected places. However, at the height of the summer season, Dubrovnik's glorious past draws thousands of visitors, with large cruise ships docking to release their masses—perhaps not a part of the trip you envisioned.

Of course, there are plenty of reasons the tourists continue to pile into town. Chief among them is the sheer beauty of the city, which can be both grand and quaint, melancholy and sun-drenched happy,

Highlights

Look for ★ to find recommended sights, activities, dining, and lodging.

★ **City Walls (Gradske zidine):** There's no better way to get an eyeful of the white city than a walk along its 15th-century walls (page 289).

★ **Stradun:** Though it's impossible to miss the Stradun, it's easy to overlook its beauty when you're moving along in a river of travelers. Stop for a coffee at one of the cafés to soak in the atmosphere on Dubrovnik's main artery (page 290).

★ **War Photo Limited:** This moving gallery hosts a permanent exhibition of photographs from Croatia's 1990s Homeland War (page 290).

★ **Pustijerna:** Dubrovnik's oldest quarter, with many medieval buildings that survived the 1667 earthquake, is also home to the stunning St. Ignatius's Church (page 295).

★ **Mount Srđ (Brdo Srđ):** Take a cable car or trek the stony path up Dubrovnik's famed hill for amazing views and a stop at a museum chronicling Dubrovnik's role in the country's war for independence (page 297).

★ **Fort Lovrijenac:** Worth the hike to the top for the outstanding views, this clifftop fort protected Dubrovnik against the Venetians (page 298).

★ **Lokrum:** This forested island is a nice spot for a swim or a hike away from the crowds (page 298).

★ **Pelješac Peninsula:** Food and wine lovers shouldn't miss this excursion near Dubrovnik for oysters, seafood, and a wine crawl (page 312).

depending on the view or the fall of the shadows. The city has impressed generations of holidaymakers (and recently *Game of Thrones* fans), though sadly Dubrovnik's self-confidence often turns into an air of coldness and over-importance, a bit like other once-grand seaside provincial towns. Look past the occasional attitude to the magnificent buildings and island-peppered sea beyond.

Of course, some of the attitude is deserved. Dubrovnik is the crown jewel of Croatia and accounts for a huge bulk of the country's tourist trade—it's the city everyone's heard of. The upsides to all this bustle are the many fine hotels and shops and the breadth of amenities you're likely to find. Of course, it's hard to see the upside when you're jam-packed with fellow travelers or left waiting for a table. When the Stradun gets too crowded, escape to less-visited sights around Dubrovnik, like Trsteno, former summer home of Dubrovnik's nobility; the sparsely populated Elafiti Islands; or a winery on the Pelješac Peninsula.

HISTORY

Dubrovnik was originally a small island inhabited by the Illyrians and the Romans. Its name, historically Ragusa, was first mentioned in AD 667. At that time it was a refuge for people fleeing invaders that came after the demise of the Roman Empire. A Slav settlement called Dubrava sprung up across the channel. The narrow waterway was filled in during the 10th and 11th centuries, the two cities merged, and the city spread all the way to the foot of Mount Srđ.

During the 9th and 10th centuries, the city was under the control of the Byzantine Empire, which helped protect the port city from invaders. In 1000, however, it came under Venetian control, then back to Byzantine in 1018, and to the Normans in 1081. By the 12th century, it was becoming a powerful and important city-state, signing trade agreements and treaties. In 1189

Dubrovnik, Ragusa's Croatian name, was used for the first time in a trade agreement (though Ragusa was used regularly to refer to the city until the early 20th century).

Dubrovnik's freedom was short-lived, however. Venice once again took control in 1232, forcing strict trading restrictions and taxes that severely diminished the city's position as an important port. It wasn't until 1358 that an armistice from Croatian-Hungarian king Louis I made Dubrovnik an independent city-state, the Ragusan Republic. Louis placed no restrictions on Dubrovnik's trade, even allowing them to do business with Venice and Serbia, often at odds with the Croatian-Hungarian nation.

The prosperity of Dubrovnik changed the city, with the last of its wooden houses demolished in the early 16th century and the town reconstructed completely in white stone. Palaces, fountains, towers, a public school, and a shipyard were all built during the town's golden era.

The time of prosperity ended with an earthquake in 1667 that destroyed buildings, killed around 4,000 people (over half the city's population at the time), and pulverized many pieces of art. The city recovered through trade, but its glory days were over. It continued to suffer blows to its position (war with Venice, an unfortunate trade agreement with France, a defeat of the navy by Napoleon's forces) until its status as city-state was taken away by Napoleon's Marshall Marmont in 1808. Six years later, Dubrovnik became a part of the Kingdom of Dalmatia, under Austrian rule.

Still, the legend of Dubrovnik continued among visitors, who raved about the city and began to come in droves by the late 19th and early 20th centuries. It continued to be a frequent destination for visitors throughout its time as a part of Yugoslavia. Although the war left its scars, Dubrovnik was quick to recover tourism based on its legendary reputation

Previous: view from the town walls of Dubrovnik; Dominican Monastery; Fort Lovrijenac

Dubrovnik

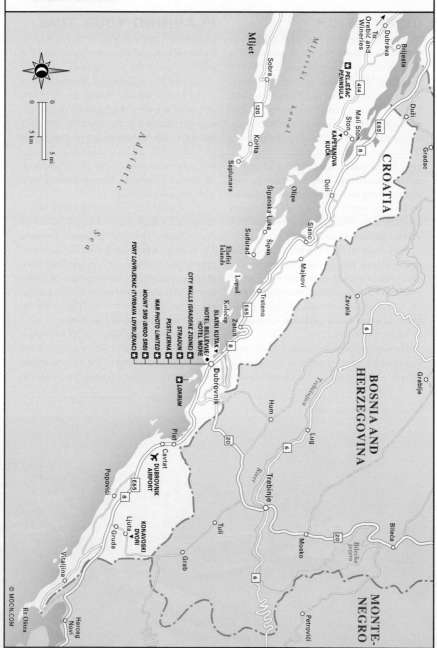

To Orebić and Wineries

Dubrava
Brijesta

Mljet

414
⊕ PELJEŠAC PENINSULA

E65
Duži

Mali Ston
Ston
▼ KAPETANOVA KUĆA

8

Gradac

CROATIA

Sobra

Mljetski kanal

120

Korita

Šipanska Luka
Olipa
Doli

Saplunara

Slano

Šipan
Sudurad
Majkovi

Zavala

Elafiti Islands

Lopud

Trsteno

E65
Zaton

6

Grablje

Kolocep

8

FORT LOVRIJENAC (TVRĐAVA LOVRIJENAC) ⊕
MOUNT SRĐ (BRDO SRĐ) ⊕
WAR PHOTO LIMITED ⊕
PUSTIJERNA ⊕
STRADUN ⊕
CITY WALLS (GRADSKE ZIDINE) ⊕
SLATKI KUTAK ▼
HOTEL BELLEVUE ● HOTEL MORE ●

Dubrovnik

⊕ LOKRUM

Hum

Lug

BOSNIA AND HERZEGOVINA

Trebišnjica River

Plat

Cavtat
✈ DUBROVNIK AIRPORT

20

6

Popovići

E65
8

Gruda
Ljuta ▼
KONAVOSKI DVORI

Tuli

Trebinje

Bileća

Vitaljina

Grab

Mosko

20

Bilećko Jezero

6

MONTE-NEGRO

Herceg Novi

Rij. Ojtra

Petovići

Adriatic Sea

0 —— 5 mi
0 —— 5 km

and the grand scale of the city that continues to seduce.

ORIENTATION

Dubrovnik stretches over five kilometers (three miles) along the coast, although the three most important sections are the Old Town, within the famous city walls in the center; Lapad to the west; and Ploče to the east. The Old Town is pedestrian-only and likely to occupy the bulk of your visit to Dubrovnik. It's peppered with sightseeing stops, shops, services, restaurants, and even a few lodgings. The city is dissected by the all-important Stradun (also referred to as Placa), a wide street running east-west. At the western end of the Stradun, you'll find the Pile Gate, outside of which buses pick up and drop off and taxis wait for their next fare.

Since many of the city's hotels are located in Lapad and Danče (west of the city but not as far as Lapad), you may find yourself around the Pile Gate often, hopping bus 6 for the 30-minute ride to Lapad. It's also in this western section where you'll find the majority of the city's better beaches.

The eastern neighborhood of Ploče, once Dubrovnik's cattle market, is a residential suburb with a handful of accommodations and a few more sightseeing stops worth your time.

PLANNING YOUR TIME

Ideally you'll have at least three full days in Dubrovnik. Spend the first day with all the other visitors at the must-see city sights and the second day relaxing on Lokrum or one of the Elafiti Islands. Spend the third day on a wine crawl on the Pelješac Peninsula, a long but doable day trip from the city. Four full days should be enough to thoroughly see Dubrovnik and its surroundings, leaving you time to travel to some of the Southern Dalmatian islands like Mljet or Korčula, both with easy connections.

If you don't like waiting for a table in restaurants, try to go outside the peak lunch and dinner hours (12:30pm-2pm and 7pm-9pm). The same goes for tourist sites, as a good portion of the visitors are brought into town from the cruise ships between 9am and 6pm. If some of the places you want to see have longer operating hours, try to visit then, when the bulk of the visitors have gone home.

There's not really any time of year when Dubrovnik is devoid of tourists, though the fewest will be visiting in the dead of winter (when the vicious *bura* is known to blow) and

panoramic view of Dubrovnik

the largest crowds are in July and August. Though the peak season can get a little wild, you do have the advantage of the excellent **Dubrovnik Summer Festival,** packed with classical concerts and theater performances, a must for culture buffs.

Itinerary Ideas

DUBROVNIK ON DAY 1

1 Head into town early for a coffee on the **Stradun** before it gets too busy.

2 Head out for a tour of Dubrovnik, starting with a walk around the **city walls.**

3 Stop for a quick look at the **Sponza Palace,** which holds the state archives and a memorial to those who died during the siege of Dubrovnik.

4 Break for lunch at **Buffet Škola** for one of the city's most famous sandwiches.

5 Continue your tour, saving the **Franciscan monastery** for later in the day when the crowds have tapered off.

6 After refreshing back at your hotel, have dinner at **Restaurant Sesame.**

DUBROVNIK ON DAY 2

1 Today head to the **market** on Gundulićeva poljana for provisions for a beach picnic.

2 From the Old Town's harbor, catch a water taxi to **Lokrum,** where you can while away the day lounging on the beach and strolling the shady paths.

3 Return to Dubrovnik to splurge on dinner at the phenomenal **Restaurant 360** under a starlit sky.

4 Alternatively, rent a speedboat or book a water taxi to **Restaurant BOWA Dubrovnik** and splurge on a private cabana for a Robinson Crusoe-does-luxe kind of day.

GOURMET JAUNT TO PELJEŠAC

Day 1

- Drive from Dubrovnik to **Orebić.**
- Hike up to the **Franciscan Monastery** and work up an appetite before having dinner in town.
- Check into the **Hotel Indijan.**

Day 2

- Have coffee and cake at **Croccantino.**
- Drive east to visit the **Grgić winery** and the other wineries around the village of Potomje. **Matuško winery** makes a good stop on your way back to Orebić.

Day 3

- Today, head to **Mali Ston** and savor a long lunch at **Kapetanova Kuća** (don't forget to order the local oysters) before heading back to Dubrovnik.

Dubrovnik Itinerary Ideas

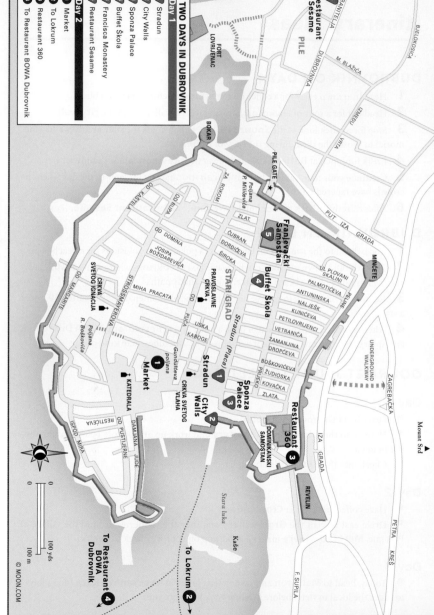

TWO DAYS IN DUBROVNIK

Day 1
1. Stradun
2. City Walls
3. Sponza Palace
4. Buffet Škola
5. Franciscа Monastery
6. Restaurant Sesame

Day 2
1. Market
2. To Lokrum
3. Restaurant 360
4. To Restaurant BOWA Dubrovnik

© MOON.COM

Gourmet Jaunt to Pelješac

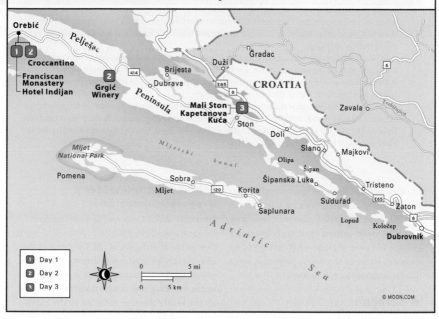

Sights

Though you can easily get a good overview of Dubrovnik in a day, there's enough here to fill up a few days, lazily wandering through the town's museums and galleries. Make sure to start with the Old Town sights, the best of the bunch.

OLD TOWN (STARI GRAD)
★ City Walls
(Gradske zidine)

Placa utica 32, entrance inside the Pile Gate to the left; www.wallsofdubrovnik.com; 8am-6:30pm Apr.-May, 8am-7:30pm June-July, 8am-6:30pm Aug.-Sept., 8am-5:30pm Oct., 10am-3pm Nov.-March; 150Kn, which includes entry to Fort Lovrijenac

Taking a walk along Dubrovnik's city walls is absolutely the best way to start your tour of the Old Town. Running for about two kilometers (one mile), the walk around will take you 1-1.5 hours, depending on your speed and the size of the crowds. Backpacks are discouraged and prohibited in some sections due to winds.

Built and tweaked from the mid-15th century until the great earthquake in 1667, the walls feature the rounded **Minčeta fortress** (built in response to the invention of gunpowder) in the northwest, the **Revelin** in the east, **St. John (Sveti Ivan)** by the harbor, and the beautiful **Bokar** (worked on by stone masons Michelozzi and Dalmatinac) in the southwest. The best views are likely from the walls that face the sea, looking toward the red-tiled roofs on one side and the sea on the other. An interesting stop under the Gornji Ugao tower of the Minčeta fortress is the recently renovated **Medieval Foundry.** For 30Kn, a caretaker

Dubrovnik in Film

While it's well-known that Dubrovnik is a frequent setting in the hit TV series Game of Thrones, there are many other places to look out for around town that have had cameo appearances in major Hollywood films.

In Star Wars: Episode VIII, look out for the scenes where Finn and Rose land on the beach and are escaping from the ensuing chase due to being parked illegally (which could happen to you in Dubrovnik if you're not careful!). You can spot **Banje Beach,** the **Minčeta Tower, Placa Ulica,** and the north wall of the city walls in the film.

The western harbor appears in Emerald City, and Dubrovnik was also one of the filming locations of Robin Hood: Origins. Rumor has it that an upcoming James Bond film will include Dubrovnik, so keep your eyes open for places you've visited. Check www.moviemaps.org for more specific info.

explains how the foundry functioned in precise archeological detail. It's a must for serious fans of history who go for substance, not show. The **Pile Gate,** where most travelers enter into the old core of Dubrovnik, is topped by a somber statue of the town's protector, Saint Blasius, welcoming you to town.

★ Stradun

This is possibly the most important spot in Dubrovnik to explain, given the confusion its name can cause the average visitor—some people call it **Placa** and some use its colloquial name, Stradun. Running from the Pile Gate to the Ploče, the Stradun (or Placa, according to street signs) is the meeting and strutting spot for all of Dubrovnik. It also divides the city into the southern side, Ragusa (derived from the Greek *laus,* for rock), inhabited by the Illyrians in the 4th century, and Dubrava, on the north, settled several centuries later by the Slavs. The Stradun, which used to be a marshy channel, was filled in the late 10th or 11th century. In 1438, Onofrio designed a fountain for either end of Dubrovnik's main street. Croatian writer Slobodan Prosperov Novak described the Stradun: "Ragusans see their homes as places where they die of boredom—while Stradun is the place where they live."

At the end of the Stradun is the busy **Luža Square (Trg Luža)**. Here you'll find the **town bell tower** *(gradski zvonik),* built in the 15th century.

Franciscan Monastery (Franjevački samostan)

Placa 2; tel. 020/321-410; 9am-6pm daily summer, 9am-5pm daily winter; 30Kn

One of the highlights of old Dubrovnik, the Franciscan Monastery is among the city's most popular attractions. The Baroque look of the building was a later addition, making up for severe damage suffered in the earthquake and fire of 1667. One of the only surviving pieces of the original late-15th-century church is the portal, the fire having also destroyed paintings by Caravaggio, Titian, and many others. The cloisters and the monastery's courtyard are perhaps the most beautiful features of the complex, packed with fragrant orange trees. In the alley between the monastery and the Church of Our Savior is the **Old Pharmacy**. The 700-year-old pharmacy is supposedly the oldest continuously operating pharmacy in Europe. For less of a crowd, try to visit the monastery at the end of the day.

★ War Photo Limited

Antuninska 6; tel. 020/322-166; www.warphotoltd. com; 10am-10pm daily May-Sept., 10am-4pm Wed.-Mon. Apr. and Oct.; 50Kn

A small but moving gallery run by New Zealand war photographer Wade Goddard, War Photo Limited showcases work by some of the world's top war photojournalists. Permanent displays chronicle the

Old Town Dubrovnik

A d r i a t i c

S e a

FORT LOVRIJENAC
(TVRĐAVA LOVRIJENAC)

SESAME
INN

BRANITELJA

PILE

To Danče, Lapad,
Hotel Bellevue,
and Hotel More

BJELOKOSICA

DUBROVNIKA

M. BLAŽIĆA

ATLAS
CLUB NAUTICA

HILTON IMPERIAL
DUBROVNIK

BUS STATION
(LAPAD)

IZMEĐU

VRTA

Bokar

BOKAR

CITY WALLS
(GRADSKE ZIDINE)

PILE GATE

CHURCH OF
OUR SAVIOR

PUT IZA GRADA

MINČETA

FELME

HOSTEL
ANGELINA

UL PLOVANI
SKALINI

PALMOTIĆEVA

ANTUNINSKA

NALJEŠK

KUNIĆEVA

PETILOVRIJENCI

VETRANIĆA

ZAMANJINA

DROPČEVA

BOŠKOVIĆEVA

ŽUDIOSKA

PRIJEKO

KOVAČKA

ZLATA.

UNDERGROUND
WALKWAY

ZAGREBAČKA

MOUNT SRĐ (BRDO SRĐ)

BUS STATION
(CAVTAT)

DUBROVNIK
CABLE CAR

IZA GRADA

ONOFRIO'S
LARGE FOUNTAIN

ZA ROKOM

OD KAŠTELA

OD PUPA

OD DOMINA

ZLAT

ĆUBRAN

ĐORĐIĆEVA

ŠIROKA

PORTUN

STARI GRAD

Stradun (Placa)

TOURIST
OFFICE

OLD
PHARMACY

FRANCISCAN
MONASTERY

HOTEL
STARI GRAD

NISHTA

WAR PHOTO
LIMITED

BUFFET
ŠKOLA

TAVELIN WINE
AND ART BAR

DOM MARINA DRŽIĆA

ST. JOSEPH'S
BOUTIQUE HOTEL

RUPE ETHNOGRAPHIC
MUSEUM

JOSIPA
BOŽIDAREVIĆA

APARTMENTS
NIVES

MIHA

PRACATA

OD PUĆA

PRAVOSLAVNE
CRKVE

PROTO

USKA

KAROGE

BARBA

RESTAURANT
FORTY-FOUR

ORTHODOX
CHURCH
MUSEUM

STROSSMAYEROVA

APARTMENTS
PLACA

Poljina

R. Boškovića

CRKVA
SVETOG IGNACIJA

OD MARGARITE

PUSTIJERNA

APARTMENTS
AMORET

CATHEDRAL

DULČIĆ-MASLE-
PULITIKA GALLERY

Gundulićeva
poljana

OLIVA
PIZZERIA

STRADUN

ST. BLAISUS'S
CHURCH

ORLANDO'S
COLUMN

LITTLE FOUNTAIN

ONOFRIO'S
LITTLE FOUNTAIN

SYNAGOGUE
AND MUSEUM

SPONZA PALACE

DOMINIKANSKI
SAMOSTAN

RESTAURANT
360

REVELIN
FORTRESS

PLOČE
GATE

RESTIĆEVA

OD PUSTIJERNE

DAMJANA

JUDE

BROD MIRA

RECTOR'S PALACE/
CULTURAL HISTORY MUSEUM

KARMEN
APARTMENTS

TVRĐAVA
SV. IVAN

MARITIME MUSEUM

Stara luka

Kaše

To Lokrum

PETRA KREŠ

F. SUPILA

VILLA
ADRIATICA

To Sveti Jakov,
Umjetnička Galerija,
and Villa Dubrovnik

To
Lazareti

Banje
Beach

0   100 yds
0   100 m

© MOON.COM

The Siege of Dubrovnik

The 1991 attack on Dubrovnik by Serb forces came out of nowhere for Dubrovnik's citizens. Not really seen as an important port and with hardly any Serb residents to speak of, Dubrovnik was attacked more to hurt Croatian morale than for any strategic purpose. The people of Dubrovnik were bombed and shot at from November 1991 until May 1992, with the Old Town sustaining plenty of damage. The fortresses of the city walls once again became practical structures as locals hid inside them for shelter and safety. The brave people of Dubrovnik held out, and the siege ended in July 1992, when the Croatian army secured a path to the beautiful city.

1990s Homeland War, and revolving exhibits bring home to the viewer the grimness of struggles in places such as Africa and the Middle East.

Synagogue and Museum

Žudioska 5; tel. 020/321-204; 8am-6pm daily summer, 9am-12pm Mon.-Fri. winter; 35Kn

The small Žudioska (Jew's Street) is home to a tiny but significant synagogue and museum dating from the 14th century and said to be the second oldest synagogue in Europe still in use. It served one of the oldest communities of Sephardic Jews in the Balkans. Inside the synagogue are a Torah, religious texts, and a Moorish carpet all brought by refugees from the Spanish Inquisition.

Unfortunately, they did not escape persecution here either. The people of Dubrovnik regularly ridiculed the Jews, barred them from drinking from all but one fountain, and mocked them in local festivals.

Sponza Palace
(Palača Sponza)

Luža; tel. 020/321-032; 9am-9pm daily summer, 10am-3pm daily winter; free

Most notable among the buildings on the Luža Square (Trg Luža) is the Sponza Palace, a customs house built in 1520. Today, the palace is home to the **Dubrovnik State Archives (Državni arhiv u Dubrovniku)** (tel. 020/321-032, www.dad.hr, 8am-3pm Mon.-Fri., 8am-1pm Sat., 15Kn), containing records dating back to the first half of the 11th century, with some on revolving display. The palace also houses a permanent exhibit,

the **Memorial Room of the Defenders of Dubrovnik (Spomen soba poginulim dubrovački braniteljima)** (9am-9pm daily summer, 10am-3pm daily winter; free), displaying pictures and portraits of those who died during the 1991-1992 siege of Dubrovnik.

St. Blasius's Church
(Crkva svetog Vlaha)

Luža 3; tel. 020/323-462; morning and evening daily; free

Across from the Sponza Palace, the present-day St. Blasius's Church stands on the spot of an earlier Romanesque structure destroyed in the earthquake of 1667. The church you see today, a mass of creamy stone carved with statues, was finished in 1714. Don't miss the sculpture of Saint Blasius with a model of Dubrovnik in his hand, a survivor from the previous, and much older, church.

Orlando's Column
(Orlandov stup)

In the middle of Luža Square you'll see a relatively unimpressive column carved with a statue of a knight and supporting a flag. Known as Orlando's Column, the monument is much more significant than it looks.

A knight who died in the 8th century, Orlando, also known as Roland, became a superstar of his day when he was immortalized and given legendary qualities in the medieval epic poem *Chanson de Roland* (Song of Roland). His admirers, mainly Northern Europeans, formed a cult, but the fever reached Dubrovnik when Sigismund, the Hungarian and Czech king who would later

Saint Blasius (Sveti Vlaho)

Saint Blasius has been the protector of Dubrovnik since the 11th century. Legend has it that a local religious authority had a vision of the saint that saved them from attack by the Venetians. As you're touring around Dubrovnik, keep an eye out for Saint Blasius, usually portrayed with a long beard, a tall bishop's hat, and a raised hand with one finger extended as if to make a point. St. Blasius Day is celebrated every February 3 in Dubrovnik, with processions carrying the reliquaries containing his head and a few other body parts.

rule Germany as well, visited the city. Orlando was promptly adopted by Dubrovnik as having fought a battle with a Saracen corsair named Spuzente ("bad breath"), even though the battle actually took place long after Orlando's death.

Considered the most important symbol of freedom for the city, Orlando's Column first had a flag hoisted above it in 1419, celebrating Dubrovnik's position as an independent city-state; it was lowered in 1808 when Napoleon's army marched into town. The statue was blown over by a strong wind in 1825—even Orlando was no match for the *bura*—and put into storage for 50 years. When he was returned, he no longer faced east against the Turks, but north, toward those that oppressed Dubrovnik's freedom, the Austrians. Today, it flies a flag that reads *libertas* (freedom).

Onofrio's Little Fountain
(Mala Onofrijeva česma)

Near Luža Square is Onofrio's Little Fountain, a much smaller work than the giant domed fountain at the other end of the Stradun. The 15th-century fountain is delicate, with decorations of cherubs and frolicking dolphins.

Rector's Palace
(Knežev dvor)

Though the building is called the Rector's Palace, it was actually more of a government building than a palace for a ruler. The rector wasn't much of a ruler anyway—the title was more honorary than one of real power, as he was given only a one-month term and was ineligible for the two subsequent years, and a few apartments in the palace for his living quarters. The palace also held a dungeon that must have made sleeping in the place a bit difficult due to prisoner noise.

The current palace was constructed in the 15th century after a couple of gunpowder explosions (the palace was also used for storing munitions) rendered the old building almost useless. The new palace is a grand affair, with lots of stone carvings and columns along the facade; Dalmatinac, a famous 15th-century stone mason and architect, was among the many craftsmen who worked on the building. The most interesting carving is a relief of Greek god Asclepius sitting in his pharmacy. The funny part of the story is that locals confused his birthplace, Epidaurus in Greece, with the nearby city of the same name, today called Cavtat, and made him its protector.

CULTURAL HISTORY MUSEUM (Gradski muzej)

Pred Dvorom 1; tel. 020/321-437; www.dumus. hr; 9am-6pm daily Apr.-Oct., 9am-4pm Mon.-Sat. Nov.-Mar.; 80Kn, or 120Kn for admission to nine city museums

Inside the palace, the Cultural History Museum has been recently renovated. Sparsely furnished rooms and lots of Baroque, mostly anonymous, paintings decorate the rooms where the rector and other political figures once sat. It is pretty and well-done, but if you are not a fan of historic buildings and period furniture, you may want to spend your time elsewhere.

Dulčić-Masle-Pulitika Gallery (Galerija Dulčić-Masle-Pulitika)

Poljana Marina Držića 1; tel. 020/323-172; 10am-8pm Tues.-Sun. summer; 120Kn includes visits to nine city museums

Close to the Rector's Palace in a refined

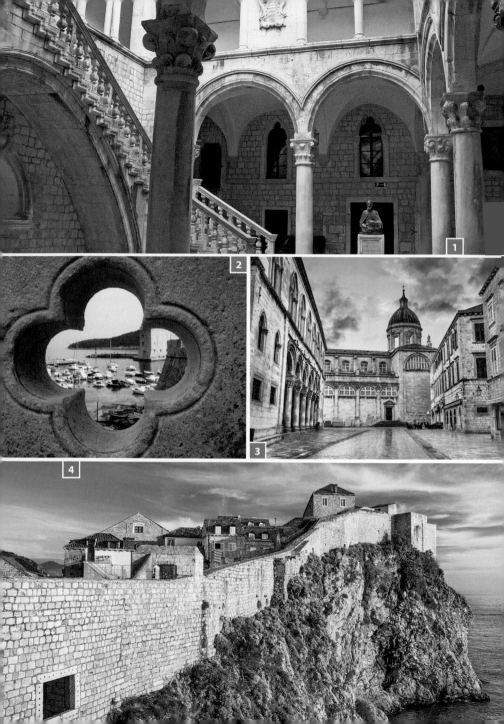

Ivan Gundulić, Poet and Playwright

Born in 1589 to a wealthy and aristocratic Dubrovnik family, Gundulić began writing plays around 1615; they were performed in front of the Rector's Palace. But Gundulić was not only a playwright and poet. Having studied law, he held numerous political positions in Dubrovnik, including judge and senator, though he died too early to be appointed rector, a position given only to men age 50 or older.

The first verse of his best-known pastoral play, *Dubrava*, serves as an unofficial motto for Dubrovnik: *"O lijepa, o draga, o slatka sloboda"* ("Oh beautiful, oh beloved, oh sweet freedom").

Ivan Gundulić died in 1638 in Dubrovnik of a high fever.

Baroque townhouse, the Dulčić-Masle-Pulitika Gallery is more worth visiting for the views over the cathedral than for the art inside. The first floor displays works by the three Dubrovnik artists for whom the gallery is named, while the second floor is home to works by Cavtat artist Vlaho Bukovac and Croatia's famed Ivan Meštrović.

Cathedral
(Katedrala)

Poljana Marina Držića; tel. 020/323-459; 9am-5:30pm Mon.-Sat., 11am-5:30pm and mass Sun.; free

Although its dome is one of Dubrovnik's postcard views, the cathedral has an interior that is more ho-hum than exciting. The original church, purportedly built by Richard the Lionhearted in the 12th century in return for the kindness he was shown after a shipwreck, was destroyed in the 1667 earthquake. Excavations following a 1979 earthquake uncovered another, possibly Byzantine, church from the 7th or 8th century under the cathedral. The Baroque structure seen today, built between 1672 and 1713, does have a visit-worthy **treasury** *(riznica)* (25Kn) that houses several oddities, including the arm, head, and lower leg of Saint Blaise in an 11th-century golden Byzantine box and a diaper purportedly belonging to baby Jesus.

_____

1: atrium of Rector's Palace 2: Old Port view
3: Dubrovnik Cathedral 4: city walls

Maritime Museum
(Pomorski muzej)

Tvrđava Sv. Ivana; tel. 020/323-904; www.dumus.hr; 9am-10pm Tues.-Sun. Apr.-Oct., 9am-4pm Tues.-Sun. Nov.-Mar.; 120Kn includes entrance to nine city museums

Near the cathedral, St. John's Fortress is where you'll find the lovely Maritime Museum, one of Dubrovnik's most important museums. Following the history of the city's seafaring, it has everything from model ships to medicine chests to the blueprints for building Gruž harbor. Given the importance of the sea to the development of Dubrovnik, it's hard to pass up this stop.

★ Pustijerna

The Pustijerna is one of Dubrovnik's most ancient quarters, with many buildings dating from before the earthquake of 1667. The neighborhood is quite medieval in feel. Here you'll find the Jesuit **St. Ignatius's Church (Crkva Sv. Ignacija)** (Ruđera Boškovića 6; tel. 020/323-500; 7am-8pm daily; free), a giant Baroque structure built in the first half of the 18th century and modeled on the Church of the Gesù in Rome. The grand staircase leading to it was also inspired by the eternal city, modeled on the Spanish Steps. The steps and the square are often used for performances during the Dubrovnik Summer Festival.

Descending the wide stairway, you'll run into **Gundulić Square (Gundulićeva poljana)**, where the morning market is held, watched over by a statue of Croatia's well-loved poet Ivan Gundulić. The reliefs around

Convents in Dubrovnik

Dubrovnik's old convents often go unnoticed by the average visitor, though the city was home to eight nunneries before the great earthquake of 1667. Today, only two are somewhat preserved—that of St. Catherine (today a music school) and the Clarist convent near Onofrio's large fountain. Many women were put inside the convents by their elders, aristocrats bent on preserving the purity of the family line. With hardly anyone for them to marry, their parents thought it better to enter a convent than sully the blood with that of a commoner. The plan backfired—by the late 17th century, the town was already promoting common families to the rank of nobility to make up for the disappearing aristocracy.

Life inside the nunnery was not much better than a prison. A law passed in 1433 required the convents to be surrounded by thick walls without windows, and sleeping quarters were locked at night.

One nun, Agnes Beneša, set fire to her convent, possibly to try to escape, in 1620. She was walled up in the Rector's Palace dungeon as a punishment but still managed to wriggle through a hole left for confession and find her way to freedom.

the statue reflect scenes from one of his most famous works, *Osman,* an epic about the Poles' victory over the Turks.

Orthodox Church Museum
(Muzej pravoslavne crkve)

Od Puča 8; tel. 020/323-283; 9am-2pm Mon.-Sat. summer; 10Kn

From Gundulić Square, take Od Puča, a street that runs parallel with the Stradun, west to the Orthodox Church Museum. The museum houses a number of delicate icons of Byzantine and Cretan origin. Next door is the Orthodox Church, built in the 19th century.

Nearby, look for **Iza Roka** (Behind Roc), where you'll come across the **Church of St. Roc** (Crkva Svetog Roka), not very important but quite interesting for an inscription written on the eastern wall of the facade. A grumpy neighbor was obviously tired of some boys breaking his window during their games and wrote in Latin, "Go in peace, and remember that you will die, you who now are playing ball."

House of Marin Držić
(Dom Marina Držića)

Široka 7; tel. 020/323-242; www.muzej-marindrzic.eu; 9am-8:30pm Tues.-Sat. Oct.-May, 10am-6pm Mon. and 9am-10pm Tues.-Sat. June-Sept.; 120Kn includes

entrance to nine city museums

The House of Marin Držić is a Gothic townhome where the slightly eccentric playwright was born in the 16th century. He was constantly at odds with local authorities, as the Dubrovnik of his day didn't think much of his plays and comedies—the only document regarding Marin Držić in the state archives is about a loan. There's not much to see here, but if you happen to catch one of his comedies at the Dubrovnik Summer Festival, where the writer is honored posthumously, and want to know more about him, this is the place to go.

Rupe Ethnographic Museum
(Etnografski muzej Rupe)

Od Rupa 3; tel. 020/412-545; www.dumus. hr; 9am-4pm Wed.-Mon. Nov.-Mar., 9am-10pm Wed.-Mon. Apr.-Oct.; 120Kn includes entrance to nine city museums in town

Supposedly the reason to come to the Rupe Ethnographic Museum is to admire the costumes and relics related to life in the rural areas around Dubrovnik. However, you'll find a stronger reason might be the sweeping views of mountains, sea, and red-tiled roofs from the top-floor display. The building was once the city's granary, a very important location during its heyday, when individuals were issued tickets allotting them a certain amount of grain. It's here where they picked up the grain stored in *rupe* (holes), hence the name.

Dominican Monastery
(Dominikanski samostan)

Sv. Dominika 4; tel. 020/322-200; www.dominikanci-dubrovnik.hr; 9am-6pm daily summer, 9am-5pm daily winter, mass 7am and 7pm Mon.-Sat., 8:30am and 7pm Sun.; 30Kn

The somewhat plain exterior of the 14th-century Dominican Monastery hides an interior decorated with a delicate Gothic and Renaissance cloister and an outstanding collection of paintings by local artists. Included in the exhibit are a painting of Dubrovnik before the 1667 earthquake and *The Miracle of St. Dominic* by turn-of-the-20th-century Cavtat artist Vlaho Bukovac, as well as works by Titian and Antonio Veneziano.

EAST OF THE CITY WALLS
Revelin Fortress
(Tvrđava Revelin)

The Revelin Fortress took almost a century to complete, with work ramped up and quickly finished in 1539 due to threats from the Ottoman Empire. Now the Revelin is a concert venue during the Dubrovnik Summer Festival and also houses a café and nightclub. Near the Revelin is the **Ploče Gate,** the eastern entrance to town, which welcomed most of the tradesmen to town in its day. Like the Pile Gate, it's guarded over by a statue of Saint Blaise.

Lazareti

Dating from the late 16th century, the buildings of the Lazareti are today part of the modern suburb of Ploče. Most of the neighborhood, which used to be a large market for cattle as well as produce, has been destroyed and paved over. But the Lazareti, built to inspect the health and goods of foreigners before they entered the city, remain untouched. The purpose of the row of gated buildings was not only to protect the health of Dubrovnik's citizens, but also to keep the city from becoming raucous at night and to ferry the tradesmen into town in an orderly fashion.

Today, the buildings house the **Art Workshop Lazareti (Art Radionica Lazareti)** (Frana Supila 8; www.arl.hr; 10am-5pm daily), which displays contemporary art in its Otok gallery. In the summer it's often the home of great concerts and nightlife.

Dubrovnik Art Gallery
(Umjetnička Galerija)

Frana Supila 23; tel. 020/426-590; www.ugdubrovnik. hr; 9am-3pm daily; 120Kn for entrance to nine city museums

Near the Lazareti is the Dubrovnik Art Gallery in a grand 1930s mansion. There's often an excellent contemporary exhibition on, and the gallery brings in a big name from the art world most summers.

NORTH OF THE CITY WALLS
★ Mount Srđ
(Brdo Srđ)

A don't-miss in the city, the best views of all are from the **Dubrovnik Cable Car (Žičara Dubrovnik)** (Petra Krešimira 4. bb; tel. 020/325-393; www.dubrovnikcablecar.com, 9am-12am daily June-Aug., 9am-8pm daily Apr. and Oct., 9am-9pm daily May and Sept., 9am-5pm daily Nov. and Feb.-Mar., 9am-4pm daily Dec.-Jan.; 150Kn return ticket). The cable car has been transporting tourists since 1969 up to Mount Srđ, where on a clear day they claim you can see for almost 60 kilometers (37 miles). It is certainly a wonderful experience as long as you buy your tickets online and go very early during the summer, as lines can get incredibly long as the day wears on.

If you don't want to pay the fare, or want to buy only a one-way ticket, there is a trail that you can hike up or down. Make sure to wear good shoes, as there are loose rocks underfoot, and take the usual hiking precautions: sunscreen, hat, and water.

Escaping the Crowds in Dubrovnik

In June and July, when masses of tourists descend on Dubrovnik from the hotels and the giant cruise ships that dock in the harbors, the crowds can get to be a little much.

The best tip for escaping the crowds is to visit the **Old Town** in the **early morning** and the **late evening,** when the critical mass has returned to their cruise ships or their package hotels and you're left to walk around without worrying if you're going to unknowingly whack someone with your backpack.

There are, of course, out-of-the-way spots around Dubrovnik (head to **Trsteno**) or just off the coast, like the **Elafiti islands** of **Šipan** (home to over 30 churches, at least six of which date from pre-Roman times), **Koločep** (only 30 minutes by ferry, with lots of secluded beaches), and **Lopud** (with plenty of sightseeing and beaches).

On a summer Sunday, head to the village of **Čilipi** (near the airport), where colorful folk performances draw large crowds—but not as large as those strolling the Stradun.

Museum of the Homeland War
(Muzej Domovinskog rata)

Imperial Fort; 8am-6pm daily summer; 8am-4pm daily winter; 30Kn

At the top of Mount Srđ you'll find the Museum of the Homeland War. The museum is located in the 19th-century Napoleonic Imperial Fort, which was defended by the local population during the Homeland War, as Croatians refer to their fight for independence during the 1990s. A well-done video, photographs, and exhibits showcase the valiant fight for the city. If you want to go even higher, climb up to the rooftop for a super view over Dubrovnik.

WEST OF THE CITY WALLS
★ Fort Lovrijenac
(Tvrđava Lovrijenac)

30Kn, or as part of the City Walls ticket

Fort Lovrijenac can be reached by climbing the stairs from Pile Beach. Set 37 meters (121 feet) above the Adriatic on a cliff, the fort was built to protect the city, particularly against the Venetian fleet. Taking centuries to construct, the fort was founded in the early 11th century but wasn't completed until the 16th. Inside the meters-thick walls are a small chapel and a beautiful courtyard that often serves as a locale for events on the Dubrovnik Summer Festival's schedule.

OFF THE COAST
★ Lokrum

Boats leave the Old Town port, Stara Luka, every 30 minutes in summer; around 150Kn one-way

Purportedly the island where King Richard the Lionhearted was shipwrecked while returning from a Crusade in 1192, likely due to a late-fall *bura*, the forested island of Lokrum lies one kilometer (0.6 mile) off the coast of Dubrovnik. The island was once home to a Benedictine monastery, but it was an Austrian who really shaped the place. In the mid-19th century, Archduke Maximilian Ferdinand von Habsburg, brother of Emperor Franz Joseph of Austria, built a summer home on the island as well as a **Botanical Garden** (Botanički vrt), still open to the public free of charge. This is a great place for a swim—there's a nice little lake at the southwest corner of the island—as well as for strolling along the paths that lead to a **Napoleonic fort** *(napoleonsko utvrđenje).*

BEACHES

The city beach at **Banje,** near the Ploče Gate, is a decent place for a swim, though a much better spot, the beach at **Sveti Jakov,** is a 20-minute walk along the Vlaha Bukovca past Villa Dubrovnik and down a long stairway

---

1: Stradun 2: alleyway in Old Town Dubrovnik
3: Dubrovnik's morning market 4: Pile Gate

(remember you'll have to hike back up). It's usually not too crowded and has a superb view of a golden Dubrovnik at sunset. Remember that hotel beaches are either private or accessed with a daily fee. In return you get to use the beach and the pool, if the hotel has one.

The beach at **Danče,** west of the Old Town, is rocky but quite clean, and the **Betina špilja** (accessed via water taxi) is a cave with a nice pebbly beach, though it doesn't have any services or cafés. **Lapad,** west of the Old Town (take bus 6 from the Pile Gate), is also filled with beaches, though it's probably nicer to take a water taxi to **Lokrum.**

Entertainment and Events

NIGHTLIFE AND BARS

D'VINO WINE BAR

Palmotićeva 4a; tel. 020/321-130; www.dvino.net; 10am-late daily

If you're looking for a low-key evening, D'Vino Wine Bar offers flights of Croatian wines or wines by the glass alongside a variety of snacks. There are over 60 by the glass selections on offer and the bar can also arrange wine tours if you want to explore the local viticulture in more depth.

DUBROVNIK BEER FACTORY

Od Puča 8; 9am-1am daily

If beer is your thing, try the Dubrovnik Beer Factory, which offers local craft beers on a tucked away patio, a great respite from a hot day of sightseeing. Prices are reasonable and many craft selections are offered on tap, which isn't that common in Croatia.

CULTURE CLUB REVELIN

Sv. Dominika 3; tel. 098/533-531; www.clubrevelin. com; 11pm-5am daily summer

Love it or hate it, Culture Club Revelin is one of the city's busiest nightclubs, with scantily clad go-go dancers, loud music, and light shows. This place can be pricey, and the crowd definitely skews younger.

LAZARETI

Lazareti complex, Frana Supila 8; tel. 020/324-633; www.lazareti.com; 9pm-4am when events are scheduled; cash only

Lazareti is a club with an edge. Set in the old quarantine barracks of Lazareti, the club hosts live concerts and good DJs throughout the year. Check with the **tourist office** (Ante Starčićeva 7, tel. 020/427-591, www. tzdubrovnik.hr) for a local events guide if the website hasn't been updated recently.

FESTIVALS AND EVENTS

DUBROVNIK SUMMER FESTIVAL

Various locations, tel. 020/412-288; info@dubrovnik-festival.hr, www.dubrovnik-festival.hr; Jul.-Aug.; 30-200Kn

The crown jewel of the city's events is the Dubrovnik Summer Festival in July and August, when classical music and plays are performed in eye-catching venues all over town. The festival usually includes opera and Shakespeare in addition to the concerts and theater performances of local playwrights like Marin Držić. Dubrovnik usually manages to draw a couple of big international names, and these tickets sell out months in advance, some as soon as the schedule comes out in April. If you haven't had that much time to plan, once you get to town you can usually pick up tickets for other performances from festival info booths on the Stradun and at the Pile Gate. During July and August, you'll also find a healthy schedule of pop and jazz performances around the Old Town.

DUBROVNIK SYMPHONY ORCHESTRA

tel. 020/417-101; www.dso.hr

If you're looking for classical music throughout the year, try the **Dubrovnik Symphony**

Game of Thrones and Dubrovnik

The fantasy TV series *Game of Thrones* has been a runaway hit worldwide, but not everyone knows that many of the settings are real and can be found in Dubrovnik. With medieval architecture worthy of a Hollywood blockbuster series, fans should keep their eyes out for a few key spots:

- **Trsteno:** The historic Renaissance gardens were used as the setting for the King's Landing Palace Gardens.

- **St. Dominika Street:** This appears in the series dozens of times, often as part of market scenes.

- **Pile:** This waterfront locale is known as Blackwater Bay in *Game of Thrones*.

- **Lokrum Island:** This beautiful escape from Dubrovnik also doubles as the city of Qarth.

If you just can't get enough *Game of Thrones* and would like to discover more locations from the series, you can take Viator's three-hour **Game of Thrones Walking Tour** (www.viator.com, around 430Kn).

Orchestra, which performs in the Revelin Fortress as well as other locations in town. With an over 90-year history, this local orchestra not only has classical concerts, but klapa, opera, and concerts with a modern twist.

Shopping

KNIJŽARA ALGEBRA
Placa 9; tel. 020/323-217; www.knjizara-algebra.hr; 8:30am-8:30pm Mon.-Sat.
You can shop for English magazines and newspapers and a good selection of books on local topics and history at Knijžara Algebra, with a convenient within-the-walls location.

OLD PHARMACY
Alley between the Franciscan monastery on Placa 2 and the Church of Our Savior
The Old Pharmacy (located in the alley between the Franciscan monastery on Placa 2 and the Church of Our Savior) can be a bit of a rip-off (think captured audience for sunscreen on a hot day), but their natural face and hand creams, made from the secret recipes of the monks at the monastery next door, are a nice purchase for the spa fan in your life. Based on herbs and flowers like rose, lavender, and rosemary, you certainly can't get them at your local department store.

DUBROVAČKA KUĆA
Od sv Dominika; tel. 020/322-092; 9am-9:30pm Mon.-Sat., 9am-7:30pm Sun. summer, call for winter hours
If you don't have a lot of time, try Dubrovačka kuća, a one-stop shop selling gourmet liquors, wines, and olive oils for souvenirs as well as books, posters, and handmade items through its partnership with the Museum of Arts and Crafts in Zagreb.

LIFE ACCORDING TO KAWA
Hvarska 2; tel. 20/696-958; 9am-12am June-Sept., 9am-7pm Oct.-May
Just outside the Ploče gate, Life According to Kawa is a Croatian design concept store. You will find high-end fashion and home items as

well as books and gourmet goods for swank souvenirs and mementos, the sort that let you casually say "I got it at this little shop in Dubrovnik" in response to where you got them.

Sports and Recreation

To see another side of Dubrovnik, it doesn't hurt to get athletic.

ADRIATIC KAYAK TOURS

Zrinsko-Frankopanska 6; tel. 020/312-770; www.adriatickayaktours.com

Even beginners can take to the seas in a kayak, with a tour to the island of Lokrum through Adriatic Kayak Tours. The firm also offers white-water rafting in nearby Montenegro and mountain biking in the Konavle.

BLUE PLANET DIVING

Masarykov put 20; tel. 091/899-973; www.blueplanet-diving.com

Scuba divers can check out Blue Planet Diving, in the Hotel Dubrovnik Palace, for trips and courses for all levels and interests. Dive sites include several wrecks, caves, and reefs around Dubrovnik.

VILLA NERETVA

Krvavac 2, Metković; tel. 020/672-200; www.hotel-villa-neretva.com

For the slightly lower-key adventure-seeker, Villa Neretva offers photo safaris and nature schools in the Neretva River delta, ending with a meal at the family-run restaurant that offers equally adventurous dishes of eel and frog.

Accommodations

Dubrovnik is not the cheapest place to find lodging, especially in the summer months. It also books up early, so it's wise to reserve your room in advance. If you do find yourself in a bind, try one of the agencies that rent private rooms such as **Gulliver** (Obala Stjepana Radića 32, tel. 020/313-313, www.gulliver. hr), across from the ferries, or **Atlas** (Svetog Đurđa 1, tel. 020/442-565, www.atlas-croatia. com), near the Pile Gate. Try to avoid the people hawking rooms at the ferry terminal and the bus stations, as the rooms are generally way off the beaten track, and they often turn out to be giant rip-offs.

INSIDE THE CITY WALLS
Under 700Kn
HOSTEL ANGELINA

Plovani skalini 17A; tel. 091/893-9089; www.hostelangelinaoldtowndubrovnik.com; 282Kn pp

Hostel Angelina is clean and friendly, with a selection of shared and private rooms and a shared kitchen. Rooms are air-conditioned and there is free Wi-Fi and a variety of free lockers for guest use.

APARTMENTS NIVES RAČIĆ

Nikole Božidarevića 7; tel. 020/323-181; www.dubrovnik-palace.com; 598Kn d

Apartments Nives Račić has two small apartments and a tiny room with beamed ceilings, some antiques, and good hospitality.

APARTMENTS PLACA

Gundulićeva Poljana 5; tel. 091/721-9202; www. dubrovnik-online.net/apartments_placa; from 700Kn d

The Apartments Placa front Gundulić Square, the site of a morning market where you can buy fresh fruits and vegetables for the day. The rooms are bright and sunny with small kitchenettes.

700-1,400Kn
APARTMENTS AMORET

Restićeva 2; tel. 020/324-005; www.dubrovnik-amoret.com; from 830Kn d

The Apartments Amoret are located in the heart of the Old Town, steps from the Stradun in a 16th-century building. Furnished tastefully with a bit of antique flair, they also have satellite TV, air-conditioning, and wireless Internet.

KARMEN APARTMENTS

Bandureva 1; tel. 020/323-433; www.karmendu.com; 710-1,032Kn

Within the city walls, one street over from the Rector's Palace and next to the hosts' swinging jazz café, where Jimi Hendrix once jammed, the Karmen Apartments are well decorated and filled with charm.

Over 1,400Kn
★ HOTEL STARI GRAD

Od Sigurate 4; tel. 020/322-244; www.hotelstarigrad.com; 2,500Kn d, including breakfast

The Hotel Stari Grad is in the heart of Old Town. The small rooms and baths are furnished with antiques, and the rooftop terrace is a great spot for breakfast or a coffee. However, the number of stairs to get up to bed will not be appreciated if you're at all out of shape.

★ ST. JOSEPH'S BOUTIQUE HOTEL

Svetoga Josipa 3; tel. 20/432-089; www.stjosephs.hr; 2,600Kn d, including breakfast

Another standout, the St. Joseph's Boutique Hotel, is located in a 16th-century-era house that has been meticulously renovated. The

six-room hotel is more like an extremely luxurious B&B, with breakfast served in your room each morning by a very attentive staff.

OUTSIDE THE CITY WALLS
Under 700Kn
SESAME INN

Don Frana Bulica 5; tel. 020/412-910; www. bbsesameinn.hr; from 699Kn d, including breakfast

Only 150 meters (about 500 feet) west of the Pile Gate, the three comfy rooms at the Sesame Inn are also close to a nice beach at Danče, and the inn has a good restaurant as well.

ORKA APARTMENTS

Lapadska obala 11; tel. 020/356-800; www.orkapartments.com; from 528Kn d

Slightly west of town in Lapad (hop on bus 6 from the Pile Gate), the Orka Apartments were built in 2007 and offer clean, no-nonsense lodgings a short trip from Dubrovnik.

SIMPLY ANGELIC APARTMENTS

Ploče; tel. 091/911-6901; www. angelicaapartmetnsdubrovnik.com; from 496Kn d

It's only a 10-minute walk from the town walls to the Simply Angelic Apartments, east of the Old Town, which have great views over the sea to the island of Lokrum. The rooms are basic but nice and are located near a small supermarket, a café, and a beach, although those with walking difficulties or knee troubles should beware of the stair climbing required to reach the apartments.

700-1,400Kn
★ VILLA ADRIATICA

Frana Supila 4; tel. 020/411-962; www.villa-adriatica.net; 1,010Kn d

Outside the Ploče Gate to the east you'll find the Villa Adriatica, an early-19th-century family home with one apartment and four sunny and bright rooms, furnished with antiques; the home has a delightful garden with lemon trees.

HOTEL ZAGREB

*Šetalište Kralja Zvonimira 27; tel. 020/438-930;
www.hotelzagreb-dubrovnik.com; 995Kn d, including
breakfast*

The Hotel Zagreb in Lapad, west of the Old Town, is located in a sunny refurbished villa with a palm- and cypress-filled garden. The rooms are solidly three-star, and the trek to Dubrovnik and the beach is fairly short.

HOTEL LAPAD

*Lapadska obala 37; tel. 020/432-922;
www.hotel-lapad.hr; 1,050Kn d, including breakfast*

The small rooms at the Hotel Lapad have been renovated in a minimalist modern style. The hotel has a small pool area overlooking the sea, but no direct access to the beach. Hop on bus 6 at the bus stop across the street for a quick trip to Dubrovnik's town gates.

VILA CURIC

*Mostarska 2F; tel. 020/437-250; www.vila-curic.hr;
1,000Kn d*

The Vila Curic in Lapad is convenient to multiple restaurants and is a short bus ride to the walled city. The 14 self-catering apartments aren't exactly high-design, but they are clean and fresh and there is a lovely pool with a view for guests to use.

Over 1,400Kn

HILTON IMPERIAL DUBROVNIK

*Marijana Blažića 2; tel. 020/320-320;
www.hilton.com; 3,200Kn d, including breakfast*

The Hilton Imperial Dubrovnik is just a quick walk from the Pile Gate. The concierge at the hotel is outstanding and can help you with recommendations, advice, and day trips to the islands. Make sure to ask for a sea-view room, as some actually face a wall.

IMPORTANNE RESORT

*Kardinala Alojzija Stepinca 31; tel. 020/440-100;
www.importanneresort.com; 1,810Kn d, including
breakfast*

The Importanne Resort is an overhaul of four hotels into one property that was re-opened in 2007. The hotel has a great beach, two seawater pools, and sports facilities, although it is a 10-minute drive to the city walls.

HOTEL MORE

*Kardinala Stepinca 33; tel. 020/494-200;
www.hotel-more.hr; 1,780Kn d, including breakfast*

The Hotel More is close to Lapad, west of the Old Town; the area has lots of restaurants and cafés. The 34-room hotel has a small pool area and a beach at the water's edge. It's about a 20-minute bus ride to the gates of Dubrovnik.

HOTEL BELLEVUE

*Pera Čingrije 7; tel. 020/330-000;
www.adriaticluxuryhotels.com; 2,280Kn d,
including breakfast*

The location of the Hotel Bellevue, practically part of a cliff face overlooking the Adriatic, is stunning, as are the well-designed public and private spaces. The hotel has a small beach below and an indoor pool. It's located west of the walls in Danče, so it's a 30- to 40-minute panoramic walk to the Old Town—though with the hotel's chic restaurant and stellar views, you may not go out for dinner after all.

HOTEL KAZBEK

*Lapdska Obala 25; tel. 020/362-900; www.
kazbekdubrovnik.com; 2,800Kn d, including breakfast*

The Hotel Kazbek in Lapad has an Old World elegance and a speedboat for hire docked in front, perfect for jaunts to surrounding islands.

★ VILLA DUBROVNIK

*Vlaha Bukovca 6; tel. 020/500-300;
www.villa-dubrovnik.hr; 4,000Kn d*

At the top of Dubrovnik's luxury accommodations, the Villa Dubrovnik is a 56-room hotel overlooking the Old Town and the island of Lokrum. The balcony-outfitted rooms are great, and the rooftop terrace is perfect for sunset viewing, but it's the wooden boat that shuttles you to and from the Old Town that will really make you feel like a movie star.

1: group of kayakers at a sea cave on the island of Lokrum 2: beach on the island of Lokrum

Food

Eating in Dubrovnik is rarely cheap and often not as good as what you'll find in other parts of Croatia, particularly in high season. That said, here are a few best bets that will at least leave you satisfied and possibly even impress you.

CAFÉS AND DESSERTS
SLATKI KUTAK
Šetalište Kralja Zvonimira 5, tel. 020/417-920, 10am-8pm daily

For the best crepes in town, hit up Slatki Kutak for dessert or even as a sweet start to the day.

FINE DINING
DUBROVNIK RESTAURANT
Lapadska obala 25; tel. 020/362-900; www.kazbekdubrovnik.com; 190Kn

An overlooked gem on the Dubrovnik restaurant scene, the Dubrovnik Restaurant, in the Hotel Kazbek, serves cuisine based on all regions of Croatia, from Istrian pasta with asparagus and black truffles to Dalmatian lamb skewers with mint sauce, and even ends the meal with a homemade version of the famous local confection Bajadera.

VAPOR
Pera Čingrije 7; tel. 020/330-000; 12pm-3pm and 6pm-10pm daily; 180Kn

Certainly the most fashionable restaurant in town, Vapor, at the Bellevue, has a knockout interior by designer Renata Štrok and an amazing view plus sophisticated spins on Mediterranean cuisine.

★ RESTAURANT 360
Sv Dominika; tel. 020/322-222; www.360dubrovnik.com; 6:30pm-11pm Tues.-Sun.; 260Kn

At the top of the list of Dubrovnik's best restaurants is Restaurant 360 (formerly Gil's), a must-book. From the local yet contemporary cuisine (black ravioli stuffed with Pag cheese, pan seared pigeon) to the stellar view overlooking the old harbor to the 6,000-bottle wine cellar, a meal here is actually worth the money.

entrance of Proto

Romantic Dining Outside Dubrovnik

For fewer tourists or just for a change of pace, heading out of Dubrovnik for lunch or dinner can be refreshing to both mind and wallet.

Gverović-Orsan (Stilkovića 43, tel. 020/891-267, www.gverovic-orsan.hr, 12pm-12am Mon.-Sat. Mar.-Dec., 100Kn), in the fishing village of Zaton Mali, is popular with low-key foodies. Black risotto is the house specialty, while marinated fish carpaccio and the salad of local *motar* (a plant that grows wild near the sea) are not to be missed. You can also take a swim while you're waiting for your meal from the beach in front. Zaton Mali is seven kilometers (four miles) northwest of Dubrovnik toward Split on the main coastal road.

In the village of Zaton Veliki, 10 kilometers (six miles) northwest of Dubrovnik, you'll find the waterfront **Konoba Ankora** (Zaton bb, tel. 020/891-031, www.restoran-ankora-dubrovnik. com, 9am-12am daily summer, 95Kn), perfect for a seafood meal at sunset.

Owned by the same group as respected Dubrovnik restaurants Proto and Atlas Club Nautika, ★ **Konavoski Dvori** (Ljuta, Konavle, tel. 020/791-039, www.esculaprestaurants.com, 12pm-12am daily, 100Kn) is set in a peaceful location next to a rushing brook. Marinated cheese, fresh trout, and meats baked under an iron bell are the specialties of the house. Konavoski Dvori is located in Konavle, 21 kilometers (13 miles) southeast of Dubrovnik toward Montenegro. If you're driving, take the road to Montenegro, and when you reach Gruda, take the road for the village of Ljuta, where the restaurant is located.

★ RESTAURANT BOWA DUBROVNIK

tel. 091/636-6111; www.bowa-dubrovnik.com; 11am-6pm May-Oct.; 250Kn

Restaurant BOWA Dubrovnik is on the nearby island of Šipan, in an isolated, idyllic cove. You can spend time on the beach or rent one of their private cabanas and swim, drink, and eat, and then do it all again. Fresh grilled fish, black seafood pasta, and rosemary gin and tonics are a few of the standouts, not to mention the gorgeous location. To get there, rent a speed boat for at least half a day or arrange a water taxi through the restaurant or your hotel. Reservations are a must.

QUICK BITES

BARBA

Boškovićeva 5; tel. 091/205-3488; 10am-1am daily; 45Kn

Barba offers cheap fish-and-chips in a clean modern space.

★ BUFFET ŠKOLA

Antuninska 1; tel. 020/321-096; 8am-2am daily summer, call for winter hours; 40Kn

Nestled in a small space off the Stradun,

Buffet Škola is famous for its sandwiches on fresh-baked bread and smoked ham and cheese snack plates. Besides the food, this place is a bit of a legend in a town overcome with new establishments.

TAVELIN WINE AND ART BAR

Iza Roka 11; tel. 099/885-4197; 11am-11pm daily; 80Kn

Tavelin Wine and Art Bar has a good selection of local wines and beers along with tapas-style snacks.

OLIVA PIZZERIA

Lučarica 5; tel. 020/324-594; www.pizza-oliva.com; 55Kn

The Oliva Pizzeria, near St. Blaise's, serves pasta, salads, and pizza by the slice for only 10Kn.

SEAFOOD

PROTO

Široka 1; tel. 020/323-234; www.esculaprestaurants. com; 11am-11pm daily; 120Kn

Proto has a good Old Town location and a nice terrace, where you should try to reserve a table in summer. The menu is mostly fish, with lots of local offerings, and even snails. The wine list is solid, too.

ATLAS CLUB NAUTIKA

Brsalje 3; tel. 020/442-526; www.nautikarestaurants. com; 12pm-12am daily mid-Jan.-mid-Dec.; five-course meal 600Kn

Proto's big brother, the Atlas Club Nautika holds Dubrovnik's prime position for a restaurant, right next to the Pile Gate, with two large terraces overlooking the sea. The best tables are numbered in the 30s on the Penatur terrace, or try tables 56 or 57 on the Lovrijenac terrace. The food here is fancy, like the shrimp soup with black truffles, though it doesn't quite live up to the hype. The view, however, does. Thrifty types might want to opt for a light lunch here instead.

TRADITIONAL
PORTUN

Od Sigurate 2; tel. 099/801-4535; 9am-11pm daily; 90Kn

Tucked in a narrow alleyway within the city walls, Portun makes classic Dalmatian food in a traditional setting. Don't miss the black risotto.

RESTAURANT FORTY-FOUR

Ul. Miha Pracata 6; tel. 095/862-2411; 11am-11pm daily; 110Kn

A great find in the old city, Restaurant Forty-Four serves traditional dishes with a modern flair. Service is good in a city where that can be a rarity, particularly in summer.

RESTAURANT SESAME

Dante Alighieria bb; tel. 020/412-910; www.sesame. hr; 8am-12am daily; 110Kn

Walk outside the city walls for about 10 minutes, heading west out of the Pile Gate, and you'll find Restaurant Sesame, in the seaside suburb of Lapad. The cozy restaurant serves breakfast as well as reasonable lunches and dinner, with dishes like seafood risotto and orange-and-almond crepes for dessert.

VEGETARIAN
NISHTA

Prijeko 30; tel. 098/186-7440; www.nishtarestaurant. com; 9am-12am Mon.-Sat., 3pm-12am Sun.; 60Kn

Nishta offers lots of tasty vegan options right in the Old Town. The vibe is international, with a menu offering curries, spring rolls, and wraps. Nishta also doles out nondairy shakes from its smoothie bar.

Information and Services

TOURS AND TOURIST INFORMATION
TOURIST OFFICE

Ante Starčićeva 7; tel. 020/427-591; www.tzdubrovnik.hr; 8am-8pm daily summer, 9am-4pm Mon.-Fri., 9am-1pm Sat. winter

Your first stop for information should be the slightly out-of-the-way branch of the Dubrovnik tourist office. A short walk from the Pile Gate, the office has much friendlier employees than their colleagues on the Stradun. Stop by to pick up maps, brochures, advice, and free monthly guides to events. The

tourist office here also has Internet access, so you can check your email.

DUBROVNIK WALKS

www.dubrovnikwalks.com; May-Oct.; 90-140Kn

If you'd like a guide to help you navigate the city, Dubrovnik Walks offers two 1.5-hour guided walking tours in English, each with two departures daily, between May and the end of October. There's no need to reserve a spot; just show up at the appointed time and place, provided on a convenient map on the website (currently in front of the club Fuego outside the Pile Gate).

OTHER SERVICES

Snail mail is most easily sent from the main **post office** (corner of Široka and Od Puča, 9am-6pm Mon.-Sat.).

Left luggage can be deposited at the **bus station** (Put Republike 29, tel. 060/305-070, 5:30am-9pm daily, 20Kn daily).

Two pharmacies, **Gruž** (Obala Pape Ivana Pavla 9, tel. 020/418-990) and **Kod Zvonika** (Placa 2, tel. 020/321-133), take turns as the city's designated all-night pharmacy.

Do your laundry at the Old Town retro **Sanja and Rosie's Launderette** (Put od Bosanske 2, www.dubrovniklaundry.com, 8am-10pm daily summer, 9am-6pm daily winter, 60Kn).

Getting There and Around

GETTING THERE
Air
DUBROVNIK AIRPORT
DBV; tel. 020/773-333; www.airport-dubrovnik.hr
If you're flying into Dubrovnik Airport, you'll need to find a way to get the 20 or so kilometers (12-13 miles) from its location, southeast of the city in Čilipi, to your hotel. Incoming flights operated by Croatia Airlines and British Airways are met by a shuttle bus (30 minutes, 30Kn), which stops near the Pile Gate and at the main bus station near the ferry terminal. On the way back, they leave from the main bus station 1.5 hours before departures. Taxis are in the 250-300Kn range, depending on the location of your hotel. You can also arrange for pickup through your lodging, usually offered for a fare comparable to or slightly less than the taxis.

Bus
Put Republike 29; tel. 060/305-070;
www.libertasdubrovnik.hr; 5:30am-10:30pm daily
By bus there are almost hourly connections with Split (4.5 hours) and around six connections daily with Zagreb (11 hours); you'll need your passport, since a portion of each journey goes through Bosnia. If you're headed to Montenegro, have your passport handy and take a bus that leaves at least once daily. The bay of Kotor, for example, is about a 2.5-hour journey.

From the main bus station, it's about a 30-minute walk to the Old Town, or hop on bus 1A or bus 3, which will take you to the Pile Gate.

Car
If you're driving to Dubrovnik, keep in mind that you'll have to pass through Bosnia, so keep your passport and papers handy. Dubrovnik is 216 kilometers (134 miles), about a 3.5-hour drive, south of Split, and 580 kilometers (360 miles), about a seven-hour drive, south of Zagreb.

Boat
Ferries (harbor tel. 020/418-989) run from the main terminal in Gruž to Rijeka, Zadar, Split, Montenegro, and the islands. Smaller catamarans and water taxis in the old harbor near the Ploče Gate will take you to Lokrum and Cavtat. In summer there are usually two ferries per day to popular destinations like Hvar and Split and multiple connections to the Elafiti Islands (most islands approximately 30 minutes, around 25Kn). Winter brings less frequent connections. Check with **Jadroagent** (Obala Stepjana Radića 32, tel. 020/419-000, www.jadrolinija.hr) about tickets, schedules, and fares.

GETTING AROUND
Bus
Around town, the **city buses** (www.libertasdubrovnik.hr) can get you where you need to go. Buy tickets from the newsstands (12Kn) or the driver (15Kn) or pick up a daily pass (30Kn) from the Libertas bus kiosk just

outside the Pile Gate. Many of the city's hotels and apartments are located in the western suburb of Lapad. Hop on bus 6 from the Pile Gate to get there.

Taxi

Taxis are usually a slow way of getting around town; the bus is often quicker. Look for taxis outside the Pile Gate. You can also phone (tel. 020/332-222) or add the app inTAXI to your smartphone; it's 27Kn to start plus 9Kn per kilometer.

Car

You don't really need a car in Dubrovnik—

traffic is awful, parking is scarce, and the Old Town, where most of the stuff you'll want to visit is located, is completely pedestrian. That said, Dubrovnik has all the major rent-a-car companies, like **Budget** (Obala Stejana Radića 24, tel. 020/418-998, www.budget.hr) and **Hertz** (Frana Supila 9, tel. 020/425-000, www.hertz.hr).

Boat

Water taxis can be a useful way to get to some of the area's more hidden beaches and an atmospheric mode of transportation as well. Pick them up at the Stara Luka (Old Port).

Around Dubrovnik

TRSTENO

7am-7pm daily summer, 8am-4pm daily winter; 50Kn
If you're a fan of gardens, you can't miss Trsteno, about 15 kilometers (nine miles) northwest of Dubrovnik. The Gučetić family built the villa and beautiful gardens at Trsteno in the early 16th century. The entrance to the noble landscape is between two ancient plane trees. Filled with Renaissance gardens of lavender and rosemary, fruit trees, and languid statues surrounded by creeping bougainvillea, Trsteno is the ideal place to unwind and enjoy nature. From the end of the garden's palace ruins (which aren't ruins at all, but actually a bit of 19th-century folly architecture) you can get a nice view of the sea and then go down the stairs to a small stretch of beach for a bit of seaside lounging. Unfortunately, the space has been neglected, but if you can see past some of the overgrowth, it's a nice stop. That said, the *Game of Thrones* producers were pretty impressed—enough to use it as a setting in the show.

To get there by car, hop on the Magistrala, heading north, and follow the signs. Buses to and from Split pick up and drop off here;

contact **Libertas** (tel. 0800-1910, www. libertasdubrovnik.com). The ride is about 40-45 minutes.

CAVTAT

On the Magistrala, 20 kilometers (12 miles) to the south of Dubrovnik, Cavtat has a long history intertwined with Dubrovnik's. Settled by the Greeks in the 3rd century BC, the city, then called Epidaurus, was actually a forerunner of Dubrovnik. Attacks by the Slavs in the 7th century forced the people to flee to Dubrovnik, at that time across a channel of water, and abandon the city. Cavtat was later an important fishing village, birthplace of many sea captains and the region's famed painter Vlaho Bukovac. In the 20th century, Cavtat became a tourist destination, with loads of concrete tourist hotels ruining the original beauty of the quiet seaside town. Cavtat is one of the few cities in the Konavle (the area south of Dubrovnik) that was not destroyed in the Homeland War. Its charming old town is worth a visit if you have the time or are looking for somewhere slightly quieter than Dubrovnik.

Sights

There are several interesting sightseeing stops in the palm tree-laden old town.

BALTAZAR BOGIŠIĆ COLLECTION (Zbirka Baltazar Bogišić)

9:30am-1pm Mon.-Sat.; 15Kn

A must for book lovers, the Baltazar Bogišić Collection displays a collection bequeathed by local scholar Baltazar Bogišić, a great lover of Slavic literature who died in 1908. There are over 20,000 books and manuscripts as well as a wonderful painting by Vlaho Bukovac that depicts the city's carnival—still celebrated in a grand tradition today—with some 80 locals portrayed in their finest costumes around the turn of the 20th century.

VLAHO BUKOVAC GALLERY

Bukovčeva 5; www.kuca-bukovac.hr; 9am-1pm and 4pm-8pm Tues.-Sat.; 20Kn

The Vlaho Bukovac Gallery, a former residence of the artist, exhibits his portraits (from which he made his living), frescoes he painted on the walls as a teenager, and other paintings, including one with his interpretation of the afterlife. There's more Vlaho Bukovac at **St. Nicholas's Church (Crkva svetog Nikole)**, with a painting above the main altar.

RAČIĆ MAUSOLEUM (Račićev mauzolej)

Između tri crkve 1; 10am-12pm and 5pm-7pm Mon.-Sat.; 20Kn

The Račić Mausoleum in the **St. Roc Cemetery (Groblje svetog Roka)** is another must-see in town. Located at the highest point in the Old Town behind the **Monastery of Our Lady of the Snow (Samostan snježne Gospe)**, the opulent grave site, built in the 1920s, is one of Ivan Meštrović's finest works. The white stone building, guarded by two austere yet tender angels, is made even more beautiful by its position among towering cypresses overlooking the sea.

Food

TAVERNA GALIJA

Vuličevićeva 1; tel. 020/478-566; www.galija.hr; 12pm-11pm daily Mar.-Oct.; 110Kn

If you find yourself in need of sustenance, try the Taverna Galija, with a stone terrace and stone-walled interior near the monastery. The menu has something for everyone, from steaming risottos to steak to grilled fish dishes.

Getting There

Catch one of over a dozen buses that depart Dubrovnik daily for Cavtat (take bus 10), or take a boat from the Old Port (Stara Luka) in Dubrovnik (50Kn). Buses and boats take about 45 minutes.

ELAFITI ISLANDS

The Elafiti (or Elaphite) Islands are a nice escape from the summer hordes of Dubrovnik—though don't expect to find them completely devoid of tourists; there are just fewer. Mostly car-free and full of great beaches for lounging, the islands are a short ferry ride from Dubrovnik, from 20 minutes to over an hour, depending on which one you choose; check with **Jadrolinija** (www.jadrolinija.hr) for times and fares.

Koločep

It takes only 20-30 minutes to reach Koločep, a small green island filled with pine forests. Historically, the island was known for its coral, though today it's mostly known for being a peaceful spot for a swim. There's a nice sandy beach in **Donje Čelo,** a village at the north end of the island.

Lopud

The boat to Lopud takes a little under an hour and lets you off at the island's only village, also named Lopud. Despite the lack of villages, the island has always been the most developed of the Elafiti. Today you'll still see some of the **former sea captains' Gothic** homes around town. West of the harbor and up a set of steps you'll find the remains of the villa belonging to Miho Pracat, a 16th-century sea merchant, who was supposedly the richest man in Dubrovnik at the time. He was also one of the kindest, leaving a vast amount of money to the poor of Dubrovnik. The city thanked him by placing his likeness in a prominent location in the Rector's Palace.

Near the ruins of Pracat's villa is the **Đorđić-Mayner Park (Perivoj Đorđić-Mayner)**, a peaceful park, and finally the ruins of a **fortress (Tvrđava)** (follow the signs), with a superb viewpoint where you can admire the surroundings.

Locals and visitors alike will agree that **Uvala Šunj,** a sandy beach 20 minutes' walk south of the village, is Lopud's best beach. Nearby is **Our Lady of Šunj (Gospa od Šunja)** (tel. 020/759-038, open sporadically, free). If the 12th-century church is open, make sure to take a look at the rather disturbing painting of a large snake swallowing a young child.

Lopud has a good selection of seafood restaurants along the Obala Iva Kuljevana, the town's main street, as well as snack bars on the Šunj beach.

Šipan

While Lopud is the most developed, Šipan is the largest; it's a little over an hour away from Dubrovnik. The island is home to dozens of churches, including several that date from before the 9th century. The first ferry stop is Suđurađ (or Sudjuradj), a village dominated by the giant walled villa of the 16th-century seafaring family Stjepović. Parts of the villa have been restored but are currently only open to tour groups.

If you want to see something the groups likely won't, hike up toward the **Church of Our Lady (Crkva velike Gospe)** (two kilometers/one mile up), which looks like a fortress, on the hill above town. On the way you'll come across the ruins of the **Bishop's House (Biskupovo)**. Inside is a fresco depicting Michelangelo, who was a friend of the

bishop of Dubrovnik Lodovico Beccadelli. Old letters prove that Beccadelli begged his friend to visit him on Šipan, but Michelangelo refused.

From Suđurađ, you can either walk to the village of **Šipanska Luka** on a seven-kilometer (four-mile) road (there are few to no cars on the island, so it's quite manageable) or get off at the second ferry stop, which debarks at Šipanska Luka. There are some more beautiful sea captains' villas from the 15th and 16th centuries, though the real draw here is the beaches, located on both sides of the harbor (the farther you walk, the prettier they get).

You can rent bikes in Šipanska Luka from the **Hotel Šipan** (Šipanska Luka 160, tel. 020/758-000, www.hotel-sipan.hr, May-Sept., 900Kn d, including breakfast). There are a couple of other good restaurants in town, such as tourist-oriented (read: English menu) **Tauris** (Šipanska Luka, tel. 020/758-088, www.sipan.info, 8am-12am daily mid-Apr.-Oct., 70-100Kn) that serves decidedly quality local specialties: fresh fish, fish stew, fish pâté, olive oil, and refreshing salads.

If you are on the island, try to arrange a water taxi to **Restaurant BOWA Dubrovnik**. Make reservations ahead of time, though.

★ PELJEŠAC PENINSULA

Just north of Dubrovnik, the Pelješac Peninsula stretches its verdant arm into the sea toward the island of Korčula. It's actually quite remote and a nice respite after busy Dubrovnik. The peninsula is also a great stop for food and wine lovers, with some of Croatia's best wines produced in its vineyards. Even from Dubrovnik or Korčula, it's possible to fit in a day trip of winery-hopping.

Orebić

A small town that relied heavily on its trading alliance with nearby Dubrovnik for several

---

1: Catholic monastery on the island of Lopud
2: grape vines in Pelješac 3: the walled city of Ston

centuries, Orebić is now home to lots of hotels catering to those who come to enjoy the nice shingle beaches on its shores.

But before you put on your bathing suit, take a look at the **Franciscan monastery (Franjevački samostan)** (9am-12pm and 5pm-7pm Mon.-Sat., 5pm-7pm Sun., 10Kn), about a half hour's walk up the hill out of town. Filled with attractive icons and paintings, most given by sailors in gratitude for safe journeys or rescues, the monastery also has a lovely view of the surroundings from its terrace.

If you're looking for a sandy beach, head 20 minutes east of the ferry terminal to **Trstenica,** great for kids and with plenty of cafés and *konobas* for refreshment.

The **Hotel Orsan** (Kralja Petra Krešimira IV 119, tel. 020/797-800, www.orebic-hotels. hr, 350Kn d, including breakfast) is not fancy; the rooms are quite outdated, and the food's not that great. The upsides? You can walk to town via a waterfront promenade, lounge by the pool, sun on the beach right in front of the hotel, and enjoy the pretty sea views for relatively little money.

For something a bit more chic, try the small boutique **Hotel Indijan** (Škvar 2, tel. 020/714-555, www.hotelindijan.hr, 997Kn d, including breakfast). The modern hotel has a beach right outside, an indoor-outdoor pool, and a solid restaurant if you don't feel like eating out. The **Boutique Hotel Adriatic** (Šetalište Kneza Domagoja 8, tel. 020/714-488, 1,200Kn d) is another great option located in an old stone villa right on the water.

There are multiple good restaurants in town and it's hard to choose a bad one. But a don't-miss in Orebić is certainly dessert or coffee at **Croccantino** (Obala Pomoraca 30, tel. 098/165-0777) for excellent cakes but also great coffee and tea and a selection of ice cream. But, seriously, the cake.

Orebić is about a two-hour drive northwest of Dubrovnik. There are several daily buses from Dubrovnik to Orebić (1.5-2 hours), usually continuing on to Korčula. In summer,

Orebić is also connected by several daily ferries (fewer in winter) to the island of Korčula, which take only about 15 minutes.

Ston and Mali Ston

The walled city of Ston, important to the protection of Dubrovnik for centuries, has a nice pre-Romanesque church just west of town, **St. Michael's Church (Crkva svetog Mihovila).** However, the real draw of the area is enjoying a meal of the oysters that come from the beds in nearby Mali Ston (the towns are less than one kilometer apart).

The small family-run hotel **Ostrea** (Mali Ston, tel. 020/754-555, www.ostrea.hr, 710Kn d, including breakfast) is right on the water, with attractively furnished rooms; it's conveniently located right next to the best restaurant in town, Kapetanova kuća, owned by the same family.

Don't leave without trying ★ **Kapetanova kuća** (Mali Ston, tel. 020/754-555, www.ostrea.hr, 9am-12am daily, 170Kn) for excellent food, including Ston oysters and even octopus burgers. The interior is nice (with the prerequisite stone walls, convivial atmosphere, and neat table settings), but it's the harborside terrace, with a calming view of the bobbing boats, that might make you drag out your meal as long as possible.

Another great option, which makes it hard to choose if you don't have time for two meals, is ★ **Konoba Mandrač** (Broce 11, tel. 091/605-4220, 11am-11:30pm daily, 150Kn) for local Ston oysters and fish caught fresh in the morning by the owner himself. With a nice waterfront setting and reasonable prices, what more can you ask for?

Ston and Mali Ston are 60 kilometers (37 miles) northwest of Dubrovnik. Buses traveling from Dubrovnik to Orebić pass through Ston and Mali Ston. They take about 1.5 hours. If you're driving from Dubrovnik, take Highway 8 toward Split and take Road 414 toward Ston and Mali Ston. It's unlikely you'll notice Road 414, so it's better to look out for signs for Ston or Orebić. The drive takes about 1.5 hours.

Wineries

Home to some of Croatia's best wineries, the Pelješac Peninsula is the perfect place for a wine crawl through the steep grape-laden vineyards. The peninsula is home to a variety of whites and reds, but it's best known for its rich Dingač, a reliable wine that can veer into world-class territory depending on the maker and the year. There are dozens of wineries in the area, but it's worthwhile to call out a few of the best. First up is the **Grgić winery** (Trstenik 78, tel. 020/748-090, www.grgic-vina.com, 9am-5pm daily) in Trstenik, about 15 kilometers (nine miles) east of Orebić, actually the Croatian branch of American Grgich Hills Winery in Napa Valley, California. Owner Mike Grgić returned to his homeland in the 1990s to start a vineyard that has quickly gained a serious reputation, particularly for its Plavac Mali. Although a forest fire consumed some of the vines—over 100,000 in the surrounding Trstenik area including other wineries—production is still going despite the damage.

In the village of Potomje, about 10 kilometers (six miles) east of Orebić, visit **Niko Bura** (Zrinsko Frankopanska 19, tel. 020/742-204, www.mokalo.hr, call for hours) for his Dingač Bura and Postup wines as well as **Vedran Kiridzija** (Potemje 40, tel. 020/742-312, call for hours) and **Goran Miličić** (tel. 020/742-031, call for hours) to sample their Dingač varieties.

The **Matuško Winery** (Potomje 5, tel. 099/213-6255, 8am-7pm daily) is a must-visit in the area for tasting their internationally acclaimed Dingač.

The area has a marked **wine route** (Pelješki vinski put, Kuna 8, tel. 020/742-139, vinskiput@net.hr), pointing out wineries and gastronomic stops in a neat little package. If you want to go it on your own, try **Dalmatinska kuća** (Borak, tel. 020/748-017, www.dalmatinskakuca.com, 12pm-12am daily Apr.-Oct., 90Kn) for local specialties and a glass of the owner's wine while dining on the restaurant's terrace.

Ljubljana

With a cultural menu to rival much larger capitals, a funky nightlife, and a strong sense of self, Ljubljana is minute in size but big on character.

The city is charming precisely because it is small. You can get intimate with Ljubljana, see the sights, and still have time left to discover a few gems of your own.

Most impressive about Ljubljana may be the tremendous mark made on its streetscapes and buildings by the country's most famous architect, Jože Plečnik. Whether you admire his style, heavily influenced by the classicists, or not, it's impossible not to appreciate the sheer amount of work he undertook during his lifetime and his vision for a grand city, even if it is quite small. Ljubljana is also full of

Highlights

Look for ★ to find recommended sights, activities, dining, and lodging.

★ **Triple Bridge (Tromostovje):** This bridge, built by architect Jože Plečnik, is a trademark of the city (page 322).

★ **Dragon Bridge (Zmajski Most):** Stopping for a photo op on this bridge, famous for its iconic dragons, is a must (page 324).

★ **Cathedral of St. Nicholas (Stolnica sveti Nikolaja):** The city's cathedral has all the things you've come to expect in European churches: frescoes, gilt, and sculptures. It also has some unexpected features, like fabulous bronze doors (page 325).

★ **Ljubljana Castle (Ljubljanski Grad):** The views from this hilltop castle complex make it worth the hike (page 326).

★ **Upper Square (Gornji trg):** The one-stop shop of the Old Town, this picturesque square and its extension, Levstik Square, are home to some of the city's most beautiful facades and churches (page 327).

★ **Tivoli Park:** Plečnik-landscaped promenades lead you to many city treasures, including the Tivoli Mansion, a small zoo, and an excellent historical museum (page 331).

© MOON.COM

good restaurants, lots of clubs and bars for evenings out, and plenty of stops to interest younger visitors. Though it's much smaller than Zagreb to the south (Ljubljana has a population of close to 270,000 in the metro area), it's more developed, hitting just the right chord between East and West.

Ljubljana hasn't been completely overrun by tourists, though it's plenty busy in the high season. It's still overlooked by lots of visitors, like Germans and Austrians traveling down to Dalmatia who just drive straight through. You can easily see the city in one day and still have time to explore it further, or get out into the countryside for a day trip. Travelers that take the time to wander the Old Town, eat in the restaurants, and browse the antiques markets and tiny galleries will find a warm, friendly, slightly quirky town, always confident in the treasure that is Ljubljana.

HISTORY

The Romans came to the area in the 1st century AD and called the city Emona; an invasion by Attila the Hun in the 5th century destroyed most of the Roman structures. The city lay fairly barren until the 12th century, when a new settlement was built below the castle by Carniolan aristocracy. In the 14th century the Hapsburgs took over and didn't let go, except during a brief reign by Napoleon when Ljubljana was capital of the Illyrian provinces between 1809 and 1813.

The age of rail travel transformed Ljubljana, making it a major center of culture and tourism. An earthquake in 1895 damaged the city's buildings, many beyond repair, but made room for an even grander city, marked by over-the-top Secessionist buildings.

Ljubljana, once a stop on the *Orient Express,* flourished until World War II. Even after inclusion in Tito's Yugoslavia, the city grew substantially as people from rural villages moved into town for factory jobs, changing the landscape of modern Ljubljana, whose suburbs are marked by huge apartment buildings.

It has always been a prosperous city, relishing in its location between East and West, accepted by both sides as their own and capitalizing on that singularity. As the capital of the first former Yugoslav republic to join the European Union (in 2004), Ljubljana is poised to use its position to even more advantage.

ORIENTATION

The Ljubljanica River divides the city into two distinct sides. To the east is Ljubljana's most ancient core, with the castle, cathedral, and medieval squares taking center stage on most visitors' itineraries. The west is the more modern side, though you'll still find a fair share of Austro-Hungarian architecture; a lot of the city's museums and galleries, as well as the University of Ljubljana, are on the western side. The two sides are linked by four bridges, three of which are architecturally interesting (the Dragon Bridge, Triple Bridge, and Cobblers' Bridge).

Further west you'll find the beautiful green spaces of Tivoli Park, while walking south along the left bank of the Ljubljanica River leads you to the Krakovo district.

PLANNING YOUR TIME

If you have two or three days to spend in Ljubljana, you won't regret it. That said, the city is very small and easily explored on foot, and it's possible to pack in the highlights in one full day.

A quick tour should hit Prešeren Square, Ljubljana Castle, and the Old Town (Mestni trg, Stari trg, and Gornji trg), with a stop at the Dragon Bridge for a photograph. Top off the day with a good dinner and at least one coffee and cake. If you have another day, fit in some of Ljubljana's excellent museums, galleries, and a bit of shopping. With a third day, spend some time in Tivoli Park and hopefully a visit to the charming quarter of Krakovo.

Previous: Triple Bridge; Dragon Bridge; Ljubljanica River

Ljubljana

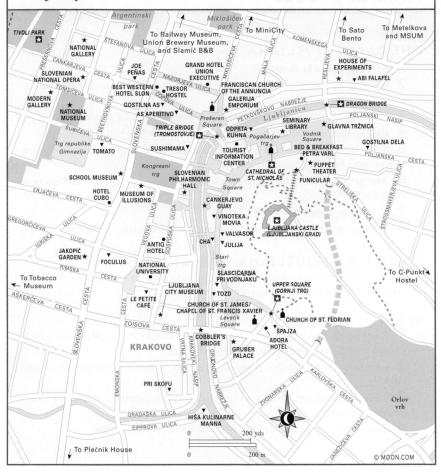

The city is beautiful throughout the year, though summer is probably the most fun, with warm evenings and long days perfect for strolling along the river and sipping wine at an outdoor café. December is also nice, with the festive decorations and holiday market making the already gingerbread-vibe city an excellent holiday getaway.

Itinerary Ideas

ONE DAY IN LJUBLJANA

1 Have breakfast at **Ek Bistro.**

2 Start your tour of Slovenia's capital city in **Prešeren Square (Prešernov trg),** named after the city's most famous poet.

3 Stop at the iconic landmark **Triple Bridge (Tromostovje)** for a selfie.

4 Head up the glass funicular to **Ljubljana Castle (Ljubljanski Grad).**

5 After a tour of the castle, head back down to the Old Town, stopping at **Upper Square (Gornji trg)** to see the city's oldest houses.

6 Afterward, you should have time for a bit of souvenir shopping and wine-tasting at **Wine Bar Suklje.**

7 Have dinner at the lovely **Julija.**

8 End the evening on the **Cankerjevo Quay,** a busy riverside street filled with cafés.

TWO DAYS IN LJUBLJANA WITH CHILDREN

Ljubljana is a perfect city to explore with the kids. It's safe, it's fairly small, and its charming, fairy tale-like qualities won't be lost on even the littlest ones.

Day 1

1 Start your day with a trip to the **School Museum (Šolski Muzej).** Make sure to book a lesson in the historical schoolhouse, given in English.

2 After lunch, let them get their energy out at the **zoo,** located inside the beautiful **Tivoli Park.**

3 Walk by the **Puppet Theater** and catch the puppets popping out of the top of the clock on the hour.

4 Tuck in for the night in one of the old jail cells at the **Hostel Celica.**

Day 2

1 Spend the morning at the **Ljubljana Castle (Ljubljanski Grad),** making sure to stop at the **Museum of Puppetry (Lutkovni muzej)** and have lunch in the castle.

2 Then check out the **Railway Museum (Železniški muzej).**

3 If they're still bursting with energy, head to **MiniCity,** where they can spend hours practicing for adult life through play at the miniature city built just for them.

Ljubljana Itinerary Ideas

Railway Museum [2]

ONE DAY IN LJUBLJANA

1. Ek Bistro
2. Prešeren Square (Prešernov trg)
3. Triple Bridge (Tromostovje)
4. Ljubliana Castle (Ljublianski Grad)
5. Upper Square (Gornji trg)
6. Wine Bar Suklje
7. Julija
8. Cankerjevo Quay

TWO DAYS IN LJUBLJANA WITH CHILDREN

DAY ONE
1. School Museum (Šolski Muzej)
2. Zoo at Tivoli Park
3. Puppet Theater
4. Hostel Celica

DAY TWO
1. Ljubliana Castle (Ljublianski Grad)
2. Railway Museum (Železniški muzej)
3. MiniCity

To [3] MiniCity

Hostel Celica [4]

Argentinski park

Tivoli Park

Miklošičev park

STEFANOVA ULICA

KOMENSKEGA ULICA

CANKARJEVA CESTA

[2] To Zoo

TOMSICEVA ULICA

COPOVA ULICA

NAZORJEVA ULICA

MILOSICEVA CESTA

MALA ULICA

RESLJEVA

Prešeren Square [2]

PETKOVŠKOVO NABREŽJE

Ljubljanica

POLJANŠKI NASIP

Ek Bistro [1]

ŠUBICEVA ULICA

BEETHOVNA

SLOVENSKA

Triple Bridge [3]

Pogačarjev trg

Vodnik Square

POLJANSKA CESTA

Trg republike Gimnazija

School Museum [1]

Kongresni trg

Town Square

Cankerjevo Quay [8]

Puppet Theater [3]

STRELIŠKA ULICA

STROSSMAYERJEVA ULICA

ERJACEVA CESTA

VEGOVA ULICA

GOSPOSKA ULICA

CANKARJEVO NABREŽJE

[4] [1]

Ljubliana Castle

TORCICEVA ULICA

IGRIŠKA ULICA

RIMSKA CESTA

Stari trg

[7] **Julija**

AŠKERCEVA CESTA

SLOVENSKA

Wine Bar Suklje [6]

ZOISOVA CESTA

COBBLER'S BRIDGE

Levstik Square

[5] **Upper Square**

EMONSKA

KRAKOVSKI NASIP

VRTNA ULICA

GRUDNOVO NABREŽJE

ZVONARSKA ULICA

KARLOVŠKA CESTA

Orlov vrh

GRADAŠKA ULICA

EIPPROVA ULICA

JANEŽIČEVA CESTA

| 0 | 200 yds |
| 0 | 200 m |

© MOON.COM

LJUBLJANA
ITINERARY IDEAS

Sights

PREŠEREN SQUARE
(Prešernov Trg)

This is the place where all of Ljubljana seems to meet, with the intersecting city streets and the groups of students on the stairs leading up to the rose-colored **Franciscan Church of the Annunciation.**

Franciscan Church of the Annunciation
(Franciskanska cerkev)

Prešernov trg 4; 8am-6pm daily; free

The Franciscan Church of the Annunciation is Prešeren Square's most striking feature. Inside the mid-17th-century church is an ornate Baroque altar by Francesco Robba, an 18th-century Italian sculptor who spent most of his life in Ljubljana. There are several services daily (7am, 8am, 9am, 10am, 11:15am, 4pm, 7pm, and 9pm).

Galerija Emporium

Trubarjeva 1; tel. 01/426-3170

Also on Prešeren Square is Galerija Emporium, formerly **Centromerkur**, Ljubljana's oldest department store. Whether you feel like shopping or not, the art nouveau building is worth a look for fans of the style, from the impressive wrought-iron entrance topped with a statue of Mercury to the winding staircases within.

But it's the statue in the square, a monument to Prešeren, that's caused the most fuss in Ljubljana's past. The classical nude by Ivan Zajcs and Maks Fabiani was once seen as scandalous for being placed so close to a church.

★ Triple Bridge
(Tromostovje)

Inspired by the bridges of Venice, the Triple Bridge is a Plečnik design that has become a city trademark. The Ljubljana-transforming architect added two delicate arched bridges on the sides of the original single bridge, creating a unique and practical effect. The central bridge, once called the Hospital Bridge, was built in 1842. Traffic was creating many problems for the busy thoroughfare, so in 1929 Plečnik had the ingenious idea to build the parallel pedestrian bridges to prevent the original bridge from being destroyed and to route traffic in a more efficient manner. The balustrade-lined Triple Bridge, along with the Dragon Bridge, is considered a symbol of the city by locals.

EAST OF PREŠEREN SQUARE
House of Experiments
(Hiša Eksperimentov)

Trubarjeva 39; tel. 01/300-6888; www.he.si; 11am-7pm Sat.-Sun., 11am-7pm Wed.-Sun. in July and Aug.; €6

If you're traveling with the kids, check out the House of Experiments, a small museum with plenty of hands-on displays teaching scientific principles. Over 50 experiment stations, including a giant bubble maker and a piano that plays music according to weight, have easy-to-follow instructions (ask for an accompanying leaflet in English) that result in exciting conclusions. In addition to the reactions, you can learn about the science behind them. Though it's aimed toward the younger set, the House of Experiments is a great place for anyone interested in science.

Metelkova

Metelkova is a community housed around the seven buildings that make up a former military barracks near the Celica hostel. Facades of the buildings are covered with street art and installations that some see as beautiful and others grotesque. The area is quiet during the

1: Triple Bridge and Preseren Square **2:** Cathedral of St. Nicholas

The Great Poet France Prešeren

France Prešeren is widely considered to be the greatest Slovenian poet and the force that shaped the country's subsequent literature. He was born in 1800 in Vrba; his parents recognized his intelligence and sent him to elementary school in Ribnica at the age of eight. He attended high school in Ljubljana and university in Vienna, where he studied law.

Prešeren had a tragic life, never winning over his one true love, never marrying the mother of his three children, losing close friends to death, and battling alcoholism. Still, all of this intense emotional upheaval helped create his beautiful, tender poetry.

The great Romanticist poet of Slovenia, Prešeren's image can be found on the Slovenian two-euro coin and at Ljubljana's busy Prešeren Square (Prešernov trg).

day and comes alive at night when the area's alternative clubs start cranking up the music.

SLOVENE ETHNOGRAPHIC MUSEUM

Metelkova 2; tel. 01/300-8700; www.etno-muzej. si; 10am-6pm Tues.-Sun.; €4.50, free 1st Sun. of the month

Though it's a bit out of the way (across the river to the northeast), the Slovene Ethnographic Museum has a good overview of Slovenian cultural history. But that's not all. A philosophical look at man and his or her place in the world is one of the permanent exhibitions. The museum has three floors to explore, captivating temporary exhibitions, and careful translations in English, making it a worthwhile stop.

MUSEUM OF CONTEMPORARY ART METELKOVA (MSUM)

Maistrova ulica 3; tel. 01/241-6800; www.mg-lj.si; 10am-6pm Tues.-Sun.; €5, free 1st Sun. of the month

The Museum of Contemporary Art Metelkova (MSUM) can be found nearby. A small museum that gets mixed reviews, it's best for die-hard fans of modern art who might actually recognize the set for one of lauded artist Marina Abramovic's performance pieces.

VODNIK SQUARE
(Vodnikov Trg)

This attractive square, built at the very end of the 19th century after the earthquake, is home to Ljubljana's Central Market, filled with colorful stands of fruits and vegetables from Monday through Saturday. It's a great place to pick up sausages, homemade sauerkraut, and Slovenian cakes from friendly local vendors, but you'll probably want to skip the stands hawking souvenirs.

★ Dragon Bridge
(Zmajski Most)

It's impossible to miss the Dragon Bridge, located near Vodnik Square. It was the first modern bridge to cross the Ljubljanica, and vehicles still use it today. Built in 1901 by Dalmatian architect Jurij Zaninović, it was originally dedicated to Emperor Franz Joseph, but the menacing green dragon statues were just too iconic for that name to catch on. Legend has it that if a virgin walks across the bridge, one of the dragons will wave its tail. A wonderful example of art nouveau architecture, the bridge is mainly important as a symbol of Ljubljana.

A short walk away is the very different **Butcher's Bridge,** where lovers go to lock in the good vibes by placing padlocks along the bridge and throwing away the key.

Central Market
(Glavna tržnica)

A trip to the Central Market (mornings Mon.-Sat.) is a nice break from museums and monuments. However, it's also an essential stop for fans of Plečnik—he designed the market, filled

The Ljubljana Dragon

the Dragon Bridge

Dragons don't really figure into much of the architecture around Slovenia and neighboring Croatia, yet the mythical creature holds an important spot in Ljubljana culture. The origins of the Ljubljana dragon are tied closely with Greek legends. The hero who stole the Golden Fleece, Jason, was running away from the king he took it from and was forced to head up the Danube River. From there, he and his men sailed to the Sava and then to the Ljubljanica River. On their journey they came across a big lake and marsh, where Jason supposedly fought and killed a vicious monster. The monster, the Ljubljana dragon, remained a part of local folklore and was adopted as a part of Ljubljana's coat of arms and as mascot of the city.

with his signature columns, that stretches through Pogačar Square and Vodnik Square next to the Cathedral of St. Nicholas.

★ Cathedral of St. Nicholas
(Stolnica sveti Nikolaja)

Dolničarjeva 1; tel. 01/234-2690; www.lj-stolnica.rkc. si; 6am-12pm and 3pm-7pm daily; free

A 1701 Baroque cathedral built on the site of an earlier 13th-century church of the same name, the grand Cathedral of St. Nicholas was designed by Italian architect Andrea Pozzo. The exterior hides the church's gilt-edged frescoes by Quaglio (18th century) and Langus (19th century), which make the cathedral like a colorful jewel box. Perhaps the biggest don't-miss, though, are the

impressive and solemn **bronze doors,** added in 1996 by artist Tone Demšar to commemorate the pope's visit and the 1,250th year of Christianity in Slovenia.

Seminary Library
(Semeniška Knjižnica)

Dolničarjeva ulica 4; tel. 01/300-1953; www.semenisce.si; €2, by arrangement only

Near the Cathedral of St. Nicholas, you will find the charming Seminary Library. Arrange a tour in advance to sneak a peek at a beautiful baroque library, dating from 1701. It was the first library in the city and if you are someone who literally worships books, you won't want to miss this chapel-like library.

Puppet Theater
(Lutkovno Gledališče)

Krekov trg 2; tel. 01/300-0970; www.lgl.si; ticket office 9am-7pm Mon.-Fri., 9am-1pm Sat., and 1 hour before each performance

It's fun to catch a show at the Puppet Theater. If you can't make a show, catch the puppets that pop out of the clock above the theater at the top of every hour 8am-8pm daily.

★ LJUBLJANA CASTLE
(Ljubljanski Grad)

tel. 01/432-7216; www.ljubljanskigrad.si; 9am-8pm daily Apr., May, and Oct., 10am-7pm daily Dec., 10am-6pm Jan., Feb., Mar., and Nov., 9am-9pm daily June-Sept.; €7.50

The hill that Ljubljana Castle sits on has always been home to forts, first occupied by the Celts, then the Illyrians, and later the Romans. The earliest part of the current structure, however, dates from the early 16th century. The highlights of the castle are the 15th-century **St. George's Chapel (Kapela sv. Jurija),** decorated with 60 colorful coats of arms from the 18th century, and the 19th-century **Lookout Tower,** where you can get a super view of Ljubljana and the Julian Alps.

There are several tours at the castle for an additional fee (purchased with castle ticket but work out to around €2 each): options include a **Time Machine tour,** with a guide and six stations with costumed actors; a **Behind Bars tour,** with replicas of torture devices and a story told by actors representing an executioner and a witch; and a **simple audio guide** option.

Also on-site are several exhibitions and museums within the complex. The **permanent exhibition** of the castle focuses on a presentation of Slovenian history from prehistory to the present. There is also a 12-minute projection, **Virtual Castle (Virtualni Grad),** allowing visitors to see how the structure has changed through the centuries. Perhaps most intriguing is the **Penitentiary (Kaznilnica),** held in the historical prison cells, which gives visitors a look at how life behind bars was in

the castle during the 19th century. Operating hours are the same for all three exhibits (10am-6pm daily Jan.-Mar. and Nov., 9am-8pm daily Apr.-May and Oct., 9am-9pm daily June-Sept., 10am-9pm daily Dec., included with castle admission).

The castle complex has a decent gift shop and an attractive **café** (9am-11pm daily summer, 10am-9pm daily winter) for a caffeine fix and two onsite restaurants (12pm-10pm Mon.-Sat.). After your tour, make sure to take time to hike around some of the peaceful leafy paths at the castle's base; the paths were designed by Plečnik in the 1930s.

Museum of Puppetry
(Lutkovni muzej)

10am-6pm daily Jan.-Mar. and Nov., 9am-8pm daily Apr.-May and Oct., 9am-9pm daily June-Sept., 10am-7pm daily Dec.; included with castle admission

The castle also houses the city's Museum of Puppetry. The museum showcases the country's puppetry history and artists, an important part of Slovenian culture, and also teaches visitors a bit about techniques used to stage shows. You can take a guided tour of the museum for an additional fee.

Funicular
(tirna vzpenjača)

lower station is at Krek Square, opposite the Central Market; 10am-8pm daily Jan.-Mar. and Nov., 9am-9pm daily Apr.-May and Oct., 9am-11pm daily June-Sept., 10am-10pm daily Dec.; €4 return ticket, less if part of castle admission

Perhaps the best part of touring the castle is the trip to get here, if you take the floor-to-ceiling glass funicular to the top. Departing every 10 minutes from Krek Square, it's the quickest way up or down but not the only one. You can also walk up the footpath called **Študentovska pot** (a continuation of the street Studentovska ulica, reached via Vodnikov trg).

OLD TOWN

The old core of Ljubljana has a storybook quality, with meticulous Baroque and medieval buildings filled with locals shopping in the small boutiques and stopping for a coffee in the area's many cafés.

Town Square
(Mestni trg)

It's worth wandering around the small galleries and boutiques on this picturesque cobbled square, dominated by the **Town Hall (Mestna hiša)**, built in the 15th century. The Town Hall assumed its current appearance during an 18th-century renovation. The best feature of the building is its beautiful Gothic courtyard with a fountain depicting Narcissus.

The jaunty Baroque facades of the buildings that line the square replaced the 12th-century square's medieval buildings, most of which were destroyed in the earthquake of 1511. Francesco Robba took his inspiration for **Robba's Fountain (Robbov Vodnjak)** from fountains he saw while visiting Rome. Built in the 18th century and Robba's final work in Ljubljana before moving to Zagreb, it represents the three rivers of Carniola (Ljubljanica, Sava, and Krka).

From here, head down to nearby Fish Square (Ribji trg), the location of Ljubljana's **oldest house** (No. 6), built in 1528.

Cankerjevo Quay
(Cankerjevo Nabrezje)

This charming riverside walk is filled with cafés and restaurants. Take a minute away from your Old Town tour to have a cup of coffee and watch the boats go by.

Cobblers' Bridge
(Čevljarski Most)

This column-lined Plečnik-designed pedestrian bridge divides Upper Square (Gornji trg) and Town Square (Mestni trg), or the old and new sides of town. Though the cobblers' huts that once lined a medieval wooden bridge here are now gone, the name keeps their memory alive. From here, you can walk down **Old Square (Stari trg),** more of a street than a square, to Upper Square.

★ Upper Square
(Gornji trg)

Upper Square is where you'll find the city's **medieval houses**, although the facades are mostly Baroque, and the 17th-century **Church of St. Florian (Cerkev sv. Florijana)** (Gornji trg 18, tel. 01/252-1727). The church was built in the late 17th century, though Plečnik left his mark here too when he moved a statue by Francesco Robba in front of what was once the main portal.

Flowing out of Upper Square is **Levstik Square (Levstikov trg),** redesigned in the 20th century, again by Plečnik. It's worth a look in the Baroque interior of the **Church of St. James (Cerkev sv. Jakoba)** (Gornji trg 18; tel. 01/252-1727; services 8am, 9:15am, 10:30am, and 5pm daily; free), whose 17th-century **Chapel of St. Francis Xavier (Kapela sv. Frančiška Ksaverija)** is probably the prettiest and most ornate church in town. Just across from the church is the rococo **Gruber Palace (Grubereva Palaca)** (Zvezdarska ulica 1; tel. 01/241-4200; call for hours) built between 1771 and 1783, which today houses the **National Archives (Narodni arhiv Slovenije).**

LEFT BANK

Though it's more modern than the Old Town that skims the base of the castle, Ljubljana's Left Bank is filled with plenty of attractive Austro-Hungarian architecture, as well as many of the city's museums, theaters, and restaurants.

Slovenian Philharmonic Hall
(Slovenska Filharmonija)

Kongresni trg 10; tel. 01/241-0800;
www.filharmonija.si

The Slovenian Philharmonic Orchestra is one of the world's oldest, originally founded in 1701. Its members have included greats such as Haydn, Brahms, and Beethoven. The Slovenian Philharmonic Hall was designed by Austrian architect Adolf Wagner and built in 1891. However, even this building did not escape Plečnik's master hand; he changed the

back facade and added onto the neo-Renaissance structure.

Museum of Illusions
(Muzej Iluzij)

Kongresni trg 13; tel. 01/320-5466; www.muzeiiluzii.si; 9am-10pm daily; €9.50

The small Museum of Illusions has three floors of displays that trick the senses, including an infinity room and a drunken walk. It's a bit expensive for such a small museum, but it is worth the stop if you have the City Pass, a ticket which entitles you to admission at a number of city museums and discounts throughout the city, which includes admission here at the time of writing.

School Museum
(Šolski Muzej)

Plečnikov trg 1; tel. 01/251-3024; www.ssolski-muzej. si; 9am-4pm Mon.-Fri. and 10am-2pm the first Saturday of every month; €1

The School Museum may sound like a drag, but its exhibits on the history of school in Slovenia over the centuries are actually quite interesting. Even better is to attend when "school" is in session. Become a pupil during the Austro-Hungarian empire and learn the meaning of Ljubljana, a famous Slovenian poem, and how to count to ten in Slovenian. Contact the museum for lesson times.

Modern Gallery
(Moderna galerija)

Tomšičeva 14; tel. 01/241-6800; www.mg-lj.si; 10am-6pm Tues.-Sun.; €5

The Modern Gallery is located in an austere renovated space that houses a small collection of modern Slovenian art.

Ljubljana City Museum
(Mestni muzej Ljubljana)

Gosposka 15; tel. 01/241-2500; www.mgml.si;

10am-6pm Tues.-Sun., 10am-9pm Thurs.; €6

The Ljubljana City Museum aims to give an overview of the city's history, including photographs, documents, and scale models of planned but never completed Plečnik designs. It's an interesting and informative stop if you have the time.

National Gallery
(Narodna galerija)

Prešernova 24; tel. 01/241-5418; www.ng-slo.si; 10am-6pm Tues.-Sun., 10am-8pm Thurs.; €7

The building of the National Gallery is worth a visit itself. The 1896 Czech-designed structure is loaded with gilt and over-the-top ceilings, a superb example of the Secessionist era, that lend added grandeur to the fine art housed here. The core of the collection centers on Slovenian art from the 13th to the 20th centuries, though it houses a solid collection of European paintings as well. The gallery has a café and a nice shop for souvenirs.

National Museum
(Narodni muzej)

Muzejska ulica 1; tel. 01/241-4400; www.narmuz-lj.si; 10am-6pm Tues.-Sun., 10am-8pm Thurs.; €6

Though it's the oldest museum in Slovenia, the exhibition at the National Museum Prešernova is relatively small. It features some Roman stone monuments, an Egyptian mummy, bronze artifacts from the Illyrians, and various artifacts, weapons, jewelry, and archaeological finds.

Railway Museum
(Železniški muzej)

Parmova 35; tel. 01/291-2641; www.slo-zelznice.si; 10am-6pm Tues.-Sun.; €3.50

Young and old should enjoy the Railway Museum. Admire the shiny steam engines, rail memorabilia, uniforms, and even art from Slovenia's history of railroading. You'll also find some trains and signaling equipment in the yard outside and a re-creation of a station master's office inside.

1: Ljubljana and its castle **2:** Upper Square **3:** basilica of St. George's Chapel in Ljubljana Castle **4:** the embankment of Ljubljanica river

Plečnik's Ljubljana

It's rare to have a city almost entirely designed and renovated by one architect. After an 1895 earthquake left the city badly damaged, Jože Plečnik led the way for Ljubljana to recreate and modernize itself.

Born in Ljubljana in 1872, Plečnik studied with the famous Viennese architect Otto Wagner, working in his office during the 1890s. He completed several structures in Vienna before moving to Prague, where the Czech president appointed him the chief architect in charge of renovating Prague Castle.

Plečnik returned to Ljubljana in 1921, transforming the city during the 1920s and 1930s. He renovated churches and the municipal cemetery, Žale, and built new bridges, waterfronts, buildings, monuments, and parks. Jože Plečnik died in Ljubljana in 1957, but there's no doubt about the strong impression he left on Ljubljana.

DISCOVERING THE ARCHITECT IN A DAY

- Start your tour in the Trnovo neighborhood at **Plečnik's house.** Today the lovingly restored space, preserved as he left it on his death, gives you a sense of the architect and the man. Cross the **Trnovo Bridge,** with its interesting pyramids mimicking the spires of the Church of St. John the Baptist and the trees growing along the bridge, also a Plečnik idea.

- Continue toward the city center on Emonska cesta, stopping at its intersection with Mirje, where even a set of old **Roman walls** were not left untouched by the architect. The most striking of his additions is the large pyramid over one of the openings in the wall.

- Back on Emonska, you'll pass the **Faculty of Architecture,** where he taught from 1945 to 1947, and a **monument** to the Illyrians he designed on French Revolution Square (Trg Francoske Revolucije).

- The nearby **Križanke theater** was not only designed by Plečnik (when he was in his 80s, no less), it was also the site of a couple of jokes on the communists who commissioned him to create it. In one of the complex's courtyards, he put in a vast amount of lighting, so much that some people questioned the idea. His excuse? The communists needed enlightening. He also placed columns decorated with the hammer and sickle directly opposite a statue of Christ in the main courtyard. Plečnik was a devout Roman Catholic, and this was likely his own way of injecting a snub at the Yugoslavian regime.

- From here, double back to **Vegova street (Vegova cesta),** a beautiful street planned by the architect. Head past **Congress Square (Kongresni trg),** which was also touched by Plečnik's skilled hand, though many features have been paved over with asphalt. To the west of the square you'll find a staircase leading to the beautiful tree-lined river **promenade.** From the river, you can see the rear facade of the **Slovenian Philharmonic Hall (Slovenska Filharmonija),** another Plečnik creation.

- Walking along the river, you should hit the **Triple Bridge (Tromostovje).** It was Plečnik who had the brilliant idea of adding two pedestrian bridges alongside the motor bridge, along with some handsome street lamps. From here, it's off to the **market,** where even the banality of buying bread did not escape his elegant and symmetrical touch.

Union Brewery Museum
(Pivovarski muzej)

Pivovarniška 2; tel. 01/471-7340;
www.union-experience.si; tours 12pm, 2pm, 4pm,
and 6pm Mon.-Fri., 2pm, 4pm, and 6pm Sat.; €14

Fans of beer or history or both will appreciate the charming Union Brewery Museum. Located in the 150-year-old Union Brewery, the displays consist of the history of brewing in Slovenia. Included in the ticket price are a tour of the brewery and a beer or iced tea.

Tobacco Museum
(Tobačni muzej)
Tobačna 1; tel. 01/477-7344; www.tobacna.si; 11am-7pm Tues.-Sat., 11am-3pm Sun.; free

Though it may not be politically correct, the Tobacco Museum is quite interesting even for nonsmokers. Not only do the displays track tobacco's history in Europe since the Middle Ages, but they also show the importance of the factory for women's emancipation in Slovenia.

★ TIVOLI PARK
A giant peaceful green space in the middle of the city, Tivoli Park is so big it makes one think that previous generations had very high hopes for Ljubljana's growth.

International Center for Graphic Arts
(Mednarodni Grafični Likovni Center)
Pod Turnom 3; tel. 01/241-3800; www.mglc-lj.si; 8am-6pm Mon.-Fri., 10am-6pm Sat.; €5

A Plečnik-landscaped promenade leads to the **Tivoli Mansion,** where the International Center for Graphic Arts resides today. The center is a must for fans of graphic and visual arts, with posters, book designs, and more, most from the second half of the 20th century.

National Museum of Contemporary History
Celovška cesta 23; tel. 01/300-9610; www.muzej-nz.si; 10am-6pm Tues.-Sun.; €4.50, free 1st Sun. of the month

The interactive and well-presented National Museum of Contemporary History is the quickest way to get up to speed on Slovenian history over the past 200 years. Particularly engaging are the exhibits around World War II and the resistance of the partisans as well as the Time Capsule room, arranged as it might have been during the Yugoslavia years and free to roam around in. A visit to this museum will leave you feeling like you have a deeper understanding of the country's past.

Zoo
Večna pot 70; tel. 01/244-2188; www.zoo-ljubljana.si; 9am-4pm daily Dec.-Feb., 9am-5pm daily Mar. and Nov., 9am-6pm daily Sept. and Oct., 9am-7pm daily Apr.-Aug.; €8

Those with small children might enjoy the zoo. The small size of the zoo is seen as an advantage by some and a disadvantage by others.

KRAKOVO
A pleasant neighborhood to walk around, dating from the 15th century, Krakovo was originally a fishing settlement and later home to the Slovenian impressionist painter Rihard Jakopič; the neighborhood still has an organic, almost country feel to it.

Jakopič Garden
Mirje 4; tel. 01/241-2506; 10am-6pm Tues.-Sun.; free

The Jakopič Garden is home to a few Roman ruins, including several additions to the ancient walls by Plečnik, but the real draw to Krakovo is its artsy, unpretentious vibe. Wander the enclave of peasant-style homes, many with gardens that supply the town market, and narrow little streets with pleasing flower and vegetable patches, and stop at one of the funky cafés.

Plečnik House
(Hiša Plečnik)
Karunova ulica 6; tel. 01/280-1604; www.mgml.si; 10am-6pm Tues.-Sun.; €6

Just beyond the borders of the Krakovo neighborhood in Trnovo, the Plečnik House was opened in 2015 after a painstaking renovation. Get to know the architect who shaped so much of Ljubljana through great stories, history, the rooms he lived in, and the garden he enjoyed.

OUTSIDE THE CITY CENTER
MiniCity
BTC City, Šmartinska 152; tel. 041/377-366; www.minicity.si; 10am-8pm Mon.-Sat., 10am-6pm Sun.; €10

Located in a large shopping mall, MiniCity is

a great place for families to visit. Stations in the miniature city include a police station, a hospital, a radio station, an airplane, a bakery, and more, where children ages 3 to 12 (it's best suited for ages 3 to 8) can play pretend for hours.

Entertainment and Events

NIGHTLIFE
Bars
Ljubljana has a great bar and club scene, with something for everyone.

KUD FRANCE PREŠEREN
Karunova 14; tel. 01/283-2288; 11am-1am daily; €3-5
Literary and artsy types might want to check out the KUD France Prešeren, home to a small café and a strong presence on Ljubljana's arts scene since 1919. Something happens here most every night, from readings and performances to concerts and workshops.

PRITLIČJE
Mestni trg 2; tel. 040/204-693; www.pritlicje.si; 9am-1am Sun.-Wed., 9am-3am Thurs.-Sat.; €2-5
Pritličje is in a great location next to the Town Hall in the Old Town. It not only serves a great selection of drinks but has a serious comic book store as well.

BAR FETICHE
Cankarjevo najbrezje 25; tel. 040/700-370; www.fetichepatisserie.com; 9am-1am daily; €3-7
Bar Fetiche has excellent cakes and specialty ice creams prepared by a Paris-trained Japanese pastry chef by day and an impressive list of gin and tonic cocktails by night.

WINE BAR SUKLJE
Breg 10; tel. 040/654-575; www.winebar.suklje. com; 9am-12am Mon.-Thur., 9am-1am Fri. and Sat., 9am-11pm Sun.; €4-8
Wine Bar Suklje, located on a riverside pedestrian zone, has 300 labels and 30 by-the-glass selections from Slovenia and beyond. The bar also offers cheese plates, hearty slices of savory pie, and crostini to nibble on while you sip.

KOLIBRI COCKTAIL BAR
Židovska Steza 2; tel. 031/336-087; www.kolibri-bar. com; 7am-1am daily; €4-9
For something distinctly different, hit up Kolibri Cocktail Bar, which serves creative cocktails, many based on historical recipes, in a cozy, kitchsy-cool atmosphere. Certainly an experience you won't have just anywhere.

ZMAVC
Rimska 21; tel. 01/251-0324; 7:30am-1am Mon.-Fri., 10am-1am Sat., 6pm-1am Sun.; €2-5
Students shouldn't miss Zmavc, a graffiti-covered bar filled with comic-strip walls, raucous fun-loving staff and customers, and a general good vibe.

NUK CAFÉ
Turjaška 1; tel. 01/320-6066, 8am-8pm Mon.-Fri., 9am-2pm Sat.; €2-4
Art and philosophy majors will appreciate NUK café, in the basement of the stunning National University Library, which affords a chance to sip coffee with the locals and lots of private nooks for deep discussions.

ROLLBAR
Hala 18; tel. 01/585-2570; www.indoor-karting.com; 8am-11pm Mon.-Thurs., 8am-1am Fri.-Sat., 8am-10pm Sun.; €3-7
At the racing-themed Rollbar in the BTC City shopping center, you can race go-karts until your inner child is satisfied.

Pubs
Beer lovers fear not: Ljubljana has dozens of pubs to choose from. For a bit of beer crawl, stroll along **Petovškovo Nabrežje** in the evening to sample a variety of beers at the many riverside bars.

Eating for Good in Ljubljana

While Ljubljana is rife with excellent places to eat, there are three spots that not only fill your stomach, but your heart as well. **Učilna Okusov (Classroom of Flavors)** (Adamič-Lundrovo nabrežje 1-7, tel. 01/292-7785, www.ucilnaokusov.si, 8am-4pm Mon.-Fri. and 8am-2pm Sat.) is a shop and tasting room near the Dragon Bridge run by three local vocational schools. You can buy a variety of regional products, some produced by the students, while supporting young people learning hospitality and retail skills. **Gostilna Dela** (Poljanska cesta 7, tel. 051/491-491, 8am-4pm Mon.-Fri.) is a tasty café with reasonable prices. Even better? The café helps employ disadvantaged and disabled youth while teaching them valuable and transferable skills for the future. An excellent taste adventure, **Skuhna** (Trubarjevo 56, www.skuhna.si, 11:30am-6pm Mon.-Wed., 12pm-10pm Thurs.-Sat.) is a restaurant on a mission to increase employment opportunities for migrants and bring people of different cultures together. The menu focuses on authentic dishes from Africa, Asia, and South America, lovingly prepared by migrants from those areas.

DAKTARI

Krekov trg 7; www.daktari.si; 7:30am-1am Mon.-Fri., 8am-1am Sat., 9am-12am Sun.; €2-6

Conveniently located near the castle funicular, Daktari offers a variety of good beers and snacks as well as Turkish coffee and brandy for any non-beer-drinking companions.

CUTTY SARK

Knafljev prehod 1; tel. 01/425-1477; www. cuttysarkpub.si; 9am-1am Mon.-Sat., noon-1am Sun.; €3-7

If you're feeling homesick, try expat hangouts Cutty Sark or Patrick's for on-tap Guinness and English-speaking companionship.

PATRICK'S

Prečna 6; tel. 01/230-1768; www.irishpub-ljubljana. si; 10am-1am Mon.-Fri., 12pm-1am Sat., 5pm-12am Sun.; €3-7

Like Cutty Sark, Patrick's is an expat hub with an English-speaking crowd to swap stories with over a beer.

Live Music and Dance Clubs
GAJO JAZZ CLUB

Beethovnova 8; tel. 01/425-3206; www.jazzclubgajo. com; 9am-1am Mon.-Fri., 9am-12am Sat.-Sun.

A solid choice for chilling out to a quality jam session, the elegant but low-key Gajo Jazz Club hosts local and international acts.

SAX PUB

Eipporva 7; tel. 01/283-1457; 10am-1am Tues.-Sat., 4pm-10pm Sun., 12pm-1am Mon.

For more party atmosphere with your jazz, Sax Pub has Thursday-night live jazz inside a graffiti-painted riverside cottage.

METELKOVO MESTO

Metelkova cesta; tel. 01/432-3378; www. metelkovamesto.org; call or see website for schedule

On the more extreme side, or at least as extreme as Ljubljana gets, Metelkovo Mesto is a former army barracks that hosts themed events, including punk, dance, and gay and lesbian. It's usually hard to find out what's going on ahead of time, so if you can't get anyone on the phone, have a look to see if it seems like your style.

ORTO BAR

Grablovičeva 1; tel. 01/232-1674; 8pm-4am daily

Packed, sweaty, and loud describe Orto Bar, a lounge swathed in red velvet serving shots and pulsing music from blues to punk.

THE ARTS
Music and Theater
LJUBLJANA CASTLE
(Ljubljanski Grad)

Studentovska ulica; tel. 01/232-9994; www.ljubljanskigradl.si

Ljubljana Castle hosts musical and theatrical

performances throughout the year. Events are held more frequently during the summer.

KRIŽANKE SUMMER THEATER
(Poletno gledališče Križank)
Miklošičeva 28; tel. 01/439-6445;
www.ljubljanafestival.si
Križanke Summer Theater is an open-air theater located on the site of a former monastery. The entire complex has a sliding roof that makes for outstanding theater and concerts, from classical to pop and jazz, in all sorts of weather.

SLOVENIAN PHILHARMONIC HALL
(Slovenska Filharmonija)
Kongresni trg 10; tel. 01/241-0800;
www.filharmonija.si
The Slovenian Philharmonic Hall is a dependable venue for solid classical performances.

SLOVENIAN NATIONAL OPERA AND BALLET THEATER
(Slovensko narodno gledališče)
Zupančičeva 1; tel. 01/425-4840
The frothy 1882 home of the Slovenian National Opera and Ballet Theater is a fitting location for Verdi, Mozart, and *Swan Lake*.

PUPPET THEATER
(Lutkovno Gledališče)
Krekov trg 2; tel. 01/300-0970; www.lgl.si; ticket office 4pm-6pm Mon.-Fri., 10am-12pm Sat.
If you're traveling with kids or you're just a kid at heart, a marionette show at the Puppet Theater is a nice way to while away an afternoon.

Cinema
No need to hunt for a special foreign-language cinema in Slovenia. Most films (with the exception of some children's films) are not dubbed, only subtitled, which means you can

easily rub shoulders with the locals and still enjoy the movie.

KINOKLUB VIČ
Trg Mladinskih Delovnih Brigad 6; tel. 01/241-8411;
www.kolosej.si
Try the old-school but renovated Kinoklub Vič for major releases and the occasional off-beat movie.

KINOTEKA
Miklošičeva 28; tel. 01/547-1580; www.kinoteka.si
For art and foreign films (fun if you speak French, less choice if you only speak English), check out Kinoteka.

KOLOSEJ
Šmartinska 152; tel. 01/520-5500; www.kolosej.si
For the standard big multiplex experience, head to BTC City, where Kolosej has a large selection of Hollywood blockbusters.

FESTIVALS AND EVENTS
The **International Festival of Documentary Film (Festival Dokumentarnega Filma)** (www.fdf.si) screens documentary films from around the world every year in late March or early April.

At the beginning of May, the **Wire Walk** (www.pohod.si), whose longest trek is 35 kilometers (about 22 miles) around the city, memorializes Ljubljana's occupation by the Italians, who surrounded the city with barbed wire during World War II.

Many museums are free on the International Day of Museums (May 18), the Museum Summer Night (usually June 16), and the Day of Culture (Dec. 3), celebrating the birthday of Prešeren.

The **Ljubljana Festival** (www.ljubljanafestival.si), held every summer from sometime in June to sometime in August, is an outstanding arts festival that brings together international chamber and symphony orchestras, visual artists, and even an

---

1: shopping for antiques at the Sunday market
2: outdoor cafe in Old Town **3:** restaurants and bars line the riverbanks

open-air cinema for dozens of cultural performances. Summer also brings the **Ljubljana Jazz Festival** (www.ljubljanajazz.si), an outstanding event that has been an annual feature for 50 years. **Trnfest** is another summer festival, bringing free concerts and performances to the Trnovo neighborhood the entire month of August.

In December, **Christmas** spirit fills Ljubljana's streets, with decorations and lots of stalls selling gifts and refreshments in the Old Town.

Shopping and Recreation

SHOPPING
English Books
OXFORD CENTER
Kopitarjeva 2; tel. 01/360-3789; 8am-7pm Mon.-Fri., 8am-1pm Sat.
For reprints of classics in English, maps, and dictionaries, head to Oxford Center, which stocks a large supply of titles for locals learning English.

KONZORCIJ
Slovenska 29; tel. 01/241-0650; 9am-7:30pm Mon.-Fri., 9am-1pm Sat.
The downtown location of Mladinska knjiga's Konzorcij has a good stock of foreign-language titles, including travel, and has free Wi-Fi.

Food and Wine
ŠTORIJA WINE SHOP
Trubarjeva 17; tel. 040/690-096; 11am-8pm Mon.-Sat.
If you'd like to pick up some souvenirs for the gourmets in your life, try the Štorija Wine Shop. While there are many wine shops in Ljubljana, Štorija is special because it focuses on smaller Slovenian winemakers you probably wouldn't be able to source back home, including the historic "orange wine."

ČOKOLADNICA CUKRČEK
Mestni trg 11; tel. 01/519-9286; www.cukrcek.si; 9am-8pm Mon.-Sat., 10am-7pm Sun.
Čokoladnica Cukrček has hundreds of attractively packaged chocolate confections, hot chocolates, and even chocolates shaped like Ljubljana's signature dragon or one of its most famous poets, Prešeren.

GLAVNA TRŽNICA
Central Market; tel. 01/300-1200; morning Mon.-Sat.
You may want to drop by the Glavna tržnica for locally produced honeys and other sundries. Some of the merchants are also the producers, which makes for a pleasant farm-to-table experience.

HONEY HOUSE
Mestni trg 7; www.honeyhouse.si; 10am-6pm Mon.-Fri., 10am-1pm Sat.
Foodies will appreciate the stash at Honey House, with everything you could imagine produced from honey, including wine and candies.

PIRANSKE SOLINE
Mestni trg 17; tel. 01/425-0190; www.soline.si; 9am-8pm Mon.-Fri., 9am-5pm Sat., 10am-3pm Sun.
Piranske soline sells a range of salt-based products, from cooking salts to bath salts, all from the famous salt pans of the coastal city of Piran. Don't pass up trying the salted chocolates.

VINOTEKA MOVIA WINE BAR AND SHOP
Mestni trg 4; tel. 051/304-590; www.movia.si; 12pm-11pm Mon.-Sat.
The best place to buy wine in town is at the Vinoteka Movia Wine Bar and Shop from the famous western Slovenia winery Movia.

Souvenirs
IDRIJSKA ČIPKA

Mestni trg 17; tel. 01/425-0051; www.idrija-lace.com; 10am-1pm and 3pm-7pm Mon.-Fri.

You can buy lace from Idrija, whose long tradition of lace-making is legendary in Slovenia, at Idrijska čipka. The lace makes a nice handicraft to take home, and the shop has souvenirs like lace Christmas ornaments, lace collars, and tablecloths.

SMILE CONCEPT STORE

Mestni trg 6; tel. 040/511-451; 10am-8pm Mon.-Sat., 10am-2pm Sun.

Also on Mestni trg, the Smile Concept Store sells unique souvenirs and crafts made by local designers.

RUSTIKA

Ljubljana Castle, Studentovska ulica; 9am-8pm daily summer, 10am-7pm daily winter

Though much of it is typical souvenir bric-a-brac, you might find something for your suitcase at Rustika inside Ljubljana Castle.

On Saturdays from June through October there is an art market in Gornji Trg, as well as one in the garden of the Slovenia Ethnographic Museum, weather permitting. Local arts and crafts from various vendors are for sale.

Antiques
SUNDAY MARKET

Cankarjevo Nabrežje; 8am-2pm Sun.

The riverside Sunday market, near the Cobblers' Bridge, is the place to find fun antiques, old postcards, and jewelry to stash in your suitcase.

SPIN VINYL ROCK N ROLL PLOŠČARNA

Gallusovo Nabrežje 13; tel. 01/251-1018; www.spinvinyl.si; 10am-7pm Mon.-Fri., 10:30am-2pm Sat.

For antiques of a different sort, Spin Vinyl Rock n Roll Ploščarna is an old-school Old Town record shop selling stacks of vinyl from the former Yugoslavia—a fun souvenir for music fans.

Fashion
DRAŽ

Gornji trg 9; tel. 01/426-6041; www.draz.si; 9am-1pm and 3pm-7pm Mon.-Fri., 10am-1pm Sat.

Though avant-garde knitting might seem like an oxymoron, Draž just might change your mind. The local fashion house designs dresses, skirts, and sweaters that are all runway-ready.

ZOOFA

Breg 12; tel. 059/978-983; www.zoofa.si; 10am-7pm Mon.-Fri., 10am-4pm Sat., 10am-2pm Sun.

Zoofa has a good selection of Slovenian-designed clothing and shoes.

Shopping Centers
BTC CITY

Šmartinska 152; tel. 01/585-1100; www.btc-city.com; 9am-9pm Mon.-Sat.

BTC City, a few kilometers northeast of the center, has 400 shops, restaurants, and bars, and also houses a cinema, a post office, and even a water park. Shops include everything you would expect to find in an urban shopping center, mostly international high street brands.

SPORTS AND RECREATION
City Tours

Ljubljana offers several excellent tours, including a two-hour **walking tour** (www.ljubljanafreetour.com) of the city's major sites for tips only, one-hour **boat tour** (depart from the Cankarjevo nabrežje dock, check with tourist office for times, €25), and a two-hour guided **bike tour** (www.ljubljanabybike.com, €25).

Recreation

The **Path of Remembrance and Comradeship (Pot spominov in tovarništva)** (www.pohod.si) is a 35-kilometer (22-mile) circuit commemorating the Italian occupation during World War II, following the perimeter that was enclosed in barbed wire. Today, it's a great trek or cycling path through the city's surroundings,

Escape Rooms

Escape rooms have become a bit of a trend worldwide, but in Slovenia they have taken over in a matter of months. With almost a dozen rooms to choose from already, it's a fun way to spend an hour or two. A group of teammates will be locked in a room (usually with a walkie-talkie for emergencies or if your team needs a hint) and start hunting for clues. One clue leads to another, often tied to local culture and history. The help of high-tech tricks brings a bit of excitement and drama to some rooms. Teams battle the clock to escape the room before time runs out. It's not only a fun activity for groups but a fun way to connect with strangers as well. **Escape Room Enigmarium** (tel. 031/334-488, www.escape-room.si, €60) was the first of its kind in Slovenia and offers multiple locations across Ljubljana with options such as Professor's Secret, Salvation Room, and the Classroom of Doom. (There's even an Escape Igloo in Kranjska Gora, 85 kilometers/53 miles northwest of Ljubljana.) You choose a room and book online; you do not need to know Slovenian to play.

passing some worthwhile stops like Plečnik's re-creation of the municipal graveyard, Žale cemetery, and Fužine castle. Follow the signs marked "POT."

SKOK SPORT CENTER

Marinovseva 8; tel. 01/512-4402; www.skok-sport.si
Skok Sport Center offers rafting, kayaking, and cycling as well as kayaking courses (from €28-60) around Ljubljana and beyond. The center also rents bicycles and canoes from around €10 a day.

BALONARSKI CENTER BARJE

Flandrova 1; tel. 01/512-9220; www.bcb.si
If you'd like to take to the skies, Balonarski Center Barje can help arrange balloon flights over the city and the countryside (from €170.)

Spectator Sports

A great source of tickets in Ljubljana, for both sporting events and concerts, is **Eventim.si** (www.eventim.si).

ŽSD STADIUM

Milčinskega ulica 2; tel. 01/438-6470
Ljubljana's soccer team, NK Olimpia, plays at ŽSD Stadium.

TIVOLI HALL
(Hala Tivoli)

Celovška cesta 25; tel. 01/431-5155
One of the most popular spectator sports these days is ice hockey; the Ljubljana team HDD Tilia Olimpija takes to the ice at Tivoli Hall. The sports hall is also home to basketball and volleyball games.

Accommodations

Ljubljana is quite expensive in terms of accommodations, particularly when it comes to value for money. But there are a few gems, if you book early. Hotels and guesthouses can be found in the center of town, in the Old Town core and around the most-frequented tourist sites, as well as out of center, so be sure to figure in time and transportation costs when deciding among your options. If you're interested in private apartments in town—a great value for families or those who like to prepare their own meals—clean and cozy flats are available from **Tour As** (www.apartmaji.si).

CENTRAL LJUBLJANA
Under €50
C-PUNKT HOSTEL

Poljanska Cesta 26c; tel. 01/474-8630; from €20 pp

The C-Punkt Hostel is about a 10-minute walk to the heart of the city. It is very clean, has a friendly staff, and is in a safe neighborhood. This hostel may not be the best in the city, but its popularity means you should book far, far in advance.

HOSTEL CELICA

Metelkova Ulica 8; tel. 01/230-9700; www.hostelcelica.com; from €25 pp

The Hostel Celica is by far one of the most interesting hostels anywhere. Located in a former military prison, most of the rooms are actually cells, all immaculately clean. The mood here is student-party central, with free Internet; it's very close to the train station and 10 minutes' walk to the center of town.

TRESOR HOSTEL

Čopova ulica 3; tel. 01/200-9060; www.hostel-tresor.si; from €20 pp

The nicest hostel in Ljubljana has to be the Tresor Hostel, located in a bank building. Not only does it meet the basic criteria for recommendation (clean, Wi-Fi, central location) but it has three common rooms and hosts cooking

workshops and jazz and DJ nights; it even rents skateboards.

€50-100
BED AND BREAKFAST
PETRA VARL

Vodnikov trg 5a; tel. 01/430-3788; petra@varl.si; €60 d, including breakfast

The Bed and Breakfast Petra Varl is a charming little bed-and-breakfast, a two-minute stroll from the center, with friendly service from the artist-owner. The room with the terrace is particularly sweet.

Over €100
★ ADORA HOTEL

Rožna ulica 7; tel. 0820/57-240; www.adorahotel.si; €125 d, including breakfast

Located in a charming old building, close to sights and restaurants, the Adora Hotel has air-conditioning, attractively decorated rooms, and quite good value for money in Ljubljana terms.

SLAMIC BED & BREAKFAST

Kersnikova Ulica 1; tel. 01/433-8233; www.slamic.si; €150 d, including breakfast

The Slamic Bed & Breakfast offers surprisingly luxe rooms, complete with cable TV, free Internet access, and hardwood floors. Located only 10 minutes' walk to either the train and bus stations or the Old Town core, the small hotel also has a popular and very good café and sweets shop on the ground floor, perfect for a leisurely breakfast before sightseeing.

ANTIQ HOTEL

Vegova 5a; tel. 01/421-3560; www.antiqpalace.com; €144 d, including breakfast

The Antiq Hotel has an excellent location on a pedestrian square in the center of town. The hotel's decor (lace-trimmed towels and antique furniture) is either homey or outdated and grandmotherly, depending on your attitude. The only downside for some travelers might be the stairs—the building has no elevator.

★ HOTEL CUBO

Slovenska cesta 15; tel. 01/425-6000;
www.hotelcubo.com; €175 d, including breakfast

The Hotel Cubo is located on the edge of the old town in an art deco building. Rooms are sleek and well-designed, but what really makes the hotel stand out are its services. An excellent onsite restaurant as well as outings you can add, like a bike with a picnic basket for two or a picnic on horseback, are lovely touches that allow you to explore the city in a different way and provide plenty of eye-candy for your photos.

BEST WESTERN HOTEL SLON

Slovenska cesta 34; tel. 01/470-1100;
www.hotelslon.com; €190 d, including breakfast

With all the amenities of big chain hotels, such as an in-hotel sauna, a restaurant, a lounge bar, and valet parking, the Best Western Hotel Slon has swank public spaces in a restored 1930s-era building. The rooms don't have the original character, but the hotel is convenient and a short walk to the Old Town, and it has free Internet access in the lobby.

LEV HOTEL

Vošnjakova ulica 1; tel. 01/433-2155;
www.union-hotels.eu; €120 d, including breakfast

While it's hard to see all five of the stars that the Lev Hotel advertises, its location on the edge of Tivoli Park is nice, and it's clean and comfortable, with free parking, a restaurant, and a bar on-site.

★ GRAND HOTEL UNION
EXECUTIVE

Miklošičeva 1; tel. 01/308-1270;
www.union-hotels.eu; €180 d

The Grand Hotel Union Executive has a perfect location in the center of old Ljubljana and a rooftop pool for those who'd like to take a dip. The hotel has a stunning art nouveau facade, and the rooms are nice and spacious.

OUT OF THE CENTER
Under €50

If you happen to be in Ljubljana during the summer, the cheapest accommodations around are the *dijaški dom* (contact the tourist office at the Triple Bridge, €15 d), or student dorms. All are well connected by bus, with stops located conveniently next to the dorms; they are also walkable, from 10 to 30 minutes from the center. The rooms are simply furnished, with one to three single beds, and it's hard to beat the price.

€50-100
PRI ZABARJU

Viška cesta; tel. 01/428-2462; www.prizabarju.si;
€90 d, including breakfast

A guesthouse option is Pri Zabarju, a cozy place with air-conditioning, parking, a restaurant of the same name, and a decadent cake place all in one convenient location. You'll need to take a bus or taxi to get to this spot, approximately four kilometers (2.5 miles) west of the center of things.

MONS HOTEL

Pot za Brdom 55; tel. 01/470-2700;
www.hotel.mons.si; €100 d

The über-modern Mons Hotel is a couple of kilometers west of the center. Be aware that sometimes the service does not live up to the hotel's four stars, and be sure to ask for a room facing the woods rather than the highway. There is a free shuttle to the center, or you can take a taxi.

Over €100
AHOTEL

Cesta Dveh Cesarjev 34; tel. 01/429-1892;
www.ahotel.si; €125 d, including breakfast

Despite the fact it's located 2.2 kilometers (1.3 miles) from the city center, the AHotel is possibly the best-value hotel for the money. With a sleek, trendy lobby and bar, sparkling minimalist rooms, and a good continental breakfast buffet, the AHotel isn't exactly luxe, but it still exceeds expectations. It's located in Trnovo, a very pretty old quarter of town, and is well connected by bus.

AUSTRIA TREND HOTEL
Dunjaska 154; tel. 01/588-2510; www.austria-trend. at/lju; €120 d

The Austria Trend Hotel offers sleek and spacious rooms. The hotel is two kilometers (just over a mile) north of town in Bežigrad, connected by shuttle or via bus to the city center.

Food

CENTRAL LJUBLJANA
Breakfast
LE PETIT CAFÉ
Trg francoske revolucije 4; tel. 01/251-2575; www.lepetit.si; 7:30am-11pm Mon.-Fri., 9am-11pm Sat.-Sun.; €8

The immensely popular Le Petit Café is a local pick for breakfast staples (eggs, toasted baguettes) in a Provence-themed café.

★ EK BISTRO
Petkovškovo nabrežje 65; tel. 041/937-534; 8am-8pm Mon.-Sat., 8am-3pm Sun.; €10

Another excellent breakfast option, the Ek Bistro offers an excellent brunch with dutch babies, eggs benedict, and more in a lovely exposed-brick-wall atmosphere.

Cafés and Desserts
SLASCICARNA PRI VODNJAKU
Stari trg 30; tel. 01/425-0712; 8am-12am daily; €3-6

The often overlooked Slascicarna Pri Vodnjaku has a super old-school atmosphere in which to sip tea and tuck into dessert.

SLASCICARNA ZVEZDA
Wolfova 14; tel. 01/420-9090; 7am-11pm Mon.-Sat., 10am-8pm Sun.; €3-6

The park-side Slascicarna Zvezda is far trendier and offers lots of ice cream, coffees, and cakes.

CHA
Stari trg 3; tel. 01/25-7010; www.cha.si; 9am-10:30pm Mon.-Fri., 9am-3pm and 6pm-10:30pm Sat.; €2-5

For real tea, from English to herbal, served in pretty porcelain for flair, try Cha.

★ TOZD
Gallusovo nabrežje 27; tel. 040/72-362; 8:30am-1am daily; €3-7

And for excellent coffee, look no further than Tozd, which morphs into a bar with good beer in the evenings.

Wine Bar
★ VINOTEKA MOVIA WINE BAR AND SHOP
Mestni trg 1; tel. 051/301 590; www.movia.si; 12pm-11pm Mon.-Sat.; €5-10

The Vinoteka Movia Wine Bar and Shop is a must stop for wine fans to sample and purchase some of Slovenia's rock-star winemakers' best wines in a cozy setting.

Upscale Street Food
★ ODPRTA KUHNA
Pogačarjev trg; www.odprtakuhna.si; 10am-9pm Fri. from early spring through late fall, weather permitting

Though it's seasonal, Odprta Kuhna is a must-try if you are in the city when this open kitchen comes to an Old Town square. Food stands from dozens of vendors elevate street food to a new level at this award-winning concept.

Fine Dining

GOSTILNA AS

Čopova 5a; tel. 01/425-8822; www.gostilnaas.si; 12pm-12am daily; €25

While Gostilna As may not be as trendy as some spots on the city's restaurant scene, it is still the establishment restaurant of Ljubljana's movers and shakers. The food is excellent, the atmosphere warm and local, and the terrace is superb for warm-weather dining.

ŠPAJZA

Gornji trg 28; tel. 01/425-3094; 12pm-11pm Mon.-Sat.; €19

Špajza has local atmosphere infused with a romantic vibe. Serving typical Slovenian dishes (think horse and venison) prepared with care as well as a good selection of fish brought in daily from Croatia, the restaurant has a nice outdoor courtyard for fair-weather dining.

VALVASOR

Stari trg 7; tel. 041/381-561; www.valvasor.net; 11:30am-11:30pm daily; €20

Valvasor snagged a spot on Gault Millau's list, but the prices are not outrageous. European staples like duck confit and foie gras are complemented by a nice wine list.

★ JULIJA

Stari trg 9; tel. 01/425-6463; www.julijarestaurant.com; 12pm-10pm daily; €19

Nearby, the bistro-like Julija serves dishes like scallops with lemon crème and gnocchi with truffles.

International

ABI FALAFEL

Trubarjeva 40; tel. 041/640-166; www.falafel.si; 10am-12am Mon.-Sat., 1pm-10pm Sun.; €4

The name, Abi Falafel, describes this miniscule spot's menu pretty well. In addition to the Middle Eastern staple, it serves hummus, burgers, and pizza.

JOE PEÑA'S

Cankarjeva 6; tel. 01/421-5800; www.joepenas.si; 10am-1am Mon.-Thurs., 10am-2am Fri.-Sat., 12pm-12am Sun.; €9

Joe Peña's has been around for a while. You can get fajitas, enchiladas, and margaritas all in a central location.

CANTINA RESTAURANTE

Wolfova 4; tel. 01/426-9325; www.cantina.si; 10am-12am daily; €10

The newer Cantina Restaurante will get you closer to the Mexican cuisine you're craving.

SUSHIMAMA

Wolfova ulica 1; tel. 01/426-9125; 11am-11pm daily; €12

The first sushi restaurant in Ljubljana, Sushimama still serves up rolls and sashimi to a trendy, mostly young crowd.

SATO BENTO

Kotnikova ulica 5; tel. 040/301-373; www.japanska-hrana.si; €10

A better value is Sato Bento, which offers great Japanese noodle bowls and sushi at an excellent price.

Local Cuisine

★ PRI SKOFU

Rečna ulica 17; tel. 01/252-7003; 12pm-11pm Tues.-Sun.; €19

In the charming Krakovo neighborhood, Pri Skofu is famous in town for its home-style cooking that is typically locally sourced.

HIŠA KULINARKE MANNA

Eipprova ul. 1/A; tel. 01/426-4508; www.restaurant-manna.com; 12pm-12am Mon.-Sat.; €30

Foodies should head straight to the cozy Hiša Kulinarke Manna for slow-food specialties like smoked duck breast with horseradish terrine, lamb with herb crust, and the house cake, Manna.

Pasta and Pizza

FOCULUS
Gregorčičeva 3; tel. 01/251-5643; 10am-12am Mon.-Sat., 12pm-12am Sun.; €8

Though the funky restaurant has sometimes less-than-stellar service, Foculus is a must-visit for fans of pizza, with over 60 varieties, including Turkish, truffle, and seafood.

AS APERITIVO
Čopova 5a; tel. 01/425-8822; www.asaperitivo.si; 9am-3am daily; €12

As Aperitivo is the more casual offshoot of the pricier Gostilna As. Turning into a popular club spot as the night wears on, it's also the destination for pastas and salads at reasonable prices in a swank setting.

Quick Bites

Ljubljana has a great selection of budget-friendly restaurants aimed at locals on their lunch break and students in need of sustenance.

GOSTILNA DELA
Poljanska cesta 7; tel. 051/491-491; 8am-4pm Mon.-Fri.; €6

Gostilna Dela is close to the Dragon Bridge and has good portions and good prices.

NOBEL BUREK
Miklošičeva 30; tel. 01/232-3392; 24 hours daily; €3

A local student haunt, conveniently located near the bus and train stations, Nobel Burek offers steaming hot *burek* and pizza 24 hours a day.

Vegetarian

Technically, the only vegetarian restaurant in town is outside the city center. However, several mainstream restaurants offer a good variety of vegetarian dishes, like the pizzeria **Foculus** (Gregorčičeva 3, tel. 01/251-5643, 10am-12am Mon.-Sat., 12pm-12am Sun., €8) and Middle Eastern **Abi Falafel** (Trubarjeva 40, tel. 041/640-166, 10am-12pm Mon.-Sat., 1pm-10pm Sun., €6), both described above.

OUT OF THE CENTER

Fine Dining

GOSTILNA KAVAL
Tacenska 95; tel. 01/512-5596; www.bid.si/kaval; 10am-11pm Mon.-Fri., 12pm-11pm Sat.-Sun.; €15

Though the cuisine is not as haute as the more central Manna, Gostilna Kaval, about seven kilometers (4.3 miles) northwest of the center, has some tasty Tuscany-inspired cuisine and a romantic terrace, with pretty reasonable prices.

★ CUBO
Šmartinska c. 55; tel. 01/521-1515; www.cubo-ljubljana.com; 11am-11pm Mon.-Fri., 12pm-11pm Sat.; €18

The swank space at Cubo, about three kilometers (1.8 miles) northeast of the center, is as stylish as its food. A Mediterranean-inspired menu and decadent desserts are gobbled up by a chic clientele.

Local Cuisine

GOSTILNA POD ROŽNIKOM
Cankarjev Vrh 1; tel. 01/251-3429; www.roznik.si; 10am-11pm Mon.-Fri., 12pm-11pm Sat.-Sun.; €19

While all its dishes aren't exactly Slovenian, Gostilna pod Rožnikom has a great selection of regional cuisine, like grilled *ražnjiči* skewers, fried sweet peppers, and Serbian salads. Located in a leafy spot near the city zoo, it also has a huge shady terrace for alfresco dining.

★ GOSTILNA KOVAČ
Pot k Savi 9; tel. 01/537-1244; www.kovac-co.si; 12pm-10pm Mon.-Fri.; €32

Worth the drive or taxi ride to the edge of town for a special meal, the Gostilna Kovač has been serving traditional Slovenian cuisine since 1849. The interior is romantic, with wood-beamed ceilings and antiques, and there's a nice terrace as well. The restaurant is about five kilometers (three miles) northeast of the center, just above the Bežigrad neighborhood.

Quick Bites

HOT HORSE

Tivoli Park; tel. 01/521-1427; www.hot-horse.si;
10am-6am Mon., 9am-6am Tues.-Sun.; €5

Though some may find it offensive, Hot Horse is a local institution, serving late-night horse burgers next to Tivoli Park. They have a veggie burger on the menu, too, though it's doubtful that many animal lovers are eating here.

Vegan

BAZILIKA

Prešernova cesta 15; tel. 041/883-488; www.bazilika. si; 7am-8pm Mon.-Fri.; €6

For healthy vegan dishes and desserts, try Bazilika.

Information and Services

VISITOR AND TRAVEL INFORMATION

TOURIST INFORMATION CENTER

Adamič-Lundrovo Nabrežje 2; tel. 01/306-1215;
www.visitljubljana.com; 8am-9pm daily June-Sept.,
8am-7pm daily Oct.-May

The Tourist Information Center, next to the Triple Bridge, not only offers maps and guidance but is the source for tours of the city. You'll also find outposts of the tourist office at the bus and train stations (8am-10pm daily June-Sept., 10am-7pm daily Oct.-May) and the airport (11am-5:30pm Mon.-Fri., 11am-4:30pm Sat.). The tourist board also offers **bike tours** for groups of three or more from mid-April to the end of October. Tours should be booked ahead with the office.

Dial 981 for an **English-speaking operator** who should be able to help you with entertainment and events around Ljubljana.

A great value for money, the **Ljubljana Card** (www.visitljubljana.com, €24.30 for 24 hours, €30.60 for 48 hours, €35.10 for 72 hours) provides admission to 15 attractions, travel on city buses, a guided city tour, and Wi-Fi access.

BANKS AND CURRENCY EXCHANGE

Handling money in Ljubljana is easier than ever since Slovenia adopted the euro. If you need to change money, almost any bank (Ljubljanska Banka is the major local bank) can help, probably at better rates than the hotels. ATMs all over town should work with your bank card.

INTERNET ACCESS AND COMMUNICATIONS

The city offers 60 minutes of free Wi-Fi per day. Visit www.wifreeljubljana.si for more details. Even easier is to buy the **Ljubljana Card** (www.visitljubljana.com) or find a café with free Wi-Fi and buy a coffee to keep you company while you keep in touch with friends back home.

LAUNDRY SERVICES

CHEMO EXPRESS

Wolfova ulica 12; www.chemoexpress.com;
tel. 01/251-4404; €10 per load

Chemo Express can dry clean or wash your dirty clothes.

OPERI SMART WASHING

Beblerjev trg 2, in the Mercator shopping center;
€3 per wash

For self-service, Operi Smart Washing also offers free Wi-Fi while you wait.

EMERGENCY SERVICES

The police can be reached by dialing 113; emergency info (ambulances and fire) is at 112. If your rental car is in distress, call 987 for roadside assistance. Minor medical emergencies can be attended to at the **Medical**

Center (Bohoričeva 4, tel. 01/232-3060) or the Klinični center Ljubljana (Zaloška cesta 2, tel. 01/522-5050). The pharmacy Ljekarna Ljubljana (Prisojna ulica 7, tel. 01/230-6230) is open 24 hours daily.

Getting There and Around

GETTING THERE
Air
LJUBLJANA JOŽE PUČNIK AIRPORT
LJU; tel. 04/206-1981; www.lju-airport.si
Several carriers fly into Ljubljana Jože Pučnik Airport, 23 kilometers (14 miles) northwest of the center. **Adria Airways** (Gosposvetska 6, tel. 01/231-3312, www.adria.si) is Slovenia's national carrier, with flights to most major cities in Europe. **Air France** (www.airfrance.com) flies to Paris every day of the week, while **EasyJet** (www.easyjet.com) offers daily service to and from London in high season.

From the airport, you can hop a city bus (departure at 10 past the hour Mon.-Fri., less frequent on weekends and holidays) or a taxi (stand in front of the terminal, tel. 04/206-1678, around €35 into town). There is also an airport shuttle (information 040/887-766, around €8), which takes about 30 minutes to the city center.

Train
TRAIN STATION
Trg Osvobodilne fronte 6; tel. 01/291-3332;
potnik.info@slo-zeleznice.si, www.slo-zeleznice.si
Rail travel isn't as glamorous as it once was, but traveling the tracks around Slovenia is reliable and relatively inexpensive. The train station is conveniently located near the city center, a 10- to 15-minute trek to the main sights. There are good international connections, and it's also a good way to see some other towns in Slovenia: Maribor (2.5 hours), Kamnik (one hour), Postojna (one hour), and Koper (2.5 hours) are all served by the trains. Contact the station for timetables and more information.

Bus
BUS STATION
Trg Osvobodilne fronte 4; tel. 01/234-4600;
avtobusna.postaja@ap-ljubljana.si,
www.ap-ljubljana.si
The bus station has both international and local connections, and is a 10- to 15-minute walk to the city center. It is a safe and reliable means of getting around and runs to more locations than the train. You can connect to cities such as Škofja Loka (45 minutes), Lake Bohinj (two hours), Kranjska Gora (two hours), and Piran (2.75 hours).

Car
All highways in Slovenia lead to Ljubljana, so it's pretty much impossible to get lost if you're coming from another country. The highway to Zagreb, the E70, takes about two hours to drive the 120 kilometers (75 miles). Driving around Ljubljana is safe and, given that it's not too big, usually manageable.

GETTING AROUND
Bus
City buses (Ljubljanski Potniški Promet, LPP, Trdinova 3, or Slovenska 55, tel. 01/434-3248, www.lpp.si) are a reliable means of getting around town if you're staying in the suburbs. Otherwise, you won't really need them, since Ljubljana's core is quite small and easily accessible on foot. The 22 bus lines run between 5am and 10:30pm daily, with a few operating until 12am and beyond. Tickets can be purchased on board (around €1) or from a newsstand or kiosk (look for signs advertising *žetoni*, or tokens).

A great deal for travelers is the **Ljubljana Card** (www.visitljubljana.com, €24.30 for

24 hours, €30.60 for 48 hours, €35.10 for 72 hours), offering free city bus transportation, admission to museums and galleries, and savings at a number of restaurants, hotels, shops, and even taxi fares all over the city. The card can be purchased online or from sales outlets around the city such as the bus and train stations, the tourist office, and many hotels.

Car

Major rental agencies such as **Avis** (www.avisalpe.si) and **Hertz** (www.hertz.si) have outlets in Ljubljana. If you're driving around, remember that white zones allow you to park for one hour with a parking ticket (available at newsstands and kiosks).

Taxi

You'll find taxi stands outside the Best Western Slon Hotel, the train station, close to Town Square, and on Prešeren Square (only at night). Each firm has different prices, though holders of the Ljubljana Card get a 20 percent discount from **Rumeni Taxi** (tel. 041/731-831).

Bicycle

The tourist office has also started a program to **rent bicycles** (8am-7pm daily Apr.-June and Sept.-Oct., 8am-9pm daily July-Aug., €1 for 2 hours, €5 all day) from outlets all over the city: in front of the Slovenian Tourist Information Center, Antiq Hotel, train station, Ljubljana Resort, Grand Hotel Union Garni, Hostel Celica, Zlata ribica, and M Hotel. Ljubljana Card holders get four hours of free bicycle use.

Around Ljubljana

IŠKI VINTGAR

Only 15 kilometers (9 miles) south of Ljubljana, a small rapid river forms a pretty spot for nature fans. A beautiful limestone gorge, filled with rapids and waterfalls and a 10-meter-high (almost 33-foot-high) solitary rock formation dubbed the Rock Man, the Iški Vintgar gorge is a great place to go for hiking, with lots of trails, including the E6 European Foot Trail. Marked with white and blue signs, the trail will eventually link Italy, Austria, Slovenia, and Croatia.

The city transit 191 **bus** from Ljubljana station (www.lpp.si, about €1) takes between 30 minutes and an hour, depending on the number of stops. Buses leave approximately every 10 minutes.

BISTRA

TECHNICAL MUSEUM OF SLOVENIA

(Tehniški Muzej Slovenije)

Bistra; tel. 01/750-6670; www.tms.si; 8am-4pm Tues.-Fri., 9am-5pm Sat., 10am-6pm Sun. Sept.-June, *10am-5pm Tues.-Fri., 9am-5pm Sat., 10am-6pm Sun. July-Aug.; €4.50*

Seriously overlooked, the lovely Technical Museum of Slovenia is located in a former Carthusian monastery in the village of Bistra, near Vrhnika, about 25 kilometers (15 miles) southwest of Ljubljana. The museum has exhibits not only on things you would associate with such a museum—printing, woodworking, and electricity—but also on fishing, hunting, and forestry. Bonuses are the bucolic location next to a lake and a collection of old cards, including Tito's.

Take a **train** from Ljubljana to Borovnica (€2.50), and then arrange a taxi with **Intertours Taxi** (tel. 080/311-311, about €5 each way).

RAKITNA

Thirty kilometers (19 miles) southwest of the capital, the small village of Rakitna has a nice Baroque church and the remains of a Roman defensive wall. The real draw, though, are the sports on offer. In winter, the flat landscape makes for great cross-country skiing on the snowy karst plateau and ice skating on the lake, while in summer you can come for swimming in the lake. The tourist association, **Rakitna Tourist Society (Turistično društvo Rakitna)** (tel. 01/365-0082), can provide information on ski and skate rentals.

The **bus** from Ljubljana (www.lpp.si, about €2) takes 1.5 to 2 hours. Dozens of buses connect Ljubljana with Rakitna daily. You can catch number 44 from Notranje Gorice via city transit.

ZBILJSKO JEZERO

Zbiljsko jezero, only 16 kilometers (10 miles) northwest of the capital, is the perfect day trip from Ljubljana. Here you can escape city hustle and bustle by renting a boat or carriage to tour around the peaceful lake, created in the 1950s. The lakeside village of Zbilje is much older, first mentioned in the 14th century. There's also a great hike following the 18th-century **Stations of the Cross (Kalvarija),** an uphill pilgrimage path dotted with over a dozen shrines.

The **bus** from Ljubljana (www.lpp.si, about €1.50) takes 30 minutes and departs approximately every 10 minutes. Take 25 from the main station and connect at the end of the line to 30.

STIČNA
STIČNA MONASTERY
(Stična Samostan)

Stična 17; tel. 01/787-7100; www.rkc.si/sticna; 8am-12pm and 2pm-5pm Tues.-Sat., 2pm-5pm Sun.; €4.50

Thirty-five kilometers (22 miles) southeast of Ljubljana, the Stična Monastery only has a few full-time residents, but the cute Baroque church and the **Slovenian Religious Museum** (Slovenski Verski muzej) are nice for visiting if you have extra time. The Cistercian monastery is one of the oldest in Slovenia, dating from the 12th century, and resembles a castle more than a monastery due to fortifications to ward off the Turks in the 15th century. Especially noteworthy are the herbal teas, produced by the monks and nuns, that claim to heal a variety of ailments; they make an interesting souvenir purchase.

The **bus** from Ljubljana (www.lpp.si, about €1.50) takes one hour from the main bus station via city transit.

Technical Museum of Slovenia

Inland Slovenia

Inland Slovenia boasts snow-capped moun-tains, ethereal lakes, rushing rivers, and a network of caves, making the region ideal for sports enthusiasts. It's also where travelers can truly explore the core of Slovenia and its culture.

You can learn more about the country's history, food, and lifestyle in its Roman ruins, herding stations, centuries-old churches and castles, and a mass of vineyards and wine routes well worth sampling. The region is also home to the quirky folk carnival celebration called the Kurentovanje.

Less-touristed towns like Maribor and Ptuj are worth a stop, and the interior hosts several decent ski runs and hot-spring spa centers, where you can ease your muscles after your adventures. The highlight

Highlights

Look for ★ to find recommended sights, activities, dining, and lodging.

★ Kurentovanje: Ptuj's colorful carnival celebration, typified by the horned mask of the mythical Kurent, is one of Slovenia's most interesting festivals (page 358).

★ Škofja Loka: An almost perfectly preserved medieval town with a 6th-century bridge, this village is the heart of rural Slovenia and an easy day trip from Ljubljana (page 367).

★ Velika Planina: Seeing the summer herding of livestock on Velika Planina is a rare experience. Stay in a mountain hut, eat your fill of fresh cheese, and then work it off with an invigorating mountain bike ride (page 368).

★ Logar Valley (Logarska Dolina): This valley of unexplainable beauty is rimmed by giant alpine peaks and culminates in Slovenia's tallest waterfall (page 369).

★ Bled: The ethereal blue lake of Bled, with a tiny church-topped island, surrounded by mountains, is one of those things you just have to see to believe (page 375).

★ Triglav National Park: Pick a sport and head to Slovenia's only national park for an adrenaline fix, followed by some serious chill-out in one of the area's idyllic hotels (page 380).

of the interior, though, is certainly Bled with its fairy-tale lake and the nearby Triglav National Park, encompassing several villages and towns, filled with rushing streams and a vast selection of outdoor pursuits for active travelers.

The wine routes of the Bela Krajina are a must for gourmets, while quieter travelers will appreciate Idrija's wonderful manor hotel and lace-making traditions. Slovenian wines are well known for their quality, and over 70 percent of the country's production reaches quality or premium status.

Whatever your preference, the interior of Slovenia offers something for everyone, from snowy slopes to rolling hills dotted with vineyards with lots of picturesque castles and churches and interesting museums in between.

PLANNING YOUR TIME

If you have only one day, head directly to Bled, the best of Slovenia's interior region. From here, your planning will depend on your interests. You could spend two days skiing or pursuing some outdoor activities around Bovec and Bohinj, or take a couple of days to slowly wind your way through the Bela Krajina and Dolenjska wine regions. Many locations are possible long day trips from Ljubljana, including Škofja Loka and Idrija.

Itinerary Ideas

HIGHLIGHTS OF INLAND SLOVENIA

Day 1
- Start your trip by touring the sights in **Maribor.**
- Have dinner in the wine cellar at the **Chateau Ramšak** and tuck in for the night in one of their luxurious tents amongst the vineyards.

Day 2
- Head to the **Žiče Carthusian monastery** in **Slovenske Konjice** and buy some herbal preparations from the monks' shop.
- Play a round of golf or wander through the vineyards before settling down for the night at **Zlati Grič**

Day 3
- Wake up early to drive an hour and a half to the **Logar Valley (Logarska Dolina)**, where you can work up an appetite hiking the park's trails.
- Head to the idyllic **Tourist Farm Lenar** for a good night's rest.

Day 4
- It's a little under two hours' drive to **Bled**, a fairy-tale setting complete with a castle and church-topped island in an unreal turquoise lake surrounded by snow-capped mountains.

Previous: Lake Bled; another view of Lake Bled; Kurent costumes at Ptuj's Kurentovanje festival

Inland Slovenia

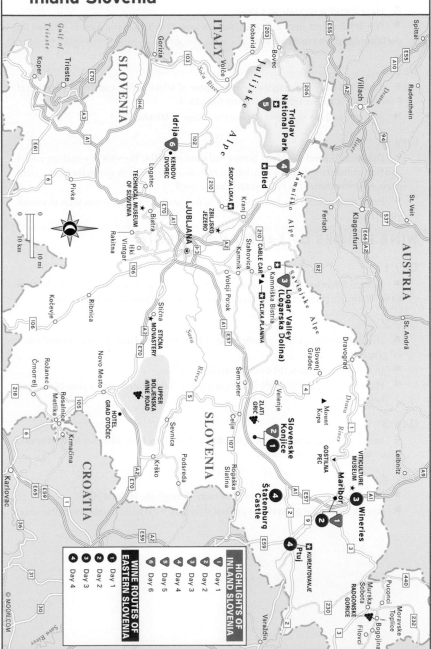

HIGHLIGHTS OF INLAND SLOVENIA
- 1 Day 1
- 2 Day 2
- 3 Day 3
- 4 Day 4
- 5 Day 5
- 6 Day 6

WINE ROUTES OF EASTERN SLOVENIA
- 1 Day 1
- 2 Day 2
- 3 Day 3
- 4 Day 4

- Spend the afternoon puttering around the lake in a *pletna* boat or a horse-drawn carriage.
- Have dinner at Restaurant 1906
- Stay at Vila Bled, once a vacation home of Josip Broz Tito, if you want to get a feel for the lakeside getaway in its heyday.

Day 5

- Today you can get sporty, trying any number of active pursuits, at Triglav National Park, which is almost around the corner from Bled.
- Stay at the alpine-style Vila Park in the village of Ukanc.

Day 6

- Drive south about two hours to the small town of Idrija. There's a lace-making school and historic mercury mine to visit, but the real reason to visit is to stay in the town's main draw, Kendov Dvorec, a 14th-century manor hotel.
- From here you can head to Ljubljana in only an hour's time, if you want to extend your trip.

WINE ROUTES OF EASTERN SLOVENIA

Day 1

- Head to Slovenske Konjice and check in at the vineyard-surrounded house at Zlati Grič. Walk on a path lined with vines down to the winery's restaurant for dinner.

Day 2

- Drive to Maribor, where your first stop is The Old Vine House to see Slovenia's oldest grapevine.
- In the afternoon, tour the city's Vinag Wine Cellar.
- Have dinner at Gostilna Pec, and end the day at Rožmarin with a glass of Riesling before bed.

Day 3

- In the morning, head just out of Maribor to tour three local wineries: Vino Horvat, Hiša vina Doppler, and Črnko.

Day 4

- End your tour near Ptuj and the wine route through the Haloze Hills.
- Stop at Štatenberg Castle for one last Slovenian meal accompanied by stellar wine.

Slovenian Wine

Slovenia's main wine-growing regions are **Podravje** (Pohorje and Pomurje regions, where you'll find the most marked wine routes), **Posavje** (Bela Krajina and Dolenjska regions), and **Primorska** (coastal region). Many of the country's 40,000 registered wineries are more hobbies and retirement occupations than anything else. Still, there's plenty of quality to be had, and given the small operations of most of the producers, it's likely you've never had the chance to try many of them—the production is just too low to export. Slovenia produces both red and white wines, though the whites are by far the best. Most of Slovenia is crisscrossed by one wine route or another. One less-traveled spot for wine lovers is the **Brda** region, bordering Italy, sure to bring lots of discoveries from the small vineyards along the roads.

Pohorje Region

This flat fertile area is at the edge of the Alps and is famous for its white wines. Covered in thick evergreen forests, it is home to one of Slovenia's larger cities, Maribor. Outside Maribor are some nice ski slopes, suited to pleasure-seekers more than professionals, but fun all the same—especially if you end your day in one of the area's steaming hot-spring pools.

MARIBOR

It's Slovenia's second-largest city, but most people see Maribor as primarily a business town, a pass-through on the way to Austria. Even the tourist office advertises a "Maribor in Two Hours" itinerary, hoping to lure people in a little longer. That may be about to change as more people are discovering the charming town and its excellent wine routes.

Maribor is actually a charming Austro-Hungarian town with a young spirit, supplied by the university students in town. And it's on the edge of wine country, serving as a good base to explore the area, with plenty of tastings and decent whites to keep fans of the grape interested.

Sights

Maribor Castle (Marborski grad) (Grajska ulica 2) was built in the 15th century by Emperor Friderik III. The highlight of the castle is Festive Hall, with an 18th-century painting on the ceiling by Austrian Johann Gebler, depicting a battle between Christian and Turkish soldiers. Franz Liszt gave a concert in the hall in 1874.

Today, the castle is home to the visit-worthy **Regional Museum of Maribor (Pokrajinski Muzej Maribor)** (Grajska ulica 2, tel. 02/228-3551, www.museum-mb. si, 10am-6pm Tues.-Sat., 10am-2pm Sun., €5). Permanent exhibitions include an overview of the region's history as well as a fascinating display of the art of pharmacy. A re-creation of a 19th-century pharmacy, displays about monastic pharmacies of the region, and a chance to smell and even touch local herbal drugs are what make the exhibition special.

The Gothic **Maribor Cathedral (Stolnica Maribor)** (Slomškov trg 20, tel. 02/251-8432, www.stolnicamaribor.com) was originally built in the 12th century in the Romanesque style. It's worth the 150-plus stair-climb to the top of its 57-meter-tall (187 feet) Bell Tower (10am-1pm Wed.-Fri. and Sun., 10am-1pm and 4pm-7pm Sat.) for the view of Maribor. The 18th-century structure replaced the original 17th-century version that was destroyed by lightning. The old tower was almost 20 meters taller.

Nearby **Rotovški Square (Rotovški trg)**, also referred to as **Main Square (Glavni**

Pohorje Region

Svečina ○ · A1 · WINERIES
E66 · A2
AUSTRIA · Dravograd ○ · Drava · 1 · VITICULTURE ★
River · MUSEUM KEBL · To Murska
Sobota
3
82 · Mount · Maribor
▲ Kopa · GOSTILNA
PEC
Slovenj ○ · E57 · 9 · KURENTOVANJE
Gradec · 4 · A1
210 · Ravne ○ · 2
Savinjske Alpe · Ptuj
LOGAR VALLEY · Kamniška · Velenje · ZLATI GRIČ · ŠTATENBURG
(LOGARSKA DOLINA) · ○ Bistria · CASTLE · E59
CABLE CAR ■ ▲ VELIKA PLANINA · PEKEL CAVE ✦ · 430
Krvavec · ROMAN NECROPOLIS · Slovenske
ARCHAEOLOGICAL PARK · Konjice
Stahovica · Šempeter ○ · Celje · 107 · Rogaška
Kranj ○ · Kamnik○ · E57 · Slatina
A2 · ○ Volčji Potok · A1 · River
SLOVENIA · CROATIA
Sava
H3
A1 · LJUBLJANA · 5
Sevnica ○ · Podsreda ○
A2 · E70 · UPPER
DOLJENSKA · ○ Krško · A2
WINE ROAD · E59
106 · 0 · 10 mi
0 · 10 km · ZAGREB
© AVALON TRAVEL · Novo Mesto ○ · E70

trg), is where the hub of Maribor's old town comes to life. Here you'll find the 16th-century Renaissance-style **Town Hall (Rotovž)**, where Hitler once stood on the balcony and proclaimed Maribor part of his territory.

The 18th-century Baroque **Aloysius church (Alojzijeva cerkev)** (tel. 02/234-6611, mass 8am Mon.-Sat., 10am Sun., free) is also worth a visit if you are around at mass time. The building has an ornate interior with rococo railings highlighted by pretty a trio of landscape paintings of the surrounding region. Three cities of the Štajerska region are depicted in these paintings behind the altar—Maribor, Celje, and Ptuj.

The center of the square is punctuated with a gilded **plague column (Kužno Znamenje)**, built by the locals in the 17th century to thank the Virgin Mary for sparing them in a plague that wiped out a third of the population.

Another must-visit if you're in town is **Lent**, which in Maribor doesn't refer to a religious calendar but to a busy riverside neighborhood. It's here that you'll find **The Old Vine House**, home to the oldest grapevine in Slovenia. There are lots of bars, restaurants, and shops to peruse as well. The neighborhood also includes **Jewish Square (Židovski trg)**, with **Jewish Tower (Židovski stolp)**, where the town's watchman used to live, now a photography museum (9am-5pm Tues.-Fri. and 1pm-5pm Sat., €3), and the **Maribor Synagogue (Sinagoga Maribor)** (Židovski trg, 8am-4pm Mon.-Fri., €1), built in the 15th century, a rarity in the former Yugoslavia.

The Jewish population settled in Maribor's Lent neighborhood in the second half of the 13th century. Due to its location next to the

Maribor's Secret God of Wine

It's only fitting that a region with so much good wine should have a statue to the Roman god of wine and fun. If you have time, search for the statue in a niche on the city's Slovenska ulica. A statue of the Virgin Mary used to be in the niche, until someone stole her, and the empty spot was filled with this jovial guy sitting on top of a barrel. Perhaps someone realized that he was a better choice, presiding over the city's main street for merrymaking.

Drava river, Lent became an area for the town's tradesmen. Streets like **Locksmith's Street (Ključavničarska ulica)** and **Leather Street (Usnjarska ulica)** are reminders of that past.

The **National Liberation Museum Maribor (Muzej Narodne Osvobotive Maribor)** (Ulica heroja Tomšiča 5, tel. 05/235-2605, www.mnom.si, 8am-5pm Mon.-Fri. and 9am-12pm Sat., €3) is set in a beautiful historic villa and displays both permanent and temporary exhibitions on the history of Maribor and the surrounding area.

The **City Park** is home to a relaxing walk around the **Three ponds (Trije ribniki)**. From City Park you can also make your way to the top of the 386-meter-high (1,266 feet) **Pyramid Hill (Piramida)**. A path lined with grapevines winds to the top, perfect for cycling or hiking. The hill was once home to Maribor Castle, built in the 12th century. In the 18th century, it was pulled down, and the stones were fashioned into a pyramid, which gives the hill its name.

Also on the outskirts of town in a leafy park is the pink and white Betnava Mansion. Here you will find the delightful **Maribor Beekeeping Association** (Streliška 150, tel. 031/261-884, 3pm-6pm Wed., free). You can taste many types of Slovenian honeys, including varieties you might not have tried, like pine needle, chestnut, and acacia. For a fee you can also sample honey brandy and honey champagne. In summer you can visit the apiary as well as look at a beehive made of glass, a fascinating way to observe the bees at work.

Wineries

Maribor is a particularly interesting stop for wine lovers and is part of the Podravje wine region. The largest wine-growing region in Slovenia, it actually produces less than smaller regions. This translates to high-quality wines, particularly fruity and flowery whites. The region often uses the technique of late harvest and ice wine harvest for their sweet wines, producing small batches that get serious respect. Popular wines are rieslings and chardonnays and a sweet local variety called Traminec. But don't count out the other whites. One local winery, Vino Horvat, is much lauded for their sauvignons.

In the Lent area, stop at **The Old Vine House (Hiša Stare trte)** (Vojašniška 8, tel. 02/251-5100, 10am-6pm daily Oct.-Apr., 10am-8pm daily May-Sept.) to see the oldest vine in Slovenia, a 400-year-old grapevine still producing today. The vine survived the Ottoman invasion and bombing during World War II and is quite famous, not only having its own house and museum but its own anthem as well, recorded by a local musical group. The 35-55 kilograms (77-121 pounds) of grapes it produces yearly are bottled into a hundred or so bottles of Žametna črnina. The museum is also a nice place to taste regional wines and purchase a few as well.

Then head to the **Vinag Wine Cellar** (Trg svobode 3, tel. 02/220-8119, tours at 11am and 4pm Sat., 4pm Sun., or by arrangement) with its 2.5 kilometers (1.5 miles) of underground tunnels that stretch below the center of the city, holding some 250,000 bottles of wine. Though the cellars were established during the mid-19th century, the oldest bottle is from 1946. Everything earlier was consumed during World War II. Arrange for tours and tastings ahead of time.

Vino Horvat (tel. 02/251-7872, www.vino-horvat.eu, call for hours) is in the hills of Maribor, close to Pyramid Hill (Piramida). They produce sparkling wines as well as whites and reds, but their strength lies in their sauvignons, some of which are award winning. A tour includes seeing the wine cellar, learning about wine production, and a tasting. If you want to take some bottles home, a case will only set you back about €8.

One of the best overall wine experiences in the area, **Chateau Ramšak** (Počehova 35, tel. 040/628-303, www.chateauramsak.com) is an old villa surrounded by vineyards. Have dinner in the chateau's restored wine cellar (they make excellent whites) or the lovely gardens before glamping under the stars in one of the property's luxurious tents. If you are lucky enough to visit during the harvest, you can get involved personally in the winemaking process.

Hiša vina Doppler (Kozjak nad Pesnico 79, tel. 02/654-3202, www.doppler.si, tours by appointment) bought their 19th-century vines from a group of Benedictine monks in 1938 and continue the winemaking tradition today. With an offering of whites, rosé, and a dry red, the location in the hills is not to be missed.

The **Črnko winery** (Jareninski vrh 5, tel. 02/640-7351, www.crnko.net, call for hours for tours) near Maribor is a great place to go to not only see the vineyards but taste the offerings in the family's wine tavern (5pm-11pm daily). As well as some of the region's specialties, chardonnay, sauvignon, and riesling, don't miss the lovely gray pinot.

In nearby Svečina, there is a **Viticulture Museum Kebl (Vinogradniški muzej Kebl)** (Slatina 13, tel. 02/656-0171, www.svecina.com, 2pm-7pm Sun. and by appointment, closed in inclement weather) next to a peaceful hiking trail. Though the museum has information about the region's winemaking, content in English is sparse to nonexistent. There is also a **Nordic Walking Trail** (www.potka.si/nw_vinotour/en) through the vineyards, with information and an English map on the website.

In the fall, usually October and November, Maribor hosts the **Old Wine Festival**

(Festival Stare trte), with tastings, colorful presentations, folk music, dancing, and even a vegetarian day. Contact the Maribor **tourist office** (Partizanska 6a, tel. 02/234-6611, www.maribor-pohorje.si) for more details.

Last but certainly not least are the region's four marked **wine routes,** encompassing dozens of stops at local wineries, many serving homemade meals as well. Detailed information, plus the possibility to book a guided tour, can be found at the Maribor tourist office.

Sports and Recreation

The Maribor area has lots of great sports for adventure enthusiasts. **SB Shop** (Pohorska 60, tel. 059/259-040, www.sb-shop.si) is a great one-stop shop for bike rentals, ropes courses, skydiving, summer sledding, and more.

In winter, the **Mariborsko Pohorje Ski Resort** (www.mariborskopohorje.si) offers over 40 kilometers (25 miles) of slopes at all levels. Popular with locals and Croatians who come up for the weekend, the region is gaining in popularity with other travelers since the overall price of a ski vacation can be much lower. Hotels around the mountain also offer a variety of wellness packages for those not interested in skiing, or as a way to wind down after a long day on the slopes.

Contact the Maribor **tourist office** (Partizanska 6a, tel. 02/234-6611, www.maribor-pohorje.si) about ski passes for the Pohorje, which are also valid for other runs in Slovenia, such as Kranjska Gora. The tourist office also rents bikes for cycling around town.

NK Maribor (Mladenska 29, tel. 02/228-4700, www.nkmaribor.com) is Slovenia's most successful soccer team, playing games at Maribor's **People's Garden (Ljudski vrt).**

Accommodations and Food

Summertime means that most college dorm rooms in town are available for rent to visitors. Contact the **tourist office** (Partizanska 6a, tel. 02/234-6611, www.maribor-pohorje.si) for more details.

Don't let the name fool you: **Youth Hostel Hotel Uni** (Volkmerjev prehod 7, tel. 02/250-6700, www.hotel-orel.si, €54 d) is more a hotel than a hostel, with clean rooms with a work area, en suite bath, and Internet access plus an excellent buffet breakfast. The hostel's sister property, **Ibis Styles** (Volkmerjev prehod 7, tel. 02/250-6700, www.hotel-orel.si, €105 d), charges twice the price and is not much nicer. Choose these properties for the location in the heart of the old town, not for the rooms or amenities.

The **Hotel Tabor Maribor** (Ulica heroja Zidanška 18, tel. 02/421-6410, www.hoteltabor-maribor.si, €73 d, including breakfast) isn't fancy, but the rooms are clean and it's only a 15-minute walk to the center. If you are an ice hockey fan, the hotel is conveniently located across from the city's rink. The family-run hotel offers free parking and Wi-Fi plus a good buffet breakfast.

Built in 2011 and located in downtown Maribor, the **Hotel City Maribor** (Ulica kneza Koclja 22, tel. 02/292-7000, www.cityhotel-mb.si, €120 d, including breakfast) has 78 rooms, some with views of the Drava river. Other reasons to choose Hotel City Maribor: a restaurant and bar with great views, free parking, and electric bike and scooter rental available from reception for seeing the town.

The **Hotel Bellevue** (Na Slemenu 35, tel. 02/607-5100, www.hotelbellvue.si, €130 d) is a four-star hotel that's really more of a three. Stay here if you want to be steps away from the ski lift. For straight touring it's not the best choice, though it does have a good wellness center, featuring a wide variety of saunas near Maribor.

For a unique overnight experience, do a spot of glamping in one of the luxurious tents at **Chateau Ramšak** (Počehova 35, tel. 040/628-303, www.chateauramsak.com, €115 d), surrounded by vineyards.

For a quick lunch, **Restaurant Bolarič (Mesarstvo, trgovina in okrepčevalnica Bolarič)** (Jurčičeva 3, tel. 02/250-5910, 8am-4pm Mon.-Fri., 7am-1pm Sat., €4) has good hot pots and breaded, fried meats with basic sides for unbelievably cheap prices, even if its official name is a mouthful.

Good burgers and steaks are available at the reasonably priced **Jack & Joe Steak and Burger Club** (Od bregu 20, tel. 051/370-621, €12). Tuck into a hearty meal in this trendy restaurant after working up an appetite on the slopes or hiking around town.

Another great option is **La Pizzeria** (Gosposka ulica 8, tel. 041/302-302, www.lapizzeria.si, 11am-11pm Mon.-Thurs., 11am-12am Fri.-Sat., €10), which offers huge tasty pizzas to rival those in neighboring Italy. Salads and desserts are also on offer at this eclectic yet modern restaurant.

For traditional Slovenian specialties, the out-of-town ★ **Gostilna Pec** (Sp. Selnica 1, tel. 02/674-0356, www.gostilnapec.si, 11am-11pm Mon.-Sat., 11am-8pm Sun., €14) is a quiet, relaxing place with a nice terrace for summer dining. Dishes like venison or pumpkin soup change with the seasons, but the quality of the food and the nice local wine list remain consistent.

In town, **Rožmarin** (Gosposka ulica 8, tel. 02/234-3180, www.rozmarin.si, 11am-10pm Mon.-Thurs., 11am-11pm Fri.-Sat., wine bar open later, €12) is the place to go for just about everything culinary and wine-related. The trendy swank space serves everything from breakfast to dinner in its restaurant, while the minimalist coffeehouse provides good coffee and the wine bar is the perfect place to hang out over a glass of wine. You can even stop at their wine store to pick up a few bottles for the trip home.

A haute cuisine addition to Maribor, ★ **Restavracija Mak** (Osojnikova ulica 20, tel. 02/620-0053, www.restavracija-mak.si, 8am-11pm Mon.-Thurs., 8am-12am Fri. and Sat., 8am-10pm Sun., €24) is slow-food restaurant extraordinaire. To fully appreciate this culinary experience that somehow hasn't caught the international attention it deserves, plan on spending four to five hours here for a meal. Infusions, savory mousses, and deconstructed desserts are all on the constantly changing menu and presented as art pieces to admire and enjoy.

Information and Services
The **tourist office** (Partizanska 6a, tel. 02/234-6611, www.maribor-pohorje.si, 9am-7pm Mon.-Fri., 10am-3pm Sat. Nov.-Mar., 9am-7pm Mon.-Fri., 9am-5pm Sat.-Sun. Apr.-Oct.) provides maps and offers guided tours around the city.

Getting There and Around
Located about 120 kilometers (75 miles) northeast of Ljubljana, Maribor is a well-connected city. The **Bus Station Maribor (Avtobusna postaja Maribor)** (Mlinska ulica 1, tel. 02/235-0212, or toll-free tel. 080-11-16) provides dozens of links to regional as well as international destinations such as Ljubljana (three hours) and Ptuj (30 minutes). Since Maribor is Slovenia's second-largest city, the **train station** (Partizanska cesta 50, tel. 02/292-2164, picmaribor-mednarodnablagajna@slo-zeleznice.si) has excellent connections, including multiple daily trains to Ptuj (45 minutes), Ljubljana (2.5 hours), Postojna (3.5 hours), and Koper (five hours). You'll also find international connections daily to cities such as Vienna, Graz, Zagreb, Budapest, and even Venice. The train from Ljubljana to Maribor is a nicer trip than the bus.

PTUJ
Ptuj is a beautiful town on the Drava River. It's overlooked by visitors most of the year, but the town swells for the city's famous Kurentovanje, or Carnival celebration, typified by the wooly horned Kurent costume. A local tradition for centuries, the Kurent is said to drive away winter and welcome spring.

Any time of the year, the town's a nice stop, and cruising the wine routes around town is a must for those who enjoy tasting local wines.

Sights
Ptuj castle (Ptuj Grad) (Grajska Raven, tel.

02/787-9230, www.pmpo.si, 9am-5pm daily mid-Oct.-Apr., 9am-6pm daily May-June and Sept.-mid-Oct., 9am-6pm Mon.-Fri., 9am-8pm Sat.-Sun. July-Aug., €6) is impossible to miss, occupying a hill in the center of town. Parts of the castle date from as early as the 11th century, though the structure has undergone almost as many additions and renovations as it has owners. Today, it is home to a small but interesting museum with exhibitions of musical instruments, weaponry, folk art on glass, and perhaps most unique of all, a display of traditional carnival costumes from the town's best-known event, the Kurentovanje.

A former **Dominican monastery (Dominikanski samostan)** (Muzejski trg 1, tel. 02/787-9230) is worth the stop if you can manage to get in; it's only open on special days like the Slovenian Day of Culture (Feb. 8). The 13th-century building and its fading frescoes are beautiful. The building exterior is very pretty, with frosting-like frills on a pink facade and four statues in its niches.

TOP EXPERIENCE

★ Kurentovanje
Ptuj is most famous for its colorful Kurentovanje festival (www.kurentovanje. net), a don't-miss if you happen to be in the area during the 10 days that lead up to Mardi Gras in February or March. There's a procession of men dressed in the horn-masked sheepskin Kurent costume, which looks like something between a devil and a wooly mammoth. The purpose of the costumes is to scare away winter and welcome spring. The festival has been held every year for half a century, though its origins date back hundreds of years, and today it draws some 100,000 visitors each February. During the day you'll find plenty of theater and musical performances to keep you entertained. At night there are balls

---

1: wine road in the Pohorje region **2:** Zlati Grič in slovenske Konjce **3:** The Old Vine House winery in Maribor

and dancing accompanied by lively folk music performances.

Wineries

Ptujska klet wine cellars (Vinarski trg 1, tel. 02/787-9810, www.pullus.si, tours reserved in advance between 9am-3pm Mon.-Fri.) has daily scheduled tours and tastings to help you sample some of the local whites. The **KK Ptuj-Haloze cellars** (Trstenjakova 6), over 400 years old, are another stop, located in a former monastery. They produce some excellent white wines, particularly rieslings and late-harvest wines known as *suhi jagodni izbor*.

Contact the **tourist office** (Slovenski trg 5, tel. 02/779-6011, www.ptuj-tourism. si) for more detailed info and maps on two **wine routes** you can take from Ptuj. One of the best around Ptuj is the **Haloze Hills** route, starting near Borl Castle. Between the villages of Podlehnik and Poljčane, stop at ★ **Štatenberg Castle** (Štatenberg 86, tel. 02/803-0216, www.dvorecstatenberg.si, 8am-12am Sat. and 10am-6pm Sunday, Apr.-Oct.), an 18th-century Baroque mansion that today is home to a good restaurant that serves superior local wines.

Accommodations and Food

Located in a renovated historic property in the center of town, the **Bed & Breakfast Šilak** (Dravska ulica 13, tel. 02/787-7447, bed-breakfast-silak.business.site, €70 d, including breakfast) is an experience in itself. The lovely family-run B&B is cozy and clean and offers free parking. The **Grand Hotel Primus** (Pot v. toplice 9, tel. 02/749-4100, www.terme-ptuj.si, €110 d) opened in late 2007. Just outside of town, it comes with a wellness center and hot-spring baths as well as a water park for the kids.

Have a coffee, or even stay overnight, at the charming **muziKafe** (Vrazov trg 1, tel. 02/787-8860, www.muzikafe.si, from €57 d, including breakfast). Centrally located, the eclectic cafe offers coffee and hot cocoa with a street-side book exchange. If you choose to stay overnight in one of the artsy and cozy rooms, there is a nice breakfast available as well.

Ribič (Dravska ulica 9, tel. 02/749-0638, 10am-11pm Tues.-Thurs. and Sun., 10am-12am Fri.-Sat., €12) has great freshwater fish and superb views from its riverside terrace.

Getting There and Around

Regular buses link Ptuj's **bus station** (Osojnikova 11, tel. 02/771-1491), about 130 kilometers (80 miles) northeast of Ljubljana, with Maribor (30 minutes) and Ljubljana (3.5 hours).

You'll need a car to travel the wine routes around town. By car from Ljubljana, take the highway toward Maribor, exiting at Slovenska Bistrica.

There are several trains daily from Ptuj's **train station** (Osojnikova 2, tel. 02/292-5702) to Maribor, about a 45-minute trip. You can also take the train to Ljubljana (three hours).

SLOVENSKE KONJICE

Slovenske Konjice is a beautiful village worthy of a laid-back detour. The 12th-century **Žiče Carthusian monastery (Žička kartuzija)** (Stare Slemene 24, tel. 03/759-3110, call for hours) is worth a visit to see the living quarters, including the dining room and kitchen, of the monks who left the cloister in the 18th century. There's a restaurant on-site for a quick bite and you shouldn't leave without at least visiting the **Viva Sana** herb shop to check out their herbal preparations.

Accommodations and Food

★ **Zlati Grič** (Stari trg 29A, tel. 03/758-0350, www.zlati-gric.si, €80 d) is a winemaking compound, complete with vineyards, a golf course, a nice restaurant (12pm-9pm daily, €10-18), and apartments in a historic building to stay a relaxing night or two. It's truly a getaway-from-it-all experience and highly recommended. It's also a great overnight on the way to Maribor or Vienna from Ljubljana.

Getting There and Around

Slovenske Konjice is most easily reached by

car. From Ljubljana, take the A1 highway east toward Celje/Maribor, and take the exit for Slovenske Konjice, a total drive of about 90 kilometers (56 miles).

MOUNT KOPA AREA

Part of the Pohorje mountain range, the area is full of alpine charm and small villages, some with an interesting stop or two.

Mežica

Fans of history or mining will enjoy experiencing an old mine in the region. Traveling 3.5 kilometers (2.1 miles) into the mountain, the train at the lead and zinc mine museum in Mežica, **Mine Museum (Podzemlje Pece)** (Glančnik 6, tel. 02/870-0180, www.podzemljepece.com, tours 11am daily Apr.-June and Sept.-Nov., 11am and 3pm daily July-Aug., €7.80), takes you through an interesting look at mining life with expert guides. Cycling enthusiasts can also rent bicycles and cycle through the mine. Another interesting option is a kayak tour of the mine. Mežica is 24 kilometers (15 miles) west of Slovenj Gradec.

Slovenj Gradec

The small town of Slovenj Gradec is worth an hour or two to check out its preserved old town and a couple of its museums and churches, particularly the **Church of St. Elizabeth (Cerkev Sv Elizabeta)** on Trg Svobode, the 15th-century **Church of the Holy Spirit (Cerkev Sv Duha),** and the **Slovenj Gradec Art Gallery (Likovnih Umetnosti Slovenj Gradec)** (Glavni trg 24, tel. 02/884-1283, www.glu-sg.si, 9am-6pm Tues.-Fri., 10am-1pm and 2pm-5pm Sat.-Sun., €2.50), a surprisingly good modern art gallery housed in the old town hall.

Also on the square, make sure to stop and visit a shop specializing in making gingerbread and candles since 1757. **Perger 1757** (Glavni trg 34, tel. 02/884-1496, www.perger1757.si, 10am-8pm Mon.-Sat.) also has a nice variety of honey products, which all make great souvenirs.

The Slovenj Gradec **tourist office** (Glavni trg 24, tel. 02/881-2116, www.slovenj-gradec.si, 9am-6pm Mon.-Fri.) is a good source of local information, including skiing and hiking at the nearby Kope ski center, which typically sees snow November to April.

Ravne

Another worthwhile stop, the village of Ravne has long been an ironworking center. Today its **Carinthian Museum of Ravne na Koroškem (Koroški pokrajinski muzej)** (Na gradu 2, tel. 02/870-6461, www.kpm.si, 10am-1pm Tues.-Thurs., €2) displays a bit about the history of ironworking and some interesting modern iron sculptures as well as exhibitions about the development and culture of the Carinthian region. Contact the **tourist office** (Trg Svobode 21, tel. 02/822-1219, www.ravne.si/tic, 8am-4pm Mon.-Fri., 8am-12pm Sat.) for more details. Ravne is 25 kilometers (15.5 miles) south of Slovenj Gradec.

Accommodations and Food

The cheapest accommodations around are the mountain huts that provide shelter, a bed, and a bath. Many of the rooms are shared; bring a sleeping bag, and be prepared to hike to get to them. These huts can be booked through the **Slovenian Tourist Board** (www.slovenia.info).

The **Tourist Farm Ravnjak** (Sele 37, tel. 041/787-090, www.kmetija-ravnjak.si, from €40 d) is a lovely farm stay with local food (available for a small upcharge) in a peaceful setting with friendly hosts. The farm also offers a complimentary sauna to guests, which is particularly nice in the winter months. The **Okrepčevalnica Orada** (Trg svobode 3, Slovenj Gradec, tel. 02/823-7098, 11am-10pm Tues.-Sun., €15) in Slovenj Gradec offers reasonably priced freshwater fish plates and can arrange for fishing trips.

Getting There and Around

Slovenj Gradec is 110 kilometers (68 miles) northeast of Ljubljana. While you'll need a car to really explore the area, Slovenj Gradec does have excellent bus connections to Ljubljana (2.5 hours). Buses from Slovenj Gradec head to the ski areas regularly in ski season.

Pomurje Region

Green fields wind along the river Mura in the Pomurje region, one of Slovenia's most agricultural areas. This translates into lots of bucolic scenery and sleepy towns. To reach some of the smaller towns, it's best to have a car. Another alternative is to travel by bicycle. Several cycling routes are well marked; they vary in length from 10 to 50 kilometers (6 to 31 miles). Pick up a map from the Murska Sobota **tourist office** (Slovenska 37, Murska Sobota, tel. 02/534-1130, www.visitpomurje. eu, 9am-5pm Mon.-Fri.).

MURSKA SOBOTA

The **castle** in Murska Sobota is a Renaissance-era structure set in the middle of a huge park. It houses the **Murska Sobota Regional Museum (Pokrajinski muzej Murska Sobota)** (Trubarjev drevored 4, tel. 02/521-1155, www.pomurski-muzej.si, 9am-5pm Tues.-Fri., 9am-3pm Sat., 2pm-6pm Sun., €3), where the most interesting exhibit is the history of the region's Jewish population, from rural life to their persecution in World War II.

Have lunch at the **Tourist Farm Vinski hram kupljen** (Okoslavci 2a, Sveti Jurij ob Ščavnici, tel. 02/568-9073, www.kupljen.si, entrees from €12, call for reservations, cash only), in the village of Okoslavci, 12 kilometers (7.5 miles) southwest of Murska Sobota, and sample the farm's homemade jellies, salamis, sausages, and peach and pear brandies. The farm can also arrange guided wine-tastings.

Murska Sobota is 182 kilometers (113 miles) northeast of Ljubljana and 41 kilometers (25 miles) east of Maribor. It is connected by bus with Maribor (2 hours) and Ljubljana (4 hours). Trains also connect the town with Ljubljana (3.5 hours), Maribor (1.5 hours), and Ptuj (1 hour).

MORAVSKE TOPLICE AND SELO

The **Hotel Livada Prestige** (Kranjčeva 12, tel. 02/512-2288, www.hotel-livada.si, €83 d, including breakfast) in Moravske Toplice, seven kilometers (four miles) northeast of Murska Sobota, offers lots of hot-spring baths, spa treatments, a restaurant, and a golf course for a nice relaxing break. While it's not the five-star hotel that it claims to be, it is good value for the money.

Near Moravske Toplice, the **St. Nicholas Chapel (Rotunda Sv. Nikolaj)** (9am-5pm daily Apr.-Nov., or ask in the village about the key, €1.70), at the edge of the village of Selo, is a striking example of Romanesque architecture. Likely built in the 13th century, the cylindrical church houses some beautifully preserved paintings, including the *Adoration of the Magi* from the beginning of the 14th century. For more information, contact the Moravske Toplice **tourist office** (tel. 02/538-1520, www.moravske-toplice.com).

The Vineyard Scarecrow

Traveling through Eastern Slovenia's vineyards, you might notice, or hear, a windmill-like structure. The *klopotec* is typical of the region, though no one knows for sure how or when it came about. Unlike a windmill, these structures are meant to make noise, and their name is quite descriptive of the sound they make.

The distinctive wooden clack is a happy noise in the region. The devices go up in vineyards in late summer to scare the birds away from the ripening grapes, and they signal that the harvest is just around the corner. Folk legends also say it helps to soften the grapes, though no one's ever proven the myth.

BOGOJINA

If you didn't get your fill of architect Jože Plečnik in Ljubljana, his addition to the **Church of the Ascension (Cerkev Gospodovega vnebovzetja)** (Bogojina 147, usually 8am-5pm daily, free) in Bogojina, about 10 kilometers (6.2 miles) east of Murska Sobota, is a beautiful combination of 20th-century and classic architecture. The church incorporates local folk pottery into its decoration, making it all the more interesting. Check with the Moravske Toplice **tourist office** (tel. 02/538-1520, www.moravske-toplice.com) for specific hours.

FILOVCI

Pomurje is well known for its pottery. The village of Filovci, about four kilometers (2.4 miles) east of Bogojina, has several famous potters who will welcome you into their studios. Check with the **tourist office** (Filovci 410, tel. 02/547-1248) to make arrangements. Also of interest in nearby Filovski Gaj are the thatched wine cellars, part of the area's typical traditional architecture that is disappearing today.

WINERIES

Ride 10-20 kilometers (6-12 miles) through the vineyards of **Radgonske gorice** (Jurkovičeva 5, Puconci, tel. 02/564-8526, www.radgonske-gorice.si, 7am-5pm Mon.-Sat., call for reservations, €6) on a train and enjoy guided tastings of the wines. The vintners claim to have produced Slovenia's first sparkling wine. Puconci is about five kilometers (three miles) north of Murska Sobota.

The Pomurje region has the **Goričko Wine Route** (Puconci 79, tel. 02/545-9673, zkstrp. puconci@siol.net), filled with both cultural and culinary stops. Contact the office for more details and a printed map.

Savinjska Valley

The green Savinjska Valley is one of Slovenia's most picturesque yet least-visited areas. Filled with medieval castles, the largest and most famous at Celje, the region has other attractions—Roman ruins, hot-spring parks, caves, and a mining museum, among others.

CELJE

The town of Celje is most visitors' first stop in the Savinjska Valley. Though the outskirts are filled with factories and blocky structures, the old core is well preserved and charming. **Celje Castle (Stari Grad Celje)** (Cestan na grad 78, tel. 03/544-3690, www.grad-celje. com, 9am-9pm daily June-Aug., 9am-7pm daily Apr., 9am-8pm daily May and Sept., 9am-6pm daily Mar. and Oct., 9am-5pm daily Nov. and Feb., 10am-4pm daily Dec.-Jan., €4), the largest in Slovenia, is an interesting outing. It's close to an hour's hike on foot, though you can take the easy way and hail a taxi. The early-13th-century structure has been added to and changed over the years. The 14th-century Frederick's Tower was built to serve as a defensive escape from attackers. Its name comes from the legend that a son named Frederick wanted to marry a woman his father disapproved of. To prevent the marriage, he imprisoned Frederick in the tower. There's not a lot to see in the castle itself, but there are some nice views, and the grounds are beautiful.

If it's displays you're after, the **Celje Regional Museum (Pokrajinski muzej Celje)** (Muzejski trg 1, tel. 03/428-0950, www.pokmuz-ce.si, 10am-6pm Tues.-Sat. Mar.-Oct., 10am-6pm Tues.-Fri., 10am-12pm Sat. Nov.-Feb., €3.50) in Celje's Stara Grofija manor house has an impressive collection of artifacts and art from prehistoric to post-World War II.

A small but well-done museum, especially

Slovenian Dialects

Slovenian is one of the most varied languages in the world. With only two million speakers, Slovenian has at least 32 different dialects, which are derived from the seven main dialects—Carinthian (spoken in the regions directly bordering Austria), Upper Carniolan, Lower Carniolan (around Ljubljana), Styrian, Pannonian (near Hungary), and Rovte. The speech is so different that it is very likely that residents of one part won't understand residents of another area, even though in written form the difference is relatively small.

While standard Slovenian, taught in schools and published in newspapers, is based on the dialect spoken in and around Ljubljana, known as Lower Carniolan, other areas speak a daily language peppered with varying vocabulary and accents. This diversity is largely due to the difficult geography of Slovenia, which isolated the various regions from one another.

Though the first printed book in Slovenian emerged in the 16th century, modern Slovenes can thank the work of early-19th-century linguist Jernej Kopitar, who published a book about the language that began to give it a standard literary form. It is interesting to note that written and spoken Slovenian are very different from each other, since the literary language is based on a form hundreds of years old.

for those who find most history museums to be too heavy, the **Museum of Recent History Celje (Muzej Novjose Zgodovine Celje)** (Prešernova ulica 17, tel. 03/428-6410, www.muzej-nz-ce.si, 9am-5pm Tues.-Fri., 9am-1pm Sat., 2pm-6pm Sun., €3) has a floor dedicated to a street as it might have been in Celje's past where you can walk through reconstructed shops and a home. There is also a dentistry museum, a memorial room to victims of the Nazis, and a small children's museum.

Accommodations and Food

The **Castle View Hostel (Sobe pod gradom)** (Mariborska 2, tel. 070/220-069, www.mc-celje.si, €18 pp) is a good youth hostel in Celje with clean, bright rooms.

In the center of town, the **Hotel Evropa** (Krekov trg 4, tel. 03/426-9000, www.hotel-evropa.si, €90 d including breakfast) is 140 years old. The rooms don't have much character but they are renovated and clean.

You can find lots of casual restaurants and bars in the town of Celje for a bite to eat. **Stari Pisker** (Savinova ulica 9, tel. 03/544-2480, www.stari-pisker.com, €9) has massive burgers, onion rings, and beer as well as a solid variety of other meat dishes.

Gostilna Pri Kmetec (Zagrad 140A, tel. 03/544-2555, www.tlacan.si, 12pm-10pm Wed.-Sat., 10am-6pm Sun., €15) offers local specialties in a superb location with a picturesque view over the town of Celje.

Getting There and Around

Celje is 46 kilometers (28.5 miles) southwest of Maribor and 73 kilometers (45 miles) northeast of Ljubljana. You can reach Celje by bus or train. There are connections by bus to cities such as Ljubljana (1.5 hours), Maribor (1.5 hours), and Ptuj (two hours). Trains connect Celje with cities such as Ljubljana (1.5 hours), Ptuj (one hour), and Maribor (45 minutes) as well as local villages like Velenje (45 minutes) and Rogaška Slatina (45 minutes). A taxi stand can be found on Krekov trg near the train station. If driving from Ljubljana, take the Maribor highway and exit at Celje. From Maribor, take the highway toward Ljubljana and exit at Celje.

ŠEMPETER

The Celje Regional Museum runs the **Roman necropolis archaeological park (Arheološki park Rimska nekropola)** (10am-3pm daily Apr., 10am-5pm daily May-Sept., 10am-4pm Sat.-Sun. Oct., €5) in Šempeter, 12 kilometers (7 miles) west of Celje. Containing over 100 Roman tombs, the outdoor museum is one of the best-preserved Roman monuments in Slovenia. Outstanding among the many family gravestones, the eight-meter-high (26 feet) Spectatius tomb, likely dating from the 2nd century AD, is covered with intricate reliefs, including a depiction of the four seasons and a gruesome Medusa head guarding the remains.

The nearby **Pekel Cave** (entry every hour on the hour 10am-4pm Sat.-Sun. Mar. and Oct., 9am-4pm daily Apr., 10am-5pm daily May-Sept., €8) has the highest underground waterfall in Slovenia at four meters (13 feet).

For more information about the necropolis and Pekel Cave, contact the Šempeter **tourist office** (Ob Rimski nekropoli 2, tel. 03/700-2056, www.td-sempeter.si).

VELENJE

Though the city of Velenje is not the most attractive in Slovenia, history fans and older children (visitors must be age 7 or older) will enjoy a visit to the **Coal-Mining Museum of Slovenia (Muzej premogovništva Slovenije)** (Stari jašek—Koroška cesta, tel. 03/587-0997, www.muzej.rlv.si, 9:30am 4:30pm Tues.-Sat., last entry 2:30pm, €11). An elevator takes visitors 160 meters (525 feet) into the ground to see what it was like to be a coal miner in the early 20th century. The museum also features a guided tour of the mines, a film on the daily life of the miners, and a coal miner's lunch. The museum accommodates individuals with disabilities, but arrangements should be made in advance for wheelchairs.

Eighteen kilometers (11 miles) northwest of Celje, Velenje is connected by bus to Slovenj Gradec (45 minutes), Celje (45 minutes), and Ljubljana (2 hours), and by train to Celje (50 minutes).

ROGAŠKA SLATINA

The **Grand Hotel Rogaška** (Stritarjeva 1, tel. 03/811-2000, www.terme-rogaska.si, €92 d) is located in a former Austro-Hungarian palace in the town of Rogaška Slatina. The rooms (the hotel bills itself as a four-star, but it is a solid three-star by most standards) do not live up to the beauty of the palace, but the setting is spectacular, and you can use the hotel's hot-spring pools and spa.

Rogaška Slatina is about 25 kilometers (15.5 miles) east of Celje and is connected to Celje by a train that takes about 45 minutes.

PODSREDA

First mentioned in the 13th century, **Podsreda castle (Grad Podsreda)** (10am-6pm Tues.-Sun. summer, €4) is a pretty Romanesque fortress, located on a hill above the village of Podsreda, with some small exhibitions of local glasswork and concerts during the summer. It's a nice way to spend an hour if you're in the area. If you find it closed, the keys are kept at the **Kozjanski Park office** (Podsreda 45, tel. 03/800-7100, kozjanski-park@kp.gov.si).

Podsreda is 20 kilometers (12 miles) south of Rogaška Slatina and about 35 kilometers (22 miles) southeast of Celje.

Savinjske Alps Region

In this region of rolling green hills that give way to rocky alpine peaks, the beauty of nature competes with pretty villages full of churches, castles, and quaint museums for travelers' attention. No matter what the season, you can take to the slopes for a bit of fresh air and exercise.

★ ŠKOFJA LOKA

Filled with old buildings and charming squares, the well-preserved medieval town of Škofja Loka has a fairy-tale quality, special even among Slovenia's picturesque villages.

Start with a tour of the town's castle and small museum. The 13th-century **Old Loka Castle (Loka Grad)** (Grajska pot 13, tel. 04/517-0400, www.loski-muzej.si, 9am-6pm Tues.-Sun., €5) houses a few nice displays, most with English descriptions. Among the permanent collections are displays of art and archaeology, though most interesting to visitors will likely be the ethnographic collection, with regional costumes and displays on local trades like lace- and hat-making.

After visiting the castle, continue wandering around the steep and winding streets, admiring the town's medieval buildings and churches, particularly the 15th-century **St. Jacob's Church (Cerkev Sv Jakob)**, whose interior was recast by Plečnik, and cross the 6th-century Capuchin Bridge. On the last weekend in June the town holds the **Path of Venus (Venerina pot)** medieval street fair, definitely worth a visit if you're in the area at the time.

Accommodations and Food

The **Kveder Guest House (Goštišče Kveder)** (Spodnja Luša 16, tel. 04/514-1499, www.kveder-sp.si, €40 d, including breakfast) is a farm that offers comfortable but basic rooms and good meals in a peaceful alpine setting. Only one kilometer away from skiing, the bed-and-breakfast can also arrange for horseback riding in the valley.

For an entire vacation in addition to a hotel room, ★ **Pri Lenart Hotel** (Podvrh 1, tel. 051/266-042, www.walkslovenia.com, €1,216 weekly pp all-inclusive) offers walking tours of the Slovenian countryside reaching into the foothills of the Julian Alps. TripAdvisor named it the top small hotel in Slovenia in 2015, and for good reason. The guest rooms are luxurious yet quaint, with high-beamed ceilings and peaceful surroundings. Depending on the walk you choose, you might wander past rushing streams, through villages stopping at artists' homes, or through a butterfly valley. The treks aren't for the out-of-shape, since you can expect to spend up to seven hours a day walking. But don't worry—the restaurant serves a three-course gourmet meal in the evenings complete with complimentary house wine at the end of a long day.

The **Kašča restaurant** (Spodnji trg 1, tel. 04/512-4300, www.gostilna kasca.si, 12pm-11pm Mon.-Sat., €11), in the basement of the medieval granary in Škofja Loka, has hearty dishes, from Slovenian meat and potato staples to pizzas.

Information and Services

The **tourist office** (Mestni trg 7, tel. 04/512-0268, www.skofjaloka.info) can organize guided tours for groups. The **town website** (www.skofjaloka.si) also provides useful information.

Getting There and Around

Škofja Loka is 21 kilometers (13 miles) northwest of Ljubljana. From the **bus station** (Kapucinski trg 13, tel. 04/517-0300, www.alpetour.si) buses run to Ljubljana (40 minutes) and Kranj (15-20 minutes). The **train station** (Kidriceva cesta 61, tel. 04/294-4174)

1: Celje Castle 2: Škofja Loka with Capuchin Bridge over the Sora river

is a few kilometers from the town center, but hourly buses link the station with the town. Trains run to Ljubljana (30 minutes), Kranj (10 minutes), and Bled (35 minutes). In town, you can easily get around on foot.

VOLČJI POTOK

Before World War II, the **Arboretum Volčji Potok** (Volčji Potok 3, tel. 01/831-2345, www. arboretum-vp.si, 8am-8pm daily summer, 8am-6pm daily winter, €5) belonged to private owners who surrounded their Baroque mansion, now destroyed, with sprawling gardens. Today, it's a great botanical garden with an outdoor café that's open in good weather. It's about 20 kilometers (12 miles) east of Škofja Loka and about 18 kilometers (11 miles) northeast of Ljubljana. From Ljubljana, take the highway toward Celje and exit at Domžale toward Radomlje, and then follow the signs for the park.

KAMNIK

The attractive little medieval town of Kamnik is small but beautiful, framed by snow-capped mountains. There's not a lot to see, though it makes a nice stop for lunch and a look around, or perhaps whiling away a few hours of a lazy day. The town's 12th-century **Small Castle (Mali Grad)** has a two-story chapel. You can visit the exterior of the castle anytime, but make arrangements through the **Tourist Information Center Kamnik (Turistično informacijski center Kamnik)** (Tomšičeva 23, tel. 01/831-8250, tic@kamnik-tourism. si, www.kamnik-tourism.si) to visit the interior and the chapel. The town also has an interesting gallery, the **Miha Maleš Gallery (Galerija Miha Maleš)** (Glavni trg 2, tel. 01/831-7647, 8am-1pm and 4pm-7pm Tues.-Sat., donation), which has an exhibition of the work of Maleš, a local 20th-century painter, as well as changing temporary exhibitions.

There are several pizzerias and taverns in town, though the **Pivnica Pri Podkvi** (Trg Svobode 1, tel. 041/961-559, 9am-10pm Mon.-Sat., €5) offers excellent value for money, particularly its daily menu, offering sturdy meat dishes and local specialties.

Located 25 kilometers (15.5 miles) north of Ljubljana, Kamnik is well connected to the capital by bus and train. With almost a dozen connections daily, the bus takes 30 minutes to an hour, depending on how many stops the bus has on its route, while the train takes close to an hour.

VELIKA PLANINA AND KRVAVEC

TOP EXPERIENCE

★ Velika Planina

Velika Planina mountain (www. velikaplanina.si), about 10 kilometers (6 miles) northeast of Kamnik, offers active recreation year-round. In summer, take the **cable car** (station in Kamniška Bistrica, 11 kilometers north of Kamnik, €11) to Velika Planina, and then walk about 30 minutes to the summer **herdsmen's settlements** (just past the Lodging House Zeleni Rob you'll see signs for the herders' settlements on **Mala Planina**) to see the sheep herders and their livestock, taste fresh milk and cheese, and visit the typical cottages in the area, which is rife with hiking and mountain-biking trails.

The herders' settlements are in use from June through September while they tend their livestock. Within the settlement there is the tiny **Preskar museum** (open daily in season) located in a hut whose style was typical before World War II, more oval than today's huts.

In winter Velika Planina has **skiing** (daily pass €19) ranging from beginner to moderate runs, and a free kindergarten program on weekends for the little ones. Ski and snowboarding gear can be rented on the slope, and information on hiking and biking trails is available on-site as well.

Krvavec

Krvavec mountain (www.rtc-krvavec.si, €28 all day), 10 kilometers (6 miles) northwest

Charcoal Makers

If you've noticed smoldering piles of sticks or leaves in the countryside, you might be asking yourself if Slovenians have fallen prey to some strange cult or discovered an incredibly inventive way to smoke a turkey. But what you're actually witnessing is a tradition that reaches back into the Iron Age—the art of charcoal-making.

How does it work? A large pile of wood is assembled and a fire is kindled through a trough at the center of the top of the pile. The wood begins to carbonize but doesn't catch fire because there isn't enough oxygen inside. After several days the wood turns to charcoal.

A process that was once quite common, it all but died out when coal mining, train transportation, and other factors caused the demand to diminish. Lately, however, it has experienced somewhat of a renaissance. The quality of the charcoal is thought to be better and fetches higher prices for those looking to perfect their barbecue. Also, the importance of keeping the tradition alive and tourism means that you can still find about 50 charcoal makers in the country, with the highest concentration east of Ljubljana.

of Kamnik, has more challenging slopes than Velika Planina.

Accommodations and Food

The Velika Planina area has several great lodging options. If your load is light—you have to carry your own luggage from the cable car—the **Jarški dom** (tel. 01/832-5571 or 041/621-732, call for reservations and rates) on Mala Planina is sort of a rural youth hostel with shared rooms and lots of convivial rustic charm. Though the experience is closer to camping than a hotel, it's hard to beat the setting.

The **cottages** (tel. 01/832-7258, www. velikaplanina.si, from €60) on Velika Planina aren't luxe, but they're comfortable and perfect for skiing holidays. You can walk to the ski lift and, after a long day on the slopes, kick back in a typical cottage, complete with a kitchen, TV, bath, and cozy bed. They're perfect for families.

On Velika Planina, the **Lodging House Zeleni Rob** (tel. 051/341-406, www. velikaplanina.si, 8am-8pm daily summer, 8am-8pm Fri.-Sun. off-season, €8) is the place to go for typical alpine meals like bread-loaf bowls of mushroom soup, bean and sauerkraut soup (locally called *jota*), and apple pie for dessert.

Getting There and Around

Two or three daily bus services connect Kamnik with Velika Planina (15-20 minutes) and Krvavec (about 20 minutes). Bus connections are too infrequent to stay in Kamnik and ski during the day on the mountains, so if you don't have a car, try arranging for lodging at Velika Planina or Krvavec to cut down on the commuting hassle.

There are about three daily buses between Kamnik and the cable car station in Kamniška Bistrica. If you're driving, follow the signs to Kamniška Bistrica-Gornji Grad.

TOP EXPERIENCE

★ LOGAR VALLEY (LOGARSKA DOLINA)

An alpine glacial valley with views of the towering Kamnik-Savinja Alps, it's hard to find the words to describe such a place, but you could try "untouched," "unspoiled," and "otherworldly" for starters. Let's also say that more than one person has described this as more breathtaking than the much more lauded (and much more crowded) Lake Bled.

Staying one day will allow you to take a short hike, see the Rinka waterfall, and eat in one of the delightful farmhouses. But you could easily spend days here, hiking farther to isolated mountain huts, allowing yourself to get knee-deep in nature so stunning you may never want to leave.

For most people, the Logar Valley (Logarska Dolina) is most beautiful (and user-friendly) in summer. But for those not afraid of a little snow and armed with the right equipment, winter can be just as magical and more solitary. In summer, if you want to seek some of that solitude, stay in the valley. When the day trekkers have departed, you can have the valley's starry skies almost to yourself.

The park is home to rare and endangered flora and fauna such as slipper orchids, Carniolan lilies, and Kamnik orchids as well as mountain eagles and peregrine falcons. If you trek up to higher elevations, you might also spot chamois and ibex.

Perhaps part of the Logar Valley's charm is its welcome. After driving a winding road hemmed in by mountains on each side, you're suddenly overcome (*verklempt* might be a better word, given how close you are to Austria here) by the wide lush green valley backed by giant rocky snow-capped mountains—sort of like entering paradise.

In high season, you'll pay at the entrance gate (Apr.-Oct. free for pedestrians and cyclists, €6 for cars). Off-season you can still enter the park, but the information center will not be open, and entrance is free. The hotels near the information center, particularly the Hotel Plesnik, should be able to provide you with information.

There's a trail that starts about one kilometer from the entrance. The valley is seven kilometers (four miles) long, and hiking the entire trail takes about two hours.

The **Rinka Information Center** (tel. 03/838-9004, www.logarskadolina.si, 9am-6pm daily May-Oct.) is about two kilometers (1.2 miles) from the gate. A couple of hotels and pensions are near the info center. The information center can provide maps and answer questions. It's also the place to arrange a guided walk, horseback riding, rock climbing, or paragliding. You can also rent bikes—either mountain or electric—at the information center.

From here you can start the **Trail of the Logar Valley** toward the waterfall. Along the way you'll pass a woodcutter's hut, a charcoal burner's hut, and a giant juniper tree.

The trail continues five kilometers (three miles) from the information center to the top of the valley, with the park's most popular attraction, the 90-meter-high (295 feet) **Rinka waterfall (Rinski Slap)**. It's the highest single waterfall in the country and became a national monument in 1987.

You can climb to the top of the waterfall; it takes about half an hour, but be careful, as it can be quite slippery. Your climb is rewarded with a view of three snow-capped peaks, all over 2,200 meters (7,200 feet)—Kranjska Rinka, Koroška Rinka, and Štajerska Rinka.

Serious hikers might also want to continue their trek up Okrešelj (elevation around 1,400 meters/4,593 feet) and Kamiško sedlo (around 1,800 meters/5,905 feet) before descending down to the village of Kamiška Bistrica. Mountain huts are available to sleep in since such a trek requires an overnight.

Accommodations and Food

You can eat and sleep at the **Frischauf Hut on Okrešlj (Frischaufov dom na Okrešlju)** (okreselj@siol.net, www.logarska-dolina.si, May-Oct., beds €22 pp), located about an hour's hike from the Rinka waterfall. The hut is a great place to sleep if you are continuing your trek through the mountains. It has 36 beds in shared rooms and 53 beds in private rooms. It's also a great place for lunch, with simple dishes like sausages, risottos, and pastas to fill you up after the climb. The communal atmosphere is also not to be missed.

★ **Tourist Farm Lenar (Turisticna Kmetija Lenar)** (Logarska dolina 11, tel. 03/838-9006, www.lenar.si, €35 pp, including breakfast) offers a handful of charming rooms, a couple of apartments, and a converted hay barn for rent. The bucolic location is idyllic, and you might imagine you are living in a storybook. Coupled with the delicious breakfast, it's hard to get a better deal.

The **Hotel Plesnik** (Logarska dolina 10, tel. 03/839-2300, www.plesnik.si, €72 d) has clean and large rooms that could do with a decor update. It's worth it to spring for a room with a balcony. The small 29-room hotel is the place to choose if extras like Wi-Fi (at certain locations in the hotel), an indoor pool, and a sauna are important factors. Skip the food, though, at least after breakfast, as you'll do better elsewhere.

Information and Services
In high season, the **Rinka Information Center** (tel. 03/838-9004, www.logarskadolina.si, 9am-6pm daily May-Oct.) can give you information on everything from maps to bike rentals and more. Off-season, try the **Hotel Plesnik** (Logarska dolina 10, tel. 03/839-2300).

Getting There and Around
The Logar Valley is 34 kilometers (21 miles) from Kamnik and is best reached by road, which can be accessed off the Ljubljana-Celje A1 highway. From Kamnik, follow the signs to Ljubno od Savinji, and then follow signs for Logarska Dolina. The drive takes about one hour.

Without a car, it is extremely difficult to reach the Logar Valley, since there are only a handful of buses each week. There is one daily bus (€7.20 each way) Monday to Friday only that connects Celje with Logarska Dolina. In July and August, there are two buses daily.

AROUND THE LOGAR VALLEY
If you're looking for fewer tourists as the Logar Valley increases in popularity, the valleys flanking Logar to the east and west are equally gorgeous.

Robanov Kot to the east is also a glacial valley, with lots of hikes and strenuous climbs as well. Information on the trails can be obtained from the **Solčava Tourist Information Center** (Solčava 29, tel. 03/839-0710, www.solcavsko.si). **Matkov Kot** lies to the west.

Located in Robanov Kot, the **Govc Vrsnik Tourist Farm** (Robanov Kot 34, tel. 03/839-5016, www.govc-vrsnik.com, €64 d, including breakfast) is a mountain chalet brimming with cheerful flower boxes. Inside, the clean and simple rooms along with excellent food make for a pleasant stay.

Dolenjska and Bela Krajina

Vineyards and castles are only two of the attractions of these southeastern Slovenian regions. The lush, picturesque valleys are perfect for a relaxing trip through the countryside.

DOLENJSKA
A string of rolling green hills hugging the Croatian border, the Dolenjska region is dotted with castles and hot-spring spas. The most charming of the region's towns is Novo Mesto, an attractive old town surrounded by bustling modern areas.

Ribnica
Though most of the 12th-century **Ribnica castle (Grad Ribnica)** (Škrabcev trg 40, tel. 01/836-9335, call for hours, €2.50), about 40 kilometers (25 miles) south of Ljubljana, was burned in World War II, the remaining arcades and towers house the excellent small **Ribnica Museum (Muzej Ribnica)**, with exhibitions of the town's well-known woodenware and pottery as well as some archaeological finds. It's not the sort of place to go out of your way to see, but if you're nearby, it makes a nice sightseeing stop.

Also in Ribnica, the **Ribnica Handicraft Center (Rokodelski Center Ribnica)** (Cesta na Ugar 6, tel. 01/836-1104, 9am-5pm Mon.-Fri., 9am-1pm Sat., €1.50) is a don't-miss for fans of local arts and crafts. Its location off the main road is a bit hard to find, but it's worth asking a friendly local for directions to see the handicrafts: wooden spoons, hand-woven baskets, and pottery. Sometimes you will catch one of the artisans working on their projects, and there is a shop that sells items at reasonable prices.

Novo Mesto

It's easy to spend half a day in the town of Novo Mesto. With several castles and churches worth looking inside, the small town also makes a great departure point for exploring the area's wine routes.

A worthwhile stop in town is the **Dolenjska Museum (Dolenjski Muzej)** (Muzejska 7, tel. 07/373-1130, www.dolenjskimuzej.si, 9am-5pm Tues.-Sat., €3), which displays artifacts from Novo Mesto's long history, dating back to the Bronze Age. The Novo Mesto **Cathedral** (Kapiteljska C. Sv. Nikolaj, 7am-7pm daily) dates from the 15th century and has a beautiful Tintoretto behind its altar.

Though there are several good places to eat in town, the best choice is likely the charming and oddly named **Don Bobi** (Kandijska cesta 14, www.don-bobi.com, 10am-11pm Mon.-Fri., 12pm-11pm Sat., €12), located in the center of the old town overlooking the river Krka. This small and cozy restaurant serves Dolenjska specialties alongside a solid wine list.

Novo Mesto's **tourist office** (Novi trg 6, tel. 07/393-9263, www.novomesto.si, 9am-7pm Mon.-Fri., 9am-4pm Sat., 9am-12pm Sun. June-Sept., 9am-6pm Mon.-Fri., 9am-2pm Sat. Oct.-May) can provide more information about the region, as well as help arrange for hotel and apartment stays and rent bicycles.

Novo Mesto's **bus station** (Topliška 1, tel. 07/332-1123) is well connected to Otočec (15 minutes) and Ljubljana (1 hour). From the **train station** (Kolodvorska 1, tel. 07/298-2100) you can connect to Metlika (1.5 hours) and Ljubljana (2 hours).

Around Novo Mesto

One of the nicest hotels in Slovenia, the ★ **Hotel Grad Otočec** (Grajska cesta 2, tel. 07/384-8600, www.grad-otocec.com, €500 d, including breakfast) is located in a castle on a small island in the Krka River, surrounded by lovely countryside. The hotel has a golf course and tennis center, and also offers information on a variety of walking trails in the area. The **restaurant** (6am-11pm daily, €18) in the castle serves good food in a hard-to-beat setting. Otočec is eight kilometers (five miles) northeast of Novo Mesto, right off the highway to Zagreb. A taxi from Novo Mesto costs around €20. Ask the hotel about transfers from the Ljubljana airport. It's also less than an hour's drive from Zagreb.

Quite possibly the best farm stay in Slovenia, the **Seruga Tourist Farm** (Sela pri Ratezu 15, tel. 07/334-6900, www.seruga.si, from €65 d, including breakfast) is bucolic perfection. The historic building, the surroundings, the excellent food, and the friendly hosts make this a wonderful getaway-from-it-all experience.

Very basic rooms are available at **Vinoteka Bizeljsko Pri Peču** (Stara vas 58, tel. 07/452-0103, €50 d, including breakfast), located north of Čatež on the road from Brežice to Bizeljsko. The Vinoteka also has a nice **restaurant** (10am-1am daily, €8-15) with a terrace and decent local wines. You'll need a car to get here.

Wine Route

The **Upper Dolenjska Wine Route** is dotted with plenty of cellars, as well as places to buy fruit vinegars and dine on local specialties such as sausages and hearty stews. Contact the Sevnica **tourist office** (Boštanj 80, tel.

1: herdsmen's settlements at Velika Planina
2: Hotel Grad Otočec 3: Lake Bled 4: Logar Valley

07/816-5462, tip@kstm.si, 9am-7pm Mon.-Fri., 10am-7pm Sat.) for a detailed map and tips.

BELA KRAJINA

Near the Croatian border lies the region of Bela Krajina. Though it is miniscule in size, its beautiful landscape, known for the white-barked birch trees that populate the area, and its strong cultural traditions make it stand out. Bela Krajina is particularly known for its folk music traditions, celebrated by several festivals. The region is well connected by buses, but the best way to see Bela Krajina is with a car or on a bicycle. The tourist offices in most towns can help you rent one.

Metlika

If you can get past the communist-era block buildings in the outer ring, the well-preserved old town in Metlika is well worth a visit. The **Metlika Castle (Metliški Grad)** (Trg Svobode 4, tel. 07/306-3370, www.belokranjski-muzej.si, 9am-5pm Mon.-Sat., 10am-2pm Sun., €4) has a small gallery, a viticulture exhibition, and the **Bela Krajina Museum (Belokranjski muzej)**, with displays chronicling the area's history from prehistoric times through World War II. Kids will enjoy the **Fire Brigade Museum (Slovenski gasilski muzej)** (Trg Svobode 5, tel. 07/305-8697, 9am-2pm Mon.-Sat., free), highlighting Bela Krajina's fire brigade, the first in Slovenia. The old fire engines, uniforms, and photographs are an interesting step back in time.

A fun lodging option in the area is the **Turistična kmetija Črnič** (Grabrovec 65, tel. 07/305-0114, www.crnic.si, €40 d, including breakfast), a farm a few kilometers outside Metlika, right off a bicycle trail. The farm offers not only cozy accommodations but good food and homemade wine.

The Metlika **tourist office** (Mestni trg 1, tel. 07/305-8331, www.metlika-turizem.si, 8am-3:30pm Mon.-Fri., 9am-12pm Sat.) can provide you with maps of wine routes in the area, marked with cellars, sights of interest, and restaurants along the way. The office can also arrange for bicycle rental.

About 17 kilometers (10.5 miles) southeast of Novo Mesto, Metlika is linked by bus and train with Novo Mesto (1 hour) and Ljubljana (2 hours).

Rosalnice

The most interesting architectural features of the region are the **Three Parishes (Tri fare)** (free), a complex of three Gothic churches surrounded by a wall in the village of Rosalnice, three kilometers (1.8 miles) east of Metlika. A lack of records has left the history of the churches somewhat unknown. Some think the churches were built by the Knights Templar in the 12th century, while others claim they were built in the 14th or 15th centuries. Whatever their true provenance, the churches have been a pilgrimage site for hundreds of years.

For more information, check with the **Metlika County office** (Mestni trg 14, Metlika, tel. 07/305-8331, www.metlika-turizem.si).

Črnomelj

Larger than charming Metlika, 12 kilometers (seven miles) to the northeast, the town of Črnomelj is also somewhat more neglected. However, the city is full of history, including a 12th-century castle and a couple of churches. The best time to visit is during the **Jurjevanje festival** (www.jurjevanje.si), held sometime between late April and late June and featuring folk music and dance performances from all over Slovenia. The oldest folk festival in Slovenia, it's been held every year since 1964.

Around Črnomelj

Near the tiny village of **Rožanec,** five kilometers (three miles) northwest of Črnomelj, there's a surprisingly well-preserved Roman-era temple to the sun god Mithras. Ask in the village for directions.

Wine Routes

The vineyards of Bela Krajina are responsible for some of Slovenia's best reds and whites.

The region is known for three types of wines: Metliška črnina, a dry red that combines four different types of grapes; Belokranjec, a dry white; and Portugalka, a young red that ripens in October (most Metlika wines are late-harvest or ice wines). Wine-tasting in the region is typically accompanied by a local flatbread called *pogača*.

One wine cellar to visit in Metlika is **Vinska Klet Metlika** (Cesta XV brigade 2, tel. 07/363-7000, www.kz-metlika.si, tasting arranged by appointment 9am-3pm Mon.-Fri., 9am-12pm Sat., from €8). The winery, Kmetijaska Zadruga Metlika works with a cooperative of up to 200 small growers to produce about a dozen regular wines and some special sweet ice wines.

In Krmačina, a smaller village down the road, you'll find a much more famous winery: The **Prus Wine Cellar** (Krmačina 6, tel. 07/305-9098, www.vinaprus.si, call for hours

and tours, €10) has won awards for many of its wines, including World Champion for some of its sauvignons and yellow muscats. A winery tour lasts one to two hours and includes tasting and a cellar tour. After the tour, you can also purchase some of the family's honeys and homemade spirits.

In Črnomelj, the **Črnomaljska Klet information center** (Ulica Mirana Jarca 2, tel. 07/306-1100) has local wines for sampling and for purchase.

In May, Metlika hosts the **Vinška vigred festival,** with lots of wine-tastings, bottles to buy as souvenirs, and colorful folk performances.

Bela Krajina has several marked wine routes, perfect for cycling on a crisp fall or spring day, sampling local wines along the way. Contact the **Bela Krajina tourist board** (tel. 07/305-6530, tic.crnomelj@ric-belakrajina.si, www.ric-belakrajina.si) for maps and information. The Metlika tourist office can also provide maps and information.

Bled and the Julian Alps

Possibly Slovenia's most beautiful region and home to Triglav National Park, the Julian Alps have something for adventure seekers, nature lovers, and everyone in between. It's a region most associated with its vistas—snow-capped mountains cut through by gorges filled with turquoise blue rushing rivers and covered with evergreen forests. In a word, it's idyllic. You'll find genteel turn-of-the-20th-century hotels around Lake Bled, harking back to a grander time, down the road from back-to-basics pensions in the middle of nowhere—both extremes providing spots to just relax and let go. The **Soča River Valley** is one of the best places for active adventures, particularly rafting the rushing streams or just admiring them from a walking path above, while towns like Idrija offer quieter

pleasures, from dining in a stately manor hotel to admiring (and perhaps purchasing) some of the town's famous lace.

★ BLED

With a medieval castle overlooking the bright-blue lake's church-topped island, rimmed with majestic evergreens and surrounded by mountains, Bled should be tops on your must-see list. One of Slovenia's most photographed spots, Bled's castle draws in the tourists, and its surroundings keep them coming back. It's perhaps among the few places in the world that surpasses its postcards.

Pilgrims have been coming to Bled since the 8th century, when the Carantanians came to worship Živa, the Slavic fertility goddess, on the island spot where the Church of the Assumption stands today.

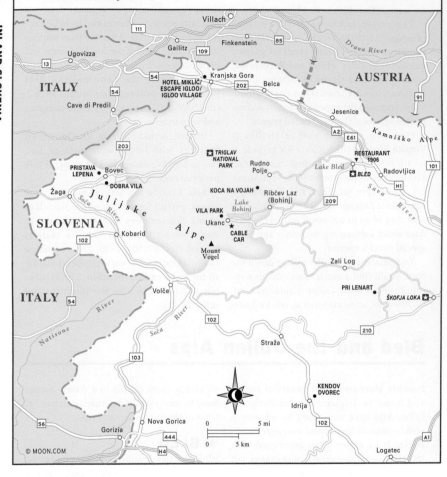

Julian Alps

Villach
111
Finkenstein
85
Gailitz
109
Drava River
Ugovizza
13
54
Kranjska Gora
HOTEL MIKLIČ/
ESCAPE IGLOO/
IGLOO VILLAGE
202
Belca
AUSTRIA
ITALY
54
Cave di Predil
Jesenice
91
A2
E61
Kamniško Alpe
203
TRIGLAV
NATIONAL
PARK
Rudno
Polje
Lake Bled
RESTAURANT
1906
BLED
Radovljica
101
PRISTAVA
LEPENA
Bovec
DOBRA VILA
KOCA NA VOJAH
Ribčev Laz
(Bohinj)
209
H1
Sava
River
Žaga
Soča
River
Julijske
VILA PARK
Lake
Bohinj
SLOVENIA
Kobarid
Alpe
Ukanc
CABLE
CAR
102
Mount
Vogel
Zali Log
ITALY
54
Volče
Soča
River
102
210
Straža
103
KENDOV
DVOREC
Idrija
56
Nova Gorica
444
Gorizia
© MOON.COM
H4
PRI LENART
ŠKOFJA LOKA
0   5 mi
0   5 km
102
A1
Logatec

Bled became a popular tourist spot in the late 1800s. By 1900, Bled had rooms for over a thousand travelers, and in the years leading up to World War II, the town continued to flourish, adding over a dozen tennis courts and a golf course.

Though Bled suffered throughout World War II, Tito gave it his stamp of approval, building a villa on the lake and constructing new hotels for a new generation of visitors.

Those hotels take some of the shine off Bled as you drive into town, but once you're past their blocky facades and the lake comes into view, you'll realize why so many come to this corner of Slovenia.

Sights

LAKE BLED PROMENADE

The lake itself is Bled's most stunning sight. The natural glacier-formed lake is rimmed by a promenade that's worth the walk before you head up to the small cliff-top castle. Allow 1-1.5 hours to walk the six-kilometer (3.7-mile) circumference, watching *pletna* boats

The Legend of Lake Bled

Once upon a time, there was a beautiful princess . . . or so the story usually goes. In Bled, the story starts almost the same way. A young aristocratic woman, married to the handsome owner of Bled castle, lived happily high above Bled's splendid lake. One day, her husband was out hunting and was killed by some robbers. Devastated, the young widow took all of her gold and had it fashioned into a bell for the church on the island in the lake, so that every time it rang, it would remind her of her sorrows.

While the bell was being transported to the island, a huge storm came up and the boat that was carrying it sank, along with the heavy bell, which disappeared below the blue water. Distraught, the woman went into a convent in Rome. After she died, the pope sent another bell to the little church on the island in Lake Bled. Ever since, pilgrims have traveled to the island, believing if they touched the bell and prayed to the Virgin Mary, their prayers would be answered. And according to the legend, the bell that sank can still be heard ringing below even today.

and swans gliding on the lake and taking in views of the island, the castle, and the surrounding mountains.

BLED CASTLE
(BLEJSKI GRAD)

Perched on a cliff some 140 meters (459 feet) above the lake, **Bled Castle (Blejski Grad)** (Grajska 25, tel. 04/578-0525, www.bljeski-grad.si, 8am-8pm daily April-June and Sept.-Oct., 8am-6pm daily Jan.-March and Jan.-Dec., 8am-9pm July and Aug., €11) offers a panoramic view and a small exhibition of the history of Bled and the castle itself.

The castle was first mentioned in the early 11th century and there are still some Romanesque remnants to be spotted around the castle. Given to a Catholic bishop in 1011, the castle was altered and changed throughout the centuries, including a heavy 20th-century renovation. In the upper courtyard, look in the Gothic chapel to see the beautiful frescoes and the paintings of those who donated the land the castle is built on to the Bishop: German Emperor Henry II and his wife.

There's also a working replica of a medieval printing press, a wine cellar (call to arrange a visit), and reenactments of medieval life by theater groups during the summer and on special occasions. The castle also has a restaurant if you're hungry. Even if you're not

into castles, the view over the lake and mountains is worth the entry fee.

You can hike up to the castle, or you can drive up and park your car in the parking lot. The steep, moderately challenging walk is around 600 meters (about a third of a mile) and takes about 20 minutes; paths from the promenade are marked "Grad."

BLED ISLAND
(BLEJSKI OTOK)

Several spots on the lake offer boat rides, including the typical gondola-like *pletna* (in front of the Health Park, Hotel Park, Mlino, and the Rowing Center, tel. 041/427-155, €12). Take one to the **Church of the Assumption (Cerkev Marijinega Vnebovzetja)** (tel. 04/576-7979, www.blejskiotok.si, 9am-7pm daily summer, €6) on the tiny island in the middle of the lake. Built in the 15th century, the church has been through two earthquakes and subsequent renovations in the 17th century that formed its current Baroque style. All that remains of the former Gothic church are a wooden statue of the Virgin Mary and a few frescoes. While the church is basic, the bell is its most storied element, so it's worth the climb to make a wish. Keep in mind that there are close to 100 steps from the boat dock up to the church.

Allow 2-3 hours for a trip to the island (including boat rides there and back).

HOT SPRINGS

Hot springs in the northeastern part of the lake are directed into three pools at the Hotels Toplice, Park, and Golf, which can be accessed for a fee.

HORSE-DRAWN CARRIAGE RIDES

You can hop in an Austrian-style *fijaker*, or horse-drawn carriage, to travel around the area, even going as far as the lake at Bohinj. Drivers don't become drivers—they are born drivers, as the tradition is handed down from father to son. It's this tradition, enforced by a local driver's association, that also dictates the uniform of all *fijaker* drivers. Carriages can be found in front of Festival Hall or by phone (tel. 04/574-1121). A carriage ride around the lake or to the castle costs about €40; up to four people fit in a *fijaker*.

VINTGAR GORGE

Four kilometers (2.4 miles) northeast of Bled, the **Vintgar Gorge** (www.vintgar.si, 8am-7pm daily, €5) winds its way through 1.6 kilometers (almost one mile) of stunning beauty. The Radovna river cuts a surreal-blue ribbon through the towering rocks to either side. Discovered in 1891, it's well worth the trip to walk the paths and footbridges and marvel at nature.

Sports and Recreation

Bled is full of dozens of sporting activities. The easiest is **hiking,** with marked walking paths throughout the area. Pick up a trail map at the **tourist office** (Cesta svobode 10, tel. 04/574-1122, www.bled.si). The surrounding rivers make for good **rafting and kayaking.** Try **Bled Rafting** (Hrastova 2, tel. 041/678-008, www.bled-rafting.si) in Bled and **3glav Adventures** (Ljubljanska 1, tel. 041/686-184, www.3glav-adventures.com) in Bohinj, which also offers hiking, diving, parachuting, and paragliding outings.

The **Golf and Country Club Bled** (Kidričeva 10c, tel. 04/537-7711, www.golfbled.si) has two courses, rents equipment,

The *Pletna*

The wooden flat-bottomed boats that ferry passengers to and from Bled Island have a long history in the region, dating back to the 12th century. Because the farmland was poor, certain families were allowed to ferry pilgrims back and forth to the island. The *pletna* got its current form at the turn of the 20th century. The boats, all seven meters long and two meters wide (23 feet long and 6.5 feet wide), carrying 20 people, likely got their name from the old German word *pleten*, which meant flat-bottomed boat. The Empress Maria Theresa gave the rights to operate a *pletna* to 20 local families. Centuries later, the skippers, called *pletnari*, still retain the tradition. Just like Bled's carriage drivers, you don't become one, you are born one.

and provides instruction if you've never played before.

Accommodations

Located at the northwest corner of the lake, the ★ **Hotel Triglav Bled** (Kolodvorska cesta 33, tel. 04/575-2610, www.hoteltriglavbled.si, €159 d, including breakfast) is removed from the hustle and bustle of Bled tourism without being too far out. The charming historic house overlooking Lake Bled has a pool, and the food is excellent.

The **Grand Hotel Toplice** (Cesta svobode 12, tel. 04/579-1000, www.hotel-toplice.com, €300 d, including breakfast) was the swankest place in town, harking back to Bled's glory days. Room rates include use of the hotel's hot-spring pools and outdoor pools and saunas. The price these days doesn't really live up to the standard, but if you want to stay where the big-wigs stayed long ago, this is the place.

The ★ **Vila Bled** (Cesta svobode 26, tel. 04/579-1500, www.vila-bled.com, €228 d, including breakfast) may have lost some of its luster since Tito lived here, but even if just for the history, this four-star hotel deserves a mention. The rooms are renovated and large, refreshingly maintaining the villa's 1950s decor. It's quite a treat to stay here.

Garni Hotel Berc (Pod Stražo 13, tel. 04/576-5658, www.berc-sp.si, €65 d, including breakfast) is just a few minutes' walk to the center of Bled. The hotel has clean wood-lined rooms, friendly service, and a hearty buffet breakfast.

The **Bledec Youth Hostel** (Grajska 17, tel. 04/574-5250, www.mlino.si, €16 pp or €46 d) is a budget option, only 10 minutes' walk to Bled Castle.

On the south side of Lake Bled, the **Garden Village Bled** (Cesta Gorenjskega odreda 1, tel. 08/389-9220, www.gardenvillagebled.com, €370) has treehouses and glamping tents, a must for families visiting the area. The property has a freshwater stream, orchards, a good restaurant, and a children's playground.

Food

For dessert and coffee, try the local cream cake on the terrace of the **Park Hotel** (Cesta svobode 15, tel. 04/579-1800, www.hotel-park-bled.com, 9am-9pm daily).

In the heart of Bled's center, **Public Bar and Vegan Kitchen Bled** (Ljubljanska cesta 4, tel. 70/270-712, 12pm-9pm Tues.-Sun., €6) has great vegan food in a country that doesn't offer a lot of vegan options. Reasonably priced and with some local beer on tap, it's a great lunch spot even if normally you are a carnivore.

Usually tourist attractions don't have the best restaurants, but the **Bled Castle Restaurant** (Ljubljanska cesta 8, tel. 04/574-1458, 6pm-12am Mon.-Fri., 12pm-12am Sat.-Sun., €20) is perfect for a romantic dinner, especially if you can snag a table overlooking the lake. Local dishes like trout or pork cutlets are served alongside a good wine selection.

Though it's a few kilometers southeast of Bled, **Gostilna Lectar** (Linhartov trg 2, tel. 04/537-4800, www.lectar.com, 12pm-11pm Wed.-Mon., €18) in Radovljica started in the 18th century making the colorful gingerbread hearts the region is known for. Today, the restaurant still houses a gingerbread museum

where you can buy souvenirs, but the real draw is the excellent food in the old house, filled with rustic cozy charm. While the restaurant serves traditional Slovenian cuisine, the owners take pride in their dishes created especially for vegetarians.

★ **Wine Bar and Restaurant Sova** (Cesta svobode 37, tel. 059/132-100, www.restavracija-sova.com, 11am-10pm daily, €25) has an outstanding menu, artistically presented. Dishes range from slow-cooked veal with local cheese to smoked goose breast carpaccio and truffle soup with boiled chestnuts, prosciutto chips, and profiterole with black chanterelles. Combined with great service and a good wine selection, it's a must-eat in Bled.

A fine dining destination perfect for a special romantic dinner, ★ **Restaurant 1906** (Kolodvorska cesta 33, tel. 04/575-2610, www.hoteltriglavbled.si, €159) specializes in Slovenian dishes made with fresh local ingredients and a gourmet touch. From a hearty game stew with polenta to a fresh lake trout with garlic croquettes and seasonal vegetables, the food can only be matched by the views from the restaurant's terrace over the lake.

Information and Services

You can get more information on Bled, including maps of walking trails, at the **tourist office** (Cesta svobode 10, tel. 04/574-1122, www.bled.si, 8am-9pm Mon.-Sat., 9am-5pm Sun. July-Aug., 8am-7pm Mon.-Sat., 11am-5pm Sun. Mar.-June and Sept.-Oct., 9am-6pm Mon.-Sat., 12pm-4pm Sun. Nov.-Feb.).

Getting There and Around

Buses leave and arrive hourly connecting Bled's **bus station** (Cesta svobode 4, tel. 04/574-1114) to Ljubljana (about 1.5 hours). Buses for Bohinj (40 minutes) depart at least a couple of times a day. You can also take a bus to Bled from Idrija and Kobarid, though connections are less frequent. The Bled tourist office (Cesta svobode 10, tel. 04/574-1122, www.bled.si) should be able to provide you with more details and current schedules, which change with the seasons. The train is not the most practical way to reach Bled, since the station is far from the center of town. Buses connect the **train station in Lesce** (Zelezniska 12, tel. 04/531-8364) with the center of Bled every 30 minutes and take about 15 minutes. By train you can connect to Ljubljana (one hour) and Kranj (25 minutes). The **Bled Jezero train station** (Koldovorska 50, tel. 04/294-2363) offers excellent connections to Bohinj (20 minutes) by an old steam train in the summer months. This station is only 1.5 kilometers (almost one mile) out of town.

Bled is 57 kilometers (35 miles) northwest of Ljubljana. If you're coming by car, simply take the E61 highway from Ljubljana.

★ TRIGLAV NATIONAL PARK

Triglav National Park is Slovenia's only national park, bordering both Austria and Italy. The park is vast, covering 3 percent of Slovenia's land mass. Unlike some national parks, there are actually towns and villages within the park itself, such as Bovec, on the very edge, which is the best place to stay if you want to raft the Soča River. Bohinj, with its famous lake, and Kranjska Gora, the country's most popular ski resort, are also part of the park.

The park gets its name from the towering Mount Triglav (2,864 meters/9,396 feet), the country's highest peak. The park encompasses most of the Julian Alps and is great not just for climbing but just about any outdoor activity you can think of. The park's **main information station** (Ljubljanska cesta 27, Bled, tel. 04/578-0200) is in Bled, but you can also get more information online (www.tnp.si).

Bohinj

While it may not be as fairy-tale beautiful as Bled, Bohinj is a pretty lake in its own right, albeit in a wilder way. It's far less touristy than Bled, and there are plenty of secluded spots to get completely away from the pack. Because the lake is part of Triglav National Park, there's very little development. The north shore, for instance, is completely natural and a great place for hiking.

The name Bohinj refers to the lake, since there's no town with that name. When people refer to Bohinj, they are thinking of the town of **Ribčev Laz,** which serves as a regional center on the eastern edge of the lake. You can find pretty much anything you need here, from a post office to a grocery store. At the opposite end, on the western shore, is the village of **Ukanc,** with a hotel, a campsite, and some shops.

There's not much to see in Bohinj besides the Gothic **Church of St. John (Cerkev Sveti Janez)** (9am-12pm and 5pm-8pm daily July-Aug., donation), in Ribčev Laz; in the off-season, ask at the tourist office (Ribčev Laz 48, tel. 04/574-1122) for its hours. The 13th-century church has been restored and altered over the years, explaining the Baroque bell tower and altars, though there are some nice 14th-century frescoes inside. The church is also a great vantage point for views of the lake.

One fun sight is the three-room **Museum of Alpine Dairy Farming** (Stara Fuzina 181, tel. 04/577-0156, 10am-12pm and 4pm-6pm Tues.-Sun. Jan-Oct.), in an abandoned village cheese dairy, built in the 19th century and in operation until 1967. There is a nice display that documents the region's dairy history, cheese-making tools, and a room that depicts a herdsman's house.

The rest of the lake's activities revolve around getting in touch with nature. Start with a panoramic view of the surrounding Julian Alps, the lake, and a 59-meter (153-foot) waterfall by taking the **cable car** (www.vogel.si, 8am-6pm daily off-season, 8am-7pm daily summer, €13.50) up Mount Vogel. The station is near the village of Ukanc, on the western end of the lake. Another nice way to see the area is the summer **steam train** that travels several weekends from May to late October. A round-trip between Bled and Bohinj costs €41 and takes about 40 minutes. Reservations can be made with the Info Center in the Ljubljana Railway office or by phone (tel. 01/291-3391). You can reserve one day before, if they have space.

SPORTS AND RECREATION

Once you've had a feel for the surroundings, jump into some sports to really make the most of Bohinj's natural advantages. **Alpinsport** (Ribčev Laz 53, 04/572-3486, www.alpinsport. si, open daily, hours vary) can organize all sorts of outings: Rafting, kayaking, canyoneering, spelunking, rock climbing, and skiing are all on the menu. If you prefer to adventure alone, they also rent bikes, canoes, kayaks, and ski equipment.

There is excellent **fly-fishing** in the Bohinj area. **Hotel Pension Stare** (Ukanc 128, tel. 04/574-6400, www.impel-bohinj.si) sells fishing tickets for the lake as well as provides guides and rents equipment for fishing in the lake, river, and streams in the area.

ACCOMMODATIONS

You can find private rooms and apartments throughout the Bohinj area at the **tourist office** (Ribčev Laz 48, tel. 04/574-1122, www. bohinj.si, 8am-8pm Mon.-Sat., 9am-7pm Sun. July-Aug., 8am-7pm Mon.-Sat., 9am-3pm Sun. Sept.-June) or pitch a tent at **Camp Zlatorog** (Ukanc 2, tel. 04/572-3482, www.aaturizem. com, €9) on the shores of Lake Bohinj near Ukanc.

The only real disadvantage to the **YH Pod Voglom** (Ribčev Laz 60, tel. 04/572-3461, podvoglom@siol.net, www.hostel-podvoglom. com, €16 pp or €38 d) is that it's five kilometers (three miles) from Ribčev Laz. The advantage, though, is the pretty location and all the activities organized through the hostel's sports center, from kayaking and rafting excursions to skiing. The hostel does have its own restaurants and also rents bikes and kayaks.

Don't let the four stars fool you (it's more of a three), but the **Hotel Bohinj** (Ribčev Laz 45, tel. 04/572-6000, info@aaturizem.com, www. aaturizam.com, €80 d) is a fresh hotel with friendly service, spacious rooms, and an incredibly central location.

The **Alpik Apartments** (Ukanc 85, tel. 041/435-555, www.alpik.com, from €99 d) offer one- and two-bedroom apartments as well as chalet rooms in a peaceful location only a few minutes' walk to the lake.

In an even quieter location in the tiny village of Ukanc, the ★ **Vila Park** (Ukanc 129, tel. 04/572-3300, €62 d) is full of friendly service and great reasonably priced lodging. Located beside a turquoise-green stream and outfitted like an alpine hut, it's well worth the rates. Ask for a room with a large balcony overlooking the mountains.

FOOD

Since most of the guesthouses in the area offer full board, there are relatively few restaurants around town. Anywhere you go, it's hard to go wrong ordering Bohinj trout if you like fish. In Ribčev Laz try **Center Pizzerija** (Ribčev Laz 50, tel. 04/572-3170, 12pm-10pm daily, €10) for pizza as well as local fish. Just outside Ribčev Laz, ★ **Koca na Vojah** (Stara Fužina 233, tel. 041/234-625, 10am-6pm daily, €10) is a small restaurant nestled in the mountains just north of the small village of Stara Fužina, serving wonderful pies and hot, steaming plates of dumplings, soups, and stews. Even farther out of town is **Gostilna Rupa** (Srednja Vas 87, tel. 04/572-3401, 10am-12am Tues.-Sun., €15), serving huge portions of meat and sauce-laden dishes in a folksy setting. There's a terrace next to a playground for kids.

INFORMATION AND SERVICES

The **tourist office** (Ribčev Laz 48, tel. 04/574-1122, www.bohinj.si, 8am-8pm Mon.-Sat., 9am-7pm Sun. July-Aug., 8am-7pm Mon.-Sat., 9am-3pm Sun. Sept.-June) is located in Ribčev Laz.

GETTING THERE AND AROUND

The best way to get to Bohinj, about 25 kilometers (15.5 miles) southwest of Bled, is by car on Road 209 (well signed for Bohinj). There are also buses that connect with Bled (40 minutes) and Ljubljana (two hours). You'll also find good train connections with Bled (20 minutes), a scenic way to see the area. Contact the tourist offices in Bohinj or in Bled for more information.

Kranjska Gora

Kranjska Gora is the country's largest ski resort, with a charming little mountain-town center. Best suited for beginning or laid-back skiing, perfect for families, it also has a lot of warm-weather sports for the sunnier months.

The area has 20 different ski lifts plus lots of cross-country skiing, snowboarding, sledding, ice-climbing, and more. The **Kranska Gora Recreational Ski Center** (Borovška 103a, tel. 04/580-9400, www.kr-gora.si) is the town's ski lift operator and source of information, rentals, instruction, and more. There's even a kindergarten that serves as a camp and fun center for the kids while the parents tackle more difficult runs.

Highly recommended off the slopes is the **Escape Igloo** (www.escape-igloo.com, minimum two people, €60 pp), a winter-only attraction that locks you in an igloo and gives you a limited amount of time to save the world based on unfolding clues.

In summer the ski center hosts summer sledding and tubing. There's also a bike park, which rents mountain bikes to use on the trails and obstacle courses made for heartstopping rides. The summer activities are open from May to September.

ACCOMMODATIONS AND FOOD

One of the nicest things about Kranjska Gora is that the town's hotels are all just across from the chairlifts, separated only by a snow covered field, so it's easy to get to the slopes in no time.

Perhaps the most interesting activity is actually a place to sleep or hang out. ★ **Igloo Village** (tel. 01/300-3845, www.eskimska-vas.si, late Dec.-Mar.) is a temporary hotel complex composed of individual igloos for overnights. The package (€100) includes snowshoeing, a cocktail, dinner in the igloo restaurant, a DJ party in the ice bar, overnight in an igloo, and breakfast. If you prefer to sleep in a heated room but want to experience the Igloo Village, the complex also offers snowshoeing and dinner with a cocktail and DJ party in the Ice Bar for €45 pp.

Located in a turn-of-the-20th-century house three kilometers (1.8 miles) from town, **Pr'Gavedarjo Hostel** (Podkoren 72, tel. 031/479-087, www.prtatko.com, from €50) is a smart family hotel, small in size but big on value. Rooms are clean and well designed, and the service is friendly.

A small family-run hotel, the **Hotel Miklic** (Vitranška 13, tel. 045/881-635, www.hotelmiklic.com, €130 d, including breakfast) has large rooms with somewhat 1980s decor and a good restaurant for après-ski sustenance. It's a five-minute walk from the hotel to the center of town.

For the very hungry, the traditional **Gostilna pri Martinu** (Borovška cesta 61, tel. 04/582-0300, 10am-11pm daily, €15) has sausages and meat-and-potato stews to satiate even the heartiest of appetites. The **Milka Restaurant** (Cvršiška cesta 45, tel. 070/169-366, €17) has beautiful views of the Julian Alps and excellent traditional dishes served in a very modern way.

GETTING THERE AND AROUND

Bus service connecting Kranjska Gora with Bled (about 1.5 hours) and Ljubljana (2.5 hours) is very reliable. In the summer there are also good connections with Bovec (two hours). Driving to Kranjska Gora from Ljubljana, take the E61 highway. Kranjska Gora is 85 kilometers (53 miles) from Ljubljana and 39 kilometers (24 miles) from Bled. Keep in mind that the road connecting Bovec and Kranjska Gora is often blocked by heavy snowfall in the winter, adding considerable traveling time between the two locations.

1: ski lift on Kranjska Gora 2: paddlers on the Soča River, Bovec 3: a suspension bridge over the Soča River in Triglav National Park 4: Lake Bohinj

Bovec

The main attraction in Bovec is the **Soča River,** rushing and careening through the forested valley. The river is the best reason for sports enthusiasts to visit, particularly in spring and summer, when it's at its best for rafting and kayaking. Bovec is on the edge of Triglav National Park, crisscrossed with hiking and biking trails. The less adventurous should be sufficiently impressed by the river's almost surreal color—a bright blue or green that's rarely seen in nature.

You'll find maps of the surrounding bike and hiking paths at the **tourist office** (Trg Golobarskih Žrtev 8, tel. 05/384-1910, info@ bovec.si, www.soca-valley.com, 9am-8pm daily July-Aug., 9am-5pm Mon.-Fri., 9am-12pm Sat.-Sun. Sept.-June). For high-quality mountain bike rentals, try **Outdoor Galaxy** (Kot1, tel. 040/605-325, www.outdoor-galaxy. com).

For rafting and kayaking, **Soča Rafting** (Trg Golobarskih Žrtev 48, tel. 05/389-6200, www.socarafting.si) or **Alpe Šport Vančar** (Trg Golobarskih Žrtev 28, tel. 05/389-6350, www.bovecsport.com) should be able to hook you up with equipment and guides down the river. Alpe Šport Vančar also has canyoneering and paragliding for the courageous.

ACCOMMODATIONS AND FOOD

It's hard to believe such a small place is home to two hotel gems. ★ **Dobra Vila** (Mala vas 112, 05/389-6400, www.dobra-vila-bovec. si, €95 d) is a funky little hotel with upscale themed rooms and super-friendly owners. Most of the rooms don't have bathtubs, just showers, though the rooms have DVD players and the hotel has a few English-language movies on hand for late-night entertainment.

The location of the ★ **Pristava Lepena** (Lepena 2, tel. 05/388-9900, www.pristava-lepena.com, €66 pp) makes you wonder if you've somehow been beamed up to the local version of heaven. Sitting in the middle of rocky snow-capped mountains, about six kilometers (3.7 miles) east of Bovec, the unassuming little cottages vary in size and sleep two to eight people, with discounts for weekly rentals. Each cottage has its own terrace and is pleasantly furnished but not likely to win any design awards. The complex has a pool, a sauna, and a very good restaurant. It is a slice of quiet, perfect relaxation. The Pristava Lepena is a great spot for dinner or lunch, particularly if the weather is good enough that you can sit on the terrace surrounded by the tranquil mountains.

The **Dobra Vila** has an excellent restaurant, but for a quick meal in the center of Bovec, try **Felix** (Mala Vas 16, €9) for sandwiches, snacks, and hamburgers.

GETTING THERE AND AROUND

Buses depart from Ljubljana to Bovec regularly, though it's a long trip, over 3.5 hours. Buses also link Bovec with Kobarid (30 minutes). The bus stop is in front of the Pizzerija Letni Vrt. Bovec is about 120 kilometers (75 miles) northwest of Ljubljana. If you're traveling by car, be aware that during winter the Vršič pass is closed, meaning that you can't get to Bovec directly from Kranjska Gora, 35 kilometers (22 miles) to the north.

Kobarid

Kobarid is most famous for its bloody World War I battle between Austrian and German and Italian forces. Today, the quiet little town's **Kobarid Museum (Kobariški muzej)** (Gregorčičeva 10, tel. 05/389-0000, www.kobariski-muzej.si, 9am-6pm daily Apr.-Sept., 10am-5pm daily Oct.-Mar., €5) has an interesting display about the battle, including a short video in English. The **Kobarid Historical Walk** (pick up a map at the Kobarid Museum) is a five-kilometer (three-mile) trek through multiple markers recounting details of the battle. Even if you're not that into history, the well-marked path itself is worth the time, with lots of pretty and peaceful views to enjoy.

ACCOMMODATIONS AND FOOD

Hotel Hvala (Trg svobode 1, tel. 05/389-9300, www.hotelhvala.si, €51 d) is a small family-run hotel. The rooms aren't anything special, but the service is friendly, the place is very clean, and the restaurant is excellent. If you come for anything, come for the freshwater fish, which is somewhat legendary—plenty of Italians cross the border just to eat here.

INFORMATION AND SERVICES

You can find more information about Kobarid and the surrounding area at the **tourist office** (Gregorčičeva 10, tel. 05/389-9200, www.kobarid.si, 9am-6pm Mon.-Fri., 9am-7pm Sat.-Sun.), located in the Kobarid Museum.

GETTING THERE AND AROUND

There are at least two buses every day from Ljubljana to Kobarid, which take about three hours. Several daily connections link Kobarid with Bovec (30 minutes). At least one daily connection makes getting to Idrija (two hours) possible from the town. Kobarid is about 115 kilometers (71 miles) northwest of Ljubljana. During the winter, the Vršič pass is closed, obliterating the direct connection with Kranjska Gora and adding time to your journey if you're linking locations in the Julian Alps.

Idrija

This town is famous for three things: its mercury mine, its lace, and its fantastic hotel. Most people start at the hotel and then explore the mine and the lace on the side.

Women in Idrija have been making lace for 300 years. A presence in town since 1876, the **Lace-Making School (Čipkarska šola)** (Prelovčeva 2, tel. 05/373-4570, www.cipkarskasola.si, 10am-1pm Mon.-Fri., €2.50 pp) has a small exhibition of lace by students of the school as well as lace for sale, which makes a lovely souvenir.

The **Idrija Mercury Mine** (Kosovelova 3, tel. 05/377-1142, www.antonijevrov.si, tours at 10am and 3pm Mon.-Fri., 10am, 3pm, and 4pm Sat.-Sun., or by arrangement, €9) is worth a visit. The oldest part of the mine, which dates from 1500, and an 18th-century underground chapel are open for visitors to see during the one-hour underground tour.

If you're a bit claustrophobic but would still like to learn about mercury mining and the region in general, the well-done **Idrija Municipal Museum (Mestni Muzej Idrija)** (Prelovčeva 9, tel. 05/372-6600, www.muzej-idrija-cerkno.si, 9am-6pm daily, €5) is a great place to put on your list in Idrija. The museum is located in the Castle Gewerkenegg, built at the beginning of the 16th century as the administrative headquarters and warehouse for the Idrija Mercury Mine. In addition to mine history, there is a presentation of the history and culture of Idrija in general, including its lace-making, forestry, and cinnabar extraction industries. And if you want to explore the history of mining even further, the museum runs the **Miner's House** (Bazoviška 4, tel. 05/372-6600, www.muzej-idrija-cerkno.si, 9am-4pm daily, €3) with a small ethnographic collection.

ACCOMMODATIONS AND FOOD

Located in a 14th-century manor, the hotel ★ **Kendov Dvorec** (Na Griču 2, tel. 05/372-5100, www.kendov-dvorec.com, €200 d including breakfast) is the town's main draw. The rooms are decorated with local antiques and Idrian lace, and the terrace is superb. A meal in the manor's cozy restaurant is certainly worth the splurge.

GETTING THERE AND AROUND

Idrija is 55 kilometers (34 miles) west of Ljubljana. By car, the trip from Ljubljana takes about an hour. By bus, you can connect with Kobarid (two hours), Bovec (1.5 hours), and Ljubljana (1.5 hours).

Coastal Slovenia and the Karst Region

While not as grand as the Croatian coast, the

Slovenian seaside offers its own charms, from historic towns with an Italian flavor to karst caves and dancing Lipizzaner horses.

For art lovers, there's stunning architecture and unique medieval frescoes, and for nature lovers, a bird sanctuary. Coastal walking paths and towns filled with winding cobblestone streets will satisfy those in search of a pretty view.

Piran, with its Venetian-influenced atmosphere and architecture, is a favorite stop in this region. The coast of Slovenia, much like Istria to the south, was ruled by the Venetians. The Italian influence is still strong, from the historic buildings to the modern cuisine and even

Highlights

Look for ★ to find recommended sights, activities, dining, and lodging.

★ **Hrastovlje:** A simple church and its macabre *Dance of Death* fresco are worth the detour from Koper to this inland village (page 393).

★ **Piran:** The pride of the Slovenian coast, the historic town of Piran is beautiful, charming, and relatively unspoiled (page 394).

★ **Postojna:** It's worth a visit for the impressive and historic Postojna Cave and also the nearby Predjama Castle, built into a rocky cliff (page 397).

★ **Lipica Stud Farm (Kobilarna Lipica):** The provenance of Vienna's famous Lipizzaner horses, this stud farm hosts performances and even gives lessons (page 399).

Coastal Slovenia and the Karst Region

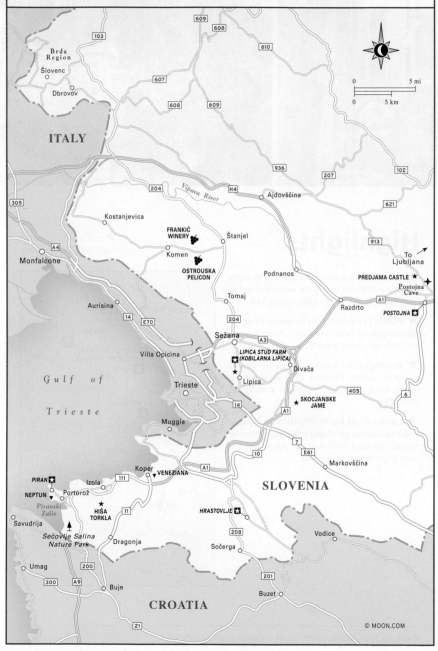

0   5 mi

0   5 km

609
608
610
103
**Brda
Region**
Šlovenc
607
Dbrovov
608   609

ITALY

936   207   102

204   *Vipava River*   H4   Ajdovščina

621

Kostanjevica

**FRANKIČ
WINERY**   Štanjel

913

Komen

To
Ljubljana

**OSTROUSKA
PELICON**   Podnanos

PREDJAMA CASTLE ★

Postojna
Cave

Tomaj

A1   **POSTOJNA**

Aurisina   204   Razdrto

305

A4

Monfalcone

14   E70   Sežana   A3

Villa Opicina   **LIPICA STUD FARM
(KOBILARNA LIPICA)**   Divača

★   Lipica

G u l f   o f   **Trieste**   405   6

T r i e s t e   **SKOCJANSKE
JAME** ★

14

Muggia   7

10   E61   Markovščina

Koper   A1

PIRAN ★   Izola   111   ▼ **VENEZIANA**

NEPTUN ▼   Portorož   **SLOVENIA**

*Piranski
Zaliv*   **HIŠA
TORKLA** ★   11   **HRASTOVLJE** ✚

Savudrija   Dragonja   208

*Sečovlje Salina
Nature Park*   Sočerga   Vodice

Umag   200   201

300   A9   Buje   Buzet

CROATIA   21

© MOON.COM

the language. Italian is still spoken as a second language by most of the region's natives.

The coast is fully booked during July and August, populated mostly by vacationing Italians.

Slightly inland from the coast is Slovene Istria, full of good wines and good food, particularly the wind-cured karst *pršut* the region is famous for, much like Croatian Istria to the south. The villages are interesting to explore, particularly Hrastovlje, whose church sports a haunting fresco of dancing skeletons celebrating death. Farther inland is a network of stalactite-filled karst caves, from those at Postojna, the most famous, to the Škocjan caves, the most dramatic. Another interesting detour is the Lipica Stud Farm, where Vienna's famous team of majestic horses has been bred for centuries.

PLANNING YOUR TIME

Fitting in a thorough tour of coastal Slovenia only takes a few nights: two nights in a coastal town, likely Piran, and a day to explore Slovene Istria while on the way to the Postojna cave and the Lipica Stud Farm. Of course, you could always extend your tour or shorten it, spending one night on your way down from Ljubljana, taking in one of the coast's interior sights, and another night on the coast, giving you a decent overview of the tiny region.

Keep in mind that you're just over the border from Italy, making for an easy day trip or even overnight to Trieste.

Itinerary Ideas

HIGHLIGHTS OF THE SLOVENIAN COAST

It's possible to see all the best of the Slovenian coast, with time for wine-tasting and leisurely meals, in four days.

Day 1

- See the famous dancing skeleton fresco at **Hrastovlje**.
- Have a late lunch at **Hiša Torkla**.
- Spend the night at the **Kempinski Palace Portorož**.

Day 2

- Head to **Piran** to explore this tiny walled medieval town and enjoy its sights and museums.
- Eat at **Fritolin pri Cantini** for good seafood in a casual setting.

Day 3

- Take a drive slightly inland to Postojna to explore the **Postojna Cave (Postojonska Jama)** and **Predjama Castle (Predjamski Grad).**
- Have dinner and spend the night at the fully restored Yugoslav-era **Hotel Jama.**

Day 4

- Visit the **Lipica Stud Farm** to see the horses.
- Spend the night at the charming **Lipizzaner Lodge Guest House.**

Coastal Slovenia Itinerary Ideas

HIGHLIGHTS OF THE SLOVENIAN COAST

1 Day 1
2 Day 2
3 Day 3
4 Day 4

A COASTAL WINE TOUR

1 Day 1: Koper to Štanjel
2 Day 2: Štanjel to Kom
3 Day 3: Komen to Brda

© MOON.COM

A COASTAL WINE TOUR

Use this three-day itinerary as a flexible starting point for your tour of coastal Slovenia's wine. With only an hour of driving between the stops, you can either just see the highlights listed here or lengthen it with more wineries, depending how much time you want to spend at tastings, lunch, and sights.

Day 1: Koper to Štanjel

- Have a tour and tasting at **VinaKoper** in Koper.
- Drive to **Štanjel,** where you will spend the night at **Hiša Posebne Sorte,** enjoying some of the guesthouse's homemade wine with dinner.

Day 2: Štanjel to Komen

- Spend the morning touring the **Štanjel Castle (Štanjel Grad)** and have a walk around the **Ferrari Garden.**
- Take a short drive to the **Frankič Winery** and the **Turistična kmetija Ostrouška Pelican** to sample local wines. Both establishments offer rooms for the night.

Day 3: Komen to Brda

- Drive to the **Brda** region, stopping at winemaker **Movia.**
- Head to **Kabaj,** where you can eat, sleep, and sample homemade wine.
- From here, you are very close to Italy if you are so inclined to visit, or you can explore the Brda wine roads further.

The Coast

The small coast of Slovenia is heavily influenced by the countries that border it. Italy has loomed large in the region since it occupied this corner of Slovenia from World War I through most of World War II. Italian replaced Slovenian in local schools, settlers from Italy were installed in the area, and Italian street signs appeared. Though Slovenian is today the language of choice, you'll still find that many locals speak Italian, and the Italian community, descendants of the settlers, is a strong influence. Signs are still printed in both Italian and Slovenian, and the Italian vibe is felt in everything from the architecture, which heralds from Venice's powerful past, to the cuisine.

The main cities on the coast are Koper, Izola, Piran, and Portorož. Koper and Izola both have charming old-town cores, though they find it hard to compete with the picturesque Piran. Portorož unfortunately revolves around package-holiday hotels and loads of souvenir shops hawking T-shirts, beach towels, and plastic bric-a-brac.

KOPER

Koper is not the most charming of Slovenia's coastal towns. Once an important harbor in its Venetian heyday, the city lost its position when the Austro-Hungarian Empire looked to other coastal towns for shipping. A port town with some great architecture from the 15th and 16th centuries, it's best used as a cheaper source of lodging than pricier coastal towns.

Sights

The old Venetian core is pretty, starting with the **Cathedral of the Assumption (Stolnica Marijinega vnebovzetja)** (Titov trg, 7am-12pm and 3pm-7pm daily, free), a Romanesque structure with a Venetian Gothic facade on the town's main square, Titov trg. One of the oldest church bells in Slovenia hangs in its bell tower (€1 to climb to the top), dating from 1333. Climbing the tower is a nice way to get a good view over Koper.

On the other side of the square is the impressive 15th-century Venetian **Praetorian Palace (Pretorska Palaca)** (Titov trg 3, 9am-8pm daily summer, 9am-5pm daily winter), once the home of the town mayor. The looming building is a mishmash of Gothic and Renaissance features and looks a bit more like a castle than a palace. A free tour of the palace is available by arrangement with the **tourist office** (Titov trg 3, tel. 05/664-6403, tic@koper.si, www.koper.si, 9am-8pm Mon.-Sat., 9am-12pm Sun. July-Aug., 9am-5pm Mon.-Fri., 9am-12pm Sat. Sept.-June), which is located inside the palace.

The **Regional Museum (Pokrajinski muzej)** (Kidričeva 19, tel. 041/556-644, www.pokrajinskimuzejkoper.si, 8am-4pm Tues.-Fri., 9am-5pm Sat. and Sun., €5-8), in the attractive 16th-century Belgramoni Tacco palace, has a few exhibits chronicling Koper's past, as well as a copy of the *Dance of Death* from the village of Hrastovlje.

Wine Route

Check with the Koper **tourist office** (Titov trg 3, tel. 05/664-6403, tic@koper.si, www.koper.si) about the Istrian wine route out of Koper, highlighting some of the area's wineries. Wine lovers will appreciate Slovene Istria's takes on Malvazija and Teran as well as the locally produced Mus we.

VinaKoper (Šmarska cesta 1, tel. 05/663-0100, www.vinakoper.si, tours and tastings arranged in advance) has been producing wine since 1947. Their wines, particularly their Malvasia, merlots, and muscat, have won multiple international awards. Arrange a tour and tasting in advance and purchase a couple of bottles to take home.

Accommodations and Food

Stay and eat at the basic but wonderful **Domačija Butul** (Manžan 10d, www.butul. net, from €30 pp). The three rooms and two apartments are simple but very clean. The guesthouse also serves amazing food even if you aren't staying here, with several tasting menus on offer (three-course menu €35). The food is way chicer than most of what you'll find around Koper. They also offer cooking classes and a variety of homemade wines.

The **Villa Domus Hostel and Student House** (Vojkovo nabrezje 12, tel. 030/468-777, www.villa-domus.si, €75 d or €17 per person in a dorm) is a modern, extraordinarily clean hostel, a 10-15-minute walk to the center of town.

In Koper, stop by **Veneziana** (Ribiški trg 9, www.casaveneziana.si, 7pm-late daily), a friendly wine bar that has an excellent wine list, great atmosphere, and snacks. The wine bar also has modern apartments (from €65) to rent to travelers.

The **Gostilna "Za gradom"** (Kraljeva ulica 10, tel. 05/628-5504, www.zagradom. com, 12pm-10pm Tues.-Sat., reservations recommended, €20) serves typical Istrian foods like *fuži* as well as lots of fresh fish.

Capra (Pristaniska ulica 3, tel. 041/602-030, www.capra.si, 9am-10pm daily, €30) brings a little dash of haute-inspired cuisine to Koper. Definitely expensive, but the artfully arranged, modern takes on traditional Mediterranean cuisine are a departure from the other restaurants in Koper.

Getting There and Around

Koper is 100 kilometers (62 miles) southwest of Ljubljana. Koper's **bus station** (Kolodvorska 11, tel. 05/639-5269) has lots of connections to other coastal towns such as Izola (15 minutes), Piran (30 minutes), and Portorož (30 minutes). A couple of daily connections (more in summer) link Koper with Ljubljana (2.5 hours), Postojna (1.5 hours), and Celje (four hours). Train travel is also possible—the **train station** (Kolodvorska 11, tel. 05/639-5263) links Koper with Ljubljana (2.5 hours) and Postojna (1.5 hours)—though connections are far less frequent than the bus.

Ciao, Italia: Side Trips to Italy

The Slovenian coast is just over the border from Italy, making a trip to another country a tempting and easy possibility. Trieste is the closest large city, once the favored destination of Yugoslav citizens on shopping expeditions, looking for brands they couldn't buy in their own country. Fifteen years ago, the city was filled with all the name-brand stores, but as many of those stores have opened in independent Slovenia, Croatia, and Bosnia, many of those in Trieste have gone out of business, replaced with a variety of Chinese discount stores. While Trieste is not the most charming place, it is another country, and is linked by frequent bus and train connections as well as day trips provided by local travel agency Kompas Tours (www.kompas.si).

More attractive is a short trip to Venice, linked with Ljubljana by the fast new *Casanova* train that takes only four hours and runs once daily. From cities on the coast, the *Prince of Venice* (Obala 41, Portorož, tel. 05/617-8000, www.kompas.si) takes passengers on boat rides between Izola and Venice (daily departures Mar.-Oct., 2.5 hours each way), and included is a guided tour of Venice. Tickets can be purchased from Kompas travel agencies all over Slovenia. Italy-based Venezia Lines (tel. 39/41-520-5473, www.venezialines.com, €69 one-way) connects Venice with Piran.

★ HRASTOVLJE

The nearby village of Hrastovlje is a beautiful detour from Koper. The 15th-century Church of the Holy Trinity (Cerkev sveti Trojice) (generally 9am-12pm and 1pm-5pm Wed.-Mon., otherwise ask for key from Rozana Rihter, tel. 031/432-231, €3) is pretty in its simplicity and its setting, surrounded by vineyards. However, the most famous feature is the *Dance of Death* painted on the inside of the church walls. The Gothic fresco portrays people from all walks of life (a baby, a king, and others) dancing with skeletons. Other church frescoes display scenes from the Bible. The church is listed as a UNESCO World Heritage site. There are only a few such death paintings in the region, making its rarity and macabre beauty all the more reason to visit the church.

Hrastovlje is 18 kilometers (11 miles) southeast of Koper. Driving from Koper, take Road 10, exiting at Črni Kal. From here follow Road 208 toward Buzet in Croatia until you see the signs for Hrastovlje. There's a parking lot not far from the church. Trains also stop near Hrastovlje, but you should check current schedules for connections from Koper. Buses stop some eight kilometers (about five miles) away in Črni Kal.

IZOLA

A relaxed fishing village most of the year, Izola becomes a popular destination in summer, frequented by a young and fairly artsy crowd. There's not too much specifically to do or see—the town's old walls were destroyed in the 19th century—but the old core has some pretty churches and villas that are nice to gawk at. Most of the old town dates from the 15th and 16th centuries, built by Izola's powerful rulers across the Adriatic, the Venetians. The tourist office (Sončno nabrežje 4, tel. 05/640-1050, tic.izola@izola.si, www.izola.si, 8am-7pm Mon.-Fri., 8am-5pm Sat.-Sun. July-Aug., 8am-7pm Mon.-Fri., 9am-12pm Sat. Sept.-June) has started a summer Street Museum program, which provides maps pointing out specific shops, art studios, and coffee shops to visit throughout the town. They eventually hope to add activities and presentations that connect with Izola's maritime traditions.

Accommodations and Food

Located in the nearby village of Korte, five kilometers (three miles) south of Izola, Guesthouse Stara šola (Korte 74, tel. 05/642-1114, www.starasola.com, €60 d) opened in 2006 in a turn-of-the-20th-century schoolhouse. It's conveniently located near Koper, Izola, and Piran, and it makes a great base, particularly if you have a car.

On the waterfront in Izola's old town is the excellently located three-star **Hotel Marina** (Veliki trg 11, tel. 05/660-4100, www.hotelmarina.si, €110 d). The rooms offer basic decor, TV, air-conditioning, and a minibar. The hotel grounds feature a nice spa with saunas and massages.

For casual dining in Izola, head to **Pizzerija Gušt** (Drevored 1. maja 5, tel. 041/675-953, 8am-12am daily, €12) for pizza and Istrian pasta dishes. For some of Izola's seafood, try **Marina** (Veliki trg 11, tel. 05/660-4100, 12pm-10pm daily, €16), which also has a nice view of the harbor.

For something more high-end, try ★ **Hiša Torkla** (Korte 44B, tel. 05/620-9657, www.hisa-torkla.si, 12pm-10pm Wed.-Sun., €10-20) in the village of Korte. Always-seasonal ingredients round out a locally focused menu, served in a cozy atmosphere with exposed stone walls. The restaurant is the best in the area.

Getting There and Around

Izola is 110 kilometers (68 miles) southwest of Ljubljana and six kilometers (almost four miles) west of Koper. Buses connect Izola with Portorož (10 minutes), Koper (15 minutes), and Piran (20 minutes) every hour or so. At least one daily connection links the town with Ljubljana (2.5 hours).

TOP EXPERIENCE

PORTOROŽ

This is Slovenia's busiest, and least attractive, seaside resort. Unless you're looking for the kind of place that attracts spring-breakers (mainly with package hotels, cheap beer, and lots of nightclubs), you can feel free to skip this stop.

If you'd like to see what's under the water around Portorož, **Nemo Divers** (Laguna Bernardin, tel. 05/674-4198, www.nemo-divers.si) can hook you up with courses in scuba diving and waterskiing, as well as diving and waterskiing excursions and pedal boat and Jet Ski rentals.

Accommodations and Food

Rizibizi (Vilfanova ulica 10, tel. 059/935-320, www.rizibizi.si, from €40 for a several-course tasting menu) is not central, but it has a great hilltop view with plenty of terrace space and Istrian truffle dishes to enjoy.

★ **Kempinski Palace Portorož** (Obala 45, tel. 05/692-7000, www.kempinski.com, €250 d, including breakfast) is one of the few truly five-star hotels this side of Dubrovnik. Located in a historic building on the promenade in the center of town, the hotel's luxe rooms, terrace with a sea view, and amazing buffet breakfast bring the Slovenian coast back to its heyday.

Getting There and Around

Portorož is 122 kilometers (76 miles) southwest of Ljubljana and six kilometers (almost four miles) south of Izola. Buses have frequent connections to towns on the coast, such as Piran (five minutes), Izola (10 minutes), and Koper (25 minutes). Less-frequent connections serve Postojna (two hours) and Ljubljana (three hours).

It takes less than an hour to walk to Piran from town. You can also rent a bicycle or scooter from **Atlas Express** (Obala 55, tel. 05/674-6772).

★ PIRAN

A medieval walled Venetian town, Piran is the prettiest city on Slovenia's coast. Filled with winding cobblestone streets, Venetian architecture, and a view of the lights of Trieste from the waterfront, Piran is mercifully unsullied by the tacky trappings of many seaside resorts.

Piran's history likely dates to a Greek settlement, before either the Romans or the Slavs inhabited the seaside town. However, it's the

---

1: Postojna cave **2:** Predjama Castle **3:** Piran waterfront **4:** Church of the Holy Trinity in Hrastovlje

Venetians, who owned the town from the 13th to 18th centuries, who left an indelible mark on the architecture and personality of Piran.

Today, the city is quickly being restored as old buildings are snatched up by EU citizens looking for vacation homes in the charming enclave.

Sights

The **Church of St. George (Stolna Cerkev Sv Jurija)** (11am-5pm daily, €1 to climb the bell tower) takes center stage in the little town, peering down from the hilltop. Today it's a mostly Baroque church, but the original structure dates from the 12th century. Climbing up the bell tower gives an even better view for snapping photos, and it's a workout to climb the almost 150 steps.

The town's **Sergej Mašera Maritime Museum (Pomorski muzej Sergej Mašera)** (Cankarjevo nabrežje 3, tel. 05/671-0040, www.pomorskimuzej.si, 9am-12pm and 5pm-9pm Tues.-Sun. July-Aug., 9am-5pm Tues.-Sun. Sept-June, €3.50) has an interesting collection of model ships, navigational instruments, sailors' uniforms, and paintings. The museum also skims the surface of Piran's salt mining, from which it made its wealth. Fans of classical music will appreciate the **Tartini Room,** celebrating 18th-century composer Giuseppe Tartini, with displays that include his death mask and one of his violins.

The **Magical World of Shells (Čarobni svet školjk)** (Tartinjev trg 15, tel. 040/758-900, www.svet-skoljk.si, 11am-6pm Tues.-Sat. Mar.-May and Oct.-Nov., 10am-8pm daily June-Sept., 11am-6pm Sat.-Sun. Dec.-Feb., €4) is a must if you appreciate shells. Over 3,000 specimens are on display, including the shell of the largest snail in the world.

Accommodations

Renovated in 2015, **Hostel Pirano** (Vodopivčeva ulica 9, www.hostelpiran.com, €50 d), in the heart of the old town, is more hotel than hostel, if you don't mind sharing a bath, though the hotel does offer some rooms with private baths.

For the best location in town, stay at the 100-year-old **Hotel Piran** (Stjenkova utica 1, tel. 05/666-7100, www.hotel-piran.si, €160 d, including breakfast) in the center of town on the waterfront. It's worth it to try to get a sea-facing room to make the most of your stay. If you can't, there's always the rather pricey rooftop bar.

Food

Try **Gostilna Park** (Župančičeva 21, tel. 059/921-751, €20), a great seafood restaurant with a cozy atmosphere. A nicer take on takeaway, **Fritolin pri Cantini** (Prvomajski trg 6, tel. 041/873-872, 12pm-9:30pm Mon.-Thu., 12pm-10pm Fri.-Sun., €15). Drinks are served at your table, but pick up the great fish dishes and fries from the counter. **Neptun** (Župančičeva 7, tel. 05/673-4111, 12pm-4pm and 6pm-12am daily, €20) is a small restaurant specializing in grilled seafood. The ambience is cozy and the menu simple, mainly fish and potatoes, but always the best quality, fresh from the sea. Also try the **Ivo Inn** (Gregorčičeva 31, tel. 05/673-2233, call for hours, €25) with marina-side terrace dining.

Getting There and Around

Piran is 119 kilometers (74 miles) southwest of Ljubljana and three kilometers (1.8 miles) north of Portorož. The town is well connected by bus to Portorož (five minutes), Izola (20 minutes), and Koper (30 minutes), with connections almost hourly during the day. There are a couple of daily connections with Postojna (two hours) and Ljubljana (three hours). If you're coming by car, parking in Piran can be an issue. The parking lot at Formace near the Grand Hotel Bernardin resort complex is a 15-minute walk, or take the free shuttle bus.

SEČOVLJE SALINA NATURE PARK

(Krajinski Park Sečovlje Salina)

If you're interested in delving into the salt-mining tradition, the **Sečovlje Salina**

Nature Park (Seča 115, tel. 05/672-1330, kpss@soline.si, www.kpss.si, 8am-9pm daily summer, 8am-5pm daily winter, €7) features a small museum and a place where you can see salt-making in action. The salt pans date from the 9th century, so the park has quite an interesting history. The marshlands park also has walking and biking routes for admiring the indigenous wildlife, such as the some 282 bird species that call the park home.

There is currently no public transportation to the park. If you're driving, take the main Lucija-Sečovlje road headed to Croatia and follow the signs for Lera, a couple of kilometers south of Piran. There are two entrances to the park; the more convenient one is at Lera, where you can also rent bikes for just a few euros a day. Another fun way to see the park is to take a **boat tour** (tel. 031/337-339, www.autentica.si), which includes a boat trip through the saltpans and a guided tour of Piran.

The Karst Region

The Karst Region (Kras) is one of Slovenia's toughest, not only geographically, with its windswept rocky base, but also historically. The area was filled with partisans who were persecuted by the Nazis, the homes burned and the people thrown into concentration camps.

The area has a rough beauty and is really a don't-miss for gourmets, who should stop to sample the area's famous wind-cured hams and earthy Teran red wine.

The limestone plateau that gives the region its name is littered with caves. The two most impressive are the Postojna Cave and the Škocjan Caves. The Postojna Cave is the more famous, but the smaller Škocjan Caves are stunning as well and much less touristed.

There aren't a lot of options for upscale accommodations in the area. If you're used to room service, it's probably best to stay in Ljubljana or one of the coastal towns and make the Kras a day trip.

★ POSTOJNA

Postojna, a modern little town, doesn't have much to offer in its center, but on the outskirts are two must-see attractions: the Postojna Cave and the magnificent Predjama Castle.

Sights
POSTOJNA CAVE
(Postojnska Jama)
Postojna Cave (tel. 05/700-0100, www.

postojnska-jama.eu, visits every hour 9am-5pm daily May-June and Sept., every hour 9am-6pm daily July-Aug., 10am, 11am, 12pm, 2pm, 3pm, and 4pm daily Apr. and Oct., 10am, 12pm, and 3pm daily Jan.-Mar. and Nov.-Dec., €27.90) is a network of 23 kilometers (14 miles) of underground rock formations that are millions of years old. Though the first recorded visit to the caves was in the 13th century, it wasn't until the 19th century when the caves became a staple for visitors. The Postojna cave is especially famous for its "human fish," a colorless lizard-type animal that lives for up to 60 years.

The Postojna Cave is the most visited attraction in Slovenia, and for good reason. The guided tour, which takes a little over an hour, combines a train ride with a bit of walking. The train itself is historic, the little double-track cars having ferried visitors into the cave for over 140 years.

Many of the first visitors, particularly in the 16th and 17th centuries, signed their names on the wall of the cave, which can still be seen in the Passage of Old Signatures. Today, of course, it would be considered destruction of property. Archduke Ferdinand I was the first to visit, in 1819, followed by a long list of nobility and political leaders, including the widow of Napoleon, Empress Marie Louise, and even Mussolini.

Toward the end of the tour, you can

also choose to visit the cave's Human Fish Museum, exhibiting a few of the captive animals as well as some related displays, for a couple of extra euros.

PREDJAMA CASTLE
(Predjamski Grad)

When you first see **Predjama Castle** (tel. 05/700-0100, www.postojnska-jama.eu, 10am-4pm daily Nov.-Mar., 10am-4pm daily Oct. and Apr., 9am-6pm daily May-June and Sept., 9am-7pm daily July-Aug., €14.90), a towering white structure carved into the rock face on a hill above the sweet little village of Predjama, nine kilometers (5.5 miles) from Postojna, you think, this is what a castle is supposed to be. And it doesn't end there; from the history of the place to the cave underneath the castle, Predjama Castle really does inspire.

The most famous of the castle's owners was the 15th-century Erazem, who some see as a handsome knight and others describe as a robber baron. Legend has it that, although the castle is accessible from only one side, Erazem had a secret passage to bring supplies so that the emperor's army could attack while he and his group held out inside. A disloyal servant and a trick played by the enemy finally brought his defeat.

In addition to learning about the history of the castle, there are also displays of equipment, displays about castle life in the late Gothic period in the dining room, and a room of hunting trophies. From May to September you can also visit the **cave** (tours at 11am, 1pm, 3pm, and 5pm, €8) under Predjama Castle, but it's closed in winter when it's home to a colony of bats.

There is a free shuttle bus between the Postojna Cave and Predjama Castle in July and August if you buy a combined ticket for both attractions.

Accommodations and Food

A tastefully renovated 1971-era hotel, the **Hotel Jama** (Jamska cesta 28, tel. 05/700-0200, www.postonska-jama.eu, €95 d including breakfast) includes park admission for its guests and has three solid restaurants to choose from. Set amongst the mountains, it is a peaceful respite after a day of touring.

Getting There and Around

The village of Postojna is 45 kilometers (28 miles) south of Ljubljana. Buses from Ljubljana (one hour) and Koper (one hour) as well as trains from Ljubljana (1.5 hours) and Koper (1.5 hours) connect with Postojna. The caves are a 1.5-kilometer (just under a mile) walk from the village.

ŠKOCJAN CAVES
(Škocjanske Jame)

Škocjan Caves (Škocjan 2, tel. 05/708-2110, www.park-skocjanske-jame.si, visits every hour 10am-5pm daily June-Sept., 10am, 12pm, 1pm, and 3:30pm daily Apr.-May and Oct., 10am and 1pm Mon.-Sat., 10am, 1pm, and 3pm Sun. Nov.-Mar., from €16) is a UNESCO World Heritage site. The 1.5-hour tour takes you through art-like stalactites before unveiling the pièce de résistance—a 146-meter-high (479-foot-high) gorge with a bright green river rushing below. Certainly some of the world's most beautiful caves, they were discovered in the 2nd century BC, though it wasn't until the 19th century when scientists began exploring them in earnest.

The tour begins with the Silent Cave, filled with giant stalactites and stalagmites, and continues to the Great Hall, a mammoth space whose ceiling looms 30 meters (98 feet) above. Following is the Murmuring Cave, which feels like you've entered an adventure movie, followed by the Gours, some pretty rock pools, out to the Schmidl hall (Schmidlova dvorana, the last part of the cave), and the exit. The paths are safe and well maintained, but there are quite a few stairs. The Škocjan Caves are much less touristy than the nearby Postojna Cave, but can still be very popular in summer.

Getting There and Around

The Škocjan caves are 25 kilometers (15.5 miles) southwest of Postojna and 75 kilometers (46.6 miles) southwest of Ljubljana. By car, take the A1 highway from Ljubljana and exit at Divača. Then follow the brown signs for the caves. If you're relying on public transportation, take a train to Divača, where a well-marked three-kilometer (1.8-mile) path leads to the cave entrance.

LIPICA

The town of Lipica was made famous by its horses, the famed Lipizzaners of Austria's Spanish Riding School.

★ Lipica Stud Farm
(Kobilarna Lipica)

The **Lipica Stud Farm** (Lipica 5, tel. 05/739-1708, www.lipica.org, 10am-6pm daily, check website for guided tours and performance schedule, €16-23) was established by the bishop of Trieste and purchased in 1580 by the Austrian archduke Karl II. The Lipizzaner breed is a mixture of indigenous horses with Spanish and Arabian lines. The white horses, which are gray and black at birth and turn white over time, are a majestic breed, whose muscular frame made them a favorite of the Austrian royalty. It's said that the rough karst landscape creates the horses' tough hooves.

If you can, see a display at the Classic Riding School, where the highly trained horses appear to be dancing rather than galloping; it's truly a don't-miss. The horses aren't carted off to Vienna anymore, but perform locally for visitors. There are daily pony rides for children and riding classes weekly for novices as well as more experienced riders.

Accommodations and Food

For budget travelers, the **Pliskovica Youth Hostel** (Pliskovica 11, tel. 05/764-0250, www.hostelkras.com, €14 pp), a few kilometers southwest of Štanjel, is an old Kras farm and full of local flavor. The **Lipizzaner Lodge Guest House** (Landol 17, Postojna, tel. 05/620-3443, www.lipizzanerlodge.com, €85 d, including breakfast) has six clean, modern rooms in a peaceful location and offers a sauna and café on site.

Osmica Kmetija Kosmina (Brje pri Komnu, tel. 05/766-7240, 9am-1am daily, €15), about 12 kilometers (7 miles) southeast of Štanjel, is a local rustic place with huge helpings of the region's famous cuisine—*pršut*, homemade sausages and cheeses, and earthy Teran wine. The **Gostilna Gombač** (Lokev 165, tel. 05/767-0466, 11am-10pm Thurs.-Mon., €20) is a good place for dinner after a visit to the Lipica Stud Farm. The house specialty is roast game.

Lipizzaner horses

The Wines of Brda: Slovenian Tuscany

In the far west of Slovenia, the region of Brda is a hilly area reminiscent of Tuscany, and almost a stone's throw to Italy. The wines of Goriška Brda have the country's highest per-hectare yield of medals and awards. There are plenty of international medals too, as well as write-ups in the most respected U.S. food and wine magazines. It's really worth the trip to head west if you're in Idrija, or north if you're on the coast, to this exciting wine region. Not only will you get to taste great wine, you'll get to sample and buy wines that are almost unattainable in the United States.

vines in Goriška Brda

The area has two well-marked wine routes that include a few sightseeing stops and places to eat. You can pick up maps from the **Brda tourist office** (Grajska cesta 10, Dobrovo, tel. 05/395-9594, tic@brda.si, www.brda.si).

Your first stop should be **Klet Brda** (Dobrovo Naslov Zadružna cesta 9, tel. 05/331-0144, www.klet-brda.si, call to arrange tasting, from €6) in the village of Dobrovo. Founded in 1957 as a cooperative, it is still owned by its members today. The winery offers whites, reds, and sparkling wines, and in 2015 won over 30 medals in international wine competitions.

Next up is Brda's rock-star winemaker, Ales Kristančić, from the **Movia Winery** (Ceglo 18, tel. 05/395-9510, www.movia.si, call to arrange tasting), owned by the family since 1820. Ales has put the winery's name on the map, and for good reason: Movia's wines are both high-quality and refreshingly surprising, from gentle, fresh whites to deep, layered reds.

Lesser-known wineries to try include **Kristančič** (Medana 1, tel. 05/395-9533, call for hours), in the village of Medana, one of the area's largest private vineyards, with about 15 cultivated hectares. It's not related to Movia, as it's a common last name in the area. Kristančič houses most of its wines in stainless-steel barrels, giving the wine a contemporary taste. His specialties are the very modern Manzoni and the more traditional Tokaj, a white almond-flavored wine, and cabernet franc, a rich red best drunk when it's aged three to five years.

Another respected local winemaker is the **Simčič family** (Ceglo 3b, tel. 05/395-9200, call for hours), in the village of Ceglo; the majority of their vineyards are technically across the Italian border. Their wines have won multiple regional awards. Don't miss their Sivi Pinot (a gray pinot), chardonnay, and Beli Pinot.

Finally, stop at the **Kabaj** (Šlovrenc 4, Dobrovo, tel. 05/395-9560, www.kabaj.si, €80 d, with breakfast), one of Slovenia's best winemakers, with their own list of international accolades. The wines go perfectly with specialties of the **winery restaurant** (12pm-3pm and 7pm-11pm Thurs.-Sun., call for reservations, €10-25), like *cotechino* sausage baked with potatoes, carrots, and leeks under a bell with homemade crème brûlée for dessert. After dinner, tuck into the cozy rooms at the winery's homestead for very sweet dreams indeed.

Reaching and exploring the Brda region is easiest by car. If you're driving, the region is south of Kobarid along the Italian-Slovenian border or north of Štanjel on the highway that runs through Nova Gorica. The main towns are Dobrovo, Šmartno, and Goriška Brda. Bus connections are possible but infrequent.

Getting There and Around

Lipica is 80 kilometers (50 miles) southwest of Ljubljana. There are no buses or trains to Lipica. The closest transportation hub is the village of Sežana; buses and trains take about two hours from Ljubljana.

ŠTANJEL

Though much of Štanjel village was damaged in World War II, the medieval core is positively charming. Artists have been slowly taking over the town with their studios, and the town is the perfect getaway for those who like to get off the tourist track, relaxing with a leisurely lunch or perusing the market, held the third Sunday of every month.

Štanjel Castle (Štanjel Grad) (Štanjel 1a, tel. 05/769-0056, www.stanjel.eu, 9am-3pm Tues.-Fri., 10am-4pm Sat.-Sun. winter, 10am-6pm Sat.-Sun. summer, €14) has a gallery of local graphic artist and painter Lojze Spacal. The castle also houses a small bar that sells light snacks and a souvenir shop. Below the castle, there's also a lovely garden, the Ferrari Garden, worth a stroll.

The **Hiše Posebne Sorte** (Kodreti 15, tel. 05/769-0000, sorta.si, €60 d.) is a cozy home and restaurant in a bucolic farm setting. Rooms are clean, the surroundings are lovely, and the food is excellent.

You can get more information from the **tourist office** (tel. 05/769-0056, www.komen.si, 11am-4pm Mon., Wed., and Sat.), located near the castle.

Štanjel is 100 kilometers (62 miles) southwest of Ljubljana and 24 kilometers (15 miles) northwest of the Škocjan caves. A couple of daily buses connect the village of Divača with Štanjel, taking about 40 minutes.

WINERIES

The wines of the Karst are the mighty, earthy Teran, a local red, and the fresh white Malvasia. Another wine with a very old tradition in the area, the lightly almond flavored Vitovska, is making a comeback. The region's **Kras Wine Route** (Vinska Cesta Kras, www.vinskacestakras.si) has a long tradition dating back to the days when the wines were highly valued by the Greeks and Romans.

There are around 170 wineries along the route, but a couple to try near Komen include the **Frankič Winery** (Brje pri Komnu 24, tel. 05/766-8771, www.frankic-peloz.si, reserve online or by phone), which also offers apartments if you would like to stay overnight, and the charming **Turistična kmetija Ostrouška Pelicon** (Coljava 5, Komen, tel. 05/766-8708, www.ostrouska-pelicon.com, 1pm-7pm Sat.-Sun. Mar.-June and Sept.-Dec.). This farm not only serves great homemade wine but excellent food as well.

If you're here the last Saturday of May, the area celebrates Teran and cellars all along the road are open for tastings of this Karst specialty.

Montenegro

Montenegro is often heralded as the next "it"

destination, now that Croatia and Slovenia have been discovered by droves of tourists.

And it's true that going to Montenegro now is a great idea, but you won't find it completely undiscovered. European and Balkan tourists, as well as a fair number of Russians, discovered this gem quite a while ago, and many Adriatic cruises make a stop at Kotor, one of the country's UNESCO World Heritage protected sites.

What you will find are people passionately in love with their country, whose ancestors fought off invaders even in the most unbelievable circumstances. But guests, on the other hand, they welcome with open arms, thrilled to show off Montenegro's treasures, and there are

Highlights

Look for ★ to find recommended sights, activities, dining, and lodging.

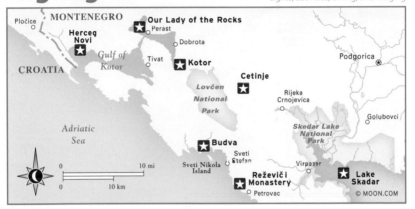

★ **Herceg Novi:** A lovely coastal town to visit, with a six-kilometer (3.7-mile) promenade to enjoy strolling, the town is also the perfect jumping off point for a number of active pursuits such as kayaking, sailing, or canyoning (page 409).

★ **Our Lady of the Rocks:** Picturesque church-topped island off the waterfront of the charming seaside village of Perast (page 413).

★ **Kotor:** The walled city of Kotor, nestled in a picture-perfect fjord, is a UNESCO world heritage site and a must-see on the Montenegrin coast (page 416).

★ **Budva:** Full of raucous party-seekers on the beaches, Budva has a few quiet spots too and

some history to enjoy when you are not sunning yourself on its 38-kilometer (23.6-mile) riviera (page 421).

★ **Reževići Monastery:** Peaceful, historic, and filled with beautiful frescoes, it sits just above the excellent beach spot, Perazica Do (page 429).

★ **Cetinje:** The cultural capital of Montenegro, this beautiful little town is filled with museums and galleries (page 431).

★ **Lake Skadar:** Lakeside beauty and wildlife paradise, the shores are also home to some of the country's best wineries (page 433).

Previous: St. George's Island, Perast **Above:** Kotor; Herceg Novi

Montenegro

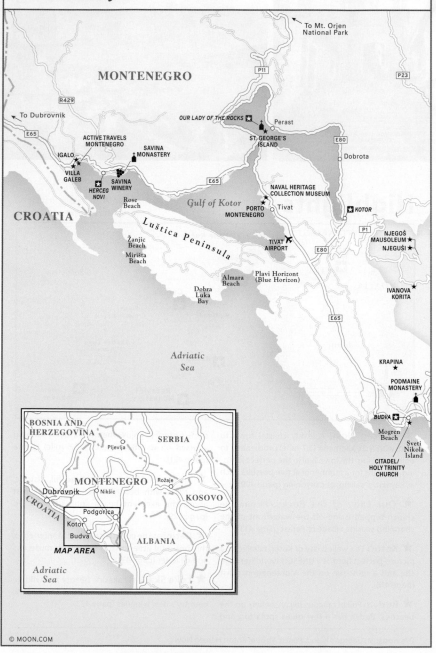

To Mt. Orjen
National Park

MONTENEGRO

P11

P23

R429

To Dubrovnik

E65

OUR LADY OF THE ROCKS ✠ ○ Perast

ACTIVE TRAVELS
MONTENEGRO

SAVINA
MONASTERY ♱

ST. GEORGE'S
ISLAND

E80

IGALO ★

○ Dobrota

VILLA
GALEB

SAVINA
WINERY

HERCEG
NOVI ✠

Rose
Beach

NAVAL HERITAGE
COLLECTION MUSEUM

E65

PORTO
MONTENEGRO

✠ KOTOR

Gulf of Kotor

○ Tivat

Luštica Peninsula

P1

NJEGOŠ
MAUSOLEUM ★

NJEGUŠI ★

Žanjic
Beach

TIVAT
AIRPORT ✈

E80

Mirišta
Beach

Almara
Beach

Plavi Horizont
(Blue Horizon)

Dobra
Luka
Bay

IVANOVA
KORITA ★

E65

Adriatic
Sea

KRAPINA ★

PODMAINE
MONASTERY ♱

BUDVA ✠

Mogren
Beach

Sveti
Nikola
Island

CITADEL/
HOLY TRINITY
CHURCH

BOSNIA AND
HERZEGOVINA

SERBIA

○ Pljevlja

MONTENEGRO

Rožaje ○

Dubrovnik ○

○ Nikšic

KOSOVO

CROATIA

Podgorica ○

Kotor ○

Budva ○

ALBANIA

MAP AREA

Adriatic
Sea

MONTENEGRO

CROATIA

© MOON.COM

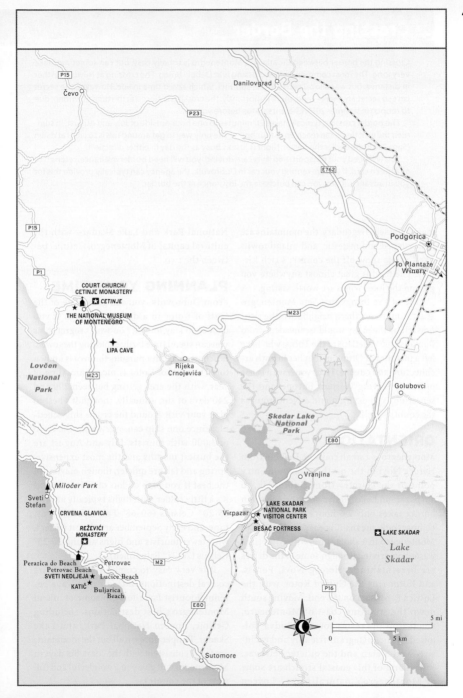

Crossing the Border

Crossing the border between Croatia and Montenegro is usually easy, but can sometimes take very long. The most common border crossing is at Debelji Brijeg. The crossing at Njivici is farther in distance, but was a local secret in the summer, which saved time in line. However, the secret isn't so secret anymore—and, more importantly, the crossing is closed at the time of writing, due to reopen in summer 2019. Check its status before you go.

The border crossing typically takes 20 minutes to one hour outside of July and August. In summer, the wait times can reach up to four hours. The only way to get around this is to cross at dawn (5am-7am), the earlier the better. Night is just as busy as the day in either direction.

You will need your passport, and if you are driving, you will need border insurance, referred to as a green card. If you are renting your car in Dubrovnik, the agency can typically provide this for you in advance. If not, you can purchase the insurance at the border.

many. The sea is legendary, the mountains are both rugged and majestic, and inland towns like Cetinje show off the country's rich history. The food is great almost anywhere you go, and the local wines are worth tasting.

One of the things that sets Montenegro apart from its northern neighbors is the richness left by the many would-be invaders, from Romans and Venetians to the Turks, who have left a plethora of Ottoman touches in both architecture and cuisine. Here you have a sense of finally leaving Western Europe, and the sensation is as exciting and adventurous as the country itself.

ORIENTATION

Montenegro is a small country. Driving from Herceg Novi in the north, a common entry point to the country from Dubrovnik, to Virpazar, on Lake Skadar near the Albanian border takes only 2.5 hours. The country's compactness means it is easy to see a lot of Montenegro in a short time, with little time wasted on driving (though some of the drives are breathtaking). Herceg Novi, Perast, and Kotor ring the Gulf of Kotor, with the Luštica Peninsula on the end. Moving south down the stunning coast of Montenegro, you'll find the resort town of Budva, followed by the Instagram-friendly and exclusive Sveti Stefan and the quieter Petrovac. Just inland of this coastal stretch are some of Montenegro's natural gems—Lovćen

National Park and Lake Skadar—with the cultural capital of Montenegro, Cetinje, between the two.

PLANNING YOUR TIME

From Dubrovnik, you can get a taste of the Gulf of Kotor in a day trip, though if you choose to stay longer, you won't regret it, as you can spend time lazily exploring the towns, beaches, and active pursuits the area is known for. The Gulf of Kotor is nice at any time of year, with the area getting between 200 and 240 days of sun annually, though it's best to plan your visit around the cruise ship schedule, since one ship can overwhelm the town of 3,000 with tourists. July and August are the busiest months and the most expensive. Spring and fall are quieter, though maybe not the best if you plan on lots of swimming, as it's a little colder with highs typically around 15-20° Celsius (60-68° Fahrenheit). May, June, and early September are almost perfect, with fewer tourists and highs around 20-25° Celsius (70-77° Fahrenheit).

It is very easy to combine Montenegro's coastal destinations, including Budva, a perennial tourist favorite, with some of inland Montenegro's best destinations, including Cetinje, Lovćen National Park, and Lake Skadar. Temperatures in all but the mountains are fairly consistent with the coast. Six days in Montenegro will give you a wonderful and full view of the country.

Itinerary Ideas

DAY TRIP FROM DUBROVNIK

One of the great things about the Gulf of Kotor is that the area is totally doable as a day trip from Dubrovnik, which is only 20 kilometers (12 miles) away. Leave **Dubrovnik** bright and early around 7am, even earlier if you are taking the trip in summer, when the border crossing can be a trip in itself. This trip is best done by car, for maximum flexibility, but there are many operators who offer tours by bus as well.

1 Head first to **Kotor,** and spend the early morning hours wandering around the town before the cruise ship tourists start to fill the streets (or plan your visit when a boat is not in port).

2 Climb up the **town walls** for a great view, a trek that will take 1.5-2 hours total.

3 Have a quick lunch at **Hoste**. Get cash from an ATM in town for your next stop, which does not have that little luxury.

4 Take off for **Perast,** driving along the fjord-like Gulf of Kotor and enjoying the scenery.

5 In Perast, park at the entrance to the town, walk down to the waterfront, and take a water taxi to **Our Lady of the Rocks**.

6 Upon return to Perast's waterfront, have an early dinner at the **Hotel Conte** in Perast before heading back toward Dubrovnik.

THE BEST OF MONTENEGRO IN SIX DAYS

See the best Montenegro has to offer on a tour of its coast, Lovćen National Park, and Lake Skadar.

Day 1: Herceg Novi

- Spend the day in **Herceg Novi**. Walk along the six-kilometer (3.7-mile) **Šetalište Pet Danica**, from the sandy beaches at **Igalo** to the **Old Town (Stari Grad)** of Herceg Novi and beyond.
- Visit the **Savina Monastery** and enjoy the panoramic views.
- Have dinner at **Oro di Terra** in the nearby village of Baošići.

Day 2: Perast to Kotor

- Head to **Perast**, taking a water taxi to **Our Lady of the Rocks** and having a water-side lunch at the **Hotel Conte**.
- Drive to **Kotor** (a beautiful drive overlooking the fjord) and spend a few hours in the UNESCO World Heritage status walled city. Have dinner in the old town.

Day 3: Lovćen National Park

- Visit the **Njegoš Mausolem**, a must-see in the park, in the morning.
- If you're not too tired from hiking up the hundreds of steps, you can **rent a bike** from the **visitors center** and tool around, or just lounge around and be lazy at your hotel.

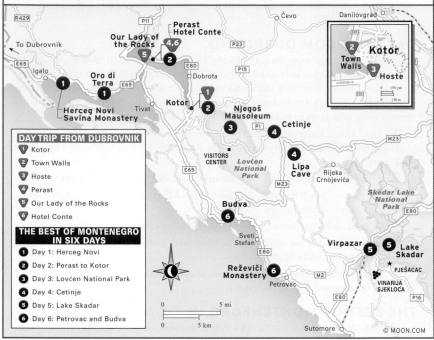

Montenegro Itinerary Ideas

DAY TRIP FROM DUBROVNIK
1. Kotor
2. Town Walls
3. Hoste
4. Perast
5. Our Lady of the Rocks
6. Hotel Conte

THE BEST OF MONTENEGRO IN SIX DAYS
1. Day 1: Herceg Novi
2. Day 2: Perast to Kotor
3. Day 3: Lovćen National Park
4. Day 4: Cetinje
5. Day 5: Lake Skadar
6. Day 6: Petrovac and Budva

Day 4: Cetinje

- Spend the morning in the historic capital of Montenegro, **Cetinje,** enjoying the museums and galleries in town.
- After lunch, if you are up for a little adventure, see the **Lipa Cave** in the afternoon.

Day 5: Lake Skadar

- Drive to **Virpazar** on Lake Skadar and take a boat tour, complete with lunch on a beach, with **Pješacac.**
- Spend your afternoon touring a local winery like **Vinarija Sjekloća** and tasting some of Montenegro's finest wines.

Day 6: Budva and Petrovac

- Spend the morning in **Budva's Old Town**, then head to **Perazica Do beach** for a waterside seafood lunch and a couple of hours of sunning and lazing on the beach.
- Head above the beach to visit the **Reževići Monastery** before heading back to Budva for dinner and a night out.

The Gulf of Kotor

The **Gulf of Kotor (Boka Kotorska)**, made up of four bays linked by narrow, mountain-lined straits, is a perfect natural harbor. The region has long been known for its shipping and seafaring, and in the Middle Ages, the area's seafaring men created its own Boka Navy, comprised of ships from Kotor and other gulf ports. Begun as a trading guild, the group became an important defense against pirates up until the 19th century.

Not as well known as Budva, but nonetheless far from undiscovered, the Gulf of Kotor is a stunning gem you should fit into your trip. Doable as a long day trip from Dubrovnik, the gulf is full of medieval fishing villages, from humble to somewhat grand; sparkling blue waters; a fjord-like bay ending in the famed town of Kotor; and quiet beaches out on the Luštica peninsula. Every type of traveler will find something to love here: Foodies will appreciate the reasonable and excellent restaurants; adventurers can trek, canyon, or kayak; and those hunting for luxury amongst the history can find designer boutiques and chic poolside lounging in the upscale development of Porto Montenegro.

Just south of the Gulf of Kotor, the coast of Montenegro slowly ebbs from busy Budva, filled to the brim with youthful beachgoers who light up its bars at night, to the luxe enclave of Sveti Stefan and those who come to photograph it. Winding further south are the beaches around Petrovac, filled with locals from both Montenegro and the region, enjoying a family vacation in the sun. While all of the Adriatic coast's towns have distinct personalities, and something for all types of travelers, it is quite easy to say that the southern coast of Montenegro is the most diverse, going from most-touristed to least, all in one small stretch of seaside.

★ HERCEG NOVI

A beautiful coastal town close to the border of Croatia, Herceg Novi is an excellent base from which to see the area. The town's ancient center, **Stari Grad (Old Town)**, is filled with a mix of architectural styles that reflect the many changes of power and influence throughout the centuries. While there aren't a lot of wide beaches here, the town has a wonderful six-kilometer (3.7-mile) promenade that hugs the sea and goes from one village to another, edged by the Mimosa trees Herceg Novi is famous for. They are so abundant that the city even has a festival dedicated to the flower, which blooms freely in this town that gets over 200 sunny days per year.

Sights
OLD TOWN
(Stari Grad)

Enter Herceg Novi's **Stari Grad** from Njegoševa ulica, a street of gleaming stones that ends at a café-lined square. From here you can climb to the 17th-century **clock tower (Sahat Kula)** (Trg Herceg Stjepana) built by the Turks when the tower served as the city's main gate. On Herceg Stjepan Square (Trg Herceg Stjepana), locally referred to as Belavista, is a lovely late-19th-century Orthodox church, the **Church of St. Archangel Michael** (Trg Herceg Stjepana, tel. 031/350-820, 7am-12am summer, 7am-9pm winter, free). Finished in 1911, the eclectic style of the building, mixing touches of Byzantine, Romanesque-Gothic, and Islamic architecture, is what makes it special.

Kanli Kula Fortress (Kanli Kula, tel. 031/323-072, 9am-7pm daily, €2), means "bloody tower." Built by the Turks in the 16th century, its original purpose was as a prison, and the prisoner's carvings can still be seen on the walls. Today it is a great viewpoint over the

Gulf of Kotor

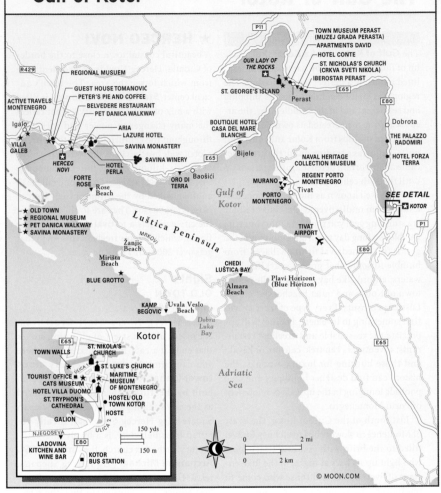

**TOWN MUSEUM PERAST
(MUZEJ GRADA PERASTA)
APARTMENTS DAVID
HOTEL CONTE
ST. NICHOLAS'S CHURCH
(CRKVA SVETI NIKOLA)
IBEROSTAR PERAST**

OUR LADY OF
THE ROCKS

ST. GEORGE'S ISLAND

Perast

Dobrota

REGIONAL MUSEUM

**GUEST HOUSE TOMANOVIĆ
PETER'S PIE AND COFFEE
BELVEDERE RESTAURANT
PET DANICA WALKWAY**

**ACTIVE TRAVELS
MONTENEGRO**

Igalo

**ARIA
LAZURE HOTEL
SAVINA MONASTERY**

**VILLA
GALEB**

**HERCEG
NOVI**

**HOTEL
PERLA**

SAVINA WINERY

**BOUTIQUE HOTEL
CASA DEL MARE
BLANCHE**

Bijele

**THE PALAZZO
RADOMIRI**

**HOTEL FORZA
TERRA**

**NAVAL HERITAGE
COLLECTION MUSEUM**

**FORTE
ROSE**

Rose
Beach

**ORO DI
TERRA**

Baošići

MURANO

**REGENT PORTO
MONTENEGRO**

Gulf of
Kotor

**PORTO
MONTENEGRO**

Tivat

SEE DETAIL

KOTOR

★ **OLD TOWN**
★ **REGIONAL MUSEUM**
★ **PET DANICA WALKWAY**
★ **SAVINA MONASTERY**

Luštica Peninsula

MRKOVI

**TIVAT
AIRPORT**

Žanjic
Beach

Mirišta
Beach

★
BLUE GROTTO

**CHEDI
LUŠTICA BAY**

Plavi Horizont
(Blue Horizon)

Almara
Beach

**KAMP
BEGOVIĆ**

Uvala Veslo
Beach

Dobra
Luka
Bay

Kotor

Adriatic
Sea

TOWN WALLS

**ST. NIKOLA'S
CHURCH**

ULICA 1

**TOURIST OFFICE
CATS MUSEUM
HOTEL VILLA DUOMO**

ST. LUKE'S CHURCH

**MARITIME
MUSEUM
OF MONTENEGRO**

**ST. TRYPHON'S
CATHEDRAL**

**HOSTEL OLD
TOWN KOTOR**

HOSTE

GALION

NJEGOSEVA

ULICA 2

0   150 yds

**LADOVINA
KITCHEN AND
WINE BAR**

**KOTOR
BUS STATION**

0   150 m

0   2 mi

0   2 km

© MOON.COM

town and serves as a venue for outdoor summer performances.

Not quite as impressive is the town's **Forte Mare** (Forte Mare, tel. 031/323-072, 9am-8pm daily, €2), built between the 14th and 17th centuries. The entry price mainly gets you some nice views and a walk around the old fort. You can also see what is left of the **Citadela** below the fortress. Built in the 18th century, it was a casualty of the 1979 earthquake.

If you are keen to visit a museum but don't want to venture out of the Old Town, try the **Josip Benković Art Gallery (Umjetnička Galerija Josip Benković)** (Ul. Marka Vojnovića 4, tel. 031/340-318, www.jbbgalerija. me, call for hours). The small gallery has an exhibition of Montenegrin artists and is associated with the regional museum, which is on the west side of town.

REGIONAL MUSEUM
(Zavičajni muzej)

On the west side of town, a small **Regional Museum (Zavičajni muzej)** (Ul. Mirka Komnenovića 9, 9am-9pm Fri.-Sat., €3) is located in a beautiful building and surrounding gardens, but the displays inside are fairly sparse.

PET DANICA WALKWAY
(Šetalište Pet Danica)

A great way to see the town and its surroundings is to walk along the **Šetalište Pet Danica**, a six-kilometer (3.7-mile) promenade that starts to the west of Herceg Novi, in Igalo, to the east in Meljine. It is named after five young girls, all named Danica, who fought and died in World War II. The route follows the path of an old railway line that connected the Montenegrin coast with Sarajevo. Today the promenade is lined with cafés, bars, and small beaches all along its edges.

SAVINA MONASTERY
(Manastir Savina)

Savina Monastery (Manastirska 21, tel. 031/345-300, 6am-8pm, free) is an orthodox monastery just east of Herceg Novi. The complex is composed of three buildings—the Great Church, the Small Church, and the Temple of St. Sava—according to legend built by St. Sava himself in the 13th century. While all of the grounds are covered with lush vegetation and have great views over the area, the Temple of St. Sava, set at the very top of the hill, has the best views of all. There is also a small treasury that can be visited for a small fee. Visitors are required to cover their legs and shoulders; garments are provided if you came ill-prepared.

On the grounds of the monastery you will see vineyards, which belong to the **Savina Winery** (Branka Ćopića 79, tel. 069/042-022, www.savina.me, call to reserve tour and tasting), and which can be toured with a prior reservation for tour and tasting.

Sports and Recreation

Herceg Novi is a great jumping-off point for many tours and sports activities. For those who would like to take a kayak tour, try **Kayak Herceg Novi** (www.kayak-hercegnovi.com) or **Montenegro Outdoors** (www.montenegrooutdoors.com), which also offers sailing classes and excursions. **Active Travels Montenegro** (www.activetravelsmontenegro.com) arranges rafting, canyoning, and trekking trips and more.

Festivals and Events

Herceg Novi is known for its **Mimosa Festival (Praznik Mimoze)** (www.hercegfest.me/praznik-mimoze), held in February during carnival season and at the height of the Mimosa tree blooms. The town comes alive with concerts, parades, performances, and, of course, displays of flowers.

Another time of year that is fun to visit is in early August during the **Montenegro Film Festival** (www.filmfestival.me), which has brought excellent European, documentary, and student films to the area for over thirty years. Much more accessible than larger festivals, it is a great treat for film buffs.

Late August brings the **Guitar Art Summer Fest** (www.hercegfest.me/festivali), an event celebrating international musicians in classical guitar.

Nightlife

Only steps away from each other in the Old Town are two really great bars. **Pub Got** (Stepenište 28 Oktobra 8, tel. 067/833-447, 8am-3am Mon.-Sat., 5pm-3am Sun.) is centrally located, and anyone looking for a good pub should head here. Local beers are also served if you like to sip brews as part of your travel experience. **Prostorija** (Stepenište 28 Oktobra 13, tel. 069/286-766, 8am-1am daily) is a friendly, artsy lounge with great music and reasonably priced drinks.

Food

Whether you are looking for breakfast, lunch, or coffee and cake any time of day, the vegetarian café and bakery ★ **Peter's Pie and Coffee** (Šetalište Pet Danica 18A, tel. 067/148-180, peterspie.wordpress.com, 8am-5pm daily, €5) won't disappoint. Start your day with an omelet or muffin, munch on a savory pie for brunch, or enjoy the daily vegetarian stew or soup (offered after 12pm) with house-baked bread. Smoothies, salads, teas, coffee, and even a nice wine list are on the menu too.

Tri Lipe (Stepinište 28. Oktobra, tel. 031/321-107, www.tri-lipe.com, 8:30am-11pm daily, €12) is extremely popular in summer due to its lovely shady terrace. Sometimes that means the food quality can suffer, but generally it is a reliable option for local meat and seafood dishes.

Oro di Terra (1a E65, Baošići, tel. 069/903-330, 8am-12am daily, €14) is located in the village of Baošići. With an extremely unique interior and some sea-view tables outside, the chef doles out tasty dishes, like their tuna steak, served with local wine.

If you are looking for a romantic atmosphere, **Belvedere Restaurant** (Manastirska 2, tel. 069/315-205, 10am-10pm daily, €12) is a mid-priced restaurant with a variety of mixed seafood and grill plates. The restaurant has a great terrace overlooking Boka Bay that elevates the solid cuisine to something special.

Accommodations

Walking distance to the Old Town, the bus station, and the beach, the **Guest House Tomanović** (Dr. Jova Bijelića 17, tel. 031/323-640, guest-house-tomanovic-me.book.direct, €30 d) is a great choice for budget travelers. The rooms are basic and a little outdated, but the owners are friendly, some apartments have lovely sea views, and there is free Wi-Fi and air-conditioning.

Possibly the best value for the price in Herceg Novi, the **Aria** (Braće Grakalica 63, tel. 068/068-765, guest-house-aria.herceg-novi.hotels-me.net, €50 d, including breakfast) is a long walk to town but only steps to the beach. The Aria has all the important boxes ticked: lovely rooms, friendly staff, and

an excellent breakfast, plus many rooms have sea-view balconies.

The ★ **Lazure** Hotel (Braće Pedišića bb, tel. 031/348-049, www.lazurehotel.com, €189 d, including breakfast) opened in 2018. The cozy 24-room hotel has three restaurants, two bars, and a beach just out front. Even better is the expert renovation of the 18th-century building, transforming rooms into modern, airy chill-out zones that are anything but cliché.

The waterfront **Hotel Perla** (Šetalište 5 Danica 98, tel. 031/345-700, www.perla.me, €166 d, including breakfast) is just a short walk along the boardwalk into the Old Town, yet far enough away from the nightlife for a good night's sleep.

A 12-room hotel, the **Boutique Hotel Casa del Mare Blanche** (Bijela bb, tel. 031/339-903, www.casadelmare.me, €180 d, including breakfast) is even quieter, and slightly out-of-town in the village of Bijela. Clean, fresh rooms, a good breakfast, and a small pool add to the coziness.

Information and Services

The main Herceg Novi **tourist office** (Trg Nikole Durkovića, tel. 031/350-820, www.hercegnovi.travel) is a good source of information on sights, activities, and accommodations in town. During the summers there are also several kiosks along the Šetalište Pet Danica.

Getting There and Around

Herceg Novi is only about 20 kilometers (12 miles) from the **Dubrovnik airport**. Depending on the time of day, the border crossing between Croatia and Montenegro at **Debelji Brijeg** can turn a short trip (under an hour) into a very long journey, with wait times reaching up to two and even three hours in the summer, so make sure to plan your trip accordingly. There is another crossing at Njivici, which is longer in distance but shorter in time during the height of the season (at the time of writing it is closed, but due to reopen in summer 2019). Up to 10 buses connect the

Dubrovnik airport with Herceg Novi daily and cost approximately €14. The travel time should be in line with car travel, though public transit only uses the main route, with the longest border crossing.

From the **Tivat airport**, there are multiple buses a day to Herceg Novi (www.busticket4. me, one hour, €3), but they aren't very frequent. Taxis will run you almost €40. A better option is to choose a hotel or guesthouse that can arrange a reasonable private transfer.

The **bus station** (Orjenski bataljon 3, tel. 031/321-225, www.busticket4.me) in Herceg Novi is a short walk to the Old Town. Multiple buses from Cetinje (2.5 hours), Budva, and Kotor (one hour), run by different carriers, all stop here, and tickets are under €10. Visit the listed website for a comprehensive schedule.

Taxi boats are a great way to get around the area, but the prices can get quite steep in summer, when demand rises. Negotiate to see what you're willing to pay and the driver is willing to accept. In the busy season, you will easily find many options in the marinas around town, with prices ranging from €20 to Rose or €75 to Tivat. One reliable option, except in the dead of winter, is **Montenegro Water Taxi** (www.watertaxi.info).

Around Herceg Novi
IGALO
Slightly to the west of Herceg Novi, reachable on foot by the Šetalište Pet Danica, is the village of **Igalo**. The walk is around 2.6 kilometers (1.6 miles) long and should take around half an hour. Known for its therapeutic muds and many sandy beaches that dip into shallow waters (only one meter/3.2 feet deep for some 250 meters/820 feet out). The town is also home to Tito's **Villa Galeb** (Sava Ilića 5, tel. 031/658-555, tours Mon., Wed., and Fri. at 6pm and 7:15pm, €3). One of the Yugoslav leader's summer homes, built in 1976, there is an entire floor of the villa dedicated to therapies for Tito's circulation problems, even though he only resided here four times in his life. The villa is a bit run-down, but it is hardly changed and the access to both state

and private rooms, including Tito's bedroom and private office, as well as the underground bomb shelter, are incredibly interesting.

MT. ORJEN NATIONAL PARK
Mt. Orjen, at 1,894 meters (6,213 feet), is the highest mountain on the Adriatic, part of the Dinaric Alps range. The mountain gets the highest rainfall in the country, which makes it a favorite for skiing in the winter. There are several treks up to Mt. Orjen that start in Herceg Novi, from one hour to five hours, with three mountain huts at various points where you can stop for rest and refreshment. A tour is a nice way to see the trek, either on foot or by mountain bike. One company to consider is **Be Active Montenegro** (www. beactive.me), who offer guided treks and mountain bike rentals.

PERAST
Small in size, but in a jewel-box sort of way, Perast is one of the most beautiful towns on the Montenegrin coast. With only 400 townspeople, but 16 churches and over a dozen Venetian-style palaces, the main draw of Perast are its tiny church-topped islands in the bay. There are no banks or ATMs in Perast, so bring cash, though most restaurants do accept credit cards.

Sights
★ OUR LADY OF THE ROCKS
(Crkva Gospe Skrpjela)
One of Montenegro's top tourist attractions, the island church of **Our Lady of the Rocks** (museum entry €1) is a must-see. You will find a variety of boat tours to the island from the entire area, but it is just in front of Perast and also accessible by taxi boat. Legend has it the island was created after a fisherman was miraculously healed and the locals began throwing rocks in the sacred spot for good luck. Dating from the 15th century, the church has a number of beautiful artifacts and paintings, but many might say it is the love stories that make the church so special (as well as its idyllic island position). You will find gold and

silver plates abound in the church, donated by families hoping to keep their loved ones safe at sea, but it is a needlepoint tapestry that is perhaps the most heartbreaking. A local woman worked on the tapestry for a quarter of a century, using her own hair for the angel's. If you look closely you can see the strands in the tapestry going from brown to gray as she waited for her love to return.

Visible from the church's island is the tiny **St. George's Island (Sveti Djordje)**. Home to a monastery, the island is not open to the public, but it is the source of a local legend. According to the story, a soldier was stationed on the island and during a skirmish, accidentally shot the girl he was in love with instead. Distraught over his mistake, he killed himself and they are reportedly both buried on the island.

ST. NICHOLAS'S CHURCH
(Crkva Sveti Nikola)
The 17th-century St. Nicholas's Church (8am-6pm daily, €1 for the treasury, €1 to climb the bell tower) is a small Catholic church that is charming, but not so impressive. The draw here is the bell tower, and the views you are rewarded with if you climb up all of the steps of the 55-meter-high (180-foot-high) tower (some parts have low ceilings that may be difficult for taller individuals).

TOWN MUSEUM PERAST
(Muzej Grada Perasta)
The small but well-executed **Town Museum Perast** (Obala Marka Martinovica, tel. 032/373-519, www.muzejperast.me, €4) has a nice selection of exhibits chronicling the town's history, maritime tradition, and costumes. The balcony of the museum, a 17th-century palace, is a great place to take photos.

Festivals and Events
On the evening of July 22, a parade of

1: Our Lady of the Rocks Church, Perast
2: St. Jerome Church in Herceg Novi 3: Kotor Bay, viewed from castle ruins in Kotor Town

decorated boats heads out toward Our Lady of the Rocks, throwing stones in the sea to celebrate the founding of the island at the **Fašinada Festival**. If you find yourself in town, make sure to snag a table at one of the restaurants along the waterfront, like the Hotel Conte, before the parade starts around 6:30pm. The festival also includes a two-day sailing regatta, the **Fašinada Cup** (www.fasinada-cup.com).

A festival to commemorate a 17th-century victory over the Turks held every May 15, the **Gadjanje Kokota** is something to be avoided by animal lovers, as the festivities are centered around the shooting of a rooster. There are also some cultural dances and processions held during the event.

Food and Accommodations
The **Apartments David** (Perast 126, tel. 067/591-271, €90 d) are located in an old 17th-century stone building in the town, easy walking distance to restaurants and the beach. The rooms are fresh, the owners friendly, and there is air-conditioning and free Wi-Fi. All units are equipped with kitchens and dining and living areas, with some units having great sea views.

The **Hotel Conte** (Obala Kapetana Marka Martinovića BB, tel. 032/373-687, www.hotelconte.me, €80 d, including breakfast) offers cozy rooms in the restaurant/hotel complex by the sea. The **restaurant** (10am-11pm daily, €18) serves great traditional cuisine, such as fish with almond or truffle sauce, grilled octopus, and lamb with polenta. The atmosphere is just as great, with dozens of outdoor tables for admiring the view toward Our Lady of the Rocks. The restaurant is the perfect place to snag a spot during the Fašinada festival.

New in 2018, the five-star ★ **Iberostar Perast** (Obala Kapetana Marka Martinovića BB, tel. 032/311-400, www.iberostar.com, €170 d) is located in a historic 18th-century palace on Perast's waterfront. The hotel has a spa, an excellent restaurant, and a speedboat that takes you on a five-minute journey to a private beach and beach club. The hotel can also arrange a number of excursions and sporting activities.

Getting There and Around

Buses from Kotor are frequent (around twice an hour), take only 30 minutes or so, and cost only €2 (www.busticket4.me). They do not technically go to Perast but stop on the main road at the top of town.

If you are parking, there are paid lots on both sides of town that cost around €2 per day. Cars are not allowed in town during the summer, but golf carts are available for a fee to shuttle you to the waterfront. Driving between Perast and Kotor is the fastest route any time of year, but you should be aware that the road is narrow and the roads can be quite busy in summer. The drive from Herceg Novi is around 45 minutes, and from Kotor less than half an hour.

★ KOTOR

Nestled between the mountains in a magical fjord-like bay, the walled city of Kotor is steeped in history from its days as an important port and home of sea captains and sailors along the Adriatic coast. Built between the 12th and 14th centuries, also known as Cattaro in Italian, the city is full of churches and palaces that have given it UNESCO World Heritage protected status. Though it's less polished than many of the popular towns along the Croatian coast, many travelers will appreciate the honesty of Kotor, in its glory and its scruffy bits. See that before it changes, as the town of around 3,000 is anything but undiscovered these days. The town's fortifications have survived the Illyrians, Romans, Byzantines, Venetians, Ottomans, and other invaders, as well as two major earthquakes. But they aren't likely to keep out the hordes of tourists who want a piece of this beautiful gem. Plan your visit around the cruise ships that stop here on their trip along the Adriatic to experience Kotor as it should be.

Sights

KOTOR TOWN WALLS
(Bedemi Grada Kotora)

There are three ways to enter the walled city of Kotor. The **Sea Gate**, built in 1555, is the most popular and most crowded way to enter. Until the 19th century, you could only enter the Sea Gate by boat, since the road and parking lot at the end of the bridge did not exist yet. Opposite the Sea Gate is the **clock tower**, built in 1602. It is said that it was tilted quite significantly to the west in the earthquake of 1667. Years of attempts to correct the tilt were fruitless, but the earthquake of 1979 knocked it back into place. Below the clock tower is a stone pyramid, called the **Pillar of Shame**, where guilty persons were embarrassed in front of the town.

The **Southern Gate**, also known as the **Gurdić Gate**, is only a five-minute walk away from the Sea Gate via the main road. It is an option to enter the town more quietly during the hustle of the tourist season. The **North Gate**, or **River Gate**, enters the city by way of a stone bridge that crosses the shortest river in Montenegro, the Škurda. Near the North Gate or near the Pjaca Salate (literally "salad plaza") are ways to enter the town walls.

Built from the 9th to the 19th centuries, the town walls (admission €3 May-Sept.) are over four kilometers (2.4 miles) long and climb up the hill over 200 meters (656 feet) to the San Giovanni fortress, where soldiers once defended Kotor. It is quite a hike, but the views are magnificent. The trek will take you around 45 minutes each way, but be aware it is a climb—around 1,350 steps to get there.

MARITIME MUSEUM OF MONTENEGRO
(Pomorski muzej Crne Gore)

The **Maritime Museum of Montenegro** (Trg Bokeljske Mornarice 391, tel. 032/304-720, www.museummaritimum.com, 8am-6pm Mon.-Sat., 9am-1pm Sun. Apr.-June and Sept., 8am-11pm Mon.-Sat., 10am-7pm Sun. July-Aug., 9am-5pm Mon.-Sat., 9am-12pm Sun. Oct.-Mar., €4) has been a city attraction since 1900. Located in an 18th-century Baroque palace, the museum's exhibits include ship models, portraits and paintings, weapons, furniture, uniforms, and maritime instruments.

ST. TRYPHON'S CATHEDRAL
(Katedrala Sveti Tripun)

St. Tryphon's Cathedral (Trg Sv. Tripuna, 8am-7pm daily, €2.50) was originally a rather humble Romanesque Catholic church dating from 1166. The current cathedral is a mix of styles due to reconstruction in the 17th century after an earthquake. The altarpiece, with Christ, the Virgin, and 18 other saints, was created by Kotor's goldsmiths in the early 15th century.

ST. LUKE'S CHURCH
(Crkva Sveti Luka)

Originally a Catholic church built in 1195, the Romanesque- and Byzantine-style **St. Luke's Church** (Crkva Sveti Luka) was given to the Orthodox church in the 19th century after almost two centuries of holding both Catholic and Orthodox services. It is the only building in Kotor that did not suffer damage in any of the city's earthquakes. The church is full of history, from the remnants of 12th-century frescoes to the church floor, made of tombstones of regular townspeople who were buried there until the 1930s.

ST. NIKOLA'S CHURCH
(Crkva Sveti Nikola)

St. Nikola's Church (Ulica 1, Trg Sv. Nikole, 8am-7pm daily, free) is a one-nave Orthodox church completed in 1909. Honoring St. Nicholas, the patron saint of sailors, there is an impressive iconostasis, a wall of icons, behind the altar. Even more unique are the large framed paintings of the four evangelists, Mark, Matthew, Luke, and John.

ST. OZANA'S CHURCH
(Blažena Ozana)

The Catholic **St. Ozana's Church** (Ulica 1, Trg od Drva, 8am-7pm daily, free), also called the Blessed Ozana (blažena Ozana), displays the preserved body of the nun the church is named after. Peaceful and extremely well-preserved (she died in 1565), Ozana is said to have saved the town from the Turks due to a vision and then spent the rest of her life in a cell devoting her life to prayer. The bronze doors of the church, a more recent addition to the 13th-century church, depict the life of Ozana and her story.

CATS MUSUEM
(Muzej mački)

If you've noticed the many cats around town, the descendants of centuries of ship cats from all over the world, you might not be surprised to find they have their own museum. The **Cats Museum** (Trg Gospa od Andjela, www.catsmuseum.org, €1) is very small—just two rooms of memorabilia—but the admission price goes to support local cats. You can even buy a bag of food in the gift shop to feed the cats you come across.

Sports and Recreation

There are two wonderful treks besides the town walls that active types may want to embark on from Kotor Town. The **Ladder of Kotor,** or the Ladder of Cattaro, is an ancient trail that once was the only connection between Kotor and the important inland town of Cetinje. Climbing up almost 1,000 meters (3,280 feet) to the Krstac pass, the trailhead starts just to the west of the Old Town. Quickly accelerating uphill, the trail has 72 switchbacks and is very well marked. You will reach the San Giovanni Fortress in around an hour, and from here you can continue to climb up the mountain or come back down along the town walls.

Škurda Canyon is a stunning trek, accessible by hiking from Kotor, but probably best traversed with a guide. Tunnels, waterfalls, and excellent views are all rewards for taking up the challenge, a 3-5-hour trip in total. **Kotor Bay Tours** (255 Dobrota, tel. 069/152-015, www.kotorbaytours.com) is a good option to try.

Festivals and Events

Kotor's **Carnival** in February is a popular and colorful event, with masked balls, processions, theater events, and concerts throughout the town for over a week. The town puts on a smaller Summer Carnival for tourists, usually in August.

Camellia Days (Dani Kamelije) is a celebration of the camellia flower, which blooms in March and April. Legend has it that in 1870 a sea captain brought a camellia back from Japan for his wife and it became a prized and popular flower in the area ever since. The festival has lovely flower displays, a ball, and a queen of sorts, the Lady of the Camellia.

In the summer, **Kotor Art** (www.kotorart. me) is a festival in four parts with international presentations in music, children's theater, philosophy, architecture, and the local *klapa* music from the end of June to mid-August.

Typically held the third Saturday of August, the **Boka Night (Bokeska noć)** is a celebration of the town, with a procession and contest for most beautifully decorated boat, followed by dancing and music, and ending with a fireworks display.

Food

For cheap and convenient eats, the **Hoste** (263 Stari Grad, www.hoste.com, 10am-10pm daily, €5) tapas bar has a variety of great wines and cocktails and small plates, including mixed salads, olives and cheese, fried calamari, and *kurkuma* (chickpea and turmeric) fritters on lentils. It's located just outside the Southern Gate (vrata Gurdića).

The charming **Ladovina Kitchen and Wine Bar** (Njegoševa 209, tel. 063/422-472, www.ladovina.me, 8am-1am Mon.-Sat., 8am-12am Sun., €12) has a lovely terrace and excellent local cuisine such as mussels, seafood pasta, steak, and a good selection of vegetarian dishes as well.

For a meal with a view, head to **Galion** (Suranj bb, tel. 032/325-054, www.galion.me, 12pm-12am daily, €25) on the Kotor harbor a short walk from the Old Town. Beef carpaccio, excellent seafood dishes, and a strong wine list—and, of course, the view—make for a special night out.

Accommodations

Possibly the only hostel in the world with a 700-year-old water spout in its kitchen, the **Hostel Old Town Kotor** (Stari Grad 284, tel. 032/325-317, www.hostel-kotor.me, from €17 pp) is located in a 13th-century building within the Old Town walls. Rooms are cozy, with exposed-stone walls, and the hostel offers bike rental, a pub crawl, and a great tour for reasonable prices. The hostel also has a few private rooms if you are done with dormitory-style accommodations.

A boutique hotel with 13 apartments, the **Hotel Villa Duomo** (Stari Grad 385, tel. 032/323-111, www.villaduomo.com, from €120 d, including breakfast) is in the heart of the Old Town in a lovely old villa. The hotel has great service and an excellent breakfast. Do be aware that though the attic room is spacious and very cool, it might not be the best choice if you aren't comfortable with a loft-style bed. Other rooms do not share this feature.

A 10-minute drive from Kotor, the **Hotel Forza Terra** (Dobrota bb, tel. 067/370-370, www.hotelforzaterra.com, €270 d, including breakfast) is a relaxing getaway from the tourist bustle of Kotor. Situated on the waterfront, the hotel has a good restaurant and bar, as well as a small pool and spa.

★ **The Palazzo Radomiri** (Dobrota 220, tel. 032/333-176, www.palazzoradomiri.com, from €180 d, including breakfast) is an excellent splurge if you are visiting Kotor. A short drive out of town keeps the place peaceful, and you can enjoy the peace on the rooftop lounge at sunset, napping or reading a book from the hotel library in a hammock, or dining on the private pier in the evening. The restored 18th-century captain's mansion has beautifully decorated rooms and a variety of activities, including a pool, complimentary morning yoga, and an eight-kilometer (five-mile) seafront promenade for a jog with a view.

Information and Services

The **Tourist Office of Kotor** (Stari Grad 328, tel. 032/325-950, www.tokotor.me, 8am-8pm daily July-Sept., 8am-2pm Mon.-Fri. Oct.-June) offers maps and information, as well as help in arranging accommodations. It is conveniently located next to the post office. Plan your visit to Kotor town by seeing when cruise ships are docked at www.crew-center.com. Planning for when the ships have departed will mean your visit to the town will be a lot quieter.

Getting There and Around

The main **bus station** (Ul. Put prvoboraca bb, tel. 032/325-809, www.autobuskastanicakotor.me, 6am-10pm daily) has hourly connections from Budva (one hour), Herceg Novi (one hour), and Tivat (20 minutes) for under €10. There are multiple operators and lines running from each of these destinations. The website listed above can give you a comprehensive schedule. Bus connections from Dubrovnik are also available but can take up to six hours depending on the line and the border wait time that day. These tickets cost around €18.

From Herceg Novi, the trip takes just over an hour by car (43 kilometers/26 miles). From Dubrovnik, plan on driving at least two hours, or even four or five at the busiest times in high season (92 kilometers/57 miles).

Within the walled city of Kotor, the best way to get around is on foot.

TIVAT AND PORTO MONTENEGRO

If you are tiring of picture-perfect cobblestone fishing villages, head to Tivat and Porto Montenegro (www.portomontenegro.com) for something completely different. A redevelopment of an old naval base, the town is dedicated to tourism, with a swank hotel and marina for the yachting set. You can visit the informative **Naval Heritage Collection Museum** (9am-4pm Mon.-Fri., 1pm-5pm Sat., €2-5) to see a history of the shipyard and Montenegro's naval past,

including two dry-docked Yugoslav submarines. You will also find a variety of **luxury shopping** and even an **English language bookstore** in town.

Tivat is also home to coastal Montenegro's **airport**, which offers connections to Belgrade, Brussels, London, and several cities in Russia. The busiest airport in the country, it has a variety of standard as well as low-cost carriers such as Eurowings and EasyJet.

Food and Accommodations

The real draw of Porto Montenegro is its five-star hotel, the ★ **Regent Porto Montenegro** (Obala bb, tel. 032/660-660, www.regenthotels.com, €310 d). The hotel has two wings: the Venezia, with rooms and suites decorated to mimic being aboard a luxury liner, and the Aqua wing, with a more modern aesthetic. The resort has a spa, several pools, a gym, tennis courts, and several bars and restaurants. The chef at the best restaurant, the ★ **Murano** (tel. 032/660-682, 7am-10pm winter, 7am-11pm summer, €35), trained at famed Noma in Copenhagen before returning to the region to show off his culinary magic. Porto Montenegro is also home to dozens of shops from international brands like Burberry and Rolex, as well as a selection of other restaurants, bars, and clubs. Prices are higher than what you might pay in other parts of Montenegro.

LUŠTICA PENINSULA

Once a pristine peninsula dotted with olive groves and picturesque fishing villages, the beauty of the Luštica Peninsula has not gone unnoticed. It is quickly becoming a hot spot for luxury developments like the Chedi Luštica Bay hotel, built to resemble one of the local villages and blend into the surroundings. The peninsula is also home to several excellent beaches.

From Oblatno on the easternmost side of the peninsula to Rose on the western tip, it is only about a 30-minute drive.

Beaches

Your impression of Luštica's **Blue Grotto (Plava Špilja)** probably depends upon when you went and which boat you took. The iridescent blue waters of the grotto can be otherworldly and an excellent experience if you are able to enjoy them in peace. In the summer, a glut of tourist boats can crowd the grotto, making it not so pleasant and even a little dangerous. Until the boat entry is better organized, try to take a boat very early or late in the day to avoid the busiest times during the summer. In other times of the year it should be reasonably quiet no matter when you go. Also check on how long the boat operator stays in the grotto. Is there time for a swim if you want one? **Montenegro Water Taxi** (www.watertaxi.info) is a good operator with a solid three-hour tour, which includes time for photos, and snorkeling or swimming.

There are multiple good beaches on the peninsula. **Žanjic beach** is long, backed by olive trees for shade, covered in tiny white pebbles, and has a variety of places to eat and drink. All this good doesn't come without hundreds (even up to a thousand) people every day in the summer, so just be aware you will have company.

Mirišta Beach is also popular, with a good beachside restaurant and an old Austro-Hungarian fortress at its tip. If you walk over there you are likely to find a more secluded spot. Or take a minute boat ride from Mirišta to Dobreč beach, a more secluded beach with loungers and its own seafood restaurant.

Uvalo Veslo is not as accessible as some of the other beaches, but if you are looking for something more remote and breathtaking, this is it. Its rocky, and there are plenty of cliffs that aren't safe for children, but it is a much more secluded spot and is great for snorkelers. If you want to hire a boat for the day, there are small beaches in **Dobra Luka Bay** that are excellent, but only reachable by water.

Another beach that is less crowded and a little more upscale is the **Almara Beach Club** (www.almara.me) in Oblatno. There is a shallow sandy beach, a variety of lounge chairs, a bar with a DJ, and a floating pier the kids love.

Plavi Horizont (Blue Horizon) beach is a wide semicircular stretch of sand backed by a pine forest and often described as the best in Montenegro, though what one likes in a beach can be very personal. The beach was threatened by a giant five-star development, but the backers had pulled out at the time of writing, meaning that Plavi Horizont will continue on its public course for the time being.

At the very end of the peninsula is the village of **Rose**, at the entrance to the Bay of Kotor, which gently buzzes in summer when a few restaurants open for the season. It is easier to reach the village by boat from Herceg Novi than by car on the peninsula.

Food and Accommodations

Kamp Begović (Ponta Veslo, tel. 069/340-430, pontaveslo@gmail.com, €5 pp) is a lovely place to camp not only for its position among the shade of dozens of olive trees, but for its position near Uvalo Veslo and other great beaches that can be accessed from the campsite. The campsite is basic (no electricity), but there are showers and toilets.

Forte Rose (Rose, tel. 067/377-311, www.forterose.me, €100 d) is a restaurant and hotel located in the precious little hamlet of Rose in an old stone fortress. The restaurant serves local specialties in an idyllic waterside setting under the shade of pines. The hotel has a few apartments and suites that are clean and fresh, with all the basic amenities like air-conditioning and a good breakfast. The hotel lists soundproofing as an amenity, but when you sleep in a fortress, would you expect anything less?

The first of seven planned hotels in Luštica Bay by the Asian luxury hotel chain Chedi, ★ **Chedi Luštica Bay** (Luštica Bay Marina, tel. 032/661-266, www.chedilusticabay.com, €240 d) opened its doors in July 2018. The hotel was planned to blend into its surroundings and resemble a typical Montenegrin coastal village. It offers restaurants and lounges, a spa, an indoor spa pool, and a three-level heated outdoor infinity pool, as well as a private beach nearby.

Getting There and Around

The best way to get to the Lustica Peninsula is by car, absolutely necessary if you want to visit the beaches easily. From Herceg Novi to the heart of the peninsula, expect to drive just under two hours, while from Kotor driving time is around one hour. Another great option is to visit the village of Rose by water taxi from Herceg Novi, which should run between €15 and €20.

Budva Coast

★ BUDVA

Budva, on the coast just south of the Gulf of Kotor, is the most-visited town in Montenegro, and for good reason. By day there is the charming Stari Grad (Old Town) to visit with loads of charm and good places to eat. The beaches are super and by night the town comes alive. As the country's most popular destination, you will find loads of fellow visitors, particularly from Russia, but also lots of spots to wine and dine in this tourist mecca.

Sights
CITADEL
(Citadela)

Located at the southern side of town is the Citadel (9am-12am June-Sept., 9am-5pm Oct.-May, €3.50), which dates from at least 1425. There is a small **museum,** but the best parts are the views. The entrance and exit of the town walls (€2) is located here, where you can walk along the ramparts for an overview of the city and some nice photographs. Be aware that there is only one way in and out, so if you are visiting during a busy season, going early in the morning is a good idea.

Built into the town walls are two small churches. **Catholic St. Mary's in Punta** (Crkva Sveti Marije, sporadically open) was built in the year 840 and is the oldest of all the churches in Budva. Today it hosts art exhibitions and concerts. **St. Sava's Church** (Crkva Sv Save, sporadically open) was named after the founder of the Serbian Orthodox church.

HOLY TRINITY CHURCH
(Crkva Svete Trojice)

When the Venetian republic fell in 1797, the Orthodox residents of Budva asked Austria to allow them to build a church. The small **Church of the Holy Trinity** (8am-12pm and 5pm-7pm daily, free) was finished in 1804. Inside there is an impressive iconostasis by Greek iconographers and vividly painted ceilings.

ST. JOHN'S CHURCH
(Crkva Sveti Ivana)

Existing in Budva since the 7th century, the **Catholic Church of St. John** (sporadically open, free) suffered significant damage in the earthquake of 1667 and has undergone several reconstructions and additions in the centuries since. One of these additions was its bell tower, visible from much of Budva, which was completed in 1867. The inside of the church, if you are lucky enough to find it open, is relatively unadorned, especially compared to its Orthodox neighbor. A 12th-century icon known as the Madonna of Budva and a 40-square-meter (430-square-foot) glass mosaic by Croatian painter Ivo Dulcić are two interesting and important works inside the church.

THE MODERN GALLERY OF BUDVA
(Moderna galerija Budva)

Behind the facade of an ancient building, the **Modern Gallery of Budva** (Cara Dušana 19, tel. 033/451-343, 8am-2pm and 5pm-9pm Mon.-Fri., free) displays contemporary regional artists and is a nice stop for art fans.

THE CITY MUSEUM OF BUDVA
(Muzej grada Budve)

The **City Museum of Budva** (Petra i Petrovića 11, tel. 033/453-308, 9am-8pm Tues.-Fri., 2pm-8pm Sat.-Sun., €3) centers around a permanent exhibition of archaeological and ethnographic displays, collected from sites around Budva dating back to the 5th century BC. Lower floors focus on ancient artifacts while the top floor displays more recent memorabilia and traditional costumes. The only downside to the museum is that there is little information to accompany the objects on display.

PODMAINE MONASTERY
(Manastir Podmaine)

The **Podmaine Monastery** (www.manastirpodmaine.org, open daily, services at 5am and 4pm Mon.-Sat., 8:30am Sun. and holidays, free), also referred to as Podostrog, is located two kilometers (1.2 miles) north of the Old Town. You can arrive at the monastery by foot or by car.

The monastery is thought to date from the 15th century. It was here that Petar Drugi Petrović Njegoš wrote parts of his famous *The Mountain Wreath*, considered by many Montenegrins as their greatest work of literature, and he also died here in 1735. There are two churches in the monastery complex. The larger church, the **Great Temple of the Assumption**, was significantly damaged in the 1979 earthquake. When it was rebuilt, around 2000, the frescoes were repainted to include former Yugoslav leader Tito on his way to hell in the Last Judgment. The smaller church, the **Little Church of the Assumption,** is located underneath the cells of the monastery, only four meters (13 feet) long by 2.5 meters (8 feet) wide. There is a terrace above the church with excellent views of the sea.

Oftentimes, monks will offer to take you around the monastery. One interesting souvenir to purchase from the monastery is a *brojanica*, a bracelet made of beads of string that are often worn on the left wrist by locals.

Beaches

The Budva Rivijera is some 38 kilometers (23.6 miles) long, with multiple beaches that are usually filled with tourists on rented loungers during the summer. Quiet it's not. If you are seeking something more mellow, head to **Sveti Nikola island,** or south towards **Petrovac.**

Just outside the Old Town walls, near the hotel Avala, is **Richard's Head (Ričardova Glava)** beach. The beach was named after actor Richard Widmark, who filmed the movie *The Long Ships* here in 1964. The beach is popular with young locals, but in the early morning it is fairly empty.

Continue past the Hotel Avala and you will find a **statue** of a naked dancer on the rocks that is a popular photo op. A little further on is the **Mogren Beach**, actually two beaches connected by a natural tunnel. The sea in front is clear and beautiful, but it can be rough when windy. You can rent two chairs and an umbrella for €15. It is crowded in summer and a little run down, but the cliffs and water off the beach are lovely and it is convenient, only 100 meters (328 feet) from the Old Town.

Slovenska Beach (Slovenska plaža) is the largest beach in Budva, but unfortunately also the most crowded and dirtiest. It does have lounge chairs for rent, plus basketball, volleyball, and restaurants and bars along the long promenade that connects to the Old Town. However, your time is likely better spent seeking out a nicer spot to sun and swim.

Sveti Nikola Island is locally known as Hawaii by the locals. Just off the shore of Budva you can buy a water taxi ticket for around €3. Though you won't find the beach undiscovered by any means, and the shores are rockier, you can get away from *some* of the crowd here. There are lounge chairs for rent and you can bring your own food or purchase from the vendors at the beach.

It's not cheap, but if you've traveled this

1: Budva 2: Sveti Stefan beach 3: Njegoš Mausoleum 4: Orthodox Cetinje Monastery

far, consider splurging on a beach package at the ★ **Dukley Beach Lounge** (www.dukleylounge.com, 9am-11pm daily July-Sept. 15, 10am-6pm daily Sept. 15-30, contact regarding other times). With a free hourly taxi boat from Budva's Old Town (in summer), the packages cost between €50-100 and come with two sunbeds, an umbrella, fluffy towels, a bottle of champagne, fresh fruit, and two bottles of water. The three beaches are pristine, each with their own vibe. If you get hungry, there is a great restaurant, and you can also book a massage. If you plan to stay all day, it may be worth the price, especially if you are not staying at a fancy hotel with its own private beach.

Festivals and Events

The **Sea Dance Festival** (www.seadancefestival.me, one weekend in late summer, usually Aug.) is held on one of the Budva Rivijera beaches (locations can change from year to year). The festival brings international, regional, and local bands to the stage for a music-filled weekend. The vibe is decidedly youthful.

Mackerel Day (first Saturday in October) has been an occasion in Budva for almost 50 years. A parade and old-fashioned sports competitions accompany a plethora of fish, wine, and local specialties just outside the town walls.

Nightlife

If you are looking for good craft beer and a cozy atmosphere, **Casper Bar** (Cara Dušana 10, tel. 033/402-290, 10am-2am daily), conveniently located in the Old Town, won't disappoint. Just down the way, **Stara Budva** (Cara Dušana, 8am-1am daily), near the Old Town walls, is a café by day and often has live acoustic acts on summer and weekend nights.

Hacienda (Mediteranska, tel. 068/227-994, hours claim always open) is a bar with a Latin vibe and great cocktails. Summer parties also include Latin dancing and plenty of ambience.

Budva is known for its big discos and party ambience. There are several to choose from

but all of them get mixed reviews. There are often complaints of being overcharged, of waiters being upset if they aren't tipped, and Serbian music nights just not being the ticket for foreign tourists. Be aware of these, and check what's on that night to avoid disappointment. **Top Hill** (Topliški Put bb, www.tophill.me, 11pm-5am July-Aug., entrance varies with show) is a well-known open-air nightclub with space for 5,000 people. The acts can be quite good, but be aware that at the time of writing there is no dance floor, just loads of standing tables where you are expected to order. It is walkable from the Old Town, which takes about an hour, so a taxi is probably a better option.

Trocadero (Mediteranska 4, tel. 069/069-086, 11pm-5am Fri.-Sat., additional days in summer, entrance varies with performance) has been on Budva's nightlife scene for 25 years, but it's still just as relevant. While the cover fee tends to be cheaper than Top Hill, and there is a dance floor, some acts can be decidedly local, depending on your music tastes. Located on the Slovenska beach.

Food

Budva is a tourist mecca with dozens of restaurants to choose from. Most are quite good, though it isn't necessarily the foodie paradise you might expect from such a touristed city.

For a quick bite, **Verde** (Velji Vinogradi bb, tel. 069/222-269, 8am-10pm daily, €5) has great sandwiches, salads, and kebabs at very reasonable prices. It's a to-go atmosphere, without any tables for sitting, but excellent for a picnic. If you are looking for good quality local cuisine, try **Kafana Rivijera** (Trg Palmi, tel. 068/299-759, 8am-11pm daily, €12), with a lovely atmosphere, some outdoor seating, and a pleasant staff. Risotto, seafood, mussels, *pašticada*, and local wine are all on offer. The modern ambience at **Forsage Gastro Lounge** (29 Novembra 24, tel. 067/001-008, 8am-11pm daily, €14) sets the scene for well-presented food. One of the best dishes on the menu is the tuna steak, done to perfection.

The Turkish restaurant ★ **Dvorište by**

Bahçe (Cara Dušana 5, tel. 068/497-173, 12pm-11pm daily, €10) is one of the nicest places to eat in central Budva. The restaurant has a giant outdoor terrace, covered with grapevines and illuminated by lanterns. The food, both Turkish and local, is excellent and the prices are very reasonable. For the best experience, try the Turkish specialties like the stew in a clay pot, kebabs, and *çökertme*.

Accommodations
STARI GRAD

The **Freedom Hostel Budva** (Cara Dušana 21, tel. 067/783-7110, €20 pp) and the **Freedom Hostel 2** (Trg Palmi Budva, tel. 067/783-7110, €20 pp) are both conveniently located walking distance from sights, restaurants, and bars. Both hostels have Wi-Fi, no smoking, air-conditioning, a shared kitchen, and cozy lounge areas. Freedom Hostel 2 is newer, has more private room options, and is a no-party hostel, the best choice if you are looking for a quiet night's sleep.

The best thing about the **Astoria Boutique Hotel** (Njegoševa 4, tel. 033/451-110, www.astoriamontenegro.com, €80 d) is its location, inside the city walls with many rooms sporting balconies overlooking the beach or the Old Town. There is also a small private beach and a roof terrace for dinner with excellent views. Guests should know that rooms are on the small side and bathrooms fairly basic. There is also an extra charge for parking and sunbeds, but the location really can't be beat.

OUTSIDE STARI GRAD

The Queen of Montenegro is undergoing a complete renovation and in spring 2019 will open as the **Falkensteiner Hotel Budva** (Ulica Narodnog fronta bb, tel. 033/685-000, www.queenmontenegro.com, €150 d, including breakfast). The hotel has indoor and outdoor pools, a spa, and restaurants, and it is a quick walk to the beach.

An excellent value for the money, the ★ **Hotel Poseidon** (Jaz Beach, tel. 069/411-240, www.poseidon-jaz.com, €112 d, including breakfast) is located on Jaz Beach, one of the nicest beaches around Budva, though the public portion can get so crowded it loses its appeal. Staying at the Hotel Poseidon solves that problem with its private portion of Jaz lined with attractive sunbeds and umbrellas, included with your stay, for a more luxurious experience on the beach. The rooms are nice and fresh and the food in the restaurants is quite good. The hotel has an arrangement with a local taxi service that can take you to Stari Grad for only €5.

★ **Dukley Hotel and Resort** (Jadranski put, Zavala Peninsula, tel. 069/170-777, www.dukleyhotels.com, €400 d, including breakfast) is a luxurious choice on the Zavala Peninsula. The hotel offers spacious rooms, three private beaches, excellent food, a spa, and a kids club. In the summer there is a free taxi boat to Budva's Stari Grad, and you can also pay for your stay with cryptocurrency.

Information and Services

Tourist information can be found at the **Budva Tourist Info Center** (Njegoševa 28, http://budva.travel, 8am-4pm Mon.-Fri., extended hours and various pop-up info centers around the area in summer), which can help with information on attractions, accommodations, and more.

Getting There and Around

Multiple buses from all around Montenegro arrive daily at the city's main **bus station** (tel. 033/456-000, www.balkanviator.com). Bus trips from Herceg Novi cost €7 and take two hours, while a trip from Kotor costs €4 and takes about 45 minutes. Buses from Petrovac and Sveti Stefan (20 minutes, €2) also arrive at this station almost hourly throughout the day.

By car, travel times from Kotor or Cetinje are only around half an hour. From Herceg Novi, it will take about an hour and a half. Well-marked parking areas are easily found in Budva.

Taxis in Budva, as in much of Montenegro, are quite likely to take you for a ride, in more than one way. Calling a reputable taxi service is the best way to not get overcharged. **Eco Taxi** (dial 19567 from a local phone, www.taxibudva.com) is one company that seems quite reliable. Alternatively, have your hotel help you get a taxi with a set fare.

Around Budva

KRAPINA

Krapina is a small village only five kilometers (three miles) from Budva. The small ethno village has an excellent fish restaurant, **Pojata** (Krapina, tel. 069/024-587, 11am-7pm daily, €15-20). Near the restaurant is a waterfall-fed swimming hole. If you are ready for something completely different than the tourist madness of Budva, this is the place to go.

SVETI STEFAN

When people say "Sveti Stefan," they are usually referring to the highly exclusive island, now an uber-posh Aman resort with an equally posh price tag, open only to paying guests. However, the area on the mainland is free. It's a great vantage point for taking photos of the picture-perfect Sveti Stefan island, and there is an edge of pink pebbly beach available for lounging without paying a day-use fee.

However, given that Sveti Stefan is Montenegro's most-photographed site and quite a treat to visit, it is worth the splurge to book a meal on the island, which grants you partial access to this exclusive paradise, quite possibly one of the most unique resorts in the world.

Famed for its pebbly beach and unspoiled fortified island village, Sveti Stefan has a very interesting history. Built with treasure from the spoils of a successful local campaign to defeat the Ottomans, Sveti Stefan dates from the 15th century. By the 1950s, though, only twenty people remained on the island, so the country nationalized what was left and opened a swank hotel in the 1960s. Some of the biggest stars of the day stayed here, including Sophia Loren, Doris Day, and Princess Margaret. After the breakup of Yugoslavia,

it became an Aman resort in 2007 and once again hosts today's top celebrities.

Sights

Budget travelers can get glimpses and tastes of Sveti Stefan from shore. Parking can be difficult, but if you can find a space, here's what you should see.

SVETI STEFAN BEACH

Sveti Stefan Beach is actually two beaches divided by the bridge heading to the island resort. The beach to the left of the bridge is free. The beach to the right belongs to the Aman resort. Its pebbles are finer, along with the price of sitting there. You can pay a day-use fee to join the exclusive side, around €100 for a set of two lounge chairs, table, and umbrella. It is lovelier in photos than in reality. If you want to see Sveti Stefan, save your money for lunch and take photos of the island from the municipal side of the beach.

MILOČER PARK

At the northern end of Sveti Stefan Beach, Park Miločer was the summer destination for the relatively short-lived dynasty of the royal Serbian Karađorđević family. Their residence, Villa Miločer, is now part of the Aman resort. Though you can't use the pristine Queen's Beach, an alcove once the favorite of Queen Marija Karađorđević, or King's Beach, both part of the Aman resort, it is worth your time to walk through the park's cypress- and olive-lined promenade. The path starts at the Olive Restaurant.

CRVENA GLAVICA

Often mistaken online for the beaches directly in front of Sveti Stefan island, this is actually a grouping of several red-rocked beaches two kilometers (1.2 miles) from Sveti Stefan in the direction of Petrovac. There are some great spots for a dip here, and not too many people, but definitely a fair share of nudists. The beaches are steep and are not recommended for children or those with mobility issues.

Food

Sveti Stefan, both the exclusive island and not, is not quite a foodie paradise, but the food is good. If you are traveling with kids, the **Olive Restaurant** (Sv Stefan bb, tel. 069/187-988, 9am-12am daily, €15) at the entrance to Miločer Park is a great choice due to the large playground next door. The views are super, and the Mediterranean cuisine hits the spot after a walk along the promenade.

If you can snag a terrace table overlooking the water, **Famelja Kentera** (Slobode 24, tel. 069/231-922, 8am-12am daily, €14) is a good choice, serving solid Mediterranean cuisine. They offer other items like burgers, but stick to the local stuff and you should be happy.

Paštrovića Dvori (Blizikuće, tel. 033/468-162, 12pm-11pm daily, €12) is a must-stop, particularly if you traveled the Croatian or Montenegrin coasts in the 1990s or early 2000s. Go there for a cozy, homey atmosphere with good local cuisine including cheese plates, grilled squid, fish, and *blitva* (swiss chard and potatoes). This is a restaurant with a view, and it is wise to try to time your meal for a little before sunset.

On the Aman Sveti Stefan there are several restaurants and bars, but most are closed from October to May, as is the main resort. The **restaurant at Vila Miločer** (Sveti Stefan, tel. 033/420-000, www.aman.com, €30) stays open all year and offers similar cuisine to the Piazza Restaurant. The **Piazza** (Sveti Stefan, tel. 033/420-000, www.aman.com, €20), on a stone terrace shaded by olive trees, is a good spot to make reservations at if you want to get on the island without breaking the bank. The Mediterranean cuisine is good—risottos, locally sourced cheese, pizzas—but maybe not what you would expect for the price or the place. The resort has just opened a new Italian restaurant, **Arva** (Sveti Stefan, tel. 033/420-000, www.aman.com, €35), based on seasonal cuisine served family style. **Nobu** (Sveti Stefan, tel. 033/420-000, www.aman.com, €40) is another option at the Aman, but reviews seem to be quite mixed as to whether it lives up to the reputation of the brand.

Accommodations

With fabulous views over Sveti Stefan island, **Vila Drago** (Slobode 32, tel. 069/032-050, www.viladrago.com, €55 d) has parking and air-conditioning, and all of the spacious rooms have balconies or terraces, many with views to the sea. There is a stairway (around 200 steps) leading down to the public beach and a restaurant for breakfast, lunch, and dinner.

The ★ **Aman Sveti Stefan** (Sveti Stefan, tel. 033/420-000, www.aman.com, €750 d, including breakfast) is the premier resort in Montenegro. The hotel has two choices for accommodations: the Aman Sveti Stefan Island (open June-Sept.) and the Vila Miločer (open year-round). The island portion consists of the original village of Sveti Stefan, with the buildings restored to house rooms, services, and restaurants. Some guests, used to the spacious and often light-filled architecture at Aman resorts around the world, may find this quite a departure from the brand's aesthetic. However, it must be appreciated that instead of constructing an "authentic" copy or demolishing a beautiful piece of history, they have transformed it. The Vila Miločer is the historic villa of the royal family and is located just behind Queen's beach.

Getting There and Around

Coming from Budva, there are several buses per hour (20 min, €2) in summer and at least an hourly bus in winter via the Mediteran Express line (tel. 033/451-567). The hourlong bus trip (€5) from Kotor departs at least hourly (more frequently in summer).

There is parking at the beach that runs around €2 per hour. The roads leading here are steep and windy, though, so drive carefully.

PETROVAC

More laid-back than Budva but still full of devil-may-care real estate development, there are some charming pockets to discover in Petrovac as well as a good selection of hotels and beaches. The town was originally settled by the Romans and there are still some remnants of their stay. The waterfront promenade and harbor are a great place to walk, and it is a nice choice for families looking for reasonably priced accommodations and a nice beach.

Sights

The small 16th-century Venetian fortress **Fort Lastva (Kaštel Lastva)**, also known as Kastio, at the northern end of the harbor, was built to discourage pirates and serve as a storehouse for exports of wine and olive oil. Today, a climb atop the fortress affords a few nice views.

In the distance you will see two small islets, **Katič** and **Sveti Nedljeja**. The latter is topped with a small church, built in thanks for the islet saving a few sailors' lives after a shipwreck. Rent a kayak, or hire a water taxi to take you to the islet should you like to visit.

There are also some **Roman mosaics** in town from the 3rd or 4th century, discovered in 1902. These are located in a rather shabby glass structure amongst an olive garden off Mirište street.

Beaches

Petrovac beach, next to the harbor, is covered in small red pebbles and is a good beach for children. It is extraordinarily crowded in summer due to the apartments and hotels backing it. The **Lućice beach** is a little quieter, 500 meters (1,640 feet) south of town in a beautiful cove. Even less crowded is **Buljarica beach**, about a 45-minute walk from Petrovac. Over two kilometers (1.2 miles) long, the beach itself is not as pretty as Lućice, but it is usually less crowded.

Festivals and Events

Petrovac Night (August) is an all-day festival of fish, wine, and sweets. Concerts from regional stars and fireworks top off the evening.

Food

Though the restaurant looks like nothing special, the best place to eat in Petrovac is ★ **Fat**

Boys Kafana (2 Ulica Br. 65, tel. 033/475-013, 12pm-11pm daily, €10). The excellent food (including burgers, kebabs, seafood, and fish soup) and the extremely friendly staff make this place a must.

Konoba Mediterraneo (Obala 17, tel. 068/462-461, www.mediterraneo.me, 12pm-12am daily, €12) has a super setting, a shady terrace courtyard on the waterfront promenade. The food is solid and usually well-prepared local fare. It is also a nice stop for coffee and cake.

Accommodations

The campsite **Camping Maslina** (Buljarica bb, tel. 068/602-040, www.campingmaslina. com, €5 pitch and €3.50 pp) has a peaceful atmosphere amongst a centuries-old olive grove. Two hundred meters (656 feet) from the beach and a half hours' walk to Petrovac, the campsite also offers toilets, showers, electricity, and Wi-Fi.

A great value, the **Hotel Danica** (Nika Andusa bb, tel. 033/462-306, www. hoteldanica.net, €50 d) is in a quiet location on the edge of a nature preserve. It is still convenient to walk to restaurants and sights, and is a short stroll to the beach.

Corso Levante Luxury Suites (Vrulje bb, tel. 069/011-003, €120) are apartments perfect for families and only a 10-minute walk to Petrovac beach. The hotel has a small swimming pool and sun area, and supermarkets are nearby to stock up your apartment fridge with snacks and drinks.

The **Hotel Riva** (Obala bb, tel. 033/461-339, www.hotelriva.me, €130 d) is located on the city's waterside promenade, close to bars and restaurants. Rooms are modern and bright. The hotel can arrange boat trips to secluded beaches, or it is a quick stroll to Petrovac beach.

The **Melia Budva Petrovac** (Nika Anjusica bb, tel. 033/472-200, www.melia. com, €100 d, including breakfast) is a brand-new hotel with two swimming pools, two restaurants and bars, a small spa and gym, and a short walk to the beach.

The **Hotel Palas** (Trg sunca 1, tel.

033/402-456, www.hgbudvanskarivijera.com, €90 d) is only open April through October. With direct access to Petrovac beach in front, during summer there is a children's play center as well as free shows (concerts, folk dances, and more) on the terrace almost every night. All rooms have a balcony and over half have a sea view. The hotel also offers two pools, including a children's pool; two restaurants; and two bars.

Information and Services

You can get more information from the **Tourist Organization Budva** (http://budva. travel) or from one of the pop-up info kiosks the organization runs in Petrovac in the summer near the main beach.

Getting There and Around

In the summer, you can get regular bus service from Budva, Herceg Novi, and Kotor to Petrovac, stopping at Petrovac's **bus station** (Rijeka Reževići bb, tel. 033/461-510). The bus station is only operational during the summer. By car, Petrovac is a one-hour trip from Kotor and a 30-minute drive from Budva on the main coastal road.

Around Petrovac
★ REŽEVIĆI MONASTERY
(Manastir Reževići)

Just 100 meters (328 feet) off the main coastal road between Sveti Stefan and Petrovac, the Reževići Monastery is a worthwhile stop on your trip. Built on the location of an ancient pagan temple, the first of the monastery's three churches, the **Church of the Assumption,** was built in 1226 by the Serbian king, Stefan the First Crowned. A second church, the **Church of the Archdeacon Stefan,** was built in the 14th century but was completely rebuilt in the early 19th century. The two smaller churches are covered in older frescoes, fading but still lovely. The largest church, the **Church of the Holy Trinity (Crkva Sv. Trojice),** was built in 1770. The church's frescoes were repainted in the 1970s and are quite stunning—depicting important figures from Serbian and Orthodox Christian history. There is little information, and all signage is in Cyrillic script, but it does not detract from the beauty. All three churches are open daily and the monastery has a small gift shop, and it is a nice gesture to find a souvenir to take home since admission is free.

You can drive to the monastery or hike from Petrovac (about one and a half hours from the center).

PERAZICA DO BEACH

In the bay below the Monastery is quite possibly the nicest beach near Petrovac, reachable by a two-kilometer (1.2-mile) walk through a forested trail that passes through several tunnels on the right side of Petrovac. Easily accessible by car as well, the pine forest-backed beach is clean and relatively uncrowded, and the water is crystal clear. A small restaurant that is quite good, offers smoothies, drinks, and meals, and lounge chairs and umbrellas are available for rent. The only thing that spoils all this perfection? The abandoned construction of a hotel that was to be named As. Though it means ace here, the irony cannot be lost on English speakers.

Inland Montenegro

Though most tourists stick to Montenegro's stunning coastline, not making a trip inland is missing the true core of Montenegro. You can appreciate the views and hiking or biking at Lovćen National Park; enjoy the plethora of museums in the picturesque little town of Cetinje, Montenegro's erstwhile capital; or spend some lazy time around Lake Skadar, which also happens to be Montenegro's best wine region.

LOVĆEN NATIONAL PARK

Easily accessed as a day trip from Kotor, Cetinje, or even Budva, Lovćen National Park was protected by the state over 50 years ago. Besides being an easily accessible park with some great views and a number of flora and fauna, the park is culturally important to Montenegrins as well. Their beloved Petar II Petrović Njegoš is enshrined here, and the mountain from which the park gets its name, Mt. Lovćen, is the "black mountain" from which the country derives its name.

Sights

IVANOVA KORITA

Located in the center of the park, this village of sorts offers accommodations and restaurants to both day-trippers and overnighters. The visitors center is also found in town. In the winter, a small ski slope is fun for kids and beginners.

NJEGOŠ MAUSOLEUM
(Njegošev Mauzolej)

Njegoš Mausoleum is the resting place of Montenegro's most-loved son, Petar II Petrović Njegoš. Climb 461 steps from the base to the austere structure built in the 1970s, guarded by a pair of large stone statues of women in folk costume. Inside, a statue of Petar II Petrović Njegoš, backed by a protective eagle, sits beneath a gilded dome. Behind the mausoleum, walk down to the viewing platform over the park.

NJEGUŠI

This small village within the park was the naissance of the Petrović dynasty. The village is also known for its excellent cheese (you will see Njeguši cheese listed on menus throughout the country). Typically vendors selling cheese and smoked ham (another local delicacy) are by the roadside should you like to pick some up for a picnic.

Food and Accommodations

The National Park (Ivanova Korita, www.nparkovi.me, visitors center open 9am-5pm daily) offers bungalows for €30 per day that accommodate up to four people as well as campsites (€3 pitch, €10 pitch in established campsite). The park's main hub in Ivanova Korita offers a picnic area, a restaurant, and a hotel, Ivanov Konak (Ivanova Korita, tel. 041/233-700, ivanov-konak-me.book.direct, €60 d) with cozy, well-kept rooms as well as tennis courts and easy access to the park.

Sports and Recreation

Running through the park is the Via Dinarica (www.via-dinarica.org), a 2,000-kilometer (1,242-mile) trail that stretches through multiple countries in the Western Balkans.

If you just want to hike or mountain bike, the visitors center can provide information and rents bikes by the day. There is a zip line just before you reach the mausoleum if you're feeling adventurous. Alternatively, Montenegro Biking (www.pedalj.me) offers a variety of tours and bike trail info.

Information and Services

The National Park Visitors Center (Ivanova Korita, www.nparkovi.me, 9am-5pm daily) can provide information and guides. They also rent bicycles, snowshoes, and walking poles for adventuring around the park.

Getting There

There is no public transportation to the park. If you are without a car, you can take a tour from one of the coastal towns (try **Globtour**, www.globtourmontenegro.com, or **Montenegro Pulse**, www.montenegropulse. com, for something more private).

The drive from Kotor is around 34 kilometers (21 miles) and takes 1.5 hours, while the trip from Cetinje (19 kilometers/12 miles) takes only 30 minutes. Cetinje is close enough that even a taxi would not be prohibitively expensive (around €25), but do agree on the price in advance.

★ CETINJE

It's easy to see why Cetinje is often referred to as the cultural capital of Montenegro. The capital of Montenegro for almost 500 years, until 1946, Cetinje is home to more museums and charming tourist attractions than its stark and somewhat shabby successor.

Sights
NJEGOŠEVA STREET
(Njegoševa Ulica)

Cetinje's main street, partly a tree-lined pedestrian zone, is the heart of the city. It is a good starting point for your explorations of the town, and well worth a stroll past the shops, restaurants, and cafés. At the southern end are two parks as well as the **Blue Palace (Plavi Dvorac)**, built by Crown Prince Danilo. Today it is home to Montenegro's president.

COURT CHURCH
(Dvorska crkva)

A tiny church built on the ruins of the original 15th-century monastery, the **Court Church** (Novice Cerovića bb, 8am-7pm daily, free) is the burial place of Cetinje's founder, Ivan Crnojević, as well as the last

king and queen of Montenegro, who fled to Italy in WWI but were returned in the late 1980s. The church is typically open and free to enter. There is a beautifully restored paneled altar with paintings of saints and religious figures.

CETINJE MONASTERY
(Cetinjski Manastir)

Make sure to dress demurely and cover your shoulders, or you won't be allowed in this monastery, built by Prince Danilo in the 18th century. Photos are also not allowed inside the monastery buildings. The church purportedly holds the hand of John the Baptist, and the monastery has a nice **treasury**, open only by arrangement.

THE NATIONAL MUSEUM OF MONTENEGRO
(Narodni Muzej Crne Gore)

The National Museum of Montenegro (Novice Cerovića 7, tel. 041/230-310, www. mnmuseum.org, 9am-5pm daily summer, 9am-4pm Mon.-Sat. winter, €10 includes admission to all six attractions) is actually a consortium of six museums and galleries around Cetinje.

The main building, the former Parliament building from the early 20th century, houses two of the museums. On the ground floor is the **History Museum (Istorijski muzej)** (Novice Cerovića 7, tel. 041/230-310, www. mnmuseum.org, 9am-5pm daily summer, 9am-4pm Mon.-Sat. winter, €3, or €10 for all six attractions), which has an overview of Montenegrin history from the Stone Age to the present. Though little information is provided in English, it is still quite informative and interesting, and staff can often answer questions you may have. Upstairs, the **Montenegrin Art Gallery (Crnagorska galerija umjetnosti)** (Novice Cerovića 7, tel. 041/230-310, www.mnmuseum.org, 9am-5pm daily summer, 9am-4pm Mon.-Sat. winter, €4, or €10 for all six attractions) has a small collection of icons including the gem on display: the bejeweled 9th-century *Our Lady of Philermos.*

Across from the History Museum is the **Njegoš Museum (Njegošev Muzej)** (Dvorski trg, tel. 041/230-310, www. mnmuseum.org, 9am-5pm daily summer, 9am-4pm Mon.-Sat. winter, €3, or €10 for all six attractions). This palace, more commonly referred to as **Biljarda (Billiards),** was the home of Montenegro's famed Petar II Petrović Njegoš. It got its name from the nation's first billiards table, which is still housed here today. Furniture, costumes, weapons, documents, and more personal effects of Njegoš are on display. Biljarda was also the headquarters of the Austrians in World War I, and nearby you can find the giant **Relief Map of Montenegro (Relefna Karta Crne Gore)** (Dvorski trg, tel. 041/230-310, www.mnmuseum.org, 9am-5pm daily summer, 9am-4pm Mon.-Sat. winter, €1, or €10 for all six attractions) they built in 1916.

The **King Nikola Museum (Muzej Kralja Nikole)** (Dvorski Trg, www.mnmuseum.org, 9am-5pm daily summer, 9am-4pm Mon.-Sat. winter, €5, or €10 for all six attractions) is in the former royal palace of the last king of Montenegro. This lovely building houses exhibits of furniture, paintings, clothing, and memorabilia from the royal family.

A large museum dedicated to modern and contemporary Montenegrin art, the **Miodrag Dado Đurić Gallery (Galerija Miodrag Dado Đurić)** (Balšića Pazar, tel. 041/230-310, www.mnmuseum.org, 9am-5pm daily summer, 9am-4pm Mon.-Sat. winter, €4, or €10 for all six attractions) is worth a stop if you are an art fan.

Festivals and Events

The **Summer in the Old Capital (Ljeto u Prijestonici)** festival (June-Sept.) draws over 30,000 visitors to the cultural performances, concerts, and theater events.

Food

The cozy yet modern atmosphere at **Metro Food** (Balšić Pazar 7, tel. 067/318-250, 8am-12am daily, €5) is a pleasant accompaniment to this centrally located restaurant. Burgers, pizzas, pastas, tasty desserts, and a decent selection of beers and wines hit the spot while touring around town.

For something a little more romantic, **Belveder Nacionalni Restaurant** (Stari Put, tel. 067/569-217, 10am-10pm daily, €12) serves traditional dishes that won't disappoint. Smoked meats and cheese plates, homemade bread, and oven-baked lamb are excellent whether enjoyed inside or outside on the terrace overlooking the mountains. It's very close to the Lipa Cave, if you are in the area.

Accommodations

Opened in 2018, the lovely **Camp Oaza Lipa** (Lipa Dobrska bb, tel. 068/033-219, from €5) is in a quiet location, has a good buffet breakfast for an additional charge, and is run by friendly staff. The owners can sometimes provide tents and mattresses if you are traveling light.

La Vecchia Casa (Ulica Vojvode Batrića 6, tel. 067/629-660, €60 d) is a sweet traditional house with several cozy rooms, surrounded by a lush garden. The guesthouse offers free Wi-Fi and is only a minute's walk away from Cetinje's main street.

Information and Services

The **Cetinje Tourist Organization** (Bajova 2, tel. 041/230-250, www.cetinje.travel) can help with information and advice.

Getting There and Around

Cetinje is easily reached by car from Kotor via Lovćen National Park on the P1 road. The trip takes about 1.25 hours (44 kilometers/27 miles). The drive from Budva to Cetinje (32 kilometers/20 miles) takes about 35 minutes. Buses from Budva (40 minutes, €4) and Kotor

(1.5 hours, €5) are frequent and arrive at the main **bus station** (Trg Golootockih Zrtava).

Around Cetinje
LIPA CAVE
(Lipska Pećina)

A karst cave dating from millions of years ago, the **Lipa Cave** (Lipska pećina bb, tel. 067/003-040, www.lipa-cave.me, tours at 10am, 12pm, and 2pm Apr., 10am, 11:30am, 1pm, 2:30pm, and 4pm May-Oct., from €10.90) is one of the largest caves in Montenegro, with over 2.5 kilometers (1.5 miles) of passages. To visit the cave, you must take one of the two official tours, the Basic Tour (€10.90) or the Extreme Tour (€50), which needs to be arranged in advance and can be customized to your preferences and fitness abilities. The cave is 6 kilometers (3.7 miles) from Cetinje and can be reached by car or taxi.

TOP EXPERIENCE

★ LAKE SKADAR

One of Europe's largest lakes, Lake Skadar spans from Montenegro into Albania. The Montenegrin side of Lake Skadar is a national park and important bird sanctuary, home to both the endangered Dalmatian pelican and the pygmy cormorant. The region is perfect for boat tours, kayaking, and hiking, and the area to the west is home to some of Montenegro's best vineyards.

Sights
VRANJINA

A good entry point for exploring the lake is Vranjina, a short drive from Podgorica. The **Lake Skadar National Park Visitors Center** (tel. 020/879-103, www.nparkovi.me, 8am-6pm daily summer, 8am-4pm Mon.-Fri. winter), located just off the main road, has a small, informative, free exhibition and provides maps, brochures, information, and fishing permits.

VIRPAZAR

The **Bešač Fortress** was built in the 15th century by the Ottomans. Used as a prison during WWII by the Italians, it has been partially restored, but much of it is still in disrepair. It is a nice walk up from the village of Virpazar for some nice views.

In December, the town's **Festival of Wine and Bleak** may sound rather, well, bleak until you learn that bleak is a type of fish found in Lake Skadar, and quite tasty too. It

Karuc village on Lake Skadar

is a great opportunity to sample fish, wine, honey, and cheese from the region in a festive atmosphere.

RIJEKA CRNOJEVIĆA

One of the most charming villages on the lake, Rijeka Crnojevića was the summer home of the last Montenegrin king. The most photographed location here is the lovely old bridge built by Prince Danilo in the 19th century.

There have been a couple of large luxury developments planned near here, which would likely change the feel of the village entirely. However, at the time of writing they are either on hold or abandoned, so enjoy this little hamlet in peace for the moment.

Wineries

On the northern side of Lake Skadar, near Podgorica, the **Plantaže Winery** (Radomira Ivanova 2, tel. 020/444-125, www.plantaze. com, tours 9am-5pm Mon.-Fri., call to schedule, from €12) is Montenegro's largest producer of wine. Twenty-nine varieties of grapes are grown at their Podgorica vineyard, though the deep red Vranac is king, taking up more than two-thirds of the vines. Tours include a trip through the vineyards on a small tourist train and wine-tasting with light appetizers.

In Virpazar, visit **Vinarija Mašanović** (Virpazar, tel. 069/063-460, masanovic. blogspot.com, call to arrange tour), a family winery with 10 generations of heritage that produces a Vranac as well as homemade brandies made from fruit trees on the vineyard including quince, apple, and plum.

Also in Virpazar, **Vinarija Sjekloća** (Limljani bb, tel. 069/020-285, www. sjeklocavino.me, call to arrange tour, €50) is a family winery with many international medals. A tour of the winery and cellars includes a tasting of three vintage wines. You can also buy wine to take home as an exclusive souvenir—they produce only a few thousand bottles a year, so it's unlikely you will be able to buy them abroad.

Sports and Recreation

One of the best ways to enjoy Lake Skadar is on the water. If you don't feel like being too active, the company **Pješacac** (Virpazar bb, tel. 021/711-004, www.pjesacac.com) has a lovely boat tour accompanied by a great meal on a private beach by the lake. Tours depart from Virpazar.

For the more active, **Undiscovered Montenegro** (Boljevići bb, Virpazar, tel. 069/770-027, www.lake-skadar.com, Apr.-Oct.) has guided hiking and kayaking tours as well as wine tours and more. Tours depart from Virpazar.

Food

While the quality of restaurants in the Lake Skadar region can vary widely, as long as you stick with fresh river fish or the restaurant's daily special, it is likely to be a good experience. Ordering something non-local like a hamburger is just setting yourself up for disappointment.

In Virpazar, **Konoba Starčevo** (Tanki rt bb, Virpazar, tel. 067/887-302, www. konobastarcevo.com, 9am-9pm daily, €8) has nice outdoor seating overlooking the lake. House specialties include fish stew and grilled carp with a fruit sauce.

Next to the old bridge in Rijeka Crnojevića, **Konoba Mostina** (Rijeka Crnojevića bb, tel. 069/843-317, 11am-10pm daily, €10) offers smoked trout, fried eel, and grilled carp as well as a few good local meat dishes and decent pizzas for the kids.

Accommodations

Simple, basic rooms can be found at the **Guesthouse Mala Venecija** (Vranjina bb, Vranjina, tel. 069/020-108, €35 d, including breakfast!). While it is no-frills, the rooms are very clean, the views over the lake are peaceful, and there's a good little on-site restaurant, and even an antique store/exhibition.

★ **Eco Resort and Winery Cermeniza** (Zabes, Virpazar, tel. 067/373-059, www. cermeniza.me, €85 d) is a group of five stone cottages that share a swimming pool and garden. Breakfast, lunch, and dinner are available by arrangement. The winery also offers tastings, tours, and more experiences for oenophiles

Even though it doesn't mention "eco in its name, the ★ **Outdoor Club OK Koral** (Orahovo, Virpazar, tel. 067/453-695, www. okkoral.me, €124 d glamping including breakfast or dinner, €9 tent pitch) is truly an ecological resort, light on the land, and all food served in a complete farm-to-table

experience. The resort also can arrange tours of local wineries.

Getting There and Around

Lake Skadar is best accessed by car. There are multiple routes around the lakes. To reach Rijeka Crnojevica from Cetinje, only about 16 kilometers (10 miles), take the highway until you see exits and signage for the village. Virpazar is easily reached via the road that hugs the lake. From Rijeka Crnojevica, it is just under an hour's drive.

Background

The Landscape

CROATIA
Geography

Croatia covers a little more than 55,000 square kilometers (21,200 square miles). The topography within its borders swings from fairly flat and fertile to rocky mountains and hilly craggy karst to the sea, where islands dot the Adriatic.

The country can be broken down into three major geographical regions. The verdant fields of Slavonia and the Baranja become increasing hilly but just as green as they reach Zagreb and Zagorje in the

northwestern part of the country. The coastal regions are isolated by very mountainous and little-developed regions of the Gorski Kotar. The hinterlands of the Adriatic are barely habitable mounds of karst rock. The sea is mostly pebbly, sometimes rocky, and filled with islands that vary from forested to almost barren.

The islands are one of the features that make the country special—it has over 1,200, and most are uninhabited. The coastline, while only 1,777 kilometers (1,104 miles) in length if measured point to point, has so many coves and indentions that the actual length covers over 4,000 kilometers (2,485 miles).

Climate

Inland Croatia and its coast vary greatly. The interior experiences a continental climate with cold, wet winters and increasingly hot summers. The coast is hot and dry in the summer and mild, often rainy, in winter.

Winds on the coast have a significant effect on daily life. In the summer the *maestral*, a breeze blowing over the sea, keeps the temperatures down and is responsible for Croatia's image as a great sailing destination. In winter the southeasterly *široko* brings in warm air, sometimes creating cloudy days, but it's the northeasterly *bura* (capable of annoying at any time of year, but most vicious in winter) that never ceases to frustrate locals. Its gusts can knock cars off bridges and make sailing dangerous. The *bura* is also responsible for plenty of cold bursts of air, unwelcomed by any sun-loving Dalmatian.

Environmental Issues

Because Croatia was relatively unindustrialized in years past, the water and air have remained relatively unpolluted, and most of the forest, which covers close to a quarter of the country, is thick and green. However, acid rain and logging are constantly threatening the forests, eating away at them year by year. And virtually every year Dalmatia's dry climate couples with the wind and a too-soon-discarded cigarette to burn broad swaths of Croatia's forests. It's estimated that the fires have destroyed about 10 percent of the forests in the last two decades.

Overfishing of the Adriatic has been a constant problem, though the Croatian fishing fleet is not entirely to blame, as it represents only a small portion of the fishing capacity. The fishing rights are shared with other nations and with an ever-increasing number of poachers using the waters illegally.

Though Croatia has emissions laws, it's obvious that their application is often less than rigorous, especially if that the car owner is willing to provide a small payment to the friendly technician at the annual checkup.

Plants and Animals

Near the eastern border of Croatia is Kopački Rit, a wetlands nature preserve filled with the area's indigenous wildlife, including cormorants, herons, lots of fish, wild pigs, and deer. The Lonjsko Polje near the town of Sisak is the place to go to see the hundreds of storks that populate the area.

Heading toward the coast, the mountainous Gorski Kotar is marked by dense forests of maple, beech, fir, and spruce. A number of deer, brown bears, and lynx populate the region.

Krka National Park is home to rare sea otters, herons, geese, and ducks as well as several nonpoisonous snake species, like the leopard snake. Paklenica National Park has two poisonous varieties of snakes as well as many large birds like peregrine falcons, hawks, and owls.

On the islands, Cres is important as a refuge for the giant griffon vulture, and most of the islands are home to wild herbs that grow out of the rocks. The coast is also known for maquis and lavender as well as juniper, olive, and fig trees, which all flourish in the dry windswept climate of the seaside region.

The Velebit Range boasts the greatest range of plant life, with over 2,500 species, including the endangered edelweiss.

SLOVENIA
Geography

Nestled between the Alps, the Adriatic Sea, and the Pannonian Plain, Slovenia only covers slightly more than 20,000 square kilometers (7,700 square miles) but packs in substantial variety within the small space. Most of the country is alpine, with plenty of snow-covered peaks and green valleys. Close to half of the country's population lives in the chilly alpine area. The coastal region is made up of sunny vine-covered hills and karst rock, home to close to 1,000 caves, while the Pannonian Plain is a fertile region dotted with hot springs.

Climate

Due to the vast differences in geography, the small country of Slovenia is home to three distinct climates. The alpine region is bitterly cold and snowy in winter and relatively mild during the summer. Still, you'll need a cozy sweater around the regions of Bled, Bohinj, and Triglav National Park even at the height of summer. The plains are more continental, with cold and wet winters and warm to hot summers. The coastal climate is sub-Mediterranean, with hot, dry summers and sometimes rainy winters.

Environmental Issues

Slovenia is the third most forested country in the European Union, with close to 60 percent of its land covered in thick woods. Still, acid rain has become a serious threat to forests along the coast, and the Sava River has been polluted by industrial waste.

Plants and Animals

Due to its diverse geography and climates, Slovenia is home to a wide range of flora and fauna. The interior of the country is dominated by beech and oak trees with pine, fir, and spruce becoming more common as the altitudes reach higher in the alpine region. You'll find the ever rarer edelweiss, alpine orchids, and the Alpine ibex, a goatlike wild animal.

Slovenia is also home to marmots, deer, and wild boars, and its rushing rivers and streams are filled with trout. The marble trout, however, is the only indigenous type of trout. In the eastern section of the country, toward Hungary, you'll find the white stork and a number of migrating birds.

The karst region is best suited to plants that flourish in the Mediterranean climate, particularly olive trees and wild herbs.

MONTENEGRO
Geography

Like Croatia and Slovenia, the tiny country of Montenegro, with a land area of just over 13,000 square kilometers (over 5,000 square miles), is blessed with an extremely varied landscape. From the mountain ranges along its borders with Serbia and Albania to a small but beautiful coastal region, it's hard to believe so much geographical diversity can be packed into such a small space. One of its most stunning features is the Bay of Kotor, a submerged river canyon, with over 1,000-meter (3,200-foot) mountains plunging to the waters below.

Climate

Montenegro's climate is almost as diverse as its landscape. With a Mediterranean climate on the coast and alpine conditions in the mountainous regions, even in the summer the two areas can vary as much as 16.5 degrees Celsius (30 degrees Fahrenheit). Winters on the coast are mild, with temperatures typically well above freezing, while the mountains will see substantial snowfall.

Environmental Issues

Montenegro has made vast improvements to its environmental standards since its independence in 2006. Though it used to have

---

1: ibex, Triglav National Park **2:** at dawn in the Julian Alps, Triglav National Park

significant pollution issues from its industrialized north to shipyard waste on the coast, the country now garners most of its income from tourism, which has forced the country into taking care of its most important resource: it's beauty.

Plants and Animals

Over 3,000 plant specimens and over half of all European bird species can be found in the little country of Montenegro. Similar to its northern neighbor Slovenia, the alpine regions of Montenegro are covered in oak, ash, and hazel trees, while the higher altitudes have an abundance of pine, spruce, and birch. The Durmitor range is known for its dense black pine forest. Along the coast, pine, cypress, and olive trees dominate the landscape. A few remaining brown bears and a small population of wolves and lynx can be found in the mountains. Snakes are abundant in Montenegro, with the horned viper and the common viper among the poisonous varieties.

History

ANCIENT CIVILIZATION

The first proven inhabitants of Croatia were a type of Neanderthal, evidenced by the Krapina man, whose bones were discovered in a cave in Zagorje at the turn of the 20th century. A better description might have been Krapina men and women, since over 800 bones were found at the site; they were x-rayed and dated at around 100,000 years old.

But the Zagorje is not the only region to have been settled by ancient peoples. There is evidence of Neolithic tribes on Hvar, and in Slavonia the discovery of the famous Vučedol Pigeon, a ritual vessel made of pottery, shows that an early culture lived near Vukovar 4,500 years ago.

The Illyrian people, a group of tribes approximately covering the geography of the former Yugoslavia, were the predominant culture from the 10th to the 4th centuries BC. They built fortresses and monuments, some of which survive today, with their iron tools, and they established cities throughout Montenegro, Croatia, and Slovenia. Friezes found in Ljubljana depict early sacrifices, battles, and sporting events. In 2016, the first known palace of the Illyrian kings, dating from the 3rd century BC, was unearthed in Risa, Montenegro.

EARLY HISTORY

The Greeks showed up on the Croatian coast in the 6th century BC, setting up trading posts like Issa (modern-day Vis) up and down the Adriatic. They often battled with the Illyrians, who proved to be their downfall despite their own waning power. In the 3rd century BC, the Illyrian King Agron, together with the Macedonians, battled the Greeks, and Agron's widow, Queen Teuta, attacked their weakened forces again. The Romans then swooped in, taking control, and by the 2nd century BC they had gained the predominant foothold in the region.

Once the 1st century AD rolled around, the Romans held all of Dalmatia, and their inland territories stretched all the way to Hungary. The Romans set up cities like Salona, which became the regional capital, and took over the Illyrian Jadera (modern-day Zadar). In Istria, Parentium (Poreč) and Polensium (Pula), as evidenced by its large amphitheater, were important centers as well. In Slovenia the major cities were Emona (Ljubljana), Celeia (Celje), and Poetovio (Ptuj). In Montenegro, Doclea (Podgorica) was the principal town.

The Adriatic coast of Croatia became important for Rome not only strategically but as a source of soldiers who were absorbed into the Roman army. The region produced two emperors for the empire—Diocletian (whose giant palace still stands in Split) and Constantine. While Croatia and Slovenia were still officially in Rome's territory, Montenegro was on the border between Diocletian and Constantine's territories.

By the 5th century, the Romans' power was slipping, and Visigoths, Huns, Lombards, Avars, and finally Slavs started eating away at the empire, until Rome's hold on Dalmatia officially ended in the 7th century. Its refugees fled to Spalato (Split) and Ragusa (Dubrovnik) for safety.

The Slavs, from which modern-day Croats and Slovenes descended, were mainly agricultural people until the 7th century, when they came to the region and started fighting the Avars. Some historians believe they were encouraged by the Byzantine Empire to serve as a balance for the Avar tribes, though it seems their loyalties waffled between both groups.

MIDDLE AGES

The early Middle Ages saw Croatia, Slovenia, and Montenegro establish brief periods of local rule, and the history from this era closely mirrors the geopolitical landscape (and complicated past) of the countries today.

It was Christianity that held Croatia together in the early Middle Ages. The Franks had fought their way down into Dalmatia by the 9th century, spreading their beliefs with them. The result was a link with the church at Rome that kept Dalmatia tied to the Pannonian provinces even though Dalmatia remained largely controlled by the Byzantine Empire.

In the 7th century, tribes in Slovenia were united under Samo's Tribal Union. Though the union disintegrated when the Slav leader Samo died, it made a fairly easy transition to a Slavic principality known as Carantania, which came under Frankish rule.

The 10th-century King Tomislav was the first ruler to officially join the inland and coastal regions of Croatia. He had a lot of things going for him, mainly approval from Rome and the military power to defeat the Hungarians when they attacked in 924. Tomislav ushered in a time of peace and stability for the country, though by the late 11th century the power to keep Croatia independent was waning. Three kings died without an heir, opening the door for Ladislas of Hungary (brother-in-law of one of those kings, Zvonimir) to take over by 1102.

The Roman Amphitheater of Pula was constructed in 27-68 AD and is among the six largest surviving Roman arenas in the world.

The takeover of Croatia by Hungary changed the economic and political landscape of the country. Since towns like Varaždin and Zagreb were conveniently located on the route between Hungary and the sea, a flourish of activity and prosperity occurred in northern Croatia. This prosperity was mostly felt by the land owners and aristocracy, however, as the feudal system kept most citizens under its thumb.

A huge blow to the area came in 1242 when the Tatars attacked. Though King Bela IV managed to escape and the Tatars were thrown out, the cities attacked suffered substantial damage, with many medieval buildings and monuments lost during the fighting.

On the coast, Dalmatia had been flip-flopping rulers since the 11th century, but as the centuries passed, most of the fights were between the Venetians and the Hungarians for control of the seaside provinces. In the end, the Venetians won, though not through military might: They bought Dalmatia from a frightened King Ladislas of Naples for 100,000 ducats at the beginning of the 15th century.

Though Venice's rule did result in some beautiful Italian architecture, the period was by and large an unfortunate one for Dalmatia and Istria. The Venetians clear-cut forests for their own use (once they were gone and the soil eroded, trees never grew back), banned trade with anyone other than themselves (driving down prices), and invested precious little in the provinces as a whole. By the end of the 18th century, the people were not only poor but starving, living off whatever they could manage to pluck from the land.

In Montenegro in the 11th century, the state of Duklja, formed with the Roman town of Doclea as its center, took over territory ranging from Dubrovnik to modern-day Albania, but by the 12th century various conflicts had caused it to diminish in power and it was absorbed by Raška, a group of Serbian tribes that had formed in the 10th century. In the 12th century the Nejmanjić dynasty gained control of Raška. Over the centuries Stefan's heirs expanded the territory to include parts of Albania, Bulgaria, Macedonia, and even Greece. During this time Duklja (which became renamed Zeta) was still considered somewhat separate, with tensions between its nobles and those of the more powerful Raška, which ruled it. By the early 15th century, Venice had gained control of Kotor and Raška was too busy with their own power struggles to notice the Ottoman threat on the horizon.

WAR WITH THE OTTOMANS

By the late 15th century, the Ottomans had taken Serbia and overran Zeta (present-day Montenegro). A small group of Zetan holdouts fled to Mt. Lovcen (Cetinje). Mt. Lovcen, referred to by the Venetians as "monte negro" (black mountain), is the origin of the country's name. The Zetans put up a strong fight and kept their holdout free of the Ottomans for nearly 30 years until they were overcome in the early 16th century. But no sooner had the Ottomans taken Cetinje than they realized they didn't really want it. The land wasn't worth anything, and the people wouldn't give up fighting. Largely left to themselves, they established a *vladika*, or prince-bishop, as ruler and continued to war intermittently with the Ottomans.

For inland Croatia, the Ottomans created havoc between the late 15th and late 17th centuries. The Ottomans had already moved into Bosnia by the 1450s, and the Croatians knew it was only a matter of time before they advanced further. In 1493, the time had come, though even a strong showing of Hungarian and Croatian forces at Krbavsko polje (near Plitvice) couldn't stop them. The coast was now open to periodic raids by the Turks, but the worst was suffered inland, as they burned towns in their way, capturing or killing residents.

When the Hungarian king was killed in a battle with the Ottomans, everyone looked to Austria, where Archduke Ferdinand I took over the Hungarian empire and tried to help the Croats. But even he wasn't much help. At the end of the 16th century, only land around

Zagreb, Karlovac, and Varaždin remained under Austro-Hungarian control; Venice had managed to retain the coast.

The Hapsburgs took advantage of the refugees, known as Vlachs, who had fled Serbia for northern Croatia, by using them to settle the lands south of Zagreb and protect the land from invasion. The tide started to turn in 1571 when the Ottomans were defeated at the Battle of Lepanto. Over the next 120 years, cities seized by the Ottomans gradually returned to Hapsburg control, and in 1699 the Treaty of Sremski Karlovci officially erased any claims of the Ottomans on Croatian and Hungarian lands.

NAPOLEON AND THE AUSTRO-HUNGARIAN EMPIRE

Venetian power was slipping, and in Montenegro that meant a shift to Russia as their benefactors in their fight against the Ottomans. In Dalmatia, Istria, and inland Croatia, the 18th century had managed to maintain the status quo, more or less, but Napoleon was about to change the political landscape of Croatia substantially.

When Venice fell to Napoleon in 1797, he gave Dalmatia to the Austrian empire, but by 1800 the entire Croatian coast and Slovenia were under French control, dubbed the Illyrian provinces, and even given a French governor, Marshal Marmont.

The short period under Napoleonic rule was marked by a return of the Slavic language and infrastructure the coastal provinces sorely needed. Napoleon's aim had been to strengthen the provinces—including Slovenians, Croatians, and Serbs—to form an identity separate from their ruling forces.

This idea was somewhat squashed with the Treaty of Vienna in 1815, when the Hapsburg empire laid claim to all of Slovenia and Croatia, putting Croatia under the jurisdiction of Hungary. But the nationalist ideas had taken on much more of a life than the new government would have liked, with the Croatian writer Ljudevit Gaj heralding a new

Illyrian movement. The Austrians and the Hungarians thought the pro-Slav sentiment was getting out of hand in the mid-19th century, and even banned the use of the word *Illyria*.

Croatians saw the 1848 revolution of Hungary against Austria as an opportunity for more independence. The Croatian Sabor bargained that in exchanged for sending the military forces under Ban Josip Jelačić in support of the emperor, Hungary would no longer have control over Croatia, and the country would maintain more autonomy. Though Jelačić and his troops' efforts did help to end the revolution in Vienna, they did not bring the war with the Hungarians to a victory; in the end it was the Russians who came to Austria's aid. After the threat was gone, Austria reneged on its promises and shut down the idea of more Croatian independence.

The bitterness that resulted was actually one of the undercurrents that formed Yugoslavia. Led by the charismatic Bishop Strossmayer, the Illyrian movement, by then called the National Party, advanced in its ideas that all Slavs are the same, not different. They theorized that the Austrians magnified their differences to keep them weaker.

During this period Montenegro enjoyed a largely stable government under the vladika (prince-bishop). Providing aid to Serbia in a war against the Ottomans in 1876 helped Montenegro establish international recognition and propelled it into the modern world. Trade expanded, the first modern roads and railways were built, and postal service was established.

WORLD WAR I

The beginning of World War I brought a period of uncertainty for Croatians and Slovenians, who figured that once again they'd be pawns in a much larger game. They initially supported the Austro-Hungarian Empire, but more and more defeats made the effort look hopeless. Before they waited for larger countries to decide their fate, they brokered a deal for the formation of a Slav state

Josip Broz Tito

Josip Broz was born in the village of Kumrovec on May 7, 1892, in the Croatian Zagorje. He was one of 15 children, and left school at the age of 12.

He fought in World War I, drafted into the Austro-Hungarian army. While fighting on the Russian front against the Serbs, he was captured and thrown in prison, where he learned Russian and began to embrace communist ideals. When Czar Nicholas II abdicated, Tito was released and immediately went to fight with Lenin's army, for which he was thrown into prison again until the communists took power later that year.

Returning to Croatia in 1920, he joined the Communist Party of Yugoslavia, and by the early 1930s was one of the party's stars. It was during this period he adopted the nickname "Tito." One of the many versions of how he got the name is that it came from the phrase *"Ti to!"* meaning "You [do] that!"—an allusion to his brusque manner. During World War II, Tito's Partisans fought against the Germans, the Ustaše, and the royalist Chetniks. The Partisans' success in tying down significant numbers of German forces helped them win Allied support, and in 1945 Tito became dictator of Yugoslavia. Tito broke with Stalin in the late 1940s, which allowed the Yugoslav peoples more freedom than any of the Eastern Bloc countries. However, Tito's reign was heavy-handed, and anyone uttering a word against the government or Tito was severely punished.

Tito died in Ljubljana on May 4, 1980, slightly more than a decade before the country he'd ruled fell apart.

(called the National Council of Slovenes, Croats, and Serbs), with its headquarters in Belgrade. The Croats knew they would have to choose between Italy and Serbia, and Serbia was their preference. Italy quickly pounced on Istria, claiming it as their territory.

The democracy was short-lived, however. The laws and power fell heavily in favor of Serbia, which was the strongest, both politically and militarily, of the three. Croat Stjepan Radić stood in opposition, pushing for a federal democracy, but the Serbs quickly squashed these hopes; Radić and two Croatian members of parliament were fatally shot in the national parliament in Belgrade in 1928, and King Aleksander declared the country a royal dictatorship.

Montenegro began World War I with its new king, Nicholas, forced into exile by the Austrians. At the end of the war, the king was deposed and Montenegro joined the new Kingdom of Slovenes, Croats, and Serbs.

WORLD WAR II

Killing Radić and instituting a royal dictatorship created several angry groups that fled the country but planned to regain independence by any means. Among these was the Ustaše Movement, led by Ante Pavelić. During Pavelić's exile in Italy, Mussolini recognized an opportunity to reassert Italian interests in Croatia through his organization. Though Pavelić claimed he and his group were protecting Croatian interests, he readily agreed to cede vast territories of Croatia, including ports like Rijeka in Istria and many Croatian islands, in return for Mussolini's support.

Other parties were organizing their own coups, such as the HSS (Croatian Peasants' Party), led by Vlatko Maček, the successor of the unfortunate Radić, and the Communist Party of Yugoslavia (KPJ), heavily supported by Moscow and led by Josip Broz Tito from 1937.

The outbreak of World War II provided the perfect opportunity for the competing political forces to fight it out. Germany invaded Yugoslavia on April 6, 1941. Pavelić and his fascist cronies used the Axis occupation of Yugoslavia as a chance to gain political control and rid themselves of their enemies, who included scores of innocent Serbs, Jews, and Roma as well as Croatian political opponents. Over the next four years, some 150,000 lives (according to the most well-researched estimates, though estimates range from 30,000 to 1 million) were lost in the concentration camp at Jasenovac.

Tito's National Liberation Partisan groups, which included Croatians, Serbs, Slovenians, and other nationalities, were fighting the Germans and Italians and gained strong support from the Allies, who saw them as the most significant opponent to the fascists. Tito set up Partisan governments wherever he maintained a victory, and when he marched into Belgrade in the fall of 1944, he was declared prime minister. The Ustaše fled Zagreb in 1945 when Germany surrendered, leading the way to a unified southern Slav state—including Slovenia, Croatia, Macedonia, Serbia, Montenegro, and Bosnia and Herzegovina—under Josip Broz Tito.

YUGOSLAVIA UNDER TITO

It quickly became apparent that Yugoslavia was an authoritarian state. Until the 1980s, Tito's heavy-handed rule opposed any hint of anti-government sentiment, obliterated political parties, and kept an iron thumb on the Roman Catholic Church. Tito broke with Stalin in 1948, and Yugoslavia gained freedoms that other Eastern Bloc countries didn't have, like the ability to have passports and travel.

Unlike its position in the former federation of states, Montenegro enjoyed a good position in Yugoslavia. Many Montenegrins held positions of power, and the country was the beneficiary of large sums of money in investment and industrialization.

Croatian and Slovenian sentiment toward Belgrade was already waning by the 1960s. The two republics were significantly more prosperous, yet their gains were doled out to the central government in Serbia and the poorer republics. Also, Belgrade kept a heavy number of Serbs in Croatian and Slovenian government and police positions, ostensibly as a program to aid the disadvantaged.

In 1971, Croatians launched a political movement known as the Croatian Spring. The leaders of the movement came from within Tito's Communist Party—high-ranking officials and the intelligentsia made up a great portion of the movement's supporters. The movement was striving for more autonomy for the republic and more personal freedoms. What they got was a swift crackdown by Tito, who jailed dozens and drove many into exile, drastically reducing the influence of the Croatians in the central and regional governments. However, the event was an indication of the underlying currents in Yugoslavian politics, and it pointed the direction in which the country was headed once Serb dominance eroded through the weakening of the Eastern bloc and the lack of economic progress.

BREAKING FREE

After Tito's death in 1980, the country was still left with his legacy of debt. Inflation skyrocketed and the economy was in a state of severe crisis.

The Slovenians were the first to take the lead toward freedom, moving to multi-party elections and calling for changes to the Yugoslav constitution in favor of more independence. Slovenia's lead was followed by Croatia, which was still reasserting itself after the purges following the Croatian Spring movement.

In January 1990, at the meeting of the Yugoslav League of Communists, the Slovenians called for autonomy for each republic. The Serbs rejected the idea, and the Slovenians and Croatians walked out of the room in defiance.

The Croatian Democratic Union (HDZ), the first noncommunist party in Croatia, was formed in May 1989 under the leadership of Franjo Tuđman. The party was vehemently anti-Yugoslav and called for secession. The not-even-a-year-old party won the elections by a landslide in the spring of 1990. In June 1991, both the Republic of Croatia and the Republic of Slovenia declared themselves independent.

Montenegro joined the Serbs in fighting

to keep Croatia, Slovenia, and Bosnia from breaking free. However, as the war went on, relations between Montenegro and Serbia became increasingly fraught.

The Serbs in Krajina, in the far east of Croatia, immediately claimed Krajina as their own, and intense fighting broke out—the start of what is known in Croatia as the Homeland War. Slovenia was also engaged in some skirmishes, though for them the war was over in 10 days. For Croatia it was a different story. Over the next three months, Croatia lost a quarter of its territory to Serb forces, Vukovar was besieged and eventually leveled to the ground, and the UN imposed an arms embargo on all of former Yugoslavia, further disadvantaging the severely underarmed Croatia, already in a desperate situation.

The tide began to turn for Croatia in 1992, when the European Commission (the executive body of the EU) formally recognized the country. The UN plan was to maintain the borders of the former federal republics in accordance with the Constitution of Yugoslavia. For years, however, the plan went nowhere, as local Serbs supported by Slobodan Milošević and the Serb-controlled Yugoslav Army rejected implementation of the UN resolutions.

When attention turned to the atrocities in Bosnia-Herzegovina, Croatia managed to obtain arms and gradually make headway until they reclaimed Maslenica, near Zadar, and entered Slavonia in 1995.

There were a number of instances in which abandoned Serb homes and villages were burned and horrific attacks on some Serbs who stayed behind were carried out. Croatia had agreed, however, to protect human rights and cooperate with the International War Crimes Tribunal, so following the end of the war in 1995, Croatia eventually agreed to keep their commitments after receiving pressure from the international community. Croatia extradited a number of its citizens accused of war crimes to stand trial.

AFTERMATH OF THE WARS OF INDEPENDENCE

Slovenia had a quick recuperation from their short war. In 2004 they entered the European Union and have already adopted the euro. Croatia has had a somewhat harder time, hampered by the decisions of Franjo Tuđman, which stifled economic growth and slowed the path to entry into the EU until 2013.

The war-torn regions of Karlovac, Maslenica, and especially eastern Slavonia were devastated in the war, and economic recovery has been slow. It has taken most Serb refugees some time to reclaim homes and land, though Croatia finally has not only allowed their return but has also rebuilt residences destroyed during the war.

After entry to the European Union, a number of Croatian young people have left Slavonia, in particular, for better job opportunities abroad.

Montenegro struggled with its union with Serbia for many years, frustrated by the sanctions placed on the countries by the United Nations, which Montenegro saw as Serbia's fault. In 2006, 55.5 percent of Montenegrins voted to end the federation of Serbia and Montenegro. Fifty-five percent was needed for it to pass.

Government and Economy

GOVERNMENT

Croatia

ORGANIZATION

Croatia's constitution was adopted on December 22, 1990, creating a parliamentary democracy. Subsequent changes have weakened the office of the president so that it is more a ceremonial position than one with much power.

The executive branch consists of the president and the prime minister. The president is elected by popular vote for a five-year term, while the prime minister is appointed by the majority party in parliament. The legislative branch is split into the Županijski Dom (House of Districts) and the Zastupnički Dom (House of Representatives), both comprising officials who are elected by popular vote (with the exception of five members of the House of Districts, who are appointed by the president) and serve a four-year term. The judicial branch is the Supreme Court, a body of judges appointed by a council elected by the House of Representatives.

POLITICAL PARTIES

Croatia has 18 political parties, though only three truly vie for power: the Social Democratic Party (SDP), the Croatian People's Party (HNS), and the Croatian Democratic Union (HDZ). Other significant parties include the Istrian Democratic Party, one of the strongest regional parties; the Croatian Party of Rights (HSP), a far-right party; and historical parties like the Croatian Peasants' Party (HSS).

Slovenia

ORGANIZATION

Slovenia's constitution was adopted on December 23, 1991, and the country is a parliamentary democracy. The executive branch of the Slovenian government is made up of the president, elected for a five-year term by popular vote, and a prime minister, generally chosen from the majority party in parliament. The legislative branch is the Državni zbor (National Assembly), with 90 members elected for four-year terms; 88 members are elected by popular vote and 2 members by ethnic minorities.

POLITICAL PARTIES

Slovenia has a multiparty system and over a dozen political parties. The strongest parties tend to be the Slovenian Democratic Party (SDS) and the Liberal Democracy of Slovenia (LDS). However, the country has several special-interest parties for groups such as pensioners, youth, and environmentalists.

Montenegro

ORGANIZATION

Montenegro gained independence from Serbia in 2006 and is a parliamentary republic. Its constitution was adopted in 2007. The head of parliament is the Prime Minister, and the President, elected to a five-year term, is head of state. The judicial branch is comprised of a constitution court of five judges with nine-year terms and a Supreme Court, whose justices are appointed for life. The legislative branch has 81 members elected to four-year terms.

POLITICAL PARTIES

The Democratic Party of Socialists (DPS) has led Montenegro for over two decades and holds almost 50 percent of seats in Parliament. Other parties include the Social Democrats (SDP), the Socialist People's Party, the Democratic Front, the Movement for Changes (PZP), Positive Montenegro (PCG), the Bosniak Party, and the Democratic Union of Albanians (DUA).

ECONOMY
Croatia

During its years as part of Yugoslavia, Croatia enjoyed a position as one of the country's most prosperous and industrious republics. Shipbuilding, aluminum, chemicals, and oil refining industries thrived. When Croatia became independent in the early 1990s, the country had an excellent opportunity to make use of its industries and attract foreign companies who would invest in the new country.

Somehow, Tuđman's team managed to sell off factories and industries for paltry sums to friends and cronies who sucked them dry of cash, stripped their assets, and sold off their real estate holdings. This business model reduced the tax base and left the industries worthless to any buyer. The rampant corruption significantly limited the amount of foreign investment, in spite of the relatively high level of economic development. Instead, the companies expanding their operations to Eastern Europe largely chose to set up local operations elsewhere in the region, severely stifling Croatia's growth.

Tourism was an important industry for Croatia, particularly in the 1960s and 1970s, though the war in the 1990s all but obliterated it for several years. In the early 1990s you could visit Trogir and Split without encountering any other visitors except a few straggling UN personnel. Many travelers were still afraid to return in the late 1990s, even though the war had ended in 1995. Around 2000 things really started to take off, with islands like Hvar and destinations like Dubrovnik gracing the pages of more than a few European and American glossies. The financial crisis of 2009 and 2010 slowed tourism, but not for long—Zagreb in particular has flourished in the numbers of visitors it attracts.

The average net monthly salary in Croatia is around 5,000Kn; in Zagreb it is somewhat higher, around 6,000Kn monthly. Unemployment is around 14 percent, much lower than in the mid-1990s when it topped 20 percent. Work in construction, brought on by a boom in real estate, has helped move these figures ever lower.

Slovenia

Along with Croatia, Slovenia was the most successful of the republics in the former Yugoslavia. Slovenia made up one-third of exports from Yugoslavia. When Slovenia became independent in 1991, it made a swift and easy transition into the European economy. Slovenia became a member of the European Union in 2004 and adopted the euro as its currency in 2007. Unemployment was around 9.3 percent in 2015.

While real GDP grew by 6.8 percent in 2007, the fastest since independence, the financial crisis of 2009 and 2010 created negative growth, and though it has improved, growth in 2015 was around -1%. Inflation was quite high after entering the Eurozone— the country has averaged 5.5% over the last 20 years. One of the major problems for Slovenia's economy in the future is dealing with an aging population; a low birth rate is doing little to alleviate the issue.

Even though Slovenia is quite verdant, agriculture makes up very little of the country's GDP. Many farmed products are consumed locally, including the region's wines, since most of the producers are too small to export effectively. Lead and zinc mining, which were once vital to the country's economy, have all but died out. Today, Slovenia is mostly involved in mid- to high-tech manufacturing.

Services make up a large part of the Slovenian economy, and tourism is increasingly becoming one of the sector's most important forces. Ljubljana has become a favorite destination of the travel columns for its charm and Prague-without-the-crowds vibe. Bled and Bohinj also draw their share of travelers, while the country's ski slopes attract a mostly local crowd, along with weekenders from neighboring Croatia.

Though the country has done better with

1: Idrija lace **2:** The fishmarket in Zadar is one of the largest and best supplied in Croatia.

foreign investors than neighboring Croatia, the privatization process in Slovenia was often marred by corruption, with more than a few political-insider purchases. Outside investment is still quite low for an EU nation. That said, the country is now working toward a favorable environment for foreign investment and is doing phenomenally well among the transition countries, largely due to an educated and motivated work force and excellent infrastructure.

Montenegro

Until the middle of the 20th century, Montenegro's economy was largely based on agriculture, though there is little arable land. During the years it was part of Yugoslavia, industry usurped agriculture. Coal mining, forestry, aluminum production (as the country boasts bauxite as one of its natural resources), and electricity generation were some of the mainstays of Yugoslavian Montenegro.

Today tourism accounts for more than 20 percent of the GDP, with the country bringing in three times the tourists of its population on a yearly basis. Forestry is still a healthy industry, since trees cover over two-fifths of the land.

Montenegro does not use all of its hydropower capability and is building an underwater cable to Italy, to be completed in 2018, in order to become an exporter of their wealth of energy production. For good or bad, the country relies heavily on foreign investment, which it has attracted by offering a low corporate tax rate. It has the highest foreign investment per capita in Europe.

Though Montenegro hopes to join the EU by 2020, they already use the euro as their domestic currency.

People and Culture

CROATIA
Demography

Croatia is home to approximately 4.5 million people. The largest city is its capital, Zagreb, with approximately 1 million people in the metro area. Split is second with around 180,000 in the city and over 200,000 when the suburbs are included. Rijeka comes in third with around 130,000. The birth rate is extremely low, about 9.6 for every 1,000 people, translating into a slightly shrinking and aging population.

Though Croats make up close to 90 percent of the population, Serbs make up 4.5 percent, with Bosnians, Italians, Hungarians, and Slovenes making up much of the remaining 5.5 percent. There is little immigration besides a small stream of Chinese who come to work in family businesses or to study.

Religion

Over 80 percent of Croatians are Roman Catholic, with Orthodox Christians, Muslims, and atheists making up much of the rest. Catholicism is important to the national identity, and you'll find churches packed on Christmas, Easter, and August 15th (Velika Gospa). However, the churches are much less full on any regular Sunday.

Catholicism was not prohibited in Tito's Yugoslavia, but it was heavily frowned upon. Schools operated on Christmas Day, and if children didn't show up, their parents would likely be brought in for questioning. People who held state jobs refrained from going to church since it wasn't helpful to one's career or job security.

When Croatia claimed its independence in 1991, attending church and defining oneself as Roman Catholic was seen as integral to being a "good Croatian." The church enjoyed lots of power in the government under Tuđman, though that has eroded in recent years.

Language

Croatian is a Slavic language, actually

classified as either Serbo-Croat or Croato-Serbian by most linguists. The language is spoken in Croatia, Bosnia and Herzegovina, and Serbia, though the vast majority of locals in each country would beg to differ.

Most Croatians speak Croatian as well as at least one other language. On the coast, this language is likely to be Italian. For older people, it's probably German. Most Croatians under 45 speak at least some, if not a lot, of English, largely due to the number of U.S. television shows broadcast locally with subtitles.

The Arts

One of the most underappreciated arts in Croatia is its rich tradition of folk music. Unfortunately, the country doesn't have a lot of places to go and see music performances outside of periodic folk festivals. Bars and clubs rarely play folk music, though a good inland Croatian wedding should always have a *tambura* band.

The *tambura* (also called the *tamburica*) is the most important instrument in Slavonian folk music. The instrument is most similar to a mandolin and was brought to the region by the Ottomans.

On the coast, the dominant folk music is the *klapa*, an a capella group of 4-10 men who sing rather sad songs. A good group can be quite impressive, and it's highly recommended to hit a *klapa* festival if you have the chance.

Though Istrian music is not as popular, it is interesting if you happen to come across some at one of the local festivals. The instruments—like the *sopila*, a type of large oboe, and the *mijeh*, a bagpipe made of a goat bladder—are what really make the music unique.

Croatian architecture is quite varied, with lots to see around the country. In Dalmatia you'll find some pre-Romanesque churches—the best example is St. Donat's Church in Zadar, built at the beginning of the 9th century. Romanesque and Gothic styles followed, with Dalmatian sculptor Juraj Dalmatinac (circa 1400-1473) at the forefront of the Gothic style, sculpting reliefs

and erecting buildings all over the Dalmatian coast. A good mix of both Renaissance and Gothic styles can be found in Šibenik's 15th-century Katedrala svetog Jakova. Other great examples of Renaissance architecture can be found all along the coast in places such as Hvar and Dubrovnik (the latter was a center for Renaissance architecture, though much of it was destroyed by the great earthquake of 1667). In northern Croatia, the Baroque style was predominant; Varaždin is the town most known for its Baroque architecture, dating from the 17th and 18th centuries. The Secessionist style (the local term for the art nouveau style) became popular in the late 19th and early 20th century. A beautiful example of Secessionist architecture is the Državni Arhiv in Zagreb, built in 1913.

The most famous Croatian painter is Vlaho Bukovac (1855-1922), a 19th-century artist from Cavtat, near Dubrovnik, who was a master of light landscapes and realistic paintings. Croatian-born sculptor Ivan Meštrović (1883-1962) has enjoyed international acclaim. Many of his works dug deep into the Croatian national spirit for inspiration. However, the most interesting and unique style of painting is naive painting; the work not only depicted rural peasant life in the first half of the 20th century but also came under fire for its political themes. Ivan Generalić (1914-1992) is the most well-known artist of this genre.

SLOVENIA
Demography

Slightly more than two million people live in Slovenia. Ljubljana, the capital, is the biggest city, with more than 250,000 people. The city is small but quite cosmopolitan given the number of embassies and consulates in town. Maribor is the second largest, with approximately 115,000 residents. Several towns hover around the 50,000 mark, like Kranj and Koper. The birth rate is extremely low, about 9.63 births for every 1,000 people.

Slovenes make up over 80 percent of the population. Italians and Hungarians are both considered indigenous minorities and are given a special status in the National Assembly, with one seat each to represent them. There are also people from the former Yugoslav republics; most are refugees who have made Slovenia their new home.

Religion

Close to 60 percent of Slovenians are Roman Catholic. Other groups include Protestants, Orthodox Christians, Muslims, and Jews. Protestantism was quite popular in the 16th century, though today its followers make up only about 1 percent of the population, located mostly in the Murska Sobota region. Jews were driven out in the 15th century and today there is a very small community of only 100 or so. Muslims make up a little over 2 percent of the population and are mostly newcomers to Slovenia, usually escaping the horrors of Bosnia during the war.

The Slovenian constitution declares the separation of church and state and maintains that all religions are equal, though it is clear that the Roman Catholic Church has more sway in affairs of the state than minority religions. That said, the church's say in Slovenia is considerably less than in neighboring Austria, Hungary, and Croatia. A 1996 visit by the pope was met with far less fanfare than in Croatia.

Language

Slovenian is a Slavic language. It is similar to Croatian but not enough that speakers from the two countries can easily understand each other (think of speakers of Spanish and Italian having a conversation). People who grew up under the Yugoslav regime speak Serbo-Croatian as a second language, but young people under 25 likely speak little or perhaps none at all.

Most Slovenes speak at least two languages. Many Slovenes speak English, as it is widely taught in schools and seen on television. German, Italian, and Hungarian are also popular second languages.

The Arts

Music is an important part of the Slovenian cultural landscape. The small country boasts five orchestras and two opera companies, and it's also home to a variety of modern bands, like the popular rock group Siddharta. However, it's the country's folk music (ljudska glasba) that is truly distinctive. Varied and rich, local folk music features not only its own rhythms and tunes, but also its own instruments, such as the cymbalom, a stringed instrument played with sticks, and the zvegla, a wooden cross flute.

Slovenia is full of architectural styles, from the pre-Romanesque, Gothic, and Baroque to more modern styles. The most abundant of these styles are likely Baroque (Ljubljana's cathedral is an example) and Secessionist architecture (Ljubljana's Miklošičeva street is teeming with it). One name stands out among all the architects—Jože Plečnik (1872-1957), whose classical and symmetrical style transformed the city of Ljubljana in the early 20th century following the 1895 earthquake.

Slovenia's folk craft tradition is definitely worth a mention; it's been an important part of the culture since medieval times. From delicate Idrija lace to wooden crafts and ironworking, Slovenia is full of quality handiwork.

Visual arts have always been important to Slovenia, with close to 50 art museums throughout the country. Churches are full of examples of Gothic frescoes (Hrastovlje's Dance of Death is one of the most famous), while Baroque sculptures, like Francesco Robba's fountains in Ljubljana, are found in cities throughout Slovenia. In the 19th century, impressionist Rihard Jakopič was the best-known painter, while most of the 20th century was dominated by the Club of Independents, a group of painters who focused on socialist realism, a Soviet-influenced style of strong lines and powerful images. Over the past 30 years, postmodernist style has prevailed, with a crop of interesting artists such as sculptor Marjetica Potrč.

MONTENEGRO

Demography

Montenegrins differ in how they identify themselves. Though close to 50 percent consider themselves as Montenegrin, a little over a quarter would describe themselves as Serbs. It is important to keep in mind that only around 55 percent of Montenegrins voted to leave Serbia in the referendum. The largest minority, around 20 percent of the population, are Bosniak Muslims. They live primarily in the northern mountain regions. Albanians make up 5 percent of the population and live along the coast.

Religion

Close to three-quarters of the population adhere to Orthodox Christianity, falling under the Serbian Orthodox Church. Around 20 percent are Muslim and less than 5 percent are Roman Catholic. Only 1.2 percent of the population claims no religion at all.

Language

Montenegrin is the official language of Montenegro, with four others in official use: Serbian, Croatian, Bosnian, and Albanian.

Although the languages (except for Albanian) are mutually intelligible, like most former Yugoslav countries, Montenegro claims theirs as distinct.

Although Montenegro has a history of links to Serbia, the pronunciation of Montenegrin is more similar to that of Croatian. Montenegro also uses a Latin alphabet, though the Cyrillic alphabet of Serbian can also be seen.

The Arts

Montenegrin literature is rooted heavily in epic folk songs sung while accompanied by the gusle (a one-stringed instrument). The greatest guslar is considered Petar Petrović Njegus, a vladika (prince-bishop) who was also one of the country's most important poets. Some claim that his most famous work, The Mountain Wreath, has inspired radical Serb nationalists throughout the years and celebrates ethnic cleansing.

Fans of historical architecture can find a variety of styles throughout the country, including pre-Romanesque, Gothic, Baroque, and Byzantine churches and buildings. Venetian architecture shines in the UNESCO World Heritage city of Kotor, known to the medieval Venetians as Cattaro.

Essentials

Getting There

CROATIA
Air
There are several international airports in Croatia, though the busiest of these is Zagreb's **Pleso Airport** (ZAG, www.zagreb-airport.hr). Many of the coastal airports, like **Pula Airport** (PUY, www.airport-pula.hr), **Rijeka Airport** (RJK, www.rijeka-airport.hr), **Zadar Airport** (ZAD, www.zadar-airport.hr), and the island of Brač's **Bol Airport** (BWK, www.airport-brac.hr), have a lot more flights available during the summer than in the off-season. **Split Airport** (SPU,

www.split-airport.hr) and **Dubrovnik Airport** (DBV, www.airport-dubrovnik.hr) are the largest coastal airports, while the small **Osijek Airport** (OSI, www.osijek-airport.hr) is useful for getting to Slavonia without a drive. All of the airport websites will direct you to flight schedules, lists of airlines, car rental companies, and information on buses and shuttles into town.

It is important to know that if you're planning to travel on to Serbia, Bosnia, or Montenegro, there are few or no direct flights. Your closest connections are in Ljubljana. There are currently no direct flights from the United States to Croatia. You'll have to connect in a large European city like London, Frankfurt, Munich, or Vienna. **Croatia Airlines** (www.croatiaairlines.hr) has the biggest selection of flights, with several daily connections between Zagreb or Split and Frankfurt or Munich. **British Airways** (www.britishairways.com) flies from London to Split and Dubrovnik. There are some great budget-carrier options from the British Isles, like **EasyJet** (www.easyjet.com), **Ryanair** (www.ryanair.com), and **Wizzair** (www.wizzair.com), though most connect to the Croatian coast and fly more frequently, or only, during the summer.

Round-trip tickets from North America, with one connection in a major European capital, run about $1,200. You can save money by being flexible on travel dates (mid-week is usually cheapest) and times (early-morning or late-evening flights tend to be in less demand).

Another option if you're on a tight budget is to get a bargain fare to a major hub like Vienna and then take the train to Croatia. You have a similar option with flights to cities like Venice and then connecting with a ferry to one of the Croatian islands or coastal ports. Of course, you should account for the time involved—trains and ferries take up to six hours plus transfers—when deciding if the savings

makes sense. On the upside, it's a nice way to fit in a stopover in another European city.

You could get the best of both worlds by connecting to Istria and Dalmatia (and sometimes Zagreb) via low-cost carriers, most of which fly out of the smaller airports around London.

For international flights, it's best to arrive 2-3 hours early. In the summer and early fall, when lines at overcrowded airports can get unruly, err on the three-hour side. Security check-ins in Croatia move along pretty smoothly, though you still may have to take off your shoes (this rule seems to change monthly) and leave the bottled water at home, since Croatia observes the liquids ban. It'll be quicker if you have your sample-size bottles in a plastic zip-top bag, pack your metal jewelry in your carry-on, and wear shoes that are easy to remove. Croatian airports are very particular about batteries in checked luggage. Remove any batteries and put them in your carry-on unless you want to unpack your bags at the check-in counter.

Land

Train travel to Croatia from Austria takes about six hours. Sometimes you'll get a new, fairly modern train, and other times you might get a train that looks like it's been riding the rails since the 1940s. If you're traveling around Europe by train, look into the **Eurail Pass** (www.eurail.com) and **Rail Europe** (www.raileurope.com), though the passes don't currently cover Croatia and Slovenia. If you're traveling frequently by train throughout Europe, it's worthwhile to buy the **Thomas Cook European Timetable** (www.thomascooktimetables.com, about $25.50), which has schedules of over 50,000 trains as well as ferry routes.

You can also take the bus to Croatia, but there's always a debate about which method is faster. Technically, the bus is quicker, but it's happened more than a few times, particularly on the routes from Austria and Germany, that the bus will detour to drop off regular passengers at or closer to their homes. This happens most often on Friday, when locals who work in Germany and Austria are on a weekend visit to their families, and it can add another hour or more to your trip.

Driving to Croatia from Austria is quite easy, particularly now that the highway between Ljubljana and Zagreb is being completed. If you're going to Istria or Kvarner, simply take the road toward Rijeka instead of Zagreb. From Italy, come through Ancona, where you can also catch a ferry to lots of points on the Dalmatian coast. From the Italian city of Bari, you can get a ferry to Dubrovnik.

Though the European Union has declared vignettes (a sticker allowing you to use a particular country's highway system) illegal, some countries continue to use them, including Slovenia. You can buy the sticker at the border or at a gas station.

Sea

Cruise ships dock regularly in and around Dubrovnik. Ship staff should be able to give you information on getting to your next destination. Ferries are available to Croatia from the Italian coast, with departures from Ancona, Bari, Pescara, Rimini, and Venice. There are several ferry companies, though the most frequent and varied is **Jadrolinija** (www.jadrolinija.hr). You will want to book your ticket in advance if you have a car and are traveling in July and August.

Traditional ferry service from the Italian coast to Split takes eight or nine hours. If you're traveling without a car, **SNAV** (www.snav.it) has high-speed ferries that take about 4.5 hours from Ancona and Pescara to Split.

SLOVENIA
Air

Slovenia's main airport is the small **Brnik Airport** (LJU, www.lju-airport.si), about 23 kilometers (14 miles) from Ljubljana. A number of carriers connect with the airport going to a surprising number of destinations, including Serbia and Bosnia, making Ljubljana better than Zagreb for connections to other countries in the region.

There are no direct flights from North America to Slovenia; you'll need to connect through a larger European city to get to there. **Adria Airways** (www.adria-airways.com), **Austrian Airlines** (www.aua-si.com), and

main bus station Zagreb

Czech Airlines (www.czechairlines.com) all fly to Ljubljana from major European hubs, while **EasyJet** (www.easyjet.com) is a good budget carrier from the British Isles to Slovenia.

There are two small airports, **Maribor Airport** (MBX, www.maribor-airport.si) and **Portorož Airport** (POW, www.portoroz-airport.si), that might also be worth checking out for other possible routes to the country.

Round-trip tickets from North America, with one connection in a major European capital, run about $1,200. You can save money by being flexible on travel dates (mid-week is usually cheapest) and times (early-morning or late-evening flights tend to be in less demand).

Booking a cheap ticket with a budget airline like **Ryanair** (www.ryanair.com) to Trieste, Italy (approximately 100 kilometers/62 miles) or Klagenfurt, Austria (approximately 80 kilometers/50 miles) and connecting with Ljubljana via train or bus is another possibility. You'll lose time with this option, so take that into consideration along with cost.

If you'd like to take advantage of a stopover in Venice, there's a high-speed train connecting Venice to Ljubljana.

Land

You can connect to any country in Europe, including other former Yugoslav republics, through **Slovenian Railways (Slovenske Železnice)** (tel. 01/291-3332, potnik.info@slo-zeleznice.si, www.slo-zeleznice.si). There's a new high-speed train, the *Casanova,* that connects Venice and Ljubljana in just four hours (about the same as driving on a day without traffic). The *Casanova* travels once daily. Most of Slovenia's trains are new and modern. If you're traveling around Europe by train, look into the **Eurail Pass** (www.eurail.com) and **Rail Europe** (www.raileurope.com), though keep in mind the passes do not cover Slovenia.

Bus service around Slovenia is reliable and safe. The **Ljubljana bus station** (Trg Osvobodilne fronte 4, avtobusna.postoja@

ap-ljubljana.si, www.ap-ljubljana.si) has connections to Slovenian and international cities. A trip to Zagreb will take about 2.5 hours.

Driving in Slovenia is easy and the routes are well marked. You can connect to Slovenia via Villach, Klagenfurt, or Graz in Austria, or Trieste in Italy. A highway links Zagreb to Ljubljana in under two hours. Slovenia currently requires vignettes for cars traveling around Slovenia. You can buy the windshield sticker at gas stations around the country. It is valid for one year and costs €35.

Sea

During the summer season, ferries run from Venice to Portorož and Piran on the Slovenian coast. If you're interested in taking to the Adriatic Sea, check out the *Prince of Venice* (http://adriatic-lines.com) and **Venezia Lines** (www.venezialines.com).

MONTENEGRO
Air

There are two airports in Montenegro, **Podgorica Airport** (www.montenegro-airports.com) and **Tivat airport** (www.montenegroairports.com), which service the coast. There are multiple connections daily to Serbia and Russia and several connections to European destinations such as Ljubljana, Frankfurt, Warsaw, and Milan. There are no buses from either airport, but taxis are fairly reliable, though it is a good idea to agree on a fare prior to departure.

Land

There are multiple bus connections daily with the main **bus station** in Dubrovnik. There are at least half a dozen daily connections to Herceg Novi and Kotor. If you drive to Montenegro, you will cross the border from Croatia just south of Dubrovnik. The border crossing can get quite lengthy in the summer.

Sea

There is one ferry from Bari, Italy, to Bar, Montenegro, operated by **Jadrolinija** (www.jadrolinija.com).

Getting Around

CROATIA

Air

Traveling by air in Croatia can save considerable time, particularly the Zagreb to Dubrovnik route, cutting off about 8-10 hours of driving time. **Croatia Airlines** (www.croatiaairlines.com) offers a good array of flights, particularly to destinations in Dalmatia. Keep in mind, though, that tickets within Croatia are best booked once you get to Croatia, unless purchased as part of your international flights. Booking these flights locally will cost at least 50 percent less than you would have paid when booking from home.

Train

Croatian Railways (Hrvatske željeznice) (www.hznet.hr) trains are fairly reliable, fairly clean (if a little old at times), and usually cheaper than taking the bus. The train offers great connections throughout inland Croatia or to destinations on the coast from Zagreb, though many coastal towns are not connected by train. The Eurail Pass does include Croatia.

Be aware that there are two categories of trains: the *putnički* (slow trains, stopping at every village along the way) and IC (intercity trains). The IC trains are more expensive but save a lot of time. You can buy tickets at the station before leaving or from the conductor on the train if you're in a hurry (you'll pay a premium, though). A red *vožnje* (timetable) is posted at every station. *Odlasci* are departures and *dolasci* are arrivals. You can also buy a timetable at larger stations or find out more information on the Croatian Railways website.

Bus

Buses connecting Croatian cities are run by multiple private companies, though the system is quite well organized. Long-distance buses are almost always air-conditioned and quite comfortable, though shorter connections might well be made on old and rather shabby buses. There are multiple connections (sometimes hourly) between Zagreb and other major Croatian cities. Smaller towns may only have one or two connections a day during the week and perhaps none on the weekends.

You'll need to buy your tickets at the counter of the bus station. One thing to keep in mind: You can only buy tickets in advance if you are getting on the bus at its original departure point. If you want to board a bus at a city along its route, you won't be able to buy your ticket until the bus pulls up at the station.

If you're traveling to the coast from Zagreb or vice versa, it's a good idea to buy your ticket a day or two in advance since they tend to sell out during the summer. If you can't find anywhere to buy a ticket, just sit on the bus and wait for the driver, who should be able to sell you one.

Tickets for buses traveling within a town (around Zagreb, for instance) can be purchased at newspaper kiosks or on the bus from the driver. Remember to insert your ticket in the machine inside the bus to validate it.

Boat

Ferries to the Croatian islands close to the coast (Rab and Cres, for example) are usually marked from the road (look for signs with a picture of a boat and the word *trajekt*). You don't need a reservation; just drive up and wait in line. If you're going on foot, it's even easier and rarely more than 30Kn for passage.

Ferries running to islands farther out run on precise timetables. You'll find most of these ferries' schedules at the **Jadrolinija** website (www.jadrolinija.com). Faster hydrofoils and catamarans link Split with islands such as Brač, Hvar, and Vis. They're more expensive but also much faster and usually worth the splurge.

Car

Traveling by car in Croatia is almost essential if you plan on seeing some more out-of-the-way destinations. It's also fairly easy, with the country's network of excellent highways connecting major cities. There are multilane highways between Zagreb and eastern Croatia toward Serbia, Zagreb and Varaždin, and on to Hungary, as well as Zagreb and Ljubljana. There's a great highway between Zagreb and Split (with plans to reach Dubrovnik), though it is quite expensive, with tolls running upward of 200Kn. There's also a highway connecting Zagreb with Rijeka, making the trip to Kvarner only two hours from the capital.

Other roads are often narrow and are not always well maintained. They can also be quite heavily trafficked, though some, like the coastal road, called the Magistrala, offer great views. It's probably best to avoid driving the Magistrala at night; at all times of day and night, remember to watch for pedestrians walking along the narrow and often cliff-hugging road.

You will need your driver's license to drive in Croatia; an International Driving Permit (available from AAA) is recommended. The rental car company will provide you with any additional documents. If a police officer stops you and asks you for your *prijava,* tell him which hotel you are staying at or give the name of the apartment or home owner, as they are supposed to register you. If you are bringing your own car to Croatia, you must have third-party insurance, usually available for purchase at or near the border.

You can buy detailed roadmaps at bookstores, some newsstands, and most gas stations.

Gas stations *(benzinska stanica)* are open at least 7am-7pm Monday-Saturday. Some

stations are closed on Sunday, but every town and major highway should have some 24-hour stations. It's best to try to fill up your tank Monday through Friday, since gas station inspections aren't conducted on weekends and holidays, making those the most likely times for employees to put water in the tank, leaving you stranded a few hundred kilometers down the road.

If you do break down, you can call **HAK** (tel. 987, www.hak.hr), the Croatian Auto Club, for 24-hour emergency roadside assistance. A tire repair shop is called a *vulkanizer* and there are often roadside signs to direct you to the closest one.

RULES OF THE ROAD

Speed limits are posted on roads and range from 40 km/h (25 mi/h) in town to 130 km/h (80 mi/h) on highways. Currently, Croatia allows a 0.05 percent blood alcohol limit for drivers, upped in 2008 from a much-criticized 0 percent limit imposed in 2004 (a local newspaper showed you technically couldn't eat a chocolate-covered cherry and drive); it's worth checking online right before departure, though, to see if any laws have changed, since there have been two changes within a few brief years.

Random breath tests and random stops by police are legal in Croatia. You should not pass a stopped bus (though you'll see lots of locals attempting to do so), nor should you drive on tram lines when the tram line is marked in yellow. A few high-traffic spots in the center of Zagreb allow for cars to share the lane with the trams. Police are allowed to collect fines on the spot, though sometimes it's anyone's guess as to whose pocket the money goes in.

Remember that you are not allowed to make a right turn on red in Croatia. If it's not green, don't go. Punishment for Croatians is the seizure of their driver's license for three months, though police are not allowed to seize foreign driver's licenses. Instead, you'd likely get a hefty fine.

CAR RENTAL

You will need your driver's license, passport, and a credit card to rent a car in Croatia.

Car rental in Croatia is very expensive: around $100 per day for a small car with unlimited mileage, including insurance. You'll find all the major rental agencies, such as **Hertz** (www.hertz.com), **Budget** (www.budget.com), and **Alamo** (www.alamo.com), in Croatia. You can either book online or at an agency in town or at the airport once you arrive. The largest European car rental agency is **Europcar** (www.europcar.com). You may also want to check out the budget **Easy Car** (www.easycar.com) for a cheaper deal.

Under most circumstances, cars rented in Croatia can be driven to Slovenia (and vice versa), though you should always check with the rental company before doing so. Sometimes there are additional fees for the privilege.

PARKING

Though driving in Croatia is relatively easy, parking rarely is. Illegally parked vehicles are often towed. Handicapped spaces are usually marked with a sign or paint; beware of parking in unsigned spaces or those with fading paint, which are difficult to see at night, leaving you an unwelcome surprise in the morning. In many of Croatia's northern and inland towns, regular spaces are marked in blue, and handicapped spaces (marked in white or yellow) are more likely to have a sign in front of them than in southern Croatia. In Zagreb and the coast, handicapped spaces are almost always marked with blue paint. Most cities have at least one parking garage.

In Zagreb you can pay for parking with your cell phone—particularly handy if you've picked up a prepaid cell phone. You send your license plate number via a text message (the number you send it to is determined by what zone you're parked in). It is charged to your cell phone immediately (either added to your bill or, if you have a prepaid card, deducted from the balance). If you don't have a cell phone, you go up to the nearest machine, insert coins, get a receipt, and put it on your dashboard. More and more locations outside of Zagreb are also adopting the pay-by-cell-phone system.

SLOVENIA
Train

If you're traveling to or from Ljubljana, train travel might be just the ticket. **Slovenian Railways (Slovenske Železnice)** (www.slo-zeleznice.si) trains are quite clean, and a lot of the fleet is relatively new. However, the rail system has few connections between smaller towns, so it often doesn't pay to use the train if you're planning on connecting to smaller destinations. IC (intercity) trains are the fastest and only a little more expensive than slower trains. If you see a boxed *R* on the timetable next to the train you would like to take, you'll need to make a reservation in order to get on the train. An *R* without a box means that you can reserve a seat, but aren't required to. It's cheapest to buy tickets at the counter, but if you have (or don't need) a reservation, you can also jump on the train and buy your ticket directly from the conductor for a slightly higher price. Slovenia is part of the Eurail network.

Bus

Most cities in Slovenia are connected by bus. Longer, more frequented routes are likely to be served by the nicest buses, while buses connecting small towns are almost sure to be somewhat older. Prices are calculated by the distance covered.

The timetables, called *vozni red,* are a bit difficult to decipher. Color-coded tables usually follow this formula: black (daily), blue (weekdays), green and orange (daily except Sun.), yellow (school hours), red (Sun. and holidays). If the timetable uses letters, look for letters instead: V (daily), D (weekdays), D+ (daily except Sun.), N (Sun.), NP (Sun. and holidays), ŠP (school hours).

You can buy tickets at the local *avtobusna postaja* (bus station) or pay when you get on the bus. You can make a seat reservation one day in advance for a small fee.

Car

Driving in Slovenia is much like driving in Croatia, only somewhat tamer. There is a major highway running between Ljubljana and Zagreb and another under construction between Ljubljana and Villach. There's also a smaller highway going to Maribor. Otherwise, plan to take rural roads, which have the advantage of offering some stunning scenery. But since they're only two-lane roads, expect the occasional traffic snarl.

Currently, you'll need to purchase a vignette (€35) to use highways in Slovenia if your rental car doesn't already have one. They are available from most any gas station off the highway. You should carry your driver's license and passport when driving, though having an International Driving Permit (available from AAA) is not a bad idea. If you are bringing your own car to Slovenia, you must have third-party insurance, usually available for purchase at or near the border.

Good road maps are available at most every gas station along the highway, though gas stations along rural roads might not have such a wide selection.

If you break down in Slovenia, you can get emergency roadside assistance by calling **Auto-Moto Zveza Slovenije (AMZS)** (tel. 1987, info.center@amzs.si, www.amzs.si), the Slovenian Auto Club. Their website is also a useful tool, with lots of information about driving in Slovenia as well as constantly updated traffic conditions.

As in Croatia, pay attention, as many road rules are ignored by overzealous drivers, and take care driving out of the city at night (especially on rural roads)—drinking and driving is a common offense.

RULES OF THE ROAD

Speed limits range between 40 km/h (25 mi/h) in work zones and some in-town sections and 130 km/h (80 mi/h) on major highways. Slovenians rarely respect these limits,

but police can induce a hefty fine if you're caught speeding.

The blood alcohol limit is 0.05 percent. You may not make a right turn on red in Slovenia. It is not permitted to use a cell phone while driving. You may not honk the horn in busy areas unless you need to avoid a traffic accident. Seatbelts are required for all occupants of the car and low-beam headlights must be kept on at all times. During the winter months (Nov.-Mar.) you are also required to carry snow chains.

As in Croatia, police are allowed to stop you for any reason. Police near small towns are particularly known for random checks and for keeping an eye out for speeding violations. Many offenses require immediate payment of the fine.

CAR RENTAL

You will need your driver's license, passport, and a credit card to rent a car in Slovenia.

You should be able to rent a car for around €50 per day, including insurance. Slovenia has all the major rental agencies, such as **Hertz** (www.hertz.com), **Budget** (www.budget.com), and **Alamo** (www.alamo.com), though rentals are very expensive. If you need to book at the last minute, Ljubljana has offices of all the major agencies. The largest European rental car agency is **Europcar** (www.europcar.com). You may also want to check out the budget **Easy Car** (www.easycar.com) for a cheaper deal.

Under most circumstances, you can drive your rental car into Croatia, though you should always check with the car rental company before doing so in case there are additional fees or paperwork involved.

PARKING

Slovenia is very small, making it somewhat easier to park compared with Croatia. However, the cities do not have a lot of garages, so you'll need to brush up on your parallel parking skills. Parking is allowed in white zones for up to one hour and in blue zones for up to 30 minutes for free.

MONTENEGRO
Train
Trains in Montenegro are extremely cheap but often extremely old. Don't expect Wi-Fi or air-conditioning. The lines connect Virpazar with Bar, Podgorica, and more.

Bus
The best method of public transit in Montenegro, buses are frequent, inexpensive, and reliable. Most offer air-conditioning.

Car
Driving in Montenegro is the best way to see the country, offering you the most flexibility. You should be aware that some roads are very narrow and occasionally precipitous, so proceed with caution.

Visas and Officialdom

CROATIA
Visas and Passports
You should have no trouble getting through immigration if you have the right paperwork. For U.S., U.K., Canadian, Australian, and New Zealand citizens, this simply means a passport; no visa is required for stays up to 90 days. EU citizens only need a national identity card for stays of up to 30 days. Citizens of other countries will want to check visa regulations for Croatia. Visit the Consular Department of the Croatian Foreign Ministry's website at www.mvp.hr for more information.

You are required to register with the police within 24 hours of your arrival. If you're staying in a hotel, hostel, or camp, or have a room booked through an agency, they should register for you (that's why they ask to photocopy your passport or record the information from it). If you are staying with friends or booked a room yourself, your hosts should technically register you, although the authorities are usually lax on this rule, particularly in touristy areas, as long as the stay is not too long. The worst consequence is getting thrown out of the country, though it's more likely they'd advise you to leave and enter again and then register properly.

Croatian Embassies and Consulates
Croatia has embassies and consulates in many countries, such as the **United States** (tel. 202/588-5899, www.croatiaemb.org), the **United Kingdom** (tel. 0870/005-6709, www. croatia.embassyhomepage.com), **Canada** (tel. 613/562-7820, www.croatiaemb.net), and **Australia** (tel. 02/6286-6988, croemb@ bigpond.com).

Foreign Embassies in Croatia
Embassies and consulates are your lifeline in case of emergency. If you have lost your passport, have a medical emergency, or run into trouble with the local law, contact your embassy or consulate for help. If you require assistance, contact the following, all in Zagreb: **U.S. embassy** (Ulica T. Jefferson 2, Buzin, tel. 01/661-2200, www.usembassy.hr); **Australian embassy** (Centar Kaptol, Nova Ves 11, tel. 01/489-1200, www.auembassy.hr); **British embassy** (I. Lučića 4, tel. 01/600-9100, www.britishembassy.gov.uk/croatia); **Canadian embassy** (Prilaz Gjure Deželića 4, tel. 01/484-1200).

Customs
All valuable items brought into Croatia (such as boats, laptops, etc.) should be declared so that you can take them back out with you when you leave. You are only allowed to bring in 200 cigarettes, one liter of alcohol, and 500 grams (about one pound) of coffee. You can even bring your pets if you have a current proof of vaccinations.

In Croatia many purchases over 500Kn are tax-free. Make sure you get the form from the store at the time of purchase (they'll need your passport number to fill it out) and you can get a refund after you get home or once you cross the border. You are not allowed to leave the country with more than 2,000Kn in cash. If you want to purchase a work of art, ask about export approval before purchasing it.

You can find more information at www.carina.hr.

Police

Croatia is quite safe and has a low rate of crime. Your biggest dangers arise from pickpockets and petty theft. Basic safety practices will help minimize risk: Take out a travel insurance policy before you leave home, don't wear flashy jewelry, and keep your bag close under your arm.

It is legal for police to perform random identity-card checks, so it is helpful to have your passport at all times, though you're unlikely to be asked for it. In any case, make a couple of photocopies of your passport's identity page, which will expedite getting a new one from your embassy or consulate. Police in Croatia are friendly. To report a crime you can dial 92 from anywhere in Croatia.

SLOVENIA
Visas and Passports

You should have no trouble getting through immigration if you have the right paperwork. For U.S., U.K., Canadian, Australian, and New Zealand citizens, this simply means a passport; no visa is required for stays up to 90 days. Citizens of the EU, Switzerland, and Croatia can visit for up to 30 days with only a national identity card. However, as visa requirements can change, it's useful to check the Slovenian Ministry of Foreign Affairs website (www.sigov.si/mzz).

Slovenian Embassies and Consulates

Slovenia has embassies and consulates in many countries such as the **United States** (tel. 202/667-5363, www.embassy.org/slovenia), the **United Kingdom** (tel. 020/7222-5400, www.slovenia.embassyhomepage.com),

Canada (tel. 613/565-5781, vot@mzz-dkp.gov.si), and **Australia** (tel. 02/6243-4830).

Foreign Embassies in Slovenia

Embassies and consulates are your lifeline in case of emergency. If you have lost your passport, have a medical emergency, or run into trouble with the local law, contact your embassy or consulate for help. If you require assistance, contact the following, all in Ljubljana: **U.S. embassy** (Prešernova 31, tel. 01/200-5500, www.usembassy.si); **Australian consulate** (Trg Republike 3/XII, tel. 01/425-4252); **British embassy** (Trg Republike 3/IV, tel. 01/200-3910, www.british-embassy.si); **Canadian consulate** (Miklošičeva 19, tel. 01/430-3570).

Customs

EU citizens are not restricted on bringing in alcohol or tobacco for personal use. Non-EU citizens are limited to 200 cigarettes or 50 cigars, two liters of wine, and one liter of alcohol.

For more information, check out www.carina.gov.si.

Police

Crime rates are quite low in Slovenia. Theft is the most common complaint, and if you find yourself a victim, you should report the incident to the police. Police in Slovenia are quite friendly and generally speak at least basic English. The emergency number for the police is 113.

MONTENEGRO
Visas and Passports

You should have no trouble getting through immigration if you have the right paperwork. For U.S., U.K., Canadian, Australian, and New Zealand citizens, this simply means a passport; no visa is required for stays up to 90 days. EU citizens only need a national identity card for stays of up to 30 days. Citizens of other countries will want to check visa regulations for Montenegro.

You are required to register with the police within 24 hours of your arrival. If you're staying in a hotel, hostel, or camp, or have a room booked through an agency, they should register for you (that's why they ask to photocopy your passport or record the information from it). If you are staying with friends or booked a room yourself, your hosts should technically register you.

Montenegrin Embassies and Consulates

Montenegro has embassies and consulates in many countries, such as the **United States** (tel. 202/234-6108, usa@mfa.gov.me), the **United Kingdom** (tel. 20/330-27-227, unitedkingdom@mfa.gov.me), **Canada** (tel. 604/638-8950, kfoy@consulofmontenegro.com), and **New Zealand** (tel. 21/107-6303, jgregovich@xtra.co.nz).

Foreign Embassies in Montenegro

Embassies and consulates are your lifeline in case of emergency. If you have lost your passport, have a medical emergency, or run into trouble with the local law, contact your embassy or consulate for help. If you require assistance, contact the following, in Podgorica: **U.S. embassy** (Dzona Dzeksona 2, Podgorica, tel. 020/410-500, me.usembassy.gov); **British embassy** (Ulcinjska 8, tel. 020/618-010, podgorica@fco.gov.uk). Canada, Australia, New Zealand, and South Africa do not have embassies in Montenegro.

Customs

You are allowed to bring up to one kilogram (2.2 pounds) of food (possibly the most unexpected customs rule in Montenegro), 200 cigarettes, one liter of wine, one liter of spirits, and up to 250 milliliters (8.4 ounces) of perfume. If you have more than €2,000 in cash or travelers checks, they should be declared. If you do not declare it and you have more than €2,000 on your departure, it may be confiscated.

Recreation

Croatia and Slovenia are definitely sporting destinations, whether your tastes run to the spectator side of things or you'd prefer to get down and dirty in some adrenaline-boosting adventure sports. Croatia in particular is known for the many athletes the country has produced, including NBA stars, European-league soccer players, Olympic medalist skiers, and a Wimbledon champion.

In general, if it's adventure sports you're after, Slovenia is the best choice, with faster rapids, higher slopes, and more rocky traverses to climb. Croatia is your destination for sailing and diving. Both countries have beautiful hiking trails.

HIKING

There's no better way than hiking to see the natural beauty of Croatia and Slovenia or to commiserate with the locals. Hiking has a long tradition in the region, with serious

hikers (often in their 60s and 70s) outfitted in proper hiking attire and walking sticks. Around Zagreb, Mount Medvednica and the hills around Samobor are littered with hiking trails and *planinarski domovi* (mountaineer's huts), where you can stop for a drink and a bite to eat at the top. Other areas to explore are the Gorski Kotar, Učka Nature Park in Kvarner, and Paklenica National Park and Plitvice Lakes National Park in Dalmatia.

In Slovenia, the Julian Alps will keep you in awe of the surrounding mountains and deep-green forests. Keep in mind that many mountaineer's huts are only open on weekends or in season, so don't depend on them for shelter or sustenance.

You can get lots more information from the **Croatian Mountaineering Association (Hrvatski planinarski savez)** (tel. 01/482-4142, hps@plsavez.hr, www.plsavez.hr) and the **Alpine Association of Slovenia**

Sailing Croatia

The absolute best way to see the Croatian coast, from Istria all the way down to deepest Dalmatia, is via sailboat. The coast and islands are loaded with small marinas, places to berth, and even restaurants with convenient places to anchor and come in for a bite. You can find remote coves and lots of great scenery.

If you're game, try **Ultra Sailing** (www.ultra-sailing.hr) for charters and courses, from beginners to families to advanced. **Nautika Centar Nava** (www.navaboats.com) is another option for charters, with a selection of yachts for the well-heeled as well. For help with navigating, check out the **Adriatic Navigator** (www.adriatic-navigator.com), which also publishes a guide available at VIP mobile phone stores and certain harbors and marinas in Croatia. Not confident in your seafaring skills? Ask the charter companies about hiring a captain to go along with the boat, and leave the navigating to someone else.

(**Planinska zveza Slovenije**) (tel. 01/434-3022, www.pzs.si).

DIVING

Scuba diving in Croatia is some of the best in the Mediterranean. The sea is clean, the water is clear, tides are generally mild, and the stone base of most of the coastline makes for great visibility. There's lots of variety, too, with spots for cave diving, reef viewing, and shipwrecks. You'll find plenty of excursions and courses at diving centers throughout the country. Particularly strong areas for diving include Mljet and Vis in the Southern Dalmatian Islands, the pristine Kornati Islands, and shipwrecks around Lošinj in the Kvarner Islands and off the coast of Rovinj in Istria.

The Croatian Port Authorities require you to buy a diving card (around 100Kn) after showing your diving license. Diving cards can be purchased at local diving centers or the *lučka kapetanija* (port captain's office) of marinas and harbors. If you don't have a license, you'll find lots of reasonable certification courses. For more information contact the **Croatian Diving Federation** (www.diving-hrs.hr).

Diving is also popular in Slovenia, though not so much as in Croatia since there are fewer dive sites. Try **Nemo Divers** (www.nemo-divers.si) in Portorož for diving courses and excursions or **3glav Adventures** (www.3glav-adventures.com) in Bohinj for diving below the surface of Lake Bled. The **Slovenian Diving Federation** (Slovenska Potaljaška Zveza, www.spz.si) is a great source of information for divers and those who would like to take a course. Cave diving is a very interesting sport, but you can only do it with a licensed guide; contact the diving federation for more information.

SKIING

Skiing in Croatia is popular both as a spectator sport (popularized further by Olympic medalist Janica Kostelić) and as an active sport. There are really only two spots for skiing: Sljeme in the hills above Zagreb and Bjelolasica in the Gorski Kotar. Don't expect any double black diamonds or superb facilities, but it does make a fun day trip or outing.

Slovenia is a much better choice for skiing. The most popular slopes are in the Kranjska Gora and Pohorje areas, though there are runs all over the country. While skiing here is no match for the Austrian slopes, it's nice, well organized, and generally very reasonably priced.

SPECTATOR SPORTS

Soccer, or football, as it is commonly known in Europe, is by far the region's favorite spectator sport. National teams occasionally play in Zagreb and Ljubljana, usually vying for qualification in a tournament such as the European or World Cups. You're more likely to catch a local game: The biggest are Zagreb's Dinamo or Split's Hajduk. In Slovenia the most successful team is NK Maribor. The season lasts from mid-August to the end of May, with a break in January and February. Tickets are relatively cheap and can be purchased on-site before the game. Only big matches between the big teams (sometimes) and national team games (almost always) require ticket purchases in advance of the actual event.

Basketball is also popular in Croatia. Its small hometown teams like Cibona have produced major NBA names like Tony Kukoč. The Croatian handball team has always been excellent and the country's pride in their success shows. A giant arena just for handball is currently being built on the outskirts of Novi Zagreb. Volleyball and water polo are also popular sports.

Accommodations

There are dozens of places to stay in Croatia, Slovenia, and Montenegro, and finding a room shouldn't pose any problem. You will want to reserve ahead during the summer on the coast (mostly to get a good room versus an overpriced mediocre one); otherwise you can probably just show up and find a room in all but the most rural locations—which may have no accommodations at all.

Should you find yourself on the coast without a room, head to one of the Tourist Information offices for help in finding a hotel or private room. Realize that the majority of these offices are in no way related to the town's tourist office. They are in fact agencies brokering rooms, many of them far from the sea and quite expensive for those who show up at the last minute. Stick to your guns about price (or location, or air-conditioning, or television, or whatever else is important to you) and they should be able to come up with something. If that fails, along Croatia's Dalmatian coast you'll often see older women and men standing by the road with signs marked *sobe* or *pension*. They'll also be found in bus stations and train stations. Be aware that some of these people may try to rip you off, and women traveling alone should avoid them altogether. If you do decide to see what they have to offer, ask to see the room before agreeing to anything, and get a commitment for a price first.

In the case of agencies or private rooms, know that you are not obligated to take the room if you don't like what you see. Politely decline and start round 2 of finding a place to stay for the night.

These private rooms and apartments are probably your best value along the coast. Overbuilding means sometimes you can strike a phenomenal deal, getting a basic room for the night for only €10-15 (70-100Kn). These super-cheap rooms won't be right on the beach, though.

Still, you'll find the best deals (and rooms) through official tourist offices and reputable agencies like the ones noted throughout this guide. The companies like Airbnb and the website Booking.com have been quickly embraced by Croatians and Slovenians renting rooms or apartments. When looking online for private rooms or apartments, check the reviews and rely on them.

Package hotels are an option for the traveler who wants to check in and not venture much farther than the hotel pool or beach. But they are not always the best deal for the traveler who likes to see what's around the area, since the price includes breakfast and a lunch or dinner (which, by the way, are rarely culinary treats in themselves). Quite a lot of European travelers frequent the package hotels.

If you're traveling in a group, renting an apartment or house is a great way to go. Check out the sites listed above as well as Home Away (www.homeaway.com) for dozens of properties in Croatia and Slovenia, particularly along the coastal regions.

HOTELS

Huge soulless concrete hotels are one of the traces of former Yugoslavia left all over Croatia and Slovenia's tourist destinations. You'll most likely find that the service, staff, and decor date from the same era as well. Though some of these complexes have received upgrades, for the most part it's best to avoid them and look for more charming places to stay.

One thing to keep in mind as you're researching hotels in Croatia and Slovenia is that in reality, hotels are typically one star lower than the rating advertised. A true five-star hotel in the region is a rare find (although more are cropping up every year). Most hotels rated five-star are in fact four-star, four-star is really three-star, and so on.

Generally, hotels rated three-star or lower will be overpriced for what you get. It's better to try to find a small boutique hotel, pension, or private room or apartment.

On the coast, most hotels offer full-board and half-board add-ons for meals. Usually it's best to forgo these options unless you're staying somewhere extremely rural.

If it's the hotel facilities you're really after, such as pools, bars by the beach, and hot springs, some of the communist leftovers actually sport nicer surroundings than they do rooms. If you're staying somewhere else, you're generally allowed to come on the resort's property—you'll know it's okay if you don't see any signs forbidding it. No one will say anything, as long as you're buying drinks and snacks at one of the outdoor cafés.

Hotels on the coast are the best deal for families who want access to a kiddie club, pools, and so on. A few new and newly renovated properties offer good value for money, while the older communist-era hotels will just make you feel like you've been ripped off.

TERME

Terme (hot-spring spas) in Croatia and Slovenia are hotels with hot-spring pools, saunas, and sometimes other facilities like spas and kiddie clubs. Unfortunately, most of these properties are severely in need of renovations, with tired furniture, threadbare carpets, and a depressing ambience.

However, the owners are making a big effort to update them; Slovenia leads with at least four good *terme,* while Croatia currently has only one worth a visit.

If it's just the hot-spring pools you're after, most of the *terme* have day passes available for purchase, so you can use the facilities without staying in the hotel.

PRIVATE ROOMS AND APARTMENTS

Sobe (private rooms) are some of the best values in Croatia and Slovenia, with the added bonus of getting to know the locals who run the place. The owners are usually friendly and very hospitable, willing to help in any way they can.

If you're looking for luxury accommodations, this is rarely the way to go, but you are almost certain to find clean, comfortable rooms and often a tasty continental breakfast. The rooms are ranked by the local tourist board, with the lowest rated having shared baths and the highest often having air-conditioning and television. However, you may want to ask for details since the ratings system sometimes seems a bit skewed.

On the coast of Croatia, rooms are available most of the year, though a lot are closed during the winter. In high season, you'll probably need to book ahead to get the best rooms. There are fewer private rooms in inland Croatia and Slovenia, but they do exist.

To find a room, check with the local tourist association or look for buildings with a small sign bearing a picture of a bed and the word *sobe,* or a homemade sign with *sobe* or *zimmer frei* (German for "room available"). You can knock on the door or ring the bell at these establishments and see what's on offer.

Apartmani (apartments) get booked a little faster than the rooms and usually have a minimum stay requirement, particularly during the high season. In this category you'll find everything from basic to quite luxurious. A local travel agent or specialty provider should be able to help you book an apartment that meets your expectations.

SEOSKI TURIZAM AND TOURIST FARMS

To really see the traditional side of Croatia and Slovenia, a rural homestay is almost prerequisite. Most of the establishments boast magnificent surroundings, which make up for the typically basic amenities, though some rural homes do have elaborate interiors.

In Croatia, you'll find *seoski turizam* (village tourism) or *agroturizam* (agro-tourism) establishments throughout, particularly in inland Croatia and Istria. You also might want to check out the Istrian Tourism Board's website (www.istra.com) for a good listing of *agroturizam* options.

In Slovenia, check out the **Slovenian Tourist Board** (www.slovenia.info) or **Hiše s tradicijo** (Houses of Tradition, www.hisestradicijo.com) for lots of charming bucolic cottages

HOSTELS

Hostels in Croatia are decent, though Slovenia's are typically better; all are generally clean and safe, and most welcome all ages. They can be a good deal, depending on the location, though baths might be a bit below standard in terms of water pressure, quality, and availability of toilet paper.

The number of Croatian hostels affiliated with **Hostelling International** (www.hihostels.com) is somewhat limited. In Slovenia there's a relatively better selection. Most hostels are open year-round, though it's wise to book ahead, particularly during the summer months.

Private hostels are a bit harder to gauge. Try a website like www.hostelz.com for reviews from other travelers.

CAMPING

Slovenia and Croatia have dozens of campgrounds (in Croatia *autokamp,* in Slovenia *kamps*), particularly in the coastal regions. Campgrounds are usually open April to October and cost only a few euros (35-50Kn) for a space and another few euros per person. Some rent tents for those who don't have them.

Most camps offer electricity, showers, laundry services, and more. Some even rent small cabins or bungalows.

It is illegal to camp in places other than a designated campsite.

Food

It's hard to pin down what constitutes typical Slovenian, Croatian, or Montenegrin food. The countries' geography and history have created a varied culinary offering, strong on regional dishes, influenced by Austrian, Italian, Hungarian, and even Turkish cuisine. What is almost always certain is that the food will be

excellent quality and the portions are likely to be huge, particularly by European standards. Many main meat and potato dishes should suffice for two people, particularly if you add a salad and dip into the bread basket, a must-have on any Croatian and Slovenian table.

TYPICAL FARE

Slovenia, Croatia, and Montenegro have some dishes and flavors that overlap, and there are certain items that are typical all over. In Slovenia and Croatia, one staple is *kremšnita,*

1: holiday house for rent 2: doing laundry the local way, Dubrovnik 3: traditional Slovenian and Croatian cuisine: mixed grilled fish and seafood with garlic oil

How to Get Good Fish

The biggest obstacle between you and an outstanding seafood meal at the coast (particularly in high season) is frozen or day-old fish. It's common for restaurants to serve the subpar fish to foreigners, who they know they'll never see again anyway, and give the best stuff to the locals.

To avoid this unfortunate but all too common scenario, ask to see the fish that's on offer, as the locals do. A platter of different types of fish will be brought out for you to choose from. Keep in mind that the eyes should be clear and never cloudy, and ask the waiter if he'll lift the gills so you can see their color, which should be a bright red. Dull or deep red means they're old or frozen.

Even if you have no idea what to look for, asking to see the fish should get you a better selection than if you hadn't seen it, and they may even think you know what you're talking about.

a custard and pastry dessert claimed by multiple towns in Slovenia and Croatia, though it is suspiciously similar to the Germanic *cremeschnitte*. *Burek* has its origins in the Ottoman Empire, but that doesn't keep it from being a staple in bakeries throughout Croatia, Slovenia, and Montenegro. The ultimate cheap sustenance, perfect after a night of clubbing, the flaky pie can be filled with cheese, potatoes, meat, or even apples. Last but not least there's *pršut* (prosciutto or cured ham). The best *pršut* tends to come from Istria and Dalmatia, where it's said that the strong winter *bura* winds help age the ham, and from Njeguši in Montenegro. A little *pršut*, cheese, and olives with fresh bread on the side is highly recommended as a starter or light lunch.

Croatia

Croatia's Zagorje region is filled with meat and potato dishes and veal, pork, or turkey prepared *zagrebački* style (stuffed with ham and cheese, then breaded and fried). Other typical dishes for the region are *purica s mlincima*, turkey baked with a decadent type of pasta, and *punjene paprika* or *sarma*, peppers stuffed with rice and meat. *Štrukli* (pastry baked with cheese and cream) is also common, either a salty version as a starter or side dish or a sweet version for dessert.

A trip to Slavonia would be incomplete without sampling some of the region's famous pork dishes and its spicy *kulen* (salami). A meal in inland Croatia and Zagorje

is frequently preceded by soup, often a clear broth with a few noodles.

Istria is very proud of its truffles, and there are few dishes that escape their touch, though often the touch is a bit heavy-handed. You can have pasta, steak, cheese, or even omelets with truffles. Istria is also known for its *fuži*, a type of pasta, and *maneštra*, a thick bean and vegetable soup.

Dalmatia is heavy on seafood, often served in a sauce called *buzara*, which has a base of garlic and white wine. Some *buzara* adds tomatoes.

Grilled fish is the most common of the seafood dishes, usually accompanied by a side of *blitva*, a vegetable similar to Swiss chard, cooked in garlic and olive oil with potatoes.

Other excellent seafood dishes are lobster or octopus *ispod peka* (baked in a brick oven) and mussels and oysters. However, don't eat *prstače* (date shells)—it's an endangered species and illegal to sell.

If you'd like something besides seafood, but still typical of Dalmatia, try *pašticada*, beef cooked in a sauce of vinegar, wine, and prunes or tomatoes. *Janjetina*, or lamb, is found at restaurants all over Dalmatia, usually off the coast and up the hills or along the old coastal road. Generally roasted on a spit, it's at its best in the spring and early summer when the lambs aren't too big and the meat is still tender. *Janjetina* is considered a delicacy (despite the basic restaurants it's usually served in) and sometimes a must-eat for those journeying to the coast.

You will also find quite a few fast-food establishments serving up *čevapčiči*, seasoned ground-meat kebabs. The dish has an Eastern origin, and while it is more typical of Bosnia, you will find it a popular staple in Croatia as well.

Slovenia

Though regional cuisine varies widely in the small country, there are a few staples that are found most everywhere. Fresh bread is de rigueur at every meal, and you'll find a heaping basket of it served alongside your meal. The second staple is soup *(juha)*, which begins most every meal, from a barley or bean soup in winter to a lighter fish soup on the coast in summer.

Pork *(svinjina)* is the most favored meat of the country, though you'll find veal *(teletina)* and beef *(govedina)* on almost every menu. *Žganci*, or a porridge of corn or buckwheat, is a common side dish.

In Slovenia's mountainous regions you'll find lots of variations on meat and potatoes, gooey dumplings, and fried doughnuts. You'll also find a fair amount of freshwater trout *(postrv)* and game *(divjačina)*. On the coast, it's fish, fish, and a little more fish.

As you edge toward Hungary in the Prekmurje region, you'll find spicy goulashes, while other regions favor heavy potato-and-bean soups. *Prekmurska gibanica*, a pastry with nuts, poppy seeds, apples, raisins, and cheese, is a filling dessert.

But if it's something more exotic you're looking for, Ljubljana is the place to go, with Asian and Italian cuisines as well as twists on the traditional.

Montenegro

As in Croatia, one of the best meat dishes is anything cooked in a clay oven, ispod saca (known as ispod peka in Croatia). Another excellent must-try is Montenegrin lamb cooked in milk.

Completely different from anything you might find to the north, kačamak is cooked cornmeal with potatoes, sometimes topped with cream cheese and sour milk.

FINDING A RESTAURANT

If you'd like to explore beyond this guide's recommendations, there are some simple rules you can follow for finding a restaurant in Croatia and Slovenia. An establishment labeled *restoran* (Croatia) or *restavracija* (Slovenia) tends to be more formal, though not always completely atmospheric. Service at these establishments tends to be very good, with professional waiters taking pride in what they do. You may have to flag down the waiter for the bill *(račun* in both Croatian and Slovenian) or mention that you're in a hurry if you want to speed up the process. It is considered rude for waiters in restaurants of this type to rush you through your meal.

A *konoba* (Croatia) or *gostišče* (Slovenia) is one step down in formality, though usually a step up in atmosphere. Frequently cozy, wood-beamed, and decorated with local farm implements, a *konoba* serves its food with warmth. Prices are in line with a *restoran* or *restavracija*.

Even less formal is the *gostiona* (Croatia) or *gostilna* (Slovenia). This is the sort of place you'll likely find local business types chowing down for lunch, and all but empty in the evenings.

This said, there's a trend to call more upmarket establishments *konoba* or *gostilna*, similar to the way a bistro in Manhattan might bring a three-figure bill. If you're looking for inexpensive but filling food, ask for a place that serves *gablec* (Croatia). It's a colloquial term that refers to a lunch menu (though literally it means a light snack), usually priced for workers on their lunch breaks.

Most restaurants open around 10am or 11am and close around 11pm. As for the day of the week they are closed, it's anyone's guess, though the most likely day is Monday for traditional restaurants or Sunday for those that cater to working types.

Pretty much every town in Croatia and Slovenia has a pizzeria with great pizzas and sometimes pasta dishes. You can also nip into a bakery for a slice of pizza to go, a sandwich, or a slice of *burek*.

Croatians and Slovenians breakfast on the light side, if at all. Most hotels and bed-and-breakfasts will offer at least a continental breakfast. Otherwise, buy a pastry and take it to a café. Since most cafés don't sell food, they won't mind you dunking your doughnut into their coffee.

DRINKING

Croatians and Slovenians adore their coffee, spending lots of time seeing and being seen in cafés all over, at all hours of the day and night. Espresso and *macchiato (kava s mlijekom)* tend to be on the strong side. If you'd like something a little lighter, order a *bijela kava* (*macchiato* with extra milk) in the capital cities. Outside the capitals, the *bijela* (white) side tends to be a little skimpy. Lots of young people drink Nescafé, in vanilla or chocolate flavors, so don't feel you're alone if the other items on offer are too strong for your tastes. You won't have any trouble locating a café in Croatia and Slovenia, where sometimes it feels like there's one every 20 meters. They're open from the early morning until late at night.

If you'd like something non-caffeinated, make sure to specify whether you want it carbonated *(gazirano)* or not *(negazirano)*. Also be aware that ordering "juice" will always get you orange juice. If you'd like apple, make sure to specify.

Croatian and Slovenian beers are lighter than their Germanic counterparts. Karlovačko and Ožujsko are the most common in Croatia, while Velebit, Tomislav, and Osiječko Crno are richer and worth a try. The most frequent Slovenian brand is Laško. Beers tend to be very reasonable, with a huge glass setting you back only a few euros (25-30Kn).

Croatians and Slovenians are very proud of their brandies. Though plum brandy is the most common, you'll also find pear brandy, herb brandy, honey brandy, and walnut brandy. Zadar in Dalmatia is famous for its cherry liqueur, *maraskino*. They are typically taken as an aperitif before a meal.

Croatian and Slovenian wines are high in quality but often are not known to Western travelers. Because most of the producers sell out their stock locally, few bottles make it to supermarket shelves out of the country. Traveling around the countryside is a great way to get to know the locals as well as pick up a few bottles of regional wines. Istria's Malvazija, a light, crisp white, should satisfy pretty much any drinker when it is drunk young. Teran, also indigenous to Istria, is an earthy red with a strong taste best suited to local palates. Other well-known Croatian wines are reds made from Plavac Mali grapes in Dalmatia and the whites of Slavonia, whose reputation is growing. Slovenia is most known for its Beli Pinot and Šipon, both white wines, and for Kraški Teran in the Karst. The country also produces Cviček, similar to a rosé, and some decent sparkling wines.

If you happen to get a low-quality wine in Croatia or Slovenia, do as the locals do and mix it with other beverages. *Bevanda* mixes white or red wine with plain water, *gemišt* mixes white wine and bubbly mineral water, while *bambus* uses cola to take the edge off a bitter red wine.

Travel Tips

OPPORTUNITIES FOR STUDY AND EMPLOYMENT

Getting a work permit in Croatia and Slovenia is difficult to impossible. However, there are a few ways to spend more time in the area.

Teaching English or teaching in an international school is probably your best bet, though even these jobs are hard to come by. Many locals have an excellent level of English, so it's rare for schools to want to deal with the paperwork required to recruit a native speaker with no residency or work permit. If you'd like to find such a job, contact local language schools or the international schools in Zagreb and Ljubljana to inquire about positions.

Volunteer work is another option, with most posts revolving around the environment. **Caput Insulae Eco Centre** in Beli, Croatia (www.caput-insulae.com), helps protect endangered griffon vultures on the island of Cres, and **Blue World** (www.blue-world.org) monitors dolphins from the island of Lošinj.

There are many language schools in Croatia. A couple to check out are the **APLO** (www.aplo-centar.com) and the **Croatian Heritage Foundation** (www.matis.hr), as well as the all-purpose www.studyabroad.com, which lists dozens of study and work programs for many countries, including Croatia and Slovenia.

ACCESS FOR TRAVELERS WITH DISABILITIES

Options for physically challenged travelers have improved in Croatia, Slovenia, and Montenegro, but the facilities are still far from what they should be to properly accommodate wheelchairs and other special needs. The older sections of town are difficult to maneuver, often with narrow cobbled streets, but even more modern parts of town often fail to have wheelchair-friendly curbs. Newer and high-end hotels, as well as airports, almost always have elevators and restrooms specially designed for wheelchairs. To avoid frustration, plan in advance as much as possible.

Your first stop should be the website of the **Society for Accessible Travel and Hospitality** (www.sath.org), which has a wonderful section of general travel tips to assist in planning. Then contact the tourist office for the cities you would like to visit to find out about sights and hotels with adapted facilities (it's a good idea to double-check this information with the venues before booking).

TRAVELING WITH CHILDREN

Traveling with kids is easy in Croatia, Slovenia, and Montenegro. People in the region love children, and generally, the farther south you go, the more they love them. You'll often see children around cafés, walking with their parents in the evening, at weddings and family events, and in restaurants, though less so due to monetary constraints on most young families.

The only thing to keep in mind, in Slovenia and Croatia and particularly Montenegro, is that with very young children, do be aware of lax safety regulations that are laxer the further south you go.

Sightseeing

Monuments and museums are open to children, often with free or discounted admission. You'll find at least one *igraonica* (play center) in most every city. While there aren't lots of spots specifically for very young children, school-age kids will appreciate sights like Rovinj's museum for the *batana* boat, the mummy at Zagreb's archaeological museum, Ljubljana's excellent children's science museum, and the many medieval castles around the area. Make the trip more interesting by creating a treasure hunt for info tidbits to get the kids more involved at the sights you visit.

Restaurants

Children are welcome in most restaurants in Croatia, Slovenia, and Montenegro. Diners are generally happy sharing their meal with children, and turn a blind eye to those that run around freely. You may even find not-too-busy waiters or waitresses entertaining them while you eat.

The only exception might be a very chic modern restaurant where small, squealing kids might draw some dirty looks. Also take into account that during the busy summer season, not all restaurant patrons are Croatian and Slovenian, and nonlocals may have different expectations of young children.

Most restaurants don't have high chairs or booster seats, so if you really need one, you may want to call ahead to find one that does, or bring your own portable one. The U.S. website **One Step Ahead** (www.onestepahead.com) has some great travel gear for little ones.

Croatian children generally eat whatever the adults are eating, and no one will mind if you ask for another plate so your kids can share your dish. Nearly every place can whip up a *tjestinine Bolognese* (pasta with meat sauce) or *Milanese* (tomato sauce without meat), some *pohani piletine* (breaded and fried chicken), or *pomfrit* (french fries) for picky eaters. For food emergencies, McDonald's can be found in Ljubljana, Maribor, Zagreb, Osijek, Varaždin, Karlovac, Rijeka, Pula, and Split.

Transportation, Accommodations, and Supplies

It's best to take a car, plane, or train when traveling around Croatia and Slovenia with young children—buses can be just too much for wiggly little souls to handle.

Most hotels levy a surcharge for children staying in your room, but are happy to provide a *kinderbet* (crib) and extra sheets and towels. On the coast, large hotels and resorts will likely have kiddie clubs or an *igraonica* where children can enjoy a program just for them.

Pharmacies sell a limited selection of baby food and supplies. You'll find a better selection in grocery stores or *drogerie marts* like the chains DM and Müller.

You're unlikely to find many changing facilities outside of shopping centers, McDonald's, highway gas stations, and airports. For young children it's best to bring some changing pads and change them in a stroller or on the seat of the car.

WOMEN TRAVELING ALONE

Croatia, Slovenia, and Montenegro are safe for female travelers, and you're unlikely to encounter any real problems. That's not to say you won't be hit on by the locals, particularly if you go to a bar or disco—it's probably better to find some traveling companions at your hotel or hostel to go out with.

Rape and violent crime are rare in all countries, but that doesn't mean you should forget about safety. Basic common sense should keep you safe: Be wary of strangers; don't drink too much; try to avoid walking on dark, empty streets alone; and don't flash money or jewelry.

GAY AND LESBIAN TRAVELERS

Attitudes toward the gay community in Croatia are still rather in the dark ages, although the younger generation is more accepting. Kissing and holding hands by couples of the same sex is almost never seen, particularly in smaller towns, where it may even cause a confrontation. The one exception to this rule is Zagreb's annual gay pride parade, a huge step for the gay community in Croatia.

There are a few havens for same-sex couples in Zagreb, including some gay bars and alternative bars that attract a laid-back crowd of straight and gay patrons. Rijeka is probably Croatia's most liberal town and has lots of bars and clubs open to same-sex couples.

Business Hours

Though we've tried to list as best we can the working hours for various restaurants, tourist offices, sightseeing destinations, and shops, it's wise to remember that hours can be somewhat flexible in Croatia, Slovenia, and Montenegro. The general rule is that this flexibility grows the smaller the town and the farther south and toward the coast you go. It's not unheard of for a tourist office to suddenly take a week's vacation or a small museum to lock its doors because it just wasn't busy. Keep a positive attitude and move on to the next place. If you're really going out of your way to visit a particular place, it's advisable to call ahead to see if they will be open. Having said that, this phenomenon is fortunately happening less and less.

For more information, check out the website www.travel.gay.hr, about traveling around Croatia; **Iskorak** (www.iskorak.hr), an organization for the advancement of gay and lesbian rights, also has a website worth a visit.

In Montenegro, there is not currently any LGBTQ establishment in the entire country. Of the three countries in this book, it is most certainly the most conservative and least tolerant towards the gay and lesbian community.

Though Slovenia is also fairly conservative when it comes to accepting gays and lesbians, particularly public opinion in rural areas, the gay community has made some amazing strides in the recent past, making the country even more tolerant than Croatia. The yearly **Ljubljana Gay and Lesbian Pride Parade (Parada ponosa)** (www.ljubljanapride.org) has been running since 2000, and a transvestite band, Sestre, was Slovenia's 2002 entry in Eurovision, a popular song contest.

In 2015 the Slovenian parliament approved a bill extending marriage rights to same-sex partners, and at the time of writing, it was still waiting for the president's signature. It is already legal for same-sex couples to adopt children in Slovenia.

TRAVEL INSURANCE

Travel insurance can come in handy in case of cancellations, missed flights, or stolen property. Before purchasing insurance, you may want to check your current policies as well as your credit cards to see what is already covered. If you need to purchase additional insurance, your own insurance company is one option, or one of dozens of companies that specialize in trip insurance. Try **Betin** (www.betins.com), **Travel Insured** (www.travelinsured.com), or **World Nomads** (www.worldnomads.com), which targets the backpacker and budget travel market.

HEALTH AND SAFETY
Health Issues

There are no immunizations required for Croatia or Slovenia, though travelers planning to spend a lot of time hiking or in wooded areas may want to consider being inoculated against tick-borne encephalitis. In lieu of getting a shot, you can also avoid heavily forested areas between April and August, wear long sleeves and long pants and a hat, and use an insect repellent with DEET.

Small medical complaints can probably be solved at the local *ljekarna* (pharmacy). Younger staff will likely speak some English, particularly in Croatia, but you can also bring a small dictionary or use the glossary in this guide to help you along.

Pharmacies are generally open 8am-8pm Monday-Friday and 8am-2pm Saturday. Neighborhood pharmacies take turns staying open 24 hours. Information should be posted at the door or window of all pharmacies or found in the local newspaper. Zagreb has several 24-hour pharmacies that are open every day of the year. These can be found at Trg bana Jelačića 3, Ilica 301 (an extremely long walk from the main square, so take a taxi), Grižanska 4, and Ozaljska 1.

For medical emergencies, go directly to the nearest *bolnica* (hospital) or call an ambulance (dial 112 in Croatia and Slovenia). EU citizens are entitled to free health care; others will want to check their countries' agreements with Croatia and Slovenia or their health insurance policy. Doctors in Croatian and Slovenian hospitals are usually wonderful and very well trained. Hospitals, particularly in large cities, are well equipped with all the necessary machines and instruments, though they are shockingly lacking in even the most basic creature comforts (occupants are often asked to bring their own toilet paper), with Croatia being far worse than Slovenia.

You may want to check out the website of the **International Society of Travel Medicine** (www.istm.org) for a list of some local clinics. The website **Travel Health Online** (www.tripprep.com) has some excellent tips and country-by-country information.

Health Insurance

If your own health insurance doesn't cover you while you're traveling, a traveler's health insurance policy is usually worth the money spent, if only for the peace of mind. Realize that in any case, you'll need to cover any costs out-of-pocket and then be reimbursed once you return home. A couple of agencies to check out when shopping for travel health insurance are **Travel Guard** (www.travelguard.com) and **STA Travel** (www.statravel.com).

CONDUCT AND CUSTOMS
Croatia

Croatians are friendly and outgoing, and you shouldn't have trouble striking up a conversation with a local. Croatians rarely split the bill; usually one person covers it with the expectation that the favor will be returned at a later date.

One thing that all Croatians are wonderful about is their hospitality. If you are invited to their home, they will likely stuff you with food and drink. Since Croatians are stingy with

Emergency Numbers

CROATIA

- Police: 92
- Fire: 93
- Ambulance: 112
- Roadside assistance: 987
- International operator: 901

SLOVENIA

- Police: 113
- Fire: 112
- Ambulance: 112
- Roadside assistance: 1987
- International operator: 115

MONTENEGRO

- Police: 122
- Ambulance: 124
- Roadside assistance: 9807

their compliments to each other, they love receiving them—don't be shy. Croatians particularly love to hear nice things about their coastline, and since it really is beautiful, you might as well go ahead and say it.

If a Croatian visits your home or apartment and you offer them a drink, they will almost invariably say no, as it is considered polite behavior. Gently insist a couple of times; that failing, bring them the drink anyway, "just in case."

There are a few things that North Americans might consider to be rude that are in fact quite normal behavior in Croatia. Elderly people will tend to try to cut in line, which is generally tolerated, if not entirely fair. Lots of diners will employ toothpicks at the table after a meal.

Some travelers complain of poor service, even at luxury establishments. You're more likely to receive this sort of treatment from older employees, a holdover from the communist regime. If you do experience it, try to have a sense of humor about it and not let it ruin your vacation.

Most Croatians eat a heavier lunch and a lighter dinner, so if you're in a little-touristed area, don't be put off by an empty restaurant in the evening.

Tipping is not common practice, though it is polite to leave a *kuna* or two after a coffee or leave around 10 percent to waitstaff in a restaurant. If you plan on returning, tipping is almost sure to bring you a higher level of service the next time around.

Smoking is commonplace in Croatia and can be positively suffocating in winter, when packed bars and cafés are overloaded with it. Though required by law to have nonsmoking areas, the tiny footprint of most establishments negates their impact.

Slovenia

Slovenians are hardworking, generally very well educated, and somewhat more reserved than the people of other Slavic countries. They consider it polite to shake hands when meeting, particularly for the first time. Close friends will kiss twice, once on each cheek.

If you're invited to dinner or to someone's home in Slovenia, it's nice to bring some flowers or a bottle of wine. Meals are considered an important part of family life and most people, young and old, meet up with their friends in cafés.

It is customary to leave a 10 percent tip in restaurants and bars; also give a small tip to taxi drivers.

Slovenia has finally passed a smoking ban in indoor places, making going out fun even in the winter.

Public restrooms are generally very clean, but don't be surprised if you need to leave a tip for the attendant. Sometimes the amount is posted. If it isn't, about €0.20 is acceptable.

Montenegro

Montenegrins are friendly and outgoing. Steer clear of conversations around politics, religion, history, or ethnicity. If you are invited to someone's home, remove your shoes at the door and bring a small gift. If you are toasting, either on the giving or receiving end, make sure to make eye contact with the other party.

In religious venues, dress modestly and walk backward out of a shrine.

Topless sunbathing is for nudist beaches only.

WHAT TO TAKE

You can buy almost anything you need in Croatia and Slovenia, but keep in mind it will likely be much more expensive than North America. Still, it's best to pack light, hopefully fitting everything into a not-too-big bag with wheels so you can pull it along behind you as you travel around. Backpacks are probably best left to serious backpackers since they tend to make you a target for thieves by labeling you a "tourist."

Try to pack light items that won't need ironing, since some small hotels might not have an iron. Layers are great, especially in some inland areas of Croatia and Slovenia where temperatures can vary vastly from day to night. A small umbrella that can fit in your bag and a light rain jacket are a good idea, especially in fall and winter. Also bring a pair of UVB-blocking sunglasses.

Perhaps most importantly, pack some comfortable rubber-soled shoes, especially for seeing the museums and monuments in the old towns, where cobblestoned streets can turn slippery for flat-soled sandals and may catch even medium-size heels between their grooves.

Though Croatians, Slovenians, and Montenegrins dress more formally than the average North American, you won't stand out in smart casual clothes and a pair of rubber-soled shoes, though the sneakers you wear to aerobics class might be out of place. Most people in the region do dress to impress, so you might want to bring along one or two outfits for more formal dinners or club-hopping to fit in with the crowd. You can leave the jacket and tie at home, though, as a collared shirt is acceptable in even the chicest establishments. That's not to say you won't see locals sporting jackets and ties, however.

Do keep in mind that staff at some churches might frown on sleeveless or low-cut tops, so dress accordingly when sightseeing.

A blow dryer is a good idea, particularly if you are staying at smaller hotels or in private rooms. Just make sure it's dual voltage, and don't forget the adapter. If you're bringing electronics like laptops or digital cameras that need recharging, make sure they are also dual voltage before packing them.

Also pack any prescription drugs you'll need for at least the length of your stay, as well as a photocopy of the drug's label or a copy of your prescription just in case you need a refill.

Most importantly, don't forget your passport, a copy of your passport in case it's lost or stolen, and your driver's license if you plan on renting a car. You don't have to have an International Driving Permit, but it's not a bad idea. They're available at AAA offices all over North America. Make sure you have a copy of your credit card numbers and the phone numbers for reporting them lost or stolen.

Holidays

CROATIA

- January 1—New Year's Day
- January 6—Epiphany
- March or April—Easter Monday
- May 1—Labor Day
- May—Corpus Christi
- June 22—Anti-Fascism Day
- June 25—Day of Croatian Statehood
- August 5—National Thanksgiving Day
- August 15—Assumption
- October 8—Independence Day
- November 1—All Saints Day
- December 25 and 26—Christmas holidays

SLOVENIA

- January 1 and 2—New Year's holidays
- February 8—Prešeren Day
- March or April—Easter Monday
- April 27—Day of Uprising Against the Occupation
- May 1 and 2—Labor Day
- May—Pentecost
- June 25—Slovenia Day
- August 15—Assumption
- October 31—Reformation Day
- November 1—All Saints Day
- December 25—Christmas Day
- December 26—Independence Day

MONTENEGRO

- January 6—Christmas Eve
- January 7—Christmas
- May 21—Independence Day
- July 13—Sovereignty Day

Information and Services

MONEY
Croatia

Croatia's currency is called the *kuna*. Bills are denominated in 5, 10, 20, 50, 100, 200, 500, and 1,000 *kuna*. Coins are available in 1, 5, 10, 20, and 50 *lipa* (100 lipa make 1 *kuna*) or 1, 2, and 5 *kuna*.

If you need to exchange money, go to a *banka* (bank) or *mjenjačnica* (exchange bureau). If you'd like to check the current rate of exchange, try the website www.xe.com. Banking hours are generally 8am-5pm Monday-Friday and 8am-12pm Saturday, though banks in larger cities may have extended hours, and those in small towns or on the coast will often close Saturdays and sometimes for lunch. Banks in coastal tourist areas may stay open until 9pm during the high season.

Most *mjenjačnice* (exchange bureaus) remain open longer than banks, and major post offices often have currency exchange counters as well. The least value for your dollar, pound, or euro is almost always given at hotels.

These days, traveler's checks are more of a burden than a blessing. To travel safely, bring credit cards and keep in a separate place the card numbers and phone number to call if a card is lost or stolen. Croatian establishments almost always accept Visa, MasterCard, and oddly enough, Diners Club, which was the first credit card available in the country, giving it a substantial market share. American Express is making serious headway, and most places take it as well. Leave your Discover card at home; only a few places will take it.

Be aware that some places, particularly small stores and businesses in smaller towns, may only take cash. Some stores and restaurants also give discounts, sometimes 10 or 20 percent, for paying with cash.

ATMs provide an easy way to get cash (though your bank is likely to charge you a usage fee for withdrawing money). ATMs are available in bigger cities and sometimes very small towns, though you shouldn't count on it. You should have no trouble using your debit card in one of these machines.

Slovenia

Slovenia adopted the euro in 2006. Bills are denominated in 5, 10, 20, 50, 100, 200, and 500 euros. Coins are available in 1, 2, 5, 10, 20, and 50 cents, plus 1 and 2 euros. Banks in Slovenia are generally open 8:30am-12:30pm and 2pm-5pm Monday-Friday. Many banks also open 8:30am-12pm on Saturday. Banks in Ljubljana will often be open the entire day, without stopping for lunch.

Using ATMs is a much easier method of getting cash than constantly exchanging money. Machines accepting Visa, Maestro, Cirrus, and MasterCard are all over the country, though you may have a tough time finding ATMs in small villages. The exchange rate offered by the banks is generally reasonable, though your bank will likely charge you a usage fee for withdrawing money.

If you do need to exchange money, banks, post offices, and exchange offices are your best bets.

Major credit cards such as American Express, Visa, MasterCard, and even Diners Club are accepted at most stores, restaurants, and hotels.

Montenegro

Montenegro uses the euro. Banks with ATMs can be found in any larger town. Some restaurants, shops, and small hotels do not accept credit cards.

COMMUNICATIONS AND MEDIA
Mail

In Croatia and Slovenia you can buy stamps at the *pošta* (post office), easily recognizable in both countries by a black horn against a yellow background. Most post offices are open 8am-7pm Monday-Friday and 8am-12pm or 1pm on Saturday. The main post offices in large cities and towns are likely to be open even longer. The Slovenian mail system is a little faster and more reliable than Croatia's, where the city of Zagreb uses a local courier service to deliver monthly utility bills. If you need to ship something quickly, try FedEx (www.fedex.com) or DHL (www.dhl.com); FedEx often works out to be the cheaper of the two. Packages shipped through any postal service should not be sealed until customs is able to take a look at them (you take the package to the desk at the post office, they have a look, and then seal it).

Telephone

To use a phone booth in Croatia and Slovenia, you'll need a telephone card (*telekarta* in Croatia, *telekartica* in Slovenia), available for sale at post offices and newspaper stands. These cards, offered in units of 25, 50, 100, 200, or 500, can be used for making local, long distance, and even international calls (buy at least a 50 for international calls). If you're calling home and not sure how long you'll be on, it might be a good idea to head to the main post office and ask for a cabin, where you make a call and pay afterward. You'll probably want to avoid direct-calling from your hotel room, though using a phone card shouldn't set you back much.

In Croatia, phone numbers can vary in length, with some numbers having six digits, though most have seven these days. In Slovenia, land-line phone numbers have seven digits, and cell phone numbers have six digits. If you're calling Croatia or Slovenia from abroad, you dial the international access code, the country code (385 for Croatia, 386 for Slovenia), the area code (drop the initial zero), and the number. If you're dialing within the country, you'll need the area code (including the initial zero) plus the number. Cell phones are preceded by 098, 095, 091, and 099 in Croatia and 031, 040, 041, and 051 in Slovenia. To call abroad from Croatia or Slovenia, dial 00, the country code (1 for the United States and Canada), the area code, and the number.

CELL PHONES

If you'd like to use your cell phone in Croatia, Slovenia, or Montenegro, before leaving home check with your service provider about procedures and costs. One of the cheapest options is to buy local SIM cards for use in GSM phones so you can make calls within Croatia and Slovenia. If you're staying in Croatia or Slovenia longer than a couple of weeks, it's probably a great investment. Before leaving home, make sure your phone won't be locked when you insert the local SIM card. Hint: Getting a phone unlocked in Croatia is relatively cheap and simple if you do get stuck (ask at a cell phone store, which typically advertise various carriers). Three SIM card providers to try in Croatia are T-Com, VIP, and Tele2, fairly new to the game and likely to be the cheapest. In Slovenia try Si.mobil.

Internet Access

In today's world it's hard to run a successful hotel or restaurant, and definitely a coffee shop, without free Wi-Fi. Gone are the days when traveling abroad meant paying for dial-up in a stuffy Internet café the size of your closet.

If your hotel doesn't have Internet access, head to the nearest café offering free Wi-Fi (and they're everywhere in Croatia and Slovenia, even on the islands, unless you're staying at one of the lighthouses), order a coffee, and connect.

English-Language Press

In Croatia, the English-language print press is almost entirely confined to the free *In Your Pocket* (www.inyourpocket.com) guides available for Zagreb, Rijeka, Zadar, Dubrovnik, and Osijek. Otherwise, head to a local kiosk or bookstore for English-language dailies and weeklies. Online you can check out Croatian news at Croatia Week (www.croatiaweek. com).

In Slovenia, *In Your Pocket* offers free guides for Ljubljana and Bled. There are some excellent expat newspapers in Slovenia, like the *Slovenia Times* (www.sloveniatimes.com), an English-language daily that can keep you in the know about virtually everything going on in Slovenia. The quarterly magazine *Ljubljana Life* (www.ljubljanalife.com) is also worth checking out.

Croatian and Slovenian Press

Croatia's main national newspapers are *Jutarnji List* (www.jutarnji.hr) and *Večernji List* (www.vecernji.hr).

In Slovenia, the major newspapers are *Delo* (www.delo.si) and *Dnevnik* (www.dnevnik.si).

MAPS AND VISITOR INFORMATION

Maps

If it's a simple city map you're searching for, most tourist offices and sometimes hotels can provide you with one that's suitable for a walk around town. You can also purchase maps at bookstores and almost all gas stations. Gas stations on highways should provide a large range, with detailed road, highway, and sometimes even city maps. If you'd like to purchase maps before leaving home, look on www.amazon.com.

A quick look at Google Maps (http://maps.google.com) can help you get your bearings, but detailed information isn't always available for Croatia and Slovenia, particularly once you're out of the big cities. Honestly the real problem here isn't Google, but the addresses themselves. You'll see addresses without a building number (indicated in Croatia by the street name followed by "bb"). The numbers weren't forgotten, they just weren't there in the first place.

Tourist Offices and Websites

A quick look at some of the main tourism websites for Croatia and Slovenia serves as a great way to fill in any blanks, ask questions, or search for tour operators and private rooms. The **Croatian National Tourist Office** (www.croatia.hr) should be your first stop for Croatian tourism info. The **Slovenian Tourist Board** (www.slovenia.info) has a feature where you can reserve all types of accommodations, from hotels to private rooms, online.

WEIGHTS AND MEASURES

Croatia, Slovenia, and Montenegro use the metric system.

The electrical system is 220 volts, 50 hertz. Most newer appliances have dual-voltage capability; if not, you'll need a voltage converter. Plugs in Croatia, Slovenia, and Montenegro are the typical European variety, two-pinned with round prongs. Plug adapters can sometimes be found for sale in airports or heavily touristed areas, but otherwise you'll spend precious time looking for one, so it's best to pick one up before leaving home.

Croatia, Slovenia, and Montenegro are in the Central European time zone, meaning that it is one hour later than the United Kingdom, six hours later than the East Coast's eastern standard time zone, nine hours later than the U.S. West Coast, 10 hours earlier than Australian central standard time, and 12 hours earlier than New Zealand. Croatia, Slovenia, and Montenegro use the 24-hour clock, especially for bus and ferry schedules, though not in conversation. Starting from midnight (0000) add one hour for each hour of the day: 0100 is 1am, 0700 is 7am, 1200 is noon, 1300 is 1pm, and 1400 is 2pm.

Resources

Glossary

CROATIAN

autobusni kolodvor: bus station
bb: stands for *bez broja* (without number); in addresses without a building number, *bb* follows the street name
bijelo vino: white wine
cesta: road
crkva: church
crno vino: red wine
dobro: good
donji grad: lower town
država: country
duplo: double
gornji grad: upper town
grad: town
gradska viječnica: town hall
hladno, hladna, hladan: cold
ime: name
jama: cave
janjetina: lamb
jezero: lake
kavana: coffee shop
konoba: bistro
ljudi: people
most: bridge
muzej: museum
obala: coast
odlično/super: great
otvoreno: open
pivo: beer
plaža: beach
Riva: waterfront promenade
samostan: monastery
seoski turizam: rural tourism
šetalište: walking path

stari grad: old town
svijet: world
trg: square
ulaz: entrance
ulica: street
vino: wine
vinska cesta: wine road
vrata: gate
vrijeme: weather
vrt: garden
vruće: hot
zatvoreno: closed
željeznički kolodvor: train station
život: life

SLOVENIAN

avtobusna postaja: bus station
belo vino: white wine
cerkev: church
cesta: road
črnina: red wine
dobro: good
država: country
dvojen: double
grad: castle
hladen: cold
ime: name
jama: cave
jezero: lake
kmečki turizem: rural tourism
ljude: people
most: bridge
muzej: museum
obala: coast
odličen: great

odprt: open
pivo: beer
plaža: beach
samostan: monastery
sprehajališče: walking path
svet: world
taverna: bistro
trg: square
ulica: street
vhod: entrance
vino: wine
vinska cesta: wine road
vrata: gate
vreme: weather
vroč: hot
vrt: garden
zaprto: closed
železniška postaja: train station
življenje: life

MONTENEGRIN

autobusni kolodvor: bus station
bb: stands for *bez broja* (without number); in addresses without a building number, *bb* follows the street name
bijelo vino: white wine
cesta: road
crkva: church
crno vino: red wine
dobro: good
donji grad: lower town
država: country
duplo: double
gornji grad: upper town
grad: town

gradska viječnica: town hall
hladno, hladna, hladan: cold
ime: name
jama: cave
janjetina: lamb
jezero: lake
kavana: coffee shop
konoba: bistro
ljudi: people
most: bridge
muzej: museum
obala: coast
odlično/super: great
otvoreno: open
pivo: beer
plaža: beach
Riva: waterfront promenade
samostan: monastery
seoski turizam: rural tourism
šetalište: walking path
stari grad: old town
svijet: world
trg: square
ulaz: entrance
ulica: street
vino: wine
vinska cesta: wine road
vrata: gate
vrijeme: weather
vrt: garden
vruće: hot
zatvoreno: closed
željeznički kolodvor: train station
život: life

Croatian Phrasebook

Croatian is not the easiest language to learn, so try using English first since most people under 40 speak at least some English. That said, Croatians are extremely happy when someone at least tries to speak Croatian. It's a sure way to break the ice and bring a smile to their faces.

PRONUNCIATION

The great thing about Croatian is that it is almost entirely phonetic. If you can master the pronunciation, you can read almost anything, even if you have no idea what it says.

Vowels

a   like the "a" in "father": *kada* kah-DAH (when)

e   like the "e" in "bed": *med* MEHD (honey)

i   like the "ee" in "sheet" or "need": *ime* EE-may (name)

o   like the beginning of the English diphthong "ou," making the pronunciation of the *o* something between that in the words "hot" and "ought" (you can also just imagine saying the letter *o* and use that pronunciation): *dobro* DO-bro (good)

u   like the "oo" in "boot" but shorter—purse your lips: *luk* LOOK (onion)

Consonants

c   like the "ts" in "dots": *starac* star-AHTS (old man)

č   referred to as a hard accent, pronounced with a confident "ch" sound like "church" or "arch": *čist* CHEEST (clean)

ć   a soft accent, like the "ch" in "chalk" but softer: *noć* NOCH (night)

đ, dž   like the "j" in "jam": *đak* JAHK (pupil)

h   like the guttural German *ach,* but softer: *hlad* HLAHD (cold)

j   like the "y" in "yellow" or "you": *jutro* YU-tro (morning)

lj   like the "lli" in "brilliant": *ljubav* lyoo-BAHV (love)

nj   like the "ni" in "lenient": *konjak* KON-yak (cognac)

r   should have a slight roll to it, like "rr": *vrlo* VRR-low (very)

š   like the "sh" in "mash": *naš* NAHSH (our)

ž   like the "s" in "treasure": *žena* ZHEH-na (woman)

BASIC AND COURTEOUS EXPRESSIONS

Hello *Bok*

Good morning *Dobro jutro*

Good afternoon *Dobar dan*

Good evening *Dobro veče*

How are you? *Kako si? Kako ste?*

Very well, thank you. *Dobro sam, hvala.*

Okay, good. *Dobro.*

Not okay, bad. *Loše.*

So-so. *Tako-tako.*

And you? *A Vi?*

Thank you. *Hvala.*

Thank you very much. *Puno Vam hvala.*

You're very kind. *Vrlo ste ljubazni.*

You're welcome. *Nema na čemu.*

Good-bye. *Doviđenja.*

See you later. *Vidimo se kasnije.*

Please. *Molim Vas/Te.*

yes *da*

no *ne*

I don't know *Ne znam.*

Just a moment, please. *Samo trenutak molim Vas.*

Excuse me, please. *Oprostite, molim Vas.*

Pleased to meet you. *Drago mi je što smo se upoznali.*

What is your name? *Kako se zovete?*

Do you speak English? *Govorite li engleski?*

I don't speak Croatian well. *Ne govorim hrvatski baš dobro.*

I don't understand. *Ne razumijem.*

How do you say . . . in Croatian? *Kako se kažete . . . na Hrvatskom?*

My name is . . . *Zovem se . . .*
Would you like . . . *Želite li . . .*
Let's go to . . . *Idemo u . . .*

TERMS OF ADDRESS

I *ja*
you (formal) *Vi*
you (familiar) *Ti*
he/him *ona*
she/her *ona*
we/us *mi*
you (plural) *vi*
they/them *oni*
Mr., sir *gospodin*
Mrs., madam *gospođa*
miss, young lady *gospodična*
wife *supruga*
husband *suprug*
friend *prijatelj*
boyfriend; girlfriend *dečko; djevojku*
son; daughter *sin; kći*
brother; sister *brat; sestra*
father; mother *otac; majka*
grandfather; grandmother *djed; baka*

TRANSPORTATION

Where is . . . ? *Gdje se nalazi . . . ?*
How far is it to . . . ? *Koliko ima do . . . ?*
from . . . to *od . . . do*
Where (which) is the way to . . . ? *Kojim putem do . . . ?*
the bus station *autobusni kolodvor*
the bus stop *autobusna stanica*
Where is this bus going? *Kamo ide ovaj autobus?*
the taxi stand *stajalište taksija*
the train station *željeznička postaja*
the boat *brod*
the airport *zračna luka*
I'd like a ticket to . . . *trebam kartu do . . .*
first (second) class *prvi (drugi) razred*
round-trip to . . . *put oko . . .*
reservation *rezervacija*
Stop here, please. *Molim Vas stanite ovdje.*
the entrance *ulaz*
the exit *izlaz*
the ticket office *prodaja karata*
(very) near; far *(vrlo) blizu; daleko*

to; toward *do; prema*
by; through *kraj, uz; kroz*
from *od*
the right *desno*
the left *lijevo*
straight ahead *ravno naprijed*
in front *ispred*
beside *pokraj*
behind *iza*
corner *ugao*
stoplight *semafor*
a turn *skretanje*
right here *upravo ovdje*
somewhere around here *negdje u blizini*
street; boulevard *ulica*
highway *autoput*
bridge; toll *most; cestarina*
address *adresa*
north; south *sjever; jug*
east; west *istok; zapad*

ACCOMMODATIONS

hotel *hotel*
Is there a room? *Imate li sobu?*
May I (may we) see it? *Mogu li (možemo li) je vidjeti?*
What is the rate? *Koja je cijena?*
Is that your best rate? *Dali je to Vaša najbolja cijena?*
Is there something cheaper? *Ima li što jeftinije?*
a single room *jednokrevetna soba*
a double room *dvokrevetna soba*
double bed *bračni krevet*
with private bath *sa privatnom kupaonicom*
hot water *topla voda*
shower *tuš*
towels *ručnici*
soap *sapun*
toilet paper *toaletni papir*
blanket *deka*
sheets *plahte*
air-conditioned *klimatizirano*
fan *ventilator*
key *ključ*
manager *upravitelj*

FOOD

I'm hungry. *Gladan sam/gladna sam.*
I'm thirsty. *Žedan sam, žedna sam.*
menu *jelovnik, meni*
order *narudžba*
glass *časa*
fork *vilica*
knife *nož*
spoon *žlica*
napkin *salvete*
breakfast *doručak*
lunch *ručak*
daily lunch special *dnevni meni*
dinner *večera*
the check *račun*
soft drink *bezalkoholno piće*
coffee *kava*
iced coffee *ledena kava*
tea *čaj*
bottled water *voda u boci*
tap water *voda iz slavine*
bottled carbonated water *gazirana
  mineralna voda u boci*
bottled uncarbonated water *negazirana
  mineralna voda u boci*
beer *pivo*
wine *vino*
white wine *bijelo vino*
red wine *crno vino*
milk *mlijeko*
juice *sok*
cream *vrhnje*
sugar *sečer*
eggs *jaja*
cheese *sir*
yogurt *jogurt*
almonds *bademi*
walnut/nut *orah*
pastry/pie *fina peciva/pite*
cake *kolač, torta*
bread *kruh*
butter *putar*
salt *sol*
pepper *paprika*
basil *bazilika*
garlic *bijeli luk, česnjak*
salad *salata*
vegetables *povrće*

artichoke *artičoka*
asparagus *šparoga*
avocado *avokado*
carrot *mrkva*
corn *kukuruz*
cucumber *krastavac*
eggplant *patliđan*
lettuce *zelena salata*
mushroom *gljiva, šampinjon*
olive *maslina*
onion *crveni luk*
pea *grašak*
potato *krumpir*
spinach *špinat*
tomato *rajčica, paradajz*
truffle *tartuf*
zucchini *tikvica*
fruit *voće*
apple *jabuka*
banana *banana*
cherry *trešnja*
fig *smokva*
grape *grožde*
lemon *limun*
lime *limeta*
orange *naranča*
peach *breskva*
pear *kruška*
plum *šljiva*
raisins *grožđice*
raspberry *malina*
strawberry *jagoda*
fish *riba*
shellfish *školjke*
anchovies *inčuni*
clam *kamenica*
crab *rak, morski rak*
mussels *dagnje*
octopus *hobotnica*
oysters *ostrige*
salmon *losos*
shrimp *škampi*
tiny squid *mala lignja*
trout *pastrva*
tuna *tunj*
meat *meso*
without meat *bez mesa*
poultry *perad*

chicken *pile/piletina*
duck *patka*
quail *prepelica*
turkey *puran, pura*
pork *svinjetina, svinjsko meso*
bacon; ham *slanina; šunka*
cured ham *pršut*
beef; steak *govedina; odrezak*
lamb *janjetina*
rabbit *zec*
chop *kotlet*
ribs *rebra*
sausage *kobasica*
croquette *kroketi*
fried *prženo*
roasted *pečeno*
barbecue; barbecued *roštilj, sa roštilja*

SHOPPING

money *novac*
money-exchange bureau *mjenjačnica*
I would like to exchange traveler's
  checks. *Želio/željela bih promjeniti putnicke*
  čekove.
What is the exchange rate? *Koji je tečaj?*
How much is the commission? *Kolika je*
  provizija?
Do you accept credit cards? *Primate li*
  kreditne kartice?
How much does it cost? *Koliko košta?*
expensive *skupo*
cheap *jeftino*
more *više*
less *manje*
a little *malo*
too much *previše*

HEALTH

Help me, please. *Molim Vas pomožite mi.*
I am ill. *Bolestan/bolesna sam.*
Call a doctor. *Zovite doktora.*
Take me to ... *Odvedite me do ...*
hospital *bolnica*
drugstore *ljekarna*
pain *bol*
fever *vrućica*
headache *glavobolja*
stomachache *bol u želucu*

burn *opeklina*
cramp *grc*
nausea *mucnina*
vomiting *povračati*
medicine *lijek*
antibiotic *antibiotik*
pill; tablet *pilulu; tubletu*
aspirin *aspirin*
ointment; cream *mast; krema*
cotton *vata*
sanitary napkins *ženski ulosci*
birth control pills *kontracepcijske pilule*
contraceptive foam *kontracepcijska pjena*
condoms *kondomi; prezervativi*
toothbrush *četkica za zube*
toothpaste *pasta za zube*
dentist *zubar*
toothache *zubobolja*

POST OFFICE AND COMMUNICATIONS

I would like to call ... *Želio bih/željela bih*
  nazvati ...
collect *na račun primatelj poziva*
station to station *od stanice do stanice*
person to person *od osobe do osobe*
credit card *kreditna kartica*
post office *pošta*
general delivery *običnom postom*
letter *pismo*
stamp *markica za pismo*
postcard *razglednica*
air mail *slanje avionom*
registered/certified *registrirano/*
  potvrđeno
money order *poštanska narudzba*
package; box *paket; kutija*
string; tape *spaga; traka*

AT THE BORDER

border *granica*
customs *carina*
immigration *imigracijski ured*
tourist card *turistička karta*
inspection *inspekcija*
passport *putovnica*
profession *zanimanje*
marital status *bračno stanje*

single *neoženjen/neudata*
married; divorced *oženjen/udat;*
  rastavljen/rastavljena
widowed *udovac/udovica*
insurance *osiguranje*
title *naziv*
driver's license *vozačka dozvola*

AT THE GAS STATION

gas station *benzinska stanica*
gasoline *benzin*
unleaded *bezolovni*
full, please *pun, molim Vas*
tire *guma*
air *zrak*
water *voda*
oil (change) *ulje (zamjeniti)*
grease *mast*
My ... doesn't work. *Moj ... ne radi.*
battery *akumulator, baterija*
radiator *radiator*
alternator *alternator*
generator *generator*
tow truck *pauk*
repair shop *automehaničarska radiona*

VERBS

to buy *kupiti*
to eat *jesti*
to climb *penjati se*
to do or make *napraviti*
to go *ići*
to love *voljeti*
to work *raditi*
to want *zeljeti*
to need *trebati*
to read *čitati*
to write *pisati*
to repair *popravljati*
to stop *stati*
to get off (the bus) *sići (sa autobusa)*
to arrive *stići*
to stay (remain) *ostati*
to stay (lodge) *nastaniti se*
to leave *otići*
to look at *gledati*
to look for *tražiti*

to give *dati*
to carry *nositi*
to have *imati*
to come *doći*

NUMBERS

zero *nula*
one *jedan*
two *dva*
three *tri*
four *četri*
five *pet*
six *šest*
seven *sedam*
eight *osam*
nine *devet*
10 *deset*
11 *jedanaest*
12 *dvanaest*
13 *trinaest*
14 *četrnaest*
15 *petnaest*
16 *šesnaest*
17 *sedamnaest*
18 *osamnaest*
19 *devetnaest*
20 *dvadeset*
21 *dvadeset i jedan*
30 *trideset*
40 *četrdeset*
50 *pedeset*
60 *šezdeset*
70 *sedamdeset*
80 *osamdeset*
90 *devedeset*
100 *sto*
101 *sto i jedan*
200 *dvijesto*
500 *petsto*
1,000 *tisuću*
10,000 *deset tisuća*
100,000 *sto tisuća*
1,000,000 *milijun*
one-half *pola, polovina*
one-third *jedna trećina*
one-fourth *jedna četvrtina*

TIME

What time is it? *Koliko je sati?*
It's one o'clock. *Jedan je sat.*
It's three in the afternoon. *Tri su popodne./Petnaest je sati.*
It's four in the morning. *Četri su ujutro.*
six-thirty *šest i trideset/pola sedam*
a quarter till eleven *petnaest do jedanaest/ deset četrdeset pet*
a quarter past five *pet i petnaest*
morning *jutro*
afternoon *popodne*
night *noć*

DAYS AND MONTHS

Monday *ponedjeljak*
Tuesday *utorak*
Wednesday *srijeda*
Thursday *četvrtak*
Friday *petak*
Saturday *subota*

Sunday *nedjelja*
day *dan*
today *danas*
tomorrow *sutra*
yesterday *jučer*
January *Siječanj*
February *Veljača*
March *Ožujak*
April *Travanj*
May *Svibanj*
June *Lipanj*
July *Srpanj*
August *Kolovoz*
September *Rujan*
October *Listopad*
November *Studeni*
December *Prosinac*
a week *tjedan*
a month *mjesec*
after *iza*
before *prije*

Slovenian Phrasebook

PRONUNCIATION

Slovenian is a mostly phonetic language, though it has many more exceptions than its neighboring Croatian. Here are a few of the most important:

- When *l* is placed at the end of a word or after any other consonant than *j*, it is pronounced as a *w*.

- When *v* is placed at the end of a word, after a vowel, or before a consonant, it is pronounced as a *w*.

- When *v* is at the beginning of a word, between consonants, or before two consecutive consonants, it is pronounced as *u*.

- If you come across a word with two vowels or consonants that are the same, like *dd*, pronounce the sound as you normally would, only slightly longer.

Vowels

a like the "a" in "father": *da* DAH (yes)
e like the "e" in "bed": *med* MEHD (honey)

i like the "ee" in "sheet" or "need": *ime* EE-may (name)
o like the beginning of the English diphthong "ou," making the pronunciation of the *o* something between the words "hot" and "ought" (you can also just imagine saying the letter *o* and use that pronunciation): *dobro* DO-bro (good)
u like the "oo" in "boot" but shorter—purse your lips: *jutro* YOO-tro (morning)

Consonants

These consonants are pronounced differently than English consonants:

c like the "ts" in "dots": *babica* BAH-bee-tsa (grandmother)
č referred to as a hard accent, pronounced with a confident "ch" sound like "church" or "arch": *čist* CHEEST (clean)
j like the "y" in "yellow" or "you": *jutro* YOO-tro (morning)

r   should have a slight roll to it, like "rr": *večer*
     VEH-CHER (evening)
š   like the "sh" in "mash": *kakšna* KAHK-shna
     (what is)
ž   like the "s" in "treasure": *žena* ZHEH-na
     (woman)

BASIC AND COURTEOUS EXPRESSIONS

Hello *Živijo*
Good morning *Dobro jutro*
Good afternoon *Dober dan*
Good evening *Dober večer*
How are you? *Kako si? Kako ste?*
Very well, thank you. *Hvala, dobro.*
Okay, good. *Dobro*
And you? *A Vi?*
Thank you. *Hvala.*
Thank you very much. *Hvala lepa.*
You're welcome. *Ni za kaj.*
Good-bye. *Nasvidenje.*
Please. *Prosim.*
yes *da*
no *ne*
Excuse me *Oprostite.*
Pleased to meet you. *Lepo da sva se
    spoznala.*
What is your name? *Kako vam je ime?*
Do you speak English? *Govorite li
    angleško?*
I don't speak Slovenian. *Ne govorim
    slovensko.*
I don't understand. *Ne razumem.*
How do you say ... in Slovenian? *Kako
    se kažete ... na Slovensko?*
My name is ... *Ime mi je ...*

TERMS OF ADDRESS

I *jaz*
you (formal) *Vi*
you (familiar) *Ti*
he/him *ona*
she/her *ona*
we/us *mi*
you (plural) *vi*
they/them *oni*
wife *soproga*
husband *soprog*

friend *prijatelj*
son; daughter *sin; hči*
brother; sister *brat; sestra*
father; mother *oče; mati*
grandfather; grandmother *ded; babica*

TRANSPORTATION

Where is ... ? *Kje je ... ?*
How do I get to ... ? *Kako pridem do ... ?*
from ... to *od ... do*
the bus station *avtobusna postaja*
Where is this bus going? *Dje ima ohod
    avtobus do?*
the taxi *taksi*
the train station *željezniška postaja*
the boat *brod*
the airport *letališče*
reservation *rezervacija*
Stop here, please. *Vstavi tukaj, prosim.*
the entrance *vhod*
the exit *izhod*
the ticket office *prodaja vozovnic*
(very) near; far *(zelo) blizu; daleč*
to *do*
by; through *po; skozi*
from *od*
the right *desno*
the left *levo*
straight ahead *naravnost*
in front *pred*
beside *poleg*
behind *zadaj*
stoplight *semafor*
a turn *zasuk*
here *tukaj*
street; boulevard *ulica*
highway *avtocesta*
bridge; toll *most; cestarina*
address *adresa*
north; south *sever; jug*
east; west *vzhod; zahod*

ACCOMMODATIONS

hotel *hotel*
Is there a room available? *Ali imate
    prosto sobo?*
May I see the room? *Si lahko ogledam
    sobo?*

What is the rate? *Kakšna je cene sobe?*
Is there something cheaper? *Imate kakšno cenejšo?*
a single room *enoposteljne sobe*
a double room *dvoposteljne sobe*
with a bath *s kopanico*
hot water *vroča voda*
with a shower *s prho*
towel *brisača*
soap *milo*
blanket *deka*
sheets *rjuhe*
fan *ventilator*
key *ključ*
manager *direktor*

FOOD

I'm hungry. *Lačen sem.*
I'm thirsty. *Žejen sem, žejna sem.*
menu *jedilnik*
order *naročilo*
glass *kozarec*
fork *vilice*
knife *nož*
spoon *žlica*
napkin *servieta*
breakfast *zajtrk*
lunch *kosilo*
dinner *obed*
the check *račun*
coffee *kava*
tea *čaj*
water *voda*
beer *pivo*
wine *vino*
white wine *belo vino*
red wine *črnina*
milk *mleko*
juice *sok*
sugar *sladkor*
eggs *jajca*
cheese *sir*
yogurt *jogurt*
walnut/nut *oreh*
pastry/pie *pita*
cake *torta*
bread *kruh*
butter *maslo*

salt *sol*
pepper *paprika*
garlic *česen*
salad *solata*
vegetables *zelenjava*
asparagus *beluš*
cucumber *kumara*
eggplant *melencana*
lettuce *solata*
olive *oliva*
pea, bean *grah*
spinach *špinača*
tomato *paradižnik*
fruit *sadje*
apple *jabolko*
banana *banana*
cherry *češnja*
fig *figa*
grape *grozd*
lemon *limona*
orange *pomaranča*
peach *breskev*
pear *hruška*
raspberry *malina*
strawberry *jagoda*
fish *riba*
shellfish *školjke*
crab *rak*
salmon *losos*
trout *postrv*
tuna *tuna*
meat *meso*
without meat *brez mesa*
chicken *piščanec*
duck *raca*
turkey *puran, pura*
pork *svinjina*
ham *šunka*
beef *govedina*
lamb *jagnje*
rabbit *zajec*
fried *pražen*
roasted *pečen*
barbecue *žar*

SHOPPING
money *denar*
money-exchange bureau *menjalnica*

bank *banka*
Can you exchange a traveler's
   check? *Mi lahko vnovčite potovalni ček?*
What is the exchange rate? *Kakšno je
   menjalno razmerje?*
Do you accept credit cards? *Ali spejemate
   kreditne kartice?*
How much does it cost? *Koliko stane?*
expensive *drago*
cheap *poceni*
more *bolj*
less *manj*
a little *malo*
too much *preveč*

HEALTH

I need help. *Potrebujem pomoč.*
I am ill. *Bolen sem.*
Call a doctor. *Zovite zdravnika.*
hospital *bolnica*
drugstore *lekarna*
pain *bolečina*
headache *glavobol*
burn *opeklina*
medicine *zdravilo*
antibiotic *antibiotik*
pill; tablet *tableta*
aspirin *aspirin*
ointment; cream *mazilo*
tampons *tamponi*
toothbrush *zobna ščetka*
toothpaste *zobna krema*
dentist *zobozdravnik*
tooth *zoba*

POST OFFICE AND COMMUNICATIONS

credit card *kreditna kartica*
post office *pošta*
letter *pismo*
stamps *znamke*
postcard *dopisnica*
air mail *zračna pošta*
string; tape *vrvica; trak*

AT THE BORDER

border *meja*
customs *carina*

immigration *imigracija*
inspection *inspekcija*
passport *potni list*
profession *poklic*
single *samski/samska*
married *poročen/poročena*
insurance *zavorovanje*
title *naslov*
driver's license *vozniško dovoljenje*

AT THE GAS STATION

gas station *bencinska črpalka*
gasoline *bencin*
unleaded *neosvinčen bencin*
full, please *poln, molim Vas*
tire *guma*
air *zrak*
water *voda*
oil (change) *olje (zamenjati)*
grease *mast*
My ... doesn't work. *Moj ... ne radi.*
battery *akumulator, baterija*
radiator *hladilnik*
alternator *alternator*
repair shop *servis*

VERBS

to buy *kupiti*
to eat *jesti*
to climb *prelaziti*
to do or make *narediti*
to go *iti*
I go *grem*
to love *ljubiti*
to work *delati*
to want *hoteti*
to read *čitati*
to write *pisati*
to repair *popravati*
to stop *ustaviti*
to arrive *priti*
to stay (remain) *ostati*
to leave *oditi*
to look at *gledati*
to look for *iskati*
to give *dati*
to carry *nesti*
to have *imeti*

NUMBERS

zero *nula*
one *ena*
two *dva*
three *tri*
four *štiri*
five *pet*
six *šest*
seven *sedem*
eight *osem*
nine *devet*
10 *deset*
11 *enajst*
12 *dvanajst*
13 *trinajst*
14 *štirinajst*
15 *petnajst*
16 *šesnajst*
17 *sedemnajst*
18 *osemnajst*
19 *devetnajst*
20 *dvajset*
21 *enaidvajset*
30 *trideset*
40 *štirideset*
50 *petdeset*
60 *šestdeset*
70 *sedemdeset*
80 *osemdeset*
90 *devedeset*
100 *sto*
101 *stoena*
200 *dvesto*
500 *petsto*
1,000 *tisoč*
10,000 *deset tisoč*
100,000 *sto tisoč*
1,000,000 *milijon*
one-half *pol*

TIME

What time is it? *Koliko je ura?*
It's one o'clock in the afternoon. *Ena polpodne.*
It's two in the morning. *Dve zjutraj.*
two-thirty *pol treh*
a quarter till one *ob tri četrt na eno*
a quarter past twelve *ob četrt čez dvanajst*
morning *jutro*
afternoon *popoldan*
night *noč*

DAYS AND MONTHS

Monday *ponedeljek*
Tuesday *torek*
Wednesday *sreda*
Thursday *četrtek*
Friday *petek*
Saturday *sobota*
Sunday *nedjelja*
day *dan*
today *danes*
tomorrow *jutri*
yesterday *včeraj*
January *Januar*
February *Februar*
March *Marec*
April *April*
May *Maj*
June *Junij*
July *Julij*
August *Avgust*
September *September*
October *Oktober*
November *November*
December *December*
a week *teden*
a month *mesec*
later *kasneje*
before *pred*

Montenegrin Phrasebook

Montenegrin is mutually intelligible with Croatian, with a few vocabulary differences. They are different in the same way American and British English might be. Though Montenegro officially recognizes the Latin alphabet, you may also see uses of Cyrillic.

PRONUNCIATION

Montenegrin is almost entirely phonetic. If you can master the pronunciation, you can read almost anything, even if you have no idea what it says. The pronunciation of Montenegrin is more or less the same as Croatian.

Vowels

a   like the "a" in "father": *kada* kah-DAH (when)

e   like the "e" in "bed": *med* MEHD (honey)

i   like the "ee" in "sheet" or "need": *ime* EE-may (name)

o   like the beginning of the English diphthong "ou," making the pronunciation of the *o* something between that in the words "hot" and "ought" (you can also just imagine saying the letter *o* and use that pronunciation): *dobro* DO-bro (good)

u   like the "oo" in "boot" but shorter—purse your lips: *luk* LOOK (onion)

Consonants

c   like the "ts" in "dots": *starac* star-AHTS (old man)

č   referred to as a hard accent, pronounced with a confident "ch" sound like "church" or "arch": *čist* CHEEST (clean)

ć   a soft accent, like the "ch" in "chalk" but softer: *noć* NOCH (night)

đ, dž   like the "j" in "jam": *đak* JAHK (pupil)

h   like the guttural German *ach,* but softer: *hlad* HLAHD (cold)

j   like the "y" in "yellow" or "you": *jutro* YU-tro (morning)

lj   like the "lli" in "brilliant": *ljubav* lyoo-BAHV (love)

nj   like the "ni" in "lenient": *konjak* KON-yak (cognac)

r   should have a slight roll to it, like "rr": *vrlo* VRR-low (very)

š   like the "sh" in "mash": *naš* NAHSH (our)

ž   like the "s" in "treasure": *žena* ZHEH-na (woman)

BASIC AND COURTEOUS EXPRESSIONS

Hello   *Halo, Zdravo*

Good morning   *Dobro jutro*

Good afternoon   *Dobar dan*

Good evening   *Dobro veče*

How are you?   *Kako si? Kako ste?*

Very well, thank you.   *Dobro sam, hvala.*

Okay, good.   *Dobro.*

Not okay, bad.   *Loše.*

So-so.   *Tako-tako.*

And you?   *A Vi?*

Thank you.   *Hvala.*

Thank you very much.   *Puno Vam hvala.*

You're very kind.   *Vrlo ste ljubazni.*

You're welcome.   *Nema na čemu.*

Good-bye.   *Doviđenja.*

See you later.   *Vidimo se kasnije.*

Please.   *Molim Vas/Te.*

yes   *da*

no   *ne*

I don't know   *Ne znam.*

Just a moment, please.   *Samo trenutak molim Vas.*

Excuse me, please.   *Oprostite, molim Vas.*

Pleased to meet you.   *Drago mi je što smo se upoznali.*

What is your name?   *Kako se zovete?*

Do you speak English?   *Govorite li engleski?*

I don't speak Montenegrin well.   *Ne govorim Crnogorskii baš dobro.*

I don't understand.   *Ne razumijem.*

How do you say . . . in Montenegrin?   *Kako se kažete . . . na Crnogorskom?*

My name is . . . *Zovem se . . .*
Would you like . . . *Želite li . . .*
Let's go to . . . *Idemo u . . .*

TERMS OF ADDRESS

I *ja*
you (formal) *Vi*
you (familiar) *Ti*
he/him *ona*
she/her *ona*
we/us *mi*
you (plural) *vi*
they/them *oni*
Mr., sir *gospodin*
Mrs., madam *gospođa*
miss, young lady *gospodična*
wife *supruga*
husband *suprug*
friend *prijatelj*
boyfriend; girlfriend *dečko; djevojka*
son; daughter *sin; kći*
brother; sister *brat; sestra*
father; mother *otac; majka*
grandfather; grandmother *djed; baka*

TRANSPORTATION

Where is . . . ? *Gdje se nalazi . . . ?*
How far is it to . . . ? *Koliko ima do . . . ?*
from . . . to *od . . . do*
Where (which) is the way to . . . ? *Kojim putem do . . . ?*
the bus station *autobusni kolodvor*
the bus stop *autobusna stanica*
Where is this bus going? *Kamo ide ovaj autobus?*
the taxi stand *stajalište taksija*
the train station *želježnička postaja*
the boat *brod*
the airport *zračna luka*
I'd like a ticket to . . . *trebam kartu do . . .*
first (second) class *prvi (drugi) razred*
round-trip to . . . *put oko . . .*
reservation *rezervacija*
Stop here, please. *Molim Vas stanite ovdje.*
the entrance *ulaz*
the exit *izlaz*
the ticket office *prodaja karata*
(very) near; far *(vrlo) blizu; daleko*

to; toward *do; prema*
by; through *kraj, uz; kroz*
from *od*
the right *desno*
the left *lijevo*
straight ahead *ravno naprijed*
in front *ispred*
beside *pokraj*
behind *iza*
corner *ugao*
stoplight *semafor*
a turn *skretanje*
right here *upravo ovdje*
somewhere around here *negdje u blizini*
street; boulevard *ulica*
highway *autoput*
bridge; toll *most; putarina*
address *adresa*
north; south *sjever; jug*
east; west *istok; zapad*

ACCOMMODATIONS

hotel *hotel*
Is there a room? *Imate li sobu?*
May I (may we) see it? *Mogu li (možemo li) je vidjeti?*
What is the rate? *Koja je cijena?*
Is that your best rate? *Dali je to Vaša najbolja cijena?*
Is there something cheaper? *Ima li što jeftinije?*
a single room *jednokrevetna soba*
a double room *dvokrevetna soba*
double bed *bračni krevet*
with private bath *sa privatnom kupaonicom*
hot water *topla voda*
shower *tuš*
towels *ručnici*
soap *sapun*
toilet paper *toaletni papir*
blanket *deka*
sheets *plahte*
air-conditioned *klimatizirano*
fan *ventilator*
key *ključ*
manager *upravitelj*

FOOD

I'm hungry. *Gladan sam/gladna sam.*
I'm thirsty. *Žedan sam, žedna sam.*
menu *jelovnik, meni*
order *narudžba*
glass *čaša*
fork *vilica*
knife *nož*
spoon *žlica*
napkin *salvete*
breakfast *doručak*
lunch *ručak*
daily lunch special *dnevni meni*
dinner *večera*
the check *račun*
soft drink *bezalkoholno piće*
coffee *kava*
iced coffee *ledena kava*
tea *čaj*
bottled water *voda u boci*
tap water *voda iz slavine*
bottled carbonated water *gazirana mineralna voda u boci*
bottled uncarbonated water *negazirana mineralna voda u boci*
beer *pivo*
wine *vino*
white wine *bijelo vino*
red wine *crno vino*
milk *mlijeko*
juice *sok*
cream *vrhnje*
sugar *sečer*
eggs *jaja*
cheese *sir*
yogurt *jogurt*
almonds *bademi*
walnut/nut *orah*
pastry/pie *fina peciva/pite*
cake *kolač, torta*
bread *hljeb*
butter *putar*
salt *sol*
pepper *paprika*
basil *bazilika*
garlic *češnjak*
salad *salata*
vegetables *povrće*

artichoke *artičoka*
asparagus *šparoga*
avocado *avokado*
carrot *mrkva, šargarepa*
corn *kukuruz*
cucumber *krastavac*
eggplant *patliđan*
lettuce *zelena salata*
mushroom *gljiva, šampinjon*
olive *maslina*
onion *crveni luk*
pea *grašak*
potato *krumpir*
spinach *spanać*
tomato *rajčica, paradajz*
truffle *tartuf*
zucchini *tikvica*
fruit *voće*
apple *jabuka*
banana *banana*
cherry *trešnja*
fig *smokva*
grape *grožde*
lemon *limun*
lime *limeta*
orange *naranča*
peach *breskva*
pear *kruška*
plum *šljiva*
raisins *grožđice*
raspberry *malina*
strawberry *jagoda*
fish *riba*
shellfish *školjke*
anchovies *inčuni*
clam *kamenica*
crab *rak, morski rak*
mussels *dagnje*
octopus *hobotnica*
oysters *ostrige*
salmon *losos*
shrimp *škampi*
tiny squid *mala lignja*
trout *pastrva*
tuna *tunj*
meat *meso*
without meat *bez mesa*
poultry *perad*

chicken *pile/piletina*
duck *patka*
quail *prepelica*
turkey *puran, pura*
pork *svinjetina, svinjsko meso*
bacon; ham *slanina; šunka*
cured ham *pršut*
beef; steak *govedina; odrezak*
lamb *janjetina*
rabbit *zec*
chop *kotlet*
ribs *rebra*
sausage *kobasica*
croquette *kroketi*
fried *prženo*
roasted *pečeno*
barbecue; barbecued *roštilj, sa roštilja*

SHOPPING
money *novac*
money-exchange bureau *mjenjačnica*
I would like to exchange traveler's checks. *Želio/željela bih promjeniti putnicke čekove.*
What is the exchange rate? *Koji je tečaj?*
How much is the commission? *Kolika je provizija?*
Do you accept credit cards? *Primate li kreditne kartice?*
How much does it cost? *Koliko košta?*
expensive *skupo*
cheap *jeftino*
more *više*
less *manje*
a little *malo*
too much *previše*

HEALTH
Help me, please. *Molim Vas pomožite mi.*
I am ill. *Bolestan/bolesna sam.*
Call a doctor. *Zovite doktora.*
Take me to . . . *Odvedite me do . . .*
hospital *bolnica*
drugstore *ljekarna*
pain *bol*
fever *vručica*
headache *glavobolja*
stomachache *bol u želucu*

burn *opeklina*
cramp *grc*
nausea *mucnina*
vomiting *povračati*
medicine *lijek*
antibiotic *antibiotik*
pill; tablet *pilula; tableta*
aspirin *aspirin*
ointment; cream *mast; krema*
cotton *vata*
sanitary napkins *ženski ulosci*
birth control pills *kontracepcijske pilule*
contraceptive foam *kontracepcijska pjena*
condoms *kondomi; prezervativi*
toothbrush *četkica za zube*
toothpaste *pasta za zube*
dentist *zubar*
toothache *zubobolja*

POST OFFICE AND COMMUNICATIONS
I would like to call . . . *Želio bih/željela bih nazvati . . .*
collect *na račun primatelj poziva*
station to station *od stanice do stanice*
person to person *od osobe do osobe*
credit card *kreditna kartica*
post office *pošta*
general delivery *običnom postom*
letter *pismo*
stamp *markica za pismo*
postcard *razglednica*
air mail *slanje avionom*
registered/certified *registrirano/ potvrđeno*
money order *poštanska narudzba*
package; box *paket; kutija*
string; tape *spaga; traka*

AT THE BORDER
border *granica*
customs *carina*
immigration *imigracijski ured*
tourist card *turistička karta*
inspection *inspekcija*
passport *putovnica*
profession *zanimanje*
marital status *bračno stanje*

single *neoženjen/neudata*
married; divorced *oženjen/udat;*
  rastavljen/rastavljena
widowed *udovac/udovica*
insurance *osiguranje*
title *naziv*
driver's license *vozačka dozvola*

AT THE GAS STATION

gas station *benzinska stanica*
gasoline *benzin*
unleaded *bezolovni*
full, please *pun, molim Vas*
tire *guma*
air *zrak*
water *voda*
oil (change) *ulje (zamjeniti)*
grease *mast*
My ... doesn't work. *Moj ... ne radi.*
battery *akumulator, baterija*
radiator *radiator*
alternator *alternator*
generator *generator*
tow truck *pauk*
repair shop *automehaničarska radiona*

VERBS

to buy *kupiti*
to eat *jesti*
to climb *penjati se*
to do or make *napraviti*
to go *ići*
to love *voljeti*
to work *raditi*
to want *zeljeti*
to need *trebati*
to read *čitati*
to write *pisati*
to repair *popravljati*
to stop *stati*
to get off (the bus) *sići (sa autobusa)*
to arrive *stići*
to stay (remain) *ostati*
to stay (lodge) *nastaniti se*
to leave *otići*
to look at *gledati*
to look for *tražiti*

to give *dati*
to carry *nositi*
to have *imati*
to come *doći*

NUMBERS

zero *nula*
one *jedan*
two *dva*
three *tri*
four *četri*
five *pet*
six *šest*
seven *sedam*
eight *osam*
nine *devet*
10 *deset*
11 *jedanaest*
12 *dvanaest*
13 *trinaest*
14 *četrnaest*
15 *petnaest*
16 *šesnaest*
17 *sedamnaest*
18 *osamnaest*
19 *devetnaest*
20 *dvadeset*
21 *dvadeset i jedan*
30 *trideset*
40 *četrdeset*
50 *pedeset*
60 *šezdeset*
70 *sedamdeset*
80 *osamdeset*
90 *devedeset*
100 *sto*
101 *sto i jedan*
200 *dvijesto*
500 *petsto*
1,000 *tisuću*
10,000 *deset tisuća*
100,000 *sto tisuća*
1,000,000 *milijun*
one-half *pola, polovina*
one-third *jedna trećina*
one-fourth *jedna četvrtina*

TIME

What time is it? *Koliko je sati?*
It's one o'clock. *Jedan je sat.*
It's three in the afternoon. *Tri su popodne./Petnaest je sati.*
It's four in the morning. *Četri su ujutro.*
six-thirty *šest i trideset/pola sedam*
a quarter till eleven *petnaest do jedanaest/ deset četrdeset pet*
a quarter past five *pet i petnaest*
morning *jutro*
afternoon *popodne*
night *noć*

DAYS AND MONTHS

Monday *ponedjeljak*
Tuesday *utorak*
Wednesday *srijeda*
Thursday *četvrtak*
Friday *petak*
Saturday *subota*
Sunday *nedjelja*

day *dan*
today *danas*
tomorrow *sutra*
yesterday *jučer*
January *januar*
February *februar*
March *mart*
April *april*
May *maj*
June *juni*
July *juli*
August *august*
September *septembar*
October *oktobar*
November *novembar*
December *decembar*
a week *tjedan*
a month *mjesec*
after *iza*
before *prije*

Suggested Reading

ARTS AND LITERATURE

Bogataj, Janez. *Handicrafts of Slovenia: Encounters with Contemporary Craftsmen.* Rokus, 2002. This beautiful tome with hundreds of color photos looks at Slovenia's traditional and modern-day crafts, from woodworking to ceramics, musical instruments, and more.

Drakulić, Slavenka. *As if I Was Not There.* Abacus, 1999. A disturbing novel about a Bosnian woman in a Serbian prison camp, it's one of the best by controversial author Drakulić. Her criticisms of her homeland in books like *Café Europa* and *How We Survived Communism and Even Laughed* have earned her much negative press in Croatia, but both books are worthwhile reads, though they can ring bitter from time to time.

Erlande-Brandenburg, Alain. *Cathedrals and Castles: Building in the Middle Ages.* Harry N. Abrams, 1995. An interesting look into how castles, cathedrals, and even city walls were designed and built. With plenty of pictures and diagrams, it's a must for architecture and history buffs as a companion to sightseeing in Croatia and Slovenia—or any European country, for that matter.

Jergović, Miljenko. *Sarajevo Marlboro.* Archipelago Books, 2004. Though this book of short stories focuses on the conflict in Bosnia, the author now lives in Zagreb and writes for a popular weekly magazine. The book is one of the best, yet saddest, you'll ever read on the war. The horrific is kept in check by a lot of dry humor, which endears the people of Sarajevo to the reader even more for their amazing strength in the face of tragedy.

Krleža, Miroslav. *On the Edge of Reason*. New Directions Publishing, 1995. This 1938 novel from one of Croatia's most respected writers blasts conformity by outlining the struggles his hero endures due to an unexpected and against-the-grain observation about a powerful businessman.

Pekić, Borislav. *How to Quiet a Vampire*. Northwestern University Press, 2003. Originally published in 1977, this novel is not just a story, but a book of philosophy and ideas. A German professor travels to a fictional Yugoslavian town where he is reminded of his service as a Nazi during World War II. It's both disturbing and thought-provoking reading from this Montenegrin political activist and writer.

Šenoa, August. *The Goldsmith's Treasure*. Spiritoso, 2005. The first Croatian historical novel, written by one of the most important authors in Croatian literature, this 1871 tome has been translated into English. Set in Zagreb in the 16th century, it is a tale of forbidden love between the daughter of a goldsmith and a nobleman's son.

Ugrešić, Dubravka. *The Museum of Unconditional Surrender*. New Directions Publishing, 2002. A deeply moving and touching book, profiling various fictional characters in vignettes that reflect on many topics, from political to emotional, but ultimately hopeful.

HISTORY AND POLITICS

Curtis, Benjamin. *A Traveller's History of Croatia*. Interlink Books, 2014. Chronicling the history of Croatia from pre-history to the present, this is the easiest read to get an overview of Croatian and some Balkan history.

Banac, Ivo. *The National Question in Yugoslavia: Origins, History, and Politics*. Cornell University Press, 1988. Examining the period just before the formation of Yugoslavia after World War I till the Vidovdan Constitution of 1921, Banac writes a scholarly and thoughtful account of the problems and underlying ideas that were never properly resolved, ultimately leading to the conflict in the 1990s. One of the best books of its kind.

Benderley, Jill. *Independent Slovenia: Origins, Movements, Prospects*. Palgrave Macmillan, 1996. A decent introduction to Slovenia's recent history, politics, economy, and a bit of culture, this book of essays written by various Slovenian scholars offers a look into the country from a local perspective.

Bracewell, Catherine Wendy. *The Uskoks of Senj: Piracy, Banditry, and Holy War in the Sixteenth-Century Adriatic*. Cornell University Press, 1992. Tracing the history and battles of the Uskoks, this well-researched book is a great look at the pirates who ruled the Adriatic in the 16th and 17th centuries.

Glenny, Misha. *The Balkans: Nationalism, War, and the Great Powers, 1804-1999*. Penguin, 2001. Tackling the very big issue of "the Balkans," Glenny wisely starts at the beginning of the 19th century, finally disputing the idea that the conflict was based on "ancient hatreds." Her arguments are sound, never prejudiced to any side, and the book is very well written, making its lengthy 742 pages go quite quickly.

Harris, Robin. *Dubrovnik: A History*. Saqi Books, 2003. Beginning her account in the 7th century, Harris weaves together the complex history of Dubrovnik along with its arts, architecture, and economic success and struggles in one easy-to-read volume. Highly recommended for fans of Dubrovnik and of history in general.

Little, Alan, and Laura Silber. *Yugoslavia: Death of a Nation*. Penguin, 1996. The authors, correspondents for the BBC and the *Financial Times*, write a gripping first-hand account of the breakup of the former

Yugoslavia. Their positions as journalists gave them access to behind-the-scenes interviews with key figures in the conflict. Another excellent book that dismisses arguments that the conflict was born of ethnic hatreds, the book is a great lesson on the region in the 1980s and 1990s.

Roberts, Elizabeth. *Realm of the Black Mountain: A History of Montenegro.* Cornell University Press, 2007. This book traces Montenegro's history from pre-Slavic times through 2006.

Tanner, Marcus. *Croatia: A Nation Forged in War.* Yale University Press, 1997. Written by a Balkan correspondent for London's *Independent* newspaper, Tanner witnessed the breakup of the Balkans firsthand. His grizzly accounts, factual and unbiased reporting, and excellent writing make for a must-read primer on the Balkan conflict.

Tomašević, Bato. *Life and Death in the Balkans.* Columbia University Press, 2008. A memoir of the author and his family, this story recounts life through multiple wars and political upheavals. It's an interesting firsthand history of modern Montenegro.

TRAVEL AND IMPRESSIONS

Eames, Andrew. *The 8:55 to Baghdad: From London to Iraq on the Trail of Agatha Christie and the Orient Express.* Overlook TP, 2006. Though the title might seem irrelevant to Slovenia and Croatia, the book includes a section where the author tracks down locals who met Christie during her journeys and also visits the Croatian location of the inspiration for her book, *Murder on the Orient Express,* based on the real-life blizzard that snowed in the famous train for more than a week. Mr. Eames is a keen observer, and his musings on Croatia and Slovenia are not to be missed.

Fortis, Abbé Alberto. *Travels into Dalmatia.* Cossimo Classics, 2007. A travelogue published in the 18th century, this book chronicles the journey of the Italian Fortis into a hitherto little-traveled land. His observations on the customs and culture of Dalmatia during this time are historically fascinating.

Novak, Slobodan Prosperov. *Dubrovnik Revisited.* VBZ, 2005. Well-known Croatian writer and former Yale professor Slobodan Prosperov Novak writes a lovely guide to Dubrovnik, seen through tender and witty eyes. Like a class with your favorite college professor, the book points out interesting tidbits and weaves literature, culture, art, and a few laughs through your tour of Dubrovnik's best-known (and sometimes overlooked) sights. If you can't find these books before you leave, you'll surely be able to pick them up at English bookstores in Croatia.

West, Rebecca. *Black Lamb and Grey Falcon.* Penguin Classics, 2007. If you buy only one book on the region, West's excellent travel book from her trip through Yugoslavia in the 1930s is a good choice—it's stunning how accurate some of her observations remain today. She's been criticized for generalizing the former Yugoslavia, but her detail on the local scenery, characters, and history as well as the underlying tension of the time makes for an absorbing read.

Internet Resources

TRAVEL INFORMATION

CROATIAN NATIONAL TOURIST BOARD

www.croatia.hr

The official site of Croatian tourism, the site should fill in all the details you need. Listing destinations and points of interest small and large, accommodations in dozens of cities and villages, and activities around the country, the site also offers an excellent events calendar. A simple search will turn up all sorts of festivals, from Istria's prized Vinistra to more obscure events.

SLOVENIAN TOURIST BOARD

www.slovenia.info

Slovenia's Tourist Board provides a website with pages and pages of information for travelers. Accommodations, events, and sights are definitely listed, but you'll also find information on wine and other themed routes, sport-fishing, and shopping. The site seems to have something for even the tiniest, most remote spot in the country. It's an excellent resource to check out before you go.

BURGER LANDMARKS

www.burger.si

If you want to have a better look at the sights you'll be visiting, this website offers 360-degree panoramas of many sights and landmarks around Slovenia and Croatia.

FIND CROATIA

www.find-croatia.com

Though the site's not very flashy, each section, whether it's about a city or island or ferry connections, is constantly updated with the latest news stories and information.

GASTRONAUT

www.gastronaut.hr

Though this site is in Croatian, a few clicks should still get you to a very comprehensive list of restaurants by town. The site's yearly ranking of the top 100 restaurants in Croatia is a reliable way to find a good to excellent place to eat in the country.

MALI PODRUM

www.mali-podrum.com

This site, in English, Croatian, and German, is devoted to Croatian wines. Though the events section is in need of an update, you'll find a list of hundreds of wineries, links to some with an online presence, and basic information on Croatian wines.

TRIP PRACTICALITIES

U.S. STATE DEPARTMENT

www.state.gov

The U.S. government provides lots of quick facts and practical info for travelers, including visa requirements, advice on immunizations, what to do if your passport is lost or stolen, and much more.

CURRENT AFFAIRS

SLOVENIA TIMES

www.sloveniatimes.com

This excellent daily news source has articles about current events in Slovenia as well as plenty of information on happenings and things of interest around the country, particularly in Ljubljana. If you'd like to talk politics with the locals, a week or so of reading will have you sounding like a native.

CROATIA WEEK

www.croatiaweek.com

An online news site with stories on current affairs, sports, politics, and more about Croatia in English.

Index

List of Maps

Photo Credits

Title page photo: Lake Bled © nataliaderiabina | dreamstime.com;
Page 2 © shann fountain alipour; page 3 © laura mellberg; page 6 © (top left) shann fountain alipour; (top right) viliamm | dreamstime.com; (bottom) gordana sermek | dreamstime.com; page 7 © (top) grafxart | dreamstime.com; (bottom left) laura mellberg; (bottom right) urospoteko | dreamstime.com; page 8 © (top) laura mellberg; page 9 © (top) laura mellberg; (bottom left) mildax | dreamstime.com; (bottom right) shann fountain alipour; pages 10-11 © andrejsafaric | dreamstime.com; page 12 (top) © simunascic | dreamstime.com; (bottom) © vanillla | dreamstime.com; page 13 © gkasabova | dreamstime.com; pages 14-15 (top) studioclover | dreamstime.com; (bottom) © goranjakus | dreamstime.com; page 16 (top) © delleved61 | dreamstime.com; (middle) © goranjakus | dreamstime.com; (bottom) © amoklv/123RF; page 17 (top) © andrejat | dreamstime.com; (bottom) © andrejsafaric | dreamstime.com; page 18 © unclejay | dreamstime.com; page 19 (top) © drfail | dreamstime.com; (bottom) © barbaracerovsek | dreamstime.com; page 20 (left) © alexey stiop | dreamstime.com; (right) jasmina | dreamstime.com; page 22 © donyanedomam | dreamstime.com; page 23 © phant | dreamstime.com; page 24 © dantautan | dreamstime.com; page 26 © kasto80 | dreamstime.com; page 27 © xbrchx | dreamstime.com; page 28 (left) © holger mette | dreamstime.com; (right) © mikolaj64 | dreamstime.com; page 29 © alexey stroganov | dreamstime.com; page 30 © shann fountain alipour; page 31 © danijel micka | dreamstime.com; page 33 © matej kastelic | dreamstime.com; page 34 © mikaks | dreamstime.com; page 35 © jasmina | dreamstime.com; page 36 © mrakhr/dreasmtime.com; page 37 © ivansmuk | dreamstime.com; page 38 (left) © biserko | dreamstime.com; (right) © madrugadaverde | dreamstime.com; page 48 © (top left) shann fountain alipour; (top right) mike clegg | dreamstime.com; (bottom) paul prescott | dreamstime.com; page 50 © (top left) ivansmuk | dreamstime.com; (top right) boris15 | dreamstime.com; (bottom) phant | dreamstime.com; page 55 © deymos | dreamstime.com; page 58 © verdeljic | dreamstime.com; page 63 © shann fountain alipour; page 65 © (top) paul prescott/123rf.com; (left middle) dominionart | dreamstime.com; (right middle) shann fountain alipour; (bottom) shann fountain alipour; page 69 © (top) boris15 | dreamstime.com; (bottom) twingomaniak | dreamstime.com; page 82 © believeinme | dreamstime.com; page 84 © (top) xbrchx | dreamstime.com; (bottom) xbrchx | dreamstime.com; page 88 © xbrchx | dreamstime.com; page 89 (left) © iveklitch | dreamstime.com; (right) xbrchx | dreamstime.com; page 94 © dreamer4787 | dreamstime.com; page 100 © (top) shann fountain alipour; (bottom) shann fountain alipour; page 112 © (top left) xbrchx | dreamstime.com; © (top right) shann fountain alipour © (bottom) xbrchx | dreamstime.com; page 114 © wolf1984 | dreamstime.com; page 117 © (top) zatletic | dreamstime.com; (bottom) xbrchx | dreamstime.com; page 123 © shann fountain alipour; page 124 © (left) xbrchx | dreamstime.com; (right) madrabothair | dreamstime.com; page 130 © (top) travelpeter | dreamstime.com; (bottom) gashgeron | dreamstime.com; page 137 © (top) phant | dreamstime.com; (right middle)volodymyr melnyk/123rf.com; (left middle) Shann fountain alipour (bottom) aaron007 | dreamstime.com; page 144 © morozena | dreamstime.com; page 151 © (top) shann fountain alipour (bottom) shann fountain alipour; page 154 © panama00 | dreamstime.com; page 160 © (top) jasmina | dreamstime.com; (left middle)shann fountain alipour; (right middle)shann fountain alipour; (bottom) rklfoto | dreamstime.com; page 163 © slavkosereda | dreamstime.com; page 164 © (left) rklfoto | dreamstime.com; (right) akwiatkowskaanna | dreamstime.com; page 169 © xbrchx | dreamstime.com; page 175 © (top) rklfoto | dreamstime.com; (left middle) jelena990 | dreamstime.com; (right middle) rklfoto | dreamstime.com; (bottom) gadzius | dreamstime.com; page 182 © (top left) dziewul | dreamstime.com; (right middle) stefan907 | dreamstime.com; (bottom) guillohmz | dreamstime.com; page 189 © (top) paul prescott | dreamstime.com; (left middle) geribody | dreamstime.com; (right middle) tyler olson/123rf.com; (bottom) padebat | dreamstime.com; page 194 © xbrchx | dreamstime.com; page 198 © lianem | dreamstime.com; page 201 © willyvend | dreamstime.com; page 203 © witr | dreamstime.com; page 204 © (left) pmartike | dreamstime.com; (right) franfoto | dreamstime.com; page 213 © (top left) dreamer4787 | dreamstime.com; (top right) delleved61 | dreamstime.com; (bottom left) rorem | dreamstime.com; (bottom right) andrejsafaric | dreamstime.com; page 218 © tadejstepisnik | dreamstime.com; page 223 © (top) phant | dreamstime.com; (bottom) franfoto | dreamstime.com; page 230 © (top) p1ko | dreamstime.com; (left middle) xbrchx | dreamstime.com; (right middle) mrakhr | dreamstime.com; (bottom) holger karius | dreamstime.com; page 237 © shann fountain alipour; page 240 © dreamer4787 | dreamstime.com; page 241 © (left) shann fountain alipour (right) shann fountain alipour; page 251 © (top left)

MAP SYMBOLS

≡≡≡	Expressway	○	City/Town	✈	Airport	⚲	Golf Course
	Primary Road	◉	State Capital	✖	Airfield	P	Parking Area
	Secondary Road	⊛	National Capital	▲	Mountain	≜	Archaeological Site
- - - -	Unpaved Road						
	Feature Trail	★	Point of Interest	✛	Unique Natural Feature	♟	Church
- - - -	Other Trail	•	Accommodation			⛽	Gas Station
············	Ferry	▼	Restaurant/Bar	🕊	Waterfall	⬭	Glacier
	Pedestrian Walkway	▪	Other Location	▲	Park	▨	Mangrove
▪▪▪▪▪	Stairs	Λ	Campground	⛷	Trailhead	▱	Reef
				✗	Skiing Area	⊡	Swamp

CONVERSION TABLES

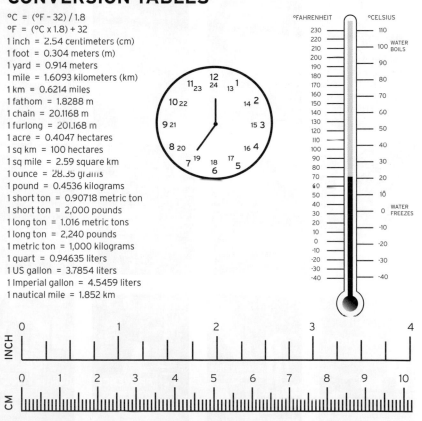

°C = (°F - 32) / 1.8
°F = (°C x 1.8) + 32
1 inch = 2.54 centimeters (cm)
1 foot = 0.304 meters (m)
1 yard = 0.914 meters
1 mile = 1.6093 kilometers (km)
1 km = 0.6214 miles
1 fathom = 1.8288 m
1 chain = 20.1168 m
1 furlong = 201.168 m
1 acre = 0.4047 hectares
1 sq km = 100 hectares
1 sq mile = 2.59 square km
1 ounce = 28.35 grams
1 pound = 0.4536 kilograms
1 short ton = 0.90718 metric ton
1 short ton = 2,000 pounds
1 long ton = 1.016 metric tons
1 long ton = 2,240 pounds
1 metric ton = 1,000 kilograms
1 quart = 0.94635 liters
1 US gallon = 3.7854 liters
1 Imperial gallon = 4.5459 liters
1 nautical mile = 1.852 km

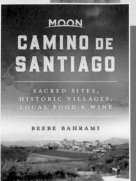

MOON

CAMINO DE SANTIAGO

SACRED SITES,
HISTORIC VILLAGES,
LOCAL FOOD & WINE

BEEBE BAHRAMI

Embark on an epic journey along the historic Camino de Santiago, stroll the most popular European cities, or chase the northern lights in Norway with Moon Travel Guides!

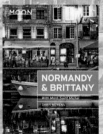

GO BIG AND GO BEYOND!

These savvy city guides include strategies to help you see the top sights and find adventure beyond the tourist crowds.

OR TAKE THINGS ONE STEP AT A TIME

NEW ENGLAND
Road Trip

BOSTON, ACADIA NATIONAL PARK, WHITE
MOUNTAINS, BERKSHIRES, NEWPORT, AND CAPE COD

JEN ROSE SMITH

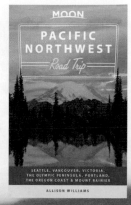

PACIFIC NORTHWEST
Road Trip

SEATTLE, VANCOUVER, VICTORIA,
THE OLYMPIC PENINSULA, PORTLAND,
THE OREGON COAST & MOUNT RAINIER

ALLISON WILLIAMS

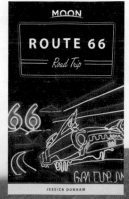

ROUTE 66
Road Trip

JESSICA DUNHAM

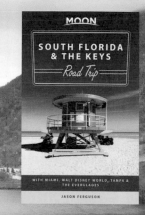

SOUTH FLORIDA & THE KEYS
Road Trip

WITH MIAMI, WALT DISNEY WORLD, TAMPA &
THE EVERGLADES

JASON FERGUSON

SOUTHWEST
Road Trip

LAS VEGAS, ZION & BRYCE, MONUMENT VALLEY,
SANTA FE & TAOS, AND THE GRAND CANYON

TIM HULL

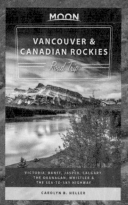

VANCOUVER & CANADIAN ROCKIES
Road Trip

VICTORIA, BANFF, JASPER, CALGARY,
THE OKANAGAN, WHISTLER &
THE SEA-TO-SKY HIGHWAY

CAROLYN B. HELLER

Road Trip USA

Covering more than 35,000 miles of blacktop stretching from east to west and north to south, *Road Trip USA* takes you deep into the heart of America.

This colorful guide covers the top road trips including historic Route 66 and is packed with maps, photos, illustrations, mile-by-mile highlights, and more!

MOON

TRIP OF A LIFETIME

ANGKOR WAT

TOM VATER

MOON

TRIP OF A LIFETIME

GALÁPAGOS ISLANDS

LISA CHO

MOON

ICELAND

JENNA GOTTLIEB

MOON

TRIP OF A LIFETIME

MACHU PICCHU

RYAN DUBÉ

MOON

MOROCCO

MOON

NEW ZEALAND

JAMIE CHRISTIAN DESPLACES

MOON

NORWAY

DAVID NIKEL

MOON

TRIP OF A LIFETIME

PATAGONIA

WAYNE BERNHARDSON

MOON

PRAGUE, VIENNA & BUDAPEST

JENNIFER WALKER

MOON

ROME, FLORENCE & VENICE

ALEXEI J. COHEN

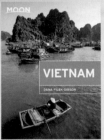

MOON

VIETNAM

DANA FILEK-GIBSON

MOON

Drive & Hike

APPALACHIAN TRAIL

THE BEST TRAIL TOWNS, DAY HIKES, AND ROAD TRIPS IN BETWEEN

TIMOTHY MALCOLM

MOON

CAMINO DE SANTIAGO

SACRED SITES, HISTORIC VILLAGES, LOCAL FOOD & WINE

BEEBE BAHRAMI

MOON

USA NATIONAL PARKS

THE COMPLETE GUIDE TO ALL

59 PARKS

BECKY LOMAX

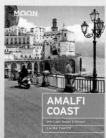

MOON CROATIA & SLOVENIA

Avalon Travel
Hachette Book Group
1700 Fourth Street
Berkeley, CA 94710, USA
www.moon.com

Editor: Ada Fung
Series Manager: Kathryn Ettinger
Copy Editor: Jessica Gould
Graphics and Production Coordinator:
   Lucie Ericksen
Cover Design: Faceout Studios, Charles Brock
Interior Design: Domini Dragoone
Moon Logo: Tim McGrath
Map Editor: Kat Bennett
Cartographers: Kat Bennett, Karin Dahl,
   Brian Shotwell
Proofreader: Elina Carmona

ISBN-13: 978-1-64049-349-0

Printing History
1st Edition — 2009
3rd Edition — June 2019
5 4 3 2 1

Front cover photo: the city walls from the Lovrijenac
   Fortress, Dubrovnik, Croatia © Giorgio Filippini /
   SIME / eStock Photo
Back cover photo: Preseren square, Ljubljana,
   Slovenia © Kasto80 | Dreamstime.com

Printed in China by RR Donnelley